T0355398

A HANDBOOK OF ESTONIAN

Nouns, Adjectives, and Verbs

Indiana University Uralic and Altaic Series
Editor: Denis Sinor
Volume 163

A HANDBOOK OF

ESTONIAN

NOUNS, ADJECTIVES AND VERBS

By HARRI WILLIAM MÜRK

Indiana University
Research Institute for Inner Asian Studies
Bloomington, Indiana
1997

ISBN 0-933070-42-X
Library of Congress Card Number: 97-069265

Indiana University Uralic and Altaic Series
Research Institute for Inner Asian Studies
Goodbody Hall
Bloomington, IN 47405

PREFACE

This handbook is a reference source on Estonian forms such as the singular and plural forms of nouns and adjectives or the various tense forms of verbs. It is aimed primarily at the non-native student. Estonian relies extensively on the different forms that a given word can exhibit for indicating the grammatical relationships among the words in a sentence or text. In addition to all of the many forms that a given word has, there are a number of different ways to derive the forms. These are usually dependent on the word itself. Thus, word forms and how they are derived are crucial to a good knowledge of Estonian.

One of the myths about Estonian is that it is a very difficult language because any given Estonian noun, adjective or verb can appear in so many different forms. For example, standard school grammars list 14 different forms in the singular for a noun or adjective. If the plural forms are added to this number then there are at least 28 forms. The large number of forms that a given word can have actually poses very few difficulties for the non-native student. All of the endings are very logical and systematic. The forms will be discussed in more detail in Part I.

More daunting, particularly for the beginner, is the fact that all words can be divided into different **classes** based on how the different forms are derived. Each class in turn can be further subdivided into many different subclasses called **types**. Each type may have a number of different **patterns**.

Initially, Estonian forms and their classes and types may seem complex but it is actually the interplay of only a handful of language phenomena which results in the seeming chaos of different patterns. Most of the patterns are easily predictable once the student has learnt the basic principles behind the whole system.

A number of current reference sources deal with Estonian word forms. The most comprehensive of these is the **Õigekeelsussõnaraamat** (Orthological Dictionary). This is the standard orthological (spelling and forms) dictionary currently used in Estonia. Ülle Viks' recent and very comprehensive **Väike Vormisõnastik** (Small Dictionary of Forms) and Saagpakk's Estonian-English dictionary also contain useful information on forms. All of these reference materials are aimed primarily at the Estonian speaker rather than the non-Estonian student of the language and are as a result not always as explicit as they need to be for non-native students.

For this reason the present handbook is more extensive than many comparable works aimed at native speakers. The materials in this handbook have been arranged in such a manner so as to make it possible to discover that underneath the seeming chaos of

Estonian forms, there is a structure that is based on logic and regularity.

In addition to non-native students of the language, native speakers unsure of many forms will also find the handbook invaluable. The general linguist wishing to find out more about the morphological system of Estonian will find it equally useful. It will provide the student with a handy tool in learning and manipulating the forms of Estonian words.

Throughout the book, technical linguistic terms have been avoided as much as possible. These may be generally unfamiliar to the majority of readers and will not be very useful to them in gaining a better understanding of the concepts. Readers with a background in linguistics or grammar will readily recognize all of the concepts in any case. The materials have also been presented in a way which often diverges from the traditional presentation found in grammar books. The emphasis has been on arranging the materials in a manner that reflects the internal structure of the language rather than trying to force it into a preexisting model.

The Handbook is divided into four parts. Part I is a précis of Estonian Forms. In this part, after a brief section describing some of the basic features of Estonian spelling and pronunciation, the various forms of the **case system** of nouns and adjectives and the forms of the **verbal system** are outlined. The précis also contains a detailed description of a series of alternations that the stems of many words exhibit known as **gradation**. Some additional minor stem alternations concommitant with gradation are also described. Because of their importance to the whole system, a short section on **syllables** is also included. In the final section of Part I, the different **classes** and **types** are described.

The formation of the comparative and superlative has not been included in this handbook, it is very regular and straightforward in any case. A few minor alternations involving palatalized and unpalatalized consonants and a vowel alternation with some irregularly formed impersonal verb forms have also not been described. They are, however, indicated in the appropriate places in the index of patterns in Part II.

Part II is an index of Estonian nouns/adjectives and verbs arranged according to the different **patterns** of forms that they exhibit.

Finally, Parts III and IV are alphabetical Estonian-English and English-Estonian glossaries cross-indexed with the index of Part II.

I am greatly indebted to a number of colleagues and friends who helped by reading and meticulously criticizing preliminary drafts. I would like to acknowledge such extensive help and encouragement from E. Johanson, C. Kramer, A. Raun, D. Sinor, A. Souza, J. Springer, S. Wayne, and S. Von Wolff.

I would also like to thank the following organizations who provided financial assistance in the final realization of this handbook:

Estonian (Toronto) Credit Union
National Estonian Foundation of Canada
Tartu College

I would also like to thank a number of Estonian Academic Societies who generously supported this project:

The Konstantin Päts Fund of Korp! Fraternitas Estica
The Jaan Tõnisson Fund of The Eesti Üliõpilaste Selts
Korp! Vironia

Korp! Amicitia
Eesti Naisüliõpilaste Selts
Korp! Fidentia
Korp! Filiae Patriae
Korp! Fraternitas Liviensis
Korp! Fraternitas Tartuensis
Korp! Indla
Korp! Revelia
Korp! Rotalia
Korp! Sakala
Korp! Ugala

Finally, I would like to thank my students, who provided the impetus for this book, whose comments were of enormous benefit in arranging the materials and for whom this handbook is dedicated.

H. W. M.

Toronto, Canada
Candlemas 1997

NOMINALS

ONE-SYLLABLE STEMS	TWO-SYLLABLE STEMS					THREE-SYLLABLE STEMS				FOUR-SYLLABLE STEMS
CLASS I	CLASS IIA	CLASS IIB	CLASS IIIA	CLASS IIIB	CLASS IV	CLASS V	CLASS VIA	CLASS VIB	CLASS VII	CLASS VIII
REGULAR	REGULAR - VOWEL PARTITIVES				REGULAR	-S STEMS			REGULAR	
TYPE 1 sUU sUU sUUd suhu -sse sUUde suude sul̇d -sid	TYPE 3 maja maja maja maJJa -sse majade maju -sid	TYPE 5 sõda sõja sõda sõTTa -sse sõdade sõdu -sid			TYPE 15 kiisu kiisu kiisut -sse kiisude kiisusid	TYPE 18 paras paraja parast parajat -sse parajate parajaid	TYPE 20 kapsas kaPsa kapsast -sse kapsaste kaPsaid	TYPE 25 hammas haMba hammast -sse hammaste haMbaid	TYPE 29 inetu inetu inetut -sse inetute inetuid	
							-R AND -L STEMS			
			TYPE 7 liLL lille liLLe liLLe -sse liLLede liLLi -sid	TYPE 12 lel̇b leiva lel̇ba lel̇ba -sse lel̇bade lel̇bu -sid			TYPE 21 tütar tüTre tütart -sse tütarde tüTreid	TYPE 26 pöial pöl̇dla pöialt -sse pöialde pöl̇dlaid	TYPE 30 raamat raamatu raamatut -sse raamatute raamatuid	TYPE 35 restoran restorani restorani restorani -sse restoranide restorane
			-J STEMS			-E STEMS I			-DA GEN.	
			TYPE 8 kiri kirja kiRja kiRja -sse kiRjade kiRju -sid		TYPE 16 pere pere peret peRRe -sse perede peresid	<==	TYPE 22 lause laUse lauset -sse lausete laUseid	TYPE 27 riie rl̇l̇de riiet -sse riiete rl̇l̇deid	TYPE 31 hõbe hõbeda hõbedat -sse hõbedate hõbedaid	
			-R AND -L STEMS				-E STEMS II		-NDA GEN.	
			TYPE 9 sõber sõbra sõPra sõPra -sse sõPrade sõPru -sid			TYPE 19 habe habeme habet -sse habemete habemeid	TYPE 23 iste iStme istet -sse iStmete iStmeid	TYPE 28 ranne raNdme rannet -sse raNdmete raNdmeid	TYPE 32 viies viienda viiendat -sse viiendate viiendaid	
	CONSONANT PARTITIVES (-D OR -T)					-U STEMS				
	TYPE 4 meri mere	TYPE 6 käsi käE			TYPE 17 õlu(t) õlle		TYPE 24 jäänu jÄÄnu		TYPE 33 kiNdel kiNdel	

meRd
meRRe -sse
merede
meresid

käTT
käTTe -sse
käte
käsi

TYPE 10
kEEl
keele
keelT
kEEldekEEle
keelte
kEEli

TYPE 13
UUs
uue
uuT
UUde -sse
uute
UUsi

IRREGULAR

TYPE 11
laPs
lapse
lasT
-sse
laste
laPsi

TYPE 14
mEEs
mehe
meeSt
-sse
meeste
mehi

ANOMALOUS TYPE

TYPE 2
aU
aU
aU
-sse
aUde
aUsid

This noun type developed historically
from a CLASS III A type.
Today it patterns like a defective
CLASS II A
and resembles externally CLASS I.

There are three items in this TYPE.

õlut
-sse
õLLede
õLLesid

<==

jäänut
-sse
jäänute
jÄÄnuid

kiNdlat
-sse
kiNdlate
kiNdlaid

-AS STEMS

TYPE 34
kuningas
kuninga
kuningat
-sse
kuningate
kuningaid

-NE STEMS

TYPE 36
raUdne
raUdse
raUdset
-sse
raUdsete
raUdseid

TYPE 38
sinine
sinise
sinist
-sse
siniste
siniseid

TYPE 41
roheline
rohelise
rohelist
rohelisse -sse
roheliste
rohelisi

-US STEMS (REGULAR)

TYPE 37
hiRmus
hiRmsa
hiRmsat
-sse
hiRmsate
hiRmsaid

TYPE 39
alus
aluse
alust
-sse
aluste
aluseid

TYPE 42
etendus
etenduse
etendust
etendusse -sse
etenduste
etendusi

-US STEM (-KSE GENITIVE)

TYPE 40
omas
omakse
omast
-sse
omaste
omaksied

VERBS

ONE-SYLLABLE STEMS	TWO-SYLLABLE STEMS					THREE-SYLLABLE STEMS				FOUR-SYLLABLE STEMS
CLASS I	CLASS IIA	CLASS IIB	CLASS IIIA	CLASS IIIB	CLASS IV	CLASS V	CLASS VIA	CLASS VIB	CLASS VII	CLASS VIII
REGULAR	REGULAR - VOWEL PARTITIVES				REGULAR		-S STEMS		REGULAR	
TYPE 1 võİma võİ võİda võİsin võİs võinud võidakse võidud	TYPE 3 elama ela elada elasin elas elanud elatakse elatud	TYPE 7 lugema loE lugeda lugesin luges lugenud loeTakse loeTud	TYPE 10 õPPima õpi õPPida õPPisin õPPis õPPinud õpitakse õpitud	TYPE 15 uSkuma usu uSkuda uSkusin uSkus uSkunud usutakse usutud	TYPE 19 pişsima pişsi pişsida pişsisin pişsis pişsinud pişsitakse pişsitud		Do not occur with verb stems		TYPE 25 kirjutama kirjuta kirjutada kirjutasin kirjutas kirjutanud kirjutatakse kirjutatud	
			CONSONANT PARTITIVES			-R AND -L STEMS			MIXED TYPE	
			TYPE 11 laUlma laula laUlda laUlsin laUlis laUlnud lauldakse lauldud	TYPE 16 aNdma anna aNda aNdsin aNdis aNdnud anTakse anTa		TYPE 20 kõnelema kõnele kõnelda kõnelesin kõneles kõnelnud kõneldakse kõneldud	TYPE 21 sUUdlema sUUdle suudelda sUUdlesin sUUdles suudelnud suudeldakse suudeldud	TYPE 23 õMblema õMble õmmelda õMblesin õMbles õmmelnud õmmeldakse õmmeldud	TYPE esitlema esitle esitleda esitlesin or esitles esitlenud esitletakse esitletud	26 esitelema esitele esiteLLa esitelin esiteli esitelnud esitellakse esiteLdud
			CONS. PART. -T AND -P				-E STEMS			
			TYPE 12 taPma tapa taPPa taPsin taPPis taPnud tapetakse tapetud	TYPE 17 taHtma taha taHta taHtsin taHtis taHtnud tahetakse tahetud			Do not occur with verb stems			
	IRREGULAR I						-A STEMS			
	TYPE 4 ajama aja ajada ajasin ajas ajanud		TYPE 13 jäTma jäta jäTTa jäTsin jäTTis jäTnud				TYPE 22 haKKama haKKa hakata haKKasin haKKas hakanud	TYPE 24 puHkama puHka puhata puHkasin puHkas puhanud		

aeTakse
aeTa

jäeTakse
jäeTa

hakatakse
hakatud

puhatakse
puhatud

IRREGULAR II

TYPE 14	TYPE 18
jooKsma	laSkma
jookse	lase
jooSta	laSta
jooKsin	laŞksin lasin
jooKsis	laŞkis lasi
jooKsnud	laSknud
jooStakse	laStakse
jooStud	laStud

-I PAST TENSE STEMS

TYPE 2	TYPE 5	TYPE 8
jÄÄma	tulema	pidama
jÄÄ	tule	peA
jÄÄda	tuLLa	pidada
jäİ	tulin	pidin
jäİn	tuli	pidi
jäänud	tulnud	pidanud
jäädakse	tullakse	---
jäädud	tuLdud	---

IRREGULAR

TYPE 6	TYPE 9
minema	nägema
mine lähe	näE
miNNa	näha
läksin	nägin
läKs	nägi
läinud	näinud
minnakse	nähakse
miNdud	näHtud

CONTENTS

PART I

PRÉCIS OF ESTONIAN FORMS

PRONUNCIATION AND SPELLING

Although Estonian spelling generally reflects actual pronunciation, there is not always a one-to-one correlation between sound and letter. There are a number of places where the spelling significantly obscures or actually hides the real pronunciation. In the following section some of these areas are outlined. Throughout the handbook standard spelling has been used with certain modifications to compensate for those areas where the spelling does not reflect the actual pronunciation adequately. These few modifications are also described here. Note that in this handbook, some letters will often be enclosed in either slashes (/ /) or square brackets ([ ]). This indicates that the sounds enclosed in the brackets are found in the pronunciation but are not necessarily indicated this way in spelling.

LENGTH

Estonian is one of the very few languages of the world where sounds can be pronounced in three lengths; short, long and extra-long. Each of the three lengths can change the meaning of a word. This is illustrated with **/ a /** and **/ n /** in the examples below:

short		long		extra-long	
sada	hundred	saada	send!	saada	to get
lina	linen	linna	city' s	linna	to the city

Short sounds are always indicated with a **single letter**
Long sounds are usually indicated with a **double letter**

The spelling conventions do not allow more than two identical letters to stand next to each other. Thus:

Extra-long sounds are also normally indicated with a **double letter**

However, double letters are not written in all places even if the actual pronunciation indicates the presence of a long or extra-long sound and:

Long and **extra-long sounds** are also very often indicated with a **single letter**

Thus, the actual lengths found in the pronunciation are often ambiguously indicated in the spelling. Even though all sounds can be pronounced in three lengths, from the spelling it seems as if there are only two lengths.

The three lengths are of central importance to the Estonian morphologic system. This unfortunately is the area where the spelling is most complicated. The conventions for indicating the three lengths in spelling are outlined below:

PRONUNCIATION AND SPELLING

Estonian sounds can be divided into two large groups based on how the three lengths are indicated in the spelling:

Sound Group 1: / p t ţ (palatalized **t**) **k /**

These are the only sounds whose three lengths are usually reflected in the spelling. The three lengths of:

/ p / are represented with the letters	**b**	**p**	**pp**
/ t / and **/ ţ /** are both represented by	**d**	**t**	**tt**
/ k / are represented with the letters	**g**	**k**	**kk**

It is very important to bear in mind that **b** and **p** are merely written variants of the same sound **/ p /**. Similarly **d** and **t** as well as **g** and **k** are letter variants of the sounds **/ t ţ /** and **/ k /** respectively. These letters are used to represent the three lengths of these sounds:

	short		long		extra-long	
	kabi	hoof	**kapi**	cupboard' s	**kappi**	cupboard (part)
unpalatalized	**mäda**	rot	**mätas**	sod	**mätta**	sod's
palatalized	**sodi**	rubbish	**koti**	bag's	**kotti**	into the bag
	suga	sley	**suka**	stocking's	**sukka**	stocking (part)

b d and **g** are always only short **/ p t ţ /** and **/ k /** sounds respectively. They can appear anywhere in a word but they appear at the beginning of a word only if it is a foreign loan-word

p t and **k** can be short, long or extra-long but only in specific environments. They are:

1) **short** at the beginning of a word or following **b d g s h p t k f š**
2) **long** when preceded by a single short vowel
3) **extra-long** usually when preceded by a double vowel,

p t and **k** are ambiguously **long** or **extra-long** when they are preceded by:

1) a double vowel or diphthong (two different vowels forming one syllable)
2) the consonant letters **m n l r**

p t and **k** are ambiguously **short** or **extra-long** when they are followed by:

1) the consonants **b d g s h p t k f š**

pp tt and **kk** are always only extra-long. They are used only if the extra-long sound is preceded by a single vowel.

These rules are illustrated in the examples below. The examples all illustrate the sound **/ k /** but similar ones can be found for **/ p /** and **/ t ţ /**:

	short		long		extra-long	
	gaas	gas				
g	**aga**	but				
	saag	saw				
			hoki	hockey	**tiiki**	pond
k	**kaas**	lid	**koiku**	cot	**auku**	hole
	katku	plague	**jänku**	bunny	**purki**	jar
	maksa	pay			**paksu**	fat
kk					**tikku**	match

Note that **/ f** and **š /** generally follow the same rules as **/ p t k /**. They are found only in foreign words. At the beginning of words they are always only short. Otherwise these two sounds are either long or extra-long.

Sound Group 2: all other consonants and vowels

The second group consists of all other consonants and vowels for which the three lengths are indicated ambiguously:

Single letters can generally be either **short** or **extra-long** while
double letters can generally be either **long** or **extra-long**

Whether a given letter represents a short, long or extra-long sound must be memorized.

These spelling conventions are particularly important in connection with certain length alternations that many words exhibit. These alternations are called gradation. The details of gradation are outlined on pages 35 - 44.

All sounds can exhibit gradation but the mixed spelling conventions make it appear as if words with the same sort of length alternations behave in different ways. For example compare the three forms of the following words in the standard spelling below (the terms nominative, genitive and partitive are explained further below):

nominative	genitive	partitive	
kapp	**kapi**	**kaPPi**	cupboard
kamm	**kammi**	**kammi**	comb
külm	**külma**	**külma**	cold

At first glance it appears from the spelling that there is an alternation between a longer **pp** and a shorter **p** in **kapp** while both **kamm** and **külm** exhibit no alternations at all.

In reality all three words have the very same length alternations in the pronunciation of the forms. In the nominative and partitive forms the **pp** **mm** and **l** are all extra-long. These alternate with a shorter version of the same sound in the genitive case.

To compensate for this defect, the standard spelling will be used here but the extra-long sounds will be indicated by writing the appropriate letter(s) with capitals. Thus the same three words in the augmented spelling where the actual alternations become apparent, will look like the following :

nominative	genitive	partitive	
kaPP	**kapi**	**kaPPi**	cupboard
kaMM	**kammi**	**kaMMi**	comb
küLm	**külma**	**küLma**	cold

More details about the different spelling conventions in conjunction with gradation are discussed on pages 38 and 40.

The following principles will guide the student in reading the forms in this index:

Short sounds- always single letter (in this index any single lower case letter)
1) **b d g** are always only short (note: **b d g** never appear as double letters)
2) single **p t k** are short in word initial position or
   next to the consonant letters **b d g s h p t k f š**.
3) all other single letters (lower case) are short sounds.

Long sounds - single or double letter (indicated with lower case letters)
4) single **p t k** are long (usually when preceded by a single short vowel)
5) all other lower case double letters are long sounds

Extra-long sounds - single or double letter (indicated with upper case letters)
6) single **P T K** are always extra-long when preceded by a double vowel,
   diphthong or the consonant letters **m n l r**
7) double **PP TT KK** are always only extra-long
8) all other upper case letters, regardless of whether they are single or double
   are extra-long sounds

PALATALIZATION

In standard Estonian the letters **d** and **t** (spelling variants of the same sound) **l n** and **s** each represent two different sounds. These sounds can be pronounced either with

1) the tip of the tongue placed against the back of the upper teeth or
2) the blade of the tongue pressed against the roof of the mouth with a
   very short ^{j} glide preceding the sound in question.

The latter mode of pronunciation is commonly called palatalization. The meaning of a word will change if the letter is pronounced as an unpalatalized or palatalized sound (see the examples below). Palatalization is not indicated in the spelling of Standard Estonian. In this handbook, however, it will be marked by placing a comma under the letter representing the palatalized sound:

d̦ ţ ļ ņ and **ş**.

Some examples of pairs of words containing both unpalatalized and palatalized sounds are found below:

unpalatalized		palatalized	
koTT	old boot	**koŢT**	bag
paLk	wages	**paĻk**	log
sAAn	I get	**sAAņ**	sleigh
kaS	question word	**kaŞS**	cat

MISSING LETTERS: the glides / j / and / w /

The Estonian sound system includes both the sounds **/ j /** (the sound found for example at the beginning of the English word **yes**) as well as **/ w /**. The Estonian alphabet, however, has only the letter **j** to represent the former sound but does not have a letter to represent **/ w /**. Thus a **/ w /** found in the pronunciation is never indicated in the spelling.

There are certain places where **/ j /** is not indicated in the spelling either even though a **/ j /** sound is present in the pronunciation. There are a number of reasons why these sounds should be represented in the spelling everywhere they occur. To compensate for this spelling defect, in this handbook **/ j /** and **/ w /** will be included in the spelling. They will be enclosed in square brackets [ ] inside the word where they are actually pronounced:

Standard spelling	augmented transcription	
juua	**jUU[w]a**	to drink
süüa	**sÜÜ[j]a**	to eat
viia	**vİİ[j]a**	to carry away,take

Thus in actual spelling the above words are written as **juua** **süüa** and **viia**. Capital letters indicate that the **UU ÜÜ** and **ii** are extra-long. The letters in the brackets indicate that a **/ j /** or **/ w /** are found in the actual pronunciation but are not included in the actual spelling.

SUMMARY

Throughout this handbook standard spelling will be used with the following three additions not used in the standard language:

1) letters representing extra-long sounds will be written as capitals
   Note that in order to distinguish capital **i** (representing extra-long **i**) from an **l** or a **1** it is written in this handbook with a dot over it **İ**

2) palatalized sounds will be indicated by placing a comma underneath the sound

3) **[j]** and **[w]** which are not found in spelling are included in the words where they occur.

THE NOMINAL CASE SYSTEM

Nouns and adjectives are usually grouped together and are known collectively as **nominals**. The various different forms of any given nominal are commonly called **cases**. English words usually have two cases, the basic form such as **house** and the possessive form such as **house's**. English pronouns such as **I, you, he, she, we** and **they** additionally have a form that is used with prepositions for example, **for me, about him, beside her, with us, to them, between you and me. I** and **me** are both cases of the first person singular pronoun. English has a relatively small number of cases for any given word. In Estonian, however, the standard grammar books recognize 14 cases. These can be divided into two basic categories: primary and secondary.

THE PRIMARY CASES

The primary cases, as their name implies, are the most important cases. They are:

1) the **naming** or **nominative case** which is comparable to the English basic form. The singular nominative is the form that is cited in the dictionary. It has no specific ending.

2) the **possessive** or **genitive case** is most comparable to the English possessive forms, **house's**. It always ends with a vowel.

3) the **partitive case** which has no direct counterpart in English. It is used to mean **some** or **part** of something. It has a number of important functions. It can end either with **t** , **d** or some vowel.

the primary cases are illustrated by the following forms of **raamat** (book):

nominative	**raamat**	book, the book
genitive	**raamatu**	book's, of the book
partitive	**raamatut**	some (part) of the book

The nominals are divided into the different **classes** and **types** on the basis of the different ways that these three cases are formed. This is discussed in the last section of Part I.

The three primary cases appear both in singular and plural forms. How the plural forms are derived from the singular primary cases is outlined in further detail later in this section.

THE STEMS

The **stems** are those forms to which the secondary case suffixes are added. The singular stem is always identical to the singular genitive and the plural stem is always identical to the plural genitive.

THE SECONDARY CASES

These cases correspond to English prepositional phrases such as **in the house, without a care, to Mary,** etc. They consist of a set of eleven suffixes that are added to the stem (either singular or plural) of a word. They are divided into four subsets:

1) **Subset 1: inside local cases**

All three case suffixes contain an **-s** element related to the word **sisi** (interior):

1) the **into case** (or **illative**) with the ending **-sse** expresses motion into
2) the **inside case** (or **inessive**) with the ending **-s** expresses location inside
3) the **out of case** (or **elative**) with the ending **-st** expresses motion out of

These are illustrated by the following forms:

illative	**raamatusse**	into the book
inessive	**raamatus**	in the book
elative	**raamatust**	out of the book

2) **Subset 2: outside local cases**

These contain an **-l** element related to the derivative suffix **-la** (place, location):

1) the **onto case** (or **allative**) with **-le** expresses motion toward or onto
2) the **on top of case** (or **adessive**) with **-l** expresses location at or on
3) the **off of case** (or **ablative**) with **-lt** expresses motion away from or off of

These three are illustrated by the following:

allative	**raamatule**	onto the book
adessive	**raamatul**	on the book
ablative	**raamatult**	off of the book

Both the **into case** (illative) and the **onto case** (allative) contain a final **-e** and express **motion toward.**

The **in** and **on** cases (inessive and adessive) consist of only **-s** and **-l** respectively and express **stationary location.**

The **out of** and **off of** cases (elative and ablative) both have a final **-t** and express **motion away from.**

3) **Subset 3: temporal cases.**

There are only two cases instead of three. They are:

1) the **becoming case** (or **translative**) with the ending **-ks** expresses a change of state (temporal motion into a new state of being).
2) the **being case** (or **essive**) with the ending **-na** expresses a state of being (temporal location).

The temporal cases are illustrated by the following two sentences:

Ta valiti **presidendiks.**	(S)he was elected president.
Ta töötas **presidendina.**	(S)he worked as the president.

While the inside and outside local cases express physical motion toward something and physical stationary location, the temporal cases express motion in time toward a certain state or condition and stationary location in time in a state or condition.

A third case to express the termination of a state of being (temporal motion out of a state) is missing in Standard Modern Estonian. However, at one time it did exist with the ending **-nt**. It is known as the **ceasing to be case** (or **excessive**). This suffix survives in Estonian in only a few words; **tagant** (away from the behind of), **kodunt** (away from home). Notice, that in these two words, while the temporal element is no longer present in the meaning of the suffix, it nonetheless retains the notion of motion away from. Note also the final **-t** parallelling the **out of** (**-st**) and **off of** (**-lt**) cases.

4) Subset 4: miscellaneous cases:

1) the **up to case** (or **terminative**) with the ending **-ni** expresses motion up to the side of something or up to the endpoint.
2) the **with case** (or **comitative**) with the ending **-ga** expresses accompaniment (with) or manner
3) the **without case** (or **abessive**) with the ending **-ta**, expresses lack of something (without)

these are illustrated by the following forms:

terminative	**kivini**	up to the rock
comitative	**kiviga**	with the rock
abessive	**kivita**	without the rock

The miscellaneous cases are uite a mixed group as far as form and function are concerned. They fit the general scheme of the inside, outside and temporal cases only very loosely.

To sum up, the 11 secondary case forming suffixes are divided into four sets arranged according to the following scheme:

secondary case suffixes	inside local cases	outside local cases	temporal cases	miscel-laneous cases
motion toward	**-sse**	**-le**	**-ks**	**-ni**
stationary location	**-s**	**-l**	**-na**	**-ga**
motion away from	**-st**	**-lt**	missing	**-ta**

The Alternate SHORT INTO case form

The regular secondary case suffix meaning **into** is **-sse**. However, many nominals (approximately 30% of the nouns and adjectives in the standard language) have two possible forms for the into case; the regular **-sse** form, and a stylistic variant called the **short into case**. While the longer **-sse** form is usually correct, for those words allowing it, the **short into case** form is preferred. The **short into case** variant form is found only in the singular. It is very exceptionally found for a few nouns in the plural as well.

The form of the **short into case** can be predicted from the shape of the primary cases. This will be discussed below in the section of classes and types. However, which words allow this form must be learnt. Standard grammars usually list the **short into case** before all of the other secondary cases. The same will be done in this handbook.

THE TERTIARY CASES

In addition to the primary and secondary cases, some words have a few irregular forms which are called tertiary cases. Only three cases are traditionally listed as such:

1) the instructive, which occurs predominately with body parts
2) the prolative, with the ending **-tsi** expressing the route used for some motion
3) the caritive ending, **-tu**, with the meaning of a characteristic lack of something

these are illustrated below:

instructive	**paĻja jalu**	barefoot
prolative	**meritsi**	by way of sea
caritive	**keeletu**	speechless

These forms only appear for a limited number of words. There are some other suffixes that occur with a very limited number of nouns which might also be considered as tertiary cases. However, these as well as the three forms mentioned above are usually considered to be adverbs in Standard Estonian grammars. They will not be included in this handbook due to their infrequent occurrence and irregular formation.

PRINCIPAL PARTS AND FORMING THE CASES

Principal parts are those forms which are used as the building blocks for predicting all of the other forms. These are the nominative, genitive and partitive singular. The behaviour of these three cases is also the basis for dividing nominals into different classes and types. In most instances it is possible to predict all of the forms of a noun or adjective on the basis of its nominative singular form. However, in the initial stages it is easier to memorize the three principal parts. From these three all other regular forms are easily derived. The formation of regular nouns and adjectives from the three principal parts will be discussed next.

Forming the nominative plural

The nominative plural is always formed by adding the plural marker **-d** to the singular stem which is always identical to the genitive singular. This is seen in the chart below:

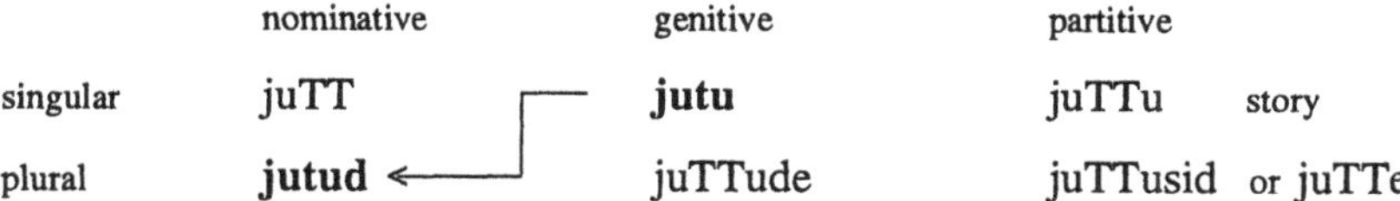

	nominative	genitive	partitive	
singular	juTT	**jutu**	juTTu	story
plural	**jutud** ←	juTTude	juTTusid or juTTe	

Forming the genitive plural

The mark of the genitive plural is **-de** (sometimes **-te**). The **-d-** (**-t-**) is the plural marker and the vowel **-e** is the marker of the genitive plural. There are two regular patterns for the formation of the genitive plural:

1) if the partitive singular ends in a vowel then the genitive plural is formed by adding **-de** to the partitive singular as illustrated below:

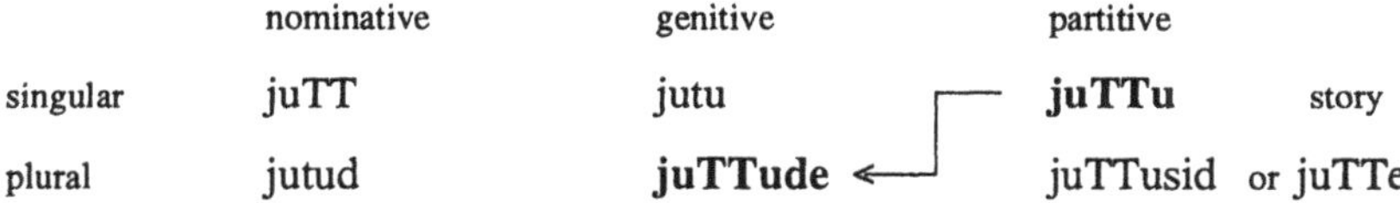

	nominative	genitive	partitive	
singular	juTT	jutu	**juTTu**	story
plural	jutud	**juTTude** ←	juTTusid or juTTe	

2) If the partitive singular ends in **-d** or **-t** (variants of the same sound) then only an **-e** needs to be added to the partitive to form the genitive plural:

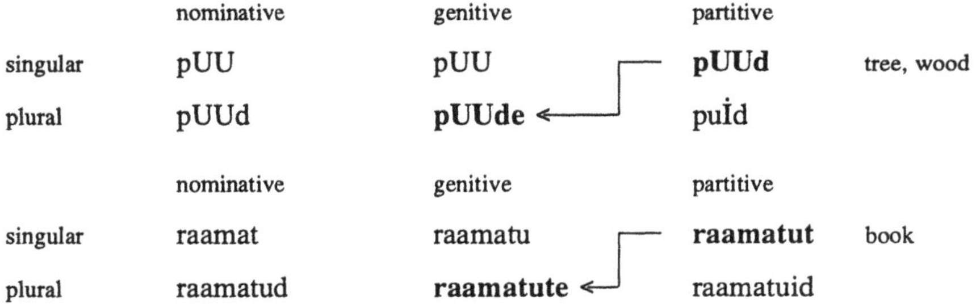

	nominative	genitive	partitive	
singular	pUU	pUU	**pUUd**	tree, wood
plural	pUUd	**pUUde** ←	puİd	

	nominative	genitive	partitive	
singular	raamat	raamatu	**raamatut**	book
plural	raamatud	**raamatute** ←	raamatuid	

Some words have slightly irregular genitive plurals. These have to be learnt.

The genitive plural of several types of nominals is based on the genitive singular rather than the partitive singular (see Classes and Types on pages 56 - 59).

	nominative	genitive	partitive	
singular	habe	**habeme**	habet	beard
plural	habemed	**habemete** ←	habemeid	

Forming the Partitive plural

The formation of the partitive plural is particularly complex. The partitive plural can end in **-id, -sid** or it can exhibit a change in the final vowel of the singular partitive. The crucial feature for determining which partitive plural endings is used is the NUMBER OF SYLLABLES IN THE GENITIVE SINGULAR:

1) If the genitive singular has an ODD NUMBER OF SYLLABLES then **-id** is added to the GENITIVE SINGULAR as illustrated below:

	nominative	genitive		partitive	
singular	hobune	**hobuse**	─┐	hobust	horse
plural	hobused	hobuste	└→	**hobuseid**	

Note that if the genitive singular ends in **-i** then the **-i** becomes **-e** when **-id** is added:

	nominative	genitive		partitive	
singular	lennuk	**lennuki**	─┐	lennukit	airplane
plural	lennukid	lennukite	└→	**lennukeid**	

2) If the genitive singular has an EVEN NUMBER OF SYLLABLES then the partitive plural is formed by either:

   a) adding **-sid** directly to the PARTITIVE SINGULAR or
   b) changing the final vowel of the PARTITIVE SINGULAR as seen below:

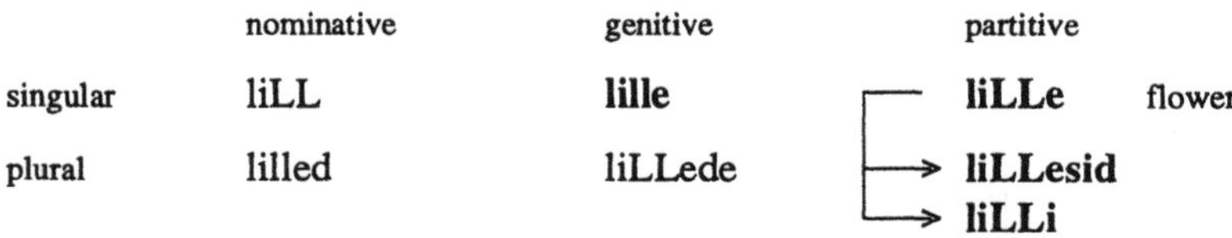

	nominative	genitive		partitive	
singular	liLL	**lille**	┌─	**liLLe**	flower
plural	lilled	liLLede	├→	**liLLesid**	
			└→	**liLLi**	

Some words, as in the above example, have a form with **-sid** as well as a form with a change in the final vowel. With these words, the shorter form with a vowel change is preferred. Other words allow only one or the other form. Which form(s) a word allows, (only **-sid** or only a vowel-changed form or both **-sid** and a vowel-changed form) is dependent on the class that the word belongs to.

SYLLABLE COUNTING FOR THE PLURAL PARTITIVE

The formation of the plural partitive crucially depends on the number of syllables in the singular genitive. In counting syllables the following two rules apply:

1) If a syllable contains an extra-long sound, that syllable will actually count as two syllables.

For example, compare the principal parts of the following two words:

nominative	**plaşku** flask	**taSku** pocket
genitive	**plaşku**	**taSku**
partitive	**plaşkut**	**taSkut**
partitive plural	**plaşkusid**	**taSkuid**

On the surface it appears that the genitive forms of both words have an even number of syllables (i.e. two). Actually, only the genitive of **plaşku** has two syllables. As expected the partitive plural of this word is **plaşkusid.**

The first syllable of **taSku,** however, has an extra-long sound in it (indicated with a capital) and extra-long syllables must be counted as two syllables. The total number of syllables of **taSku** is therefore three and its plural partitive is, as we would expect for words with an odd number of syllables, **taSkuid**. This is another example where the spelling hides information crucial to the learner.

However

2) Syllables containing extra-long sounds count as two syllable only if they occur in the last syllable or next-to-last syllable of a word of the genitive singular.

For example the genitive of **diÏvan** (sofa) is **diÏvani**. The syllable containing the extra-long sound is not found in the last or next-to-last syllable and so the genitive **diÏvani** counts for three syllables and not four. Its plural partitive is **diÏvaneid** as expected with an odd number of syllables.

Partitive Plural Vowel Changes

Only those words whose genitive singular has an even number of syllables ending in **-i -e -u** or **-a** form their partitive plural by changing the stem vowel. Words which have some other stem vowel in the singular will not allow a vowel change.

The **-i -e** and **-u** stems regularly change their stem vowel to **-e -i** and **-e** respectively in forming the partitive plural.

Words with a singular partitive ending in **-a** can change the vowel to either **-u -i** or **-e** in the partitive plural. These vowel changes must be memorized. Over half of the words in this group exhibit the **-a** > **-u** alternation, slightly less than half exhibit the **-a** > **-i** alternation and only a handful exhibit the **-a** > **-e** alternation.

The vowel changes are illustrated in the chart below and again it is initially easier to memorize these forms rather than try to predict them:

partitive vowel		the forms		
singular	plural	singular	plural	
-i ⟶	-e	**poTTi**	**poTTe**	pot
-e ⟶	-i	**liLLe**	**liLLi**	flower
-u ⟶	-e	**juTTu**	**juTTe**	story
-a ⟶	-u	**saUna**	**saUnu**	sauna
-a ⟶	-i	**kiNga**	**kiNgi**	shoe
-a ⟶	-e	**muna**	**mune**	egg

Forming the Secondary Cases

The secondary cases are all very easily formed by adding the various suffixes to either the singular or plural stem. The resultant forms are all adverbial in nature and express mainly directionality, location, and manner. The suffixes remain unchanged whether they are added to the singular or plural stems:

singular	**majasse**	into the house
plural	**majadesse**	into the houses

The Alternate SHORT INTO Case

Only stems whose genitive consists of an even number of syllables will allow a **short into case** form. The actual form of the **short into case** for these words is dependent on the class that the word belongs to. The various possible forms will be discussed below in the section on classes and types. It is easier to memorize this form along with the three principal parts.

The Alternate -i PLURAL

In addition to the usual regular plural forms with **-de (-te)**, many nouns and adjectives (but not all) have stylistic alternate plural forms called the **-i** plural. These forms are derived from the partitive plural through a set of rules discussed in detail below:

1) For words with **-id** in the partitive plural, the **-i** plural stem is formed by removing the final **-d** from the partitive plural.

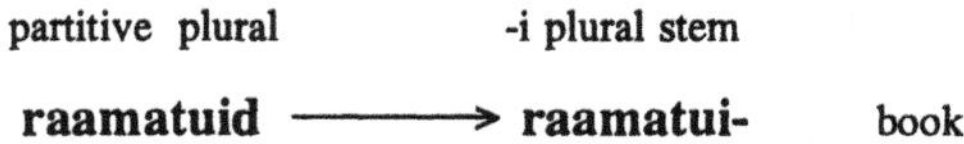

2) For words with a vowel change in the partitive plurals, the **-i** plural stem is identical to the partitive plural.

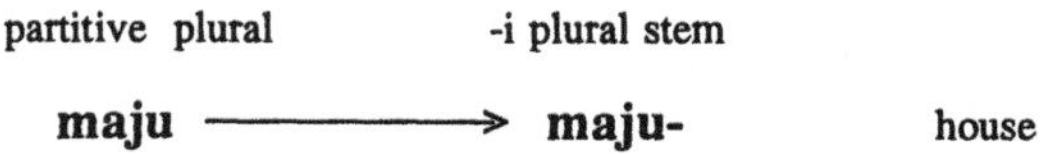

continued on page 18

KÄÄNDSÕNADE VORMID - THE NOMINAL PARADIGM

case name Estonian	English	meaning/ function	forms singular	plural regular -de plural	alternate -i plural
		PEAKÄÄNDED - PRIMARY CASES			
nimetav	nominative	naming	**kaPP**	**kapid**	
omastav	genitive	possessing	**kapi**	**kaPPide**	
osastav	partitive	part of	**kaPPi**	**kaPPisid**	**kaPPe**
tüved	stems		**kapi-**	**kaPPide-**	kape-
		ÜLDKÄÄNDED - SECONDARY CASES			
		sisekohakäänded - inside local cases			
lühike sisseütlev	short illative	into	**kaPPi**	--	
sisseütlev	illative	into	**kapisse**	**kaPPidesse**	kapesse
seesütlev	inessive	inside	**kapis**	**kaPPides**	kapes
seestütlev	elative	out of	**kapist**	**kaPPidest**	kapest
		väliskohakäänded - outside local cases			
alaleütlev	allative	onto	**kapile**	**kaPPidele**	kapele
alalütlev	adessive	on top of	**kapil**	**kaPPidel**	kapel
alaltütlev	ablative	off of	**kapilt**	**kapPidelt**	kapelt
		ajakäänded - temporal cases			
saav	translative	becoming	**kapiks**	**kaPPideks**	kapeks
olev	essive	being	**kapina**	**kaPPidena**	-i plural forms are not used with the last four cases.
lakkav	excessive	ceasing	(-nt)		
		segakäänded - miscellaneous cases			
rajav	terminative	up to	**kapini**	**kaPPideni**	
kaasaütlev	comitative	with	**kapiga**	**kaPPidega**	
ilmaütlev	abessive	without	**kapita**	**kaPPideta**	

3) If however, the genitive singular is in the weak grade (see section on Gradation on page 36 for a detailed description of the weak grade) then the **-i** plural will have the same vowel as the partitive plural but will be in the weak grade like the genitive singular.

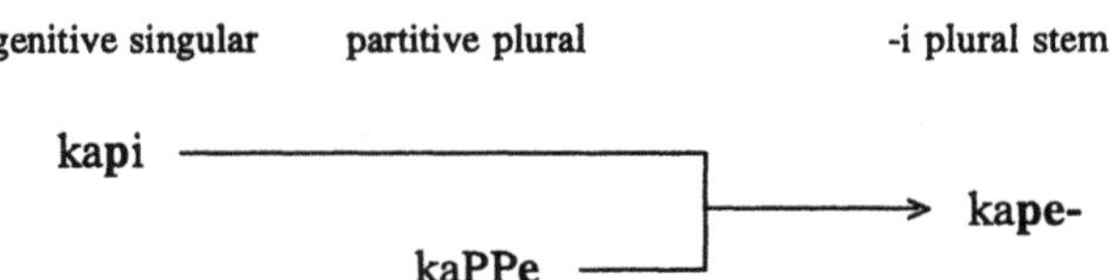

The **-i** plural form is not possible for those words that have only **-sid** as their partitive plural ending.

The regular **-de** plural forms are always correct. The alternate **-i** plural forms of those words that allow it, are generally confined only to the written language. Only on very rare occasions do they appear in the spoken language. A handful of nouns and adjectives also have an **-i** plural genitive form.

The **-i** plural is included in this handbook for the sake of completeness, but beginners are not required to master these forms.

THE NOMINAL PARADIGM

The chart on page 17 sets out the full set of forms for the word **kaPP** (cupboard). Forms in bold are those forms that are commonly used.

The schematic chart on the next page shows the derivation of the two major categories of nominals; those with an even or odd number of syllables in the genitive stem.

FORMING THE CASES

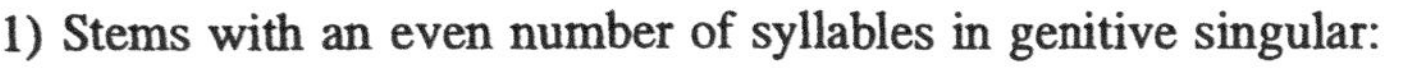
1) Stems with an even number of syllables in genitive singular:

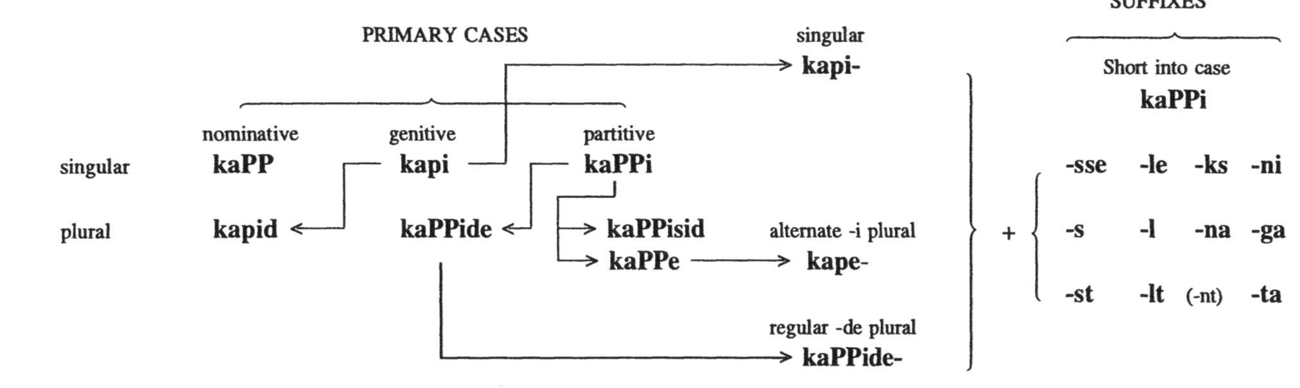

2) Stems with an odd number of Syllables in genitive singular:

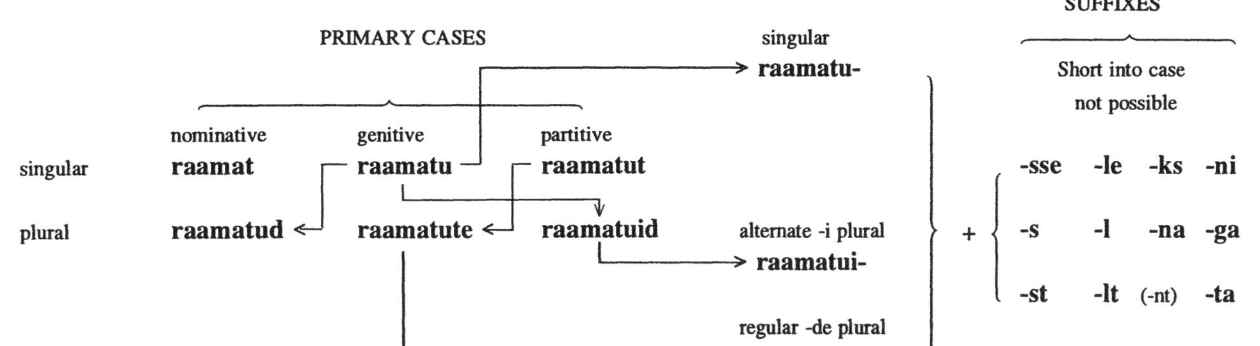

THE VERBAL SYSTEM

Verbal forms are divided into two large groups based on the types of endings or suffixes that they exhibit and how they are used in a sentence. The two groups are:

Finite Forms
These are forms which have suffixes that usually agree with the grammatical subject of the sentence and are used as the main verb in the sentence. They are collectively called the finite forms: **I go, she goes** etc.

Infinitival Forms
The other group consists of those verbal forms that have case endings. Traditionally, they have been called by a variety of names but here they will be referred to collectively as infinitival forms. Infinitival forms are used when a speaker wishes to use a verb as a part of speech other than the main verb. For example infinitival verbal forms are used in place of nouns, adjectives and adverbs in a sentence.

Each of these large groups is in turn subdivided into a number of smaller groups depending on their meanings and how they are used in a sentence. Finite and Infinitival forms will be discussed in more detail below.

Four important features of verbal forms are voice, tense, number and person:

Voice
In Estonian **voice** refers to whether the subject or agent of an action is known or unknown. If the subject is explicit in the context then personal forms of the verb are used. If the subject or agent is unknown then impersonal forms are used. The impersonal forms are most similar to French **on** as in **on chante** (someone sings) or German **man** as in **man singt**. Personal and impersonal forms are illustrated by the finite forms below:

Personal forms are used when we know who the singer is:

mina laUlsin	I sang	**meie laUlsime**	we sang
sina laUlsid	you (singular) sang	**teie laUlsite**	you (plural) sang
tema laUlis	he/she sang	**nemad laUlsid**	they sang

Impersonal forms are used when we do not know, do not care or perhaps do not want to say who the singer is:

laUldi someone (unknown) sang

Tense

English divides the time or tense of actions into three unequal parts; past, present and future. In Estonian time is divided into only two equal parts; actions either have taken place or they have not yet taken place. The former is referred to as the **past tense** and the latter for lack of a better name can be called the **non-past**.

Number and Person

Number refers to singular or plural. All persons are either singular or plural.
Person refers to any specific form that corresponds to a pronoun or noun.

1) **mina** and **meie** (I and we) are referred to as the first person,
2) **sina** and **teie** (you singular and plural) are the second person and
3) **tema** and **nemad** (he / she / it and they) as well as all other nouns are generally referred to as the third person.

THE FINITE FORMS

The finite forms are those verbal forms that appear as the main verb in a sentence. These forms are characterized by a number of markers and suffixes which are discussed below:

Voice: personal/impersonal markers

Personal forms of verbs are forms that indicate which person (first, second or third) is the subject or agent of the action. There is no specific marker to indicate that a verb form is personal. The lack of a marker altogether actually means that the form is personal.

In contrast, impersonal forms, indicating that the subject is unimportant and not named, are characterized by the impersonal marker **-t(a)-** after the stem. Since no person is explicitly indicated, impersonal forms by definition will not have a personal ending.

Tense/Mood markers

Finite verb forms are divided into five groups called **tense/moods** which are indicated with a marker placed after the verbal stem. The five tense/moods and their markers are:

1) **non-past indicative** used to indicate an action that has not yet taken place;
   - **Ø** for first and second person forms (no tense/mood suffix)
   - **Ø** for all negative non-past forms (no tense/mood suffix)
   - **-b-** for third person singular (he/she/it) form
   - **-va-** for third person plural (they) form
   - **-kse** for impersonal forms

2) **past indicative** used for actions which have taken place;
   - **-s(i)-** for most personal forms
   - **-i-** for the personal forms of some irregular verbs
   - **-nud** for past tense personal negative forms
   - **-i-** for impersonal forms
   - **-tud** for past tense impersonal negative forms

3) **conditional** used in hypothetic situations. This form can also be used to make direct commands more polite;
   -ks(i)- is the conditional marker (not to be confused with **-kse** above)

4) **hearsay** forms used for actions that are alleged to be happening
   -vat is the hearsay marker

5) **imperative** or command forms. Unlike English, Estonian has command forms for all persons and numbers. **-g-** (or **-k-**) is the imperative marker

Personal Endings

The **non-past, past** and **conditional** moods of the personal verbs in addition to the tense/mood markers also usually have personal endings. These are a series of suffixes that agree with the subject and indicate who or what is involved in the action. These endings are used only with personal forms. Impersonal forms by definition lack personal endings. The personal endings are:

-n	to indicate that the subject is **mina** (I)
-d	for the subject **sina** (you singular)
-me	for subject **meie** (we)
-te	for subject **teie** (you plural)
Ø	for subject **tema** (he/she) and **nemad** (they)

The **tema** (he/she) and **nemad** (they) forms have no personal suffixes. The **tema** form is indicated with only a bare tense/mood marker followed by no ending. For the **nemad** form the tense/mood marker is followed by the plural marker **-d**.

The **imperative** forms generally have the tense/mood marker **-g** (**-k**). While no specific personal endings are added, the shape of the imperative ending can change according to the person. The possible suffixes are:

-gu	if the subject is **mina** (I)
Ø	when the subject is **sina** (you) only the bare verbal stem is used
-gem	for subject **meie** (we)
-ge	for subject **teie** (you plural)
-gu	for subject **tema** (he/she) and **nemad** (they)

For the **mina** (I) , **tema** (he/she) and **nemad** (they) forms, the subject must be explicitly included.

Personal endings are not used with the **hearsay** (**-vat**) tense/mood forms but the subject must be mentioned explicitly.

Thus the finite verb form can consist of one element from one or more of the following categories in the following order;

1)	verbal stem	
2)	impersonal marker	**Ø -ta-**
3)	tense/mood marker	**Ø -b- -v- -si- -i- -ksi- -vat- -kse -g/k-**
4)	plural marker	**-d**
5)	personal ending	**Ø -n -d -me -te**

The Negative Forms

The negative forms are characterized by the negative particle **ei** preceding the verbal stem with its tense/mood markers. The negative forms (with the exception of the negative imperatives) do not vary according to the person of the subject. Note that the past tense/mood marker for the personal is the ending **-nud**. The negative of the imperative uses the negative particle **ära** which has a full gamut of imperative endings. The negative forms are listed under the tense/moods in the chart below.

These patterns are summarized in the chart on the following page which list the personal and impersonal finite forms in the positive and negative for the verb **elama** (to live):

THE INFINITIVAL FORMS

The infinitivals are those verb forms that can be used to replace other parts of speech in a sentence. They are divided into five groups according to the part of speech they replace. These are:

1) the true infinitives,
2) the nominal verb (or gerund),
3) the verbal adjectives (or participles),
4) the verbal noun, and
5) the verbal adverbs.

The True Infinitives

English has only one form that is commonly called the infinitive. It is characterized by the preposition **to**, for example in the sentence **I want to sing, to sing** is the infinitive.

In Estonian the infinitive can appear in a number of different case forms not all of which have direct equivalents in English. The usual marker of the infinitive is **-ma** to which various case endings can be added.

The following case forms are most commonly used with the infinitive:

1) **Partitive -da**

The partitive form of the infinitive has the ending **-da** (sometimes **-ta** or merely **-a**) without the general **-ma** infinitive marker. This form is usually called the **-da** infinitive in standard grammars.

THE VERBAL SYSTEM

Personal Forms - positive

	non-past					past					conditional					hearsay					imperative (command)				
	stem	voice	tense/mood	number	person	stem	voice	tense/mood	number	person	stem	voice	tense/mood	number	person	stem	voice	tense/mood	number	person	stem	voice	tense/mood	number	person
mina	**ela**	-	-	-	**n**	**ela**	-	**si**	-	**n**	**ela**	-	**ksi**	-	**n**	**ela**	-	**vat**	-	-	**ela**	-	**gu**	-	-
sina	**ela**	-	-	-	**d**	**ela**	-	**si**	-	**d**	**ela**	-	**ksi**	-	**d**	**ela**	-	**vat**	-	-	**ela**	-	-	-	-
tema	**ela**	-	**b**	-	-	**ela**	-	**s**	-	-	**ela**	-	**ks**	-	-	**ela**	-	**vat**	-	-	**ela**	-	**gu**	-	-
meie	**ela**	-	-	-	**me**	**ela**	-	**si**	-	**me**	**ela**	-	**ksi**	-	**me**	**ela**	-	**vat**	-	-	**ela**	-	**ge**	-	**m**
teie	**ela**	-	-	-	**te**	**ela**	-	**si**	-	**te**	**ela**	-	**ksi**	-	**te**	**ela**	-	**vat**	-	-	**ela**	-	**ge**	-	-
nemad	**ela**	-	**va**	**d**	-	**ela**	-	**si**	**d**	-	**ela**	-	**ksi**	**d**	-	**ela**	-	**vat**	-	-	**ela**	-	**gu**	-	-

Impersonal forms - positive

	stem	voice	tense/mood	number	person	stem	voice	tense/mood	number	person	stem	voice	tense/mood	number	person	stem	voice	tense/mood	number	person	stem	voice	tense/mood	number	person
	ela	**ta**	**kse**	-	-	**ela**	**t**	**i**	-	-	**ela**	**ta**	**ks**	-	-	**ela**	**ta**	**vat**	-	-	**ela**	**ta**	**gu**	-	-

Personal Forms - negative

personal negative forms are not marked for person except for imperative

	stem	voice	tense/mood	number	person	stem	voice	tense/mood	number	person	stem	voice	tense/mood	number	person	stem	voice	tense/mood	number	person	imperative
mina	ei **ela**	-	-	-	-	ei **ela**	-	**nud**	-	-	ei **ela**	-	**ks**	-	-	ei **ela**	-	**vat**	-	-	**äRgu elagu**
sina	ei **ela**	-	-	-	-	ei **ela**	-	**nud**	-	-	ei **ela**	-	**ks**	-	-	ei **ela**	-	**vat**	-	-	**ära ela**
tema	ei **ela**	-	-	-	-	ei **ela**	-	**nud**	-	-	ei **ela**	-	**ks**	-	-	ei **ela**	-	**vat**	-	-	**äRgu elagu**
meie	ei **ela**	-	-	-	-	ei **ela**	-	**nud**	-	-	ei **ela**	-	**ks**	-	-	ei **ela**	-	**vat**	-	-	**äRgem elagem**
teie	ei **ela**	-	-	-	-	ei **ela**	-	**nud**	-	-	ei **ela**	-	**ks**	-	-	ei **ela**	-	**vat**	-	-	**äRge elagu**
nemad	ei **ela**	-	-	-	-	ei **ela**	-	**nud**	-	-	ei **ela**	-	**ks**	-	-	ei **ela**	-	**vat**	-	-	**äRgu elagu**

Impersonal Forms - negative

	stem	voice	tense/mood	number	person	stem	voice	tense/mood	number	person	stem	voice	tense/mood	number	person	stem	voice	tense/mood	number	person	imperative
	ei **ela**	**ta**	-	-	-	ei **ela**	**t**	**ud**	-	-	ei **ela**	**ta**	**ks**	-	-	ei **ela**	**ta**	**vat**	-	-	**äRgu elatagu**

2) **Into Case (illative) -ma**
The bare **-ma** infinitive ending by itself with no other ending is in reality the **short INTO case** form. This is the form used to list the verb in Estonian Dictionaries. It is known as the **-ma** infinitive in standard grammars.

3) **Inside Case (inessive) - mas**

4) **Out of Case (elative) -mast**

The case of the infinitive is determined by the main verb according to which case a noun would normally appear with that verb. Thus:

The **partitive (-da)** infinite would be used with those verbs that would normally allow a partitive noun complement while

The **into case (-ma), inside case (-mas),** and **out of case (-mast)** infinitives would be used with those verbs requiring motion-toward, stationary-location or motion-away-from case complements respectively.

The following sentence pairs illustrate this:

Nominal complement		Verbal complement	
	Verbs with **partitive** complement:		
Ma tahan **raamatut**	I want a book.	Ma tahan **laUlda**	I want to sing
	Verbs with **motion-toward** ending:		
Ma läksin **kOOli**	I went to school.	Ma läksin **laUlma**	I went to sing
Ma jäİn **kOOli**	I stayed in (into) school.	Ma jäİn **laUlma**	I stayed to sing
(kOOli is the short into case form)			
	Verbs with **stationary-location** endings:		
Ma olen **koolis**	I am in school	Ma olen **laUlmas**	I am singing
Ma käİn **koolis**	I attend (go to) school	Ma käİn **laUlmas**	I go singing
	Verbs with **motion-away-from** endings:		
Ma tulen **koolist**	I come from school.	Ma tulen **laUlmast**	I come from singing.

5) **Becoming case -maks**
Other case forms also exist. An innovative but seldom used infinitive is the **becoming case** with the ending **-maks**. It means for the purpose of doing something. It has as its closest parallel the **becoming case**.

Ma tulin Eestisse **õPPimaks** eesti keelt. I came to Estonia in order to learn Estonian.

6) **Without cases -mata and -matu**
The remaining two cases of the infinite are the **without form** (**abessive**) with the ending **-mata** meaning undone and the tertiary case ending **-matu** (**caritive**) meaning something that is undoable. The former is used as an adverb of manner or as an indeclinable adjective while the latter is used as a regular adjective:

Ma tulin **sõna lausumata.**	I came without uttering a word
Tasumata arved jõudsid minuni.	The unpaid bills caught up with me
Lugematud korrad	Uncountable times

Impersonal Infinitives
The impersonal infinitives are seldom used and appear in only two cases as illustrated below:

into case	**laUldama**	to be sung
caritive	**laUldamatu**	unsingable

The impersonal into case form is restricted in its use. It is only used with the verb **pidama** (must), which is the only verb in Estonian that lacks actual impersonal forms. The impersonal caritive is very often synonymous with the personal caritive.

The Nominal Verb
Traditionally known as the gerund, in Estonian the suffix is **-mine**. It indicates the abstract concept embodied by the verb; thus **laUlma** (to sing) **laUlmine** (singing). The nominal verb has all of the regular case endings both in the singular and plural, although the plural forms are not normally used. The form is neither personal or impersonal.

The Verbal Adjectives
Also called participles, these are verb forms used as adjectives. In Estonian there are four forms; two personal forms, two impersonal forms, two non-past forms and two past forms. This is summarized below:

		personal	impersonal
non-past	nominative	**õPPiv**	**õpitav**
	genitive	**õPPiva**	**õpitava**
	partitive	**õPPivat**	**õpitavat**
	meaning	who is learning	which is being learned which will be learned which is to be learned
past	indeclinable	**õPPinud**	**õpitud**
	meaning	who has learned	which was learned

The non-past participles agree in number and case with the noun that they modify while the two past participle forms are always indeclinable (they do not have case endings).

The Verbal Noun

Like the verbal adjectives (participles), the verbal noun also appears in four forms. The non-past personal verbal noun has the ending **-ja** and is equivalent to the English **-er/-or** (the doer). The impersonal non-past noun is identical to the comparable adjective (participle) and the past verbal nouns are almost identical to the comparable adjectives without the final **-d**. All four forms have the full gamut of case endings as summarized in the following chart:

		personal	impersonal
non-past	nominative	**õPPija**	**õpitav**
	genitive	**õPPija**	**õpitava**
	partitive	**õPPijat**	**õpitavat**
	meaning	the learner the one who is learning	that which is being learned that which will be learned that which is to be learned
past	nominative	**õPPinu**	**õpitu**
	genitive	**õPPinu**	**õpitu**
	partitive	**õPPinut**	**õpitut**
	meaning	the one who has learned	that which has been learned

The Verbal Adverbs

The last set of infinitivals are those verbal forms that are used as adverbs. These are summarized in the following chart. There is no form for the non-past impersonal:

	personal	impersonal
non-past	**õPPides**	---
meaning	while studying	
past	**õPPinud**	**õpitud**
meaning	after having studied	after having been studied

PRINCIPAL PARTS AND FORMING VERBS

Personal Forms

Verbs, like the nominals, also have three primary forms that must be memorized. On the basis of these forms, the other verb forms can be predicted. The verbal primary forms are closely parallelled by the nominal primary forms.

The verbs have no primary form comparable to the nominative singular of the nominals. The non-past verbal stem is closely parallelled by the genitive/stem of the nominal while the **-da** infinitive is comparable to the nominal partitive singular. The third primary verbal form, the **-ma** infinitive, is actually the **into case** of the infinitive. This last form has generally been the form that is used in the dictionaries to cite the verb.

The close similarities between the nominal and verbal primary forms can be seen in the table below:

PRIMARY FORMS

	nominative	genitive/stem	partitive	short into case	
nominals	**oSt**	**ostu**	**oStu**	**oStu**	a purchase
verbs	---	**osta**	**oSta**	**oStma**	to buy
		non-past stem	partitive (-da infinitive)	into case (-ma infinitive)	

the into case (**-ma**) of the infinitive is usually cited first in listing verbal forms, thus:

into case	non-past stem	partitive
oStma	**osta**	**oSta**
(-ma infinitive)		(-da infinitive)

The formation of the various personal verbal forms from the three primary forms of the verb **õPPima** (to study) is summarized on the next page. For the finite forms only the **mina** or first person singular form will be listed:

A handful of verbs have irregular **-da** infinitive forms and/or **-nud** forms. Some verbs have an irregular past tense form with just **-i** instead of **-s(i)**. Finally, a few verbal nouns (**-ja** form) are slightly irregular. All of these irregular forms must be memorized.

Formation of the Impersonal

For the majority of verbs the impersonal forms are relatively straightforward. The impersonal is regularly formed by removing the **-da** (or **-ta**) of the infinitive partitive and replacing it with the appropriate impersonal and tense/mood suffixes:

	into case	non-past stem	partitive	present impersonal
personal	kirjutama	kirjuta	**kirjutada** to write	
impersonal			→ **kirjuta** + **takse** =	**kirjutatakse**
personal	pesema	pese	**peSta** to wash	
impersonal			→ **peS** + **takse** =	**peStakse**
personal	haKKama	haKKa	**hakata** to begin	
impersonal			→ **haka** + **takse** =	**hakatakse**

Exceptions to the General Rule

The impersonal forms, however, also present some irregularities particularly with many very common verbs.

FORMING THE FINITE FORMS

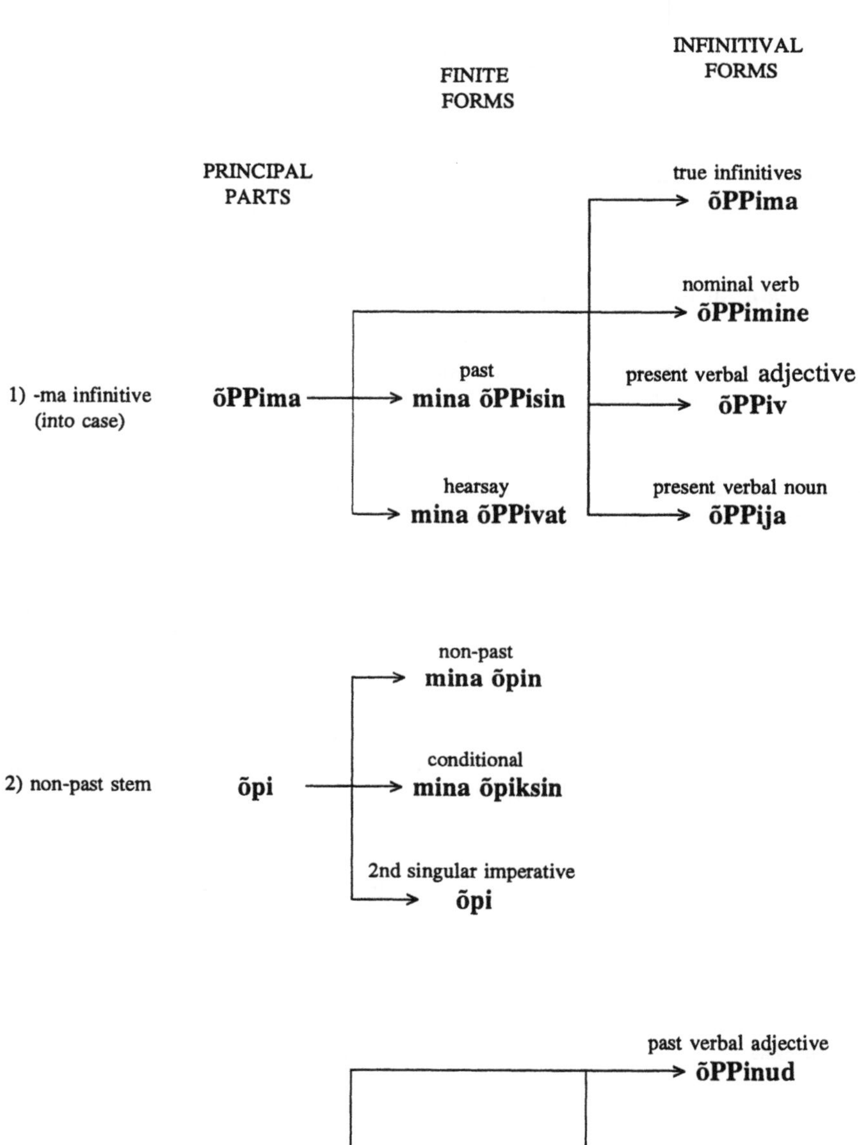

INFINITIVAL FORMS
FINITE FORMS
PRINCIPAL PARTS
true infinitives
õPPima
nominal verb
õPPimine
1) -ma infinitive
(into case)
õPPima
past
mina õPPisin
present verbal adjective
õPPiv
hearsay
mina õPPivat
present verbal noun
õPPija
non-past
mina õpin
2) non-past stem
õpi
conditional
mina õpiksin
2nd singular imperative
õpi
past verbal adjective
õPPinud
3) -da infinitive
(partitive case)
õPPida
all other imperatives
õPPige
present verbal adverb
õPPides

Exception 1) Stems with weak grade forms
If the partitive suffix **-da** is preceded by a vowel then it is important to check the non-past stem. If the non-past stem is in the weak grade (see section on gradation page 36) that is, if it is shorter than the **-da** infinitive stem, then the non-past stem must be used as the base for the impersonal. This is illustrated by the two examples below:

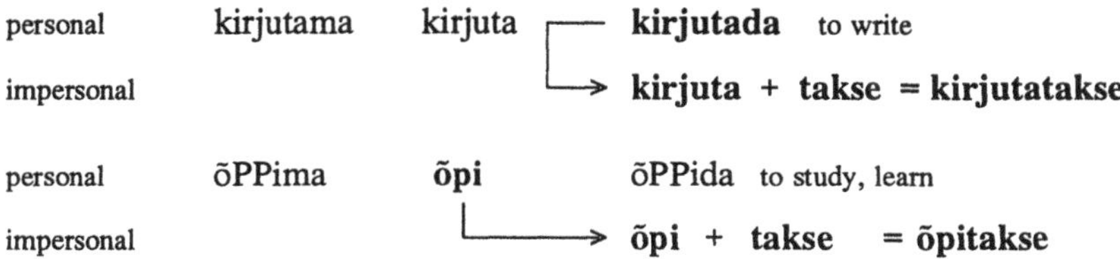

For the verb **kirjutama** the two stems are identical in length. For this verb the impersonal is regular and based on the **-da** stem. However, for the verb **õPPima,** the non-past stem is in the weak grade, it is shorter than the **-da** infinitive stem and for such verbs the non-past stem provides the stem for the impersonal.

Exception 2) Stems ending in -n -l -r
If the partitive suffix **-da** is preceded by the consonants **n l** or **r** then the impersonal marker will be **-da** instead of **-ta.**

personal	laUlma	laula	**laUlda**	to sing
impersonal			→ **laUl + dakse**	= **laUldakse**

Exception 3) Stems ending in -d or -t
One large group of irregular verbs are those whose stem ends in either **-d** or **-t.** This is best determined by looking at the stem form preceding the suffix ending of the **-ma** infinitive, for example, **võTma** (to take) **aNdma** (to give) **nuTma** (to cry). All of these verbs have certain irregularities in the impersonal forms.

Exception 4) Irregular verbs
Finally, there is a handful of common verbs that have irregular impersonal forms. They are usually those verbs that have irregular **-da** infinitive forms such as **oLLa** (to be) **tuLLa** (to come) or **sÜÜa** (to eat).

On the following two pages all of the verbs forms are laid out for the verb **õPPima** (to study, learn)

PÖÖRDSÕNADE VORMID

TEGUSÕNA KÄÄNDELISED VORMID - INFINITIVAL FORMS

infinitive	nominal	noun	adjective	adverb
				ISIKULISED VORMID
--	**õPPimine**	**õPPija**	**õPPiv**	**õPPides**
--	**õPPimise**	**õPPija**	**õPPiva**	
õPPida	**õPPimist**	**õPPijat**	**õPPivat**	
õPPima	etc.	etc.	etc.	
õPPimas				
õPPimast				
õPPimaks				
õPPimata				
õPPimatu				
				ISIKULISED MINEVIKU VORMID
		õPPinu	**õPPinud**	**õPPinud**
		õPPinu	indeclinable	
		õPPinut		
		etc.		
				UMBISIKULISED VORMID
õpitama		**õpitav**	**õpitav**	--
õpitamatu		**õpitava**	**õpitava**	
		õpitavat	**õpitavat**	
		etc.	etc.	
				UMBISIKULISED MINEVIKU VORMID
		õpitu	**õpitud**	**õpitud**
		õpitu	indeclinable	
		õpitut		
		etc.		

VERBAL FORMS

TEGUSÕNA PÖÖRDELISED VORMID - FINITE FORMS

	non-past	conditional	hearsay	imperative
PERSONAL NON-PAST FORMS		jaatavad - positive		
mina	**õpin**	**õpiksin**	**õPPivat**	**õPPigu**
sina	**õpid**	**õpiksid**	**õPPivat**	**õpi**
tema	**õpib**	**õpiks**	**õPPivat**	**õPPigu**
meie	**õpime**	**õpiksime**	**õPPivat**	**õPPigem**
teie	**õpite**	**õpiksite**	**õPPivat**	**õPPige**
nemad	**õpivad**	**õpiksid**	**õPPivat**	**õPPigu**
		eitavad - negative		
mina	**ei õpi**	**ei õpiks**	**ei õPPivat**	**äRgu õPPigu**
				ära õpi
				äRgu õPPigu
				äRgem õPPigem
				äRge õPPige
				äRgu õPPigu

PERSONAL PAST FORMS — jaatavad - positive

mina	**õPPisin**
sina	**õPPisid**
tema	**õPPis**
meie	**õPPisime**
teie	**õPPisite**
nemad	**õPPisid**

eitav - negative

mina	**ei õPPinud**

IMPERSONAL NON-PAST FORMS — jaatavad - positive

non-past	conditional	hearsay	imperative
õpitakse	**õpitaks**	**õpitavat**	**õpitagu**
	eitavad - negative		
ei õpita	**ei õpitaks**	**ei õpitavat**	**äRgu õpitagu**

IMPERSONAL PAST FORMS — jaatav - positive

õpiti

eitav - negative

ei õpitud

Special Constructions with -nud

A set of constructions consisting of various forms of the verb olema (to be) and the past verbal adjective forms, most usually the **-nud** form, are usually listed separately as a series of compound tenses of the finite verb forms. They are the equivalent of the English perfect (have done) and pluperfect (had done) tense forms:

ma olen laulnud	I have sung
etc.	I have been singing
ma olin laulnud	I had sung
etc.	I had been singing

These constructions should be treated as special **-nud** constructions rather than actual tenses. They have not been included in the verb charts in this handbook.

GRADATION

Word stems exhibit a number of internal alternations but it is actually the interplay of these few alternations which results in the seeming chaos of different patterns. Most of the patterns are easily predictable once the student has learnt the basic principles behind the whole system. The most important of these alternations is known as **Gradation**. In the next section gradation as well as some other minor alternations which occur in conjunction with it will be described.

Gradation is a characteristic feature of Estonian where the stem of a word can have two variants. One variant will be used as the stem of one set of forms and the other will be the stem of another set of forms. The two variants exhibit an alternation in one of the sounds within the stem itself.

All of the examples cited in this section to illustrate the various types of gradation are nouns. However, it must be noted that unless otherwise stated, the same phenomena are exhibited by verb stems as well.

In the following examples the partitive and genitive/stem of nouns and adjectives are listed to show each alternation.

For verbs the same alternations are best seen by comparing the **-da** (partitive) infinitive and the non-past stem. These are the verbal forms which correspond to the partitive and genitive of nouns and adjectives respectively:

There are three types of gradation;

1) **qualitative gradation**, where there is an actual change in one of the stem consonants
2) **quantitative gradation,** where there is a change in the length of one of the consonants or vowels in the stem.
3) **double gradation,** where both qualitative and quantitative gradation occur simultaneously.

Qualitative Gradation

This type of gradation occurs with some (but not all) words that have a single **-b- -d-** or **-g-** in between two short vowels. The consonants will alternate either with some other sound or will drop out altogether. Not very many words exhibit these alternations, however, most of the ones that do are among the most common words in the language.

The forms containing the **-b-** **-d-** or **-g-** are said to be in the STRONG GRADE while the forms containing the other sound or nothing are in the WEAK GRADE.

strong grade		weak grade		strong grade		
sõda	nominative	**sõja**	genitive	**sõda**	partitive	war
õde	nominative	**õE**	genitive	**õde**	partitive	sister

All possible examples of plain qualitative gradation alternations are listed below.

QUALITATIVE GRADATION

STRONG	WEAK	STRONG	WEAK	
B	b ~ --	**tuba**	**toA**	room
	b ~ v	**tõbe**	**tõve**	disease
D	d ~ --	**õde**	**õE**	sister
	d ~ j	**sõda**	**sõja**	war
G	g ~ --	**jõge**	**jõE**	river

Quantitative Gradation

With this type of gradation an extra-long sound will alternate with either a long or a short variant of the same sound. All sounds, with the exception of **/ j / / w /** and **/ v /**, can exhibit quantitative gradation. The forms containing the extra-long sounds are said to be in the STRONG GRADE and the forms containing the shorter variant of the same sound are said to be in the WEAK GRADE:

strong grade		weak grade		strong grade		
kaPP	nominative	**kapi**	genitive	**kaPPi**	partitive	cupboard
küLm	nominative	**külma**	genitive	**küLma**	partitive	cold

Capitals represent extra-long sounds. Lower case letters are either long or short sounds.

Quantitative gradation is still a very productive process in Standard Estonian. New loan-words will automatically undergo quantitative gradation if they have the appropriate syllable structure. All of the possible alternations are listed on page 40:

Quantitative gradation in reality is a feature of the syllable rather than individual sounds. The actual alternation usually affects the final sound of the main-stressed syllable preceding the genitive stem vowel. All sounds can exhibit quantitative gradation because a syllable can end in any sound. The syllables that can exhibit this type of gradation must fulfil the following two conditions:

1) the syllable must be heavy, (it must end in a consonant or in a long vowel)
2) the syllable must be a stressed syllable (usually first) in the word

The following examples will illustrate this type of gradation. The three primary forms as they appear in the spelling are followed by the actual syllabification of the genitive stem in [ ] square brackets:

⁝ = syllable boundary of genitive stem

nominative	genitive	partitive	⁝ = syllable boundary of genitive stem	
sAAļ	**saaļi**	**sAAļi**	[**saa** ⁝ li]	hall
kaMM	**kammi**	**kaMMi**	[**kam** ⁝ mi]	comb
saUn	**sauna**	**saUna**	[**sau** ⁝ na]	sauna
küLm	**külma**	**küLma**	[**kül** ⁝ ma]	cold

In all of the above examples the bold-faced sound at the end of the initial heavy syllable of the genitive/stem (in the right hand column) is the sound that exhibits the qualitative alternation which is illustrated by the three forms on the left.

Because of spelling conventions the situation is obscured for those words containing a single **p** **t** or **k** . In many instances **p** **t** and **k** are written as single letters but in reality they straddle a syllable boundary.

stem	actual syllable division	
kapi	[**kap** ⁝ pi]	cupboard
lõke	[**lõk** ⁝ ke]	bonfire
sööKi	[**söökk** ⁝ ki]	food

The syllable structure often also determines whether the extra-long sound will alternate with a long or short variant. Only the alternations listed below are possible:

Extra-Long Alternates with Long

Alternations between extra-long and long sounds are possible:

1) with any consonant (except **/ f /** and **/ š /**) when preceded by a short vowel and not followed by any other consonant:

nominative	genitive	partitive	
ke**PP**	kepi	ke**PP**i	stick
ke**LL**	kella	ke**LL**a	clock

2) with any vowel:

nominative	genitive	partitive	
k**OO**l	kooli	k**OO**li	school

3) with the foreign sounds **/ f /** and **/ š /** regardless of what precedes them:

nominative	genitive	partitive	
še**FF**	šefi	še**FF**i	boss
sei**F**	seifi	sei**F**i	safe

Extra-Long Alternates with Short
Alternations between extra-long and short sounds are possible:

1) with any consonant (except **/ f /** and **/ š /**) when preceded by a short vowel and followed by another consonant:

nominative	genitive	partitive	
ke**L**m	kelmi	ke**L**mi	rogue
pa**K**s	paksu	pa**K**su	fat

2) with **/ p t ţ k /** and **/ s /** when preceded by a long vowel, diphthong or consonant:

nominative	genitive	partitive	
see**P**	seebi	see**P**i	soap
poi**SS**	poisi	poi**SS**i	boy

3) with any diphthong (two vowels forming one syllable nucleus). The extra length is exhibited by the second vowel of the diphthong:

nominative	genitive	partitive	
sa**U**n	sauna	sa**U**na	sauna

Gradation and Spelling
It is clear from the above examples that there is a certain inconsistency in representing the length alternations in the spelling. Because of the mixed spelling conventions (see Pronunciation and Spelling on pages 5 and 6), the same basic alternation is indicated in a number of different ways in the spelling depending on which sound in the stem exhibits the alternation. The table on page 40 lists whether quantitative gradation is indicated in the spelling or not and where the syllable boundary falls.

Double Gradation
Some words exhibit both qualitative as well as quantitative gradation. The strong grade forms will contain both an extra-long sound as well as a **-b- -d- -ḑ-** (**-t-**) or **-g-** (**-k-**). The weak grade forms will contain a shorter counterpart of the extra-long sound and there will be another sound or nothing in the position of the **-b- -d- -ḑ-** (**-t-**) or **-g-** (**-k-**). The distribution of the strong and weak forms of the two types of alternations coincide.

A list of all possible double gradation alternations is found on page 41. Note the qualitative and quantitative alternations in each of the examples. Words with **/ j /** and **/ w /** that do not appear in the spelling are indicated with square brackets [ ] (page 7).

-S Alternations

Sometimes **-s-** is also subject to qualitative gradation. In addition to the qualitative alternation itself, words with **-s** alternations also exhibit a variety of other irregularities. Gradation with **-s** is restricted to only a few nouns and adjectives (there are no verbs exhibiting these alternations). The alternations are best seen by comparing the nominative form with the genitive as in the examples below (note that the partitive of all of these nouns and adjectives ends in **-t**)

In the charts below note that ⊡ and ▫ represent an extra-long and a shorter version respectively of any consonant or vowel.

GRADATION WITH -S

	nominative strong grade	genitive weak grade	partitive strong grade	
Qualitative Gradation with -s				
s ~ --	**käsi**	**käE**	**käTT**	hand
s ~ j	**paras**	**paraja**	**parajat**	suitable (this word only)
Double Gradation with -s and -ş				
Us ~ uw	**UUs**	**uu[w]e**	**uuT**	new
İs ~ ij	**hİİs**	**hii[j]e**	**hiiT**	sacred grove
Rs ~ rr	**kõRs**	**kõrre**	**kõrT**	straw
⊡ s ~ ▫ h	**mEEs**	**mehe**	**meesT**	man (this word only)
⊡ ş ~ ▫	**pAAş**	**paE**	**paaT**	limestone
⊡ ş ~ ▫ n	**kAAş**	**kaane**	**kaanT**	lid

An Anomalous -S alternation

There are a number of words in which qualitative gradation with **-s** and quantitative gradation do not coincide, i.e. **-s-** appears in otherwise weak grade forms while it is absent in the strong grade forms. The alternation is illustrated by the example below.

Strong Grade	Weak Grade	Strong Grade	Weak Grade	
⊡	~ ▫ s	**kaUni** (gen)	**kaunis** (nom)	beautiful

Because the **-s** alternation does not coincide with the quantitative gradation in these words, it is traditionally not considered an example of qualitative gradation.

QUANTITATIVE GRADATION

CONSONANTS

extra-long vs. long			extra-long vs. short		
Strong grade	Weak grade		Strong grade	Weak grade	
gradation IS indicated in spelling - Syllable division splits consonant					
kaPPa	**kapa**	beer stein	**seePi**	**seebi**	soap
juTTu	**jutu**	story	**sööTa**	**sööda**	bait
juŢTi	**juţi**	line	**peeŢi**	**peeḑi**	beet
soKKi	**soki**	sock	**sööKi**	**söögi**	food
			poiSSi	**poisi**	boy
			avanŞSi	**avanşi**	pay advance
šeFFi	**šefi**	chef			
duŠŠi	**duši**	shower			

gradation IS NOT indicated in spelling

Syllable division splits consonant			syllable division splits consonant cluster		
			liPsu	**lipsu**	tie
			maTka	**matka**	hike
			maŢsi	**maţsi**	peasant
			paKsu	**paksu**	fat
kaMMi	**kammi**	comb	**hüMni**	**hümni**	hymn
kaNNu	**kannu**	pitcher	**bloNdi**	**blondi**	blond
muŅNi	**muŋni**	penis	this alternation not found for ŋ		
toSSu	**tossu**	smoke	**käSna**	**käsna**	sponge
kaŞSi	**kaşsi**	cat	**kaŞti**	**kaşti**	box
tšeHHi	**tšehhi**	Czech	**maHvi**	**mahvi**	puff
liLLe	**lille**	flower	**küLma**	**külma**	cold
kuĻLi	**kuļli**	gull	**küĻvi**	**küļvi**	planting
naRRi	**narri**	fool	**moRni**	**morni**	sullen
seiFi	**seifi**	safe			
borŠi	**borši**	borscht, beet soup			

VOWELS

presence of gradation IS NOT indicated in spelling
syllable division occurs after vowels of first syllable

AAsa	**aasa**	meadow	**heİna**	**heina**	hay
nEEru	**neeru**	kidney	also ai oi ui õi äi öi		
pIIri	**piiri**	border	**paEla**	**paela**	ribbon
sOOla	**soola**	salt	also oe õe äe		
kUUli	**kuuli**	bullet	**saUna**	**sauna**	sauna
sÕÕri	**sõõri**	circle	also iu õu äu		
lÄÄni	**lääni**	province	**seAdu**	**seadu**	arrangement
sÖÖri	**sööri**	sire	this alternation not found for the following		
ÜÜri	**üüri**	rent	diphthongs: üi öe oa ao eo õo äo		

DOUBLE GRADATION

Note again that ⊡ and □ represent an extra-long and shorter version of any consonant or vowel.

	STRONG		WEAK	STRONG	WEAK	
	⊡ b	~	□ v	**leİba**	**leiva**	bread
B	Ub	~	uw	**kUUbe**	**kuu**[w]**e**	coat
	Mb	~	mm	**kuMba**	**kumma**	which of two
	⊡ d	~	□	**sAAdu**	**saO**	haycock
	⊡ ḑ	~	□	**pOOḑi**	**poE**	store
	⊡ nd	~	□ n	**sUUnda**	**suuna**	direction
	⊡ ld	~	□ l	**kEEldu**	**keelu**	prohibition
	⊡ rd	~	□ r	**kEErdu**	**keeru**	twist
	Ud	~	uw	**lUUda**	**luu**[w]**a**	broom
D Ḑ (T)	İd	~	ij	**hİİdu**	**hii**[j]**u**	giant
	Nd	~	nn	**liNdu**	**linnu**	bird
	Ņd	~	ņn	**tuŅdi**	**tuņni**	hour
	Ld	~	ll	**kiLdu**	**killu**	splinter
	Ļd	~	ļl	**moĻdi**	**moļli**	trough
	Rd	~	rr	**koRda**	**korra**	turn
	Ht	~	h	**jaHti**	**jahi**	hunt
	⊡ g	~	□	**rOOga**	**roA**	food
	⊡ lg	~	□ l	**hİİlge** (gen)	**hiile** (nom)	shining
	⊡ rg	~	□ r	**vEErgu**	**veeru**	column
	Ug	~	v	**haUg**	**havi**	pike (this word only)
	Ug	~	uw	**hUUga**	**huu**[w]**a**	droning
G (K)	İg	~	ij	**raİga**	**rai**[j]**a**	scab
	Lg	~	l	**jaLga**	**jala**	foot
	Rg	~	r	**kuRge**	**kure**	crane (bird)
	Ļg	~	ļj	**seĻga**	**seļja**	back
	Rg	~	rj	**jäRge**	**järje**	sequel
	Hk	~	h	**naHka**	**naha**	skin
	Sk	~	s	**kuuSke**	**kuuse**	fir

Weakening and Strengthening Gradation

There are two patterns of alternations involving the various types of gradation:

1) **Weakening Gradation**

In one pattern the nominative and partitive forms are in the strong grade while the genitive and non-past stems are in the weak grade resulting in a strong ~ weak ~ strong alternation. This is called the weakening pattern as the genitive and non-past stems are weaker than the nominative and partitive:

	strong grade		weak grade		strong grade		
nominal	**sõda**	nominative	**sõja**	genitive	**sõda**	partitive	war
verb	---		**saja**	non-past	**sadada**	partitive	rain
	sadama	into case					

2) **Strengthening Gradation**

The other pattern is the reverse of the above one. The nominative and partitive are in the weak grade and the genitive and non-past stems are in the strong grade resulting in a weak ~ strong ~ weak pattern. This is called the strengthening pattern as the genitive is stronger than the nominative and partitive.

	weak grade		strong grade		weak grade		
nominal	**komme**	nominative	**koMbe**	genitive	**kommet**	partitive	custom
verb	---		**tõMba**	non-past	**tõmmata**	partitive	pull
			tõMbama	into case			

The partitive plural of nouns and adjectives will always be in the strong grade while the **-ma** form and the past tense forms for verbs will always be in the strong grade regardless of the type of alternation.

The two patterns of weakening and strengthening gradation are illustrated in the chart on the next page. The weakening and strengthening patterns of nominals are illustrated by **kaPP** (cupboard) and **lammas** (sheep), the verbal patterns are illustrated with **õPPima** (study, learn) and **haKKama** (start). The strong grade is shaded in:

All three types of gradation discussed earlier can occur in either the weakening or strengthening patterns.

WEAKENING AND STRENGTHENING GRADATION

NOMINALS

	WEAKENING		STRENGTHENING	
	singular	plural	singular	plural
nominative	**kaPP**	**kaPid**	**lammas**	**laMbad**
genitive	**kapi**	**kaPPide**	**laMba**	**lammaste**
partitive	**kaPPi**	**kaPPe**	**lammast**	**laMbaid**
into	**kapisse**	**kaPPidesse**	**laMbasse**	**lammastesse**
in	**kapis**	**kaPPides**	**laMbas**	**lammastes**
out of	**kapist**	**kaPPidest**	**laMbast**	**lammastest**
onto	**kapile**	**kaPPidele**	**laMbale**	**lammastele**
on	**kapil**	**kaPPidel**	**laMbal**	**lammastel**
off of	**kapilt**	**kaPPidelt**	**laMbalt**	**lammastelt**
becoming	**kapiks**	**kaPPideks**	**laMbaks**	**lammasteks**
as	**kapina**	**kaPPidena**	**laMbana**	**lammastena**
ceasing				
up to	**kapini**	**kaPPideni**	**laMbani**	**lammasteni**
with	**kapiga**	**kaPPidega**	**laMbaga**	**lammastega**
without	**kapita**	**kaPPideta**	**laMbata**	**lammasteta**

VERBS

	WEAKENING		STRENGTHENING	
	infinitivals	finite forms	infinitivals	finite forms
non-past		**õpin** **õpid** **õpib** **etc.**		**haKKan** **haKKad** **haKKab** **etc.**
past participle	**õPPinud**		**hakanud**	
conditional		**õpiksin** **õpiksid** **õpiks** **etc.**		**haKKaksin** **haKKaksid** **haKKaks** **etc.**
present stem	**õpi**		**haKKa**	
-da infintive	**õPPida**		**hakata**	
imperative		**õPPigem** **õPPige** **õPPigu**		**hakakem** **hakake** **hakaku**
-ma infinitive	**õPPima**		**haKKama**	
past		**õPPisin** **õPPisid** **õPPis** **etc.**		**haKKasin** **haKKasid** **haKKas** **etc.**

Vowel Alternations
In addition to the different types of gradation in either weakening or strengthening patterns, there are three minor vowel alternations that result from the complete loss of **b d g** and **s** through qualitative gradation. These are described below.

1) Vowel Shortening
When a long or extra-long vowel ends up in front of a single short vowel through loss of **b d g** or **s** because of gradation, the extra-long vowel will shorten in the weak grade:

strong		weak		
pOOd̦	nominative	**poE**	genitive	store

2) Vowel Lowering
When a single **i ü** or **u** ends up next to another single vowel through loss of **b d g** or **s** because of gradation, the sound will become **e ö** and **o** respectively.

nominative	genitive	
kadu	**kaO**	loss
pidu	**peO**	party
sugu	**sOO**	sex, gender
kude	**koE**	tissue

3) Automatic Mono-syllable Lengthening
This is a relatively minor feature. All words of one syllable are automatically extra-long. When **b d g** or **s** disappears resulting in a one-syllable word, the vowel at the end of the syllable will automatically become extra-long.

strong grade		weak grade		strong grade		
õde	nominative	**õE**	genitive	**õde**	partitive	sister

These three vowel alternations will not occur if the weak grade form contains a [j] or [w] not indicated by the spelling:

UUs	**uu[w]e**	new
hÏIs	**hii[j]e**	sacred grove.

In conjunction with gradation, these vowel alternations result in a large number of different possible patterns of forms, which makes the morphologic system seem more complicated than it really is.

SYLLABLES

Both historically and in terms of the modern standard language one of the most important features for determining which class any given nominal or verb in Estonian belongs to is the syllable. Thus, before actually looking at the Classes and Types in the next section it is useful to have an understanding of the syllable.

There are two aspects of the syllable that are significant. They are:

1) the **number of syllables** in the stem
2) the **type of syllables** in the stem

These two features will be outlined below:

NUMBER OF SYLLABLES IN THE STEMS

The inflected vocabulary (nouns, adjectives and verbs) of Estonian is divided into four large groups based on the number of syllables in the stem:

the **genitive** form for nominals (nouns and adjectives), and;
the **non-past** stem for verbs

NOMINAL GENITIVE STEM		VERBAL NON-PAST STEM	

1) **one-syllable stems** ending in an extra-long vowel or diphthong:

mAA	land	**kEE**	boil
peA	head	**kaE**	behold

2) **two-syllable stems**:

elu	life	**ela**	live
laulu	song	**laula**	sing
sohva	sofa	**pişsi**	pee

3) **three-syllable stems** (an extra-long syllable will count as two syllables):

raamatu	book	**kirjuta**	write
aaSta	year	**juLge**	dare
laMba	sheep	**haKKa**	start

4) **four-syllable stems**

telefoni	telephone	**esitele**	introduce

To determine the number of syllables in a stem, the following three principles must be followed:

1) **Principle I**:
   Counting syllables starts from the end of the word.

2) **Principle II:**
   Going from the right (end) to the left, count all syllables until the first syllable containing either a long or extra-long sound. This is usually indicated in the spelling with a double letter. It will also be a stressed syllable.

The second principle is particularly important for long foreign words. For example:

elektroentsefalogrammi electroencephalogram (gen)

To determine what group of nouns this word will behave like, syllable counting starts from the end. The first syllable with a long or extra-long sound is the second one from the end. Thus everything in front of **-grammi** is ignored. Only these two syllables are counted and this long word behaves like all normal two-syllable nouns of the same syllable structure.

3) **Principle III:**
   A syllable containing an extra-long sound will count as two syllables only if it is in the last or next to last syllable of a stem. Syllables with extra-long sounds further away from the end count only as one syllable.

For example, the genitive of **raSke** (difficult) is **raSke** with an extra-long sound in the next to last syllable of the genitive. This syllable has to count as two. The partitive plural is **raSkeid**. The plural partitive ending **-id** is only possible with three-syllable nominals.

The genitive of **eKsam** (exam) is **eKsami** and the partitive plural is **eKsameid**. The syllable containing the extra-long sound does not precede the final genitive vowel. Thus the genitive **eKsami** must count for three syllables like **raSke** and not four. This is important particularly for nominals (see also pages 14 and 15).

NOMINAL SUFFIXES AND SYLLABLE COUNTING

An unusual feature of counting syllables occurs in connection with certain derivational suffixes. These are suffixes that can change the part of speech of a word, for example, **õNN** (luck, fortune) > **õnnelik** (fortunate).

These suffixes are divided into two groups:

1) **syllable count-sensitive suffixes:**
   these are suffixes which require all of the syllables of the stem to be counted.

For example, when **-ik** (one of the more productive suffixes) is added to a stem ALL of the syllables of the resultant word must be counted. When **-ik** is added to a stem resulting in an odd number of syllables then the partitive plural ends in **-id**:

vih	+ **ik** =	**vihik**	**vihiku**	(genitive - three syllables)	notebook
			vihikuid	(partitive plural - id)	

When **-ik** is added to a stem resulting in an even number of syllables then the partitive plural ends in a vowel:

enam	+ **ik** =	**enamiK**	**enamiku**	(genitive - four syllables)	majority
			enamiKKe	(partitive plural - vowel change)	

2) **syllable count-insensitive suffixes:**
these suffixes, in contrast, ignore the number of syllables in the stem. Only the number of syllables of the suffix itself are counted.

For example **-ja** (person -er form) has an odd number of syllables, so the plural partitive allows only **-id** regardless of the number of syllables of the word it is attached to:

luge	+ **ja** =	**lugeja**	**lugeja**	(genitive - three syllables)	reader
			lugejaid	(partitive plural)	
kirjuta	+ **ja** =	**kirjutaja**	**kirjutaja**	(genitive - four syllables)	writer
			kirjutajaid	(partitive plural)	

The following is a partial list of the two types of suffixes:

syllable count sensitive (all syllables counted)		syllable count insensitive (only syllables of suffix counted)	
-ik	**-ne**	**-ja**	**-lane -line -mine**
-elm	**-us**	**-v**	**-vus** etc.
		compound suffixes with -ne and -us are all syllable count insensitive	

TYPE OF SYLLABLES IN THE STEMS

The four major groups can be further divided into various classes based on the types of syllables that the word consists of. In Estonian there are two types of syllables:

1) **Light syllables** are those that end in one short vowel as illustrated with these nonsense syllables:

a pi tu trä be bli etc.

2) **heavy syllables** are all other syllable structures, i.e. those that end in more than one vowel or in a consonant as ilustrated with these nonsense syllables.

lat plae lõP EE roost kraap kii etc.

A misleading aspect of the spelling of long **p t** and **k** should be kept in mind here at all times. These long sounds are always spelt with only one letter instead of two, for example:

kapi cupboard **küte** heating **lõke** bonfire

At first glance it appears that the first syllable of each of these words is light. In reality the consonants in the middle of the words are long and a syllable boundary actually splits the long **p t** and **k** so that part of the consonant sound belongs to the preceding syllable and part of it belongs to the next one. The correct syllable structure for these words is actually:

[kap ⁝ pi] [küt ⁝ te] [lõk ⁝ ke]

⁝ indicates the syllable break

Thus the first syllable of such words is heavy and not light as the spelling makes it appear.

On the basis of these two features (that is, the number and type of syllables in the stem), all Estonian nouns, adjectives and verbs are divided into eight distinct classes. Each class is further subdivided into a variety of types and patterns. The classes and types are described in detail in the next section. All of the patterns are listed in detail in Part II.

CLASSES AND TYPES

The nominals and verbs in Estonian share many features in terms of **Classes** and **Types**. Therefore, both may be treated together as forming one inflectional system. In this last section of Part I this large system will be described. Wherever possible the correspondences between nominals and verbs and their classes and types will be pointed out.

Based on the number and type of syllables that a word consists of, Estonian nominals and verbs can be divided into eight basic paradigm **Classes**. Each Class in turn may have a number of **Types**. In this section a description of the characteristc elements of each class and type is given. This includes specific details about such features as the forms of the nominative, genitive and partitive cases and the primary verbal forms.

Altogether there are 42 types for nominals and 26 types for verbs. All of the classes and types are set out in chart form. These are inserted in the pocket at the back of the book. The charts have also been set up so that they will reflect the various correspondences between the types and classes as well as the correspondences between the nominals and verbs as much as possible.

The nominal and verb charts list the main forms in vertical columns in the following way:

NOMINALS				VERBS		
singular nominative	**raamat**	book		into case -ma	**õPPima**	study
genitive	**raamatu**			non-past stem	**õpi**	
partitive	**raamatut**			partitive -da	**õPPida**	
alternate into case if allowed	**-sse** *			past (1st pers)	**õPPisin**	
				past (3rd pers)	**õPPis**	
plural genitive	**raamatute**			-nud form	**õPPinud**	
partitive	**raamatuid**			non-past impersonal	**õpitakse**	
				-tud form	**õpitud**	

(* -sse indicates that only a long form is allowed)

PATTERNS

In the following section, all of the major types, arranged according to their class, are described. Most types may additionally exhibit a number of different patterns. These result from the different stem vowels that a word may exhibit or from the fact that a given word may exhibit one or more alternative forms. Irregularities in the spelling conventions will also result in different patterns. All of these patterns are listed separately in the index of part II and will not be discussed in detail in this section.

CLASS I

This small class consists of one-syllable words ending in an extra-long vowel or diphthong. Class I nominals have only one type. Verbs have two types.

Regular Types

NOMINALS

mAA land **kUU** month
peA head **sUU** mouth

1) nominative: ends in long vowel
2) genitive: identical to nominative
3) partitive: **-d** added to genitive

nominative	genitive	partitive
sUU	**sUU**	**sUUd**

4) short into case: possible for some in this type. Irregularly formed with **-h-** ; **suhu**
5) partitive plural: may be **-id**, or **-sid**. Some words allow both

VERBS

kEEma boil **vİİma** take
mÜÜma sell **käİma** attend

1) into case: ends in long vowel
2) non-past: identical to into case
3) partitive: often irregular

into case	stem	partitive
käİma	**käİ**	**käİa**

4) past tense: regular with **-s**

mina käİsin I attended
tema kaİs he/she attended

5) impersonal forms: usually irregular

-i past tense Type

jÄÄma remain **jOOma** drink
sÖÖma eat **sAAma** receive

1) partitive: usually irregular
2) irregular **-i** past tense forms

jõİn I drank
jõİ he/she drank

3) impersonal forms: usually irregular

Anomalous Type

aU (honour) and **nõU** (dish; advice) look like they belong to Class I. They actually behave like Class II nouns. There are no verbs of this type.

1) nominative, genitive and partitive forms are identical.

nominative	genitive	partitive
aU	**aU**	**aU**

CLASS II A

This class consists of two-syllable words both of whose syllables are light. They fall into two basic types, regular and consonant-stem partitives. In addition to the two regular types, verbs also have two irregular types.

Regular Vowel Partitive Types

NOMINALS

elu	life	**kivi**	stone
kala	fish	**maja**	house

1) nominative, genitive and partitive: always identical.

nominative	genitive	partitive
maja	**maja**	**maja**

2) short into case: possible for many middle consonant doubled: **maJJa**
3) partitive plural: **-sid** .
   Stems with **-a** have two variants **-sid** and vowel change.

A few words ending in **-i** in the nominative exhibit **-e** in the other forms: **nimi** name

nominative	genitive	partitive
nimi	**nime**	**nime**

VERBS

elama	live	**asuma**	settle
magama	sleep	**sobima**	suit

1) into case, non-past and partitive stems: always identical.

into case	stem	partitive
elama	**ela**	**elada**

2) all other forms: always regular
   There is only one stem to which all regular verbal endings are added.

Irregular Type

represented by one verb which has an irregular impersonal stem: **ajama** to drive

aeTakse someone drives

Consonant Partitive Type

meri sea **tuli** fire

1) nominative: **-i**
2) other forms: **-e**
3) partitive: stem vowel dropped
   -d (or **-t**) added to stem consonant

nominative	genitive	partitive
meri	**mere**	**meRd**

4) short into case: regular, middle consonant doubled: **meRRe**

Note that Class II nominatives never end in **-e**. For nominative ending in **-e** see Class IV, V and VII.

tulema come **panema** put

1) partitive: stem consonant doubled and **-a** added

into case	stem	partitive
tulema	**tule**	**tuLLa**

2) past tense forms: with **-i**

tulin I came
tuli he/she came

Irregular Type

Two verbs: **olema** to be
minema to go

CLASS II B

The words belonging to this class behave in all respects like words of Class II A except that they additionally exhibit weakening qualitative gradation. Only certain words with intervocalic **b d** or **g** fall into this class. In the descriptions below only one example of each major types will be given. The genitive and non-past stems and any forms derived from these are in the weak grade. All Class II B types correspond to Class II A types.

Regular Vowel Partitive Types

NOMINALS

nominative	genitive	partitive	
sõda	**sõja**	**sõda**	war

A few **-i** nominatives with **-e** elsewhere

nominative	genitive	partitive	
tõbi	**tõve**	**tõbe**	disease

VERBS

into case	stem	partitive	
lugema	**loE**	**lugeda**	read

One verb has an **-i** past tense form:

into case	stem	partitive	
pidama	**peA**	**pidada**	must

Consonant Partitive Types

nominative	genitive	partitive	
käsi	**käE**	**käTT**	hand

into case	stem	partitive	
nägema	**näE**	**näha**	see

CLASS III A

Usually one-syllable words ending in a consonant (one heavy syllable) belong to this class. All Class III words, both nominals and verbs, are characterized by the presence of weakening quantitative gradation. There are a number of types in this class.

Irregular Type (stem vowel appears in all forms)

This is an irregular type that is exhibited only by verbs. It is irregular in that the stem vowel is present in all forms. Class III words usually lose the vowel in some forms.

NOMINALS

VERBS

õPPima study **iStuma** sit
tantsima dance **marSSima** march

1) into case and partitive stems: stem vowel, **-i** or **-u** (rarely **-e**), present
2) non-past: extra-long sound shortened

into case	stem	partitive
õPPima	**õpi**	**õPPida**

3) past tense: regular **-s**
4) Impersonal: formed on non-past stem

Regular Type (stem vowel not present in all forms)

NOMINALS

saUn	sauna	**liLL**	flower
meTs	forest	**kaPP**	cupboard

1) nominative: extra-long sound and no stem vowel.
2) genitive: extra-long sound shortened and stem vowel added
3) partitive: extra-long sound and stem vowel both present

nominative	genitive	partitive
meTs	**metsa**	**meTsa**
kaPP	**kapi**	**kaPPi**

4) short into case: always identical to partitive
5) partitive plural: vowel change preferred. **-sid** also allowed

-J Stems

This type consists of anomalous nominatives ending in **-i**. In the nominative, the stem consonant **-j** has turned into **-i** making it look like a Class II nominative. In all other respects these stems behave like Class III nominals. The extra-long sound is not present in the nominative.

kiri	letter	**ahi**	stove
asi	thing	**kuri**	angry

1) nominative: irregular with **-i**

nominative	genitive	partitive
kiri	**kirja**	**kiRja**
ahi	**ahju**	**aHju**

2) all other forms: like regular Class III nominals

VERBS

laUlma	sing	**maiTsma**	taste
seİsma	stand	**kUUlma**	hear

1) into case and partitive stems: identical and both have extra-long sound
2) non-past stem: shortens extra-long sound and adds stem vowel **-a** (rarely **-e**)

into case	stem	partitive
laUlma	**laula**	**laUlda**

3) past tense: regular **-s**
4) impersonal forms: regular

Class III verbs have no stems corresponding to the **-J** and **-R** **-L** stems of Class III nominals.

-T Stems

Most verbs whose into case and partitive stems end in **-t** (and sometimes **-p**) have irregularly formed impersonal forms. These verbs all have the stem vowel **-a**.

nuTma	cry	**oStma**	buy
sõiTma	ride	**taPma**	kill

1) all personal forms: regular

into case	stem	partitive
nuTma	**nuta**	**nuTTa**

2) Impersonal forms: non-past stem vowel **-a** changed to **-e** and impersonal endings added to this form

nutetakse someone cries

NOMINALS

-R and -L Stems

These are stems with **-r** (there are a few **-l** stems as well in this type) which also exhibit an irregular nominative. The **-r** and **-l** have turned into **-er** and **-el** respectively making these nominatives look like some Class VI nominatives. The extra-long sound is not present in the nominative.

1) nominative: irregular with **-er** or **-el**

sõber	friend	**vigel**	hoe
põder	elk	**teder**	grouse

nominative	genitive	partitive
sõber	**sõbra**	**sõPra**
vigel	**vigla**	**viKla**

2) all other forms: like regular Class III nominals

VERBS

Irregular Stems

A couple of verbs with **-t** such as **jäTma** (to leave something behind) have completely irregular impersonal forms:

into case	stem	partitive
jäTma	**jäta**	**jäTTa**

Impersonal forms:

jäeTakse someone leaves something behind

Consonant Stem Partitive Type

These nominals correspond to Class II Consonant partitive stems.

kEEl tongue **nOOr** young

1) nominative: regular
2) genitive: regular, stem vowel **-e**

nominative	genitive	partitive
kEEl	**keele**	**keelT**

3) partitive: stem vowel dropped and **-t** added to stem consonant
4) short into case: like genitive with extra-length: **kEEle** or with ending **-de** added to nominative: **kEElde**

Irregular Consonant Partitive Types

NOMINALS

A couple of nominals have irregular genitive and/or partitive forms.

nominative	genitive	partitive	
laPs	**lapse**	**laST**	child
uKs	**ukse**	**uSt**	door

1) partitive: irregular, ends in **-t**
2) short into case: not possible

VERBS

Only a couple of verbs such as **jooKsma** (run) correspond to these stems. In most respects they behave like regular Class III verbs except for the partitive form:

into case	stem	partitive
jooKsma	**jookse**	**jooSta**

CLASS III B

The words belonging to this class behave in all respects like words of Class III A but they additionally exhibit weakening double gradation. Only major types will be listed and no details will be given. Like Class II B, only certain words with **b d** or **g** fall into this class. Not all Class III A types have corresponding Class III B types.

Stem Vowel Appears in all Forms

NOMINALS

VERBS

into case	stem	partitive	
uSkuma	**usu**	**uSkuda**	believe

Regular Vowel Partitive Types (stem vowel not always present)

nominative	genitive	partitive	
leİb	**leiva**	**leİba**	bread

-D Stems

into case	stem	partitive	
aNdma	**anna**	**aNda**	give

-T Stems

into case	stem	partitive	
taHtma	**taha**	**taHta**	want

Consonant Partitive Types

nominative	genitive	partitive	
UUs	**uu[w]e**	**uuT**	new

Irregular Consonant Partitive

nominative	genitive	partitive	
mEEs	**mehe**	**meeSt**	man

into case	stem	partitive	
laSkma	**lase**	**laSta**	shoot

CLASS IV

Two-syllable words with a heavy first syllable and a light second syllable belong here. Words of this class do not exhibit gradation:

NOMINALS

sohva sofa **kiisu** kitty-cat
lilla purple **auto** car

1) nominative and genitive: identical
2) partitive: **-t** added to genitive

nominative	genitive	partitive
auto	**auto**	**autot**

3) short into case: not possible
4) plural genitive: **-de**
5) partitive plural: always only **-sid.**

-E Stem

The nominative ends in **-e.** It resembles Class II nominals (two light syllables).

pere family **kere** body

1) nominative, genitive and partitive singular and plural like above:

nominative	genitive	partitive
pere	**pere**	**peret**

2) short into case: usually not possible

Irregular (-U Stem) Type

1) one irregular word only: **õlu** beer

	nominative	genitive	partitive
singular	**õlu**	**õlle**	**õlut**
plural	**õlled**	**õLLede**	**õLLesid**

VERBS

pişsima pee
only a couple of verbs in this class. In this index only this one verb.

1) into case, non-past and partitive stems: identical.

into case	stem	partitive
pişsima	**pişsi**	**pişsida**

2) regular in all respects

CLASS V

The words in this class are the remnants of a small class that at one time consisted of two-syllable words whose first syllable was light and second syllable was heavy. Today it consists of the irregular words **paras** (suitable) and **süda** (heart) as well as a handful of two-syllable words ending in **-e** both of whose syllables are light such as **habe** (beard). The stem consists of three syllables.

Similarly there is only a handful of verbs remaining in this class. They are characterized by stems with **-ele-**. The first syllable will be light (compare Class VI and VIII)

NOMINALS

habe	beard	**ese**	object
side	bandage	**tase**	level

1) genitive: **-me** added to nominative
2) partitive: **-t** added to nominative

nominative	genitive	partitive
habe	**habeme**	**habet**

3) short into case: not possible
4) genitive plural: irregular, **-te** added to genitive singular.
5) partitive plural: regular, **-id** added to genitive singular.

VERBS

kõnelema speak
only a handful of verbs in this class.

1) into case and non-past: identical
2) partitive: **-e** dropped after **-l** and **-da** added

into case	stem	partitive
kõnelema	**kõnele**	**kõnelda**

3) all other forms: regular

Note that Class IV **-E** stems (**pere**) and **-U** stems (**õlu**) were originally Class V words and historically correspond to Class VI **-E** (**-e** genitive) and **-U** stems respectively.

In Class V, **paras** corresponds to the **-S** stems of Class VI while **süda** and **habe** type words correspond to **-E** (**-m** or **-n** genitive) stems of Class VI. The verbs of class V correspond to Class VI **-L** and **-R** stems.

CLASS VI A

This class consists of two-syllable words. Once both syllables were heavy. Today, this class consists of a number of types according to the final sound of the second syllable. Both nominals and verbs of all Class VI types are characterized by the presence of strengthening quantitative gradation. The following stem types are found:

The first syllable will always be heavy and the second syllable can end with:

STEM ENDING	NOMINALS		VERBS	
-S	**kapsas**	cabbage	not found	
-R **-L** or **-N**	**tütar**	daughter	**sUUdlema**	kiss
-E (**-e** in genitive)	**lause**	sentence	not found	
-E (**-m** or **-n** in genitive)	**iste**	seat	not found	
-U (for nominals)	**jäänu**	survivor	not found	
-A (for verbs)	not found		**haKKama**	start to do

in an earlier stage of the language there were more verb types in this Class

Stems ending in -S

NOMINALS

kapsas cabbage **põõsas** bush
saabas boot **ratas** wheel

1) nominative: has final **-s**
2) genitive: **-s** droppped and first syllable lengthened (three syllables)
3) partitive: **-t** added to nominative

nominative	genitive	partitive
kapsas	**kaPsa**	**kapsast**

4) short into case: never possible
5) plural genitive: regular
6) partitive plural: regular, always only **-id** added to genitive.

VERBS

no **-S** stem verbs found in modern Estonian

Stems ending in -R -L or -N (-re or -le for verbs)

NOMINALS

tütar daughter **küünal** candle
peenar flowerbed **aken** window

1) nominative: has final **-r** **-l** or **-n** (**aken** window is the only **-n** stem)
2) genitive: vowel before consonant dropped first syllable lengthened and vowel, usually **-e** , added.
3) partitive: **-t** added to nominative

nominative	genitive	partitive
tütar	**tüTre**	**tütart**

4) short into case: never possible
5) plural genitive: irregularly **-de** added to nominative.
6) partitive plural: regular always only **-id** added to genitive.

VERBS

sUUdlema kiss **võiTlema** battle
mAAdlema wrestle **suPlema** bathe

1) into case and non-past stems: identical. Both have extra-long sound in first syllable.
2) partitive: **-le** becomes **-el** in front of **-da**. Extra-length disappears

into case	stem	partitive
sUUdlema	**sUUdle**	**suudelda**

3) all other forms: regular

Stems ending in -E (genitive retains -e)

NOMINALS

lause	sentence	**arve**	bill
saade	broadcast	**lõke**	bonfire

1) nominative: always ends in **-e**
2) genitive: first syllable lengthened.
3) partitive: **-t** added to nominative

nominative	genitive	partitive
lause	**laUse**	**lauset**

4) short into case: never possible
5) plural genitive: regular
6) partitive plural: regular always only **-id** added to genitive

VERBS

no **-E** stem verbs found in modern Estonian

Stems ending in -E (genitive inserts -m or -n)

köide	binding	**iste**	seat
liige	member	**kaste**	sauce

1) nominative: ends in **-e** (like the previous type in the nominative)
2) genitive: final nominative **-e** dropped, nasal consonant plus **-e** added to end and length added to first syllable
3) partitive: **-t** added to nominative

nominative	genitive	partitive
iste	**iStme**	**istet**

4) short into case: never possible
5) plural genitive: irregularly **-te** added to genitive singular.
6) partitive plural: regular always only **-id**.

no **-E (genitive -m -n)** stem verbs found in modern Estonian

Nominal stems ending in -U

saanu receiver **jäänu** survivor

A small type consisting of modified -nud forms. They behave like **-e** stem types (see above).

1) nominative: always ends in **-u**.
2) genitive: first syllable lengthened
3) partitive: **-t** added to nominative

nominative	genitive	partitive
saanu	**sAAnu**	**saanut**

4) short into case: never possible
5) plural genitive: regular
6) partitive plural: regular always only **-id**.

Verbal stems ending in -A

haKKama start **aRvama** suppose
aiTama help **lõiKama** cut

This is the most common type of Class VI verb.

1) into case stem: always vowel **-a**.
2) non-past stem: identical to nominative. Both have extra-long sound in first syllable.
3) Extra-length disappears in partitive. Partitive ending **-ta**

into case	stem	partitive
haKKama	**haKKa**	**hakata**

4) all other forms: regular.

CLASS VI B

As with Class II B and III B, the words belonging to this class behave in all respects like words of Class VI A except that they additionally exhibit weakening double gradation. All Class VI A types have corresponding Class VI B types with the exception of the nominal **-U** stems. Since in all other respects these words behave like Class VI A no details will be given. Only major types will be listed.

Stems Ending in -S

NOMINALS

nominative	genitive	partitive	
hamma	**haMba**	**hammast**	tooth

VERBS

no **-S** stem verbs found in modern Estonian

Stems Ending in -R -L or N (-re or -le for verbs)

nominative	genitive	partitive	
pöi[j]al	**pöİdla**	**pöi[j]alt**	thumb

into case	stem	partitive	
õMblema	**õMble**	**õmmelda**	sew

Stems Ending in -E (genitive retains -e)

nominative	genitive	partitive	
rii[j]e	**rİİde**	**rii[j]et**	cloth

no -E stems verbs found in modern Estonian

Stems Ending in -E (genitive -m or -n)

nominative	genitive	partitive	
ranne	**raNdme**	**rannet**	wrist

no -E stems verbs found in modern Estonian

Nominals stems ending in -U

no Class VIB -U stem nominals found in modern Estonian

Verbal stems ending in -A

into case	stem	partitive	
puHkama	**puHka**	**puhata**	rest

CLASS VII

Three-syllable words that end in a vowel belong to this class. However, since the nominative of most Class VII types have lost their stem vowels (and sometimes some of the stem consonants) it is better to look at the genitive form to determine which words fall into this Class. A syllable containing an extra-long sound preceding the final vowel of the word counts as two syllables. This Class has a number of Types:

Regular Type (stem vowel present in all forms)

NOMINALS

inetu ugly **arvuti** computer
aaSta year **raSke** difficult

1) nominative: ends in vowel
2) genitive: identical to nominative
3) partitive: **-t** added to genitive

nominative	genitive	partitive
inetu	**inetu**	**inetut**
aaSta	**aaSta**	**aaStat**

4) short into case: is never possible
5) genitive plural: regular
6) partitive plural: regular with **-id**

VERBS

kirjutama write **olenema** depend on
juLgema dare **uInuma** fall asleep

1) all stems are identical and in all respects these verbs are regular

into case	stem	partitive
kirjutama	**kirjuta**	**kirjutada**
juLgema	**juLge**	**juLgeda**

Consonant Nominative Type

raamat book **orav** squirrel
vihik notebook **pliiats** pencil

1) stem vowel missing from nominative.
2) genitive: stem vowel added
3) partitive: **-t** added to genitive

nominative	genitive	partitive
raamat	**raamatu**	**raamatut**

4) all other forms: regular

Mixed Type -(E)LE Verbs

This type consists of a set of verbs all of which contain a stem final **-le**.

into case	stem	partitive
esitlema	**esitle**	**esitleda**

1) past tense: regularly formed with **-s**

mina esitlesin I introduced
tema esitles he/she introduced

These verbs can behave according to regular Class VII verbs or to Class VIII. (see below).

NOMINALS

-DA Stems

hõbe	silver	**kare**	rough
libe	slippery	**kade**	jealous

1) nominative: resembles either Class II or certain Class IV and V **-e** stems.
2) genitive: **-da** added to nominative
3) partitive: **-t** added to genitive

nominative	genitive	partitive
hõbe	**hobeda**	**hõbedat**

4) all other forms: regular

-NDA Stems

These words are all ordinal numbers

viies	fifth	**kuues**	sixth
kolmas	third	**kaheksas**	eighth

1) nominative: ends in **-s**.
2) genitive: **-s** removed, **-nda** added
3) partitive: **-t** added to genitive

nominative	genitive	partitive
viies	**viienda**	**viiendat**

4) all other forms: regular

Truncated Stem

kiNdel	sure	**suHkur**	sugar
rüüTel	knight	**nuKKer**	sad

1) nominative: ends in vowel plus consonant - stem always has extra length.
2) genitive: vowel in front of consonant dropped and another added to end
3) partitive: **-t** added to genitive

nominative	genitive	partitive
kiNdel	**kiNdla**	**kiNdlat**

4) all other forms: regular

-AS Types

kuningas king **maasikas** strawberry
angerjas eel **innukas** eager

1) nominative: always ends in **-as**
2) genitive stem: **-s** dropped
3) partitive: **-t** added to genitive

nominative	genitive	partitive
kuningas	**kuninga**	**kuningat**

4) all other forms: regular

CLASS VIII

The nominals of this class consist of three syllable nominals ending in a consonant. All of them are foreign loan-words. Verbs have one type characterized by **-ele**.

NOMINALS

restoran restaurant **pensionär** pensioner
admiral admiral **telefon** telephone

1) nominative: three syllables, ending in a consonant
2) genitive and partitive: identical.

nominative	genitive	partitive
restoran	**restorani**	**restorani**

3) short into case: possible for many identical to genitive and partitive
4) genitive plural: regular
5) partitive plural: vowel change (or **-sid** also allowed)

VERBS

Mixed Type -ELE Verbs

All Class VIII verbs can also be conjugated like Class VII (see above). Class VIII forms tend to be restricted to the literary language. In the spoken language these verbs appear most usually as Class VI verbs.

1) an extra vowel (-e) added to stem.
2) partitive: irregular

into case	stem	partitive
esitelema	**esitele**	**esiteLLa**

3) past tense: formed with **-i**

mina esitelin I introduced
tema esiteli he/she introduced

4) impersonal forms: regular

-NE and -US Nominals

A large group of nominals deserves special attention. These are all nominals with the derivative suffixes **-NE** and **-US**. Except for the nominative, both types generally behave in the same way. Depending on the number of syllables in the genitive singular, these words belong either to Class VII or Class VIII

CLASS VII -NE and -US Nominals (odd number of syllables)

The gentive singluar of Class VII words consists of an odd number of syllables and thus the partitive plural adds **-id** directly to the genitive stem.

-NE

sinine	blue	**hobune**	horse
higine	sweaty	**rebane**	fox

1) nominative: marked with **-ne**
2) genitive: **-ne** replaced with **-se**
3) partitive: stem vowel dropped and **-t** added to the consonant.

nominative	genitive	partitive
sinine	**sinise**	**sinist**

4) short into case: not possible
5) genitive plural: regular
6) partitive plural: **-id** added to genitive

-US

alus	foundation	**katus**	roof
madrus	sailor	**sügis**	autumn

1) nominative: marked with **-us** (sometimes **-es** or **-is**)
2) genitive: **-e** added to nominative
3) partitive: stem vowel dropped and **-t** added to the consonant.

nominative	genitive	partitive
katus	**katuse**	**katust**

4) short into case: not possible
5) genitive plural: regular
6) partitive plural: **-id** added to genitive

Alternate Types of Class VII -NE and -US Words

With a few words **-ne** (and **-se**) are added to a consonant, rather than a vowel as is usual. Similarly, with some **-us** words, the **-u-** is dropped in the genitive resulting in genitive forms where **-se** follows a consonant. To ease pronunciation the partitive **-t** will be added to the genitive without dropping the stem vowel. All of these words contain an extra-long sound in the syllable preceding the suffix.

raUdne	iron (adj)	**piKne**	lightning
UUdne	novel (adj)	**eHtne**	genuine

1) nominative: marked with **-ne**
2) genitive: **-ne** replaced with **-se**
3) partitive: **-t** added to genitive

nominative	genitive	partitive
raUdne	**raUdse**	**raUdset**

4) short into case: not possible
5) genitive plural: regular
6) partitive plural: **-id** added to genitive

hiRmus	horrible	**rÕÕmus**	joyful
täHtis	important	**kUUlus**	famous

1) nominative: marked with **-us** or **-is**
2) genitive: irregularly **-a**
3) partitive: **-t** added to genitive

nominative	genitive	partitive
rÕÕmus	**rÕÕmsa**	**rÕÕmsat**

4) short into case: not possible
5) genitive plural: regular
6) partitive plural: **-id** added to genitive

A handful of **-us** words exhibit a unique alternation between **-s** and **-ks**. **-ks** will appear in those forms based on the genitive singular and **-s** will be in the other forms. These few words all have an odd number of syllables:

-NE

not found for -ne words

-US (-ks genitive)

omas kith and kin **jUUs** hair

1) nominative: marked with **-us**
2) genitive: **-s** replaced with **-kse**
3) partitive: **-t** added to the nominative

nominative	genitive	partitive
omas	**omakse**	**omast**

4) short into case: not possible
5) genitive plural: regular
6) partitive plural: **-id** added to genitive

CLASS VIII -NE and -US Nominals (even number of syllables)

In all respects these words behave like regular Class VII -NE and -US words except for the partitive plural. The genitive singular of Class VIII words consists of an even number of syllables and thus the partive plural is formed by changing the stem vowel **-e** to **-i**. These words also allow a short into form.

igavene eternal **salajane** secret
roheline green **esimene** first

1) nominative: marked with **-ne**
2) genitive: **-ne** replaced with **-se**
3) partitive: genitive stem vowel dropped **-t** added to the consonant.

nominative	genitive	partitive
roheline	**rohelise**	**rohelist**

4) short into case: double stem **-s-** e.g. **rohelisse**
5) genitive plural: regular
6) partitive plural: change stem vowel to **-i**. e.g. **rohelisi**

armastus love **kingitus** gift
mugavus comfort **üritus** event

1) nominative: marked with **-us** (never **-es** or **-is**)
2) genitive: **-e** added to nominative
3) partitive: stem vowel dropped and **-t** added to the consonant.

nominative	genitive	partitive
armastus	**armastuse**	**armastust**

4) short into case: double stem **-s-** e.g. **armastusse**
5) genitive plural: regular
6) partitive plural: change stem vowel to **-i**. e.g. **armastusi**

PART II

INDEX OF CLASSES, TYPES AND PATTERNS

INTRODUCTION

Part II of the Handbook of Estonian Nouns Adjectives and Verbs is an index of forms containing information on approximately 10,000 Estonian (non-compound) words. They have been arranged according to their paradigmatic Classes and Types.

Each Type in turn can consist of a number of different patterns of forms. The various patterns behave like the major types in all essential ways. They are set apart by the minor differences that they exhibit. There are a variety of reasons for this; the stem vowels of the patterns may be different, one or another variant form may be missing or the vagaries of the spelling conventions may be the cause of the differences.

Each pattern constitutes one main entry in the index. For each pattern all the important forms of a typical word are listed.

For **nominals** (nouns and adjectives):

1) The six primary case forms are listed. These are the nominative, genitive and partitive in both the singular and plural.
2) The alternate short INTO case form if it is allowed. If no form is found under the INTO case form then it is assumed that only the regular **-sse** INTO case form is allowed for the words that fall into this pattern. This form is normally found only in the singular.
3) The singular and plural stems are also listed. The secondary case suffixes are attached to these stems. They are not listed in the entry.
3) The alternate **-i** plural stem if it is allowed.

A typical nominal entry is set out in the following way:

14A maja ***house*** **maja 14A**

	nominative	genitive	partitive	into case	stems
singular	**maja**	**maja**	**maja**	**maJJa**	**maja-**
plural	**majad**	**majade**	**maju** majasid		**majade-** (maju-)

Also like maja: kava *programme*

The SHORT INTO CASE is not commonly used with the following items:

ala *area*	kõva ^ *hard*	paha ^ *bad*	sõna *word*
kala *fish*	lava *stage*	pala *morsel*	vana ^ *old*
kana *hen*	lina *linen*	sama ^ *same*	

Below each main entry, all of the words that behave in the same pattern are listed with a simple English gloss. The short INTO case of many words are not commonly used although they are theoretically possible. For those patterns allowing a short INTO case form, the words are divided into two groups according to whether they are commonly used or not. This division is not hard and fast. Usage may vary from speaker to speaker in this respect.

Unless otherwise marked, all entries in the nominal section should be considered as nouns. For adjectives a small superscript ^{A} is placed after the Estonian word.

For the **verbs**

1) The **-ma** into case infinitive (the dictionary form).
2) The non-past stem (also the second person singular imperative).
3) The **-da** infinitive (partitive of the infinitive).
4) The first and third person singular non-past forms. All non-past forms are based on the first person form.
5) The first and third person singular past forms. Except for the third person all other past tense forms are based on the first person past form. Because the third singular form sometimes differs slightly from the other non-past forms it has been listed separately.
6) The stem as well as the non-past and past tense forms of the impersonal.
7) All four participles (verbal adjectives).
8) Two imperative forms; the second person plural imperative and the seldom used impersonal imperative are listed.

A typical entry for a verb is set out in the following way:

284 lugema ^{t} ***read; count*** **lugema 284**

	into case	stem	partitive	1 person	3 person	participles	imperative
personal	**lugema**	**loE-**	**lugeda**	**loEn**	**loEb**	**lugev**	**lugege!**
past		**lugesi-**		**lugesin**	**luges**	**lugenud**	
impersonal		**loeTa-**		**loeTakse**		**loeTav**	**loeTagu!**
past				**loeTi**		**loeTud**	

Also like lugema: pugema ^{i} *suck up to; creep*

Again below each main entry, all of the words that behave in the same pattern are listed with a simple English gloss.

Most verbs in Estonian are either exclusively intransitive (they do not have an object) or transitive (they must have an object). Superscript ^{i} and ^{t} indicate intransitive and transitive verbs respectively. A handful of verbs are not marked with one or the other. In these instances the verb can be both transitive as well as intransitive.

For both nominals and verbs, **bold-faced** forms are the regularly used forms. Forms that are formally accepted but not generally used are in smaller non-bold-faced script. Forms that are theoretically possible but rarely or never used are enclosed in ( ) parentheses.

Each main entry in the index is prefaced by a number. This is the index number for that pattern. Every Estonian word listed in the glossaries of Parts III and IV has an index number which allows the student to locate the appropriate pattern in the index for any noun, adjective or verb quickly.

Many patterns are further divided into subsidiary patterns labelled **A B C** etc. The letter division is based on minor spelling differences and not on any actual differences.

13A aju *brain* **aju 13A**

	nominative	genitive	partitive	short into	stem
singular	**aju**	**aju**	**aju**	**aJJu**	**aju-**
plural	**ajud**	**ajude**	**ajusid**		**ajude-**

13B abi *help* **abi 13B**

	nominative	genitive	partitive	short into	stem
singular	**abi**	**abi**	**abi**	**aPPi**	**abi-**
plural	**abid**	**abide**	**abisid**		**abide-**

13C häda *trouble, problem, hardship* **häda 13C**

	nominative	genitive	partitive	short into	stem
singular	**häda**	**häda**	**häda**	**häTTa**	**häda-**
plural	**hädad**	**hädade**	**hädasid**		**hädade-**

13D segu *mixture* **segu 13D**

	nominative	genitive	partitive	short into	stem
singular	**segu**	**segu**	**segu**	**seKKu**	**segu-**
plural	**segud**	**segude**	**segusid**		**segude-**

For example all of the words indexed under pattern **13** behave in exactly the same way. For this pattern the short INTO case is formed by lengthening the middle consonant of the stem from short to extra-long. Because **b d** and **g** are treated differently from other letters, the spelling of this form can exhibit differences depending on what the middle letter of the stem is. The words falling into pattern 13 are therefore subdivided into smaller groups according to the middle consonant and how it appears in the short INTO case.

In order to conserve space not all words in the glossaries have been listed in the index under their appropriate pattern. For the most part international words have been omitted. All patterns however, are represented.

INTRODUCTION

Main headings in the index include a number (1 2 3 or 4). This refers to the number of syllables in the stems belonging to that class. Thus for example, the first heading on the next page indicates that the words in the ensuing section are all one-syllable nominals belonging to Class I:

NOMINALS - 1 - CLASS I

TYPE 1 - Regular

1 kraE *collar* kraE 1

	nominative	genitive	partitive	short into	stem
singular	**kraE**	**kraE**	**kraEd**		**kraE-**
plural	**kraEd**	**kraEde**	**kraEsid**		**kraEde-**

Also like kraE:
argOO *slang*
avarİİ *accident*
bürOO *office*
depOO *depot*
galerİİ *gallery*
garantİİ *guarantee*
halvAA *halvah*
intervjUU *interview*
kaE *cataract (eye)*
kaİ *quay*
kakaO *cocoa*
kantseleİ *office*
kanUU *canoe*
kanvAA *canvas*
kEE *necklace*
klİİd (pl) *bran*
koİ *berth; moth*
kompanİİ *company*
lEE *hearth*
levkoİ *gillyflower*
loterİİ *lottery*
maİ *May*
meiereİ *dairy*
menÜÜ *menu*
metrOO *subway*
miljÖÖ *milieu*
nivOO *level*
papagoİ *parrot*
partİİ *consignment; round*
patareİ *battery*
pEE *ass (buttocks)*
pİİ *tooth*
platOO *plateau*
plİİ *lead*
poİ *buoy*
politseİ *police*
prİİ ^A *free of charge*
rÜÜ *robe*
sÜÜ *blame*
žürİİ *jury*
taİ *lean meat*
tEE *tea*
trikOO *bathing suit*
trİo *trio*
täİ *louse*
võİ *butter*
väİ *son-in-law*

2 tEE *road* tEE 2

	nominative	genitive	partitive	short into	stem
singular	**tEE**	**tEE**	**tEEd**		**tEE-**
plural	**tEEd**	**tEEde**	**teİd** tEEsid		**tEEde-** (teİ-)

Also like tEE:
allEE *avenue*
armEE *army*
assamblEE *assembly*
ateljEE *studio*
bidEE *bidet*
dekoltEE *décolletage*
essEE *essay*
frotEE *terry cloth*
fuajEE *foyer*
idEE *idea*
kabarEE *cabaret*
klišEE *cliché*
kombinEE *camiknickers*
komitEE *committee*
kupEE *compartment (train)*
orhidEE *orchid*
palEE *palace*
portjEE *doorkeeper*
portrEE *portrait*
pürEE *purée*
relEE *relay*
resümEE *summary*
süžEE *subject matter*
želEE *jelly*
trofEE *trophy*
turnEE *tour*
varietEE variety show

3 kUU *moon; month* kUU 3

	nominative	genitive	partitive	short into	stem
singular	**kUU**	**kUU**	**kUUd**		**kUU-**
plural	**kUUd**	**kUUde** kuude	**kuİd** kUUsid		**kUUde** kuude- kuİ-

Also like kUU: vÖÖ *belt*

4 jÄÄ *ice* jÄÄ 4

	nominative	genitive	partitive	short into	stem
singular	**jÄÄ**	**jÄÄ**	**jÄÄd**	(jähe)	**jÄÄ-**
plural	**jÄÄd**	**jÄÄde**	**jäİd**		**jÄÄde**
		jääde	jÄÄsid		jääde-
					jäİ-

5 sOO *marsh* sOO 5

	nominative	genitive	partitive	short into	stem
singular	**sOO**	**sOO**	**sOOd**	(sohu)	**sOO-**
plural	**sOOd**	**sOOde**	**soİd**		**sOOde**
		soode	sOOsid		soode-
					soİ-

6 sUU *mouth* sUU 6

	nominative	genitive	partitive	short into	stem
singular	**sUU**	**sUU**	**sUUd**	**suhu**	**sUU-**
plural	**sUUd**	**sUUde**	**suİd**		**sUUde**
		suude	sUUsid		suude-
					suİ-

7 pUU *tree* pUU 7

	nominative	genitive	partitive	short into	stem
singular	**pUU**	**pUU**	**pUUd**		**pUU-**
plural	**pUUd**	**pUUde**	**puİd**		**pUUde**
		puude			puude-
					puİ-

Also like pUU: lUU *bone* mUU ^ *other* trUU ^ *faithful*

8 tÖÖ *work* tÖÖ 8

	nominative	genitive	partitive	short into	stem
singular	**tÖÖ**	**tÖÖ**	**tÖÖd**	(töhe)	**tÖÖ-**
plural	**tÖÖd**	**tÖÖde**	**töİd**		**tÖÖde**
		tööde			tööde-
					töİ-

Also like tÖÖ: ÖÖ *night*

9 mAA *land, earth, ground* mAA 9

	nominative	genitive	partitive	short into	stem
singular	**mAA**	**mAA**	**mAAd**	**maha**	**mAA-**
plural	**mAAd**	**mAAde**	**maİd**		**mAAde**
		maade			maade-
					maİ-

10 heA - hÄÄ [A] ***good*** **heA - hÄÄ 10**

	nominative	genitive	partitive	short into	stem
singular	**heA**	**heA**	**heAd**		**heA-**
	hÄÄ	hÄÄ	hÄÄd		hÄÄ-
plural	**heAd**	**heAde**	**häİd**		**heAde-**
	hÄÄd	hÄÄde			hÄÄde-
		hääde			hääde-
					häİ-

11 peA - pÄÄ ***head*** **peA - pÄÄ 11**

	nominative	genitive	partitive	short into	stem
singular	**peA**	**peA**	**peAd**	**pähe**	**peA-**
	pÄÄ	pÄÄ	pÄÄd		pÄÄ-
plural	**peAd**	**peAde**	**päİd**		**peAde-**
	pÄÄd	pÄÄde			pÄÄde-
		pääde			pääde-
					päİ-

ANOMALOUS CLASS

TYPE 2 - Anomalous

12 aU ***honour*** **aU 12**

	nominative	genitive	partitive	short into	stem
singular	**aU**	**aU**	**aU**		**aU-**
plural	**aUd**	**aUde**	**aUsid**		**aUde-**

Also like aU: nõU *vessel, dish*; *advice, councel*

NOMINALS - 2 - CLASS II A

TYPE 3 - Regular - Vowel Partitives

13A aju *brain* **aju 13A**

	nominative	genitive	partitive	short into	stem
singular	**aju**	**aju**	**aju**	**aJJu**	**aju-**
plural	**ajud**	**ajude**	**ajusid**		**ajude-**

Also like aju:
arutelu *discussion*
ava *opening*
elu *life*
haru *branch; department*
ihu *body*
kera *sphere*
keskustelu *conversation*
kino *cinema*
kõla *sound*
kõri *throat*
käru *wheel-barrow*
küla *village*
loeTelu *enumeration*
maru *tempest*
mõtiskelu *meditation*
mälu *memory*
nina *nose*
oja *brook*
pesu *wash*
pori *mud*
rivi *line; row*
savi *clay*
talu *farm*
taru *bee hive*
tuju *mood*
tüli *quarrel*
usutelu *interview*
vilu ^ *cool*
võru *hoop*
võsa *undergrowth*
õnnitelu *congratulations*

The SHORT INTO CASE is not commonly used with the following items:

aru *reason*
eha *sunset glow*
ema *mother*
heli *sound*
himu *desire*
iha *lust*
ila *saliva*
ilu *beauty*
isa *father*
isu *appetite*
iva *grain*
jahu *flour*
jama *nonsense*
janu *thirst*
kaja *echo*
kama *sour milk grain mix*
kari *reef*
karu *bear*
kasu *use*
kesa *fallow*
kilo *kilo*
kilu *sprat*
kisa *clamour*
koha *pike-perch*
koli *junk*
koma *comma*
koni *cigarette stub*
kuju *shape*
kulu *expense*
kuma *glow*
kõmu *sensation*
käli *sister-in-law(wife's sister)*
kära *uproar*
köha *cough*
küna *trough*
lelu *toy*
liha *meat*
lima *slime*
lisa *addition*
loru *lout*
lõvi *lion*
lüli *link*
melu *din*
menu *success*
muru *lawn*
musi *kiss*
muşu *kiss*
mõju *influence*
mõla *paddle*
mõnu *enjoyment*
mõra *flaw*
mõru ^ *bitter*
mära *mare*
möla *nonsense*
müra *fracas*
nari *plank-bed*
nisa *teat*
nisu *wheat*
nohu *cold*
noşu *mug (nose)*
näru *tatter*
nüri ^ *blunt*
olud (pl) *circumstances*
onu *uncle*
ora *spike*
paju *willow*
pilu *hem-stitch*
plära *gibberish*
poju *sonny*
poni *pony*
puna *redness*
puru *crumb*
raha *money*
rahu *peace; reef*
raja *frontier*
raju *tempest*
ravi *treatment (cure)*
reha *rake*
risu *litter*
roju *cur; scrag*
runo *runic song*
räni *silicon*
salu *grove*
semu *pal*
sisu *contents*
sula *thaw*
suli *crook*
sumu *mist*
sära *radiance*
taju *perception*
tala *girder*
tanu *cap (woman's)*
tara *fence*
tasu *payment*
tava *custom*
tila *spout*
tina *tin*
tola *dolt*
toru *tube, pipe*
tulu *profit*
tuvi *pigeon*
tõru *acorn*
tänu *thanks*
türa *cock (penis)*
vaha *wax*
valu *pain; metal die*
vara *wealth*
varu *supply*
viha *anger*
visa ^ *persistent*
võlu *charm*
võra *crown of tree*
võsu *shoot*
välu *glade*
õli *oil*
äri *shop; business*

13B abi *help* — abi 13B

	nominative	genitive	partitive	short into	stem
singular	**abi**	**abi**	**abi**	**aPPi**	**abi-**
plural	**abid**	**abide**	**abisid**		**abide-**

Also like abi: klubi *club* kubu *truss* naba *pole (geological)*

The SHORT INTO CASE is not commonly used with the following items:

abu *waist*	käba *float*	rabi *rabbi*	sõba *blanket*
hobi *hobby*	käbi *cone (pine, fir etc)*	reba *haunch*	taba *padlock*
häbi *shame*	libu *harlot*	rebu *egg (yolk)*	tiba *droplet*
klibu *stone shingle*	loba *gibberish*	riba *strip*	tibu *chick*
koba *clamp*	lõbu *fun*	ribi *rib*	tobu *dunce*
krabi *crab*	naba *navel*	ribu *trash*	vibu *bow (archery)*

13C häda *trouble, problem, hardship* — häda 13C

	nominative	genitive	partitive	short into	stem
singular	**häda**	**häda**	**häda**	**häTTa**	**häda-**
plural	**hädad**	**hädade**	**hädasid**		**hädade-**

Also like häda:	muda *mud*	pidu *party (social event)*	rodu *line, row*
ida *east*	pada *spades (cards)*	redu *hiding place*	udu *fog*

The SHORT INTO CASE is not commonly used with the following items:

edu *success*	kõdi *tickle*	oda *spear*	tädi *aunt*
idu *sprout*	küdi *husband's brother*	rõdu *balcony*	vidu *mistiness*
kodu *home*	mõdu *mead*	sudu *smog*	õdu *comfort*
kudu *spawn*	mäda *pus*	tudi *doddering old fool*	üdi *marrow*

13D segu *mixture* — segu 13D

	nominative	genitive	partitive	short into	stem
singular	**segu**	**segu**	**segu**	**seKKu**	**segu-**
plural	**segud**	**segude**	**segusid**		**segude-**

Also like segu: kagu *southeast* kogu *whole;bulk;collection* prügi *garbage*

The SHORT INTO CASE is not commonly used with the following items:

higi *sweat*	möga *nonsense*	pugu *gizzard*	säga *sheatfish*
iga ^ *every*	nagi *coat rack*	soga *mud*	tragi ^ *spry*
logu *rattletrap*	pigi *pitch*		

14A maja *house* — maja 14A

	nominative	genitive	partitive	short into	stem
singular	**maja**	**maja**	**maja**	**maJJa**	**maja-**
plural	**majad**	**majade**	**maju**		**majade-**
			majasid		maju-

Also like maja: kava *programme*

The SHORT INTO CASE is not commonly used with the following items:

ala *area*	kõva ^ *hard*	paha ^ *bad*	sõna *word*
kala *fish*	lava *stage*	pala *morsel*	vana ^ *old*
kana *hen*	lina *linen*	sama ^ *same*	

14B raba *moor* — raba 14B

	nominative	genitive	partitive	short into	stem
singular	**raba**	**raba**	**raba**	**raPPa**	**raba-**
plural	**rabad**	**rabade**	**rabu**		**rabade-**
			rabasid		rabu-

Also like raba: saba *tail*

The SHORT INTO CASE is not commonly used with the following item:

vaba ^ *free*

14C vaga ^ *pious* — vaga 14C

	nominative	genitive	partitive	short into	stem
singular	**vaga**	**vaga**	**vaga**	(vaKKa)	**vaga-**
plural	**vagad**	**vagade**	**vagu**		**vagade-**
			vagasid		vagu-

15 pesa *nest* — pesa 15

	nominative	genitive	partitive	short into	stem
singular	**pesa**	**pesa**	**pesa**	**peSSa**	**pesa-**
plural	**pesad**	**pesade**	**pesi**		**pesade-**
			pesasid		pesi-

Also like pesa: keha *body* osa *part*

The SHORT INTO CASE is not commonly used with the following items:

kena ^ *nice*	püha ^ *holy*	tera *blade (knife); grain*
oma ^ *own*	püha *holiday*	

16 muna ***egg*** **muna 16**

	nominative	genitive	partitive	short into	stem
singular	**muna**	**muna**	**muna**	(muNNa)	**muna-**
plural	**munad**	**munade**	**mune**		**munade-**
			munasid		mune-

17 kivi ***stone*** **kivi 17**

	nominative	genitive	partitive	short into	stem
singular	**kivi**	**kivi**	**kivi**	**kiVVi**	**kivi-**
plural	**kivid**	**kivide**	**kive**		**kivide-**
			kivisid		kive-

The SHORT INTO CASE is not commonly used with the following items:

huvi *interest* kruvi *screw*

18 nimi ***name*** **nimi 18**

	nominative	genitive	partitive	short into	stem
singular	**nimi**	**nime**	**nime**	**niMMe**	**nime-**
plural	**nimed**	**nimede**	**nimesid**		**nimede-**

Also like nimi: süli *lap* tüvi *trunk; stem (grammar)*

The SHORT INTO CASE is not commonly used with the following items:

hani *goose* lõhi *salmon* lävi *doorsill* suvi *summer*

TYPE 4 - Regular - Consonant Partitives

19 kusi ***urine*** **kusi 19**

	nominative	genitive	partitive	short into	stem
singular	**kusi**	**kuse**	**kuSt**		**kuse-**
plural	**kused**	**kusede**	**kusesid**		**kusede-**

20 meri ***sea*** **meri 20**

	nominative	genitive	partitive	short into	stem
singular	**meri**	**mere**	**meRd**	**meRRe**	**mere-**
plural	**mered**	**merede**	**meresid**		**merede-**

Also like meri: tuli *fire* uni *sleep* veri *blood*

21 lumi ***snow*** **lumi 21**

	nominative	genitive	partitive	short into	stem
singular	**lumi**	**lume**	**luNd**	**luMMe**	**lume-**
plural	**lumed**	**lumede**	**lumesid**		**lumede-**

22 mõni [A] ***some*** **mõni 22**

	nominative	genitive	partitive	short into	stem
singular	**mõni**	**mõne**	**mõNd**	**mõNda**	**mõne-**
			mõNda		
plural	**mõned**	**mõnede**	**mõnesid**		**mõnede-**

NOMINALS - 2 - CLASS II B

TYPE 5 - Regular - Vowel Partitives

23 nõbu *cousin* **nõbu 23**

	nominative	genitive	partitive	short into	stem
singular	**nõbu**	**nõO**	**nõbu**	(nõPPu)	**nõO-**
plural	**nõOd**	**nõbude**	**nõbusid**		**nõbude-**

24 kubu *truss* **kubu 24**

	nominative	genitive	partitive	short into	stem
singular	**kubu**	**kOO**	**kubu**	(kuPPu)	**kOO-**
plural	**kOOd**	**kubude**	**kubusid**		**kubude-**

25 tõde *truth* **tõde 25**

	nominative	genitive	partitive	short into	stem
singular	**tõde**	**tõE**	**tõde**	(tõTTe)	**tõE-**
plural	**tõEd**	**tõdede**	**tõdesid**		**tõdede-**

Also like tõde: õde *sister*

26 kude *tissue* **kude 26**

	nominative	genitive	partitive	short into	stem
singular	**kude**	**koE**	**kude**	(kuTTe)	**koE-**
plural	**koEd**	**kudede**	**kudesid**		**kudede-**

27 ladu *warehouse* **ladu 27**

	nominative	genitive	partitive	short into	stem
singular	**ladu**	**laO**	**ladu**	**laTTu**	**laO-**
plural	**laOd**	**ladude**	**ladusid**		**ladude-**

The SHORT INTO CASE is not commonly used with the following items:

kadu *loss* madu *viper* nadu *husband's sister* vedu *haulage*

28 pidu *party (social event)* **pidu 28**

	nominative	genitive	partitive	short into	stem
singular	**pidu**	**peO**	**pidu**	**piTTu**	**peO-**
plural	**peOd**	**pidude**	**pidusid**		**pidude-**

29 koda *chamber; corridor* **koda 29**

	nominative	genitive	partitive	short into	stem
singular	**koda**	**koja**	**koda**	**koTTa**	**koja-**
plural	**kojad**	**kodade**	**kodasid**		**kodade-**

The SHORT INTO CASE is not commonly used with:

sadu *rainfall*

30 iga *age* **iga 30**

	nominative	genitive	partitive	short into	stem
singular	**iga**	**eA**	**iga**	**iKKa**	**eA-**
plural	**eAd**	**igade**	**igasid**		**igade-**

31 nägu *face* **nägu 31**

	nominative	genitive	partitive	short into	stem
singular	**nägu**	**näO**	**nägu**	**näKKu**	**näO-**
plural	**näOd**	**nägude**	**nägusid**		**nägude-**

Also like nägu: magu *stomach* pragu *crack* vagu *furrow*
jagu *share* nõgu *hollow*

The SHORT INTO CASE is not commonly used with the following items:

agu *daybreak* hagu *brushwood* kägu *cuckoo* tegu *act; deed*

32 ligu *soak* **ligu 32**

	nominative	genitive	partitive	short into	stem
singular	**ligu**	**leO**	**ligu**	**liKKu**	**leO-**
plural	**leOd**	**ligude**	**ligusid**		**ligude-**

The SHORT INTO CASE is not commonly used with:

tigu *snail*

33 lugu *tale* lugu 33

	nominative	genitive	partitive	short into	stem
singular	**lugu**	**lOO**	**lugu**	**luKKu**	**lOO-**
plural	**lOOd**	**lugude**	**lugusid**		**lugude-**

The SHORT INTO CASE is not commonly used with:

sugu *sex; gender*

34 pügi *shearing* pügi 34

	nominative	genitive	partitive	short into	stem
singular	**pügi**	**pöE**	**pügi**	(püKKi)	**pöE-**
plural	**pöEd**	**pügide**	**pügisid**		**pügide-**

35 rida *row* rida 35

	nominative	genitive	partitive	short into	stem
singular	**rida**	**reA**	**rida**	**riTTa**	**reA-**
plural	**reAd**	**ridade**	**ridu**		**ridade-**
			ridasid		(reO-)

36 pada *pot* pada 36

	nominative	genitive	partitive	short into	stem
singular	**pada**	**paja**	**pada**	**paTTa**	**paja-**
plural	**pajad**	**padade**	**padu**		**padade-**
			padasid		(paju-)

Also like pada: sõda *war*

The SHORT INTO CASE is not commonly used with the following items:

rada *path* sada *hundred*

37 siga *pig* siga 37

	nominative	genitive	partitive	short into	stem
singular	**siga**	**seA**	**siga**	(siKKa)	**seA-**
plural	**seAd**	**sigade**	**sigu**		**sigade**
			sigasid		(seO-)

Also like siga: viga *mistake*

38 tuba *room* tuba 38

	nominative	genitive	partitive	short into	stem
singular	**tuba**	**toA**	**tuba**	**tuPPa**	**toa-**
plural	**toAd**	**tubade**	**tube**		**tubade-**
			tubasid		(toE-)

The SHORT INTO CASE is not commonly used with the following items:

luba *permission* uba *bean*

39 suga *sley* suga 39

	nominative	genitive	partitive	short into	stem
singular	**suga**	**soA**	**suga**	**suKKa**	**soA-**
plural	**soAd**	**sugade**	**suge**		**sugade-**
			sugasid		(soE-)

The SHORT INTO CASE is not commonly used with the following items:

juga *cascade* nuga *knife*

40 tõbi *disease* tõbi 40

	nominative	genitive	partitive	short into	stem
singular	**tõbi**	**tõve**	**tõbe**	**tõPPe**	**tõve-**
plural	**tõved**	**tõbede**	**tõbesid**		**tõbede-**

41 regi *sleigh* regi 41

	nominative	genitive	partitive	short into	stem
singular	**regi**	**rEE**	**rege**	**reKKe**	**rEE-**
plural	**rEEd**	**regede**	**regesid**		**regede-**

42 jõgi *river* jõgi 42

	nominative	genitive	partitive	short into	stem
singular	**jõgi**	**jõE**	**jõge**	**jõKKe**	**jõE-**
plural	**jõEd**	**jõgede**	**jõgesid**		**jõgede-**

Also like jõgi: lagi *ceiling* mägi *hill* vägi *army*

The SHORT INTO CASE is not commonly used with:

nõgi *soot*

43 tugi ***support*** **tugi 43**

	nominative	genitive	partitive	short into	stem
singular	**tugi**	**toE**	**tuge**	(tuKKe)	**toE-**
plural	**toEd**	**tugede**	**tugesid**		**tugede-**

TYPE 6 - Regular - Consonant Partitives

44 tõsi ***truth, earnestness*** **tõsi 44**

	nominative	genitive	partitive	short into	stem
singular	**tõsi**	**tõE**	**tõTT**		**tõE-**
plural	**tõEd**	**tõte**	**tõsi**		**tõte-**
					(tõsi-)

45 käsi ***hand*** **käsi 45**

	nominative	genitive	partitive	short into	stem
singular	**käsi**	**käE**	**käTT**	**käTTe**	**käE-**
plural	**käEd**	**käte**	**käsi**		**käte-**
					(käsi-)

46 vesi ***water*** **vesi 46**

	nominative	genitive	partitive	short into	stem
singular	**vesi**	**vEE**	**veTT**	**veTTe**	**vEE-**
plural	**vEEd**	**vete**	**vesi**		**vete-**
					(vesi-)

Also like vesi: esi *forefront*

The SHORT INTO CASE is not commonly used with:

mesi *honey*

47 susi ***wolf*** **susi 47**

	nominative	genitive	partitive	short into	stem
singular	**susi**	**soE**	**suTT**	(suTTe)	**soE-**
plural	**soEd**	**sute**	**susi**		**sute-**
					(susi-)

48 süsi ***coal*** **süsi 48**

	nominative	genitive	partitive	short into	stem
singular	**süsi**	**söE**	**süTT**	**süTTe**	**söE-**
plural	**söEd**	**süte**	**süsi**		**süte-**
					(süsi-)

NOMINALS - 2 - CLASS III A

TYPE 7 - Regular - Vowel Partitives

49A jAAm *station* — jAAm 49A

	nominative	genitive	partitive	short into	stem
singular	**jAAm**	**jaama**	**jAAma**	**jAAma**	**jaama-**
plural	**jaamad**	**jAAmade**	**jAAmu**		**jAAmade-**
			jAAmasid		(jaamu-)

Also like jAAm: hAAv *wound* liNN *city*

The SHORT INTO CASE is not commonly used with the following items:

AAs *noose; meadow*
haLL *frost*
kÕÕm *dandruff*
lİİv *sand*
lÕÕm *blaze*
mÕÕn *ebb*
pİİm *milk*
pİİn *torment*
vAAl *whale*
vİİn *liquor, vodka*
viLL *wool*
viMM *grudge*

49B kaEl *neck* — kaEl 49B

	nominative	genitive	partitive	short into	stem
singular	**kaEl**	**kaela**	**kaEla**	**kaEla**	**kaela-**
plural	**kaelad**	**kaElade**	**kaElu**		**kaElade-**
			kaElasid		(kaelu-)

Also like kaEl:
hõLm *tail of coat/dress*
iLm *weather*
kauSt *folder*
kõnTs *sludge*
kõRv *ear*
käİl *ship's prow*
laEv *ship*
laİ[j] ^ *wide*
naSv *sandbank*
paUn *knapsack*
põRn *spleen*
raSv *lard*
saUn *sauna*
vaRn *clothes-rack*
vaTs *belly*

The SHORT INTO CASE is not commonly used with the following items:

haRv ^ *rare*
kaRv *hair*
kihlad (pl) *engagement*
kiHv *fang*
kõHn ^ *thin*
käİ[j] *grindstone*
leİn *mourning*
lõHn *aroma*
lõNg *yarn*
lõuSt *ugly face*
lõõTs *bellows*
maHl *juice*
maKs *liver*
malTs *orache*
maTk *hike*
mõHn *bump*
mõRv *murder*
nõLv *slope*
paHn *litter*
piHl *mountain ash*
piiTs *whip*
põnTs *thud*
põTk *shank*
raUn *stoney spot*
riHm *belt*
riHv *grit, shingle; flute*
riiSt *tool*
saaSt *pollution*
saİ[j] *white bread*
saNg *handle*
sõEl *sieve*
sõIr *type of cheese*
taEl *tinder*
taHm *soot*
taRn *sedge*
tauSt *background*
tõLv *battledore*
tõRv *tar*
vaEv *hardship*
vaİ[j] *peg*
viHm *rain*
viRn *pile*
virTs *manure (liquid)*
võHm *energy, strength*
väİn *strait*
õRn ^ *tender*
äİ[j] *father-in-law*

49C kaPP *wooden drinking mug* kaPP 49C

	nominative	genitive	partitive	short into	stem
singular	**kaPP**	**kapa**	**kaPPa**	**kaPPa**	**kapa-**
plural	**kapad**	**kaPPade**	**kaPPu**		**kaPPade-**
			kaPPasid		(kapu-)

Also like kaPP: laKK *loft* vaKK *bushel*

The SHORT INTO CASE is not commonly used with the following items:

laKK *mane* siTT *shit* taPP *slaughter*

49D kamP *gang* kamP 49D

	nominative	genitive	partitive	short into	stem
singular	**kamP**	**kamba**	**kamPa**	**kamPa**	**kamba-**
plural	**kambad**	**kamPade**	**kamPu**		**kamPade-**
			kamPasid		(kambu-)

The SHORT INTO CASE is not commonly used with the following items:

kauP *wares, commodity* laiP *corpse* lauP *forehead* vaiP *rug*

49E aiT *storehouse* aiT 49E

	nominative	genitive	partitive	short into	stem
singular	**aiT**	**aida**	**aiTa**	**aiTa**	**aida-**
plural	**aidad**	**aiTade**	**aiTu**		**aiTade-**
			aiTasid		(aidu-)

Also like aiT: laTv *top of tree* lauT *barn* riiT *pyre*

The SHORT INTO CASE is not commonly used with the following items:

krõõT *hag* lõTv ^ *limp* piiT *jamb* riTv *pole*
laaT *fair*

49F paiK *place* paiK 49F

	nominative	genitive	partitive	short into	stem
singular	**paiK**	**paiga**	**paiKa**	**paiKa**	**paiga-**
plural	**paigad**	**paiKade**	**paiKu**		**paiKade-**
			paiKasid		(paigu-)

Also like paiK: panK *bank (financial)*

The SHORT INTO CASE is not commonly used with the following items:

jäiK ^ *stark* palK *pay* salK *lock of hair* tilK *drop*
marK *mark (currency)* panK *lump of earth* seiK *circumstance* tõiK *fact*
mõõK *sword* *coastal cliff* tarK ^ *wise* virK ^ *diligent*
nõrK ^ *weak* rauK *old decrepit person*

49G varSS *foal* varSS 49G

	nominative	genitive	partitive	short into	stem
singular	**varSS**	**varsa**	**varSSa**	(varSSa)	**varsa-**
plural	**varsad**	**varSSade**	**varSSu**		**varSSade-**
			varSSasid		(varsu-)

50 seİn *wall* seİn 50

	nominative	genitive	partitive	short into	stem
singular	**seİn**	**seina**	**seİna**	**seİna**	**seina-**
plural	**seinad**	**seinte**	**seİnu**		**seinte-**
		seİnade	seİnasid		seİnade-
					(seinu-)

The SHORT INTO CASE is not commonly used with the following items:

aİs *shaft*	kaEr *oat*	naEl *nail; pound*	paEl *ribbon*
heİn *hay*	kaUn *pod*	nõEl *needle*	õUn *apple*

51 saKs *gentleman, gentlewoman; noble* saKs 51

	nominative	genitive	partitive	short into	stem
singular	**saKs**	**saksa**	**saKsa**	(saKsa)	**saksa-**
plural	**saksad**	**saKste**	**saKsu**		**saKste-**
		saKsade	saKsasid		saKsade-
					(saksu-)

Also like saKs: viTs *switch*

52 paU[w] *bead* paU[w] 52

	nominative	genitive	partitive	short into	stem
singular	**paU[w]**	**pau[w]a**	**paU[w]a**	(paU[w]a)	**pau[w]a-**
plural	**pau[w]ad**	**paU[w]ade**	**paU[w]asid**		**paU[w]ade-**

Also like paU[w]: saU[w] *crook (shepherd's)*

53A pUUs *hip* pUUs 53A

	nominative	genitive	partitive	short into	stem
singular	**pUUs**	**puusa**	**pUUsa**	**pUUsa**	**puusa-**
plural	**puusad**	**pUUsade**	**pUUsi**		**pUUsade-**
			pUUsasid		(puusi-)

Also like pUUs: sOOl *salt*

The SHORT INTO CASE is not commonly used with the following items:

heLL ^ *tender*	krUUs *gravel*	nuNN *nun*	tUUm *nucleus*
hOOr *whore*	kUUm ^ *hot*	nUUm *fattening (animals)*	vÄÄr ^ *incorrect*
jÄÄr *ram*	lOOm *animal*	rUUn *gelding*	äMM *mother-in-law*
keLL *clock*	mOOn *provisions*	tuMM *mute*	äSS *ace (cards)*
koNN *frog*	mÄÄr *extent*		

53B meTs *forest* — meTs 53B

	nominative	genitive	partitive	short into	stem
singular	**meTs**	**metsa**	**meTsa**	**meTsa**	**metsa-**
plural	**metsad**	**meTsade**	**meTsi**		**meTsade-**
			meTsasid		(metsi-)

Also like meTs: päEv *day* rüHm *group* seRv *edge* suRm *death*

The SHORT INTO CASE is not commonly used with the following items:

juLm ^ *cruel*
keHv ^ *poor*
keSt *husk*
kiNg *shoe*
konTs *heel*
kuİv ^ *dry*
kujuteLm *imagination*
kuRn *strainer*
käRn *scab*
käSn *sponge*
küLm ^ *cold*
leHm *cow*
leSt *flounder*
muSt ^ *black; dirty*
mäLv *skin (for tanning)*
poHl *whortleberry*
pulmad (pl) *wedding*
puNg *bud*
päRn *linden tree*
reLv *weapon*
roİm *crime*
soNg *hernia*
süSt *canoe*
tuİm ^ *numb*
verSt *mile*

53C moKK *lip* — moKK 53C

	nominative	genitive	partitive	short into	stem
singular	**moKK**	**moka**	**moKKa**	**moKKa**	**moka-**
plural	**mokad**	**moKKade**	**moKKi**		**moKKade-**
			moKKasid		(moki-)

Also like moKK: piKK ^ *long*

The SHORT INTO CASE is not commonly used with the following items:

koKK *cook*
koPP *scoop*
käPP *paw*
lePP *alder*
noKK *beak*
nuKK *corner*
päKK *ball of thumb, foot*
sePP *smith*
suKK *stocking*
tuKK *tuft of hair*

53D pumP *pump* — pumP 53D

	nominative	genitive	partitive	short into	stem
singular	**pumP**	**pumba**	**pumPa**	(pumPa)	**pumba-**
plural	**pumbad**	**pumPade**	**pumPi**		**pumPade-**
			pumPasid		(pumbi-)

Also like pumP: kolP *skull* tulP *post*

53E nooT *seine* — nooT 53E

	nominative	genitive	partitive	short into	stem
singular	**nooT**	**nooda**	**nooTa**	**nooTa**	**nooda-**
plural	**noodad**	**nooTade**	**nooTi**		**nooTade-**
			nooTasid		(noodi-)

The SHORT INTO CASE is not commonly used with the following items:

hurT *greyhound* sööT *fodder* vänT *crank*

53F nurK *corner* — nurK 53F

	nominative	genitive	partitive	short into	stem
singular	**nurK**	**nurga**	**nurKa**	**nurKa**	**nurga-**
plural	**nurgad**	**nurKade**	**nurKi**		**nurKade-**
			nurKasid		(nurgi-)

Also like nurK: hulK *quantity*

The SHORT INTO CASE is not commonly used with the following items:

julK *turd*	munK *monk*	pulK *stick*	ränK ^ *grave*
lünK *gap*	pelK ^ *mere*	ronK *raven*	rünK *rock*

53G kärSS *snout* — kärSS 53G

	nominative	genitive	partitive	short into	stem
singular	**kärSS**	**kärsa**	**kärSSa**	(kärSSa)	**kärsa-**
plural	**kärsad**	**kärSSade**	**kärSSi**		**kärSSade-**
			kärSSasid		(kärsi-)

54 koEr *dog* — koEr 54

	nominative	genitive	partitive	short into	stem
singular	**koEr**	**koera**	**koEra**	(koEra)	**koera-**
plural	**koerad**	**koerte**	**koEri**		**koerte**
		koErade	koErasid		koErade-
					(koeri)

55 oTs *tip* — oTs 55

	nominative	genitive	partitive	short into	stem
singular	**oTs**	**otsa**	**oTsa**	**oTsa**	**otsa-**
plural	**otsad**	**oTste**	**oTsi**		**oTste**
		oTsade	oTsasid		oTsade-
					(otsi-)

Also like oTs: oKs *branch*

56 siLm *eye* — siLm 56

	nominative	genitive	partitive	short into	stem
singular	**siLm**	**silma**	**siLma**	**siLma**	**silma-**
plural	**silmad**	**siLmade**	**siLmi**	**siLmi**	**siLmade-**
		siLme	siLmasid		(siLme-)
					(silmi-)

57 nuİ[j] *cudgel* — nuİ[j] 57

	nominative	genitive	partitive	short into	stem
singular	**nuİ[j]**	**nui[j]a**	**nuİ[j]a**	(nuİ[j]a)	**nui[j]a-**
plural	**nui[j]ad**	**nuİ[j]ade**	**nuİ[j]e**		**nuİ[j]ade-**
			nuİ[j]asid		(nui[j]e-)

58A hOOv *courtyard* hOOv 58A

	nominative	genitive	partitive	short into	stem
singular	**hOOv**	**hoovi**	**hOOvi**	**hOOvi**	**hoovi-**
plural	**hoovid**	**hOOvide**	**hOOve** hOOvisid		**hOOvide-** (hoove-)

Also like hOOv:
agentUUr *agency*
arhİİv *archives*
bAAr *bar*
bAAş *base*
baĻL *ball (social)*
brošÜÜr *brochure*
buŞS *bus*
episOOd *episode*
fAAş *phase*
filiAAl *branch office*
garAAž *garage*
garderOOb *cloak-room*
griĻL *barbecue*
haĻL ^A^ *grey*
haĻL *hall*
hoteĻL *hotel*
häĻL *cradle*
ideAAl *ideal*
karjÄÄr *quarry; career*
katalOOg *catalogue*
klAAş *glass*
klaŞS *class*
kollektİİv *collective*
kOOļ *school*
kooperatİİv *cooperative*
kOOr *choir*
korporatsiOOn *student club*
kostÜÜm *suit*
krAAv *ditch*
kraHH *crash*
krİİs *crisis*
krUUş *mug*
kUUr *shed*
kÜÜn *hay shed*
latrİİn *latrine*
lavİİn *avalanche*
lEEr *confirmation; camp*
liFt *elevator*
lokAAl *pub*
lOOž *box in theatre*
loŞS *castle*
marinAAd *marinade*
moteĻL *motel*
oŅN *hut*
pAAr *pair*
panderoĻL *printed matter*
panEEl *panel*
paŅN *pan*
paradİİs *paradise*
plAAž *beach*
porTfeĻL *briefcase*
prAAm *ferry*
prograMM *program(me)*
protokoĻL *minutes*
prUUŋ ^A^ *brown*
pUUr *cage*
rAAļ *computer*
rAAm *frame*
raŞS *race (genetic)*
rİİm *rhyme*
rİİv *bolt; garter*
rOOļ *steering-wheel*
ruĻL *roll*
rUUm *room*
sAAļ *hall*
sAAŋ *sleigh*
sfÄÄr *sphere*
seiF *safe (for valuables)*
skEEm *diagram*
spirAAl *spiral*
stsEEn *scene*
taĻL *stall*
taŞS *cup*
televisiOOn *television*
tirAAž *tirage*
toĻL *customs*
tOOļ *chair*
tOOş *box*
traMM *streetcar*
treŅN *training*
troĻL *trolley bus*
trOOŋ *throne*
tsensUUr *censorship*
tsOOn *zone*
tUUb *tube*
tüŅN *barrel*
tÜÜr *rudder*
vAAş *vase*
vaŅN *bath*
viĻL *blister*
vitrİİn display-case

The SHORT INTO CASE is not commonly used with the following items:

AAdreŞS *address*
afÄÄr *affair*
akvareĻL *water-colour*
ananaSS *pineapple*
angİİn *tonsillitis*
anteŅN *antenna*
antikvAAr *antiquary*
apriĻL *April*
arbUUs *water-melon*
arEEn *arena*
arhitektUUr *architecture*
armatUUr *fixture*
arOOm *aroma*
aspirİİn *aspirin*
balerİİn *ballerina*
ballAAd *ballad*
ballOOn *balloon*
banAAn *banana*
barjÄÄr *barrier*
baŞS *bass*
batsiĻL *germ*
bEEž ^A^ *beige*
bensİİn *gasoline*
betOOn *concrete*
bisneSS *business*
blUUs *blues (jazz)*
borŠ *borscht*
dAAm *lady*
delfİİn *dolphine*
delikateŞS *delicacy*
detektİİv *detective*
diapositİİv *photo slide*
diEEs *sharp in music*
dOOş *dose*
dotatsiOOn *subsidy*
dreŞS *track-suit*
džiinid (pl) *jeans*
žäSS *jazz*
ekrAAn *screen*
estofİİl *Estophile*
fOOr *traffic light*
foreĻL *trout*
fotograaF *photographer*
furgOOn *van*
fÖÖn *hair-dryer*
gAAş *gas*
garnitUUr *trimmings*
gEEl *gel*
gEEŋ *gene*
glasUUr *glaze*
graMM *gram(me)*
gravÜÜr *engraving*
griMM *stage make-up*
gurmAAn *gourmet*
harF *harp*
ikOOn *icon*
illusiOOn *illusion*
insulİİn *insuline*
intrİİg *intrigue*
invalİİd *invalid*
isolatsiOOn *insulation*
joŅN *stubbornness*
jOOḑ *iodine*
juŅN *turd*
kAAŋ *leech*
kaMM *comb*
kaŋdidatUUr *candidacy*
kanEEl *cinnamon*
kaŅN *toy*
karameĻL *candy*
karbonAAd *chop*
karusseĻL *merry-go-round*
kaŞS *cat*
kassİİr *cashier*
kİİl *dragon-fly*
kİİn *gadfly; chopper*

58A hOOv *courtyard* continued **continued hOOv 58A**

kisseĻL *cold berry soup*
kitaRR *guitar*
koĻL *bogy*
kollEEg *colleague*
koMM *candy*
kompaŞS *compass*
komteSS *countess*
kOOḑ *code*
korAAl *hymn*
korrektUUr *proof-reading*
krAAḑ *degree*
krAAm *stuff*
krAAŋ *tap*
krEEm *cream*
kristaĻL *crystal*
krOOļ *crawl (swimming)*
krOOŋ *crown*
kroŞS *cross-country race*
kulişsid (pl) *stage-setting*
kuĻL *hawk*
kuluaarid (pl) *lobby area*
kultUUr *culture*
kuMM *tire; rubber*
kursİİv *italics*
kUUļ *bullet*
kUUr *course of treatment*
käärid (pl) *scissors*
lAAḑ *manner*
lEEŋ *back of chair*
lektÜÜr *reading matter*
lİİm *glue*
lİİn *line*
likÖÖr *liqueur*
limonAAd *soft drink*
loĻL [A] *stupid*
lOOr *veil*
lOOş *lottery ticket*
lÕÕr *flue*
lÜÜs *sluice*
mAAļ *painting (art)*
magistrAAl *main line*
majonEEs *mayonnaise*
majorAAn *marjoram*
maĻL *protractor*
mannekEEn *fashion model*
margarİİn *margarine*
marmelAAd *marmalade*
maŞS *mass*
massAAž *massage*
memuaarid *memoires*
meŞS *fair; Catholic mass*
metaĻL *metal*
montAAž *fitting*
montÖÖr *fitter*
mOOŋ *poppy*
mOOş *jam*
muĻL *bubble*
muŋnid (pl) *balls; testicles*
mUUļ *jetty*
mõMM *teddy bear*
mäMM *mush*
mÜÜr *wall*
narkomAAn *drug addict*
naRR *fool*
nartsiŞS *narcissus*
noveĻL *short story*
nuĻL *zero*
nÖÖr *string*
harF *harp*
objektİİv *lens*
OOd *ode*
originAAl *original*
paĻL *ball (toy)*
parAAd *parade*
parfÜÜm *perfume*
parOOl *password*
partitUUr *score in music*
paŞS *passport*
pastiĻL *pastille*
patrOOn *patron*
patruĻL *patrol*
pedAAl *pedal*
pelargOOn *geranium*
perrOOn *platform*
peterseĻL *parsley*
pİİm *beam*
pİİr *border*
piĻL *pill; instrument*
plAAŋ *plan*
ploMM *filling in tooth*
plOOm *plum*
pluŞS *plus*
plUUs *blouse*
poMM *bomb*
pOOl *spool*
pOOr *pore*
pOOş *pose*
prEEş *brooch*
preservatİİv *condom*
priļlid (pl) *eye glasses*
problEEm *problem*
prOOv *rehearsal*
protEEs *denture*
protseŞS *lawsuit*
puĻL *bull*
puŅN *pustule*
puŞS *sheath-knife*
pUUr *drill*
püŞS *gun*
pÜÜr *pillowcase*
redaktsiOOn *edition*
refrÄÄn *refrain*
registratUUr *registry*
reklAAm *advertisement*
reljeeF *embossment*
repertuAAr *repertoire*
režİİm *regime*
režissÖÖr *film director*
retsensiOOn *review*
revÄÄr *lapel*
rİİs *rice*
rituAAl *ritual*
rivAAl *rival*
romAAn *novel*
rOOş *rose*
rosmarİİn *rosemary*
rubİİn *ruby*
rulAAd *roulade*
ruMM *rum*
rÖÖv *robbery*
sabotAAž *sabotage*
saĻL *scarf*
sandAAl *sandal*
sapÖÖr *sapper*
sardeĻL *wiener*
sardİİn *sardine*
satİİr *satire*
serenAAd *serenade*
servİİs *set of dishes*
sessiOOn *session*
sİİd *silk*
sİİl *hedgehog*
skandAAl *scandal*
skulptUUr *sculpture*
sOOv *wish*
stAAr *star (actor)*
stAAž *seniority*
stažÖÖr *apprentice*
stİİl *style*
streŞS *stress*
sukAAd *candied peel*
suŞS *slipper*
suvenİİr *souvenir*
sõŅN *bull*
sÕÕr *circle*
süstEEm *system*
šablOOn *stencil*
šamAAn *shaman*
šampOOn *shampoo*
šantAAž *blackmail*
šokolAAd *chocolate*
želatİİn *gelatine*
žurnAAl *magazine*
talAAr *robe of office*
taMM *dam*
tariiF *tariff*
tEEs *thesis*
tekstİİl *textile*
telegraMM *telegram*
temperatUUr *temperature*
terraŞS *terrace*
tiĻL *dill; cock (penis)*
tiŞS *tit*
toĻL *inch*
toŅN *tonne*
tOOŋ *tone*
topAAs *topaz*
traditsiOOn *tradition*
treļlid (pl) *grating*
trikotAAž *knitted goods*
troĻL *troll*
troŞS *cable*
truMM *drum*
tseHH *department*
turnİİr *tournament*
tuŞS *fart*
tUUr *round*
tüĻL *tulle*
uŞS *snake*
vaktsİİn *vaccine*
vaĻL *rampart*
vİİl *file*
vİİs *manner; melody*
vinEEr *plywood*
viŅN *pimple*
vitamİİn *vitamin*
vitrAAž *stained glass*
vuRR *top*
võĻL *shaft*
ÜÜr *rent*

58B koRv *basket* koRv 58B

	nominative	genitive	partitive	short into	stem
singular	**koRv**	**korvi**	**koRvi**	**koRvi**	**korvi-**
plural	**korvid**	**koRvide**	**koRve**		**koRvide-**
			koRvisid		(korve-)

Also like koRv:	koNg *cell (prison)*	poŞt *mail; pole; sentry*	säNg *bed*
aKt *deed*	konkurenTs *competition*	proviŋTs *province*	šaHt *mine shaft*
bassei̇n *swimming-pool*	kontaKt *contact*	puŢs *cunt*	toPs *mug*
faRm *farm*	kontraŞt *contrast*	reseRv *reserve*	toRm *storm*
foNd *stock; supply*	körTs *tavern*	riNg *circle*	toRn *tower*
kaŋTs *stronghold*	looŢs *pilot boat*	riŞt *cross*	tsisteRn *cistern*
kaRm ^ *harsh*	maŞt *mast*	roNg *train*	uRn *urn*
kartoNg *cardboard box*	näRv *nerve*	saloNg *parlour*	vaNg *prisoner*
kaŞt *crate*	paragraHv *paragraph*	saŢs *lot of goods*	voRm *uniform*
konfliKt *conflict*	paŢs *plait*	seļTs *society (organization)*	äHm *excitement*

The SHORT INTO CASE is not commonly used with the following items:

aferiSt *fortune-hunter*	keĻm *rogue*	läRm *noise*	praoSt *provost*
aHv *monkey*	keţsid (pl) *sneakers*	lörTs *slush*	prinTs *prince*
akoRd *musical chord*	kiHvt ^ *terrific*	maHv *puff*	priŢs *syringe*
aKt *nude (art)*	kiPs *gypsum*	mai̇s *corn*	projeKt *project*
alaRm *alarm*	kiruRg *surgeon*	maĻm *cast-iron*	pronKs *bronze*
ambulaŋTs *dispensary*	kitarriSt *guitarist*	manifeSt *manifesto*	proteŞt *protest*
aplaUs *applause*	kiTš *kitsch*	mansaRd *attic*	pujeNg *peony*
arhiteKt *architect*	klaHv *piano key*	maSk *mask*	punKt *point*
aRm *scar*	klaTš *gossip*	maŢs *peasant*	päRm *yeast*
arSt *doctor*	kloŢs *block (toy)*	maTš *match*	päŢs *loaf*
artiSt *artiste*	kloUn *clown*	moRn ^ *sullen*	rangid (pl) *hames*
bloNd ^ *blonde*	koHv *coffee*	muHv *muff*	reHv *tire*
briDž *bridge (game)*	koKs *coke (coal)*	mumPs *mumps*	rei̇s *trip*
böRs *stock exchange*	kombai̇n *combine*	märTs *March*	reŞt *remnant; grate*
büŞt *bust*	kompleKt *set*	müŢs *hat*	retsePt *recipe; prescription*
disai̇n *design*	konseRv *canned food*	naPs *shot of liquor*	rüTm *rhythm*
fiĻm *film*	konspeKt *précis*	niPs *flick*	saHvt *juice*
floKs *phlox*	konverenTs *conference*	noRm *norm*	saĻm *verse*
flötiSt *flautist*	kraHv *count (person)*	nöPs *button*	saĻv *ointment*
gai̇d *girl guide*	kroHv *plaster*	object *object; thing*	saRm *charm*
goNg *gong*	kuŋSt *art*	oraNž ^ *orange (colour)*	saRž *serge*
hüMn *anthem*	kupoNg *coupon*	orgaSm *orgasm*	sei̇b *sheave*
infarKt *heart attack*	kuRv *curve*	paĻm *palm tree*	seKs *sex*
inteļligenTs *intelligentsia*	küĻv *sowing*	paradoKs *paradox*	sekuNd *second of time*
juHm ^ *doltish*	legeNd *legend*	paUs *pause*	seRv *serve in sport*
juriSt *jurist*	leHv *bow (ribbon)*	piRn *pear*	siRm *screen*
jõHv *horsehair*	lei̇l *steam in sauna*	piŢs *liquor shot; lace*	siŢs *cotton print*
kaNg *crow-bar; archway*	liHv *elegance*	plaŢs *square*	skiTs *sketch*
kapuuTs *hood*	linolEum *linoleum*	plaTvoRm *platform*	släNg *slang*
kaUr *loon*	liŢs *prostitute*	pojeNg *peony*	smaraGd *emerald*
keeKs *pound cake*	loRd *lord (aristocrat)*	poKs *boxing*	sorTs *sorcerer*
keKs *show-off*	luŞt *pleasure*	poPs *cotter*	souSt *gravy*

58B koRv *basket* continued **continued koRv 58B**

speŢs *specialist*
staŋTs *metal punch*
steNd *stand*
süŞt *injection*
šaRž *caricature*
žaNr *genre*
žeŞt *gesture*
taKt *tact*
taloNg *voucher*
tangid (pl) *pliers*
taUd *epidemic*
teŞt *test*
toŢs *girl*
traHv *penalty*
traksid (pl) *suspenders*
troŢs *defiance*
trööŞt *consolation*
tšelliSt *cellist*
tuHm ^ *dim*
turiSt *tourist*
tuuŞt *wisp*
täRn *asterisk*
tööŋTs ^ *blunt*
uŋTs *ounce*
vaĻm *fable*
vaļTs *roller*
veİn *wine*
veŞt *vest*
viKs ^ *alert*
viKs *shoe polish*
volaNg *flounce*
vorSt *sausage*
vuŋTs *moustache*
võļTs ^ *counterfeit*
võĻv *vault*
väRv *colour*
vürSt *prince*
vürTs *spice*

58C poŢT *pot* poŢT 58C

	nominative	genitive	partitive	short into	stem
singular	**poŢT**	**poţi**	**poŢTi**	**poŢTi**	**poţi-**
plural	**poţid**	**poŢTide**	**poŢTe** poŢTisid		**poŢTide-** (poţe-)

Also like poŢT:
bloKK *bloc*
duŠŠ *shower bath*
etaPP *stage, level*
galoPP *gallop*
griPP *flu(e), influenza*
gruPP *group*
heKK *hedge*
hüŢT *hut*
kaPP *cupboard*
kloseŢT *toilet*
koŢT *bag*
leŢT *counter (table)*
maPP *folder*
niŠŠ *niche*
paKK *package*
paPP *cardboard*
püŢT *tub*
seKK *sack*
soPP *nook*
šoKK *shock*
truPP *troupe*
trüKK *print*
tualeŢT *toilet*

The SHORT INTO CASE is not commonly used with the following items:

afiŠŠ *placard*
balleŢT *ballet*
bareŢT *beret*
brikeŢT *briquette*
eskaloPP *escalope*
etikeŢT *label*
guaŠŠ *gouache*
haKK *jackdaw*
jaKK *jacket*
juPP *stub*
juŢT *streak*
kasseŢT *cassette*
kePP *stick*
keŢT *chain*
kiŢT *putty*
klaPP *valve*
kompoŢT *stewed fruit*
kraŢT *hob-goblin*
kreveŢT *shrimp*
kušeŢT *couch*
küŢT *hunter*
laKK *varnish*
laPP *patch*
laŢT *lath*
loKK *curl*
loŢT *double chin*
luŢT *artificial nipple*
makeŢT *model*
maKK *tape-recorder*
maŢT *mat; checkmate*
muŢT *mole*
naPP ^ *scarce*
niPP *trick*
nuKK *knob*
näKK *mermaid*
omleŢT *omelette*
oŢT *bear (arhaic)*
parkeŢT *parquet*
peKK *fat*
peŢT *buttermilk*
pintseŢT *tweezers*
pleKK *tin; stain*
ploKK *pulley block*
puKK *ram*
päŢT *tramp; slipper*
püŢT *grebe*
rakeŢT *rocket*
roŢT *rat*
ruleŢT *roulette*
räŢT *kerchief*
saKK *jag*
saPP *bile*
silueŢT *silouette*
soKK *sock*
soneŢT *sonnet*
sproŢT *sprat*
suPP *soup*
šašlõKK *shishkebab*
šiKK ^ *chic*
tableŢT *tablet, pill*
taŢT *snot*
teKK *blanket; ship's deck*
trePP *stairs*
tšeKK *cheque*
tuŠŠ *Indian ink; flourish*
tuŢT *tuft*
täPP *spot*
tüKK *piece*
vaPP *coat of arms*
vaŢT *watt; cotton-wool*
voKK *spinning-wheel*
vuŢT *quail*

5D karP *box* — karP 58D

	nominative	genitive	partitive	short into	stem
singular	**karP**	**karbi**	**karPi**	**karPi**	**karbi-**
plural	**karbid**	**karPide**	**karPe**		**karPide-**
			karPisid		(karbe-)

Also like karP:	klomP *lump*	lomP *puddle*	staaP *headquarters*
klimP *dumpling*	kramP *cramp*	siļP *syllable*	tüüP *type*

The SHORT INTO CASE is not commonly used with the following items:

hooP *blow; hit*	kramP *staple for paper*	luuP *magnifying glass*	seeP *soap*
horoskooP *horoscope*	kruubid (pl) *pearl-barley*	mikroskooP *microscope*	sirP *sickle*
keeP *cloak*	kuļP *ladle*	nööP *button*	trumP *trump*
kiļP *shield*	kuuP *cube*	printsiiP *principle*	tuļP *tulip*
korP *curd cake*	lamP *lamp*	rooP *poker*	vorP *weal from beating*

58E paaŢ *boat* — paaŢ 58E

	nominative	genitive	partitive	short into	stem
singular	**paaŢ**	**paaḑi**	**paaŢi**	**paaŢi**	**paaḑi-**
plural	**paaḑid**	**paaŢide**	**paaŢe**		**paaŢide-**
			paaŢisid		(paaḑe-)

Also like paaŢ:	instituuT *institute*	paŋT *hostage*	puļT *lectern*
antikvariaaT *bookshop*	internaaT *hostel*	parlameŋT *parliament*	vaaŢ *barrel*
hasarT *risk*	kaŋT *region*	poļT *bolt*	voļT *fold*

The SHORT INTO CASE is not commonly used with the following items:

advokaaT *lawyer*	kurT ^ *deaf*	piļT *picture*	starT *start in sport*
aļT *alto*	kUUrorT *resort*	plaaŢ *record*	süiT *suite*
dirigeŋT *conductor*	liŋT *ribbon*	pliiT *stove*	süļT *head cheese*
flööŢ *flute*	loŋT *trunk (animal)*	preseŋT *tarpaulin*	tapeeŢ *wall-paper*
huŋT *wolf*	masuuT *fuel oil*	presideŋT *president*	testameŋT *will (testament)*
idiooT *idiot*	muskaaT *nutmeg*	pruŋT *plug*	tiŋT *ink; smelt*
insuļT *stroke (brain)*	müŋT *coin*	pruuŢ *fiancée*	toŋT *ghost*
kaarT *card*	müüT *myth*	raŋT *brim*	torT *torte*
kleiT *dress*	natÜÜrmorT *still life*	reŋT *rent*	traaŢ *wire*
konkureŋT *competitor*	niiT *thread*	saŋT ^ *cripple*	viļT *felt*
koŋT *bone*	nooŢ *note, music*	siļT *signboard*	viŋT *finch; thread*
konTserT *concert*	parT *duck*	skauT *boy scout*	voļT *volt*
kriiT *chalk*	pasteeŢ *paté*	sorT *sort*	vääŢ *vine*
kruŋT *plot of land*	peeŢ *beet*	sporT *sport*	vööŢ *stripe*

58F purK *can; jar* — purK 58F

	nominative	genitive	partitive	short into	stem
singular	**purK**	**purgi**	**purKi**	**purKi**	**purgi-**
plural	**purgid**	**purKide**	**purKe** purKisid		**purKide-** (purge-)

Also like purK:	kartoteeK *card file*	parK *park*	teļK *tent*
aPteeK *drugstore*	kööK *kitchen*	pruuK *usage*	tiiK *pond*
haaK *hook*	liiK *species*	riiK *state*	viiK *draw (game); crease*

The SHORT INTO CASE is not commonly used with the following items:

hüpoteeK *mortgage*	leeK *flame*	neļK *clove; carnation*	püüK *catch*
jooK *drink*	linK *latch*	nirK *weasel*	rubriiK *newspaper column*
jäļK ^ *repulsive*	luuK *shutter*	noļK *callow youth*	saaK *crop*
jääK *residue*	lööK *blow (hit)*	orK *spike*	sinK *ham*
kaļK ^ *hard-hearted*	maaK *ore*	paaK *tank*	sodiaaK *zodiac*
kiļK *tipsiness*	marK *trade-mark; stamp*	paļK *log*	soļK *slop*
kinK *gift*	minK *make-up*	piiK *lance*	streiK *strike*
koļK *thrashing*	mosaiiK *mosaic*	pinK *bench*	särK *shirt*
kooK *cake*	muļK *native of Mulgimaa*	planK *application form*	sööK *meal*
korK *cork*	märK *mark*	praaK *reject*	taļK *talc*
kreeK *bullace*	mürK *poison*	prinK ^ *firm*	tsinK *zinc*
kurK *cucumber*	müüK *sale*	puuK *tick*	tõļK *interpreter*

58G kauSS *bowl* — kauSS 58G

	nominative	genitive	partitive	short into	stem
singular	**kauSS**	**kausi**	**kauSSi**	**kauSSi**	**kausi-**
plural	**kausid**	**kauSSide**	**kauSSe** kauSSisid		**kauSSide-** (kause-)

Also like kauSS: bilanSS *balance* konKurSS *contest*

The SHORT INTO CASE is not commonly used with the following items:

avanŞS *advance-payment*	kurSS *exchange rate*	puļSS *pulse*	seanSS *sitting*
farSS *farce*	marSS *march*	renessanSS *Renaissance*	šanSS *chance*
hirSS *millet*	morSS *berry drink*	reveranSS *curtsey*	vaļSS *waltz*
kirSS *cherry*	nüanSS *nuance*	romanSS *romance*	värSS *verse*

58H kabineŢ *study office* — kabineŢ 58H

	nominative	genitive	partitive	short into	stem
singular	**kabineŢ**	**kabineţi**	**kabineŢTi**	**kabineŢTi**	**kabineţi-**
plural	**kabineţid**	**kabineŢTide**	**kabineŢTe** kabineŢTisid		**kabineŢTide-** (kabineţe-)

The SHORT INTO CASE is not commonly used with the following items:

komPveK *candy*	lilipuŢ *dwarf*	piiSkoP *bishop*	siKsaK zigzag
koTleŢ *meat-ball*	pahareŢ *demon*	sigareŢ *cigarette*	tabureŢ *stool*

59 poiSS *boy* — poiSS 59

	nominative	genitive	partitive	short into	stem
singular	**poiSS**	**poisi**	**poiSSi**	**poiSSi**	**poisi-**
plural	**poisid**	**poiste**	**poiSSe**		**poiste-**
		poiSSide	poiSSisid		poiSSide-
					(poise-)

60 püksid (pl) *pants* — püKsid 60

	nominative	genitive	partitive	short into	stem
singular	**püKs**	**püksi**	**püKsi**	**püKsi**	**püksi-**
plural	**püksid**	**püKste**	**püKse**		**püKste-**
		püKside	püKsisid		püKside-
					(pükse-)

61A kaNN *jug* — kaNN 61A

	nominative	genitive	partitive	short into	stem
singular	**kaNN**	**kannu**	**kaNNu**	**kaNNu**	**kannu-**
plural	**kannud**	**kaNNude**	**kaNNe**		**kaNNude-**
			kaNNusid		(kanne-)

Also like kaNN: kÜÜr *stoop* rOOd *company (army)* vOOl *current*

The SHORT INTO CASE is not commonly used with the following items:

huLL ᴬ *crazy*
kAAl *weight*
kİİl *wedge; keel*
kOOn *snout*
lOOm *characteristic*
mäSS *rebellion*
möLL *uproar*
nEEr *kidney*
pEEr *fart*
pÄÄs *escape*
rÕÕm *joy*
saMM *step, footstep*
sÕÕm *gulp*
tİIr *turn; shooting-range*
vEEr *slope*
vİIl *slice*
vİIv *moment*
vOOr *turn (in game)*
vuRR *moustache*
võMM *cop*

61B kaEv *well* — kaEv 61B

	nominative	genitive	partitive	short into	stem
singular	**kaEv**	**kaevu**	**kaEvu**	**kaEvu**	**kaevu-**
plural	**kaevud**	**kaEvude**	**kaEve**		**kaEvude-**
			kaEvusid		(kaeve-)

Also like kaEv:
hõİm *tribe*
kemPs *outhouse*
kinTs *haunch*
kirSt *coffin*
kiRn *churn*
komPs *bundle*
korTs *wrinkle*
lõKs *trap*
raEv *rage*
vaİm *spirit*

The SHORT INTO CASE is not commonly used with the following items:

aEr *oar*
aİm *inkling*
aRm *mercy*
aRv *number*
aUr *steam*
haİs *stink*
hiRm *fear*
jooKs *run*
juuSt *cheese*
jõulud (pl) *Christmas*
jäTk *extension*
kaLm *grave*
kalTs *rag*
kaSv *growth*
kaTk *plague*
keKs *hopscotch*
konKs *hook*
konTs *stub*
koPs *lung*
kriiPs *line*
kuLm *brow*
küHm *hump*
laaSt *chip*
laEn *loan*

61B kaEv *well* continued | **continued kaEv 61B**

laİm *slander*	naEr *laugh*	paRm *horsefly*	tanTs *dance*
laUl *song*	narTs *rag*	põRm *earthly remains*	toLm *dust*
liNg *sling*	näTs *chewing gum*	rämPs *trash*	tuPs *tassel*
liPs *tie*	nÄÄl *wife's brother*	seİs *standing*	tõUs *ascent*
lonKs *gulp*	oİm *temple (head)*	siLm *lamprey*	vaEn *enmity*
luTs *burbot*	oSt *purchase*	suiTs *smoke*	vaiSt *instinct*
maKs *payment*	paaSt *fasting*	sõİm *invective*	viNg *carbon monoxide*
mäNg *game*	paİs *dam*	sääSt *savings*	vurTs *carbonated drink*
müKs *nudge*	paKs ^A^ *fat*	tangud (pl) *barley*	võİm *power*

61C luKK *lock* | luKK 61C

	nominative	genitive	partitive	short into	stem
singular	**luKK**	**luku**	**luKKu**	**luKKu**	**luku-**
plural	**lukud**	**luKKude**	**luKKe**		**luKKude-**
			luKKusid		(luke-)

Also like luKK: lõPP *end* näPP *finger* tiPP *tip* viTT *cunt*

The SHORT INTO CASE is not commonly used with the following items:

juTT *story*	nuPP *knob*	paTT *sin*	ruTT *haste*
liPP *flag*	nuTT *crying*	päkapiKK *elf*	tiKK *match (fire)*
nuKK *doll*	paKK *chopping block*	roPP ^A^ *dirty*	täKK *stallion*

61D kimP *bundle* | kimP 61D

	nominative	genitive	partitive	short into	stem
singular	**kimP**	**kimbu**	**kimPu**	**kimPu**	**kimbu-**
plural	**kimbud**	**kimPude**	**kimPe**		**kimPude-**
			kimPusid		(kimbe-)

Also like kimP: pamP *bundle* piiP *pipe for smoking*

The SHORT INTO CASE is not commonly used with the following items:

kirP *flea*	temP *prank*	triiP *stripe*	vemP *prank*
taiP *wit*	tomP *lump*		

61E liiT *alliance* | liiT 61E

	nominative	genitive	partitive	short into	stem
singular	**liiT**	**liidu**	**liiTu**	**liiTu**	**liidu-**
plural	**liidud**	**liiTude**	**liiTe**		**liiTude-**
			liiTusid		(liide-)

The SHORT INTO CASE is not commonly used with the following items:

koiT *dawn*	puiT *timber*	sõiT *ride*	toiT *food*
mõõT *measure*	ruuT *square*	sööT *pass*	võiT *victory*
niiT *meadow*			

61F auK *hole* auK 61F

	nominative	genitive	partitive	short into	stem
singular	**auK**	**augu**	**auKu**	**auKu**	**augu-**
plural	**augud**	**auKude**	**auKe**		**auKude-**
			auKusid		(auge-)

Also like auK: järK *phase* kurK *throat* võrK *net*
jõuK *gang*

The SHORT INTO CASE is not commonly used with the following items:

erK ^ *brisk*
karK *crutch*
kelK *sled*
kinK *mound*
kooK *hook*
käiK *walkway*
kÜÜslauK *garlic*
laiK *stain*
loiK *puddle*
lõiK *slice*
murulauK *chive*
märK *signal*
pauK *bang*
pilK *glance*
planK *plank*
polK *regiment*
salK *squad*
silK *herring*
sälK *notch*
tõuK *larva*
vaiK *resin*
valK *protein*
välK *lightning*

61G kaiSS *bossom* kaiSS 61G

	nominative	genitive	partitive	short into	stem
singular	**kaiSS**	**kaisu**	**kaiSSu**	**kaiSSu**	**kaisu-**
plural	**kaisud**	**kaiSSude**	**kaiSSe**		**kaiSSude-**
			kaiSSusid		(kaise-)

62 üMbriK *envelope* üMbriK 62

	nominative	genitive	partitive	short into	stem
singular	**üMbriK**	**üMbriku**	**üMbriKKu**	**üMbriKKu**	**üMbriku-**
plural	**üMbrikud**	**üMbrike**	**üMbriKKe**		**üMbrike**
		üMbriKKude	üMbriKKusid		üMbriKKude-

Also like üMbriK:
aNdmestiK *corpus of data*
hariliK ^ *ordinary*
imeliK ^ *strange*
järjestiK *succession*
koMbestiK *customs*
kärestiK *rapids*
laevastiK *fleet*
lugemiK *reader (book)*
mineviK *past*
märKmiK *notebook*
nimestiK *list of names*
oleviK *present*
piduliK ^ *festive*
pIInliK ^ *embarrassing*
rahvastiK *population*
sõnastiK *glossary*
tagumiK *buttocks*
tuleviK *future*
tähestiK *alphabet*
tänavastiK *street network*
tühimiK *void*
vahemiK *interval*
veStmiK *phrase-book*

The SHORT INTO CASE is not commonly used with the following items:

aEdniK *gardener*
alandliK ^ *humble*
ametliK ^ *official*
ametniK *official*
antagoniStliK ^ *antagonistic*
aRgliK ^ *timid*
aristokraaTliK ^ *aristocratic*
armuliK ^ *merciful*
aşjaliK ^ *businesslike*
askeeTliK ^ *ascetic*
asuniK *settler*
ateiStliK ^ *atheistic*
atleeTliK ^ *athletic*
auKliK ^ *full of holes*
avaliK ^ *public*
daamiliK ^ *ladylike*
EEskujuliK ^ *exemplary*
EEsriNdliK ^ *progressive*
egoiStliK ^ *egoistic(al)*
eKsliK ^ *erroneous*
elajaliK ^ *beastly*
elaniK *inhabitant*
enamiK *majority*
ennatliK ^ *ill-advised*
entusiaStliK ^ *enthusiastic*
erakliK ^ *reclusive*
erandliK ^ *irregular*
esindusliK ^ *dignified*
eTTevaaTliK ^ *careful*
habemiK *bearded man*
haPniK *oxygen*
hariduslíK ^ *educational*
haRjumusliK ^ *habitual*
hIIglasliK ^ *gigantic*
hukatusliK ^ *disastrous*
häbeliK ^ *shy*
hämariK *dusk*
idealiStliK ^ *idealistic*
idiooTliK ^ *idiotic*
igaviK *eternity*

62 üMbriK *envelope* continued **continued üMbriK 62**

ilmaliK ^ *secular*
ilmastiK *climate*
inimliK ^ *humane*
isaliK ^ *fatherly*
isamAAliK ^ *patriotic*
isikliK ^ *personal*
juhusliK ^ *incidental*
jumaliK ^ *divine*
järvestiK *lake system*
kaEbliK ^ *plaintive*
kaheksandiK *an eighth*
kahjuliK ^ *harmful*
kanarbiK *heather*
kaNgelasliK ^ *heroic*
kannatliK ^ *patient*
karTliK ^ *timid*
kasuliK ^ *useful*
kasvandiK *ward (child)*
kasvatusliK ^ *educational*
katkendliK ^ *fragmentary*
kaubandusliK ^ *commercial*
keİgarliK ^ *dandyish*
keSkmiK *central part*
killustiK *broken stones*
kilPlasliK ^ *foolish*
kiRgliK ^ *passionate*
kirikliK ^ *ecclesiastical*
kirjaliK ^ *written*
kirjandusliK ^ *literary*
kirjaniK *author*
kiŞkjaliK ^ *rapacious*
kiusatusliK ^ *tempting*
klahvistiK *piano keyboard*
kodaniK *citizen*
kodanliK ^ *bourgeois*
kohaliK ^ *local*
koHtuliK ^ *judicial*
koHtuniK *judge*
kohustusliK ^ *obligatory*
kolmandiK *third*
konarliK ^ *uneven*
korraliK ^ *orderly*
kramPliK ^ *convulsive*
kriStliK ^ *Christian*
kuningliK ^ *regal*
kuŋStliK ^ *artificial*
kuŋStniK *artist*
kuratliK ^ *devilish*
kuRbliK ^ *melancholy*
kuristiK *precipice*

kuuendiK *sixth*
kõLbliK ^ *suitable morally*
kõrgendiK *plateau*
kõRgustiK *uplands*
kõrTsmiK *tavern keeper*
küMnendiK *tenth*
künKliK ^ *hilly*
laEvniK *shipowner*
lagendiK *plain*
lapseliK ^ *childlike*
lehestiK *foliage*
leİdliK ^ *resourceful*
lepistiK *alder grove*
lePliK ^ *tolerant*
lihuniK *butcher*
liiderliK ^ *licentious*
lOOdusliK ^ *nature*
loomuliK ^ *natural*
luKsusliK ^ *luxurious*
luŞtliK ^ *jolly*
luuStiK *skeleton*
lõPliK ^ *final*
lämmastiK *nitrogen*
lühinägeliK ^ *near-sighted*
lünKliK ^ *having gaps*
mAAkoNdliK ^ *provincial*
maaStiK *landscape*
madaliK *shallow*
majandusliK ^ *economic*
maŢsliK ^ *peasant-like*
meheliK ^ *manly*
meiSterliK ^ *masterful*
mesiniK *bee-keeper*
meTsniK *forester*
mureliK ^ *worried*
muuTliK ^ *changeable*
mõİsniK *squire*
mõistatusliK ^ *puzzling*
mõiStliK ^ *reasonable*
mõTliK ^ *pensive*
mädaniK *abscess*
mäeStiK *mountain range*
mÄÄrustiK *regulations*
naiseliK ^ *womanly*
neļjandiK *fourth*
nOOrusliK ^ *youthful*
nõİdusliK ^ *bewitching*
nõUdliK ^ *demanding*
nõUniK *councillor*
näİliK ^ *seeming*

näiTliK ^ *visual*
oHtliK ^ *dangerous*
omaniK *owner*
optimiStliK ^ *optimistic*
orjaliK ^ *slavish*
osaniK *share holder*
oSkusliK ^ *skilled*
oTsmiK *forehead*
palaviK *fever*
paŞliK ^ *appropriate*
peLgliK ^ *timid*
perekoNdliK ^ *family*
peţisliK ^ *deceitful*
peTliK ^ *deceptive*
peTTurliK ^ *deceitful*
pİİrkoNdliK ^ *district*
piKliK ^ *oblong*
piļTliK ^ *figurative*
piļTniK *photographer*
poisiliK ^ *boyish*
politseİniK *police officer*
pOOḑniK *storekeeper*
proualiK ^ *lady-like*
publitsiStliK ^ *essayistic*
puraviK *boletus*
puuduliK ^ *deficient*
põgeniK *refugee*
põhjaliK ^ *thorough*
põletiK *inflammation*
põLgliK ^ *contemptuous*
põõsastiK *shrubbery*
päriliK ^ *hereditary*
pärimusliK ^ *traditional*
pÄÄsmiK *pass*
pühaliK ^ *solemn*
pÜÜdliK ^ *diligent*
raamistiK *framework*
rahandusliK ^ *financial*
rahuliK ^ *peaceful*
raHvaliK ^ *folksy*
raHvusliK *national*
raiesmiK *clearing*
raiestiK *clearing*
raTsaniK *horseman*
raugaliK ^ *senile*
realiStliK ^ *realistic*
reeTliK ^ *treacherous*
riiKliK ^ *state*
riKKaliK ^ *abundant*
rägastiK *thicket*

rüüTelliK ^ *chivalrous*
saarestiK *archipelago*
saaTusliK ^ *fateful*
sajandiK *hundredth*
saladusliK ^ *mysterious*
salaliK ^ *secretive*
saMbliK *lichen*
saNgarliK ^ *heroic*
sarapiK *hazel tree grove*
seAdusliK ^ *lawful*
seiTsmendiK *seventh*
seļTskoNdliK ^ *social*
sihiliK ^ *intentional*
sisaliK *lizard*
sulestiK *plumage*
suŅdusliK ^ *compulsory*
sureliK ^ *mortal*
sõbraliK ^ *friendly*
sõnakuuleliK ^ *obedient*
sääStliK ^ *economical*
südamiK *core*
südamliK ^ *cordial*
sündmustiK *plot*
süsiniK *carbon*
taEvaliK ^ *heavenly*
tagasihoİdliK ^ *modest*
tagurliK ^ *reactionary*
taHtliK ^ *intentional*
taimestiK *vegetation*
taiPliK ^ *quick-witted*
taluniK *farmer*
talupoEgliK ^ *peasant-like*
tarandiK *enclosure*
tarviliK ^ *necessary*
tasandiK *plain*
teAdliK ^ *aware*
teAdusliK ^ *scientific*
teaTmiK *reference book*
tegeliK ^ *actual*
tegevustiK *action*
tendenTsliK ^ *tendentious*
teraviK *point*
terviKliK ^ *integral*
tervisliK ^ *wholesome*
toeStiK *props*
tooTliK ^ *productive*
torustiK *plumbing*
troŢsliK ^ *defiant*
tulestiK *lighting*
tuNdliK ^ *sensitive*

62 üMbriK *envelope* continued **continued üMbriK 62**

tähelepaneliK ^ *attentive*	vaimuliK ^ *ecclesiastical*	videviK *dusk*	välimiK *exterior*
täieliK ^ *complete*	vaiStliK ^ *instinctive*	viiendiK *fifth*	väStriK *wagtail*
täl̇usliK ^ *complete*	vajaliK ^ *necessary*	viirastusliK ^ *hallucinatory*	väärTusliK ^ *valuable*
tänuliK ^ *thankful*	valeliK ^ *deceitful*	viStriK *pimple*	õEliK ^ *sisterly*
tööStusliK ^ *industrial*	valimiK *selection*	voliniK *trustee*	õl̇gusliK ^ *legal*
ulatusliK ^ *extensive*	valuliK ^ *painful*	vOOrusliK ^ *virtuous*	õnneliK ^ *happy*
usaldusliK ^ *confidential*	varandusliK ^ *property*	võhikliK ^ *ignorant(inexpert)*	õpetliK ^ *instructive*
uSkliK ^ *religious*	vastandliK ^ *opposite*	võimaliK ^ *possible*	äMbliK *spider*
uudishimuliK ^ *curious*	vedeliK *fluid*	võLgniK *debtor*	ÄÄrmusliK ^ *extreme*
vabadiK *cotter*	vel̇driK *eccentric*	võl̥vistiK *vaulting*	üheksandiK *ninth*
vaenuliK ^ *hostile*	vennaliK ^ *brotherly*	võrestiK *trellis*	ühiskoNdliK ^ *social*
vaHtriK *maple grove*	vesiniK *hydrogen*	võsastiK *undergrowth*	üllatusliK ^ *surprising*

63A liLL *flower* liLL 63A

	nominative	genitive	partitive	short into	stem
singular	**liLL**	**lille**	**liLLe**	(liLLe)	**lille-**
plural	**lilled**	**liLLede**	**liLLi**		**liLLede-**
			liLLesid		(lilli-)

The SHORT INTO CASE is not commonly used with the following items:

aMM *wet-nurse*	meMM *mommy*	nõMM *heath*	taLL *lamb*
eMM *mommy*	nEEm *cape*	põLL *apron*	taMM *oak*
leLL *uncle*			

63B haNg *snowdrift* haNg 63B

	nominative	genitive	partitive	short into	stem
singular	**haNg**	**hange**	**haNge**	**haNge**	**hange-**
plural	**hanged**	**haNgede**	**haNgi**		**haNgede-**
			haNgesid		(hangi-)

Also like haNg:	koLm *three*	põU[w] *bosom*	õNg *hook*
hiNg *soul*	paNg *bucket*	sõl̇m *manger*	õU[w] *yard*
jäRv *lake*	piLv *cloud*	sõRm *finger*	

The SHORT INTO CASE is not commonly used with the following items:

heTk *moment*	lõl̇m *warp*	reTk *journey*	tol̇m *texture*
hiNg *hinge*	lääTs *lens*	räl̇m *herring*	ul̇m *fin*
hiRv *deer*	mäLv *sternum*	saLm *strait*	veimed (pl)*bride's presents to guests*
kiTs *goat*	nuRm *meadow*	saRv *horn*	
kõU[w] *thunder*	paRv *raft*	tal̇m *plant*	väiTs *knife*

63C tuPP *sheath* — tuPP 63C

	nominative	genitive	partitive	short into	stem
singular	**tuPP**	**tupe**	**tuPPe**	**tuPPe**	**tupe-**
plural	**tuped**	**tuPPede**	**tuPPi**		**tuPPede-**
			tuPPesid		(tupi-)

Also like tuPP: rüPP *lap*

The SHORT INTO CASE is not commonly used with the following items:

kuKK *cock (bird)* tiTT *baby* uTT *ewe*

63D eiT *old crone* — eiT 63D

	nominative	genitive	partitive	short into	stem
singular	**eiT**	**eide**	**eiTe**	(eiTe)	**eide-**
plural	**eided**	**eiTede**	**eiTi**		**eiTede-**
			eiTesid		(eidi-)

63E kiiK *swing* — kiiK 63E

	nominative	genitive	partitive	short into	stem
singular	**kiiK**	**kiige**	**kiiKe**	(kiiKe)	**kiige-**
plural	**kiiged**	**kiiKede**	**kiiKi**		**kiiKede-**
			kiiKesid		(kiigi-)

Also like kiiK: luiK *swan*

64 kõiK [A; PRONOUN] *all (sing) everything (pl) everybody* — kõiK 64

	nominative	genitive	partitive	short into	stem
singular	**kõiK**	**kõige**	**kõiKe**	(kõiKe)	**kõige-**
plural	**kõiK**	**kõigi**	**kõiKi**		**kõigi-**
		kõiKide	kõiKisid		kõikide-

65 sõĻm *knot* — sõĻm 65

	nominative	genitive	partitive	short into	stem
singular	**sõĻm**	**sõlme**	**sõLme**	**sõLme**	**sõlme-**
plural	**sõlmed**	**sõLmede**	**sõĻmi**		**sõLmede-**
			sõLmesid		(sõļmi-)

The SHORT INTO CASE is not commonly used with the following items:

saĻv *corn-bin* õŅN *happiness*

66 põĻv - põli *knee; generatrion* põĻv - põli 66

	nominative	genitive	partitive	short into	stem
singular	**põĻv - põli**	**põlve**	**põLve**	**põLve**	**põlve-**
plural	**põlved**	**põLvede**	**põĻvi**		**põLvede-**
			põLvesid		(põļvi-)

The SHORT INTO CASE is not commonly used with

taĻv - tali *winter*

67 tõri *horn* tõri 67

	nominative	genitive	partitive	short into	stem
singular	**tõri**	**tõrve**	**tõRve**	**tõRve**	**tõrve-**
plural	**tõrved**	**tõRvede**	**tõRvi**		**tõRvede-**
			tõRvesid		(tõrvi-)

TYPE 8 - J Stems

68A kiri *letter* kiri 68A

	nominative	genitive	partitive	short into	stem
singular	**kiri**	**kirja**	**kiRja**	**kiRja**	**kirja-**
plural	**kirjad**	**kiRjade**	**kiRju**		**kiRjade-**
			kiRjasid		(kirju-)

Also like kiri: kari *herd* põhi *north; bottom* sari *series*
hari *ridge*

The SHORT INTO CASE is not commonly used with the following items:

hari *brush* mari *berry*

68B kabi *hoof* kabi 68B

	nominative	genitive	partitive	short into	stem
singular	**kabi**	**kabja**	**kaPja**	**kaPja**	**kabja-**
plural	**kabjad**	**kaPjade**	**kaPju**		**kaPjade-**
			kaPjasid		(kabju-)

69A neli *four* neli 69A

	nominative	genitive	partitive	short into	stem
singular	**neli**	**neļja**	**neĻja**	**neĻja**	**neļja-**
plural	**neļjad**	**neĻjade**	**neĻju**		**neĻjade-**
			neĻjasid		(neļju-)

The SHORT INTO CASE is not commonly used with the following items:

asi *thing* kali *light ale* vili *crop* väli *field*
igihali *evergreen* nali *joke*

69B padi *pillow* **padi 69B**

	nominative	genitive	partitive	short into	stem
singular	**padi**	**paḑja**	**paȚja**	(paȚja)	**paḑja-**
plural	**paḑjad**	**paȚjade**	**paȚju** paȚjasid		**paȚjade-** (paḑju-)

70 saajad ***(pl) bridegroom's family*** **saajad 70**

	nominative	genitive	partitive	short into	stem
singular	saE	saaja	sAAja	(sAAja)	saaja-
plural	**saajad**	**sAAjade**	**sAAju** sAAjasid		**sAAjade-** (saaju-)

71A turi ***upper back*** **turi 71A**

	nominative	genitive	partitive	short into	stem
singular	**turi**	**turja**	**tuRja**	**tuRja**	**turja-**
plural	**turjad**	**tuRjade**	**tuRje** tuRjasid		**tuRjade-** (turje-)

Also like turi: kuhi *heap*

The SHORT INTO CASE is not commonly used with the following items:

kuri ^ *angry, mean* ohi *rein* ori *slave* tühi ^ *empty*

71B lubi ***lime (mineral)*** **lubi 71B**

	nominative	genitive	partitive	short into	stem
singular	**lubi**	**lubja**	**luPja**	(luPja)	**lubja-**
plural	**lubjad**	**luPjade**	**luPje** luPjasid		**luPjade-** (lubje-)

72A osi ***horsetail (plant)*** **osi 72A**

	nominative	genitive	partitive	short into	stem
singular	**osi**	**oşja**	**oŞja**	**oŞja**	**oşja-**
plural	**oşjad**	**oŞjade**	**oŞje** oŞjasid		**oŞjade-** (oşje-)

72B hudi ***cudgel*** **hudi 72B**

	nominative	genitive	partitive	short into	stem
singular	**hudi**	**huḑja**	**huȚja**	(huȚja)	**huḑja-**
plural	**huḑjad**	**huȚjade**	**huȚje** huȚjasid		**huȚjade-** (huḑje-)

73 soE [A] ***warm*** **soE 73**

	nominative	genitive	partitive	short into	stem
singular	**soE**	**sooja**	**sOOja**	**sOOja**	**sooja-**
plural	**soojad**	**sOOjade**	**sOOje**		**sOOjade-**
			sOOjasid		(sooje-)

74 vari ***shadow*** **vari 74**

	nominative	genitive	partitive	short into	stem
singular	**vari**	**varju**	**vaRju**	**vaRju**	**varju-**
plural	**varjud**	**vaRjude**	**vaRje**		**vaRjude-**
			vaRjasid		(varje-)

Also like vari: ahi *stove*

The SHORT INTO CASE is not commonly used with:

kahi *damage*

75 vali [A] ***loud*** **vali 75**

	nominative	genitive	partitive	short into	stem
singular	**vali**	**vaļju**	**vaĻju**	(vaĻju)	**vaļju-**
plural	**vaļjud**	**vaĻjude**	**vaĻje**		**vaĻjude-**
			vaĻjusid		(vaļje-)

76 puri ***sail*** **puri 76**

	nominative	genitive	partitive	short into	stem
singular	**puri**	**purje**	**puRje**	(puRje)	**purje-**
plural	**purjed**	**puRjede**	**puRjesid**		**puRjede-**

77 veli ***brother*** **veli 77**

	nominative	genitive	partitive	short into	stem
singular	**veli**	**veļje**	**veĻje**	(veĻje)	**veļje-**
plural	**veļjed**	**veĻjede**	**veĻjesid**		**veĻjede-**

TYPE 9 - R and L Stems

78A sõber ***friend*** **sõber 78A**

	nominative	genitive	partitive	short into	stem
singular	**sõber**	**sõbra**	**sõPra**	(sõPra)	**sõbra-**
plural	**sõbrad**	**sõPrade**	**sõPru**		**sõPrade-**
			sõPrasid		(sõbru-)

78B ader *plough* **ader 78B**

	nominative	genitive	partitive	short into	stem
singular	**ader**	**adra**	**aTra**	(aTra)	**adra-**
plural	**adrad**	**aTrade**	**aTru**		**aTrade-**
			aTrasid		(adru-)

Also like ader: nõder ^ *feeble* põder *elk*

78C vagel *maggot* **vagel 78C**

	nominative	genitive	partitive	short into	stem
singular	**vagel**	**vagla**	**vaKla**	(vaKla)	**vagla-**
plural	**vaglad**	**vaKlade**	**vaKlu**		**vaKlade-**
			vaKlasid		(vaglu-)

79A kubel *bubble* **kubel 79A**

	nominative	genitive	partitive	short into	stem
singular	**kubel**	**kubla**	**kuPla**	(kuPla)	**kubla-**
plural	**kublad**	**kuPlade**	**kuPli**		**kuPlade-**
			kuPlasid		(kubli-)

79B oder *barley* **oder 79B**

	nominative	genitive	partitive	short into	stem
singular	**oder**	**odra**	**oTra**	(oTra)	**odra-**
plural	**odrad**	**oTrade**	**oTri**		**oTrade-**
			oTrasid		(odri-)

79C mäger *badger* **mäger 79C**

	nominative	genitive	partitive	short into	stem
singular	**mäger**	**mägra**	**mäKra**	(mäKra)	**mägra-**
plural	**mägrad**	**mäKrade**	**mäKri**		**mäKrade-**
			mäKrasid		(mägri-)

80 puder *porridge* **puder 80**

	nominative	genitive	partitive	short into	stem
singular	**puder**	**pudru**	**puTru**	(puTru)	**pudru-**
plural	**pudrud**	**puTrude**	**puTre**		**puTrude-**
			puTrusid		(pudre-)

81A teder ***grouse*** **teder 81A**

	nominative	genitive	partitive	short into	stem
singular	**teder**	**tedre**	**teTre**	(teTre)	**tedre-**
plural	**tedred**	**teTrede**	**teTri**		**teTrede-**
			teTresid		(tedri-)

81B koger ***Yellow fish*** **koger 81B**

	nominative	genitive	partitive	short into	stem
singular	**koger**	**kogre**	**koKre**	(koKre)	**kogre-**
plural	**kogred**	**koKrede**	**koKri**		**koKrede-**
			koKresid		(kogri-)

TYPE 10 - Regular - Consonant Partitives

82 kEEl ***tongue; language*** **kEEl 82**

	nominative	genitive	partitive	short into	stem
singular	**kEEl**	**keele**	**keelT**	**kEEle**	**keele-**
				kEElde	
plural	**keeled**	**keelte**	**kEEli**		**keelte-**
					(keeli-)

Also like kEEl:	hÄÄl *voice*	mEEl *mind*	tUUl *wind*
hOOl *care*	jOOn *line*	sUUr ^ *big*	vEEr *edge*
hUUl *lip*	jUUr *root*	sÄÄr *shank*	ÄÄr *edge*

The SHORT INTO CASE is not commonly used with the following items:

hIIr *mouse*	nOOl *arrow*	pOOl *half*	sOOl *intestine*
kAAr *arc*	nOOr ^ *young*	sAAr *island; ash-tree*	sOOn *vein*
kIIr *ray*	pEEn ^ *fine*	sEEn *mushroom*	vOOr *drumlin*
kOOr *peel; cream (dairy)*			

83 lEEm ***broth*** **lEEm 83**

	nominative	genitive	partitive	short into	stem
singular	**lEEm**	**leeme**	**leenT**	**lEEme**	**leeme-**
				lEEnde	
plural	**leemed**	**leente**	**lEEmi**		**leente-**
					(leemi-)

TYPE 11 - Irregular - Consonant Partitives

84 uKs *door* **uKs 84**

	nominative	genitive	partitive	short into	stem
singular	**uKs**	**ukse**	**uSt**		**ukse-**
plural	**uksed**	**uste**	**uKsi**		**uste-** (uksi-)

85 laPs *child* **laPs 85**

	nominative	genitive	partitive	short into	stem
singular	**laPs**	**lapse**	**laSt**		**lapse-**
plural	**lapsed**	**laste**	**laPsi**		**laste-** (lapsi-)

NOMINALS - 2 - CLASS III B

TYPE 12 - Regular - Vowel Partitives

86A hAAb *aspen* — hAAb 86A

	nominative	genitive	partitive	short into	stem
singular	**hAAb**	**haava**	**hAAba**	(hAAba)	**haava-**
plural	**haavad**	**hAAbade**	**hAAbu**		**hAAbade-**
			hAAbasid		(haavu-)

Also like hAAb: tÏÏb *wing*

86B leİb *bread* — leİb 86B

	nominative	genitive	partitive	short into	stem
singular	**leİb**	**leiva**	**leİba**	(leİba)	**leiva-**
plural	**leivad**	**leİbade**	**leİbu**		**leİbade-**
			leİbasid		(leivu-)

Also like leİb: haLb [A] *nasty*

87 raMb [A] *feeble* — raMb 87

	nominative	genitive	partitive	short into	stem
singular	**raMb**	**ramma**	**raMba**	(raMba)	**ramma-**
plural	**rammad**	**raMbade**	**raMbu**		**raMbade-**
			raMbasid		(rammu-)

Also like raMb: saMb *sturgeon* viMb *bream (fish)*

88A laUd *table* — laUd 88A

	nominative	genitive	partitive	short into	stem
singular	**laUd**	**lau[w]a**	**laUda**	**laUda**	**lau[w]a-**
plural	**lau[w]ad**	**laUdade**	**laUdu**		**laUdade-**
			laUdasid		

Also like laUd: haUd *grave* raUd *iron*

The SHORT INTO CASE is not commonly used with:

põUd *drought*

88B nõİd *witch; shaman* — nõİd 88B

	nominative	genitive	partitive	short into	stem
singular	**nõİd**	**nõi[j]a**	**nõİda**	(nõİda)	**nõi[j]a-**
plural	**nõi[j]ad**	**nõİdade**	**nõİdu**		**nõİdade-**
			nõİdasid		(nõi[j]u-)

89A pİİrd *sley* — pİİrd 89A

	nominative	genitive	partitive	short into	stem
singular	**pİİrd**	**piira**	**pİİrda**	(pİİrda)	**piira-**
plural	**piirad**	**pİİrdade**	**pİİrdu**		**pİİrdade-**
			pİİrdasid		(piiru-)

89B piHt *waist* — piHt 89B

	nominative	genitive	partitive	short into	stem
singular	**piHt**	**piha**	**piHta**	**piHta**	**piha-**
plural	**pihad**	**piHtade**	**piHtu**		**piHtade-**
			piHtasid		(pihu-)

The SHORT INTO CASE is not commonly used with:

viHt *whisk in sauna*

90 aEd *garden* — aEd 90

	nominative	genitive	partitive	short into	stem
singular	**aEd**	**ai[j]a**	**aEda**	**aEda**	**ai[j]a-**
plural	**ai[j]ad**	**aEdade**	**aEdu**		**aEdade-**
			aEdasid		(ai[j]u-)

91 taLd *sole (of foot)* — taLd 91

	nominative	genitive	partitive	short into	stem
singular	**taLd**	**talla**	**taLda**	**taLda**	**talla-**
plural	**tallad**	**taLdade**	**taLdu**		**taLdade-**
			taLdasid		(tallu-)

The SHORT INTO CASE is not commonly used with the following items:

siLd *bridge; quay* tõLd *coach* vaLd *township*

92 hiNd *feeble* — hiNd 92

	nominative	genitive	partitive	short into	stem
singular	**hiNd**	**hinna**	**hiNda**	**hiNda**	**hinna-**
plural	**hinnad**	**hiNdade**	**hiNdu**		**hiNdade-**
			hiNdasid		(hinnu-)

Also like hiNd: kaNd *heel* raNd *beach*

The SHORT INTO CASE is not commonly used with:

piNd *surface*

93 mõRd ***weir*** **mõRd 93**

	nominative	genitive	partitive	short into	stem
singular	**mõRd**	**mõrra**	**mõRda**	(mõRda)	**mõrra-**
plural	**mõrrad**	**mõRdade**	**mõRdu**		**mõRdade-**
			mõRdasid		(mõrru-)

94A lõUg ***chin*** **lõUg 94A**

	nominative	genitive	partitive	short into	stem
singular	**lõUg**	**lõu[w]a**	**lõUga**	(lõUga)	**lõu[w]a-**
plural	**lõu[w]ad**	**lõUgade**	**lõUgu**		**lõUgade-**
			lõUgasid		

94B sİİg ***whitefish*** **sİİg 94B**

	nominative	genitive	partitive	short into	stem
singular	**sİİg**	**sii[j]a**	**sİİga**	(sİİga)	**sii[j]a-**
plural	**sii[j]ad**	**sİİgade**	**sİİgu**		**sİİgade-**
			sİİgasid		

Also like sİİg: lİİg *excess*

95A võLg ***debt*** **võLg 95A**

	nominative	genitive	partitive	short into	stem
singular	**võLg**	**võla**	**võLga**	**võLga**	**võla-**
plural	**võlad**	**võLgade**	**võLgu**		**võLgade-**
			võLgasid		(võlu-)

Also like võLg õLg *shoulder*

The SHORT INTO CASE is not commonly used with the following:

aRg ^ *cowardly* sõRg *cloven hoof*

95B naHk ***skin; hide*** **naHk 95B**

	nominative	genitive	partitive	short into	stem
singular	**naHk**	**naha**	**naHka**	**naHka**	**naha-**
plural	**nahad**	**naHkade**	**naHku**		**naHkade-**
			naHkasid		(nahu-)

The SHORT INTO CASE is not commonly used with the following items:

aSk *sorcery* laiSk ^ *lazy* piiSk *droplet* rööSk ^ *fresh*
kiiSk *ruff (fish)* paSk *shit* raiSk *carrion* saHk *plough*

96 sinirAAg *roller (bird)* sinirAAg 96

	nominative	genitive	partitive	short into	stem
singular	**sinirAAg**	**sinirAA**	**sinirAAga**	(sinirAAga)	**sinirAA-**
plural	**sinirAAd**	**sinirAAgade**	**sinirAAgu**		**sinirAAgade-**
			sinirAAgasid		(siniraO-)

97 lÕÕg *leash* lÕÕg 97

	nominative	genitive	partitive	short into	stem
singular	**lÕÕg**	**lõA**	**lÕÕga**	(lÕÕga)	**lõA-**
plural	**lõAd**	**lÕÕgade**	**lÕÕgu**		**lÕÕgade-**
			lÕÕgasid		(lõO-)

98 aEg *time* aEg 98

	nominative	genitive	partitive	short into	stem
singular	**aEg**	**aja**	**aEga**	(aEga)	**aja-**
plural	**ajad**	**aEgade**	**aEgu**		**aEgade-**
			aEgasid		(aju-)

99 riNd *chest; breast* riNd 99

	nominative	genitive	partitive	short into	stem
singular	**riNd**	**rinna**	**riNda**	**riNda**	**rinna-**
plural	**rinnad**	**riNdade**	**riNdu**	**riNdu**	**riNdade-**
			riNdasid		rinnu-

100 jaLg *feeble* jaLg 100

	nominative	genitive	partitive	short into	stem
singular	**jaLg**	**jala**	**jaLga**	**jaLga**	**jala-**
plural	**jalad**	**jaLgade**	**jaLgu**	**jaLgu**	**jaLgade-**
			jaLgasid		jalu-

101A hOOb *lever* hOOb 101A

	nominative	genitive	partitive	short into	stem
singular	**hOOb**	**hoova**	**hOOba**	(hOOba)	**hoova-**
plural	**hoovad**	**hOObade**	**hOObi**		**hOObade-**
			hOObasid		(hoovi-)

101B kuRb [A] *sad* — kuRb 101B

	nominative	genitive	partitive	short into	stem
singular	**kuRb**	**kurva**	**kuRba**	(kuRba)	**kurva-**
plural	**kurvad**	**kuRbade**	**kuRbi**		**kuRbade-**
			kuRbasid		(kurvi-)

Also like kuRb: koİb *shank* kü̈Rb *penis* uRb *catkin*

102 kuMb *which of two* — kuMb 102

	nominative	genitive	partitive	short into	stem
singular	**kuMb**	**kumma**	**kuMba**	**kuMba**	**kumma-**
plural	**kummad**	**kuMbade**	**kuMbi**		**kuMbade-**
			kuMbasid		(kummi-)

Also like kuMb:

eMb-kuMb	emma-kumma	eMba-kuMba	etc.	*either or*
kuMbki	kummagi	kuMbagi	etc.	*either of two*

103 lUUd *broom* — lUUd 103

	nominative	genitive	partitive	short into	stem
singular	**lUUd**	**luu[w]a**	**lUUda**	(lUUda)	**luu[w]a-**
plural	**luu[w]ad**	**lUUdade**	**lUUdi**		**lUUdade-**
			lUUdasid		

104A sUUnd *direction* — sUUnd 104A

	nominative	genitive	partitive	short into	stem
singular	**sUUnd**	**suuna**	**sUUnda**	**sUUnda**	**suuna-**
plural	**suunad**	**sUUndade**	**sUUndi**		**sUUndade-**
			sUUndasid		(suuni-)

104B koHt *place* — koHt 104B

	nominative	genitive	partitive	short into	stem
singular	**koHt**	**koha**	**koHta**	**koHta**	**koha-**
plural	**kohad**	**koHtade**	**koHti**		**koHtade-**
			koHtasid		(kohi-)

Also like koHt: luHt *wetland*

105 muLd *lever* muLd 105

	nominative	genitive	partitive	short into	stem
singular	**muLd**	**mulla**	**muLda**	**muLda**	**mulla-**
plural	**mullad**	**muLdade**	**muLdi**		**muLdade-**
			muLdasid		(mulli-)

The SHORT INTO CASE is not commonly used with the following items:

kuLd *gold* süLd *fathom*

106 -koNd *collective* -koNd 106

	nominative	genitive	partitive	short into	stem
singular	**-koNd**	**-konna**	**-koNda**	**-koNda**	**-konna-**
plural	**-konnad**	**-koNdade**	**-koNdi**		**-koNdade-**
			-koNdasid		(-konni-)

Also like -koNd:

elaniKKoNd *population*
erakoNd *political party*
haritlaskoNd *intelligentsia*
inimkoNd *humanity*
juHtkoNd *management*
keSkkoNd *environment*
kihelkoNd *parish*
kümmekoNd *ten or so*
leİbkoNd *household*
lugejaskoNd *readership*
mAAkoNd *province*
mEEskoNd *men's team*
naİskoNd *women's team*
osakoNd *department*
perekoNd *family*
pİIrkoNd *district*
põĻvkoNd *generation*
riNgkoNd *set of people*
saaTkoNd *embassy*
seḷTskoNd *coterie*
tEEkoNd *way*
toİmkoNd *committee*
tuTvuskoNd *acquiantances*
valijaskoNd *electorate*
vilistlaskoNd *alumni*
võiStkoNd *mixed team*
õHkkoNd *atmosphere*
õpetajaskoNd *teaching staff*
õpilaskoNd *student body*
ühiskoNd *society*
ülikoNd *suit*
üMbruskoNd *environs*

The SHORT INTO CASE is not commonly used with the following items:

häNd *tail* mäNd *whisk* veNd *brother*

107 koRd *order* koRd 107

	nominative	genitive	partitive	short into	stem
singular	**koRd**	**korra**	**koRda**	**koRda**	**korra-**
plural	**korrad**	**koRdade**	**koRdi**		**koRdade-**
			koRdasid		(korri-)

108 hUUg *droning* hUUg 108

	nominative	genitive	partitive	short into	stem
singular	**hUUg**	**huu[w]a**	**hUUga**	(hUUga)	**huu[w]a-**
plural	**huu[w]ad**	**hUUgade**	**hUUgi**		**hUUgade-**
			hUUgasid		(huui-)

109 leHk *stink* — leHk 109

	nominative	genitive	partitive	short into	stem
singular	**leHk**	**leha**	**leHka**	(leHka)	**leha-**
plural	**lehad**	**leHkade**	**leHki**		**leHkade-**
			leHkasid		(lehi-)

Also like leHk: suuSk *ski*, turSk *cod*, üSk *womb*, morSk *walrus*, tuHk *ash*

110 rOOg *food* — rOOg 110

	nominative	genitive	partitive	short into	stem
singular	**rOOg**	**roA**	**rOOga**	(rOOga)	**roA-**
plural	**roAd**	**rOOgade**	**rOOgi**		**rOOgade-**
			rOOgasid		(roİ-)

111 pöİd *instep* — pöİd 111

	nominative	genitive	partitive	short into	stem
singular	**pöİd**	**pöi[j]a**	**pöİda**	(pöİda)	**pöi[j]a-**
plural	**pöi[j]ad**	**pöİdade**	**pöİdi**		**pöİdade-**
			pöİdasid		(pöi[j]e-)

112 näĻg *famine; hunger* — näĻg 112

	nominative	genitive	partitive	short into	stem
singular	**näĻg**	**näļja**	**näĻga**	**näĻga**	**näļja-**
plural	**näļjad**	**näĻgade**	**näĻgi**		**näĻgade-**
			näĻgasid		(näļje-)

The SHORT INTO CASE is not commonly used with the following items:

häRg *ox*, mäRg [A] *wet*, päRg *wreath*, seĻg *back*

113 poEg *son* — poEg 113

	nominative	genitive	partitive	short into	stem
singular	**poEg**	**poja**	**poEga**	(poEga)	**poja-**
plural	**pojad**	**poEgade**	**poEgi**		**poEgade-**
			poEgasid		(poje-)

114 koĻb *flask* — koĻb 114

	nominative	genitive	partitive	short into	stem
singular	**koĻb**	**koļvi**	**koĻbi**	(koĻbi)	**koļvi-**
plural	**koļvid**	**koĻbide**	**koĻbe**		**koĻbide-**
			koĻbisid		(koļve-)

Also like koĻb: teİb *dace*

115 mOOḑ *fashion* mOOḑ 115

	nominative	genitive	partitive	short into	stem
singular	**mOOḑ**	**moE**	**mOOḑi**	**mOOḑi**	**moE-**
plural	**moEd**	**mOOḑide**	**mOOḑe**		**mOOḑide-**
			mOOḑisid		

Also like mOOḑ: pOOḑ *store*

The SHORT INTO CASE is not commonly used with the following items:

prAAḑ *roast* rAAḑ *town council*

116 jaHt *hunt; yacht* jaHt 116

	nominative	genitive	partitive	short into	stem
singular	**jaHt**	**jahi**	**jaHti**	(jaHti)	**jahi-**
plural	**jahid**	**jaHtide**	**jaHte**		**jaHtide-**
			jaHtisid		(jahe-)

Also like jaHt:
juHt *leader*
kiHt *layer*
konTraHt *contract*
piHt *confession*
praHt *rubbish*
rüHt *carriage of person*
siHt *aim*
taHt *wick*
vaHt *guard*
viHt *skein; weight (scales)*

117 moḺd *trough* moḺd 117

	nominative	genitive	partitive	short into	stem
singular	**moḺd**	**moḷli**	**moḺdi**	(moḺdi)	**moḷli-**
plural	**moḷlid**	**moḺdide**	**moḺde**		**moḺdide-**
			moḺdisid		(moḷle-)

118 tuŅd *hour; class, lesson* tuŅd 118

	nominative	genitive	partitive	short into	stem
singular	**tuŅd**	**tuņni**	**tuŅdi**	**tuŅdi**	**tuņni-**
plural	**tuņnid**	**tuŅdide**	**tuŅde**		**tuŅdide-**
			tuŅdisid		(tuņne-)

The SHORT INTO CASE is not commonly used with the following items:

aŅd *yield* mäŅd *pine* süŅd *birth*

119 sAAg *saw* sAAg 119

	nominative	genitive	partitive	short into	stem
singular	**sAAg**	**saE**	**sAAgi**	(sAAgi)	**saE-**
plural	**saEd**	**sAAgide**	**sAAge**		**sAAgide-**
			sAAgisid		

120A jäRg *footstool* jäRg 120A

	nominative	genitive	partitive	short into	stem
singular	**jäRg**	**järi**	**jäRgi**	**jäRgi**	**järi-**
plural	**järid**	**jäRgide**	**jäRge**		**jäRgide-**
			jäRgisid		(järe-)

120B väHk *crab; cancer* väHk 120B

	nominative	genitive	partitive	short into	stem
singular	**väHk**	**vähi**	**väHki**	**väHki**	**vähi-**
plural	**vähid**	**väHkide**	**väHke**		**väHkide-**
			väHkisid		(vähe-)

The SHORT INTO CASE is not commonly used with the following items:

nuHk *spy* soHk *fraud* valSk *spurious*

121 oRb *orphan* oRb 121

	nominative	genitive	partitive	short into	stem
singular	**oRb**	**orvu**	**oRbu**	(oRbu)	**orvu-**
plural	**orvud**	**oRbude**	**oRbe**		**oRbude-**
			oRbusid		(orve-)

122 aMb *archery bow* aMb 122

	nominative	genitive	partitive	short into	stem
singular	**aMb**	**ammu**	**aMbu**	(aMbu)	**ammu-**
plural	**ammud**	**aMbude**	**aMbe**		**aMbude-**
			aMbusid		(amme-)

123A rİİd *quarrel* rİİd 123A

	nominative	genitive	partitive	short into	stem
singular	**rİİd**	**rii[j]u**	**rİİdu**	**rİİdu**	**rii[j]u-**
plural	**rii[j]ud**	**rİİdude**	**rİİde**		**rİİdude-**
			rİİdusid		(rii[j]e-)

The SHORT INTO CASE is not commonly used with the following items:

hİİd giant hÜÜd *exclamation*

123B hoİd *storage* hoİd 123B

	nominative	genitive	partitive	short into	stem
singular	**hoİd**	**hoi[j]u**	**hoİdu**	**hoİdu**	**hoi[j]u-**
plural	**hoi[j]ud**	**hoİdude**	**hoİde**		**hoİdude-**
			hoİdusid		(hoi[j]e-)

The SHORT INTO CASE is not commonly used with the following items:

laİd *islet* leİd *find* loİd *apathetic* neİd *maiden*

124A kEErd *twist* — kEErd 124A

	nominative	genitive	partitive	short into	stem
singular	**kEErd**	**keeru**	**kEErdu**	**kEErdu**	**keeru-**
plural	**keerud**	**kEErdude**	**kEErde**		**kEErdude-**
			kEErdusid		(keere-)

The SHORT INTO CASE is not commonly used with:

kEEld *prohibition*

124B kõHt *belly* — kõHt 124B

	nominative	genitive	partitive	short into	stem
singular	**kõHt**	**kõhu**	**kõHtu**	**kõHtu**	**kõhu-**
plural	**kõhud**	**kõHtude**	**kõHte**		**kõHtude-**
			kõHtusid		(kõhe-)

Also like kõHt: oHt *danger*

The SHORT INTO CASE is not commonly used with the following items:

juHt *instance* maHt *capacity* toHt *birch-bark* vaHt *foam*

125 sAAd *haycock* — sAAd 125

	nominative	genitive	partitive	short into	stem
singular	**sAAd**	**saO**	**sAAdu**	(sAAdu)	**saO-**
plural	**saOd**	**sAAdude**	**sAAde**		**sAAdude-**
			sAAdusid		

126 rOOd *fish-bone* — rOOd 126

	nominative	genitive	partitive	short into	stem
singular	**rOOd**	**rOO**	**rOOdu**	(rOOdu)	**rOO-**
plural	**rOOd**	**rOOdude**	**rOOde**		**rOOdude-**
			rOOdusid		

127 jõUd *strength* — jõUd 127

	nominative	genitive	partitive	short into	stem
singular	**jõUd**	**jõU**	**jõUdu**	(jõUdu)	**jõU-**
plural	**jõUd**	**jõUdude**	**jõUde**		**jõUdude-**
			jõUdusid		

Also like jõUd: kiUd *fibre*

128 kiLd *splinter of glass* kiLd 128

	nominative	genitive	partitive	short into	stem
singular	**kiLd**	**killu**	**kiLdu**	(kiLdu)	**killu-**
plural	**killud**	**kiLdude**	**kiLde**		**kiLdude-**
			kiLdusid		(kille-)

Also like kiLd: põLd *field*

129 leNd *flight* leNd 129

	nominative	genitive	partitive	short into	stem
singular	**leNd**	**lennu**	**leNdu**	**leNdu**	**lennu-**
plural	**lennud**	**leNdude**	**leNde**		**leNdude-**
			leNdusid		(lenne-)

Also like leNd: käNd *stump of tree*

The SHORT INTO CASE is not commonly used with the following items:

iNd *enthusiasm* liNd *bird* piNd *sliver*

130 muRd *fracture* muRd 130

	nominative	genitive	partitive	short into	stem
singular	**muRd**	**murru**	**muRdu**	(muRdu)	**murru-**
plural	**murrud**	**muRdude**	**muRde**		**muRdude-**
			muRdusid		(murre-)

131A vEErg *column* vEErg 131A

	nominative	genitive	partitive	short into	stem
singular	**vEErg**	**veeru**	**vEErgu**	**vEErgu**	**veeru-**
plural	**veerud**	**vEErgude**	**vEErge**		**vEErgude-**
			vEErgusid		(veere-)

The SHORT INTO CASE is not commonly used with the following items:

pEErg *torch* vIIrg *line*

131B uRg *burrow* uRg 131B

	nominative	genitive	partitive	short into	stem
singular	**uRg**	**uru**	**uRgu**	**uRgu**	**uru-**
plural	**urud**	**uRgude**	**uRge**		**uRgude-**
			uRgusid		(ure-)

Also like uRg: oRg *valley*

The SHORT INTO CASE is not commonly used with the following items:

haLg *log* peIg *fiancé* suLg *parenthesis* tuRg *market*
kuLg *course (progress)* põLg *banishment*

131C õHk *air* õHk 131C

	nominative	genitive	partitive	short into	stem
singular	**õHk**	**õhu**	**õHku**	**õHku**	**õhu-**
plural	**õhud**	**õHkude**	**õHke** õHkusid		**õHkude-** (õhe-)

Also like õHk:

laHk *parting*	loHk *hollow*	põHk *litter*	uSk *belief*
	piHk *palm (hand)*		

The SHORT INTO CASE is not commonly used with the following items:

järSk ^ *steep*	luiSk *whetstone*	puHk *occasion*	tõHk *polecat*
käSk *command*	lõHk *split*	rõHk *pressure*	uiSk *skate*
laSk *shot*	muHk *bump on skin*	rõhud (pl) *copper chains*	viHk *sheaf*
liiSk *lot*	mürSk *artillery shell*	tuiSk *blizzard*	viiSk *bast shoe*

132 rAAg *twig* rAAg 132

	nominative	genitive	partitive	short into	stem
singular	**rAAg**	**raO**	**rAAgu**	(rAAgu)	**raO-**
plural	**raOd**	**rAAgude**	**rAAge** rAAgusid		**rAAgude-**

133 hOOg *momentum* hOOg 133

	nominative	genitive	partitive	short into	stem
singular	**hOOg**	**hOO**	**hOOgu**	**hOOgu**	**hOO-**
plural	**hOOd**	**hOOgude**	**hOOge** hOOgusid		**hOOgude-**

The SHORT INTO CASE is not commonly used with the following items:

rOOg *reed* vOOg *billow*

134 tõUg *breed* tõUg 134

	nominative	genitive	partitive	short into	stem
singular	**tõUg**	**tõU**	**tõUgu**	**tõUgu**	**tõU-**
plural	**tõUd**	**tõUgude**	**tõUge** tõUgusid		**tõUgude-**

The SHORT INTO CASE is not commonly used with the following items:

laUg *eyelid* siUg *snake*

135 peLg *fear* peLg 135

	nominative	genitive	partitive	short into	stem
singular	**peLg**	**peļju**	**peLgu**	(peLgu)	**peļju-**
plural	**peļjud**	**peLgude**	**peLge** peLgusid		**peLgude-** (peļje-)

136 kUUb *coat* **kUUb 136**

	nominative	genitive	partitive	short into	stem
singular	**kUUb**	**kuu[w]e**	**kUUbe**	(kUUbe)	**kuu[w]e-**
plural	**kuu[w]ed**	**kUUbede**	**kUUbi**		**kUUbede-**
			kUUbesid		

137 kõRb *uninhabited woodland* **kõRb 137**

	nominative	genitive	partitive	short into	stem
singular	**kõRb**	**kõrve**	**kõRbe**	**kõRbe**	**kõrve-**
plural	**kõrved**	**kõRbede**	**kõRbi**		**kõRbede-**
			kõRbesid		(kõrvi-)

138 iMb *maiden* **iMb 138**

	nominative	genitive	partitive	short into	stem
singular	**iMb**	**imme**	**iMbe**	(iMbe)	**imme-**
plural	**immed**	**iMbede**	**iMbi**		**iMbede-**
			iMbesid		(immi-)

139 leHt *leaf; page; newspaper* **leHt 139**

	nominative	genitive	partitive	short into	stem
singular	**leHt**	**lehe**	**leHte**	**leHte**	**lehe-**
plural	**lehed**	**leHtede**	**leHti**		**leHtede-**
			leHtesid		(lehi-)

Also like leHt: laHt *bay*

The SHORT INTO CASE is not commonly used with:

täHt *star*

140A kuRg *crane (bird)* **kuRg 140A**

	nominative	genitive	partitive	short into	stem
singular	**kuRg**	**kure**	**kuRge**	(kuRge)	**kure-**
plural	**kured**	**kuRgede**	**kuRgi**		**kuRgede-**
			kuRgesid		(kuri-)

Also like kuRg: kiRg *passion*

140B kuuSk *fir* **kuuSk 140B**

	nominative	genitive	partitive	short into	stem
singular	**kuuSk**	**kuuse**	**kuuSke**	(kuuSke)	**kuuse-**
plural	**kuused**	**kuuSkede**	**kuuSki**		**kuuSkede-**
			kuuSkesid		(kuusi-)

Also like kuuSk: leSk *widow(er)* sääSk *mosquito*

141 jäRg *sequel* jäRg 141

	nominative	genitive	partitive	short into	stem
singular	**jäRg**	**järje**	**jäRge**	**jäRge**	**järje-**
plural	**järjed**	**jäRgede**	**jäRgi** jäRgesid		**jäRgede-**

Also like jäRg: küL̦g *side*

The SHORT INTO CASE is not commonly used with the following items:

jäL̦g *track* säRg *roach (fish)* teL̦g *axis, axle* tel̦jed (pl) *loom*
käRg *honeycomb* süL̦g *spittle*

142A sõL̦g *Estonian brooch* sõL̦g 142A

	nominative	genitive	partitive	short into	stem
singular	**sõL̦g**	**sõle**	**sõLge**	(sõLge)	**sõle-**
plural	**sõled**	**sõLgede**	**sõL̦gi** sõLgesid		**sõLgede-** (sõl̦i-)

like sõL̦g: suL̦g *feather* õL̦g *straw*

142B koŞk *waterfall* koŞk 142B

	nominative	genitive	partitive	short into	stem
singular	**koŞk**	**kose**	**koSke**	**koSke**	**kose-**
plural	**kosed**	**koSkede**	**koŞki** koSkesid		**koSkede-** (koşi-)

Also like koŞk: põŞk *cheek*

The SHORT INTO CASE is not commonly used with the following items:

kaŞk *birch* vaŞk *copper*

TYPE 13 - Consonant Partitives

143A UUs [A] *new* UUs 143A

	nominative	genitive	partitive	short into	stem
singular	**UUs**	**uu[w]e**	**uuT**	**UUde**	**uu[w]e-**
plural	**uu[w]ed**	**uute**	**UUsi**		**uute-** (uusi-)

Also like UUs: kUUs *six*

143B vİİs *five* — vİİs 143B

	nominative	genitive	partitive	short into	stem
singular	**vİİs**	**vii[j]e**	**viiT**	**vİİde**	**vii[j]e-**
plural	**vii[j]ed**	**viite**	**vİİsi**		**viite-** (viisi-)

Also like vİİs: hİİs *sacred grove*

The SHORT INTO CASE is not commonly used with the following items:

nİİs *heddle*

143C täİs [A] *full* — täİs 143C

	nominative	genitive	partitive	short into	stem
singular	**täİs**	**täi[j]e**	**täiT**	**täİde**	**täi[j]e-**
plural	**täi[j]ed**	**täite**	**täİsi**		**täite-** (täisi-)

The SHORT INTO CASE is not commonly used with the following items:

köİs *rope* põİs *bladder* reİs *thigh* õİs *blossom*

144 kõRs *straw* — kõRs 144

	nominative	genitive	partitive	short into	stem
singular	**kõRs**	**kõrre**	**kõrT**	(kõRde)	**kõrre-**
plural	**kõrred**	**kõrte**	**kõRsi**		**kõrte-** (kõrsi-)

Also like kõRs: tõRs *vat* vaRs *stem* õRs *perch*

145 pAAş *limestone* — pAAş 145

	nominative	genitive	partitive	short into	stem
singular	**pAAş**	**paE**	**paaT**	(pAAde)	**paE-**
plural	**paEd**	**paate**	**pAAşi**		**paate-** (paaşi-)

TYPE 14 - Irregular - Consonant Partitives

146 lAAş *virgin forest* — lAAş 146

	nominative	genitive	partitive	short into	stem
singular	**lAAş**	**laane**	**laanT**	**lAAnde**	**laane-**
plural	**laaned**	**laante**	**lAAşi**		**laante-** (laaşi-)

Also like lAAş: lÄÄş *west* ÕÕş *cavity*

The SHORT INTO CASE is not commonly used with the following items:

kAAş *lid* kÜÜş *finger or toe nail*

147 mEEs ***man*** **mEEs 147**

	nominative	genitive	partitive	short into	stem
singular	**mEEs**	**mehe**	**meesT**		**mehe-**
plural	**mehed**	**meeste**	**mehi**		**meeste-** (mehi-)

148 haUg ***pike*** **haUg 148**

	nominative	genitive	partitive	short into	stem
singular	**haUg**	**havi** **haugi**	**haUgi**	(haUgi)	**havi-** **haugi-**
plural	**havid** **haugid**	**haUgide**	**haUge**		**haUgide-** (have-)

149 kaKs ***two*** **kaKs 149**

	nominative	genitive	partitive	short into	stem
singular	**kaKs**	**kahe**	**kaHt** **kaHte**	**kaHte**	**kahe-**
plural	**kahed**	**kaHtede**	**kahesid**		**kaHtede-**

Also like kaKs: üKs *one*

150 rehi ***drying barn*** **rehi 150**

	nominative	genitive	partitive	short into	stem
singular	**rehi**	**rehe**	**reHt** **reHte**	**reHte**	**rehe-**
plural	**rehed**	**reHtede**	**reHti**		**reHtede-** (rehi)

151 rohi ***grass; medicine*** **rohi 151**

	nominative	genitive	partitive	short into	stem
singular	**rohi**	**rohu**	**roHtu**	(roHtu)	**rohu-**
plural	**rohud**	**roHtude**	**roHtusid** roHte		**roHtude-**

TYPE 15 - Regular

152 auto *car* — auto 152

	nominative	genitive	partitive	short into	stem
singular	**auto**	**auto**	**autot**		**auto-**
plural	**autod**	**autode**	**autosid**		**autode-**

Also like auto:
adru *seaweed*
aku *automobile battery*
aula *assembly hall*
beebi *baby*
bruto *gross*
draama *drama*
džoki *jockey*
džuudo *judo*
firma *company*
foto *photo*
gorilla *gorilla*
Hansa *Hanseatic League*
hapu ^ *sour*
hertsoginna *duchess*
hoki *hockey*
härra *gentleman*
influentsa *influenza*
jope *jacket*
juuli *July*
juuni *June*
juura *jurisprudence*
jänki *Yankee*
jäŋku *bunny*
kaabu (man's) *hat*
kaasa *companion*
kabli *hoe*
kahju *harm*
kaļju *cliff*
kaļka *tracing paper*
kalla *calla lily*
kasiino *casino*
kassa *cash desk*
kellu *trowel*
kiisu *pussy-cat*
kirju ^ *multi-coloured*
kirka *pick(axe)*
kiţsi ^ *stingy*
kliima *climate*
knopka *thumbtack*
koļju *skull*
kompu *candy*
kraana *crane (machine)*
kraHvinna *countess*
krõhva *hag*
kummi *rubber*
kunde *client*
kuninganna *queen*
kuţsu *puppy*
lagle *brant goose*
lahja ^ *meagre*
leedi *lady*
lepatriinu *ladybug*
lible *blade of grass*
libreto *libretto*
liiga *league*
lilla ^ *purple; faggot, gay*
lita *bitch*
loto *lotto*
läila ^ *insipid*
mamma *mommy*
mammi *mommy*
manna *semolina*
marli *gauze*
morse *Morse*
moto *motto*
nafta *oil*
neiu *maiden*
noku *little boy's penis*
noţsu *piggy*
paļju ^ *plenty*
papa *daddy*
pasta *paste (food)*
peiu *fiancé*
pepu *bum (rear end)*
plaşku *flask*
plika *girl*
preili *miss*
primadonna *prima donna*
prisma *prism*
proosa *prose*
propaganda *propaganda*
proua *Mrs.*
puţka *booth*
raļli *sports rally*
ratsu *horse (mount)*
reuma *rheumatism*
rişti *clubs in cards*
roosa ^ *pink*
rosoļje *beet salad*
ruutu *diamonds in cards*
salto *somersault*
sebra *zebra*
setu *orthodox SE Estonian*
skaala *scale*
sohva *sofa*
sooda *soda*
soolo *solo*
sperma *sperm*
summa *sum*
sõtse *aunt (father's sister)*
šampanja *champagne*
šerri *sherry*
taara *packing material*
takso *taxi*
teema *theme*
tempo *tempo*
terrakota *terra cotta*
tita *baby*
trauma *trauma*
troļli *trolley*
tšello *cello*
tubli ^ *good*
tuhkatriinu *Cinderella*
tuuba *tuba*
tõmmu ^ *swarthy*
vagiina *vagina*
valuuta *currency*
vaniļje *vanilla*
vedru *spring*
veranda *verandah*
veto *veto*
viisa *visa*
villa *villa*
viski *whisky*
vürStinna *princess*
ärtu *hearts in cards*

TYPE 16 - E Stems

153 ime *miracle* — ime 153

	nominative	genitive	partitive	short into	stem
singular	**ime**	**ime**	**imet**		**ime-**
plural	**imed**	**imede**	**imesid**		**imede-**

Also like ime:	kõne *speech*	pahe *evil*	vale *lie (deception)*
hüve *advantage*	lohe *dragon; kite*	rahe *hail*	vene *boat*
jume *complexion*	lõhe *salmon; fissure*	side *communication*	vile *whistle*
kabe *checkers*	male *chess*	vahe *difference*	vine *haze*
kile *membrane*	mure *worry*	vale ^ *false, wrong*	võre *grate*

154 pere *family* — pere 154

	nominative	genitive	partitive	short into	stem
singular	**pere**	**pere**	**peret**	**peRRe**	**pere-**
plural	**pered**	**perede**	**peresid**		**perede-**

Also like pere: kere *body* tare *cabin*

TYPE 17 - U Stem

155 õlu(t) *beer* — õlu(t) 155

	nominative	genitive	partitive	short into	stem
singular	**õlu(t)**	**õlle**	**õlut**		**õlle-**
plural	**õlled**	**õLLede**	**õLLesid**		**õLLede-**

NOMINALS - 3 - CLASS V

TYPE 18 -S Stem

156 paras *suitable* paras 156

	nominative	genitive	partitive	short into	stem
singular	**paras**	**paraja**	**parajat** parast		**paraja-**
plural	**parajad**	**parajate**	**parajaid**		**parajate-** (parajai-)

TYPE 19 - E (m or n genitive) Stems

157 habe *beard* habe 157

	nominative	genitive	partitive	short into	stem
singular	**habe**	**habeme**	**habet**		**habeme-**
plural	**habemed**	**habemete**	**habemeid**		**habemete-** (habemei-)

Also like habe:

ase *site*	häbemed (pl) *female genitals*	lade *layer*	säde *spark*
ese *object*	ige *gum (teeth)*	sademed (pl) *precipitation*	tase *level*
häbe *vulva*	jäse *limb*	side *bandage*	varemed (pl) *ruins*
	kube *groin*		

158 süda *heart* süda 158

	nominative	genitive	partitive	short into	stem
singular	**süda**	**südame**	**südant**		**südame-**
plural	**südamed**	**südamete**	**südameid**		**südamete-** (südamei-)

NOMINALS - 3 - CLASS VI A

TYPE 20 -S Stems

159A põõsas *bush* — põõsas 159A

	nominative	genitive	partitive	short into	stem
singular	**põõsas**	**pÕÕsa**	**põõsast**		**pÕÕsa-**
plural	**pÕÕsad**	**põõsaste**	**pÕÕsaid**		**põõsaste-** (pÕÕsai-)

Also like põõsas:
kiivas [A] *jealous*
saarmas *otter*
siiras [A] *sincere*
võllas *gallows*
võõras [A] *strange*
võõras *stranger; guest*
üllas [A] *noble*

159B kapsas *cabbage* — kapsas 159B

	nominative	genitive	partitive	short into	stem
singular	**kapsas**	**kaPsa**	**kapsast**		**kaPsa-**
plural	**kaPsad**	**kapsaste**	**kaPsaid**		**kapsaste-** (kaPsai-)

Also like kapsas:
haljas [A] *verdant*
kangas *woven material*
kitsas [A] *narrow*
kotkas *eagle*
kärmas [A] *nimble*
mai[j]as [A] *fond of sweets*
narmas *fringe*
oinas *ram*
paljas [A] *bare (naked)*
rahvas *people*
rõivas *clothing*
rõngas *ring (circle)*
rästas *thrush*
räästas *eaves*
säinas *ide (fish)*
tainas *dough*
taltsas [A] *tame*
uljas [A] *daring*
väljad (pl) *bridel*

159C ketas *disk* — ketas 159C

	nominative	genitive	partitive	short into	stem
singular	**ketas**	**keTTa**	**ketast**		**keTTa-**
plural	**keTTad**	**ketaste**	**keTTaid**		**ketaste-** (keTTai-)

Also like ketas:
kikas *cock (bird)*
mätas *sod*
okas *thorn*
ratas *wheel*
rikas [A] *rich*

159D ablas [A] *voracious* — ablas 159D

	nominative	genitive	partitive	short into	stem
singular	**ablas**	**aPla**	**ablast**		**aPla-**
plural	**aPlad**	**ablaste**	**aPlaid**		**ablaste-** (aPlai-)

Also like ablas:
habras [A] *fragile*
kobras *beaver*
koobas *cave*
kubjas *overseer*
kõblas *hoe*
pilbas *splinter*
reibas [A] *lively*
roobas *track (railway)*
rööbas *track (railway)*
saabas *boot*
tõbras *beast*

159E kaigas *stick* — kaigas 159E

	nominative	genitive	partitive	short into	stem
singular	**kaigas**	**kaiKa**	**kaigast**		**kaiKa-**
plural	**kaiKad**	**kaigaste**	**kaiKaid**		**kaigaste-**
					(kaiKai-)

Also like kaigas: laegas *chest (box)*, rüngas *crag*, vilgas [A] *quick*, küngas *hillock*, mädarõigas *horse-radish*, tüügas *stump*, võigas [A] *hideous*

159F põrsas *piglet* — põrsas 159F

	nominative	genitive	partitive	short into	stem
singular	**põrsas**	**põrSSa**	**põrsast**		**põrSSa-**
		põRsa			**põRsa-**
plural	**põrSSad**	**põrsaste**	**põrSSaid**		**põrsaste-**
	põRsad		**põRsaid**		(põrSSai-)
					(põRsai-)

160 taevas *heaven* — taevas 160

	nominative	genitive	partitive	short into	stem
singular	**taevas**	**taEva**	**taevast**	**taEva**	**taEva-**
plural	**taEvad**	**taevaste**	**taEvaid**		**taevaste-**
					(taEvai-)

161A toores [A] *raw* — toores 161A

	nominative	genitive	partitive	short into	stem
singular	**toores**	**tOOre**	**toorest**		**tOOre-**
plural	**tOOred**	**tooreste**	**tOOreid**		**tooreste-**
					(tOOrei-)

Also like toores: köömes *triviality*

161B hernes *pea* — hernes 161B

	nominative	genitive	partitive	short into	stem
singular	**hernes**	**heRne**	**hernest**		**heRne-**
plural	**heRned**	**herneste**	**heRneid**		**herneste-**
					(heRnei-)

Also like hernes: helmes *bead*

161C täpes *speck* — täpes 161C

	nominative	genitive	partitive	short into	stem
singular	**täpes**	**täPPe**	**täpest**		**täPPe-**
plural	**täPPed**	**täpeste**	**täPPeid**		**täpeste-**
					(täPPei-)

162 kärbes *fly* — kärbes 162

	nominative	genitive	partitive	short into	stem
singular	**kärbes**	**käRbse**	**kärbest**		**käRbse-**
plural	**käRbsed**	**kärbeste**	**käRbseid**		**kärbeste-** (käRbsei-)

163A rukis *rye* — rukis 163A

	nominative	genitive	partitive	short into	stem
singular	**rukis**	**ruKKi**	**rukist**		**ruKKi-**
plural	**ruKKid**	**rukiste**	**ruKKeid**		**rukiste-** (ruKKei-)

163B aļdis [A] *prone to* — aļdis 163B

	nominative	genitive	partitive	short into	stem
singular	**aļdis**	**aļTi**	**aļdist**		**aļTi-**
plural	**aļTid**	**aļdiste**	**aļTeid**		**aļdiste-** (aļTei-)

164A kaļlis [A] *dear* — kaļlis 164A

	nominative	genitive	partitive	short into	stem
singular	**kaļlis**	**kaĻLi**	**kaļlist**		**kaĻLi-**
plural	**kaĻLid**	**kaļliste** **kaĻLite**	**kaĻLeid**		**kaļliste-** **kaĻLite-** (kaĻLei-)

164B kaunis [A] *beautiful* — kaunis 164B

	nominative	genitive	partitive	short into	stem
singular	**kaunis**	**kaUni**	**kaunist**		**kaUni-**
plural	**kaUnid**	**kauniste** **kaUnite**	**kaUneid**		**kauniste-** **kaUnite-** (kaUnei-)

Also like kaunis: naeris *turnip*

165A hoolas [A] *diligent* — hoolas 165A

	nominative	genitive	partitive	short into	stem
singular	**hoolas**	**hOOlsa**	**hOOlsat** **hoolast**		**hOOlsa-**
plural	**hOOlsad**	**hOOlsate**	**hOOlsaid**		**hOOlsate-** (hOOlsai-)

165B armas [A] ***beloved*** **armas 165B**

	nominative	genitive	partitive	short into	stem
singular	**armas**	**aRmsa**	**aRmsat** **armast**		**aRmsa-**
plural	**aRmsad**	**aRmsate**	**aRmsaid**		**aRmsate-** (aRmsai-)

Also like armas valvas [A] *vigilant* võimas [A] *powerful*

165C ergas [A] ***alert*** **ergas 165C**

	nominative	genitive	partitive	short into	stem
singular	**ergas**	**erKsa**	**erKsat** **ergast**		**erKsa-**
plural	**erKsad**	**erKsate**	**erKsaid**		**erKsate-** (erKsai-)

166A õõnes [A] ***hollow*** **õõnes 166A**

	nominative	genitive	partitive	short into	stem
singular	**õõnes**	**ÕÕnsa**	**ÕÕnsat** **õõnest**		**ÕÕnsa-**
plural	**ÕÕnsad**	**ÕÕnsate**	**ÕÕnsaid**		**ÕÕnsate-** (ÕÕnsai-)

166B tõrges [A] ***stubborn*** **tõrges 166B**

	nominative	genitive	partitive	short into	stem
singular	**tõrges**	**tõrKsa**	**tõrKsat** **tõrgest**		**tõrKsa-**
plural	**tõrKsad**	**tõrKsate**	**tõrKsaid**		**tõrKsate-** (tõrKsai-)

167 õilis [A] ***noble*** **õilis 167**

	nominative	genitive	partitive	short into	stem
singular	**õilis**	**õİlsa**	**õİlsat** **õilist**		**õİlsa-**
plural	**õİlsad**	**õİlsate**	**õİlsaid**		**õİlsate-** (õİlsai-)

168A ihnus [A] ***miserly*** **ihnus 168A**

	nominative	genitive	partitive	short into	stem
singular	**ihnus**	**iHnsa**	**iHnsat** **ihnust**		**iHnsa-**
plural	**iHnsad**	**iHnsate**	**iHnsaid**		**iHnsate-** (iHnsai-)

168B hõlbus [A] *easy* — **hõlbus 168B**

	nominative	genitive	partitive	short into	stem
singular	**hõlbus**	**hõlPsa**	**hõlPsat**		**hõlPsa-**
			hõlbust		
plural	**hõlPsad**	**hõlPsate**	**hõlPsaid**		**hõlPsate-**
					(hõlPsai-)

169 ainus [A] *sole, only* — **ainus 169**

	nominative	genitive	partitive	short into	stem
singular	**ainus**	**aİnu**	**ainust**		**aİnsa-**
	aİnus	**aİnsa**	**aİnsat**		
plural	**aİnsad**	**aİnsate**	**aİnsaid**		**aİnsate-**
					(aİnsai-)

TYPE 21 - R and L Stems

170A küünal *candle* — **küünal 170A**

	nominative	genitive	partitive	short into	stem
singular	**küünal**	**kÜÜnla**	**küünalt**		**kÜÜnla-**
plural	**kÜÜnlad**	**küünalde**	**kÜÜnlaid**		**küünalde-**
					(kÜÜnlai-)

170B kaenal *underarm* — **kaenal 170B**

	nominative	genitive	partitive	short into	stem
singular	**kaenal**	**kaEnla**	**kaenalt**		**kaEnla-**
plural	**kaEnlad**	**kaenalde**	**kaEnlaid**		**kaenalde-**
					(kaEnlai-)

Also like kaenal: süstal *syringe* tungal *torch*

170C kukal *back of head* — **kukal 170C**

	nominative	genitive	partitive	short into	stem
singular	**kukal**	**kuKla**	**kukalt**		**kuKla-**
plural	**kuKlad**	**kukalde**	**kuKlaid**		**kukalde-**
					(kuKlai-)

171A peenar *flowerbed* — **peenar 171A**

	nominative	genitive	partitive	short into	stem
singular	**peenar**	**pEEnra**	**peenart**		**pEEnra-**
plural	**pEEnrad**	**peenarde**	**pEEnraid**		**peenarde-**
					(pEEnrai-)

Also like peenar: küünar *elbow*

171B sõstar *currant* — sõstar 171B

	nominative	genitive	partitive	short into	stem
singular	**sõstar**	**sõStra**	**sõstart**		**sõStra-**
plural	**sõStrad**	**sõstarde**	**sõStraid**		**sõstarde-**
					(sõStrai-)

171C pipar *pepper* — pipar 171C

	nominative	genitive	partitive	short into	stem
singular	**pipar**	**piPra**	**pipart**		**piPra-**
plural	**piPrad**	**piparde**	**piPraid**		**piparde-**
					(piPrai-)

Also like pipar: karikakar *daisy* tatar *buckwheat*

171D pundar *bundle* — pundar 171D

	nominative	genitive	partitive	short into	stem
singular	**pundar**	**punTra**	**pundart**		**punTra-**
plural	**punTrad**	**pundarde**	**punTraid**		**pundarde-**
					(punTrai-)

172 aken *window* — aken 172

	nominative	genitive	partitive	short into	stem
singular	**aken**	**aKna**	**akent**		**aKna-**
plural	**aKnad**	**akende**	**aKnaid**		**akende-**
					(aKnai-)

173A katel *kettle* — katel 173A

	nominative	genitive	partitive	short into	stem
singular	**katel**	**kaTla**	**katelt**		**kaTla-**
plural	**kaTlad**	**katelde**	**kaTlaid**		**katelde-**
					(kaTlai-)

173B pastel *moccasin* — pastel 173B

	nominative	genitive	partitive	short into	stem
singular	**pastel**	**paStla**	**pastelt**		**paStla-**
plural	**paStlad**	**pastelde**	**paStlaid**		**pastelde-**
					(paStlai-)

Also like pastel: astel *sting*

174 kaker ***present from guest*** **kaker 174**

	nominative	genitive	partitive	short into	stem
singular	**kaker**	**kaKra**	**kakert**		**kaKra-**
plural	**kaKrad**	**kakerde**	**kaKraid**		**kakerde-** (kaKrai-)

175 lemmel ***duckweed*** **lemmel 175**

	nominative	genitive	partitive	short into	stem
singular	**lemmel**	**leMle**	**lemmelt**		**leMle-**
plural	**leMled**	**lemmelde**	**leMleid**		**lemmelde-** (leMlei-)

176 tütar ***daughter*** **tütar 176**

	nominative	genitive	partitive	short into	stem
singular	**tütar**	**tüTre**	**tütart**		**tüTre-**
plural	**tüTred**	**tütarde**	**tüTreid**		**tütarde-** (tüTrei-)

TYPE 22 - E (-e genitive) Stems

177A hoone ***edifice*** **hoone 177A**

	nominative	genitive	partitive	short into	stem
singular	**hoone**	**hOOne**	**hoonet**		**hOOne-**
plural	**hOOned**	**hoonete**	**hOOneid**		**hoonete-** (hOOnei-)

Also like hoone:
kiire ^ *fast*
luule *poetry*
luure *espionage*
meene *souvenir*
seede *digestion*
teene *service*
tiine ^ *pregnant of animals*

177B arve ***bill*** **arve 177B**

	nominative	genitive	partitive	short into	stem
singular	**arve**	**aRve**	**arvet**		**aRve-**
plural	**aRved**	**arvete**	**aRveid**		**arvete-** (aRvei-)

Also like arve:
ahne ^ *greedy*
aine *substance*
aste *step (pace)*
eine *meal*
häire *disturbance*
ihne ^ *stingy*
ilme *facial expression*
kaine ^ *sober*
kaitse *defence (shelter)*
kaste *dew*
katse *attempt*
kutse *invitation*
kärme ^ *nimble*
laine *wave*
lause *sentence*
maine *reputation*
maitse *taste*
mulje *impression*
mõiste *notion*
nõtke *bending*
okse *vomit*
olme *living conditions*
paise *boil*
palve *prayer*
peİ[j]ed (pl) *funereal wake*
perse *arse (buttocks)*
pinge *tension*
piste *stitch*
päiTsed (pl) *bridle*
rooste *rust*
selve *self-service*
surve *pressure*
terve ^ *whole, healthy*
toime *effect*
tõrje *pest control*
ulme *fantasy*
valve *watch (guard)*
vaste *equivalent*
verme *gash*
vihje *hint*
võime *ability*
võrse *sprout*

177C hape *acid* hape 177C

	nominative	genitive	partitive	short into	stem
singular	**hape**	**haPPe**	**hapet**		**haPPe-**
plural	**haPPed**	**hapete**	**haPPeid**		**hapete-** (haPPei-)

Also like hape:	küte *heating of house*	sete *sediment*	täpe *speck*
hüpe *jump*	lõke *bonfire*	teke *origin*	võte *method*
ike *yoke*	läte *spring of water*	tõke *obstacle*	äke *harrow*
kate *covering*	mõte *thought*	täke *notch*	

177D kärbe *omission in text* kärbe 177D

	nominative	genitive	partitive	short into	stem
singular	**kärbe**	**kärPe**	**kärbet**		**kärPe-**
plural	**kärPed**	**kärbete**	**kärPeid**		**kärbete-** (kärPei-)

Also like kärbe: raibe *carcass*

177E aade *idea; principle* aade 177E

	nominative	genitive	partitive	short into	stem
singular	**aade**	**aaTe**	**aadet**		**aaTe-**
plural	**aaTed**	**aadete**	**aaTeid**		**aadete-** (aaTei-)

Also like aade:	luide *dune*	teade *message*	viide *allusion*
heide *casting*	näide *example*	toode *product*	väide *statement*
köide *volume (book)*	saade *broadcast*	vaade *view*	välde *duration*
loode *embryo*			

177F lõige *pattern* lõige 177F

	nominative	genitive	partitive	short into	stem
singular	**lõige**	**lõiKe**	**lõiget**		**lõiKe-**
plural	**lõiKed**	**lõigete**	**lõiKeid**		**lõigete-** (lõiKei-)

Also like lõige:	pilge *ridicule*	tõlge *translation*	võnge *vibration*
läige *gloss*	torge *prick of needle*	tõuge *push*	välge *flashing*

178 lõuna *south; lunch; noon* lõuna 178

	nominative	genitive	partitive	short into	stem
singular	**lõuna**	**lõUna**	**lõunat**		**lõUna-**
plural	**lõUnad**	**lõunate**	**lõUnaid**		**lõunate-** (lõUnai-)

TYPE 23 - E (m or n genitive) Stems

179A koole *ford* koole 179A

	nominative	genitive	partitive	short into	stem
singular	**koole**	**kOOlme**	**koolet**		**kOOlme-**
plural	**kOOlmed**	**kOOlmete**	**kOOlmeid**		**kOOlmete-**
					(kOOlmei-)

Also like koole: pääse *admission ticket* riise *debris* sööre *nostril*
nääre *gland* pööre *switch (change)*

179B rake *harness* rake 179B

	nominative	genitive	partitive	short into	stem
singular	**rake**	**raKme**	**raket**		**raKme-**
plural	**raKmed**	**raKmete**	**raKmeid**		**raKmete-**
					(raKmei-)

179C iste *seat* iste 179C

	nominative	genitive	partitive	short into	stem
singular	**iste**	**iStme**	**istet**		**iStme-**
plural	**iStmed**	**iStmete**	**iStmeid**		**iStmete-**
					(iStmei-)

Also like ite: kaitse *defence (device)* pritse *spatter* seade *fixture*
aste *step; stair* kaste *sauce* ripse *eyelash* seitse *seven*

179D köide *bandage, fetter* köide 179D

	nominative	genitive	partitive	short into	stem
singular	**köide**	**köiTme**	**köidet**		**köiTme-**
plural	**köiTmed**	**köiTmete**	**köiTmeid**		**köiTmete-**
					(köiTmei-)

Also like köide: heide *waste material* jääTmed (pl) *refuse* meeTmed (pl) measures
teaTmed (pl) *data*

179E liige *member* liige 179E

	nominative	genitive	partitive	short into	stem
singular	**liige**	**liiKme**	**liiget**		**liiKme-**
plural	**liiKmed**	**liiKmete**	**liiKmeid**		**liiKmete-**
					(liiKmei-)

Also like liige: märge *note*

180 luka ***tooth, projection*** **luka 180**

	nominative	genitive	partitive	short into	stem
singular	**luka**	**luKme**	**lukat**		**luKme-**
plural	**luKmed**	**luKmete**	**luKmeid**		**luKmete-** (luKmei-)

181 võţi ***key*** **võţi 181**

	nominative	genitive	partitive	short into	stem
singular	**võţi**	**võŢme**	**võţit**		**võŢme-**
plural	**võŢmed**	**võŢmete**	**võŢmeid**		**võŢmete-** (võŢmei-)

182 mitu ***(numeral) many*** **mitu 182**

	nominative	genitive	partitive	short into	stem
singular	**mitu**	**miTme**	**mitut**		**miTme-**
plural	**miTmed**	**miTmete**	**miTmeid**		**miTmete-** (miTmei-)

183A seeme ***seed*** **seeme 183A**

	nominative	genitive	partitive	short into	stem
singular	**seeme**	**sEEmne**	**seemet**		**sEEmne-**
plural	**sEEmned**	**sEEmnete**	**sEEmneid**		**sEEmnete-** (sEEmnei-)

183B kümme ***ten*** **kümme 183B**

	nominative	genitive	partitive	short into	stem
singular	**kümme**	**küMne**	**kümmet**		**küMne-**
plural	**küMned**	**küMnete**	**küMneid**		**küMnete-** (küMnei-)

184 -kümmend ***tens (e.g. thirteen, etc ; twenty, thirty etc.)*** **-kümmend 184**

	nominative	genitive	partitive	short into	stem
singular	**-kümmend**	**-küMne**	**-kümmet**		**-küMne-**
plural	**-küMned**	**-küMnete**	**-küMneid**		**-küMnete-** (-küMnei-)

185 kööme - köömen ***caraway-seed*** **kööme(n) 185**

	nominative	genitive	partitive	short into	stem
singular	**kööme**	**kÖÖmne**	**köömet**		**kÖÖmne-**
	köömen		**kÖÖmnet**		
plural	**kÖÖmned**	**kÖÖmnete**	**kÖÖmneid**		**kÖÖmnete-** (kÖÖmnei-)

TYPE 24 - U Stems

186 jäänu *surviver* jäänu 186

	nominative	genitive	partitive	short into	stem
singular	**jäänu**	**jÄÄnu**	**jäänut**		**jÄÄnu-**
plural	**jÄÄnud**	**jäänute**	**jÄÄnuid**		**jäänute-** (jÄÄnui-)

Also like jäänu: läinu *departed* poonu *hanged person* saanu *recipient*

NOMINALS - 3 - CLASS VI B

TYPE 25 - S Stems

187 teivas *stake* **teivas 187**

	nominative	genitive	partitive	short into	stem
singular	**teivas**	**teİba**	**teivast**		**teİba-**
plural	**teİbad**	**teivaste**	**teİbaid**		**teivaste-** (teİbai-)

Also like teivas: turvas *peat* varvas *toe*

188 hammas *tooth* **hammas 188**

	nominative	genitive	partitive	short into	stem
singular	**hammas**	**haMba**	**hammast**		**haMba-**
plural	**haMbad**	**hammaste**	**haMbaid**		**hammaste-** (haMbai-)

Also like hammas: lammas *sheep* sammas *column (pillar)*

189 kuu[w]as *axe handle* **kuu[w]as 189**

	nominative	genitive	partitive	short into	stem
singular	**kuu[w]as**	**kUUda**	**kuu[w]ast**		**kUUda-**
plural	**kUUdad**	**kuu[w]aste**	**kUUdaid**		**kuu[w]aste-** (kUUdai-)

190 puhas ^A *clean* **puhas 190**

	nominative	genitive	partitive	short into	stem
singular	**puhas**	**puHta**	**puhast**		**puHta-**
plural	**puHtad**	**puhaste**	**puHtaid**		**puhaste-** (puHtai-)

Also like puhas: ahas ^A *narrow*

191 kallas *shore* **kallas 191**

	nominative	genitive	partitive	short into	stem
singular	**kallas**	**kaLda**	**kallast**		**kaLda-**
plural	**kaLdad**	**kallaste**	**kaLdaid**		**kallaste-** (kaLdai-)

192 kinnas *glove; mitten* **kinnas 192**

	nominative	genitive	partitive	short into	stem
singular	**kinnas**	**kiNda**	**kinnast**		**kiNda-**
plural	**kiNdad**	**kinnaste**	**kiNdaid**		**kinnaste-** (kiNdai-)

193 harras [A] *devout* **harras 193**

	nominative	genitive	partitive	short into	stem
singular	**harras**	**haRda**	**harrast**		**haRda-**
plural	**haRdad**	**harraste**	**haRdaid**		**harraste-** (haRdai-)

Also like harras: härras [A] *woeful* parras *shipboard* varras *skewer*

194 varas *thief* **varas 194**

	nominative	genitive	partitive	short into	stem
singular	**varas**	**vaRga**	**varast**		**vaRga-**
plural	**vaRgad**	**varaste**	**vaRgaid**		**varaste-** (vaRgai-)

195 helves *flake* **helves 195**

	nominative	genitive	partitive	short into	stem
singular	**helves**	**heLbe**	**helvest**		**heLbe-**
plural	**heLbed**	**helveste**	**heLbeid**		**helveste-** (heLbei-)

196 lemmes *shred* **lemmes 196**

	nominative	genitive	partitive	short into	stem
singular	**lemmes**	**leMbe**	**lemmest**		**leMbe-**
plural	**leMbed**	**lemmeste**	**leMbeid**		**lemmeste-** (leMbei-)

197 hüļjes *seal (animal)* **hüļjes 197**

	nominative	genitive	partitive	short into	stem
singular	**hüļjes**	**hüĻge**	**hüļjest**		**hüĻge-**
plural	**hüĻged**	**hüļjeste**	**hüĻgeid**		**hüļjeste-** (hüĻgei-)

198 kohus ***court of law*** **kohus 198**

	nominative	genitive	partitive	short into	stem
singular	**kohus**	**koHtu**	**kohut**		**koHtu-**
plural	**koHtud**	**koHtute**	**koHtuid**		**koHtute-** (koHtui-)

199 süņnis [A] ***decent*** **süņnis 199**

	nominative	genitive	partitive	short into	stem
singular	**süņnis**	**süŅdsa**	**süņnist** **süŅdsat**		**süŅdsa-**
plural	**süŅdsad**	**süŅdsate**	**süŅdsaid**		**süŅdsate-** (süŅdsai-)

Also like süņnis: õņnis [A] *blessed*

TYPE 26 - R and L Stems

200 sammal ***moss*** **sammal 200**

	nominative	genitive	partitive	short into	stem
singular	**sammal**	**saMbla**	**sammalt**		**saMbla-**
plural	**saMblad**	**sammalde**	**saMblaid**		**sammalde-** (saMblai-)

Also like sammal: vemmal *scamp*

201 pöi[j]al ***thumb*** **pöi[j]al 201**

	nominative	genitive	partitive	short into	stem
singular	**pöi[j]al**	**pöİdla**	**pöi[j]alt**		**pöİdla-**
plural	**pöİdlad**	**pöi[j]alde**	**pöİdlaid**		**pöi[j]alde-** (pöİdlai-)

202 pannal ***buckle*** **pannal 202**

	nominative	genitive	partitive	short into	stem
singular	**pannal**	**paNdla**	**pannalt**		**paNdla-**
plural	**paNdlad**	**pannalde**	**paNdlaid**		**pannalde-** (paNdlai-)

203 õnnar ***coccyx*** **õnnar 203**

	nominative	genitive	partitive	short into	stem
singular	**õnnar**	**õNdra**	**õnnart**		**õNdra-**
plural	**õNdrad**	**õnnarde**	**õNdraid**		**õnnarde-** (õNdrai-)

204 kinner *hollow behind knee* **kinner 204**

	nominative	genitive	partitive	short into	stem
singular	**kinner**	**kiNdra**	**kinnert**		**kiNdra-**
plural	**kiNdrad**	**kinnerde**	**kiNdraid**		**kinnerde-** (kiNdrai-)

205 kannel *zither* **kannel 205**

	nominative	genitive	partitive	short into	stem
singular	**kannel**	**kaNdle**	**kannelt**		**kaNdle-**
plural	**kaNdled**	**kannelde**	**kaNdleid**		**kannelde-** (kaNdlei-)

206 vaher *maple* **vaher 206**

	nominative	genitive	partitive	short into	stem
singular	**vaher**	**vaHtra**	**vahert** **vaHtrat**		**vaHtra-**
plural	**vaHtrad**	**vaHtrate**	**vaHtraid**		**vaHtrate-** (vaHtrai-)

207 manner *continent* **manner 207**

	nominative	genitive	partitive	short into	stem
singular	**manner**	**maNdri**	**mannert** **maNdrit**		**maNdri-**
plural	**maNdrid**	**maNdrite**	**maNdreid**		**maNdrite-** (maNdrei-)

TYPE 27 -E (-e genitive) Stems

208A iive *population growth* **iive 208A**

	nominative	genitive	partitive	short into	stem
singular	**iive**	**İİbe**	**iivet**		**İİbe-**
plural	**İİbed**	**iivete**	**İİbeid**		**iivete-** (İİbei-)

Also like iive: löőve *rash*

208B teave *information* **teave 208B**

	nominative	genitive	partitive	short into	stem
singular	**teave**	**teAbe**	**teavet**		**teAbe-**
plural	**teAbed**	**teavete**	**teAbeid**		**teavete-** (teAbei-)

Also like teave: helve *flake* käive *circulation* tarve *need*

209 komme *custom* **komme 209**

	nominative	genitive	partitive	short into	stem
singular	**komme**	**koMbe**	**kommet**		**koMbe-**
plural	**koMbed**	**kommete**	**koMbeid**		**kommete-** (koMbei-)

Also like komme: tõmme *jerk* umme *whitlow*

210A puu[w]e *defect* **puu[w]e 210A**

	nominative	genitive	partitive	short into	stem
singular	**puu[w]e**	**pUUde**	**puu[w]et**		**pUUde-**
plural	**pUUded**	**puu[w]ete**	**pUUdeid**		**puu[w]ete-** (pUUdei-)

210B nõu[w]e *requirement* **nõu[w]e 210B**

	nominative	genitive	partitive	short into	stem
singular	**nõu[w]e**	**nõUde**	**nõu[w]et**		**nõUde-**
plural	**nõUded**	**nõu[w]ete**	**nõUdeid**		**nõu[w]ete-** (nõUdei-)

210C rii[j]e *clothing* **rii[j]e 210C**

	nominative	genitive	partitive	short into	stem
singular	**rii[j]e**	**rİİde**	**rii[j]et**		**rİİde-**
plural	**rİİded**	**rii[j]ete**	**rİİdeid**		**rii[j]ete-** (rİİdei-)

Also like rii[j]e: hüü[j]e *shout, call* püü[j]e *attempt*

210D või[j]e *ointment* **või[j]e 210D**

	nominative	genitive	partitive	short into	stem
singular	**või[j]e**	**võİde**	**või[j]et**		**võİde-**
plural	**võİded**	**või[j]ete**	**võİdeid**		**või[j]ete-** (võİdei-)

Also like või[j]e: roi[j]e *rib* tai[j]e *art*

211A aare *treasure* **aare 211A**

	nominative	genitive	partitive	short into	stem
singular	**aare**	**AArde**	**aaret**		**AArde-**
plural	**AArded**	**aarete**	**AArdeid**		**aarete-** (AArdei-)

Also like aare: kääne *case (grammar)* määre *lubricant* pööre *upheaval*
haare *grasp* maare *mineral resource*

211B ehe *ornament* — ehe 211B

	nominative	genitive	partitive	short into	stem
singular	**ehe**	**eHte**	**ehet**		**eHte-**
plural	**eHted**	**ehete**	**eHteid**		**ehete-**
					(eHtei-)

Also like ehe: nähe *phenomenon* suhe *relationship* tahe *will (desire)*

212 loE *north-west* — loE 212

	nominative	genitive	partitive	short into	stem
singular	**loE**	**lOOde**	**loeT**		**lOOde-**
plural	**lOOded**	**loeTe**	**lOOdeid**		**loeTe-**
					(lOOdei-)

213 kolle *hearth* — kolle 213

	nominative	genitive	partitive	short into	stem
singular	**kolle**	**koLde**	**kollet**		**koLde-**
plural	**koLded**	**kollete**	**koLdeid**		**kollete-**
					(koLdei-)

214 tunne *feeling* — tunne 214

	nominative	genitive	partitive	short into	stem
singular	**tunne**	**tuNde**	**tunnet**		**tuNde-**
plural	**tuNded**	**tunnete**	**tuNdeid**		**tunnete-**
					(tuNdei-)

Also like tunne: enne *omen* kanne *carrying* ränne *migration*
anne *endowment (talent)* hinne *marks, grades* rinne *front* vanne *oath*

215 murre *major dialect; fracture* — murre 215

	nominative	genitive	partitive	short into	stem
singular	**murre**	**muRde**	**murret**		**muRde-**
plural	**muRded**	**murrete**	**muRdeid**		**murrete-**
					(muRdei-)

Also like murre: purre *foot-bridge* tarre *jelly* võrre *proportion*
kirre *north-east*

216 mui[j]e *smirk* — mui[j]e 216

	nominative	genitive	partitive	short into	stem
singular	**mui[j]e**	**muİge**	**mui[j]et**		**muİge-**
plural	**muİged**	**mui[j]ete**	**muİgeid**		**mui[j]ete-**
					(muİgei-)

Also like mui[j]e: oi[j]e *groan*

217A hiile *shining* **hiile 217A**

	nominative	genitive	partitive	short into	stem
singular	**hiile**	**hİİlge**	**hiilet**		**hİİlge-**
plural	**hİİlged**	**hiilete**	**hİİlgeid**		**hiilete-** (hİİlgei-)

217B pale *countenance* **pale 217B**

	nominative	genitive	partitive	short into	stem
singular	**pale**	**paLge**	**palet**		**paLge-**
plural	**paLged**	**palete**	**paLgeid**		**palete-** (paLgei-)

217C hõise *shout* **hõise 217C**

	nominative	genitive	partitive	short into	stem
singular	**hõise**	**hõiSke**	**hõiset**		**hõiSke-**
plural	**hõiSked**	**hõisete**	**hõiSkeid**		**hõisete-** (hõiSkei-)

Also like hõise: nihe *shift* ohe *sigh* purse *spurt* vise *throw*

218 ürje *beginning* **ürje 218**

	nominative	genitive	partitive	short into	stem
singular	**ürje**	**üRge**	**ürjet**		**üRge-**
plural	**üRged**	**ürjete**	**üRgeid**		**ürjete-** (üRgei-)

TYPE 28 -E (-m or -n genitive) Stems

219A suu[w]e *river mouth* **suu[w]e 219A**

	nominative	genitive	partitive	short into	stem
singular	**suu[w]e**	**sUUdme**	**suu[w]et**		**sUUdme-**
plural	**sUUdmed**	**sUUdmete**	**sUUdmeid**		**sUUdmete-** (sUUdmei-)

219B hau[w]e *brood* **hau[w]e 219B**

	nominative	genitive	partitive	short into	stem
singular	**hau[w]e**	**haUdme**	**hau[w]et**		**haUdme-**
plural	**haUdmed**	**haUdmete**	**haUdmeid**		**haUdmete-** (haUdmei-)

219C rai[j]e *offal* **rai[j]e 219C**

	nominative	genitive	partitive	short into	stem
singular	**rai[j]e**	**raİdme**	**rai[j]et**		**raİdme-**
plural	**raİdmed**	**raİdmete**	**raİdmeid**		**raİdmete-** (raİdmei-)

220 juhe *conducting wire* **juhe 220**

	nominative	genitive	partitive	short into	stem
singular	**juhe**	**juHtme**	**juhet**		**juHtme-**
plural	**juHtmed**	**juHtmete**	**juHtmeid**		**juHtmete-** (juHtmei-)

221 ranne *wrist* **ranne 221**

	nominative	genitive	partitive	short into	stem
singular	**ranne**	**raNdme**	**rannet**		**raNdme-**
plural	**raNdmed**	**raNdmete**	**raNdmeid**		**raNdmete-** (raNdmei-)

Also like ranne: aNdmed (pl) *data*

222 murre *fracture* **murre 222**

	nominative	genitive	partitive	short into	stem
singular	**murre**	**muRdme**	**murret**		**muRdme-**
plural	**muRdmed**	**muRdmete**	**muRdmeid**		**muRdmete-** (muRdmei-)

223 säi[j]e *strand (of yarn or rope)* **säi[j]e 223**

	nominative	genitive	partitive	short into	stem
singular	**säi[j]e**	**säİgme**	**säi[j]et**		**säİgme-**
plural	**säİgmed**	**säİgmete**	**säİgmeid**		**säİgmete-** (säİgmei-)

224 mähe *diaper* **mähe 224**

	nominative	genitive	partitive	short into	stem
singular	**mähe**	**mäHkme**	**mähet**		**mäHkme-**
plural	**mäHkmed**	**mäHkmete**	**mäHkmeid**		**mäHkmete-** (mäHkmei-)

Also like mähe: püHkmed (pl) *sweepings*

TYPE 29 - Regular

225A alasi *anvil* — alasi 225A

	nominative	genitive	partitive	short into	stem
singular	**alasi**	**alasi**	**alasit**		**alasi-**
plural	**alasid**	**alasite**	**alaseid**		**alasite-** (alasei-)

Also like alasi:	kõdisti *clitoris*	osuti *pointer*	tuimasti *anaesthetic*
arvuti *computer*	kõristi *rattle*	pehmendi *softener*	uinuti *soporific*
ilmuti *film developer*	käiviti *ignition switch*	piserdi *sprinkler*	valgendi *whitener*
kiŋniti *fastener*	lükati *slide rule*	põleti *burner*	võimendi *amplifier*
kustuti *fire extinguisher*	lüliti *switch*	rahusti *sedative*	välguti *camera flash*

225B veŞki *mill* — veŞki 225B

	nominative	genitive	partitive	short into	stem
singular	**veŞki**	**veŞki**	**veŞkit**		**veŞki-**
plural	**veŞkid**	**veŞkite**	**veŞkeid**		**veŞkite-** (veŞkei-)

Also like veŞki:	neiTsi *virgin*	ploTski *cigarette*	tegelinSki *go-getter*
miNgi *some; a certain*	pasaTski *crook*	ruPskid (pl) *tripe*	väeTi *feeble*

226 vOOḑi *bed* — vOOḑi 226

	nominative	genitive	partitive	short into	stem
singular	**vOOḑi**	**vOOḑi**	**vOOḑit**	**vOOḑi**	**vOOḑi-**
plural	**vOOḑid**	**vOOḑite**	**vOOḑeid**		**vOOḑite-** (vOOḑei-)

227A inetu [A] *ugly* — inetu 227A

	nominative	genitive	partitive	short into	stem
singular	**inetu**	**inetu**	**inetut**		**inetu-**
plural	**inetud**	**inetute**	**inetuid**		**inetute-** (inetui-)

Also like inetu:	aLLakirjutanu *undersigned*	armetu [A] *pitiful*	asula *settlement*
abitu [A] *helpless*	alusetu [A] *groundless*	armutu [A] *pitiless*	asutaja *founder*
aEgumatu [A] *ageless*	ammendamatu [A] *inexhaustible*	arvustaja *critic*	auStaja *admirer*
ajastu *epoch*	aNdetu [A] *untalented*	arvutu [A] *countless*	avastaja *discoverer*
aKtsia *share*	annetaja *donor*	asendaja *substitute*	botaanika *botany*
alatu [A] *vile*	aRbuja *soothsayer*	asendamatu [A] *indispensable*	butafOOria *kitsch*
algataja *instigator*	armastaja *lover*	aşjatu [A] *futile*	dressEErija *animal trainer*

227A inetu *ugly* continued

edasilüKKamatu ^ *urgent*
ehitaja *builder*
eKsimatu ^ *infallible*
elamu *dwelling*
elutu ^ *lifeless*
ennustaja *foreteller*
eramu *detached house*
esindaja *representative*
esineja *performer*
eTTevaaTamatu ^ *careless*
eTTeüTleja *prompter*
fantAAsia *imagination*
graafika *graphic art*
grammatika *grammar*
hageja *plaintiff*
halvatu ^ *paralytic*
haRjumatu ^ *unaccustomed*
helitu ^ *soundless*
hiNdamatu ^ *priceless*
hingetu ^ *lifeless*
hoiustaja *depositor*
hOOldaja *guardian*
hooletu ^ *careless*
hOOļimatu ^ *inconsiderate*
hooPleja *braggart*
häbematu ^ *impudent*
häbitu ^ *shameless*
hävitaja *destroyer*
häälestaja *tuner*
hääletaja *voter*
ilmetu ^ *expressionless*
ilutu ^ *plain*
imetaja *mammal*
jagamatu ^ *indivisible*
jOObunu *drunk*
joonestaja *draughtsperson*
joonistaja *drawer (person)*
juhataja *manager*
juhendaja *adviser*
jutlustaja *preacher*
jutustaja *narrator*
jõuetu ^ *powerless*
jäļjetu ^ *traceless*
järelejäTmatu ^ *incessant*
kaalutu ^ *weightless*
kaamera *movie camera*
kaasitaja *singer at wedding*
kadunu *deceased*
kaEbaja *complainant*
kaheksa *eight*
kahjutu ^ *harmless*
kaHtleja *sceptic*
kahvatu ^ *pale*
kaiTsetu ^ *defenceless*
kaļmistu *graveyard*
kanala *hen-house*
kannataja *sufferer*
kannatamatu ^ *impatient*
kaoTaja *loser*
karTmatu ^ *fearless*
kasutu ^ *useless*
kaSvaja *tumour*
kasvataja *educator*
kasvatamatu ^ *ill-bred*
keeletu ^ *speechless*
keevitaja *welder*
keHtetu ^ *invalid*
keTraja *spinner*
kiiTleja *boaster*
kirjutaja *writer*
kiruRgia *surgery*
kodutu ^ *homeless*
kogenematu ^ *inexperienced*
koguja *collector*
koHkumatu ^ *dauntless*
kohmetu ^ *numbed*
komÖÖdia *comedy*
kooPia *copy*
koristaja *cleaner (person)*
korratu ^ *disorderly*
korTsumatu ^ *crease-proof*
kosmeetika *cosmetics*
kriitika *criticism*
kroHvija *plasterer*
kroonika *chronicle*
kuduja *weaver*
kuRnaja *oppressor*
kUUlaja *listener*
kõiKumatu ^ *unwavering*
kõlatu ^ *soundless*
kõLbmatu ^ *useless*
kõlvatu ^ *immoral*
kõneleja *speaker*
käratu ^ *noiseless*
kärsitu ^ *impatient*
külastaja *visitor*
lAAḑija *stevedore*
laEnaja *borrower*
laenutaja *lender*
laevatamatu ^ *unnavigable*
lahendamatu ^ *insoluble*
laHkunu *the departed*
lahustumatu ^ *insoluble*
lahutamatu ^ *inseparable*
laiSkleja *idler*
laiTmatu ^ *irreproachable*
laKKamatu ^ *ceaseless*
lavastaja *producer*
leelutaja *leelu singer*
leİnaja *mourner*
leiutaja *inventor*
lepitamatu ^ *irreconcilable*
lePPimatu ^ *implacable*
liiKumatu ^ *motionless*
lİİlia *lily*
looTusetu ^ *hopeless*
lubamatu ^ *improper*
lugeja *reader*
lugematu ^ *countless*
lunastaja *Saviour*
luuletaja *poet*
lUUraja *scout*
lõpetaja *graduate*
lõPmatu ^ *endless*
lõputu ^ *endless*
läbituNgimatu ^ *impenetrable*
mAAdleja *wrestler*
mAAnia *mania*
maiTsetu ^ *tasteless*
maletaja *chess-player*
manala *land of the dead*
maNdunu *degenerate*
mannetu ^ *helpless*
matEEria *substance*
maTkaja *hiker*
meeletu ^ *frantic*
mesila *apiary*
minia *daughter-in-law*
muRdumatu ^ *unbreakable*
muretu ^ *carefree*
muusika *music*
muuTumatu ^ *unchangeable*
mõiStmatu ^ *irrational*
mõjutu ^ *ineffective*
mõTlematu ^ *thoughtless*
mõTTetu ^ *senseless*
mõõTmatu ^ *immeasurable*
mäSSaja *rebel*
mÄÄramatu ^ *indefinite*
määratu ^ *immense*
nimetu ^ *nameless*
nimistu *list of names*
näHtamatu ^ *invisible*
näiTaja *indicator*
näiTleja *actor*
ohjeldamatu ^ *unrestrained*
ohutu ^ *safe*
olematu ^ *non-existent*
olija *one who is present*
ooTamatu ^ *unexpected*
oSkamatu ^ *unskilled*
paaritu ^ *odd (number)*
paİndumatu ^ *inflexible*
palitu *coat*
paluja *applicant*
parandaja *repairer*
parandamatu ^ *incorrigible*
paratamatu ^ *inevitable*
parOOdia *parody*
pesula *laundry house*
pİİnaja *tormentor*
pİİramatu ^ *unlimited*
piiritu ^ *boundless*
pilvitu ^ *cloudless*
poliitika *politics*
pOOldaja *supporter*
prEEmia *bonus*
pugeja *bootlicker*
puHkaja *one who rests*
pUUduja *absentee*
puuTumatu ^ *intact*
põeTaja *nurse*
põhjala *Northland*
põhjatu ^ *bottomless*
põhjendamatu ^ *unjustified*
pärija *heir*
püsimatu ^ *restless*
rAAdio *radio*
rahatu ^ *penniless*
rahula *cemetery*
rahuldamatu ^ *insatiable*
rahutu ^ *restless*
ravimatu ^ *incurable*
reİsija *traveller*
riStleja *cruiser*
rOOmaja *reptile*
rõhuja *oppressor*
rõhutu ^ *unstressed*
rõõmutu ^ *cheerless*
saamatu ^ *clumsy*

continued inetu 227A

227A inetu ***ugly*** **continued**

saLgamatu ^ *undeniable*
saĻLimatu ^ *intolerant*
sEEdimatu ^ *indigestible*
seiKleja *adventurer*
seletamatu ^ *inexplicable*
seLgusetu ^ *obscure*
seOsetu ^ *disjointed*
sigala *pigsty*
sihitu ^ *aimless*
silmakirjatseja *hypocrite*
sisutu ^ *pointless*
skuMbria *makerel*
sobimatu ^ *unsuitable*
stUUdio *studio*
suitsetaja *smoker*
suŅdimatu ^ *unconstrained*
suPleja *bather*
surematu ^ *immortal*
surija *dying person*
suusataja *skier*
suvila *summer cottage*
suvitaja *vacationer*
sõlTumatu ^ *independent*
südametu ^ *heartless*
süŅdsusetu ^ *indecent*
tagala *home front*
taHtmatu ^ *involuntary*
tahumatu ^ *uncouth*
taiPamatu ^ *dim-witted*
takistamatu ^ *unhindered*
taktitu ^ *tactless*
talitaja *tender (person)*
taltsutaja *tamer*
talumatu ^ *unbearable*

taņTsija *dancer*
taRbetu ^ *useless*
taRbija *consumer*
tasuja *avenger*
teAdmatu ^ *unknown*
teadustaja *announcer*
teAdvusetu ^ *unconscious*
tEEnija *servant*
tEEnimatu ^ *unwarranted*
teenindaja *attendant*
teenistuja *employee*
teeSkleja *pretender*
tegevusetu ^ *idle*
teĻLija *subscriber*
temaatika *subject matter*
teOOria *theory*
toeTaja *supporter*
tohutu ^ *enormous*
toimetaja *editor*
toonela *underworld*
toriseja *grumbler*
toRmaja *forward (sport)*
tragÖÖdia *tragedy*
trUUdusetu ^ *unfaithful*
tujutu ^ *spiritless*
tuNdetu ^ *unfeeling*
tuNdmatu ^ *unknown*
tuņnistaja *witness*
tuuPija *crammer*
tõļKija *translator*
täHtsusetu ^ *unimportant*
täİskaSvanu *adult*
tänamatu ^ *ungrateful*
tööTaja *employee*

tüdimatu ^ *untiring*
uisutaja *skater*
ujuja *swimmer*
ujula *swimming-pool*
unetu ^ *sleepless*
unistaja *dreamer*
unustamatu ^ *unforgettable*
uPPuja *drowning person*
uralistika *Uralic studies*
uSkmatu ^ *incredulous*
uSkumatu ^ *incredible*
uuendaja *innovator*
UUrija *investigator*
vahendaja *intermediary*
vahetu ^ *immediate*
vaİdlematu ^ *indisputable*
valaja *caster (moulder)*
valamu *sink*
vaLdaja *proprietor*
valetaja *liar*
valgustaja *enlightener*
valija *voter*
valitseja *ruler*
vallatu ^ *mischievous*
vallutaja *conqueror*
valutu ^ *painless*
vanKumatu ^ *unshakable*
vaRjamatu ^ *unconcealed*
varustaja *supplier*
vaterdaja *prattler*
veHkleja *fencer*
veiderdaja *buffoon*
veretu ^ *bloodless*
viiuldaja *fiddler*

viļjatu ^ *barren*
vilumatu ^ *inexperienced*
vormitu ^ *shapeless*
võimatu ^ *impossible*
võİmetu ^ *incapable*
võİmleja *gymnast*
võiTleja *champion (hero)*
võiTmatu ^ *invincible*
võļTsija *forger*
võRdlematu ^ *incomparable*
võrratu ^ *incomparable*
võrreldamatu ^ *incomparable*
võõrustaja *host*
väļjendamatu ^ *inexpressible*
väļTimatu ^ *unavoidable*
värvitu ^ *colourless*
väsimatu ^ *untiring*
vääritu ^ *undignified*
väärTusetu ^ *worthless*
õhutaja *instigator*
õigustamatu ^ *unjustified*
õMbleja *seamstress*
õngitseja *angler*
õnnetu ^ *unhappy*
õpetaja *teacher*
õPPija *learner*
äritseja *dealer (trafficker)*
äşsitaja *provoker*
ääretu ^ *boundless*
üheksa *nine*
ühistu *co-operative*
üleannetu ^ *naughty*
ületamatu ^ *unsurpassable*
ümmardaja *handmaiden*

227B aaSta *year*

	nominative	genitive	partitive	short into	stem
singular	**aaSta**	**aaSta**	**aaStat**		**aaSta-**
plural	**aaStad**	**aaState**	**aaStaid**		**aaState-** (aaStai-)

Also like aaSta:
aŅdja *giver*
aStma *asthma*
auTu ^ *dishonourable*
haİge ^ *sick*
haİgla *hospital*
hallelUUja *hallelujah*

heLde ^ *generous*
heLge ^ *radiant*
iLge ^ *loathsome*
jOObnu *drunk (noun)*
jooKsva *rheumatism*
juLge ^ *bold*
kaiTsja *defender*

kaŅdja *carrier*
kaNge ^ *stiff*
kaRge ^ *fresh*
kaUge ^ *distant*
keRge ^ *light-weight, easy*
kiRju ^ *multi-coloured*
kõRge ^ *high*

käİmla *toilet*
laHke ^ *kind*
laUlja *singer*
lEEbe ^ *mild*
leHtla *arbour*
leİge ^ *lukewarm*
liNdla *poultry house*

227B aaSta *year* continued **continued aaSta 227B**

lOOja *Creator*
lÄÄge ^ *insipid*
lüPsja *milker*
mAArdla *mineral deposit*
mõRsja *bride*
mÜÜja *seller*
niiSke ^ *moist*
niiTja *mower*
nõTke ^ *supple*
nõuTu ^ *perplexed*
näoTu ^ *unseemly*
näTske ^ *chewy*
oŞtja *buyer*
parAAdna *main entrance*
parKla *parking-lot*

peHme ^ *soft*
priSke ^ *vigorous*
pääStja *Saviour*
raNge ^ *strict*
raSke ^ *difficult, heavy*
rEEde *Friday*
roHke ^ *plentiful*
roHtla *grass-land*
rõSke ^ *damp*
rõUged (pl) *smallpox*
sAAja *recipient*
saaTja *sender*
seLge ^ *clear*
siRge ^ *straight*
siTke ^ *tough*

suRnu *dead person*
sõiTja *passenger*
sõUdja *rower*
sööKla *cafeteria*
süNge ^ *gloomy*
süüTu ^ *innocent*
taHke ^ *solid*
taLgud (pl) *building bee*
tanKla *filling station*
taSku *pocket*
toiTja *feeder*
tooTja *producer*
tuNdra *tundra*
tööTu ^ *unemployed*
tüüTu ^ *tiresome*

uHke ^ *proud*
vaHva *outstanding*
vaLge ^ *white*
vaNgla *prison*
veaTu ^ *faultless*
viNge ^ *piercing*
vinTske ^ *tough of meat*
viRge ^ *wide-awake*
võİmla *gymnasium*
võiTja *winner*
väNge ^ *rank*
värSke ^ *fresh*
õHtu *evening*
õİge ^ *right*
üLbe *arrogant*

228 põRgu *hell* põRgu 228

	nominative	genitive	partitive	short into	stem
singular	**põRgu**	**põRgu**	**põRgut**	**põRgu**	**põRgu-**
plural	**põRgud**	**põRgute**	**põRguid**		**põRgute-** (põRgui-)

TYPE 30 - Truncated Nominative Stems (vowel genitive)

229A agul *slum* agul 229A

	nominative	genitive	partitive	short into	stem
singular	**agul**	**aguli**	**agulit**		**aguli-**
plural	**agulid**	**agulite**	**aguleid**		**agulite-** (agulei-)

Also like agul:
aiand *garden farm*
ajend *inducement*
akumulaaTor *car battery*
aLbum *album*
alev *town*
alTar *altar*
amet *profession*
arStim *remedy*
asend *position*
auTor *author*
baKter *bacteria*
dİivan *divan, sofa*
diKtor *announcer*
eKsam *examination*
elund *anatomiacl organ*
erand *exception*

eTTur *pawn*
haavand *ulcer*
heKtar *hectare*
hulKur *vagabond*
hUUmor *humour*
hÄÄrber *manor house*
igand *relic*
iHnur *miser*
indeks *index*
iNgver *ginger*
initsiaaTor *initiator*
inspeKtor *inspector*
instruKtor *instructor*
isolaaTor *insulator*
istung *session*
isur *İzhorian*
jalatsid (pl) *footwear*

jaluts *foot of bed*
jaUram *twaddler*
jOOmar *drunkard*
joRjen *dahlia*
juhend *instruction*
juHtum *incident*
jUUbel *jubilee anniversary*
juuKsur *hairdresser*
kAAmel *camel*
kabel *chapel*
kaEvur *miner*
kaHjum *loss*
kaHjur *pest*
kahur *cannon*
kajut *cabin in ship*
kalev *broadcloth*
kalkulaaTor *calculator*

kalKun *turkey*
kaLLur *dumper*
kalor *calorie*
kalur *fisherman*
kamPsun *cardigan*
kanal *canal*
kanep *hemp/cannabis*
kanTsler *chancellor*
kaPral *corporal*
kaPron *kapron*
kaPten *captain*
karaKter *character*
kaRbol *carbolic*
karburaaTor *carburettor*
karTul *potato*
kaStan *chestnut*
kaStrul *saucepan*

229A agul *slum* continued

katkend *extract*
kauTsjon *bail*
kavand *outline*
keeFir *kefir*
keİgar *dandy*
keLner *waiter*
ketšup *ketchup*
kiNdral *general*
kirjand *essay*
klarnet *clarinet*
klaver *piano*
konduKtor *conductor*
koNsul *consul*
konteİner *container*
konTor *office*
konveİer *conveyer*
kOOlon *colon*
koPter *helicopter*
kornet *cornet*
korreKtor *proof-reader*
korTer *apartment*
kroket *croquet*
kujur *sculptor*
kuLLer *courier*
kummel *camomile*
kummut *chest of drawers*
kuvar *video monitor*
kvarTal *city block*
kviiTung *receipt*
kvOOrum *quorum*
käpard *bungler*
kÖÖsner *furrier*
laadung *load*
laeKur *treasurer*
laiSkur *sluggard*
laNgevaRjur *parachutist*
laser *laser*
laSkur *marksman*
leİbur *baker*
leİdur *inventor*
leKtor *lecturer*
leNdur *flier*
lennuk *airplane*
lisand *addition*
logard *loafer*
lOOrber *laurel*
loosung *slogan*
lõuend *canvas*
lühend *abbreviation*
madrats *mattress*
magnet *magnet*
majand *farm*
major *major*
malend *chess-man*
maRmor *marble*
marSSal *marshal*
medal *medal*
meeTer *metre*
meetod *method*
melon *melon*
miKser *mixer*
miljard *billion*
miĻjon *million*
minut *minute*
mooTor *motor*
mudel *model*
muistend *folk-tale*
munand *testicle*
mustand *draft copy*
mõRvar *murderer*
naİlon *nylon*
neenets *Nenets*
nekrut *conscript*
niiduk *mower*
nooruk *young man*
notar *notary*
novaaTor *innovator*
näidend *play*
oKsjon *auction*
oKtav *octave*
olend *creature*
omand *property*
ooPer *opera*
oraaTor *orator*
oRder *order*
orel *organ*
oRgan *organ*
organisaaTor *organizer*
paber *paper*
padrun *cartridge*
pagar *baker*
pagas *baggage*
pakend *packing*
palKon *balcony*
panKur *banker*
parTner *partner*
parun *baron*
paStor *pastor*
peeKon *bacon*
peTTur *cheat*
pidur *brake*
pİİson *bison*
pilet *ticket*
piljard *billiards*
pinal *pencil-case*
pitsat *seal*
piTser *seal*
plAAner *glider*
plakat *poster*
plEEnum *plenum*
pliiats *pencil*
porgand *carrot*
porTsjon *helping*
poStskriPtum *postscript*
prinTer *computer printer*
profeSSor *professor*
prohvet *prophet*
projeKtor *projector*
propeLLer *propeller*
propusk *permit*
prožeKtor *spotlight*
pudel *bottle*
puding *pudding*
puhtand *clean copy*
puhvet *canteen*
puLdan *sailcloth*
puljong *bouillon*
pulverisaaTor *pulverizer*
purPur *purple dye*
puSkar *moonshine*
pärand *heritage*
püStol *pistol*
rabaRber *rhubarb*
radar *radar*
radiaaTor *radiator*
rakend *team (horses)*
raport *report*
ravim *remedy*
redel *ladder*
reeTur *traitor*
reformaaTor *reformer*
registraaTor *registrar*
regulaaTor *regulator*
reket *tennis racket*
rekord *record*
reKtor *rector*
reporTer *reporter*
reproduKtor *loudspeaker*
restauraaTor *restorer*
riisling *Riesling*
riiul *shelf*
ripats *pendant*
robot *robot*
roİmar *criminal*
ruuPor *megaphone*
räNdur *wanderer*
rönTgen *X-ray*
saFran *saffron*
sajand *century*
salat *salad*
samet *velvet*
saNgar *hero*
sarlakid (pl) *scarlet fever*
sedel *label*
sEEsam *sesame*
seisund *status*
seKser *plate of cold cuts*
seKtor *sector*
sekund *second of time*
seLLer *celery*
senaaTor *senator*
senat *senate*
sidrun *lemon*
sidur *clutch in car*
sigar *cigar*
sigur *chicory*
siirup *syrup*
siMMan *village hop*
sinel *overcoat*
sinep *mustard*
sinod *synod*
sirel *lilac*
skulPtor *sculptor*
slAAlom *skiing downhill*
smoking *tuxedo*
soldat *soldier*
soPran *soprano*
spiiker *speaker (parliament)*
spinat *spinach*
sprinTer *sprinter*
standard *standard*
starTer *starter*
stİİmul *stimulus*
stjuuard *steward*
stoPPer *stop-watch*
sulam *alloy*
suLgur *stopper*
sõdur *soldier*
sõiduk *vehicle*
sõnum *message*

continued agul 229A

229A agul *slum* continued **continued agul 229A**

süMbol *symbol*
sümPtom *symptom*
süntaks *syntax*
šaaKal *jackal*
šveiTser *doorkeeper*
tabel *table (chart)*
taİdur *artist*
tarind *construction*
tasand *level*
teAdur *researcher*
teFlon *teflon*
tegur *factor*
teisend *version*
teleks *telex*
teler *television set*
televİİsor *television set*
tenor *tenor*
teRmin *term*
teRRor *terror*
tikand *embroidery*

tiSler *cabinet-maker*
toHman *dupe*
tomat *tomato*
topend *wad*
trAAler *trawler*
traKtor *tractor*
transformaaTor *transformer*
trapets *trapeze*
trEEner *trainer*
treİal *lathe operator*
triĻjon *trillion*
trompet *trumpet*
trüKKal *printer*
tseNsor *censor*
tsenTrum *centre*
tsüKlon *cyclone*
tudeng *student*
tuNNel *tunnel*
tuuPur *crammer*
tõstuk *hoist*

täiend *complement*
tööStur *industrialist*
ultimaaTum *ultimatum*
uluk *wild animal*
univeRsum *universe*
usund *religion*
vaaKum *vacuum*
vader *godparent*
vagun *carriage*
vahend *means*
vaKsal *train station*
valem *formula*
vaLvur *guard*
vanur *old person*
varjend *shelter*
varjund *tinge*
vastand *opposite*
vedur *locomotive*
veerand *quarter*
velvet *velvet*

ventilaaTor *fan*
vermut *vermouth*
vigur *stunt*
viiking *Viking*
vİİner *wiener*
viiruk *incense*
viiul *violin*
vikat *scythe*
virgats *express messenger*
visand *outline*
voRmel *formula*
vuSSer *bungler*
vuTlar *case*
võlur *wizard*
võrrand *equation*
võsaviLLem *wolf*
võsund *runner (plant)*
väļjend *expression*
väRval *dyer*
ühend *compound*

229B tõEnd *proof* tõEnd 229B

	nominative	genitive	partitive	short into	stem
singular	**tõEnd**	**tõEndi**	**tõEndit**		**tõEndi-**
plural	**tõEndid**	**tõEndite**	**tõEndeid**		**tõEndite-** (tõEndei-)

Also like tõEnd:
loEnd *enumeration*
kiosK *kiosk*
peaTs *head of bed*
päRl *pearl*
žaNr *genre*
veoK *vehicle*
vÖÖnd *zone*

230 kurat *devil* kurat 230

	nominative	genitive	partitive	short into	stem
singular	**kurat**	**kuradi**	**kuradit**		**kuradi-**
plural	**kuradid**	**kuradite**	**kuradeid**		**kuradite-** (kuradei-)

231A agar [A] *eager* agar 231A

	nominative	genitive	partitive	short into	stem
singular	**agar**	**agara**	**agarat**		**agara-**
plural	**agarad**	**agarate**	**agaraid**		**agarate-** (agarai-)

Also like agar:
aabits *ABC-book*
ahel *chain*
ahvatlev [A] *enticing*
ahven *perch*
alam *subordinate*
alistuv [A] *submissive*
aLLuv *subordinate*
ammendav [A] *exhaustive*
anum *receptacle*
aRmsam *sweetheart*
auStav [A] *respectful*
avar [A] *spacious*
edel *south-west*
edev [A] *vain*
EElnev [A] *preceding*

231A agar *eager* continued

eiTav [A] *negative*
elav [A] *lively*
elus [A] *living*
emand *matron*
enam *more*
erinev [A] *different*
hAArav [A] *thrilling*
halvem [A] *worse*
helin *sound of bell*
hİIlgav [A] *shining*
humal *hop (beer)*
huRmav [A] *charming*
huvitav [A] *interesting*
hÕÕguv [A] *glowing*
häbistav [A] *shameful*
hämar [A] *dusky*
hämmastav [A] *astonishing*
hävitav [A] *destructive*
igav [A] *boring*
ilus [A] *beautiful*
imal [A] *insipid*
isand *lord (master)*
İSSand *Lord (God)*
jaaTav [A] *affirmative*
jagatav [A] *divisible*
jOOdav [A] *drinkable*
joovastav [A] *intoxicating*
judin *shudder*
Jumal *God*
jutustav [A] *narrative*
jäRgnev [A] *subsequent*
jÄÄdav [A] *permanent*
kAAluv [A] *weighty*
kahin *rustle*
kaĻLim [A] *darling*
kamar *rind of meat*
kamin *fireplace*
kammits *fetter*
kanTav [A] *portable*
karastav [A] *refreshing*
kardetav [A] *dangerous*
kardin *curtain*
karistatav [A] *punishable*
kaval [A] *sly*
keHtiv [A] *valid*
kihar *curl*
kirev [A] *dazzling*
klirin *clatter*
klopits *beater*
klõbin *clatter*

kobar *cluster*
kodar *spoke*
kogus [A] *massive*
kohev [A] *fluffy*
kohin *murmur*
kohutav [A] *dreadful*
kolin *clatter*
koRduv [A] *recurrent*
korgits *corkscrew*
kosutav [A] *refreshing*
krabin *rustle*
krigin *crunch*
kriiSkav [A] *shrill*
kruvits *screw-driver*
kujutletav [A] *imaginary*
kuRnav [A] *gruelling*
kUUldav [A] *audible*
kõbin *rustle*
kõbus [A] *hale and hearty*
kõiKuv [A] *unsteady*
kõlav [A] *sonorous*
kõlin *tinkle*
kõmin *rumble*
kõrvits *pumpkin*
kõver [A] *crooked*
kähar [A] *curly*
käİdav [A] *practicable*
köeTav [A] *heatable*
kübar *hat*
küsitav [A] *questionable*
küsiv [A] *interrogative*
kütkestav [A] *captivating*
ladus [A] *fluent*
lagrits *liquorice*
lahustuv [A] *soluble*
latern *lantern*
leHkav [A] *stinking*
lihav [A] *plump*
liigutav [A] *touching*
liiKuv [A] *mobile*
lodev [A] *slack*
loeTav [A] *readable*
looKlev [A] *meandering*
lõbus [A] *fun*
lõHkev [A] *explosive*
lõHnav [A] *fragrant*
lõiKav [A] *cutting*
lähem [A] *nearer*
lähim [A] *nearest*
läiKiv [A] *glossy*

lämmatav [A] *suffocating*
lühem [A] *shorter*
madal [A] *low*
madar *bedstraw (plant)*
magus [A] *sweet*
malev *brigade*
maMMon *Mammon*
masendav [A] *depressing*
masin *machine*
mEEldiv [A] *pleasing*
meelitav [A] *flattering*
mugav [A] *comfortable*
mugul *tuber*
mõistetav [A] *understandable*
mõjuv [A] *effective*
mõnus [A] *cosy*
märgatav [A] *noticeable*
mÄÄrav [A] *decisive*
mühin *rumbling*
mürin *rumble*
mÜÜdav [A] *saleable*
naarits *mink*
naKKav [A] *infectious*
nigel [A] *puny*
norin *snore*
nukits *small horn*
nurin *grumbling*
nõgus [A] *concave*
nõuTav [A] *required*
nädal *week*
nägus [A] *pretty*
näHtav [A] *visible*
näpits *tweezers*
odav [A] *cheap*
orav *squirrel*
osav [A] *skilful*
otsustav [A] *decisive*
pabul *animal droppings*
padin *babble*
pagan *pagan*
pahem [A] *worse*
pahur [A] *sulky*
paİnduv [A] *flexible*
palav [A] *hot*
parem [A] *better*
parim [A] *best*
pasun *trumpet*
pidev [A] *continual*
pİIsav [A] *sufficient*
pikem [A] *longer*

continued agar 231A

pilKav [A] *mocking*
pimestav [A] *blinding*
pisar *tear*
pisem [A] *smaller*
pisim [A] *tiniest*
pladin *splash*
plagin *clatter*
pomin *mutter*
põdur [A] *sickly*
põgus [A] *brief*
põiKlev [A] *evasive*
põlastav [A] *disdainful*
põletav [A] *burning*
põnev [A] *exciting*
põrand *floor*
põrin *buzz*
pädev [A] *competent*
päritav [A] *hereditary*
püsiv [A] *persistent*
rabav [A] *striking*
ragin *crackle*
rahuldav [A] *satisfactory*
rammus [A] *robust*
ranits *satchel*
ravitav [A] *curable*
rebitav [A] *tearable*
rosin *raisin*
rumal [A] *stupid*
rõhuv [A] *oppressive*
räbal *tatter*
rätsep *tailor*
saaTan *Satan*
sadam *harbour*
sadul *saddle*
sahin *rustle*
seeditav [A] *digestible*
seļTsiv [A] *sociable*
sibul *onion*
siduv [A] *binding*
sisin *sizzle*
sobiv [A] *suitable*
solin *splash*
soLvav [A] *insulting*
soovitav [A] *desirable*
sorav [A] *fluent*
sosin *whisper*
sujuv [A] *fluent*
sumin *drone*
suRmav [A] *deadly*
sõlTuv [A] *dependent*

231A agar ***eager*** **continued** — **continued agar 231A**

särav ^A *sparkling*
sÖÖdav ^A *edible*
sügav ^A *deep*
sütitav ^A *inspiring*
süŢTiv ^A *inflammable*
tabav ^A *striking*
tajutav ^A *perceptible*
talutav ^A *tolerable*
tasuv ^A *profitable*
teaTav ^A *certain; a certain*
tegev ^A *active*
teoStatav ^A *feasible*
terav ^A *sharp*
torin *grumble*
tosin *dozen*
tugev ^A *strong*
tuharad (pl) *buttocks*
tulev ^A *coming*
tulus ^A *profitable*
tuNgiv ^A *urgent*
tunnustav ^A *approving*
tõhus ^A *efficient*
täbar ^A *awkward*
täiendav ^A *supplementary*
tänav *street*
tülin *trouble*
udar *udder*
unelm *day-dream*
urin *growl*
usaldatav ^A *trustworthy*
usin ^A *diligent*
uStav ^A *faithful*
usutav ^A *plausible*
vabandatav ^A *excusable*
vadin *prattle*
vahelduv ^A *alternating*
vaieldav ^A *debatable*
vaiKiv ^A *silent*
vaimustav ^A *inspiring*
vaLdav ^A *predominant*
valus ^A *painful*
vanem *parent*
vapustav ^A *shocking*
varem ^A *earlier*
vasar *hammer*
vasem ^A *left*
vaStav ^A *corresponding*
vastutav ^A *responsible*
vedel ^A *liquid*
veeTlev ^A *charming*
venitatav ^A *elastic*
veTruv ^A *springy*
vihatav ^A *hateful*
vilets ^A *shabby*
virin *whimper*
vOOlav ^A *flowing*
vulin *gurgle*
vurin *whir*
võbin *quiver*
võluv ^A *charming*
võRdlev ^A *comparative*
võrreldav ^A *comparable*
vägev ^A *mighty*
vähem ^A *lesser*
vähim ^A *smallest*
väļditav ^A *avoidable*
värav *gate*
väsitav ^A *tiring*
õdus ^A *cosy*
õhem ^A *thinner*
õhin *zeal*
õiTsev ^A *blossoming*
õnar *groove*
ärev ^A *agitated*
ärrituv ^A *irritable*
ülem *superior*
ülev ^A *elated*
ülim ^A *supreme*
ümar ^A *rounded*
ümin *hum*

231B aUs ^A *hones* — aUs 231B

	nominative	genitive	partitive	short into	stem
singular	**aUs**	**aUsa**	**aUsat**		**aUsa-**
plural	**aUsad**	**aUsate**	**aUsaid**		**aUsate-** (aUsai-)

Also like aUs:
jÄÄv ^A *constant*
kEEv ^A *boiling*
lOOv ^A *creative*
mõİs *estate*
näİv ^A *apparent*
õEl *wicked*

232 mõlema ^A *both* — mõlema 232

	nominative	genitive	partitive	short into	stem
singular	---	**mõlema**	**mõlemat**		**mõlema-**
plural	**mõlemad**	**mõlemate**	**mõlemaid**		**mõlemate-** (mõlemai-)

233A kevad *spring* — kevad 233A

	nominative	genitive	partitive	short into	stem
singular	**kevad**	**kevade**	**kevadet**		**kevade-**
plural	**kevaded**	**kevadete**	**kevadeid**		**kevadete-** (kevadei-)

233B küPs *ripe* — küPs 233B

	nominative	genitive	partitive	short into	stem
singular	**küPs**	**küPse**	**küPset**		**küPse-**
plural	**küPsed**	**küPsete**	**küPseid**		**küPsete-** (küPsei-)

Also like küPs: kõRb *desert*

234A raamat *book* — raamat 234A

	nominative	genitive	partitive	short into	stem
singular	**raamat**	**raamatu**	**raamatut**		**raamatu-**
plural	**raamatud**	**raamatute**	**raamatuid**		**raamatute-** (raamatui-)

Also like raamat:
aisting *sense (perception)*
areng *evolution*
aurik *steamer*
botaanik *botanist*
boţikud (pl) *overshoes*
erak *recluse*
esik *entrance hall*
graafik *graphic artist*
haarang *raid*
hinnang *evaluation*
hoiak *posture*
hommik *morning*
huŋnik *pile*
hurtsik *hut*
häving *destruction*
häälik *sound (language)*
hüvang *well-being*
imik *baby*
isik *person*
jooḑik *drunkard*
jooksik *fugitive*
jooming *drinking party*
kaarik *cart*
kaasik *birch grove*
kaevik *trench*
kaksik *twin*
kallak *slope*
kaŋdik *tray*
kasarm *barracks*
kaustik *notebook*
keemik *chemist*
kemmerg *outhouse*
kirik *church*
klaşsik *classic*
kliinik *clinic*
kohvik *café*
koidik *dawn*
koļmik *triplet*
koomik *comedian*
koorik *crust*
kopsik *dipper*
kriitik *critic*
kuivik *rusk*
kuubik *cube*
kuusik *fir grove*
kõnnak *gait*
kämping *camp grounds*
käpik *mitten*
käänak *bend in road*
külmik *refrigerator*
küülik *domestic rabbit*
küünik *cynic*
lahing *battle*
lapsik [A] *childish*
laulik *songster*
lausik *flat*
lehvik *fan*
leitsak *overwhelming heat*
lemmik *favourite*
lepik *alder grove*
leping *treaty*
levik *distribution*
linik *place-mat*
lipik *tag*
lombak *cripple*
loojang *sunset*
looming *creative work*
looţsik *boat*
lööming *fight*
lüpsik *milk pail*
mannerg *can*
meţsik [A] *wild*
minek *departure*
murrak *minor dialect*
muusik *musician*
mäŋnik *pine grove*
naştik *ringed snake*
nauding *delight*
nuuştik *wash-cloth*
olek *state of being*
padrik *thicket*
paļling *serve (sports)*
paļmik *plait*
peļdik *outhouse*
peŋtsik [A] *queer*
persik *peach*
pihik *bodice*
pimik *dark-room*
pintsak *blazer*
pisik *germ*
pistik *plug*
poliitik *politician*
pooļik [A] *half-finished*
publik *audience*
puhang *gust*
päevik *diary*
pääsik *pass*
päästik *trigger*
pööning *attic*
löörang *turn*
pühak *saint*
püksikud (pl) *shorts*
raŋnik *coast*
riştik *clover*
romaŋtik *romantic*
rännak *wanderings*
räştik *viper*
räţik *towel*
röövik *caterpillar*
rünnak *attack*
saadik *ambassador*
sarvik *demon*
seelik *skirt*
seisak *standstill*
seļjak *ridge*
sepik *whole wheat bread*
smoking *tuxedo*
solvang *insult*
soosik *favourite*
soosing *patronage*
sõŋnik *manure*
särgik *singlet*
säärik *boot*
sööming *feasting*
süştik *shuttle*
taldrik *plate*
tammik *oak grove*
tehing *transaction*
tehnik *technician*
teisik *double*
teļling *scaffold*
tervik *whole*
tihnik *thicket*
toimik *file (document)*
toiming *operation*
toodang *production*
treening *training*
treeningud (pl)*training suit*
truşsikud (pl) *underpants*
tulek *arrival*
tupik *dead end*
tuulik *windmill*
tõrvik *torch*

234A raamat ***book*** **continued** **continued raamat 234A**

tõusik *upstart*
tähik *receipt*
täring *die*
tüdruk *girl*
tühik *void*
uinak *nap*
ummik *deadlock*
vabrik *factory*
vadak *whey*
valang *downpour*
valik *choice*
vanik *garland*
vasak [A] *left*
vaştik [A] *repugnant*
vihik *exercise book*
vildak [A] *slanting*
virsik *peach*
voļdik *folder*
vooļik *hose*
võhik *ignoramus*
võļtsing *forgery*
väļjak *square*
värving *hue (colour)*
õitseng *blossoming*
õpik *textbook*
õpingud (pl) *studies*
ööbik *nightingale*
ühik *unit*
ühing *workers' union*
üksik *single*
ümbrik *envelope*
ürik *historical document*

234B soEng *hair style* soEng 234B

	nominative	genitive	partitive	short into	stem
singular	**soEng**	**soEngu**	**soEngut**		**soEngu-**
plural	**soEngud**	**soEngute**	**soEnguid**		**soEngute-** (soEngui-)

Also like soEng: laEng *charge* loEng *lecture*

TYPE 31 - Truncated Nominative Stems (-da genitive)

235 hõbe *silver* hõbe 235

	nominative	genitive	partitive	short into	stem
singular	**hõbe**	**hõbeda**	**hõbedat**		**hõbeda-**
plural	**hõbedad**	**hõbedate**	**hõbedaid**		**hõbedate-** (hõbedai-)

Also like hõbe:
ere [A] *bright*
hale [A] *sorrowful*
hele [A] *bright*
hõre [A] *sparse*
jahe [A] *cool*
jube [A] *ghastly*
jäle [A] *disgusting*
jäme [A] *thick*
kade [A] *envious*
kare [A] *rough*
kibe [A] *bitter*
kile [A] *piercing*
kole [A] *horrible*
krobe [A] *rough*
kröbe [A] *crisp*
kõhe [A] *uneasy*
kõle [A] *bleak*
käre [A] *severe*
lage [A] *bare*
lahe [A] *affable*
lame [A] *flat*
libe [A] *slippery*
mage [A] *unsalted*
mahe [A] *mild*
nobe [A] *nimble*
nõme [A] *ignorant (stupid)*
pime [A] *dark*
pime [A] *blind*
rase [A] *pregnant*
rõve [A] *obscene*
rüve [A] *impure*
sage [A] *frequent*
sale [A] *slim*
sile [A] *smooth*
tahe [A] *dry*
tige [A] *angry*
tihe [A] *dense*
tobe [A] *dumb*
tore [A] *splendid*
tume [A] *dark of colour*
tüse [A] *stout*
väle [A] *nimble*
äge [A] *impetuous*

236 läheda [A] *nearby* läheda 236

	nominative	genitive	partitive	short into	stem
singular	---	**läheda**	**lähedat**		**läheda-**
plural	**lähedad**	**lähedate**	**lähedaid**		**lähedate-** (lähedai-)

Also like läheda: ligida [A] *nearby (see ligidane)*

TYPE 32 Truncated Nominative Stems (-nda genitive)

237A sajas ^A *hundredth* — sajas 237A

	nominative	genitive	partitive	short into	stem
singular	**sajas**	**sajanda**	**sajandat**		**sajanda-**
plural	**sajandad**	**sajandate**	**sajandaid**		**sajandate-** (sajandai-)

237B üheksas ^A *nineth* — üheksas 237B

	nominative	genitive	partitive	short into	stem
singular	**üheksas**	**üheksanda**	**üheksandat**		**üheksanda-**
plural	**üheksandad**	**üheksandate**	**üheksandaid**		**üheksandate-** (üheksandai-)

Also like üheksas: kaheksas ^A *eighth* miljardes ^A *billionth* tuhandes ^A *thousandth*

237C küMnes ^A *tenth* — küMnes 237C

	nominative	genitive	partitive	short into	stem
singular	**küMnes**	**küMnenda**	**küMnendat**		**küMnenda-**
plural	**küMnendad**	**küMnendate**	**küMnendaid**		**küMnendate-** (küMnendai-)

Also like küMnes: seiTsmes ^A *seventh* miLjones ^A *millionth*

238A vii[j]es ^A *fifth* — vii[j]es 238A

	nominative	genitive	partitive	short into	stem
singular	**vii[j]es**	**vii[j]enda**	**vii[j]endat** (vii[j]et)		**vii[j]enda-**
plural	**vii[j]endad**	**vii[j]endate**	**vii[j]endaid**		**vii[j]endate-** (vii[j]endai-)

Also like viies: kolmas ^A *third* kuu[w]es ^A *sixth* neljas ^A *fourth*

238B miTmes ^A *which? (ordinal number)* — miTmes 238B

	nominative	genitive	partitive	short into	stem
singular	**miTmes**	**miTmenda**	**miTmendat** (miTmet)		**miTmenda-**
plural	**miTmendad**	**miTmendate**	**miTmendaid**		**miTmendate-** (miTmendai-)

239 tuhat *hundredth* — tuhat 239

	nominative	genitive	partitive	short into	stem
singular	**tuhat**	**tuhande**	**tuhat**		**tuhande-**
plural	**tuhanded**	**tuhandete**	**tuhandeid**		**tuhandete-** (tuhandei-)

TYPE 33 - Truncated Genitive Stems

240A AAdel *nobleman* AAdel 240A

	nominative	genitive	partitive	short into	stem
singular	**AAdel**	**AAdli**	**AAdlit**		**AAdli-**
plural	**AAdlid**	**AAdlite**	**AAdleid**		**AAdlite-** (AAdlei-)

aaKer *acre*
aHter *stern of ship*
ansaMbel *ensemble*
apoStel *apostle*
aPteeKer *druggist*
aSter *aster*
auSter *oyster*
detseMber *December*
dİİsel *diesel*
džemPer *jumper*
džuNgel *jungle*
EEsel *donkey*
eeTer *ether*
eleKter *electricity*
filTer *filter*
geİser *geyser*
hAAmer *hammer*
hAAvel *pellet*
hÖÖvel *plane*
iNgel *angel*
jüNger *disciple*
kAAbel *cable*
kAAder *personnel*
kaaTer *hangover; launch*
kaHvel *fork*
kaleNder *calendar*
kalİİber *calibre*
kaMber *chamber*
kamPer *camphor*
kanTsel *pulpit*
katEEder *department*
keİser *emperor*

keLder *cellar*
kiiKer *telescope*
kİİver *helmet*
klaMber *clip*
kliiSter *paste (glue)*
klooSter *cloister, monastery*
koHver *suitcase*
kondiiTer *confectioner*
koriaNder *coriander*
kraaTer *crater*
kriNgel *knot-shaped pastry*
köSter *parish clerk*
küHvel *shovel*
lAAger *camp*
laveNdel *lavender*
leeTrid (pl) *measles*
leHter *funnel*
liiPer *tie in railroad*
liiTer *litre*
mAAler *painter (artist)*
magiSter *master (university)*
maNdel *almond; tonsil*
maNder *continent*
manTel *coat*
manÖÖver *manoeuvre*
meiSter *master (expert)*
miniSter *minister*
muNder *uniform*
muSkel *muscle*
muSter *pattern*
märTer *martyr*
möLder *miller*

mÖÖbel *furniture*
nAAber *neighbour*
nOObel [A] *grand*
noveMber *November*
nuMber *number*
nUUdel *noodle*
oHver *sacrifice; victim*
oktOOber *October*
orkeSter *orchestra*
paHtel *palette-knife*
paRdel *shaver*
pEEgel *mirror*
peeKer *goblet*
peiTel *chisel*
peNdel *pendulum*
pİİbel *Bible*
pinTsel *paintbrush*
plaaSter *plaster (surgical)*
preeSter *priest*
psühhiaaTer *psychiatrist*
puLber *powder*
punKer *bunker*
pUUdel *poodle*
pUUder *face powder*
päHkel *nut*
rabaRber *rhubarb*
rEEgel *rule*
regiSter *register*
renTsel *gutter*
revoLver *revolver*
rÖÖvel *robber*
rüüTel *knight*

saHtel *drawer*
saHver *pantry*
sEEder *cedar*
semeSter *semester*
septeMber *September*
sİİber *damper*
siNdel *shingle (roof)*
sirKel *compasses*
spaaTel *spatula*
spaRgel *asparagus*
speKter *spectrum*
striTsel *coffee cake*
sviiTer *sweater*
šniTsel *cutlet*
taHvel *black-board*
teaTer *theatre*
tEEner *servant*
temPel *temple; stamp*
tİİger *tiger*
tiiTel *title*
tuHvel *slipper*
tuuKer *diver*
uHmer *mortar*
vaHvel *wafer*
vanKer *wagon*
vimPel *pennant*
vinKel *right angel*
viSpel *whisk*
vOOder *lining*
väRvel *waistband*
vÄÄvel *sulphur*
äMber *pail*

240B kiTTel *smock* kiTTel 240B

	nominative	genitive	partitive	short into	stem
singular	**kiTTel**	**kiTli**	**kiTlit**		**kiTli-**
plural	**kiTlid**	**kiTlite**	**kiTleid**		**kiTlite-** (kiTlei-)

Also like kiTTel:
binoKKel *binoculars*
daTTel *date fruit*
kaHHel *glazed tile*

koPPel *enclosure*
kuKKel *bun*
kuPPel *dome*
liTTer *sequin*

muTTer *nut (bolt)*
niKKel *nickel*
paPPel *poplar*
snePPer *Yale lock*

spiKKer *cheat-sheet*
šiFFer *cipher*
teKKel *student's cap*
tsüKKel *cycle*

241A kiNdel [A] *sure* — kiNdel 241A

	nominative	genitive	partitive	short into	stem
singular	**kiNdel**	**kiNdla**	**kiNdlat**		**kiNdla-**
plural	**kiNdlad**	**kiNdlate**	**kiNdlaid**		**kiNdlate-** (kiNdlai-)

Also like kiNdel:	kAAren *raven*	pOOgen *bow; sheet*	vAAgen *platter*
haİsev [A] *stinking*	keStev [A] *durable*	taİgen *dough*	vaStlad (pl) *Shrove-tide*
iseteAdev [A] *self-confident*	korSten *chimney*	toiTev [A] *nourishing*	veİder [A] *odd (strange)*
jooKsev [A] *running*	maiTsev [A] *tasty*	tooTev [A] *productive*	värTen *bobbin*
jõHker [A] *brutal*	oHter [A] *abundant*	tuNdel *feeler*	

241B nuKKer [A] *melancholy* — nuKKer 241B

	nominative	genitive	partitive	short into	stem
singular	**nuKKer**	**nuKra**	**nuKrat**		**nuKra-**
plural	**nuKrad**	**nuKrate**	**nuKraid**		**nuKrate-** (nuKrai-)

Also like nuKKer: toTTer [A] *idiotic* vaPPer [A] *brave*

242A suHkur *sugar* — suHkur 242A

	nominative	genitive	partitive	short into	stem
singular	**suHkur**	**suHkru**	**suHkrut**		**suHkru-**
plural	**suHkrud**	**suHkrute**	**suHkruid**		**suHkrute-** (suHkrui-)

Also like suHkur: anKur *anchor* kaNgur *weaver* tuHkur [A] *ashen*

242B kuKKur *pouch* — kuKKur 242B

	nominative	**genitive**	**partitive**	**short into**	**stem**
singular	**kuKKur**	**kuKru**	**kuKrut**		**kuKru-**
plural	**kuKrud**	**kuKrute**	**kuKruid**		**kuKrute-** (kuKrui-)

TYPE 34 Truncated Genitive Stems (-as nominative)

243A pirukas *patty, pie* — pirukas 243A

	nominative	genitive	partitive	short into	stem
singular	**pirukas**	**piruka**	**pirukat**		**piruka-**
plural	**pirukad**	**pirukate**	**pirukaid**		**pirukate-** (pirukai-)

Also like pirukas:	arukas [A] *sensible*	haļlikas [A] *greyish*	iLmekas [A] *expressive*
aļlikas *spring, source*	arvukas [A] *numerous*	harakas *magpie*	innukas [A] *fervent*
aNdekas [A] *talented*	edukas [A] *successful*	heeringas *herring*	isekas [A] *selfish*
angerjas *eel*	elajas *beast*	hooļikas [A] *careful*	jalakas *elm*

243A pirukas ***patty, pie*** **continued** | **continued pirukas 243A**

joŋnakas ^A^ *stubborn*
jutukas ^A^ *talkative*
jõhvikas *cranberry*
jõmpsikas *urchin*
kaabakas *scoundrel*
kaaļikas *turnip*
kaalukas ^A^ *weighty*
kadakas *juniper*
kajakas *sea-gull*
kaŋnikad (pl) *buttocks*
karikas *goblet*
kasukas *fur coat*
keerukas ^A^ *intricate*
kehakas ^A^ *stout*
kellukas *bell-flower*
keļmikas ^A^ *roguish*
kiilakas ^A^ *bald-headed*
kogukas ^A^ *bulky*
kohmakas ^A^ *clumsy*
kollakas ^A^ *yellowish*
kulukas ^A^ *costly*
kuningas *king*
kuţsikas *puppy*
kuulekas ^A^ *obedient*
kõlakas *gossip*
küürakas ^A^ *hunchback*
labidas *shovel*
laţikas *bream (fish)*
liblikas *butterfly*
lillakas ^A^ *purplish*

lohakas ^A^ *sloppy*
loļlakas ^A^ *simpleton*
lombakas ^A^ *crippled*
lopsakas ^A^ *lush*
lusikas *spoon*
luşţakas ^A^ *pleasurable*
luţikas *bedbug*
lärmakas ^A^ *noisy*
maasikas *strawberry*
mahlakas ^A^ *juicy*
mahukas ^A^ *roomy*
maiTsekas ^A^ *tasteful*
majakas *lighthouse*
mardikas *beetle*
menukas ^A^ *successful*
miļlimaļlikas *jelly-fish*
muļlikas *heifer*
murakas *cloudberry*
muşţikas *blueberry*
mõjukas ^A^ *influential*
mõrtsukas *murderer*
mõõdukas ^A^ *moderate*
mölakas *oaf*
naļjakas ^A^ *funny*
narvakas *native of Narva*
nimekas ^A^ *renowned*
ninakas ^A^ *snooty*
nupukas ^A^ *quick-witted*
närakas *rag*
oblikas *sorrel*

ohakas *thistle*
orikas *barrow (pig)*
oTstaRbekas ^A^ *expedient*
parukas *wig*
pedajas *pine*
pihlakas *mountain ash*
pirtsakas ^A^ *petulant*
prussakas *cockroach*
pruuŋikas ^A^ *brownish*
punakas ^A^ *reddish*
purjekas *sailboat*
putukas *insect*
põrnikas *beetle*
raevukas ^A^ *enraged*
remmelgas *willow*
riiakas ^A^ *quarrelsome*
riisikas *milk mushroom*
rinnakas ^A^ *broad-chested*
rinnakas ^A^ *full-breasted*
rohekas ^A^ *greenish*
roosakas ^A^ *pinkish*
rusikas *fist*
ruumikas ^A^ *roomy*
sarikas *rafter*
sarmikas ^A^ *charming*
saţikas *crab-louse*
sihvakas ^A^ *slender*
sinakas ^A^ *bluish*
sinikas *whortleberry*
sipelgas *ant*

sisukas ^A^ *substantial*
siţikas *beetle*
soolikas *intestine*
sõjakas ^A^ *warlike*
särtsakas ^A^ *peppy*
taibukas ^A^ *intelligent*
toomingas *bird-cherry tree*
tormakas ^A^ *impetuous*
totakas ^A^ *brainless*
tubakas *tobacco*
tujukas ^A^ *moody*
tulikas *buttercup*
turakas *blockhead*
turtsakas ^A^ *peevish*
tülikas ^A^ *troublesome*
ulakas ^A^ *hooligan*
upsakas ^A^ *arrogant*
vaarikas *raspberry*
vaimukas ^A^ *witty*
varrukas *sleeve*
vasikas *calf*
veţikas *alga*
viilukas *slice*
viisakas ^A^ *polite*
vildakas ^A^ *slanting*
viļjakas ^A^ *fertile*
võidukas ^A^ *victorious*
värvikas ^A^ *colourful*
väärikas ^A^ *dignified*
ääḑikas *vinegar*

243B eaKas ^A^ *elderly* — eaKas 243B

	nominative	genitive	partitive	short into	stem
singular	**eaKas**	**eaKa**	**eaKat**		**eaKa-**
plural	**eaKad**	**eaKate**	**eaKaid**		**eaKate-** (eaKai-)

Also like eaKas:
haĻdjas *fairy*
jõuKas ^A^ *prosperous*
kõrKjas *bulrush*
moeKas ^A^ *stylish*
näļKjas *slug*
taKjas *burdock*
toeKas ^A^ *sturdy*
tööKas ^A^ *industrious*
väRdjas *freak*

244 vaĻmis ^A^ *finished; ripe* — vaĻmis 244

	nominative	genitive	partitive	short into	stem
singular	**vaĻmis**	**vaĻmi**	**vaĻmit**		**vaĻmi-**
plural	**vaĻmid**	**vaĻmite**	**vaĻmeid**		**vaĻmite-** (vaĻmei-)

NOMINALS - 4 - CLASS VIII

TYPE 35 - Regular

245 restoran *restaurant* restoran 245

	nominative	genitive	partitive	short into	stem
singular	**restoran**	**restorani**	**restorani**	**restorani**	**restorani-**
plural	**restoranid**	**restoranide**	**restorane**		**restoranide**
			restoranisid		restorane-

Also like restoran	karahvin *carafe*	koridor *corridor*	tehnikum *technical college*
garnison *garrison*	komisjon *commission*	seminar *seminar*	

The SHORT INTO CASE is not commonly used with the following items:

admiral *admiral*	karavan *caravan*	mikrofon *microphone*	portsigar *cigarette-case*
alkohol *alcohol*	kardemon *cardamom*	miljardär *multi-millionaire*	postiljon *mailman*
antibiootikum *antibiotic*	karneval *carnival*	miljonär *millionaire*	prokurör *prosecutor*
apelsin *orange (fruit)*	kaunitar *female beauty*	misjonär *missionary*	pullover *pullover*
bariton *baritone*	kavaler *beau*	molekul *molecule*	revisjon *audit*
bädminton *badminton*	kolonel *colonel*	monopol *monopoly*	saksofon *saxophone*
eksemplar *copy of a book*	komandör *commander*	muusikal *musical*	sanitar *orderly*
elektron *electron*	kontrolör *inspector*	mänedžer *manager*	sekretär *secretary*
festival *festival*	ksülofon *xylophone*	narkootikum *narcotics*	spinnaker *spinnaker*
följeton *feuilleton*	kuberner *governor*	ohvitser *officer*	šampinjon *mushroom*
grammofon *gramophone*	magnetofon *tape-recorder*	palderjan *valerian*	talisman *talisman*
honorar *royalty*	makaron *macaroni*	pataljon *battalion*	telefon *telephone*
insener *engineer*	maksimum *maximum*	paviljon *pavilion*	tikerber *gooseberry*
inventar *inventory*	martsipan *marzipan*	peNsionär *pensioner*	tärpentin *turpentine*
juubilar *jubilarian*	materjal *material*	personal *personnel*	veteran *veteran*
kapital *capital*	miinimum *minimum*	portselan *porcelain*	vürstitar *princess*

246 mUUseum *museum* mUUseum 246

	nominative	genitive	partitive	short into	stem
singular	**mUUseum**	**mUUseumi**	**mUUseumi**	**mUUseumi**	**mUUseumi-**
plural	**mUUseumid**	**mUUseumide**	**mUUseume**		**mUUseumide-**
			mUUseumisid		(mUUseume-)
or:					
singular	**mUUseum**	**mUUseumi**	**mUUseumit**		**mUUseumi-**
plural	**mUUseumid**	**mUUseumite**	**mUUseumeid**		**mUUseumite-**
					(mUUseumei-)

Also like mUUseum:	herbAArium *herbarium*	lektOOrium *lecture-hall*	paNsion *boarding-house*
akvAArium *aquarium*	impEErium *empire*	lüTseum *lyceum*	planetAArium *planetarium*
ambulatOOrium *dispensary*	konsistOOrium *consistory*	ministEErium *ministry*	sanatOOrium *sanatorium*
auditOOrium *auditorium*	krematOOrium *crematorium*	observatOOrium *observatory*	stAAdion *stadium*
gümnAAsium *high school*	laboratOOrium *laboratory*	ooKean *ocean*	territOOrium *territory*

The SHORT INTO CASE is not commonly used with the following items:

akoRdion *accordion*
alumIInium *aluminium*
evangEElium *Gospel*
fOOlium *foil*
jaaguar *jaguar*
jaanuar *January*
kaļTsium *calcium*
naaTrium *sodium*
ooPium *opium*
peNsion *pension*
petrOOleum *kerosene*
rAAdium *radium*
reeKviem *requiem*
stAAdium *phase*
stipeŅdium *scholarship*
stsenAArium *scenario*
sümpOOsion *symposium*
tÜÜmian *thyme*
vaaKuum *vacuum*
vEEbruar *February*

-NE AND -US NOMINALS - 3 - CLASS VII

TYPE 36 - Vowel Stem Partitives

247 raUdne ^ ***iron*** **raUdne 247**

	nominative	genitive	partitive	short into	stem
singular	**raUdne**	**raUdse**	**raUdset**		**raUdse-**
plural	**raUdsed**	**raUdsete**	**raUdseid**		**raUdsete-** (raUdsei-)

Also like raUdne:
absoluuTne ^ *absolute*
abstraKtne ^ *abstract*
absuRdne ^ *absurd*
agressİİvne ^ *aggressive*
aktİİvne ^ *active*
aktuAAlne ^ *topical*
akuuTne ^ *acute*
alkohOOlne ^ *alcoholic*
amorAAlne ^ *immoral*
anonÜÜmne ^ *anonymous*
antiiKne ^ *antique*
antipaaTne ^ *antipathetic*
apaaTne ^ *apathetic*
aromaaTne ^ *aromatic*
automaaTne ^ *automatic*
autonOOmne ^ *autonomous*
autoriteeTne ^ *authoritative*
barbAArne ^ *barbaric*
brutAAlne ^ *brutal*
defektİİvne ^ *defective*
defeKtne ^ *faulty*
dekoratİİvne ^ *decorative*
delikaaTne ^ *delicate*
detaİlne ^ *detailed*
diagonAAlne ^ *diagonal*
diskreeTne ^ *discreet*
efektİİvne ^ *effective*
eİlne ^ *yesterday's*
elaStne ^ *elastic*
eleganTne ^ *elegant*
fakultatİİvne ^ *optional*
familiAArne ^ *familiar*
feodAAlne ^ *feudal*
fiktİİvne ^ *fictitious*
formAAlne ^ *formal*
föderAAlne ^ *federal*
hoMne ^ *tomorrow*
horisontAAlne ^ *horizontal*
ideAAlne ^ *ideal*
illegAAlne ^ *illegal*
iLmne ^ *evident*
immUUnne ^ *immune*
individuAAlne ^ *individual*
instinktİİvne ^ *instinctive*
inteļligenTne ^ *intelligent*
intensİİvne ^ *intensive*
intİİmne ^ *intimate*
kaNgekaElne ^ *obstinate*
kapitAAlne ^ *capital*
kaUdne ^ *indirect*
kollektİİvne ^ *collective*
koloniAAlne ^ *colonial*
kolossAAlne ^ *colossal*
kompaKtne ^ *compact*
kompetenTne ^ *competent*
kompleKsne ^ *complex*
konkreeTne ^ *concrete*
kontraStne ^ *contrastive*
kriminAAlne ^ *criminal*
kuLdne ^ *golden*
kultUUrne ^ *cultured*
kvalitatİİvne ^ *qualitative*
kvaliteeTne ^ *good-quality*
legendAArne ^ *legendary*
liberAAlne ^ *liberal*
lİİgne ^ *excessive*
maksimAAlne ^ *maximum*
massİİvne ^ *massive*
materiAAlne ^ *material*
melanhOOlne ^ *melancholic*
minerAAlne ^ *mineral*
minimAAlne ^ *minimal*
modeRnne ^ *modern*
monotOOnne ^ *monotonous*
morAAlne ^ *moral*
muiStne ^ *ancient*
musikAAlne ^ *musical*
naİİvne ^ *naive*
naturAAlne ^ *natural*
neutrAAlne ^ *neutral*
normAAlne ^ *normal*
nÜÜdne ^ *present*
objektİİvne ^ *objective*
operatİİvne ^ *operative*
optimAAlne ^ *optimum*
originAAlne ^ *original*
ovAAlne ^ *oval*
parallEElne ^ *parallel*
peAlsed (pl) *greens (plants)*
perfeKtne ^ *perfect*
piKne *lightning*
pOOrne ^ *porous*
populAArne ^ *popular*
portatİİvne ^ *portable*
positİİvne ^ *positive*
postUUmne ^ *posthumous*
potentsiAAlne ^ *potential*
primitİİvne ^ *primitive*
produktİİvne ^ *productive*
progressİİvne ^ *progressive*
radikAAlne ^ *radical*
reAAlne ^ *practicable*
regulAArne ^ *regular*
relatİİvne ^ *relative*
resoluuTne ^ *resolute*
riskanTne ^ *risky*
sanatOOrne ^ *sanatory*
seAlne ^ *there*
seksuAAlne ^ *sexual*
sİİnne ^ *local*
skandAAlne ^ *scandalous*
solidAArne ^ *unanimous*
solİİdne ^ *respectable*
sotsiAAlne ^ *social*
spetsiAAlne ^ *special*
spirAAlne ^ *spiral*
spontAAnne ^ *spontaneous*
stabİİlne ^ *stable*
sterİİlne ^ *sterile*
stİİlne ^ *stylish*
subjektİİvne ^ *subjective*
suverÄÄnne ^ *sovereign*
sümbOOlne ^ *symbolic*
sümpaaTne ^ *sympathetic*
taİmne ^ *vegetable*
teatrAAlne ^ *theatrical*
territoriAAlne ^ *territorial*
totAAlne ^ *total*
tsentrAAlne ^ *central*
täPne ^ *precise*
uMbne ^ *stuffy*
universAAlne ^ *universal*
uRbne ^ *porous*
UUdne ^ *novel*
vaiKne ^ *quiet*
vaİmne ^ *spiritual*
vakanTne ^ *vacant*
vaŞkne ^ *copper*
vaStne ^ *new*
vaStne *larva*
verbAAlne ^ *verbal*
vertikAAlne ^ *vertical*
vİİmne ^ *final*
violeTne ^ *violet*
visuAAlne ^ *visual*
vulgAArne ^ *vulgar*
võRdne ^ *equal*
õUdne ^ *ghastly*
üHtne ^ *united*
üKsköiKne ^ *indifferent*
üRgne ^ *primeval*

248 kaprÏIsne ^A^ ***capricious*** **kaprÏIsne 248**

	nominative	genitive	partitive	short into	stem
singular	**kaprÏIsne**	**kapriiSSe**	**kapriiSSet**		**kapriiSSe-**
plural	**kapriiSSed**	**kapriiSSete**	**kapriiSSeid**		**kapriiSSete-** (kapriiSSei-)

Also like kaprÏIsne: tuberkulOOsne ^A^ *tubercular* virtuOOsne ^A^ *masterly*

249 eHtne ^A^ ***genuine*** **eHtne 249**

	nominative	genitive	partitive	short into	stem
singular	**eHtne**	**eHtsa**	**eHtsat**		**eHtsa-**
plural	**eHtsad**	**eHtsate**	**eHtsaid**		**eHtsate-** (eHtsai-)

Also like eHtne: liHtne ^A^ *simple* piNgne ^A^ *strenuous* sOOdne ^A^ *favourable*
hOOgne ^A^ *brisk* mOOdne ^A^ *fashionable*

TYPE 37

250A hiRmus ^A^ ***horrible*** **hiRmus 250A**

	nominative	genitive	partitive	short into	stem
singular	**hiRmus**	**hiRmsa**	**hiRmsat**		**hiRmsa-**
plural	**hiRmsad**	**hiRmsate**	**hiRmsaid**		**hiRmsate-** (hiRmsai-)

Also like hiRmus: kUUlus ^A^ *famous* sOOdus ^A^ *opportune* täHtis ^A^ *important*
hõlPus ^A^ *easy* rÕÕmus ^A^ *joyful*

250B täPPis ^A^ ***precise*** **täPPis 250B**

	nominative	genitive	partitive	short into	stem
singular	**täPPis**	**täPsa**	**täPsat**		**täPsa-**
plural	**täPsad**	**täPsate**	**täPsaid**		**täPsate-** (täPsai-)

TYPE 38 - Regular (Consonant Stem Partitives)

251 hobune ***horse*** **hobune 251**

	nominative	genitive	partitive	short into	stem
singular	**hobune**	**hobuse**	**hobust**		**hobuse-**
plural	**hobused**	**hobuste**	**hobuseid**		**hobuste-** (hobusei-)

Also like hobune: higine ^A^ *sweaty* jahune ^A^ *floury* kivine ^A^ *stony*
ammune ^A^ *remote in time* hiline ^A^ *late* kaljune ^A^ *craggy* kodune ^A^ *homy*
aurune ^A^ *steamy* hubane ^A^ *cosy* karjane *herder* kohene ^A^ *instantaneous*
emane ^A^ *female* isane ^A^ *male* karvane ^A^ *hairy* kollane ^A^ *yellow*

251 hobune *horse* continued **continued hobune 251**

koņdine [A] *bony*
kärnane [A] *scabby*
labane [A] *vulgar*
liivane [A] *sandy*
limane [A] *slimy*
linane [A] *linen*
lumine [A] *snowy*
mahlane [A] *juicy*
mehine [A] *manly*
metsane [A] *forested*
miļline [A] *what kind of*
mudane [A] *muddy*
mädane [A] *festering*
mägine [A] *hilly*
näļjane [A] *hungry*
närune [A] *lousy*
omane [A] *characteristic*
otsene [A] *frank*
pahane [A] *annoyed*
pakane [A] *severe cold*
patune [A] *sinful*
pilvine [A] *cloudy*
porine [A] *muddy*
punane [A] *red*
põline [A] *ancient*
põuane [A] *droughty*
päevane [A] *daily*
pöörane [A] *frantic*
rasvane [A] *greasy*
rebane *fox*
roojane [A] *filthy*
räpane [A] *slovenly*
sajune [A] *rainy*
samane [A] *identical*
sapine [A] *crabby*
savine [A] *clayey*
seebine [A] *soapy*
segane [A] *confused*
senine [A] *hitherto existing*
siidine [A] *silky*
sinine [A] *blue*
sitane [A] *shitty*
sogane [A] *muddy*
soolane [A] *salty*
suitsune [A] *smoky*
sulane *farm-hand*
suvine [A] *summery*
säärane [A] *such*
tahmane [A] *sooty*
taļvine [A] *wintry*
tasane [A] *even*
taţine [A] *snotty*
tihane *titmouse*
tiirane [A] *horny (sexual)*
tiņdine [A] *inky*
tolmune [A] *dusty*
tormine [A] *stormy*
tuline [A] *hot*
tusane [A] *sulky*
tuuline [A] *windy*
tõbine [A] *sickly*
tõrvane [A] *tarry*
tõsine [A] *serious*
tänane [A] *today's*
tühine [A] *trivial*
udune [A] *foggy*
uimane [A] *dazed*
unine [A] *sleepy*
vahune [A] *foamy*
vaigune [A] *resinous*
varane [A] *early*
vastane *opponent*
vastane [A] *contrary*
vastastikune [A] *mutual*
verine [A] *bloody*
vesine [A] *watery*
vigane [A] *defective*
vihane [A] *angry*
vihmane [A] *rainy*
viimane [A] *final*
villane [A] *woollen*
vähene [A] *scanty*
väline [A] *external*
värvine [A] *paint-covered*
vürtsine [A] *spicy*
õline [A] *oily*
ähmane [A] *faint*
äşjane [A] *recent*
ühine [A] *common*
ülane *wood anemone*
ülearune [A] *superfluous*

252 jäİne [A] *icy* jäİne 252

	nominative	genitive	partitive	short into	stem
singular	**jäİne**	**jäİse**	**jäiSt**		**jäİse-**
plural	**jäİsed**	**jäİSte**	**jäİseid**		**jäİSte-** (jäİsei-)

Also like jäİne:
kUUne [A] *month-old*
luİne [A] *bony*
maİne [A] *earthly*
paEne [A] *limestone*
puİne [A] *wooden*
soİne [A] *swampy*
taİne [A] *lean of meat*
vaEne [A] *poor*
öİne [A] *night*

TYPE 39 - Regular (Consonant Stem Partitives)

253 alus *foundation* alus 253

	nominative	genitive	partitive	short into	stem
singular	**alus**	**aluse**	**alust**		**aluse-**
plural	**alused**	**aluste**	**aluseid**		**aluste-** (alusei-)

Also like alus:
annus *dose*
eelis *advantage*
eksliibris *ex libris*
emis *sow*
hoidis *tinned food*
hoius *deposit in bank*
iiris *iris*
ilves *lynx*
jalas *runner of sled*
jalus *stirrup*
joonis *drawing*
juhis *instruction*
juhus *opportunity*
jänes *hare*
jäänus *remains*

253 alus *foundation* continued **continued alus 253**

kaelus *collar*
kannus *spur*
kAos *chaos*
katus *roof*
keedis *preserves*
keeris *eddy*
kerjus *beggar*
kleebis *sticker*
kogus *amount*
kohus *duty*
koonus *cone*
korjus *carcass*
korrus *storey in building*
kuļjus *sleigh-bell*
kõõlus *sinew*
käţis *cuff*
kääbus *dwarf*
käänis *lapel*
küņnis *threshold*
küpsis *cookie*
kütus *fuel*
küünis *claw*
lahas *splint*
lahus *solution*
lehis *larch*
lihas *muscle*
liiges *joint*
linnased (pl) *malt*
linnus *stronghold*
loomus *knitting start*
lurjus *scoundrel*
lõhmus *linden*
lõngus *gang member*
lõpus *gill*
lähised (pl) *approaches*
madrus *sailor*
manus *accessory*
matus *funeral*
miinus *minus*
mähis *wrapping*
märgis *imprint*
näidis *sample*
ollus *substance*
otsus *decision*
panus *contribution*
peţis *swindler*
pinnas *ground cover*
pistis *bribe*
poolus *pole*
pööris *whirl*
püünis *trap*
redis *radish*
seadis *device*
silmus *noose*
soomus *scale*
sõrmus *ring*
sügis *autumn*
taies *work of art*
teenus *service*
tehas *factory*
teksased (pl) *blue jeans*
teļlis *brick*
teņnis *tennis*
teras *steel*
termos *thermos*
tervis *health*
trükis *printed matter*
tunnus *feature*
tõmmis *galley proof*
tähis *sign*
täidis *filling*
uudis *news*
vanus *age*
vares *crow*
vastus *answer*
veeris *margin*
viļlis *jeep*
võimus *authority*
ääris *edging*
ümbris *wrapper*

254 pÜÜs *trap* pÜÜs 254

	nominative	genitive	partitive	short into	stem
singular	**pÜÜs**	**pÜÜse**	**püüSt**		**pÜÜse-**
plural	**pÜÜsed**	**püüSte**	**pÜÜseid**		**püüSte-** (pÜÜsei-)

Also like pÜÜs: veİs *ox*, käİsed (pl) *sleeves*, seOs *connection*, teOs *work of art*

TYPE 40

255 omas *near and dear; kith and kin* omas 255

	nominative	genitive	partitive	short into	stem
singular	**omas**	**omakse**	**omast**		**omakse-**
plural	**omaksed**	**omaste**	**omakseid**		**omaste-** (omaksei-)

256 jUUs *hair (usually plural)* jUUs 256

	nominative	genitive	partitive	short into	stem
singular	**jUUs**	**juuKse**	**juuSt**		**juuKse-**
plural	**juuKsed**	**juuSte**	**juuKseid**		**juuSte-** (juuKsei-)

Also like juuKsed: nõOs *first cousin*, õEs *sister*

-NE AND -US NOMINALS - 4 - CLASS VIII

TYPE 41

257A inimene *human being* — inimene 257A

	nominative	genitive	partitive	short into	stem
singular	**inimene**	**inimese**	**inimest**	**inimesse**	**inimese-**
plural	**inimesed**	**inimeste**	**inimesi**		**inimeste-** (inimesi-)

Also like inimene:
ajutine ^ *temporary*
alatine ^ *perpetual*
edasine ^ *further*
esimene ^ *first*
haruldane ^ *uncommon*
hiļjutine ^ *recent*
igavene ^ *eternal*
kevadine ^ *spring*
laialdane ^ *extensive*
ligidane ^ *close*
lähedane ^ *near*
mõningane ^ *some*
pikaldane ^ *sluggish*
pikergune ^ *oblong*
sagedane ^ *frequent*
salajane ^ *secret*
sügisene ^ *autumnal*
tulevane ^ *future*
tänavune ^ *this year's*
varajane ^ *early*
virmalised *northern lights*
üksildane ^ *lonely*
ümmargune ^ *round*

257B aaStane ^ *year-old* — aaStane 257B

	nominative	genitive	partitive	short into	stem
singular	**aaStane**	**aaStase**	**aaStast**	**aaStasse**	**aaStase-**
plural	**aaStased**	**aaStaste**	**aaStasi**		**aaStaste-** aaStasi-

Also like aaStane:
eŅdine ^ *former*
kaŢkine ^ *broken*
keSkne ^ *central*
kiŅNine ^ *closed*
laHtine ^ *open*
piPrane ^ *spicy*
praEgune ^ *present-day*
vilTune ^ *slanting*
õHtune ^ *evening*
üĻdine ^ *general*
ülekoHtune ^ *unfair*

Also like 257A ajutine are words with the following compound suffixes with -ne:

257C -lane (< -la + -ine) *inhabitand of* — -lane 257C

aafriklane *African*
AAsialane *Asian*
aEglane ^ *slow*
ajalOOlane *historian*
albAAnlane *Albanian*
ameeriklane *American*
arAAblane *Arab*
argentİİnlane *Argentinian*
armEEnlane *Armenian*
austerlane *Austrian*
austrAAllane *Australian*
baļTlane *Balt*
beLglane *Belgian*
bohEEmlane *Bohemian*
bolİİvlane *Bolivian*
brasİİllane *Brazilian*
bulgAArlane *Bulgarian*
eeStlane *Estonian*
egiPtlane *Egyptian*
eurooPlane *European*
grusİİnlane *Georgian*
grÖÖnlane *Greenlander*
haİglane ^ *sickly*
haritlane *intellectual*
herilane *wasp*
hİİdlane *Hiiumaa native*
hİİglane *giant*
hİİnlane *Chinese*
hispAAnlane *Spaniard*
hollandlane *Netherlander*
İİrlane *Irish*
indiAAnlane *Amerindian*
indonEEslane *Indonesian*
iNgerlane *Ingrian*
iNglane *English*
irAAnlane *Iranian*
iSlandlane *Icelander*
itAAllane *Italian*
jaaPanlane *Japanese*
jäRglane *successor*
järvalane *Järvamaa native*
kAAslane *companion*
kaHtlane ^ *dubious*
kanadalane *Canadian*
kaNgelane *hero*
karjalane *Karelian*
karSklane *abstainer*
katoliiKlane *Catholic*
kaukAAslane *Caucasian*
kiHnlane *Kihnu native*
kihulane *midge*
kilPlane *foolish person*
kodanlane *bourgeois*
korEalane *Korean*
kosilane *wooer*
kreeKlane *Greek*
kriStlane *Christian*
laPlane *Laplander*
leedulane *Lithuanian*
liiTlane *ally*

257C -lane (< -la +-ine) continued **continued -lane 257C**

lİİvlane *Livonian*
liNlane *city dweller*
läTlane *Latvian*
mehhiklane *Mexican*
mesilane *bee*
meTslane *savage*
moldAAvlane *Moldavian*
moRdvalane *Mordvin*
mudilane *toddler*
muhamEEdlane *Muslim*
muStlane *Gipsy*
mUUlane *foreigner*
mägilane *highlander*
pagulane *exile*
perUUlane *Peruvian*
pranTslane *French*
proviņTslane *provincial*
raNdlane *native of shore*
rooTslane *Swede*
ruHnlane *native of Ruhnu*
rumEEnlane *Romanian*
saKslane *German*
saMblane ^ *mossy*
siberlane *Siberian*
slAAvlane *Slav*
sOOmlane *Finn*
sporTlane *sportsman*
sugulane *relative (blood)*
sÜÜdlane *culprit*
šoTlane *Scot*
šveiTslane *Swiss*
tAAnlane *Dane*
tagurlane *reactionary*
taĻLinlane *Tallinner*
tarTlane *native of Tartu*
tatarlane *Tatar*
teAdlane *scientist*
tegelane *public figure*
tiibetlane *Tibetan*
tšİİllane *Chilean*
täİdlanev ^ *plump*
türKlane *Turk*
ukraİnlane *Ukrainian*
vaḑjalane *Vote*
vaEnlane *enemy*
vaRblane *sparrow*
venelane *Russian*
vePslane *Vepsian*
vilistlane *alumnus/alumna*
virulane *native of Virumaa*
võLglane *debtor*
võrulane *native ofVõrumaa*
vägilane *hero*
väiKlane ^ *petty*
õİglane ^ *just*
õpetlane *scholar*
õpilane *student*
ÄÄrmuslane *extremist*
üHtlane ^ *uniform*
üksiklane *hermit*

257D -line (< -l +-ine) -line 257D

abiline *helper*
aİneline ^ *material*
ajalOOline ^ *historic(al)*
akadeemiline ^ *academic*
akrobaatiline ^ *acrobatic*
alaline ^ *permanent*
aLgeline ^ *rudimentary*
analoogiline ^ *analogous*
antarktiline ^ *Antarctic*
apoliitiline ^ *apolitical*
arhaİline ^ *archaic*
arhitektuuriline ^ *architectural*
arktiline ^ *Arctic*
aStmeline ^ *gradual*
diplomaatiline ^ *diplomatic*
dogmaatiline ^ *dogmatic*
dramaatiline ^ *dramatic*
dünaamiline ^ *dynamic*
EElkoolieAline *pre-schooler*
eepiline ^ *epic*
eetiline ^ *ethical*
eksootiline ^ *exotic*
eluline ^ *vital*
epideemiline ^ *epidemic*
eriline ^ *particular*
esteetiline ^ *aesthetic*
faktiline ^ *factual*
fanaatiline ^ *fanatical*
fantastiline ^ *fantastic*
filosoofiline ^ *philosophical*
flegmaatiline ^ *phlegmatic*
füüsiline ^ *physical*
graatsiline ^ *graceful*
haMbuline ^ *toothed*
heinaline *haymaker*
heliline ^ *sonant*
heroİline ^ *heroic*
hingeline ^ *spiritual*
hinnaline ^ *valuable*
hügieeniline ^ *hygienic*
hüsteeriline ^ *hysterical*
idiomaatiline ^ *idiomatic*
idüļliline ^ *idyllic*
irooniline ^ *ironic(al)*
jooneline ^ *lined*
jooniline ^ *lined*
juriidiline ^ *juridical*
jõUline ^ *robust*
järguline ^ *phasic*
kahemõTTeline ^ *ambiguous*
katastroofiline ^ *catastrophic*
kategooriline ^ *categorical*
kaTseline ^ *experimental*
keeleline ^ *linguistic*
keemiline ^ *chemical*
keeruline ^ *complicated*
kehaline ^ *physical*
keraamiline ^ *ceramic*
kihiline ^ *layered*
kirurgiline ^ *surgical*
klaşsikaline ^ *classical*
koomiline ^ *comic*
kosmeetiline ^ *cosmetic*
kosmiline ^ *cosmic*
kriitiline ^ *critical*
krobeline ^ *rough*
krooniline ^ *chronic*
kultuuriline ^ *cultural*
kummaline ^ *strange*
kuņstiline ^ *artistic*
kuTseline ^ *professional*
kõLbeline ^ *moral*
kõmuline ^ *sensational*
kõrvaline ^ *secondary*
küüniline ^ *cynical*
lakooniline ^ *laconic*
lihaseline ^ *muscular*
lilleline ^ *flowery*
loogiline ^ *logical*
lUUleline ^ *poetic*
lüüriline ^ *lyrical*
maagiline ^ *magical*
maaļiline ^ *picturesque*
magnetiline ^ *magnetic*
maksuline ^ *liable to a fee*
marjuline *berry-picker*
maşsiline ^ *mass*
mehaaniline ^ *mechanical*
meloodiline ^ *melodious*
metaļliline ^ *metallic*
metoodiline ^ *methodical*
muRdeline ^ *dialectal*
muStriline ^ *patterned*
muusikaline ^ *musical*
mässuline ^ *rebellious*
mässuline ^ *insurgent*
müstiline ^ *mysterious*
müütiline ^ *mythical*
nurgeline ^ *angular*
närviline ^ *nervous*
oivaline ^ *marvellous*
oKKaline ^ *thorny*
oluline ^ *essential*
optiline ^ *optic*
orgaaniline ^ *organic*
osaline ^ *participant*
osaline ^ *partial*
paaniline ^ *panic-stricken*
pakiline ^ *urgent*
palgaline *employee*
patriootiline ^ *patriotic*
pedagoogiline ^ *pedagogical*
perioodiline ^ *periodic*
piNgeline ^ *strenuous*
pinnaline ^ *superficial*
plaştiline ^ *plastic*
plekiline ^ *stained*
poeetiline ^ *poetic*
praktiline ^ *practical*
proosaline ^ *prosaic*
psüühiline ^ *psychic*
põhiline ^ *fundamental*
pÕÕrdeline ^ *decisive*
raşsiline ^ *racial*
roheline ^ *green*
romaņtiline ^ *romantic*
rutuline ^ *hurried*
ruuduline ^ *checked*

257D -line (< -l +-ine) continued **continued -line 257D**

rõhuline ^ *stressed*
rütmiline ^ *rhythmic*
sakiline ^ *jagged*
seeneline *mushroom-picker*
seļtsiline *companion*
siKsakiline ^ *zigzag*
skemaatiline ^ *schematic*
skeptiline ^ *sceptical*
soome-ugriline ^ *Finno-Ugric*
spetsiifiline ^ *specific*
statistiline ^ *statistical*
stiihiline ^ *elemental*
stiililine ^ *stylistic*
struktuuriline ^ *structural*
suHteline ^ *relative*
sUUline ^ *oral*
suureline ^ *haughty*
suuTeline ^ *able*
sõjaline ^ *military*
sõnaline ^ *verbal*
sümmeetriline ^ *symmetrical*
sünteetiline ^ *synthetic*
süstemaatiline ^ *systematic*
šablooniline ^ *trite*
taktiline ^ *tactful*
taOline ^ *such*
tasuline ^ *done for pay*
tavaline ^ *usual*
tEEneline ^ *merited*
tehniline ^ *technical*
teİsmeline ^ *teenage*
temaatiline ^ *topical*
teoreetiline ^ *theoretic*
teraline ^ *granular*
tormiline ^ *stormy*
traagiline ^ *tragic*
triibuline ^ *striped*
troopiline ^ *tropical*
tuNdeline ^ *emotional*
tupsuline ^ *tasselled*
tõEline ^ *true*
tähestikuline ^ *alphabetical*
tähniline ^ *speckled*
täkiline ^ *notched*
täpiline ^ *spotted*
tÖÖline *worker*
tüüpiline ^ *typical*
usuline ^ *religious*
utoopiline ^ *Utopian*
vaevaline ^ *arduous*
vallaline ^ *unmarried*
valuline ^ *painful*
varjuline ^ *shady*
viiruline ^ *lined*
vulkaaniline ^ *volcanic*
võimeline ^ *able*
võRdeline ^ *proportional*
värviline ^ *coloured*
vääriline ^ *worthy*
vööḑiline ^ *striped*
õhuline ^ *airy*
äkiline ^ *abrupt*
ökoloogiline ^ *ecological*
üüriline *tenant*

257E -mine (<-ma + -ine) *-ing (verbal ending)* -mine 257E

alandamine *humiliation*
alistumine *submission*
anastamine *usurpation*
asutamine *founding*
edutamine *promotion*
eemaldamine *removal*
eemaldumine *withdrawal*
eraldamine *separation*
esinemine *performance*
hangeldamine *trafficking*
hiNdamine *appreciation*
hiNgamine *breathing*
hiRnumine *neighing*
huKKamine *execution*
hÕÕrumine *friction*
hÄÄldamine *pronunciation*
hääletamine *voting*
iLmumine *appearance*
internEErimine *internment*
jagamine *division*
joonestamine *draughting*
joonistamine *drawing*
juHtimine *leadership*
kEEldumine *refusal*
kogunemine *gathering*
koHtamine *encounter*
koHtumine *rendezvous*
kolimine *movinghousehold*
kontroĻLimine *inspection*
koRdamine *repetition*
koRdumine *recurrence*
korrutamine *multiplication*
krOOņimine *coronation*
kudumine *weaving*
kuramEErimine *courtship*
kõrvaldamine *removal*
käiTumine *behaviour*
laienemine *widening*
lihtsustamine *simplification*
liiKumine *movement*
liiTmine *addition*
lOOmine *creation*
lOOşimine *lottery*
lugemine *reading*
lähenemine *approach*
lüPsmine *milking*
maksustamine *taxation*
maNdumine *degeneration*
maTmine *burial*
mõiStmine *comprehension*
mõnitamine *mocking*
mõõTmine *measuring*
mÄÄramine *determining*
müristamine *thundering*
nõUdmine *demand*
nägemine *sight*
omandamine *acquisition*
omastamine *appropriation*
onanEErimine *masturbation*
ooTamine *waiting*
paİsumine *expansion*
paKKumine *offer*
paranemine *healing*
parKimine *parking*
peiTmine *hiding*
pUUdumine *absence*
põgenemine *escape*
põletamine *burning*
põLvnemine *origin*
pÄÄsemine *escape*
pÖÖramine *turning*
pühitsemine *celebration*
raiSkamine *waste*
reeTmine *betrayal*
registrEErimine *registration*
reİsimine *travelling*
relvastumine *arming*
revidEErimine *revision*
rõhumine *oppression*
sAAbumine *arrival*
saaTmine *sending*
salvestamine *recording*
sEEdimine *digestion*
seKKumine *intervention*
sonimine *delirium*
suHtumine *attitude*
suitsetamine *smoking*
surumine *pressing*
suusatamine *skiing*
süŞtimine *injection*
tAAndumine *retreat*
taaStamine *restoration*
tagumine *pounding*
taHtmine *want*
taPmine *killing*
taRbimine *consumption*
teAdmine *knowledge*
tegemine *doing*
tegemine *making*
teĻLimine *subscription*
tooTmine *production*
tulemine *coming*
tuletamine *derivation*
täiTmine *filling*
vahetamine *exchange*
valimine *elections*
vEEnmine *convincing*
veHklemine *fencing*
võİmlemine *gymnastics*
võnKumine *vibration*
võRdlemine *comparison*
õiendamine *rectification*
õnnestumine *success*
õņnistamine *blessing*
ärKamine *wakening*

257F -mine (-m + -ine) — -mine 257F

alumine ^ *bottom-most*
EElmine ^ *previous*
jäRgmine ^ *next*
keSkmine ^ *average*
peAmine ^ *main*
sEEsmine ^ *internal*
sisemine ^ *inner*
tagumine ^ *hindmost*
tiPmine ^ *topmost*
ÄÄrmine ^ *outermost*
ülemine ^ *uppermost*

257G -ke or -kene *small, dear (diminutive ending)* — -ke or -kene 257G

pääsuke or **pääsukene** ***swallow***

	nominative	genitive	partitive	short into	stem
singular	**pääsuke** pääsukene	**pääsukese**	**pääsukest**	**pääsukesse**	**pääsukese-**
plural	**pääsukesed**	**pääsukeste**	**pääsukesi**		**pääsukeste-** (pääsukesi-)

Also like pääauke(ne):
hiireke(ne) *mouse*
kaŋnike(ne) *violet*
kooruke(ne) *crust*
kullake(ne) *darling*
kuuļike(ne) *pellet*
kõhnuke(ne) ^ *slender*
leevike(ne) *bullfinch*
linnuke(ne) *birdie*
lohuke(ne) *dimple*
lõoKe(ne) *lark (bird)*
lühike(ne) ^ *short*
natuke(ne) ^ *little, a bit*
osake(ne) *particle*
peenike(ne) ^ *slender*
pisike(ne) ^ *tiny*
poisike(ne) *boy*
raasuke(ne) *morsel*
titake(ne) *baby*
täheke(ne) *starlet*
tükike(ne) *morsel*
vaEseke(ne) *poor thing*
õhuke(ne) ^ *thin*
üürike(ne) ^ *fleeting*

258 naine *woman* — naine 258

	nominative	genitive	partitive	short into	stem
singular	**naine**	**naise**	**naiSt**	**naİse**	**naise-**
plural	**naised**	**naiste**	**naİsi**		**naiste-** (naİsi-)

Also like naine: teine ^ *second;* pOOlteiSt *one and half*

259 päiKe or päiKene *sun* — päiKe or päiKene 259

	nominative	genitive	partitive	short into	stem
singular	**päiKe** päiKene	**päiKse** päiKese	**päiKest**	**päiKesse**	**päiKse-** päiKese-
plural	**päiKsed** päiKesed	**päiKeste**	**päiKseid** päiKesi		**päiKeste-** (päiKsei-) (päiKesi-)

Also like päiKe(ne): väiKe(ne) ^ *small* äiKe(ne) *thunder-storm*

TYPE 42

260A armastus *love* — armastus 260A

	nominative	genitive	partitive	short into	stem
singular	**armastus**	**armastuse**	**armastust**	**armastusse**	**armastuse-**
plural	**armastused**	**armastuste**	**armastusi**		**armastuste-** (armastusi-)

Also like armastus:
aevastus *sneeze*
agarus *eagerness*
aiandus *gardening*
alatus *villainy*
algatus *initiative*
aLLuvus *subordination*
aNdekus *aptitude*
aNdumus *devotion*
annetus *donation*
aretus *breeding*
armetus *wretchedness*
arukus *common sense*
arutlus *discussion*
aRvamus *opinion*
arvestus *calculation*
arvustus *criticism*
askeldus *bustle*
asundus *colony*
asutus *institution*
avaldus *declaration*
avarus *expanse*
avastus *discovery*
avaus *opening*
edevus *vanity*
ehitis *building (structure)*
ehitus *building (structure)*
ehmatus *scare*
eKsimus *mistake*
eksitus *error*
elamus *experience*
elatis *livelihood*
elevus *excitement*
enamus *majority*
ennustus *forecast*
ergutus *encouragement*
erinevus *difference*
erutus *excitement*
esitus *presentation*
etendus *performance*
fanaatilisus *fanaticism*
gEEnius *genius*
haigutus *yawn*
halastus *mercy*
haļlitus *mould*
halvatus *paralysis*
hammustus *bite*
haridus *education*
haRjumus *habit*
harjutus *exercise*
harrastus *hobby*
haruldus *rarity*
heegeldus *crocheting*
heledus *brightness*
heļlitus *caress*
hoiatus *warning*
hooletus *carelessness*
hOOļitsus *tending*
hukatus *ruination*
hõrgutis *delicacy*
häbematus *impudence*
hämmastus *astonishment*
hämmeldus *bewilderment*
hävitus *destruction*
hääletus *voting*
hüvitus *compensation*
igatsus *yearning*
igavus *boredom*
iiveldus *nausea*
ikaldus *crop failure*
iludus *beautiful person*
imestus *wonder*
imetlus *admiration*
inetus *ugliness*
innukus *fervency*
innustus *fervour*
irvitus *sneer*
isekus *selfishness*
iseloomustus*characterization*
iseärasus *peculiarity*
isiksus *personality*
istandus *plantation*
jagatis *quotient*
jahedus *coolness*
jahmatus *dismay*
joonistus *drawing*
joovastus *intoxication*
juhatus *management*
juHtumus *occurrence*
julgustus *encouragement*
julTumus *insolence*
jutustus *narrative*
juubeldus *rejoicing*
juuretis *leaven*
jämedus *thickness*
järeldus *conclusion*
järjestus *arrangement*
kaalutlus *consideration*
kadedus *envy*
kaevandus *mine*
kahandus *diminution*
kahemõTTelisus *ambiguity*
kahetsus *regret*
kahjustus *injury*
kahtlustus *suspicion*
kahvatus *pallor*
kaisutus *embrace*
kalandus *fishing industry*
kalastus *fishing*
kaLduvus *inclination*
kannatamatus *impatience*
kannatus *patience*
karedus *roughness*
karistus *punishment*
karjandus *herding*
karjatus *shout*
kasvatus *upbringing*
katkestus *interruption*
katsetus *experimenting*
kaTsumus *ordeal*
kaubandus *commerce*
kaUnidus *beauty*
kaunistus *adornment*
kavalus *slyness*
kavatsus *intention*
kehastus *embodiment*
keHtivus *validity*
kergendus *relief*
kibedus *bitterness*
kİİndumus *affection*
kiiritus *irradiation*
kiļjatus *shriek*
kimbatus *perplexity*
kiNdlusetus *uncertainty*
kindlustus *insurance*
kingitus *gift*
kiņnitus *assurance*
kirjandus *literature*
kirjastus *publishing house*
kirjeldus *description*
kirjutus *writing*
kitsendus *restriction*
kiţsidus *stinginess*
kiţsikus *difficulty*
kiusatus *temptation*
klõpsatus *click*
kodanlus *bourgeoisie*
kodundus *home economics*
kogemus *experience*
kogudus *congregation*
kohmakus *clumsiness*
kohmetus *numbness*
kohustus *obligation*
koledus *horror*
koletis *monster*
komistus *stumble*
koputus *knock*
korjandus *collection*
korraldus *order*
korratus *disorder*
koştitus *treat*
kriimustus *scratch*
kritseldus *scribble*
kujustus *depiction*
kujutlus *idea*
kulutus *expenditure*
kummardus *bow over*
kurvastus *grief*

260A armastus *love* continued

kuTsumus *vocation*
kUUldavus *audibility*
kuulekus *obedie*
kuulutus *advertisement*
kUUluvus *membership*
kõlavus *sonority*
kõlvatus *moral impropriety*
kõnelus *talk*
kärsitus *impatience*
käsitlus *treatment*
käsitsus *handling*
käsitus *interpretation*
käsutus *beck and call*
küllastus *satiation*
külmutus *refrigeration*
küsimus *question*
küsitlus *quiz*
labasus *vulgarity*
ladusus *fluency*
laevandus *shipping*
lahendus *solution*
lahutus *divorce*
laiendus *widening*
lainetus *waves*
lavastus *staged production*
lehvitus *wave of hand*
leiutis *invention*
lennundus *aviation*
lepitus *reconciliation*
liialdus *exaggeration*
liigitus *classification*
liigutus *gesture*
loeTavus *readability*
lohakus *sloppiness*
lohutus *consolation*
looTusetus *hopelessness*
lubadus *promise*
luuletus *poem*
lõbustus *entertainment*
lõbusus *gaiety*
lõõgastus *relaxation*
lähedus *nearness*
läkitus *summons*
lühidus *brevity*
mahedus *mildness*
maHtuvus *capacity*
majandus *economics*
majutus *housing*
maKsumus *cost*
manitsus *admonition*
masendus *depression*
meeletus *frenzy*
mehisus *manliness*
mesindus *apiculture*
metsandus *forestry*
minestus *faint*
moodustis *formation*
moonutus *distortion*
mugavus *comfort*
muļjutus *contusion*
muudatus *change*
mõistatus *riddle*
mõnitus *mockery*
mõTlematus *thoughtlessness*
mõTTetus *senselessness*
mõõdukus *moderation*
mälestis *memorial*
mälestus *memory*
määratlus *definition*
mürgitus *poisoning*
naeratus *smile*
nihestus *dislocation*
nikastus *sprain*
nimetus *name*
noogutus *nod*
noomitus *reprimand*
nõmedus *ignorance*
nägemus *vision*
näHtavus *visibility*
närvilisus *nervousness*
nöRdimus *indignation*
odavus *cheapness*
ohatis *rash*
ohutus *safety*
olemus *essence*
oletus *supposition*
omadus *quality*
omandus *possession*
osavus *skill*
oSkamatus *incompetence*
otsekohesus *frankness*
pagendus *banishment*
pagulus *state of exile*
pahandus *mischief*
pahvatus *outburst*
paİndumatus *inflexibility*
paİnduvus *flexibility*
paistetus *swelling*
palavus *heat*
paleus *ideal*
palistus *hemming*
palvetus *praying*
pangandus *banking*
parandus *repair*
paratamatus *inevitability*
paremus *superiority*
peegeldus *reflection*
peTTumus *disappointment*
pidustus *festivity*
piiritus *spirit alcohol*
pikendus *extension*
pilgutus *wink*
pimedus *darkness*
pimendus *darkening*
pinevus *tenseness*
pingutus *exertion*
plahvatus *explosion*
plaştilisus *plasticity*
pommitus *bombing*
puhastus *cleaning*
puudutus *touch*
põhjendus *justification*
põlastus *disdain*
põllundus *agriculture*
põnevus *excitement*
põrutus *contusion*
päevitus *suntan*
pärandus *legacy*
pärimus *tradition*
pööritus *dizziness*
pühendus *dedication*
püsimatus *restlessness*
püsivus *persistence*
rahandus *finance*
rahuldus *satisfaction*
rahutus *restlessness*
rajatis *construction*
raksatus *crack*
raputus *shake*
rasedus *pregnancy*
rebestus *tear*
relvastus *armament*
riietus *clothing*
rivistus *line-up*
rohelus *greenery*
roİdumus *weariness*
rumalus *stupidity*
rõivastus *clothing*
rõvedus *obscenity*
saadetis *missive*
saagikus *yield*
saavutus *achievement*
sagedus *frequency*
saladus *secret*
saledus *slimness*
saĻLimatus *intolerance*
samasus *sameness*
sillutis *pavement*
sirutus *stretch*
sisemus *interior*
sisustus *furnishings*
soodustus *advantages*
soojendus *warming*
soovitus *recommendation*
sugulus *relationship*
sukeldus *diving*
sulpsatus *splash*
surematus *immortality*
suremus *mortality*
surutis *press*
suurendus *enlargement*
sõlTumatus *independence*
sõnastus *wording*
säilitus *preservation*
säritus *exposure (photo)*
sätendus *glisten*
söövitus *etching*
sügavus *depth*
sügelus *itch*
süüdistus *accusation*
tabamus *hit*
tagatis *guarantee*
taibukus *intelligence*
takistus *hindrance*
talitus *tending*
tarretis *jelly*
tarvidus *need*
tarvitus *use*
teAdmatus *ignorance*
teenistus *employ*
tegevus *activity*
teĻLimus *order*
teravus *sharpness*
tervitus *greeting*
tigedus *anger*
tihedus *density*
tiisikus *tuberculosis*
tiNgimus *condition*
toimetus *editorial office*
toitlustus *catering*

260A armastus *love* continued | **continued armastus 260A**

toredus *splendour*
tugevus *strength*
tulemus *result*
tunnetus *perception*
tuŋnistus *testimony*
tunnustus *acknowledgement*
turustus *marketing*
tuulutus *airing*
tõElisus *reality*
tõEnäOlisus *probability*
tõlgendus *interpretation*
tõļgitsus *interpretation*
tõrelus *chiding*
tõsidus *seriousness*
tähendus *meaning*
täiendus *addition*
täiustus *elaboration*
tänamatus *ingratitude*
täpsustus *specification*
tüdimus *weariness*
tühisus *triviality*
tülgastus *disgust*
tüļPimus *boredom*
tüsedus *stoutness*
ulakus *hooliganism*
ulatus *extent*
unetus *sleeplessness*
unistus *dream (wish)*
unisus *sleepiness*
upsakus *arrogance*
uputus *flood*
usaldus *trust*
usinus *diligence*
uSkumus *belief*
uStavus *faithfulness*
usutlus *interview*
uuendus *renewal*
UUrimus *research*
vabadus *freedom*
vabandus *apology*
vaheldus *change*
vahetus *exchange*
vahistus *arrest*
vaimukus *wit*
vaimustus *enthusiasm*
vajadus *need*
valitsus *government*
vallandus *dismissal*
vaļlatus *mischief*
vallutus *conquest*
vanadus *old age*
vangistus *imprisonment*
vapustus *shock*
varandus *possessions*
varjutus *eclipse*
varustus *outfit*
vaştikus *repugnance*
vastutus *responsibility*
vEEndumus *conviction*
veTruvus *elasticity*
vigastus *injury*
viimistlus *finishing touches*
viirastus *hallucination*
viisakus *politeness*
viivitus *delay*
viletsus *poverty*
viļjakus *fertility*
viļjelus *cultivation*
vilumatus *inexperience*
vilumus *experience*
viperus *mishap*
virvendus *rippling*
visadus *persistence*
volitus *authorization*
vormilisus *formality*
võhiklus *ignorance*
võimalus *opportunity*
võimatus *impossibility*
võimelisus *ability*
võİmetus *inability*
võiTmatus *invincibility*
võLgnevus *indebtedness*
võpatus *wince*
vägevus *might*
vähemus *minority*
vähesus *shortage*
väledus *nimbleness*
välgatus *flash*
välimus *appearance*
välistus *exclusion*
väļjastus *issuing*
väļjendus *expression*
väļTimatus *inevitability*
väsimus *fatigue*
vääratus *error*
väärikus *dignity*
vääristus *refinement*
õhetus *flush in face*
õhutus *instigation*
õİglusetus *injustice*
õigustus *justification*
õlitus *oiling*
õnnetus *misfortune*
õŋnistus *blessing*
õŋnitlus *congratulations*
õpetus *instruction*
õõtsutus *swaying*
ägedus *impetuosity*
ähvardus *threat*
äkilisus *abruptness*
äpardus *failure*
äratus *wakening*
ärevus *agitation*
ärritus *irritation*
ühendus *union*
üksildus *loneliness*
üksindus *solitude*
üļdistus *generalization*
ülemus *authorities*
ülendus *promotion*
ülistus *glorification*
üllatus *surprise*
ümarus *roundness*
üritus *event*

260B aHnus *greed* | aHnus 260B

	nominative	genitive	partitive	short into	stem
singular	**aHnus**	**aHnuse**	**aHnust**	**aHnusse**	**aHnuse-**
plural	**aHnused**	**aHnuste**	**aHnusi**		**aHnuste-** (aHnusi-)

Also like aHnus:
aİnsus *singular*
aktİİvsus *activity*
aKtus *ceremony*
alandliKKus *humility*
aLgus *beginning*
aPlus *voracity*
aRgliKKus *timidness*
aRgus *cowardice*
aRmsus *belovedness*
aTlas *atlas*
auStus *respect*
aUsus *honesty*
avaliKKus *public (noun)*
brutAAlsus *brutality*
diskreeTsus *discretion*
EEldus *assumption*
eePos *epic (noun)*
eeStlus *Estonianism*
efektİİvsus *efficiency*
eiTus *negation*
elaStsus *elasticity*
eleganTsus *elegance*
eMbus *embrace*
formAAlsus *formality*
glOObus *globe*
haİgus *disease*
haLdus *administrative area*
heAdus *goodness*
heiTlus *struggle*
heLdus *generosity*
hİİlgus *shine*
hiNgus *breath*
hOOldus *maintenance*
hOOvus *current in water*
humAAnsus *humaneness*
hÕÕgus *glow*
häbeliKKus *shyness*
iHnsus *stinginess*
iHnus *miserliness*

260B aHnus *greed* continued **continued aHnus 260B**

inteļligenTsus *intelligence*
intensİİvsus *intensity*
intİİmsus *intimacy*
invalİİdsus *invalidism*
iseseİsvus *independence*
jaaTus *affirmation*
jaoTus *distribution*
juLgus *boldness*
juLmus *cruelty*
juTlus *sermon*
jUUrdlus *investigation*
jõHkrus *brutality*
jõuKus *prosperity*
jäiKus *starkness*
järSkus *steepness*
jääTis *ice-cream*
kaEbus *grievance*
kaHtlus *doubt*
kaKlus *fight*
kaKtus *cactus*
kaNgekaElsus *obstinacy*
kaNgelasliKKus *heroism*
kaNgus *stiffness*
kannatliKKus *patience*
kaoTus *loss*
kaRmus *harshness*
karSkus *abstinence*
karTliKKus *timidity*
karTus *fear*
kasuliKKus *usefulness*
kaUgus *distance*
kauPlus *shop*
keHvus *poverty*
keĻmus *roguery*
keRgus *lightness*
keRjus *beggary*
keSkus *centre*
keStus *duration*
keStvus *durability*
kiHlus *engagement*
kİİrgus *radiation*
kİİrus *speed*
kiiTus *praise*
kiNdlus *fortress*
kiTsus *narrowness*
kodakoNdsus *citizenship*
koErus *mischief*
kollektİİvsus *collectivity*
kOOndis *association*
kOOndus *gathering*
kOOnus *cone*
kOOrmus *burden*
korPus *corps*
korraliKKus *orderliness*
krooKus *crocus*
kuİvus *dryness*
kulTus *cult*
kuRbus *sorrow*
kuRjus *evil*
kuRsus *course*
kUUldus *rumour*
kUUlsus *fame*
kUUmus *heat*
kõHklus *hesitation*
kõLblus *morality*
kõRgus *height*
kõrKus *haughtiness*
käEndus *bail*
käiTis *enterprise*
käSklus *command*
küLLus *abundance*
küLmus *coldness*
laiTus *reproof*
laİus *width*
laNgus *decline*
lePliKKus *tolerance*
liHtsus *simplicity*
liiKlus *traffic*
loEndus *enumeration*
loİdus *apathy*
loĻLus *stupidity*
lonTrus *hooligan*
lOOdus *nature*
lOOmus *disposition*
looTus *hope*
luKsus *luxury*
lõiKus *operation*
läMbus *suffocation*
mAAdlus *wrestling*
maKsvus *validity*
mEElsus *mentality*
meiSterliKKus *mastery*
miTmus *plural*
muİnsus *antiquity*
muStus *dirt*
muuTus *change*
mõiStus *reason (intelligence)*
mäEndus *mining*
märKus *remark*
mÄÄrus *regulation*
nAAbrus *neighbourhood*
naKKus *infection*
naPPus *scarcity*
naRRus *foolishness*
nEEdus *curse*
niiSkus *moisture*
nOOrus *youth*
nOOrusliKKus *youthfulness*
nuHtlus *nuisance*
nuKrus *melancholy*
nõİdus *witchcraft*
nõrKus *weakness*
nõTrus *infirmity*
nõUdliKKus *strictness*
nõuKus *ingenuity*
näHtus *phenomenon*
näiTus *exhibition*
objektİİvsus *objectivity*
ooTus *expectation*
originAAlsus *originality*
oRjus *slavery*
oSkus *skill*
paKsus *fatness*
peaTus *stop*
pEEnsus *subtlety*
pEEnus *finesse*
peHmus *softness*
peiTus *hide-and-go-seek*
peTTus *deception*
pİİnliKKus *embarrassment*
piKKus *length*
pOOlus *pole*
populAArsus *popularity*
prİİus *freedom*
puHkus *vacation*
puHtus *cleanliness*
pUUdus *shortage*
põhjaliKKus *thoroughness*
põHjus *cause*
põLgus *contempt*
pühaliKKus *solemnity*
pÜÜdliKKus *diligence*
pÜÜdlus *aspiration*
raHvus *nationality*
raNgus *strictness*
raSkus *difficulty*
raSkus *weight*
relatİİvsus *relativity*
riKKus *wealth*
roHkus *plenty*
sAAdus *product*
saaTus *fate*
seAdlus *decree*
seAdus *law*
seiKlus *adventure*
seİsus *social position*
seLgus *clarity*
sİİrus *sincerity*
siTkus *toughness*
skauTlus *scouting*
solİİdsus *respectability*
sOOjus *warmth*
staaTus *status*
stabİİlsus *stability*
sterİİlsus *sterility*
suŅdus *compulsion*
suPlus *bathing*
sUUdlus *kiss*
sUUrus *size*
sõPrus *friendship*
südamliKKus *cordiality*
süNdmus *event*
süNgus *gloom*
süüTus *innocence*
šamPus *champagne*
taİdlus *amateur activities*
taoTlus *application*
tarKus *wisdom*
tarviliKKus *necessity*
teAdliKKus *awareness*
teAdus *science*
teAdvus *consciousness*
teeSklus *pretence*
tegeliKKus *reality*
teoTus *abuse*
teRvis *health*
toeTus *support*
tOOrus *brutality*
tooTliKKus *productivity*
toTrus *idiocy*
trUUdus *faithfulness*
tsirKus *circus*
tuİmus *numbness*
tuNdliKKus *sensitivity*
tuNdmus *feeling*
tuTvus *acquaintance*
tõEndus *proof*
tõEnäOsus *probability*
tõeStus *proof*
tõMbus *draught*

260B aHnus *greed* continued | **continued aHnus 260B**

tõoTus *promise*
täHtsus *importance*
täİdlus *plumpness*
täİuslíKKus *completeness*
tänuliKKus *gratitude*
täPsus *precision*
tööKus *diligence*
tööStus *industry*
tüHjus *emptiness*
tüüFus *typhus*
uHkus *pride*
uĻjus *daring*
UUdsus *novelty*
UUdus *newness*
vaaTlus *observation*
vaaTus *act of play*
vaEgus *deficiency*
vaEsus *poverty*
vaHvus *bravery*
vaİdlus *argument*
vaiKus *silence*
vaLdus *possession*
vaLgus *light*
vaĻjus *loudness*
vaLvsus *vigilance*
vaPrus *bravery*
vaRgus *theft*
veeTlus *charm*
veİdrus *eccentricity*
veNdlus *brotherhood*
veOndus *transport*
veStlus *chat*
vİİrus *virus*
virKus *diligence*
virtuOOsliKKus *virtuosity*
vOOlus *stream*
vOOrus *virtue*
vOOrusliKKus *virtuousness*
võimaliKKus *possibility*
võİmsus *potency*
võiStlus *competition*
võiTlus *fight*
võRdlus *comparison*
võRdsus *equality*
väeTis *fertilizer*
väeTus *fertilizing*
väiKlus *pettiness*
välTus *duration*
värSkus *freshness*
väRvus *colour*
väärTus *value*
õElus *wickedness*
õİglus *justice*
õİgsus *correctness*
õİgus *right*
õİlsus *noble-mindedness*
õMblus *seam*
õŅdsus *bliss*
õPPus *training*
õRnus *tenderness*
õUdus *horror*
ÕÕnsus *cavity*
ÄÄrmus *extremity*
ökonOOmsus *economy*
üHtsus *unity*
üKsluİsus *monotonous*
üKsus *unit*
üLbus *arrogance*
üĻdsus *general public*
üLLus *high-mindedness*
üMbrus *surroundings*
üTlus *saying*

VERBS - 1 - CLASS I

TYPE 1 - Regular

261A kEEma [i] *be cooking, be boiling* — kEEma 261A

	into case	stem	partitive	indicative		participle	imperative
personal	kEEma	kEE	kEEda	kEEn	kEEb	kEEv	keegu!
past		keesi-		keesin	kEEs	keenud	
impersonal		kEEda		kEEdakse		kEEdav	kEEdagu!
past				kEEdi		kEEdud	

261B näİma [i] *seem* — näİma 261B

	into case	stem	partitive	indicative		participle	imperative
personal	näİma	näİ	näİda	näİn	näİb	näİv	näigu!
past		näisi-		näisin	näİs	näinud	
impersonal		näİda		näİdakse		näİdav	näİdagu!
past				näİdi		näİdud	

Also like näİma: naİma [t] *marry*

262 kaEma [t] *behold* — kaEma 262

	into case	stem	partitive	indicative		participle	imperative
personal	kaEma	kaE	kaEda	kaEn	kaEb	kaEv	kaEgu!
past		kaEsi-		kaEsin	kaEs	keEnud	
impersonal		kaeTa		kaeTakse		kaeTav	kaeTagu!
past				kaeTi		kaeTud	

Also like kaEma: treİma [t] *turn on lathe*

263 võİma *be able; can* — võİma 263

	into case	stem	partitive	indicative		participle	imperative
personal	võİma	võİ	võİda võİ[j]a	võİn	võİb	võİv	võigu!
past		võisi-		võisin	võİs	võinud	
impersonal		võİda		võİdakse või[j]akse		võİdav	võİdagu!
past				võİdi		võİdud	

264A vİİma [t] *take* **vİİma 264A**

	into case	stem	partitive	indicative		participle	imperative
personal	**vİİma**	**vİİ**	**vİİ[j]a**	**vİİn**	**vİİb**	**vİİv**	**käigu!**
past		**viisi-**		**viisin**	**vİİs**	**viinud**	
impersonal		**vİİda**		**käi[j]akse**		**vİİdav**	**vİİdagu!**
past				**vİİdi**		**vİİdud**	

Also like vİİma: mÜÜma ' *sell*

264B käİma [i] *go; walk; attend; visit; frequent* **käİma 264B**

	into case	stem	partitive	indicative		participle	imperative
personal	**käİma**	**käİ**	**käİ[j]a**	**käİn**	**käİb**	**käİv**	**käigu!**
past		**käisi-**		**käisin**	**käİs**	**käinud**	
impersonal		**käİda**		**käi[j]akse**		**käİdav**	**käİdagu!**
past				**käİdi**		**käİdud**	

265 pOOma [t] *hang (a person)* **pOOma 265**

	into case	stem	partitive	indicative		participle	imperative
personal	**pOOma**	**pOO**	**pUU[w]a**	**pOOn**	**pOOb**	**pOOv**	**poogu!**
past		**poosi-**		**poosin**	**pOOs**	**poonud**	
impersonal		**pOOda**		**puu[w]akse**		**pOOdav**	**pOOdagu!**
past				**pOOdi**		**pOOdud**	

TYPE 2 -İ Past Tense Stems

266 jÄÄma [i] *remain; become* **jÄÄma 266**

	into case	stem	partitive	indicative		participle	imperative
personal	**jÄÄma**	**jÄÄ**	**jÄÄda**	**jÄÄn**	**jÄÄb**	**jÄÄv**	**jäägu!**
past		**jäİ-**		**jäİn**	**jäİ**	**jäänud**	
impersonal		**jÄÄda**		**jÄÄdakse**		**jÄÄdav**	**jÄÄdagu!**
past				**jÄÄdi**		**jÄÄdud**	

Also like jÄÄma: sAAma [t] *get; receive* sAAma [i] *become; be able*

267 jOOma [t] *drink* **jOOma 267**

	into case	stem	partitive	indicative		participle	imperative
personal	**jOOma**	**jOO**	**jUU[w]a**	**jOOn**	**jOOb**	**jOOv**	**joogu!**
past		**jõİ-**		**jõİn**	**jõİ**	**joonud**	
impersonal		**jOOda**		**juu[w]akse**		**jOOdav**	**jOOdagu!**
past				**jOOdi**		**jOOdud**	

Also like jOOma: lOOma [t] *create* tOOma [t] *bring*

268 sÖÖma [t] ***eat*** **sÖÖma 268**

	into case	stem	partitive	indicative		participle	imperative
personal	**sÖÖma**	**sÖÖ**	**sÜÜ[j]a**	**sÖÖn**	**sÖÖb**	**sÖÖv**	**söögu!**
past		**sõİ-**		**sõİn**	**sõİ**	**söönud**	
impersonal		**sÖÖda**		**süü[j]akse**		**sÖÖdav**	**sÖÖdagu!**
past				**sÖÖdi**		**sÖÖdud**	

Also like sÖÖma: lÖÖma [t] *hit*

VERBS - 2 - CLASS II A

TYPE 3 - Regular - Vowel Partitives

269 elama [i] *live; dwell* elama 269

	into case	stem	partitive	indicative		participle	imperative
personal	**elama**	**ela**	**elada**	**elan**	**elab**	**elav**	**elagu!**
past		**elasi-**		**elasin**	**elas**	**elanud**	
impersonal		**elata**		**elatakse**		**elatav**	**elatagu!**
past				**elati**		**elatud**	

Also like elama:
anuma *implore*
asuma [i] *settle*
avama [t] *open*
hajuma [i] *dissipate*
harima [t] *educate*
hävima [i] *perish*
ihuma [t] *whet*
imema [t] *suck*
jagama [t] *divide*
jaguma [i] *be divisible*
kajama [i] *resound*
kerima [t] *wind*
kirema [i] *crow*
kiruma [t] *cuss*
kisama [i] *bawl*
kogema [t] *experience*
koguma [t] *collect*
kolama [i] *knock about*
kolima [i] *move household*
kosima [t] *woo*
kosuma [i] *recover*

kruvima [t] *screw*
kuluma [i] *wear out*
kõlama [i] *resound*
köhima [i] *cough*
küsima [t] *ask*
lamama [i] *lie about (recline)*
lasuma [i] *lie on (recline)*
lebama [i] *rest*
levima [i] *be disseminated*
lisama [t] *add*
lubama [t] *allow; promise*
läbima [t] *pass through*
lävima [i] *associate with*
magama [i] *sleep*
munema *lay eggs*
mõjuma [i] *influence*
mürama [i] *romp*
norima *pick a quarrel*
närima [t] *chew*
omama [t] *possess*
paluma [t] *request*
puhuma *blow*

punuma [t] *weave*
purema [t] *bite*
põlema [i] *burn*
pärima [t] *inherit; inquire*
pügama [t] *crop*
püsima [i] *endure*
rajama [t] *establish*
ravima [t] *treat (medicine)*
rebima [t] *tear*
ronima [i] *climb*
rusuma [t] *oppress*
rõhuma [t] *oppress*
sasima [t] *tousle*
segama [t] *mix*
sobima [i] *suit*
sonima [i] *be delirious*
sorima *rummage*
sujuma [i] *progress smoothly*
sulama [i] *melt*
suruma [t] *press*
sõdima [i] *wage war*
särama [i] *sparkle*

sügama [t] *scratch*
tabama [t] *catch*
tagama [t] *guarantee*
tajuma [t] *perceive*
taluma [t] *bear*
tasuma [t] *repay*
tirima [t] *tug*
trügima [i] *elbow one's way*
tõdema [t] *arrive at truth*
tänama [t] *thank*
ujuma [i] *swim*
vajama [t] *need*
vajuma [i] *sink*
valama [t] *pour*
valima [t] *choose*
vanuma [i] *become matted*
venima [i] *be drawn out*
viluma [i] *become experienced*
võluma [t] *charm*
väsima [i] *become tired*
õgima [t] *devour*
ägama [i] *groan*

TYPE 4 - Irregular - Vowel Partitives

270 ajama [t] *drive* ajama 270

	into case	stem	partitive	indicative		participle	imperative
personal	**ajama**	**aja**	**ajada**	**ajan**	**ajab**	**ajav**	**ajagu!**
past		**ajasi-**		**ajasin**	**ajas**	**ajanud**	
impersonal		**aeTa**		**aeTakse**		**aeTav**	**aeTagu!**
past				**aeTi**		**aeTud**	

TYPE 5 - Regular -İ Past Tense Stems

271 panema [t] *put; set* panema 271

	into case	stem	partitive	indicative		participle	imperative
personal	**panema**	**pane**	**paNNa**	**panen**	**paneb**	**panev**	**paNgu!**
past		**pani-**		**panin**	**pani**	**pannud**	
impersonal		**paNda**		**pannakse**		**paNdav**	**paNdagu!**
past				**paNdi**		**paNdud**	

Also like panema: surema [i] *die* tulema [i] *come*

272 pesema [t] *wash* pesema 272

	into case	stem	partitive	indicative		participle	imperative
personal	**pesema**	**pese**	**peSta**	**pesen**	**peseb**	**pesev**	**peSku!**
past		**pesi-**		**pesin**	**pesi**	**peSnud**	
impersonal		**peSta**		**peStakse**		**peStav**	**peStagu!**
past				**peSti**		**peStud**	

Also like pesema: kusema [i] *urinate*

TYPE 6 - Irregular -İ Past Tense Stems

273 olema [i] *be, exist* olema 273

	into case	stem	partitive	indicative		participle	imperative
personal	**olema**	**ole**	**oLLa**	**olen**	**oN**	**olev**	**oLgu!**
				3rd plural	oN		
past		**oli-**		**olin**	**oli**	**olnud**	
impersonal		**oLda**		**ollakse**		**oLdav**	**oLdagu!**
past				**oLdi**		**oLdud**	

274 minema [i] *go* minema 274

	into case	stem	partitive	indicative		participle	imperative
personal	**minema**	**mine!**	**miNNa**			**minev**	**miNgu!**
		lähe-		**lähen**	**läheb**		
past		**läksi-**		**läksin**	**läKs**	**läinud**	
impersonal		**miNda**		**minnakse**		**miNdav**	**miNdagu!**
past				**miNdi**		**miNdud**	

VERBS - 2 - CLASS II B

TYPE 7 - Regular - Vowel Partitives

275 põdema [i] ***be ill with*** **põdema 275**

	into case	stem	partitive	indicative		participle	imperative
personal	**põdema**	**põE**	**põdeda**	**põEn**	**põEb**	**põdev**	**põdegu!**
past		**põdesi-**		**põdesin**	**põdes**	**põdenud**	
impersonal		**põeTa**		**põeTakse**		**põeTav**	**põeTagu!**
past				**põeTi**		**põeTud**	

276 vedama [t] ***haul*** **vedama 276**

	into case	stem	partitive	indicative		participle	imperative
personal	**vedama**	**veA**	**vedada**	**veAn**	**veAb**	**vedav**	**vedagu!**
past		**vedasi-**		**vedasin**	**vedas**	**vedanud**	
impersonal		**veeTa**		**veeTakse**		**veeTav**	**veeTagu!**
past				**veeTi**		**veeTud**	

277 pidama [t] ***hold*** **pidama 277**

	into case	stem	partitive	indicative		participle	imperative
personal	**pidama**	**peA**	**pidada**	**peAn**	**peAb**	**pidav**	**pidagu!**
past		**pidasi-**		**pidasin**	**pidas**	**pidanud**	
impersonal		**peeTa**		**peeTakse**		**peeTav**	**peeTagu!**
past				**peeTi**		**peeTud**	

278 kudema [i] ***spawn*** **kudema 278**

	into case	stem	partitive	indicative		participle	imperative
personal	**kudema**	**koE**	**kudeda**	**koEn**	**koEb**	**kudev**	**kudegu!**
past		**kudesi-**		**kudesin**	**kudes**	**kudenud**	
impersonal		**koeTa**		**koeTakse**		**koeTav**	**koeTagu!**
past				**koeTi**		**koeTud**	

279 küdema [i] *be burning* — küdema 279

	into case	stem	partitive	indicative		participle	imperative
personal	**küdema**	**köE**	**küdeda**	**köEn**	**köEb**	**küdev**	**küdegu!**
past		**küdesi-**		**küdesin**	**küdes**	**küdenud**	
impersonal		**köeTa**		**köeTakse**		**köeTav**	**köeTagu!**
past				**köeTi**		**köeTud**	

280 kaduma [i] *get lost* — kaduma 280

	into case	stem	partitive	indicative		participle	imperative
personal	**kaduma**	**kaO**	**kaduda**	**kaON**	**kaOb**	**kaduv**	**kadugu!**
past		**kadusi-**		**kadusin**	**kadus**	**kadunud**	
impersonal		**kaoTa**		**kaoTakse**		**kaoTav**	**kaoTagu!**
past				**kaoTi**		**kaoTud**	

Also like kaduma: laduma [t] *pile up*

281 siduma [t] *tie* — siduma 281

	into case	stem	partitive	indicative		participle	imperative
personal	**siduma**	**seO**	**siduda**	**seOn**	**seOb**	**siduv**	**sidugu!**
past		**sidusi-**		**sidusin**	**sidus**	**sidunud**	
impersonal		**seoTa**		**seoTakse**		**seoTav**	**seoTagu!**
past				**seoTi**		**seoTud**	

282 sadama [i] *rain* — sadama 282

	into case	stem	partitive	indicative		participle	imperative
personal	**sadama**	**saja**	**sadada**	**sajan**	**sajab**	**sadav**	**sadagu!**
past		**sadasi-**		**sadasin**	**sadas**	**sadanud**	
impersonal		**sajata**		**sajaTakse**		**sajatav**	**sajaTagu!**
past				**sajaTi**			**sajaTud**

283 kuduma [t] *weave* — kuduma 283

	into case	stem	partitive	indicative		participle	imperative
personal	**kuduma**	**kOO**	**kududa**	**kOOn**	**kOOb**	**kuduv**	**kudugu!**
		kuju		kujun	kujub		
past		**kudusi-**		**kudusin**	**kudus**	**kudunud**	
impersonal		**kooTa**		**kooTakse**		**kooTav**	**kooTagu!**
		kujuta		kujutakse		kujutav	kujutagu!
past				**kooTi**		**kooTud**	
				kujuti		kujutud	

284 lugema ***read; count*** **lugema 284**

	into case	stem	partitive	indicative		participle	imperative
personal	**lugema**	**loE**	**lugeda**	**loEn**	**loEb**	**lugev**	**lugegu!**
past		**lugesi-**		**lugesin**	**luges**	**lugenud**	
impersonal		**loeTa**		**loeTakse**		**loeTav**	**loeTagu!**
past				**loeTi**		**loeTud**	

Also like lugema: pugema [i] *suck up to; creep*

285 taguma [t] ***pound*** **taguma 285**

	into case	stem	partitive	indicative		participle	imperative
personal	**taguma**	**taO**	**taguda**	**taOn**	**taOb**	**taguv**	**tagugu!**
past		**tagusi-**		**tagusin**	**tagus**	**tagunud**	
impersonal		**taoTa**		**taoTakse**		**taoTav**	**taoTagu!**
past				**taoTi**		**taoTud**	

286 pügama [t] ***crop*** **pügama 286**

	into case	stem	partitive	indicative		participle	imperative
personal	**pügama**	**pöA**	**pügada**	**pöAn**	**pöAb**	**pügav**	**pügagu!**
past		**pügasi-**		**pügasin**	**pügas**	**püganud**	
impersonal		**pöeTa**		**pöeTakse**		**pöeTav**	**pöeTagu!**
past				**pöeTi**		**pöeTud**	

287 liguma [i] ***soak*** **liguma 287**

	into case	stem	partitive	indicative		participle	imperative
personal	**liguma**	**leO**	**liguda**	**leOn**	**leOb**	**liguv**	**ligugu!**
past		**ligusi-**		**ligusin**	**ligus**	**ligunud**	
impersonal		**leoTa**		**leoTakse**		**leoTav**	**leoTagu!**
past				**leoTi**		**leoTud**	

TYPE 8 - Regular -İ Past Tense Stems

288 pidama ***must, have to*** **pidama 288**

	into case	stem	partitive	indicative		participle	imperative
personal	**pidama**	**peA**	**pidada**	**peAn**	**peAb**	**pidav**	**pidagu!**
past		**pidi-**		**pidin**	**pidi**	**pidanud**	
impersonal		--		--		--	--
past				--		--	

TYPE 9 - Irregular -İ Past Tense Stems

289 nägema *see* **nägema 289**

	into case	stem	partitive	indicative		participle	imperative
personal	**nägema**	**näE-**	**näha**	**näEn**	**näEb**	**nägev**	**näHku!**
past		**nägi-**		**nägin**	**nägi**	**näinud**	
impersonal		**näHta**		**nähakse**		**näHtav**	**näHtagu!**
past				**näHti**		**näHtud**	

290 tegema [t] *do; make* **tegema 290**

	into case	stem	partitive	indicative		participle	imperative
personal	**tegema**	**tEE-**	**teha**	**tEEn**	**tEEb**	**tegev**	**teHku!**
past		**tegi-**		**tegin**	**tegi**	**teinud**	
impersonal		**teHta**		**tehakse**		**teHtav**	**teHtagu!**
past				**teHti**		**teHtud**	

VERBS - 2 - CLASS III A

TYPE 10 - Regular - Vowel Partitives

291A kaMMima ' *comb* — kaMMima 291A

	into case	stem	partitive	indicative		participle	imperative
personal	**kaMMima**	**kammi**	**kaMMida**	**kammin**	**kammib**	**kaMMiv**	**kaMMigu!**
past		**kaMMisi-**		**kaMMisin**	**kaMMis**	**kaMMinud**	
impersonal		**kammita**		**kammitakse**		**kammitav**	**kammitagu!**
past				**kammiti**		**kammitud**	

Also like kaMMima:	lAAḑima ' *load*	protokoĻLima ' *take minutes*	taŞSima ' *haul*
aMMuma i *moo*	lİİmima ' *glue*	protseŞSima *litigate*	tEEnima ' *serve*
driĻLima ' *drill*	lOOrima ' *veil*	prUUļima ' *brew*	teĻLima ' *order*
hİİlima i *sneak*	lOOşima ' *raffle*	pUUrima ' *drill*	toĻLima ' *impose duty*
hOOļima i *care for*	mAAļima *paint (art)*	pÄÄsema i *escape*	trAAļima ' *trawl*
hÕÕruma ' *rub*	mäŞSima ' *wrap*	rAAmima ' *frame*	trEEnima i *train*
joŅNima i *sulk*	mÄÄgima i *bleat*	reklAAmima ' *advertise*	trİİvima i *drift*
jUUrima ' *uproot*	mÄÄrima ' *lubricate*	rİİmima *rhyme*	tÜÜrima ' *steer*
kAAluma ' *weigh*	naRRima ' *tease*	rİİsuma ' *plunder*	UUrima ' *investigate*
kİİluma ' *wedge*	nOOmima ' *reprimand*	rİİvima ' *grate*	vaŞSima ' *muddle*
klAArima ' *clarify*	nuŞSima ' *fuck*	ruĻLima ' *roll*	vEErema i *roll*
kontroĻLima ' *inspect*	paĻLima ' *serve in sport*	rÖÖvima ' *rob*	vİİlima i *shirk*
kOOrima ' *peel*	paŞSima ' *try on*	saĻLima ' *tolerate*	vOOļima ' *carve*
krAAmima ' *clean up*	pİİluma ' *peer*	saMMuma i *pace*	vOOrima i *move in crowd*
krOOņima ' *crown*	prAAļima i *boast*	sOOsima ' *favour*	vuŞSima ' *bungle*
kÄÄrima i *ferment*	preŞSima ' *press*	sOOvima ' *wish*	vÄÄrima ' *deserve*
kÜÜrima ' *scrub*	prOOvima ' *try*	tAAruma i *stagger*	ÜÜrima ' *rent*

291B Also like kaMMima all verbs ending in -EErima — -EErima 291B

blamEErima ' *disgrace*	grimEErima ' *make up*	onanEErima i *masturbate*	restaurEErima ' *restore*
deklamEErima ' *recite*	imponEErima ' *impress*	pitsEErima ' *seal*	retsensEErima ' *review*
dirigEErima ' *conduct*	konkurEErima i *compete*	polEErima ' *polish*	šantažEErima ' *blackmail*
dressEErima *train animal*	konstatEErima ' *state*	propagEErima ' *advocate*	taksEErima ' *appraise*
eksponEErima ' *exhibit*	kuramEErima i *court*	realisEErima ' *cash in*	tsitEErima ' *quote*
fantasEErima *imagine*	marinEErima ' *marinade*	redigEErima ' *revise*	vatEErima ' *quilt*
garnEErima ' *garnish*	montEErima ' *mount*	referEErima ' *make report*	vEErima ' *spell*

291C aStuma i *step* — aStuma 291C

	into case	stem	partitive	indicative		participle	imperative
personal	**aStuma**	**astu**	**aStuda**	**astun**	**astub**	**aStuv**	**aStugu!**
past		**aStusi-**		**aStusin**	**aStus**	**aStunud**	
impersonal		**astuta**		**astutakse**		**astutav**	**astutagu!**
past				**astuti**		**astutud**	

Also like aStuma:	aiStima ' *sense*	eKsima i *lose one's way*	haİsema i *stink*

291C aStuma [i] *step* continued | **continued aStuma [i] 291C**

hiRnuma [i] *neigh*
hõĻjuma [i] *hover*
häİrima [t] *disturb*
iStuma [i] *be seated; sit down*
kaRjuma [i] *scream*
kaSvama [i] *grow*
kaTsuma [t] *touch*
keKsima [i] *skip*
kiĻjuma [i] *shriek*
kiTkuma [t] *pluck*
kiUnuma [i] *whimper*
klaTšima [t] *gossip*
kläHvima [i] *yelp*
koKsima [t] *tap*
konseRvima [t] *preserve*
konspeKtima [t] *take notes*
kraaKsuma [i] *croak*
kraŢsima [t] *scratch*
kriiKsuma [i] *creak*
kriuKsuma [i] *squeak*
kroHvima [t] *plaster*
krooKsuma [i] *croak*
kräUnuma [i] *caterwaul*
kuİvama [i] *dry*
kuStuma [i] *be extinguished*
kuTsuma [t] *invite*
kõmPsima [i] *plod*
küPsema [i] *bake; ripen*
laKsuma [i] *flap*
laUsuma [t] *utter*
leHvima [i] *flutter*
liHvima [t] *polish*
liŋTšima [t] *lynch*
loKsuma [i] *shake*
luKsuma [i] *hiccough*
maİnima [t] *mention*
maiTsema [t] *taste*
maTkima [t] *imitate*
muĻjuma [t] *bruise*
mäNgima *play*
mäŢsima [t] *hush up*
noRmima [t] *standardize*
nuuKsuma [i] *sob*
nõEluma [t] *darn*
nõTkuma [i] *bend*
oŢsima [t] *seek*
paaStuma [i] *fast*
paĻmima [t] *plait*
piiKsuma [i] *cheep*
piuKsuma [i] *squeak*
poKsima [i] *box*
priŢsima [t] *spray*
põİmima [t] *twine*
põKsuma [i] *throb*
päĻvima [t] *deserve*
raaŢsima [t] *have the heart*
raİuma [t] *chop*
reİsima [i] *travel*
riSkima [t] *risk*
riŞtima [t] *christen*
röŞtima [t] *toast*
seRvima [t] *serve in sport*
sirTsuma [i] *chirp*
suiTsema [i] *smoke*
sõEluma [t] *sieve*
sõĻmima [t] *knot*
sõTkuma [t] *knead*
säİlima [i] *preserve*
süŞtima [t] *inject*
taŋTsima [i] *dance*
taRnima [t] *supply*
taUnima [t] *condemn*
tiKsuma [i] *tick*
tiNgima *bargain*
toİmima [i] *operate*
traHvima [t] *fine*
troŢsima *defy*
trööŞtima [t] *console*
tuHnima [i] *rummage*
tuKsuma [i] *throb*
tuNgima [i] *force one's way*
turTsuma [i] *fume*
tõRjuma [t] *repel*
vaļTsima [t] *mill*
vaŋTsima [i] *trudge*
viiTsima *feel like doing*
viKsima [t] *polish*
viNguma [i] *whine*
voRmima [t] *shape*
võļTsima [t] *forge*
väRvima [t] *paint*
õiTsema [i] *bloom*
õõTsuma [i] *sway*

291D õPPima [t] *study; learn* | õPPima 291D

	into case	stem	partitive	indicative		participle	imperative
personal	**õPPima**	**õpi**	**õPPida**	**õpin**	**õpib**	**õPPiv**	**õPPigu!**
past		**õPPisi-**		**õPPisin**	**õPPis**	**õPPinud**	
impersonal		**õpita**		**õpitakse**		**õpitav**	**õpitagu!**
past				**õpiti**		**õpitud**	

Also like õPPima:
haKKima [t] *mince*
kiPPuma [i] *be anxious*
kiŢTima [t] *putty*
kloPPima [t] *beat*
kuKKuma [i] *fall; cuckoo*
laKKİma [t] *varnish*
laKKuma [t] *lick*
laPPima [t] *patch*
leKKima [i] *leak*
lePPima [i] *be content with*
loKKima [t] *curl*
lõPPema [i] *end*
lüKKima [t] *string*
niKKuma [t] *fuck*
noKKima [t] *peck*
noPPima [t] *pick*
paKKima [t] *pack*
paKKuma [t] *offer*
retuŠŠima [t] *retouch*
riKKuma [t] *spoil*
riPPuma [i] *hang*
saTTuma [i] *happen upon*
seŢTima [i] *be deposited*
siTTuma *shit*
stePPima [i] *tap-dance*
teKKima [i] *arise*
tiKKima [t] *embroider*
tiKKuma [i] *intrude*
tiPPima [t] *type*
toPPima [t] *cram*
trüKKima [t] *print*
tuKKuma [i] *doze*
tuŠŠima [t] *ink Indian ink*
uPPuma [i] *drown*
veKKima [t] *preserve*

291E kaaPima [t] *scrape* kaaPima 291E

	into case	stem	partitive	indicative		participle	imperative
personal	**kaaPima**	**kaabi**	**kaaPida**	**kaabin**	**kaabib**	**kaaPiv**	**kaaPigu!**
past		**kaaPisi-**		**kaaPisin**	**kaaPis**	**kaaPinud**	
impersonal		**kaabita**		**kaabitakse**		**kaabitav**	**kaabitagu!**
past				**kaabiti**		**kaabitud**	

Also like kaaPima:	kraaPima [t] *scrape*	looPima [t] *hurl*	tramPima [i] *stamp*
kleePima [t] *stick (glue)*	kõmPima [i] *plod*	nööPima [t] *button*	tuuPima [t] *cram*
komPima [i] *grope*	kärPima [t] *prune*	tamPima [t] *stamp*	

291F nauTima [t] *enjoy* nauTima 291F

	into case	stem	partitive	indicative		participle	imperative
personal	**nauTima**	**naudi**	**nauTida**	**naudin**	**naudib**	**nauTiv**	**nauTigu!**
past		**nauTisi-**		**nauTisin**	**nauTis**	**nauTinud**	
impersonal		**naudita**		**nauditakse**		**nauditav**	**nauditagu!**
past				**nauditi**		**nauditud**	

Also like nauTima:	kruŋTima [t] *prime*	raporTima [t] *report*	starTima [i] *start*
aborTima [t] *abort*	magneeTima [t] *magnetize*	remoŋTima [t] *repair*	tapeeŢima [t] *wall-paper*
aSfalTima [t] *asphalt*	neeŢima [t] *rivet*	remoŋTima [t] *redecorate*	transporTima [t] *transport*
eksporTima [t] *export*	neŋTima [t] *state*	reŋTima [t] *rent*	tsemeŋTima [t] *cement*
flirTima [i] *flirt*	paŋTima [t] *pawn*	sorTima [t] *sort*	voļTima [t] *fold*
imporTima [t] *import*	priŋTima [t] *print*	sporTima [i] *do sports*	väļTima [t] *avoid*

291G kiiKuma [i] *swing; rock* kiiKuma 291G

	into case	stem	partitive	indicative		participle	imperative
personal	**kiiKuma**	**kiigu**	**kiiKuda**	**kiigun**	**kiigub**	**kiiKuv**	**kiiKugu!**
past		**kiiKusi-**		**kiiKusin**	**kiiKus**	**kiiKunud**	
impersonal		**kiiguta**		**kiigutakse**		**kiigutav**	**kiigutagu!**
past				**kiiguti**		**kiigutud**	

Also like kiiKuma:	kõiKuma [i] *sway*	pooKima [t] *graft*	torKima [t] *prick of needle*
haaKima [t] *hook*	liiKuma [i] *move*	praaKima [t] *cull*	triiKima [t] *iron*
hanKima [t] *procure*	lonKima [i] *saunter*	pruuKima [t] *use*	tuiKuma [i] *stagger*
hauKuma [i] *bark*	läiKima [i] *sparkle*	rääKima *speak*	tõļKima [t] *translate*
heļKima [i] *shimmer*	minKima [t] *make up*	rööKima [i] *bawl*	tõrKuma [i] *resist*
hulKuma [i] *roam*	märKima [t] *make a note*	soļKima [t] *soil*	vanKuma [i] *totter*
keļKima [i] *brag*	nööKima [t] *chaff*	streiKima [i] *strike*	vilKuma [i] *blink*
kinKima [t] *give as present*	parKima [t] *park; tan hide*	sälKima [t] *notch*	võnKuma [i] *rock*
koļKima [t] *thrash*	pauKuma [i] *bang*	sörKima [i] *trot*	välKuma [i] *flash*
krooKima [t] *gather ruff*	pleeKima [i] *bleach*	tanKima [t] *fill up*	ööKima [i] *retch*

291H marSSima ' *march* — **marSSima 291H**

	into case	stem	partitive	indicative		participle	imperative
personal	**marSSima**	**marsi**	**marSSida**	**marsin**	**marsib**	**marSSiv**	**marSSigu!**
past		**marSSisi-**		**marSSisin**	**marSSis**	**marSSinud**	
impersonal		**marsita**		**marsitakse**		**marsitav**	**marsitagu!**
past				**marsiti**		**marsitud**	

Also like marSSima: purSSima ' *speak badly* va]SSima ' *waltz*

291İ filTrima ' *filter* — **filTrima 291İ**

	into case	stem	partitive	indicative		participle	imperative
personal	**filTrima**	**filtri**	**filTrida**	**filtrin**	**filtrib**	**filTriv**	**filTrigu!**
past		**filTrisi-**		**filTrisin**	**filTris**	**filTrinud**	
impersonal		**filtrita**		**filtritakse**		**filtritav**	**filtritagu!**
past				**filtriti**		**filtritud**	

TYPE 11 - Regular - Consonant Partitives

292A mÖÖnma *concede* — **mÖÖnma 292A**

	into case	stem	partitive	indicative		participle	imperative
personal	**mÖÖnma**	**möönа**	**mÖÖnda**	**möönan**	**möönab**	**mÖÖnev**	**mÖÖngu!**
past		**mÖÖnsi-**		**mÖÖnsin**	**mÖÖnis**	**mÖÖnnud**	
impersonal		**mÖÖnda**		**mÖÖndakse**		**mÖÖndav**	**mÖÖndagu!**
past				**mÖÖndi**		**mÖÖndud**	

Also like mÖÖnma: vEEnma ' *convince*

292B laUlma *sing* — **laUlma 292B**

	into case	stem	partitive	indicative		participle	imperative
personal	**laUlma**	**laula**	**laUlda**	**laulan**	**laulab**	**laUlev**	**laUlgu!**
past		**laUlsi-**		**laUlsin**	**laUlis**	**laUlnud**	
impersonal		**laUlda**		**laUldakse**		**laUldav**	**laUldagu!**
past				**laUldi**			**laUldud**

Also like laUlma: naErma *laugh*

293A maKsma ' *pay* — **maKsma 293A**

	into case	stem	partitive	indicative		participle	imperative
personal	**maKsma**	**maksa**	**maKsta**	**maksan**	**maksab**	**maKsev**	**maKsku!**
past		**maKsi-**		**maKsin**	**maKsis**	**maKsnud**	
impersonal		**maKSta**		**maKstakse**		**maKstav**	**maKstagu!**
past				**maKsti**		**maKstud**	

Also like maKsma: lüPsma ' *milk* maksma ' *cost* peKsma ' *beat*

293B seİsma [i] ***stand*** **seİsma 293B**

	into case	stem	partitive	indicative		participle	imperative
personal	**seİsma**	**seisa**	**seiSta**	**seisan**	**seisab**	**seİsev**	**seiSku!**
past		**seİsi-**		**seİsin**	**seİsis**	**seİsnud**	
impersonal		**seiSta**		**seiStakse**		**seiStav**	**seiStagu!**
past				**seiSti**		**seiStud**	

294 kUUlma [t] ***hear*** **kUUlma 294**

	into case	stem	partitive	indicative		participle	imperative
personal	**kUUlma**	**kuule**	**kUUlda**	**kuulen**	**kuuleb**	**kUUlev**	**kUUlgu!**
past		**kUUlsi-**		**kUUlsin**	**kUUlis**	**kUUlnud**	
impersonal		**kUUlda**		**kUUldakse**		**kUUldav**	**kUUldagu!**
past				**kUUldi**			**kUUldud**

295 kaiTsma [t] ***defend*** **kaiTsma 295**

	into case	stem	partitive	indicative		participle	imperative
personal	**kaiTsma** kaiTsema	**kaitse**	**kaiTsta**	**kaitsen**	**kaitseb**	**kaiTsev**	**kaiTsku!**
past		**kaiTsesi-**		**kaiTsesin**	**kaiTses**	**kaiTsnud**	
impersonal		**kaiTsta**		**kaiTstakse**		**kaiTstav**	**kaiTstagu!**
past				**kaiTsti**		**kaiTstud**	

Also like kaiTsma: maiTsma *taste*

296A nAAsma [i] ***return*** **nAAsma 296A**

	into case	stem	partitive	indicative		participle	imperative
personal	**nAAsma**	**naase**	**naaSta**	**naasen**	**naaseb**	**nAAsev**	**naaSku!**
past		**nAAsi-**		**nAAsin**	**nAAsis**	**nAAsnud**	
impersonal		**naaSta**		**naaStakse**		**naaStav**	**naaStagu!**
past				**naaSti**		**naaStud**	

296B tõUsma [i] ***rise*** **tõUsma 296B**

	into case	stem	partitive	indicative		participle	imperative
personal	**tõUsma**	**tõuse**	**tõuSta**	**tõusen**	**tõuseb**	**tõUsev**	**tõuSku!**
past		**tõUsi-**		**tõUsin**	**tõUsis**	**tõUsnud**	
impersonal		**tõuSta**		**tõuStakse**		**tõuStav**	**tõuStagu!**
past				**tõuSti**		**tõuStud**	

TYPE 12 - Consonant Partitives (-p and -t stems)

297A oStma ' *buy* — **oStma 297A**

	into case	stem	partitive	indicative		participle	imperative
personal	**oStma**	**osta**	**oSta**	**ostan**	**ostab**	**oStev**	**oStku!**
past		**oStsi-**		**oStsin**	**oStis**	**oStnud**	
impersonal		**osteta**		**ostetakse**		**ostetav**	**ostetagu!**
past				**osteti**		**ostetud**	

Also like oStma: haiStma ' *smell*; kaStma ' *water plants*; keStma ' *endure*; koStma ' *be heard*; mõiStma ' *understand*; paiStma ' *be visible*; piStma ' *stick (put)*; pääStma ' *save*; sääStma ' *save*; tõStma ' *lift*; veStma ' *tell story*; *whittle*

297B nuTma *cry* — **nuTma 297B**

	into case	stem	partitive	indicative		participle	imperative
personal	**nuTma**	**nuta**	**nuTTa**	**nutan**	**nutab**	**nuTTev**	**nuTku!**
past		**nuTsi-**		**nuTsin**	**nuTTis**	**nuTnud**	
impersonal		**nuteta**		**nutetakse**		**nutetav**	**nutetagu!**
past				**nuteti**		**nutetud**	

Also like nuTma: peTma ' *deceive*

297C karTma ' *fear* — **karTma 297C**

	into case	stem	partitive	indicative		participle	imperative
personal	**karTma**	**karda**	**karTa**	**kardan**	**kardab**	**karTev**	**karTku!**
past		**karTsi-**		**karTsin**	**karTis**	**karTnud**	
impersonal		**kardeta**		**kardetakse**		**kardetav**	**kardetagu!**
past				**kardeti**		**kardetud**	

Also like karTma: heiTma ' *cast*; jooTma ' *water animal*; keeTma ' *boil*; kiiTma ' *praise*; koiTma ' *dawn*; kurTma *complain*; köiTma ' *fascinate*; laiTma ' *find fault with*; liiTma ' *join*; loiTma ' *flare*; looTma *hope*; muuTma ' *change*; mõõTma ' *measure*; niiTma ' *mow*; peiTma ' *hide*; reeTma ' *betray*; saaTma ' *send*; suuTma ' *be able*; sõiTma ' *ride*; sööTma ' *feed*; toiTma ' *feed*; tooTma ' *produce*; täiTma ' *fill*; veeTma ' *spend time*; viiTma ' *idle away*; võiTma *win*; väiTma ' *stat*

298 taPma ' *kill* — **taPma 298**

	into case	stem	partitive	indicative		participle	imperative
personal	**taPma**	**tapa**	**taPPa**	**tapan**	**tapab**	**taPPev**	**taPku!**
past		**taPsi-**		**taPsin**	**taPPis**	**taPnud**	
impersonal		**tapeta**		**tapetakse**		**tapetav**	**tapetagu!**
past				**tapeti**		**tapetud**	

299 lõPma [i] ***end; die (of animals)*** **lõPma 299**

	into case	stem	partitive	indicative		participle	imperative
personal	**lõPma**	**lõpe**	**lõPPa**	**lõpen**	**lõpeb**	**lõPPev**	**lõPku!**
past		**lõPsi-**		**lõPsin**	**lõPPis**	**lõPnud**	
impersonal		**lõpeta**		**lõpetakse**		**lõpetav**	**lõpetagu!**
past				**lõpeti**		**lõpetud**	

TYPE 13 - Irregular - Consonant Partitives

300 jäTma [t] ***leave behind*** **jäTma 300**

	into case	stem	partitive	indicative		participle	imperative
personal	**jäTma**	**jäta**	**jäTTa**	**jätan**	**jätab**	**jäTTev**	**jäTku!**
past		**jäTsi-**		**jäTsin**	**jäTTis**	**jäTnud**	
impersonal		**jäeTa**		**jäeTakse**		**jäeTav**	**jäeTagu!**
past				**jäeTi**		**jäeTud**	

Also like jäTma: kaTma [t] *cover* maTma [t] *bury* võTma [t] *take (pick up)*

301 küTma [t] ***heat (house, saun, etc.)*** **küTma 301**

	into case	stem	partitive	indicative		participle	imperative
personal	**küTma**	**küta**	**küTTa**	**kütan**	**kütab**	**küTTev**	**küTku!**
past		**küTsi-**		**küTsin**	**küTTis**	**küTnud**	
impersonal		**köeTa**		**köeTakse**		**köeTav**	**köeTagu!**
past				**köeTi**		**köeTud**	

TYPE 14 - Irregular - Consonant Partitives

302 jooKsma [i] ***run*** **jooKsma 302**

	into case	stem	partitive	indicative		participle	imperative
personal	**jooKsma**	**jookse**	**jooSta**	**jooksen**	**jookseb**	**jooKsev**	**jooKsku!**
past		**jooKsi**		**jooKsin**	**jooKsis**	**jooKsnud**	
impersonal		**jooSta**		**jooStakse**		**jooStav**	**jooStagu!**
past				**jooSti**		**jooStud**	

VERBS - 2 - CLASS III B

TYPE 15 - Regular - Vowel Partitives

303 häĻbima [i] ***deviate from; stray from*** **häĻbima 303**

	into case	stem	partitive	indicative		participle	imperative
personal	**häĻbima**	**häļvi**	**häĻbida**	**häļvin**	**häļvib**	**häĻbiv**	**häĻbigu!**
past		**häĻbisi-**		**häĻbisin**	**häĻbis**	**häĻbinud**	
impersonal		**häļvita**		**häļvitakse**		**häļvitav**	**häļvitagu!**
past				**häļviti**			**häļvitud**

304 aMbuma ***shoot with bow*** **aMbuma 304**

	into case	stem	partitive	indicative		participle	imperative
personal	**aMbuma**	**ammu**	**aMbuda**	**ammun**	**ammub**	**aMbuv**	**aMbugu!**
past		**aMbusi-**		**aMbusin**	**aMbus**	**aMbunud**	
impersonal		**ammuta**		**ammutakse**		**ammutav**	**ammutagu!**
past				**ammuti**		**ammutud**	

305 prAAḑima [t] ***fry*** **prAAḑima 305**

	into case	stem	partitive	indicative		participle	imperative
personal	**prAAḑima**	**praE**	**prAAḑida**	**praEn**	**praEb**	**prAAḑiv**	**prAAḑigu!**
past		**prAAḑisi-**		**prAAḑisin**	**prAAḑis**	**prAAḑinud**	
impersonal		**praeTa**		**praeTakse**		**praeTav**	**praeTagu!**
past				**praeTi**		**praeTud**	

Also like prAAḑima: lAAḑima [t] *load*

306 haUduma [t] ***brood; hatch out*** **haUduma 306**

	into case	stem	partitive	indicative		participle	imperative
personal	**haUduma**	**haU**	**haUduda**	**haUn**	**haUb**	**haUduv**	**haUdugu!**
past		**haUdusi-**		**haUdusin**	**haUdus**	**haUdunud**	
impersonal		**hauTa**		**hauTakse**		**hauTav**	**hauTagu!**
past				**hauTi**		**hauTud**	

307 nõİduma [t] *conjure* nõİduma 307

	into case	stem	partitive	indicative		participle	imperative
personal	**nõİduma**	**nõi[j]u**	**nõİduda**	**nõi[j]un**	**nõi[j]ub**	**nõİduv**	**nõİdugu!**
past		**nõİdusi-**		**nõİdusin**	**nõİdus**	**nõİdunud**	
impersonal		**nõi[j]uta**			**nõi[j]utakse**	**nõi[j]utav**	**nõiutagu!**
past					**nõi[j]uti**	**nõi[j]utud**	

308A kÜÜndima [i] *extend* kÜÜndima 308A

	into case	stem	partitive	indicative		participle	imperative
personal	**kÜÜndima**	**küüni**	**kÜÜndida**	**küünin**	**küünib**	**kÜÜndiv**	**kÜÜndigu!**
past		**kÜÜndisi-**		**kÜÜndisin**	**kÜÜndis**	**kÜÜndinud**	
impersonal		**küünita**			**küünitakse**	**küünitav**	**küünitagu!**
past					**küüniti**	**küünitud**	

308B eHtima [t] *adorn, decorate* eHtima 308B

	into case	stem	partitive	indicative		participle	imperative
personal	**eHtima**	**ehi**	**eHtida**	**ehin**	**ehib**	**eHtiv**	**eHtigu!**
past		**eHtisi-**		**eHtisin**	**eHtis**	**eHtinud**	
impersonal		**ehita**			**ehitakse**	**ehitav**	**ehitagu!**
past					**ehiti**	**ehitud**	

Also like eHtima: piHtima [t] *confess* toHtima [t] *be allowed* uHtuma [i] *wash ashore*
juHtima [t] *lead* siHtima [t] *aim* täHtima [t] *register a letter* vaHtima [t] *stare at*
maHtuma [i] *fit*

309 piLduma [t] *toss* piLduma 309

	into case	stem	partitive	indicative		participle	imperative
personal	**piLduma**	**pillu**	**piLduda**	**pillun**	**pillub**	**piLduv**	**piLdugu!**
past		**piLdusi-**		**piLdusin**	**piLdus**	**piLdunud**	
impersonal		**pilluta**			**pillutakse**	**pillutav**	**pillutagu!**
past					**pilluti**	**pillutud**	

310 kõŅdima [i] *walk* kõŅdima 310

	into case	stem	partitive	indicative		participle	imperative
personal	**kõŅdima**	**kõŋni**	**kõŅdida**	**kõŋnin**	**kõŋnib**	**kõŅdiv**	**kõŅdigu!**
past		**kõŅdisi**		**kõŅdisin**	**kõŅdis**	**kõŅdinud**	
impersonal		**kõŋnita**			**kõŋnitakse**	**kõŋnitav**	**kõŋnitagu!**
past					**kõŋniti**	**kõŋnitud**	

Also like kõŅdima: suŅdima [t] *compel* süŅdima [i] *be born* vaNduma [i] *swear*

311 sAAgima [t] *saw* sAAgima 311

	into case	stem	partitive	indicative		participle	imperative
personal	**sAAgima**	**saE**	**sAAgida**	**saEn**	**saEb**	**sAAgiv**	**sAAgigu!**
past		**sAAgisi-**		**sAAgisin**	**sAAgis**	**sAAginud**	
impersonal		**saeTa**		**saeTakse**		**saeTav**	**saeTagu!**
past				**saeTi**		**saeTud**	

312 näUguma [i] *mew* näUguma 312

	into case	stem	partitive	indicative		participle	imperative
personal	**näUguma**	**näU**	**näUguda**	**näUn**	**näUb**	**näUguv**	**näUgugu!**
past		**näUgusi-**		**näUgusin**	**näUgus**	**näUgunud**	
impersonal		**näuTa**		**näuTakse**		**näuTav**	**näuTagu!**
past				**näuTi**		**näuTud**	

313A uLguma [i] *howl* uLguma 313A

	into case	stem	partitive	indicative		participle	imperative
personal	**uLguma**	**ulu**	**uLguda**	**ulun**	**ulub**	**uLguv**	**uLgugu!**
past		**uLgusi-**		**uLgusin**	**uLgus**	**uLgunud**	
impersonal		**uluta**		**ulutakse**		**ulutav**	**ulutagu!**
past				**uluti**		**ulutud**	

Also like uLguma: nüĻgima [t] *skin* suLgema [t] *enclose*

313B uSkuma [t] *believe* uSkuma 313B

	into case	stem	partitive	indicative		participle	imperative
personal	**uSkuma**	**usu**	**uSkuda**	**usun**	**usub**	**uSkuv**	**uSkugu!**
past		**uSkusi-**	**uSkusin**	**uSkus**	**uSkunud**		
impersonal		**usuta**		**usutakse**		**usutav**	**usutagu!**
past				**usuti**		**usutud**	

Also like uSkuma: lõHkuma [t] *break* nüHkima [t] *scrub* veHkima [i] *swing*
kiSkuma [t] *tear at* mäHkima [t] *wrap* püHkima [t] *sweep* äHkima [i] *pant*
käŞkima [t] *command* nuHkima [t] *spy* röHkima [i] *grunt*

TYPE 16 - Regular - Consonant Partitives

314 teAdma ^{t} *know (a fact)* — teAdma 314

	into case	stem	partitive	indicative		participle	imperative
personal	**teAdma**	**teA**	**teAda**	**teAn**	**teAb**	**teAdev**	**teAdku!**
past		**teAdsi-**		**teAdsin**	**teAdis**	**teAdnud**	
impersonal		**teaTa**		**teaTakse**		**teaTav**	**teaTagu!**
past				**teaTi**		**teaTud**	

Also like teAdma: seAdma ^{t} *arrange*

315 nEEdma ^{t} *curse* — nEEdma 315

	into case	stem	partitive	indicative		participle	imperative
personal	**nEEdma**	**neA**	**nEEda**	**neAn**	**neAb**	**nEEdev**	**nEEdku!**
past		**nEEdsi-**		**nEEdsin**	**nEEdis**	**nEEdnud**	
impersonal		**neeTa**		**neeTakse**		**neeTav**	**neeTagu!**
past				**neeTi**		**neeTud**	

316A jõUdma *manage to do; arrive* — jõUdma 316A

	into case	stem	partitive	indicative		participle	imperative
personal	**jõUdma**	**jõu[w]a**	**jõUda**	**jõu[w]an**	**jõu[w]ab**	**jõUdev**	**jõUdku!**
past		**jõUdsi-**		**jõUdsin**	**jõUdis**	**jõUdnud**	
impersonal		**jõuTa**		**jõuTakse**		**jõuTav**	**jõuTagu!**
past				**jõuTi**		**jõuTud**	

Also like jõUdma: nõUdma ^{t} *demand* sõUdma *row*

316B hÜÜdma *call out* — hÜÜdma 316B

	into case	stem	partitive	indicative		participle	imperative
personal	**hÜÜdma** ^{t}	**hüü[j]a**	**hÜÜda**	**hüü[j]an**	**hüü[j]an**	**hÜÜdev**	**hÜÜdku!**
past		**hÜÜdsi-**		**hÜÜdsin**	**hÜÜdis**	**hÜÜdnud**	
impersonal		**hüüTa**		**hüüTakse**		**hüüTav**	**hüüTagu!**
past				**hüüTi**		**hüüTud**	

Also like hÜÜdma: pÜÜdma ^{t} *catch; try*

316C hoİdma ^{t} *call out* — hoİdma 316C

	into case	stem	partitive	indicative		participle	imperative
personal	**hoİdma**	**hoi[j]a**	**hoİda**	**hoi[j]an**	**hoi[j]an**	**hoİdev**	**hoİdku!**
past		**hoİdsi-**	**hoİdsin**	**hoİdis**	**hoİdnud**		
impersonal		**hoiTa**		**hoiTakse**		**hoiTav**	**hoiTagu!**
past				**hoiTi hoiTud**			

Also like hoİdma: leİdma ^{t} *find*

317 aNdma [t] ***give*** **aNdma 317**

	into case	stem	partitive	indicative		participle	imperative
personal	**aNdma**	**anna**	**aNda**	**annan**	**annab**	**aNdev**	**aNdku!**
past		**aNdsi-**		**aNdsin**	**aNdis**	**aNdnud**	
impersonal		**anTa**		**anTakse**		**anTav**	**anTagu!**
past				**anTi**		**anTud**	

Also like aNdma: kaNdma [t] *carry* küNdma [t] *plough*

318 muRdma [t] ***fracture*** **muRdma 318**

	into case	stem	partitive	indicative		participle	imperative
personal	**muRdma**	**murra**	**muRda**	**murran**	**murrab**	**muRdev**	**muRdku!**
past		**muRdsi-**		**muRdsin**	**muRdis**	**muRdnud**	
impersonal		**murTa**		**murTakse**		**murTav**	**murTagu!**
past				**murTi**		**murTud**	

319 tuNdma [t] ***know (a person)*** **tuNdma 319**

	into case	stem	partitive	indicative		participle	imperative
personal	**tuNdma**	**tunne**	**tuNda**	**tunnen**	**tunneb**	**tuNdev**	**tuNdku!**
past		**tuNdsi-**		**tuNdsin**	**tuNdis**	**tuNdnud**	
impersonal		**tunTa**		**tunTakse**		**tunTav**	**tunTagu!**
past				**tunTi**		**tunTud**	

TYPE 17 - Consonant Partitives (-t stems)

320 taHtma [t] ***want*** **taHtma 320**

	into case	stem	partitive	indicative		participle	imperative
personal	**taHtma**	**taha**	**taHta**	**tahan**	**tahab**	**taHtev**	**taHtku!**
past		**taHtsi-**		**taHtsin**	**taHtis**	**taHtnud**	
impersonal		**taheta**		**tahetakse**		**tahetav**	**tahetagu!**
past				**taheti**		**tahetud**	

Also like taHtma: uHtma [i] *wash ashore*

TYPE 18 - Irregular - Consonant Partitives

321 käSkma - käŞkima ^{t} *command* käSkma - käŞkima 321

	into case	stem	partitive	indicative		participle	imperative
personal	**käSk(i)ma**	**käse**	**käSta**	**käsen**	**käseb**	**käŞkiv**	**käSku!**
		käsi	**käŞkida**	**käsin**	**käsib**		**käŞkigu!**
past		**käŞk(i)si-**		**käŞk(i)sin**	**käŞkis**	**käSknud**	
impersonal		**käSta**		**käStakse**		**käStav**	**käStagu!**
past				**käSti**		**käStud**	

322 mõSkma ^{t} *wash* mõSkma 322

	into case	stem	partitive	indicative		participle	imperative
personal	**mõSkma**	**mõse**	**mõSta**	**mõsen**	**mõseb**	**mõSkev**	**mõSku!**
past		**mõŞksi-**		**mõŞksin**	**mõŞkis**	**mõSknud**	
impersonal		**mõSta**		**mõStakse**		**mõStav**	**mõStagu!**
past				**mõSti**		**mõStud**	

323 laSkma ^{t} *shoot* laSkma 323

	into case	stem	partitive	indicative		participle	imperative
personal	**laSkma**	**lase**	**laSta**	**lasen**	**laseb**	**laSkev**	**laSku!**
past		**laŞksi-**		**laŞksin**	**laŞkis**	**laSknud**	
		lasi-		**lasin**	**lasi**		
impersonal		**laSta**		**laStakse**		**laStav**	**laStagu!**
past				**laSti**		**laStud**	

TYPE 19 - Regular

324 pişsima *piss* **pişsima 324**

	into case	stem	partitive	indicative		participle	imperative
personal	**pişsima**	**pişsi**	**pişsida**	**pişsin**	**pişsib**	**pişsiv**	**pişsigu!**
past		**pişsisi-**		**pişsisin**	**pişsis**	**pişsinud**	
impersonal		**pişsita**		**pişsitakse**		**pişsitav**	**pişsitagu!**
past				**pişsiti**			**pişsitud**

VERBS - 3 - CLASS V

TYPE 20 -L Stems

325 kõnelema [i] ***speak, talk, chat*** **kõnelema 325**

	into case	stem	partitive	indicative		participle	imperative
personal	**kõnelema**	**kõnele**	**kõnelda**	**kõnelen**	**kõneleb**	**kõnelev**	**kõnelgu!**
past		**kõnelesi-**		**kõnelesin**	**kõneles**	**kõnelnud**	
impersonal		**kõnelda**		**kõneldakse**		**kõneldav**	**kõneldagu!**
past				**kõneldi**		**kõneldud**	

Also like kõnelema:
kibelema [i] *fidget*
kihelema [i] *tingle*
kogelema [i] *stammer*
logelema [i] *loaf*
muhelema [i] *smile smugly*
nägelema [i] *wrangle*
purelema [i] *squabble*
rabelema [i] *struggle*
rüselema [i] *romp*
sädelema [i] *sparkle*
sügelema [i] *itch*
sülelema [i] *cuddle*
tegelema [i] *be engaged in*
tõrelema [i] *chide*
vedelema [i] *idle about*
viljelema [t] *cultivate*
virelema *be in poor health*

VERBS - 3 - CLASS VI A

TYPE 21 -L and -R Stems

326A sUUdlema [t] *kiss* — sUUdlema 326A

	into case	stem	partitive	indicative		participle	imperative
personal	**sUUdlema**	**sUUdle**	**suudelda**	**sUUdlen**	**sUUdleb**	**sUUdlev**	**suudelgu!**
past		**sUUdlesi-**		**sUUdlesin**	**sUUdles**	**suudelnud**	
impersonal		**suudelda**		**suudeldakse**		**suudeldav**	**suudeldagu!**
past				**suudeldi**		**suudeldud**	

Also like sUUdlema: mAAdlema [i] *wrestle*, riNglema [i] *circulate*, vÄÄnlema [i] *writhe*, kEErlema [i] *revolve*, pÖÖrlema [i] *revolve*, tİİrlema [i] *spin*

326B vaEvlema [t] *be tormented* — vaEvlema 326B

	into case	stem	partitive	indicative		participle	imperative
personal	**vaEvlema**	**vaEvle**	**vaevelda**	**vaEvlen**	**vaEvleb**	**vaEvlev**	**vaevelgu!**
past		**vaEvlesi-**		**vaEvlesin**	**vaEvles**	**vaevelnud**	
impersonal		**vaevelda**		**vaeveldakse**		**vaeveldav**	**vaeveldagu!**
past				**vaeveldi**		**vaeveldud**	

Also like vaEvlema: riStlema [i] *cruise*, tuNglema [i] *crowd*, võİmlema [i] *do gymnastics*, kePslema [i] *gambol*, toLmlema [i] *release pollen*, veStlema [i] *chat*, võiStlema [i] *compete*

326C suPlema [i] *bathe* — suPlema 326C

	into case	stem	partitive	indicative		participle	imperative
personal	**suPlema**	**suPle**	**supelda**	**suPlen**	**suPleb**	**suPlev**	**supelgu!**
past		**suPlesi-**		**suPlesin**	**suPles**	**supelnud**	
impersonal		**supelda**		**supeldakse**		**supeldav**	**supeldagu!**
past				**supeldi**		**supeldud**	

Also like suPlema: eTlema [i] *recite*, hüPlema [i] *jump about*, kaKlema [i] *fight*, taPlema [i] *battle*

326D hooPlema [i] *brag* — hooPlema 326D

	into case	stem	partitive	indicative		participle	imperative
personal	**hooPlema**	**hooPle**	**hoobelda**	**hooPlen**	**hooPleb**	**hooPlev**	**hoobelgu!**
past		**hooPlesi-**		**hooPlesin**	**hooPles**	**hoobelnud**	
impersonal		**hoobelda**		**hoobeldakse**		**hoobeldav**	**hoobeldagu!**
past				**hoobeldi**		**hoobeldud**	

Also like hooPlema: kauPlema *barter*

326E võiTlema [i] *do battle* **võiTlema 326E**

	into case	stem	partitive	indicative		participle	imperative
personal	**võiTlema**	**võiTle**	**võidelda**	**võiTlen**	**võiTleb**	**võiTlev**	**võidelgu!**
past		**võiTlesi-**		**võiTlesin**	**võiTles**	**võidelnud**	
impersonal		**võidelda**		**võideldakse**		**võideldav**	**võideldagu!**
past				**võideldi**		**võideldud**	

Also like võiTlema: kiiTlema [i] *boast* tööTlema [t] *process* veeTlema [t] *charm*
heiTlema [i] *struggle* näiTlema [i] *act in theatre* vaaTlema [t] *observe*

326F seiKlema [i] *seek adventure* **seiKlema 326F**

	into case	stem	partitive	indicative		participle	imperative
personal	**seiKlema**	**seiKle**	**seigelda**	**seiKlen**	**seiKleb**	**seiKlev**	**seigelgu!**
past		**seiKlesi-**		**seiKlesin**	**seiKles**	**seigelnud**	
impersonal		**seigelda**		**seigeldakse**		**seigeldav**	**seigeldagu!**
past				**seigeldi**		**seigeldud**	

Also like seiKlema: puiKlema [i] *evade* põiKlema [i] *evade* tõuKlema [i] *jostle*
looKlema [i] *meander*

326G [i] mäSlema *rave* **mäSlema 326G**

	into case	stem	partitive	indicative		participle	imperative
personal	**mäSlema**	**mäSle**	**mässelda**	**mäSlen**	**mäSleb**	**mäSlev**	**mässelgu!**
past		**mäSlesi-**		**mäSlesin**	**mäSles**	**mässelnud**	
impersonal		**mässelda**		**mässeldakse**		**mässeldav**	**mässeldagu!**
past				**mässeldi**		**mässeldud**	

TYPE 22 -A Stems

327A hAArama [t] *seize* **hAArama 327A**

	into case	stem	partitive	indicative		participle	imperative
personal	**hAArama**	**hAAra**	**haarata**	**hAAran**	**hAArab**	**hAArav**	**haaraku!**
past		**hAArasi-**		**hAArasin**	**hAAras**	**haaranud**	
impersonal		**haarata**		**haaratakse**		**haaratav**	**haaratagu!**
past				**haarati**		**haaratud**	

Also like hAArama: kOOrmama [t] *burden* möLLama [i] *create uproar* rIIvama [t] *graze*
hAAvama [t] *wound* kUUlama [t] *listen to* nEElama [t] *swallow* rOOmama [i] *crawl*
hIIvama [t] *heave anchor* kÄÄnama [t] *turn* nUUmama [t] *fatten animals* sOOlama [t] *salt*
hOOvama [i] *stream* lUUrama [t] *spy* pIInama [t] *torment* sUUnama [t] *direct; aim*
huLLama [i] *frolic* lÕÕmama [i] *blaze* pIIrama [t] *limit* taLLama *tread*
kaLLama [t] *pour* mÕÕnama [i] *ebb* pIIsama [i] *suffice* viNNama [t] *draw*
kEElama [t] *forbid* mäSSama [i] *rebel* piLLama [t] *drop* vOOlama [i] *flow*
kEErama [t] *wind* mÄÄrama [t] *determine* pÖÖrama [t] *turn* vÄÄnama [t] *sprain*

327B aRvama [t] *suppose* aRvama 327B

	into case	stem	partitive	indicative		participle	imperative
personal	**aRvama**	**aRva**	**arvata**	**aRvan**	**aRvab**	**aRvav**	**arvaku!**
past		**aRvasi-**		**aRvasin**	**aRvas**	**arvanud**	
impersonal		**arvata**		**arvatakse**		**arvatav**	**arvatagu!**
past				**arvati**		**arvatud**	

Also like aRvama:	koRvama [t] *compensate*	müKsama [t] *nudge*	soLvama [t] *insult*
aİmama [t] *have an inkling*	kuHjama [t] *heap up*	naPsama [t] *grab at*	sulPsama [i] *splash*
aUrama [i] *steam*	kuRnama [t] *oppress*	nuRjama [t] *bring to nought*	suRmama [t] *execute*
hiNgama [i] *breathe*	küLvama [t] *sow*	nõElama [t] *sting of snake*	sõİmama *revile*
hõİvama [t] *occupy*	laaStama [t] *ravage*	oRjama *slave*	toLmama [i] *be dusty*
hõLmama [t] *comprise*	laEnama [t] *borrow*	paHvama [i] *blurt out*	toRmama [i] *storm*
jäTkama [t] *continue*	laİmama [t] *slander*	puiStama [t] *strew*	tõRvama [t] *tar*
kaEvama [t] *dig*	leİnama [t] *mourn*	riStama [t] *cross*	vaEvama [t] *trouble*
kaHlama [i] *wade*	lõHnama [i] *smell*	rüüStama [t] *ravage*	vaLvama [t] *guard*
kaHmama [t] *grab*	läRmama [i] *be noisy*	saaStama [t] *pollute*	vaRjama [t] *conceal*
keRjama [t] *beg*	maTkama [i] *hike*	siLmama [t] *sight*	vaStama *answer*
kiUsama [t] *tease*	muStama [t] *blacken*	siUnama [t] *curse*	viHjama *hint*
koRjama [t] *gather*	mõRvama [t] *murder*		

327C haKKama [i] *start to do* haKKama 327C

	into case	stem	partitive	indicative		participle	imperative
personal	**haKKama**	**haKKa**	**hakata**	**haKKan**	**haKKab**	**haKKav**	**hakaku!**
past		**haKKasi-**		**haKKasin**	**haKKas**	**hakanud**	
impersonal		**hakata**		**hakatakse**		**hakatav**	**hakatagu!**
past				**hakati**		**hakatud**	

Also like haKKama:	hüPPama [i] *jump*	lüKKama [t] *push*	ruTTama [i] *hurry*
huKKama [t] *execute*	laKKama [i] *cease*	näPPama [t] *pilfer*	tõTTama [i] *hurry*

327D viiPama [i] *beakon* viiPama 327D

	into case	stem	partitive	indicative		participle	imperative
personal	**viiPama**	**viiPa**	**viibata**	**viiPan**	**viiPab**	**viiPav**	**viibaku!**
past		**viiPasi-**		**viiPasin**	**viiPas**	**viibanud**	
impersonal		**viibata**		**viibatakse**		**viibatav**	**viibatagu!**
past				**viibati**		**viibatud**	

Also like viiPama:	luPjama [t] *whitewash*	rüüPama [t] *sip*	trumPama *trump*
komPama [i] *grope*	pumPama [t] *pump*	taiPama [t] *realize*	võõPama [t] *paint*

327E aiTama *help* aiTama 327E

	into case	stem	partitive	indicative		participle	imperative
personal	**aiTama**	**aiTa**	**aidata**	**aiTan**	**aiTab**	**aiTav**	**aidaku!**
past		**aiTasi-**		**aiTasin**	**aiTas**	**aidanud**	
impersonal		**aidata**		**aidatakse**		**aidatav**	**aidatagu!**
past				**aidati**		**aidatud**	

Also like aiTama: ooTama ' *wait* uiTama ' *roam* viiTama ' *refer*
keTrama ' *spin* süüTama ' *ignite* vaaTama ' *look at* vänTama ' *crank*
näiTama ' *show* tüüTama ' *pester*

327F lõiKama ' *cut* lõiKama 327F

	into case	stem	partitive	indicative		participle	imperative
personal	**lõiKama**	**lõiKa**	**lõigata**	**lõiKan**	**lõiKab**	**lõiKav**	**lõigaku!**
past		**lõiKasi-**		**lõiKasin**	**lõiKas**	**lõiganud**	
impersonal		**lõigata**		**lõigatakse**		**lõigatav**	**lõigatagu!**
past				**lõigati**		**lõigatud**	

Also like lõiKama: märKama ' *notice* põiKama ' *swerve* tõuKama ' *push*
hõiKama *shout* palKama ' *employ* põrKama ' *collide* tärKama ' *sprout*
lonKama ' *limp* pilKama ' *mock* torKama ' *stab* ärKama ' *waken*

VERBS - 3 - CLASS VI B

TYPE 23 -L Stems

328 tİİblema [i] ***flit*** — **tİİblema 328**

	into case	stem	partitive	indicative		participle	imperative
personal	**tİİblema**	**tİİble**	**tiivelda**	**tİİblen**	**tİİbleb**	**tİİblev**	**tiivelgu!**
past		**tİİblesi-**		**tİİblesin**	**tİİbles**	**tiivelnud**	
impersonal		**tiivelda**		**tiiveldakse**		**tiiveldav**	**tiiveldagu!**
past				**tiiveldi**		**tiiveldud**	

Also like tİİblema: kaEblema [i] *bewail*

329 õMblema [t] ***sew*** — **õMblema 329**

	into case	stem	partitive	indicative		participle	imperative
personal	**õMblema**	**õMble**	**õmmelda**	**õMblen**	**õMbleb**	**õMblev**	**õmmelgu!**
past		**õMblesi-**		**õMblesin**	**õMbles**	**õmmelnud**	
impersonal		**õmmelda**		**õmmeldakse**		**õmmeldav**	**õmmeldagu!**
past				**õmmeldi**		**õmmeldud**	

Also like õMblema: küMblema [i] *bathe* tõMblema [i] *twitch*

330A rİİdlema [i] ***scold*** — **rİİdlema 330A**

	into case	stem	partitive	indicative		participle	imperative
personal	**rİİdlema**	**rİİdle**	**rii[j]elda**	**rİİdlen**	**rİİdleb**	**rİİdlev**	**rii[j]elgu!**
past		**rİİdlesi-**		**rİİdlesin**	**rİİdles**	**rii[j]elnud**	
impersonal		**rii[j]elda**		**rii[j]eldakse**		**rii[j]eldav**	**rii[j]eldagu!**
past				**rii[j]eldi**		**rii[j]eldud**	

Also like rİİdlema: pÜÜdlema [i] *aspire*

330B vaİdlema [i] ***argue*** — **vaİdlema 330B**

	into case	stem	partitive	indicative		participle	imperative
personal	**vaİdlema**	**vaİdle**	**vai[j]elda**	**vaİdlen**	**vaİdleb**	**vaİdlev**	**vai[j]elgu!**
past		**vaİdlesi-**		**vaİdlesin**	**vaİdles**	**vai[j]elnud**	
impersonal		**vai[j]elda**		**vai[j]eldakse**		**vai[j]eldav**	**vai[j]eldagu!**
past				**vai[j]eldi**		**vai[j]eldud**	

331A jUUrdlema ***ponder; investigate*** **jUUrdlema 331A**

	into case	stem	partitive	indicative		participle	imperative
personal	**jUUrdlema** [t]	**jUUrdle**	**juurelda**	**jUUrdlen**	**jUUrdleb**	**jUUrdlev**	**juurelgu!**
past		**jUUrdlesi-**		**jUUrdlesin**	**jUUrdles**	**juurelnud**	
impersonal		**juurelda**		**juureldakse**		**juureldav**	**juureldagu!**
past				**juureldi**		**juureldud**	

331B kaHtlema [t] ***doubt*** **kaHtlema 331B**

	into case	stem	partitive	indicative		participle	imperative
personal	**kaHtlema**	**kaHtle**	**kahelda**	**kaHtlen**	**kaHtelb**	**kaHtlev**	**kahelgu!**
past		**kaHtlesi-**		**kaHtlesin**	**kaHtles**	**kahelnud**	
impersonal		**kahelda**		**kaheldakse**		**kaheldav**	**kaheldagu!**
past				**kaheldi**		**kaheldud**	

Also like kaHtlema: koHtlema [t] *treat* nuHtlema [i] *punish* suHtlema [i] *associate with* viHtlema *whisk in sauna*

332 leNdlema [i] ***flutter*** **leNdlema 332**

	into case	stem	partitive	indicative		participle	imperative
personal	**leNdlema**	**leNdle**	**lennelda**	**leNdlen**	**leNdleb**	**leNdlev**	**lennelgu!**
past		**leNdlesi-**		**leNdlesin**	**leNdles**	**lennelnud**	
impersonal		**lennelda**		**lenneldakse**		**lenneldav**	**lenneldagu!**
past				**lenneldi**		**lenneldud**	

333 võRdlema [t] ***compare*** **võRdlema 333**

	into case	stem	partitive	indicative		participle	imperative
personal	**võRdlema**	**võRdle**	**võrrelda**	**võRdlen**	**võRdleb**	**võRdlev**	**võrrelgu!**
past		**võRdlesi-**		**võRdlesin**	**võRdles**	**võrrelnud**	
impersonal		**võrrelda**		**võrreldakse**		**võrreldav**	**võrreldagu!**
past				**võrreldi**		**võrreldud**	

334 liUglema [i] ***glide*** **liUglema 334**

	into case	stem	partitive	indicative		participle	imperative
personal	**liUglema**	**liUgle**	**liu[w]elda**	**liUglen**	**liUgleb**	**liUglev**	**liu[w]elgu!**
past		**liUglesi-**		**liUglesin**	**liUgles**	**liu[w]elnud**	
impersonal		**liu[w]elda**		**liu[w]eldakse**		**liu[w]eldav**	**liu[w]eldagu!**
past				**liu[w]eldi**		**liu[w]eldud**	

335 aEglema [i] *dawdle* — aEglema 335

	into case	stem	partitive	indicative		participle	imperative
personal	**aEglema**	**aEgle**	**ajelda**	**aEglen**	**aEgleb**	**aEglev**	**ajelgu!**
past		**aEglesi-**		**aEglesin**	**aEgles**	**ajelnud**	
impersonal		**ajelda**		**ajeldakse**		**ajeldav**	**ajeldagu!**
past				**ajeldi**		**ajeldud**	

336 teeSklema *pretend* — teeSklema 336

	into case	stem	partitive	indicative		participle	imperative
personal	**teeSklema**	**teeSkle**	**teeselda**	**teeSklen**	**teeSkleb**	**teeSklev**	**teeselgu!**
past		**teeSklesi-**		**teeSklesin**	**teeSkles**	**teeselnud**	
impersonal		**teeselda**		**teeseldakse**		**teeseldav**	**teeseldagu!**
past				**teeseldi**		**teeseldud**	

Also like teeSklema: kõHklema [i] *hesitate*, puSklema [i] *butt*, viSklema [i] *toss and turn*, kiSklema [i] *fight*, laiSklema [i] *laze about*, veHklema [i] *fence*

337 mõTlema [t] *think* — mõTlema 337

	into case	stem	partitive	indicative		participle	imperative
personal	**mõTlema**	**mõTle**	**mõtelda** **mõElda**	**mõTlen**	**mõTleb**	**mõTlev**	**mõtelgu!** **mõElgu!**
past		**mõTlesi-**		**mõTlesin**	**mõTles**	**mõtelnud** **mõElnud**	
impersonal		**mõtelda** **mõElda**		**mõteldakse** **mõEldakse**		**mõteldav** **mõEldav**	**mõteldagu!** **mõEldagu!**
past				**mõteldi** **mõEldi**		**mõteldud** **mõEldud**	

338 üTlema [t] *say* — üTlema 338

	into case	stem	partitive	indicative		participle	imperative
personal	**üTlema**	**üTle**	**ütelda** **öElda**	**üTlen**	**üTleb**	**üTlev**	**ütelgu!** **öElgu!**
past		**üTlesi-**		**üTlesin**	**üTles**	**ütelnud** **öElnud**	
impersonal		**ütelda** **öElda**		**üteldakse** **öEldakse**		**üteldav** **öEldav**	**üteldagu!** **öEldagu!**
past				**üteldi** **öEldi**		**üteldud** **öEldud**	

TYPE 24 -A Stems

339A hOObama [t] *lever* — hOObama 339A

	into case	stem	partitive	indicative		participle	imperative
personal	**hOObama**	**hOOba**	**hoovata**	**hOOban**	**hOObab**	**hOObav**	**hoovaku!**
past		**hOObasi-**		**hOObasin**	**hOObas**	**hoovanud**	
impersonal		**hoovata**		**hoovatakse**		**hoovatav**	**hoovatagu!**
past				**hoovati**		**hoovatud**	

339B kaEbama *complain* — kaEbama 339B

	into case	stem	partitive	indicative		participle	imperative
personal	**kaEbama**	**kaEba**	**kaevata**	**kaEban**	**kaEbab**	**kaEvav**	**kaevaku!**
past		**kaEbasi-**		**kaEbasin**	**kaEbas**	**kaevanud**	
impersonal		**kaevata**		**kaevatakse**		**kaevatav**	**kaevatagu!**
past				**kaevati**		**kaevatud**	

Also like kaEbama: kõLbama [i] *be good for* väRbama [t] *enlist*

340 tõMbama [t] *pull* — tõMbama 340

	into case	stem	partitive	indicative		participle	imperative
personal	**tõMbama** [t]	**tõMba**	**tõmmata**	**tõMban**	**tõMbab**	**tõMbav**	**tõmmaku!**
past		**tõMbasi-**		**tõMbasin**	**tõMbas**	**tõmmanud**	
impersonal		**tõmmata**		**tõmmatakse**		**tõmmatav**	**tõmmatagu!**
past				**tõmmati**		**tõmmatud**	

Also like tõMbama: eMbama [t] *embrace*

341A sİİrdama [t] *transplant (organs)* — sİİrdama 341A

	into case	stem	partitive	indicative		participle	imperative
personal	**sİİrdama**	**sİİrda**	**siirata**	**sİİrdan**	**sİİrdab**	**sİİrdav**	**siiraku!**
past		**sİİrdasi-**		**sİİrdasin**	**sİİrdas**	**siiranud**	
impersonal		**siirata**		**siiratakse**		**siiratav**	**siiratagu!**
past				**siirati**		**siiratud**	

341B koHtama [t] *meet* — koHtama 341B

	into case	stem	partitive	indicative		participle	imperative
personal	**koHtama**	**koHta**	**kohata**	**koHtan**	**koHtab**	**koHtav**	**kohaku!**
past		**koHtasi-**		**koHtasin**	**koHtas**	**kohanud**	
impersonal		**kohata**		**kohatakse**		**kohatav**	**kohatagu!**
past				**kohati**		**kohatud**	

342 haLdama [t] *administer* **haLdama 342**

	into case	stem	partitive	indicative		participle	imperative
personal	**haLdama**	**haLda**	**hallata**	**haLdan**	**haLdab**	**haLdav**	**hallaku!**
past		**haLdasi-**		**haLdasin**	**haLdas**	**hallanud**	
impersonal		**hallata**		**hallatakse**		**hallatav**	**hallatagu!**
past				**hallati**		**hallatud**	

Also like haLdama: kuLdama [t] *gild* muLdama [t] *earth* vaLdama [t] *possess*

343 leNdama [i] *fly* **leNdama 343**

	into case	stem	partitive	indicative		participle	imperative
personal	**leNdama**	**leNda**	**lennata**	**leNdan**	**leNdab**	**leNdav**	**lennaku!**
past		**leNdasi-**		**leNdasin**	**leNdas**	**lennanud**	
impersonal		**lennata**		**lennatakse**		**lennatav**	**lennatagu!**
past				**lennati**		**lennatud**	

Also like leNdama: räNdama [i] *wander* rüNdama [t] *attack* uNdama [i] *hum*
hiNdama [t] *value*

344 koRdama [t] *repeat* **koRdama 344**

	into case	stem	partitive	indicative		participle	imperative
personal	**koRdama**	**koRda**	**korrata**	**koRdan**	**koRdab**	**koRdav**	**korraku!**
past		**koRdasi-**		**koRdasin**	**koRdas**	**korranud**	
impersonal		**korrata**		**korratakse**		**korratav**	**korratagu!**
past				**korrati**			**korratud**

345A lõUgama [i] *bawl* **lõUgama 345A**

	into case	stem	partitive	indicative		participle	imperative
personal	**lõUgama**	**lõUga**	**lõu[w]ata**	**lõUgan**	**lõUgab**	**lõUgav**	**lõu[w]aku!**
past		**lõUgasi-**		**lõUgasin**	**lõUgas**	**lõu[w]anud**	
impersonal		**lõu[w]ata**		**lõu[w]atakse**		**lõu[w]atav**	**lõu[w]atagu!**
past				**lõu[w]ati**		**lõu[w]atud**	

345B muİgama [i] *smirk* **muİgama 345B**

	into case	stem	partitive	indicative		participle	imperative
personal	**muİgama**	**muİga**	**mui[j]ata**	**muİgan**	**muİgab**	**muİgav**	**mui[j]aku!**
past		**muİgasi-**		**muİgasin**	**muİgas**	**mui[j]anud**	
impersonal		**mui[j]ata**		**mui[j]atakse**		**mui[j]atav**	**mui[j]atagu!**
past				**mui[j]ati**		**mui[j]atud**	

Also like muİgama: möİrgama [i] *roar* oİgama [i] *groan* ruİgama [i] *grunt*

346 hüLgama [t] *abandon* — hüLgama 346

	into case	stem	partitive	indicative		participle	imperative
personal	**hüLgama**	**hüLga**	**hüļjata**	**hüLgan**	**hüLgab**	**hüLgav**	**hüļjaku!**
past		**hüLgasi-**		**hüLgasin**	**hüLgas**	**hüļjanud**	
impersonal		**hüļjata**		**hüļjatakse**		**hüļjatav**	**hüļjatagu!**
past				**hüļjati**		**hüļjatud**	

Also like hüLgama [t]   peLgama [t] *be afraid*

347 päRgama [t] *wreathe* — päRgama 347

	into case	stem	partitive	indicative		participle	imperative
personal	**päRgama**	**päRga**	**pärjata**	**päRgan**	**päRgab**	**päRgav**	**pärjaku!**
past		**päRgasi-**		**päRgasin**	**päRgas**	**pärjanud**	
impersonal		**pärjata**		**pärjatakse**		**pärjatav**	**pärjatagu!**
past				**pärjati**		**pärjatud**	

348A hİİlgama [i] *shine* — hİİlgama 348A

	into case	stem	partitive	indicative		participle	imperative
personal	**hİİlgama**	**hİİlga**	**hiilata**	**hİİlgan**	**hİİlgab**	**hİİlgav**	**hiilaku!**
past		**hİİlgasi-**		**hİİlgasin**	**hİİlgas**	**hiilanud**	
impersonal		**hiilata**		**hiilatakse**		**hiilatav**	**hiilatagu!**
past				**hiilati**		**hiilatud**	

Also like hİİlgama: kİİrgama [i] *radiate*

348B aLgama [i] *begin; start* — aLgama 348B

	into case	stem	partitive	indicative		participle	imperative
personal	**aLgama**	**aLga**	**alata**	**aLgan**	**aLgab**	**aLgav**	**alaku!**
past		**aLgasi-**		**aLgasin**	**aLgas**	**alanud**	
impersonal		**alata**		**alatakse**		**alatav**	**alatagu!**
past				**alati**		**alatud**	

Also like aLgama: kaRgama [i] *leap*   põLgama [t] *despise*   saLgama [t] *disown*

348C oSkama [t] *know how to* **oSkama 348C**

	into case	stem	partitive	indicative		participle	imperative
personal	**oSkama**	**oSka**	**osata**	**oSkan**	**oSkab**	**oSkav**	**osaku!**
past		**oSkasi-**		**oSkasin**	**oSkas**	**osanud**	
impersonal		**osata**		**osatakse**		**osatav**	**osatagu!**
past				**osati**		**osatud**	

Also like oSkama:	luiSkama [t] *whet*	oHkama [i] *sigh*	raiSkama [t] *waste*
heiSkama [t] *hoist*	luiSkama [i] *fib*	paiSkama [t] *fling*	tuiSkama [i] *drift snow*
hõiSkama [i] *cheer*	lõHkama [t] *explode*	puHkama [i] *rest*	viHkama [t] *hate*
kriiSkama [i] *screech*	norSkama [i] *snore*	purSkama [t] *spurt*	viSkama [t] *throw*
laHkama [t] *dissect*	nuuSkama [t] *blow nose*		

VERBS - 3 - CLASS VII

TYPE 25 - Regular

349A osalema [i] ***participate*** **osalema 349A**

	into case	stem	partitive	indicative		participle	imperative
personal	**osalema**	**osale**	**osaleda**	**osalen**	**osaleb**	**osalev**	**osalegu!**
past		**osalesi-**		**osalesin**	**osales**	**osalenud**	
impersonal		**osaleta**		**osaletakse**		**osaletav**	**osaletagu!**
past				**osaleti**		**osaletud**	

Also like osalema: ebalema [i] *waver; doubt* ihalema [t] *covet* mõnulema [i] *luxuriate*

349B taRbima [t] ***use, consume (of consumer items)*** **taRbima 349B**

	into case	stem	partitive	indicative		participle	imperative
personal	**taRbima**	**taRbi**	**taRbida**	**taRbin**	**taRbib**	**taRbiv**	**taRbigu!**
past		**taRbisi-**		**taRbisin**	**taRbis**	**taRbinud**	
impersonal		**taRbita**		**taRbitakse**		**taRbitav**	**taRbitagu!**
past				**taRbiti**		**taRbitud**	

Also like taRbima:	kuLgema [i] *proceed*	näĻgima [i] *starve*	teKKima [i] *arise*
jäĻgima [t] *follow*	kõRbema [i] *scorch*	närTsima [i] *wither*	vaĻmima [i] *ripen*
jäRgima [t] *conform to*	käİbima [i] *circulate*	poEgima *give birth*	veŢTima [i] *be waterlogged*
kaTkema [i] *break off*	laNgema [i] *fall*	puHkema [i] *burst out*	vİIbima [i] *stay for a time*
keHtima [i] *be valid*	lõHkema [i] *explode*	süŢTima [i] *ignite*	ÖÖbima [i] *spend the night*
kerKima [i] *rise*	mEEldima [i] *be pleasing*		

Also like 349A osalema and 349B taRbima verbs with the derivative endings:

349C all verbs ending in -isema *(imitation of sound)* **-isema 349C**

halisema [i] *lament*	kõmisema [i] *rumble*	nurisema [i] *grumble*	särisema [i] *sizzle*
helisema [i] *ring (bell)*	kähisema [i] *speak hoarsely*	pladisema [i] *splash*	torisema [i] *grumble*
kahisema [i] *rustle*	kärisema [i] *tear*	podisema [i] *simmer*	urisema [i] *growl*
kihisema [i] *seethe*	libisema [i] *slip*	pomisema [i] *mutter*	vabisema [i] *tremble*
klirisema [i] *clatter*	lobisema [i] *prattle*	põrisema [i] *buzz*	varisema [i] *collapse*
klobisema [i] *rattle*	logisema [i] *wobble*	ragisema [i] *crackle*	virisema [i] *whimper*
kohisema [i] *murmur*	lohisema [i] *drag*	sahisema [i] *rustle*	vuhisema [i] *whiz*
kolisema [i] *clatter*	lõdisema [i] *shiver*	sisisema [i] *sizzle*	vulisema [i] *gurgle*
krabisema [i] *rustle*	mühisema [i] *rumble*	solisema [i] *splash*	vurisema [i] *whirr*
krigisema [i] *crunch*	mürisema [i] *rumble*	sulisema [i] *babble (brook)*	võbisema [i] *quiver*
kubisema [i] *teem*	nagisema [i] *creak*	sumisema [i] *drone*	värisema [i] *tremble*
kõlisema [i] *tinkle*	norisema [i] *snore*	susisema [i] *hiss*	ümisema [i] *hum*

349D all verbs ending in -nema *become* -nema 349D

alanema [i] *decrease*
arenema [i] *evolve*
avanema [i] *open*
edenema [i] *progress*
erinema [i] *differ*
esinema [i] *perform*
halvenema [i] *worsen*
harunema [i] *branch off*
harvenema [i] *thin out*
hilinema [i] *be late*
hõrenema [i] *become sparse*
häbenema [i] *be ashamed*
idanema [i] *germinate*
iganema [i] *become obsolete*
jagunema [i] *be divided*
jahenema [i] *become cool*
janunema [i] *be thirsty*
kahanema [i] *diminish*
kaļlinema *become expensive*
kaugenema [i] *recede*
kergenema [i] *lighten (weight)*
kiirenema [i] *speed up*
killunema *become splintered*
kitsenema *become narrower*
kivinema [i] *petrify*
kodunema [i] *get used to*
kogunema [i] *gather together*
kohanema [i] *adapt oneself*
kuivenema [i] *dry up*
kujunema [i] *take shape*
kuumenema [i] *heat up*
kõdunema [i] *decay*
kõrgenema *become elevated*
kõvenema [i] *intensify*
külmenema *become colder*
lagunema [i] *fall to pieces*
laienema [i] *widen*
liginema [i] *approach*
ligunema [i] *soak*
lõdvenema [i] *slacken*
lõhenema [i] *split apart*
lähenema [i] *come closer*
lühenema [i] *shorten*
mõranema [i] *crack*
mädanema [i] *fester*
nõrgenema [i] *weaken*
nürinema [i] *become blunt*
olenema [i] *depend on*
paksenema [i] *fatten*
paļjunema [i] *increase*
paranema [i] *heal*
pehmenema [i] *soften*
pikenema [i] *lengthen*
pimenema [i] *darken*
pragunema [i] *crack*
pudenema [i] *crumble*
purunema [i] *shatter*
põgenema [i] *escape*
põhinema [i] *be based on*
põhjenema [i] *be based on*
pärinema [i] *derive*
rahunema [i] *calm down*
raskenema *become difficult*
rebenema [i] *tear*
sagenema *become frequent*
sarnanema [i] *resemble*
segunema [i] *mingle*
siginema [i] *breed*
sisenema [i] *enter*
soojenema [i] *become warmer*
suurenema [i] *become larger*
süvenema [i] *concentrate on*
taganema [i] *retreat*
tahenema [i] *become dry*
teravnema *become sharper*
tervenema *become healthier*
tihenema [i] *become denser*
tugevnema [i] *strengthen*
tuginema [i] *rely on*
tulenema [i] *result from*
tumenema [i] *darken colour*
täienema *become complete*
tüdinema [i] *become bored*
tühjenema [i] *become empty*
ununema [i] *become forgotten*
uuenema [i] *become renewed*
vabanema [i] *become free*
valgenema [i] *become lighter*
vananema [i] *age*
vähenema [i] *lessen*
ägenema [i] *become violent*
ühinema [i] unite

EElnema [i] *precede*
haPnema [i] *become sour*
haRgnema [i] *fork*
iLmnema [i] *become evident*
jäRgnema [i] *ensue*
kAAsnema [i] *be concurrent*
kOOsnema [i] *consist of*
paiKnema [i] *be situated*
pİİrnema [i] *border*
põLvnema [i] *originate*
seİsnema [i] *consist of*
võLgnema [i] *owe*

349E all verbs ending in -tsema *be; do* -tsema 349E

ahnitsema *be greedy*
asetsema [i] *be located*
haletsema [i] *bemoan*
hooļitsema [i] *attend to*
häälitsema [i] *make sounds*
igatsema [t] *yearn*
immitsema [i] *ooze*
kahetsema [t] *regret*
kavatsema [t] *intend*
käratsema [i] *be rowdy*
käsitsema [t] *handle*
leegitsema [i] *blaze*
lehitsema [t] *leaf*
lipitsema [i] *fawn*
lõbutsema [i] *enjoy oneself*
manitsema [i] *admonish*
muretsema [i] *worry*
muretsema [t] *procure*
mäletsema [i] *ruminate*
märatsema [i] *rage*
nukrutsema [i] *be melancholy*
närvitsema [i] *be nervous*
peenutsema [i] *be over-refined*
pesitsema [i] *nest*
pidutsema [i] *party*
plaaņitsema [t] *plan*
puļbitsema [i] *seethe*
põrnitsema [i] *scowl*
pühitsema [t] *celebrate*
raevutsema [i] *rage*
sepitsema [t] *scheme*
silmitsema [t] *eye*
skandaalitsema [t] *fuss*
suvatsema *deign*
sõbrutsema [i] *be friends*
sõrmitsema *finger*
tarvitsema [i] *need*
tavatsema [i] *be in the habit*
tegutsema [i] *act; do*
tõļgitsema [t] *interpret*
tülitsema [i] *quarrel*
valitsema [t] *rule*
varitsema [t] *lie waiting for*
võidutsema [i] *exult in triumph*
võimutsema [i] *exult in power*
õngitsema *fish*
äritsema [i] *traffic*
ümbritsema [t] *surround*

349F verbs in -tama [t] -Tama - dama *make (causative)* -tama -Tama -dama 349F

abistama [t] *help*
aerutama [i] *row*
aevastama [i] *sneeze*
alandama [t] *humiliate*
algatama [t] *instigate*
alistama [t] *subdue*
allutama [t] *subordinate*
alustama [t] *commence*
ammendama [t] *exhaust*
ammutama [t] *deplete*
anastama [t] *usurp*
andestama [t] *forgive*
annetama [t] *donate*
arendama [t] *evolve*
aretama [t] *breed*
armastama [t] *love*

349F -tama -Tama - dama continued **continued -tama -Tama - dama 349F**

arutama ' *discuss*
arvestama ' *consider*
arvustama ' *critique*
arvutama ' *calculate*
asendama ' *substitute*
asetama ' *place*
askeldama ^{i} *bustle*
asustama ' *colonize*
asutama ' *found*
augustama ' *perforate*
auStama ' *respect*
avaldama ' *make known*
avardama ' *broaden*
avastama ' *discover*
edendama ' *further*
edutama ' *promote*
edvistama ^{i} *flirt*
EEldama ' *assume*
eelistama ' *prefer*
eemaldama ' *remove*
eestindama ' *translate into Est.*
eestistama ' *Estonianize*
ehitama ' *build*
ehmatama ' *startle*
eine(s)tama ^{i} *dine*
eiTama ' *deny*
eksitama ' *mislead*
elustama ' *revive*
ennetama ' *forestall*
eŋnistama ' *restore*
ennustama ' *foretell*
eraldama ' *separate*
ergutama ' *encourage*
eristama ' *distinguish*
erutama ' *excite*
esindama ' *represent*
esitama ' *present*
etendama ' *perform*
evitama ' *put to use*
haigutama ^{i} *yawn*
hajutama ' *dissipate*
halastama ^{i} *have mercy on*
haļjendama ^{i} *be erdant*
haļlitama ^{i} *be mouldy*
halvendama ' *worsen*
hammustama ' *bite*
hangeldama ^{i} *deal in*
hapendama ' *make sour*
harjutama ' *practice*

harrastama ' *do as hobby*
harutama ' *unravel*
harvendama ' *thin out*
hauTama ' *stew*
heegeldama ' *crochet*
heidutama ' *discourage*
helistama ^{i} *telephone*
helistama ' *ring (bell)*
heļlitama ' *pamper*
higistama ^{i} *sweat*
hingeldama ^{i} *pant*
hingestama ' *animate*
hirmutama ' *frighten*
hoiatama ' *warn*
hoiustama ' *deposit in bank*
hOOldama ' *care of*
huvitama ' *interest*
hõrendama ' *make sparse*
häbistama ' *shame*
hädaldama ^{i} *fuss*
hämmastama ' *astonish*
hämmeldama ' *bewilder*
hävitama ' *destroy*
hÄÄldama ' *pronounce*
häälestama ' *tune*
hääletama *ote*
hääletama ^{i} *hitch-hike*
hööveldama ' *plane*
hüpitama ' *dandle*
hüvitama ' *compensate*
hüüatama ^{i} *cry out*
ihaldama ' *crave*
iiveldama ^{i} *be nauseous*
ilmutama ' *develop film*
ilustama ' *beautify*
imestama *wonder at*
imetama ' *suckle*
innustama ' *fill with fervour*
irvitama ^{i} *sneer*
istutama ' *plant*
iţsitama ^{i} *giggle*
jaaTama *affirm*
jahmatama ' *dismay*
jahutama ' *cool off*
jahvatama ' *grind*
jalutama ^{i} *stroll*
jaoTama ' *distribute*
joobnustama ' *intoxicate*
joonestama ' *draw (draft)*

joonistama ' *draw a picture*
joovastama ' *intoxicate*
jorutama ^{i} *loll while droning*
juhatama ' *direct*
juhatama ' *lead*
juhendama ' *advise*
julgustama ' *encourage*
jumaldama ' *adore*
jutlustama ^{i} *preach*
jutustama ' *narrate a story*
juubeldama ^{i} *rejoice*
juurutama ' *inculcate*
jõļlitama ' *goggle*
jälitama ' *pursue*
jäļjendama ' *copy*
järeldama ' *conclude*
järjestama ' *arrange in order*
jäädvustama ' *record*
kaagutama ^{i} *cackle*
kaardistama ' *map*
kaarutama ' *turn over*
kadestama ' *envy*
kaelustama ' *hug*
kaevandama ' *mine*
kahandama ' *diminish*
kahistama ' *rustle*
kahjustama ' *harm*
kahtlustama ' *suspect*
kaisutama ' *embrace*
kajastama ' *express*
kalastama *fish*
kaļlistama ' *caress*
kallutama ' *tilt*
kangutama ' *wrench*
kannatama *suffer*
kaoTama ' *lose*
karastama ' *refresh*
karistama ' *punish*
karjatama ^{i} *cry out*
karjatama ' *pasture*
kasutama ' *use*
kasvatama ' *raise (grow)*
katkestama ' *interrupt*
katsetama ' *experiment*
kaubastama ' *market*
kaunistama ' *adorn*
kavandama ' *outline*
keelustama ' *ban*
keerutama ' *twist*

keevitama ' *weld*
kehastama ' *embody*
kehitama ' *shrug shoulders*
kehtestama ' *enact*
kelgutama ^{i} *sled*
kepsutama ^{i} *gambol*
kergendama ' *lighten (weight)*
kergitama ' *raise (lift)*
keskendama ' *concentrate*
kestendama ^{i} *be chapped*
kibestama ' *embitter*
kibrutama ' *pucker*
kihistama ^{i} *snigger*
kihutama ' *incite*
kiigutama *rock*
kiirendama ' *speed up*
kiiritama ' *irradiate*
kiirustama *hurry*
kiļjatama ^{i} *give a shriek*
killustama ' *become splintered*
kimbutama ' *harass*
kindlustama ' *insure*
kiŋnistama ' *fasten*
kiŋnitama ' *certify*
kipitama ^{i} *prickle*
kiristama ' *gnash*
kirjastama ' *publish*
kirjeldama ' *describe*
kirjutama ' *write*
kirtsutama ' *wrinkle*
kisendama ^{i} *yell*
kitsendama ' *restrict*
kliisterdama ' *paste*
klobistama ' *rattle*
kobestama ' *loosen soil*
kodustama ' *domesticate*
kohandama ' *adapt*
kohendama ' *arrange*
kohmetama ^{i} *numb fast*
kohustama ' *oblige*
kohutama ' *terrify*
kokutama ^{i} *stutter*
kolistama ' *clatter*
kolletama *turn yellow*
komberdama ^{i} *hobble*
komistama ^{i} *stumble*
kooļitama ' *school*
koolutama ' *curve*
kOOndama ' *rally*

koonerdama [i] *be stingy*
kOOskölastama ' *co-ordinate*
kooStama ' *compose*
koputama [i] *knock*
koristama ' *tidy up*
korraldama ' *organize*
korrastama ' *put into order*
korrutama ' *multiply*
kortsutama ' *wrinkle*
koştitama ' *entertain guest*
kosutama ' *refresh*
kraavitama ' *drain*
krabistama ' *rustle*
krigistama ' *crunch*
kriimustama ' *scratch*
kriipsutama ' *draw lines*
kritseldama ' *scribble*
kudrutama [i] *coo*
kugistama ' *gulp down*
kuivatama ' *dry*
kuivendama ' *drain land*
kujundama ' *shape*
kujustama ' *depict*
kujutama ' *depict*
kukutama ' *overthrow*
kulutama ' *spend (use up)*
kummardama *bow*
kummitama ' *haunt*
kupatama ' *parboil*
kuristama *gargle*
kurvastama *grieve*
kustutama ' *extinguish*
kuulatama *eavesdrop*
kuulutama ' *advertise*
kuumendama ' *heat*
kuumutama ' *make hot*
kõdistama ' *tickle*
kõditama ' *tickle*
kõigutama ' *sway*
kõlgutama ' *dangle*
kõlistama ' *tinkle*
kõnetama ' *address someone*
kõrgendama ' *elevate*
kõrvaldama ' *remove*
kõrvetama ' *scorch*
kõrvutama ' *compare*
kõvendama ' *intensify*
kõverdama ' *curve*
käEndama ' *bail*

kägistama ' *strangle*
kähardama ' *curl*
käivitama ' *start up*
käristama ' *tear*
käsitama ' *comprehend*
käsutama ' *order about*
kühveldama ' *shovel*
kükitama [i] *squat*
külastama ' *isit*
külmetama ' *freeze*
külmutama ' *refrigerate*
küpsetama ' *bake*
kütkestama ' *captivate*
küüditama ' *deport*
küünistama ' *claw*
küürutama [i] *stoop*
laaberdama [i] *be rowdy*
laamendama [i] *bluster*
labastama ' *ulgarize*
laenutama ' *hire out*
laevatama [i] *navigate*
lahendama ' *solve*
lahjendama ' *dilute*
lahustama ' *dissolve*
lahutama ' *divorce*
laiendama ' *widen*
lainetama [i] *undulate*
laksutama ' *click*
lammutama ' *tear down*
langetama ' *lower*
laoStama ' *ruin*
laoTama ' *spread out*
lapsendama ' *adopt*
lavastama ' *stage*
leeritama ' *confirm (church)*
leevendama ' *soothe*
lehvitama ' *wave*
leiutama ' *invent*
leoTama ' *soak*
lepitama ' *reconcile*
levitama ' *disseminate*
libistama ' *slide*
lihtsustama ' *simplify*
liialdama ' *exaggerate*
liigitama ' *classify*
liigutama ' *move*
liivatama ' *sand*
linastama ' *screen a film*
liŋdistama ' *tape*

linnastama ' *urbanize*
liputama ' *wag (tail)*
loEndama ' *enumerate*
lohistama ' *drag*
lohutama ' *console*
loksutama ' *shake (liquid)*
looritama ' *eil*
loovutama ' *relinquish*
loputama ' *rinse*
lotendama [i] *droop*
lukustama ' *lock*
lunastama ' *redeem*
luuletama ' *write poetry*
lõbustama ' *entertain*
lõdistama ' *make shiver*
lõdvendama ' *slacken*
lõhestama ' *split apart*
lõhnastama ' *scent*
lõpetama ' *finish*
lõunastama [i] *dine (noon)*
lõunatama ' *dine (noon)*
lõõritama [i] *warble*
lähendama ' *bring closer*
läkastama [i] *have coughing fit*
läkitama ' *dispatch*
lämmatama ' *suffocate*
lömastama ' *squash*
lömitama [i] *grovel*
lühendama ' *shorten*
lülitama ' *switch*
mAAndama ' *ground (electric)*
mAAndama ' *land airplane*
madaldama ' *lower*
magustama ' *sweeten*
mahutama ' *fit*
maitsestama ' *season(spices)*
majandama ' *finance*
majutama ' *house*
maksustama ' *tax*
maletama [i] *play chess*
manööverdama ' *manoeuvre*
margistama ' *affix stamp*
masendama ' *depress*
matsutama ' *smack (lips)*
meelitama ' *coax*
meenutama ' *call to mind*
mehitama ' *man*
minestama [i] *faint*
miTmekesistama ' *diversify*

moodustama ' *form*
mOOndama ' *transform*
moonutama ' *distort*
moşsitama *pout*
mulgustama ' *perforate*
muşutama ' *kiss*
mõistatama ' *guess*
mõjustama ' *influence*
mõjutama ' *influence*
mõlgutama ' *meditate*
mõnitama ' *mock*
mõtestama ' *give meaning*
mälestama ' *commemorate*
mäletama ' *remember*
märgistama ' *imprint*
mürgeldama [i] *kick up ruckus*
mürgitama ' *poison*
müristama [i] *thunder*
naelutama ' *nail*
naeratama [i] *smile*
nakatama ' *infect*
naljatama [i] *joke*
narmendama [i] *fray*
nihestama ' *dislocate*
nihutama ' *shift*
niisutama ' *irrigate*
nikastama ' *sprain*
nimetama ' *name*
noodistama ' *set to music*
noogutama ' *nod*
noorendama ' *rejuvenate*
norutama [i] *mope*
nummerdama ' *number*
nuputama ' *devise*
nuusutama ' *smell (sniff)*
nõksatama [i] *jerk*
nõrgendama ' *weaken*
näiTlikustama ' *make graphic*
näljutama ' *starve*
näpistama ' *pinch*
näägutama ' *nag*
ohjeldama ' *restrain*
ohustama ' *endanger*
ohverdama ' *sacrifice*
oksendama *omit*
oletama ' *suppose*
omandama ' *acquire*
omastama ' *appropriate*
omistama ' attribute

349F -tama -Tama - dama continued

orjastama ˈ *enslave*
osatama ˈ *mimic*
osutama ˈ *indicate*
otsustama ˈ *decide*
pagendama ˈ *banish*
pahandama ˈ *annoy*
pahteldama ˈ *putty*
pahvatama ˈ *blurt out*
paigutama ˈ *place*
painutama ˈ *bend*
paistetama ˈ *swell*
paisutama ˈ *dam up*
paiTama ˈ *stroke (pet)*
pakatama ˈ *burst into bloom*
palistama ˈ *hem*
paljastama ˈ *bare*
paljundama ˈ *duplicate*
palvetama ˈ *pray*
parandama ˈ *repair*
parvetama ˈ *raft*
pasandama *have diarrhoea*
pasundama *blare*
patsutama ˈ *pat*
patustama ˈ *sin*
paugutama ˈ *bang*
peaTama ˈ *stop*
peegeldama ˈ *reflect*
peenendama ˈ *make finer*
peeretama ˈ *fart*
peesitama ˈ *sunbathe*
pehmendama ˈ *soften*
peibutama ˈ *decoy*
peletama ˈ *frighten*
pesitama ˈ *nest*
pidurdama ˈ *brake*
pigistama ˈ *squeeze*
pihustama ˈ *pulverize*
piiksatama ˈ *squeak*
piitsutama ˈ *whip (punish)*
pikendama ˈ *prolong*
pildistama ˈ *photograph*
pilgutama ˈ *blink*
pilutama ˈ *hem-stitch*
pimendama ˈ *darken*
pimestama ˈ *blind*
pingutama ˈ *strain*
piserdama ˈ *sprinkle*
pişsitama ˈ *take child to pee*
plahvatama ˈ *explode*

plaksutama *clap*
pleegitama ˈ *bleach*
poeTama ˈ *slip through*
polsterdama ˈ *upholster*
pommitama ˈ *bomb*
pOOldama ˈ *favour*
pooljitama ˈ *halve*
poputama ˈ *pamper*
praoTama ˈ *open slightly*
pruuŋistama ˈ *brown*
ptruuTama *whoa*
pudendama ˈ *crumble*
pudistama ˈ *lisp*
pudistama ˈ *crumble*
puhastama ˈ *clean*
punastama ˈ *blush*
punetama ˈ *glow red*
purjetama ˈ *sail*
purjutama ˈ *booze up*
purustama ˈ *shatter*
puşsitama ˈ *knife*
puuderdama ˈ *powder face*
puudutama ˈ *touch*
põeTama ˈ *nurse*
põhjendama ˈ *justify*
põhjustama ˈ *cause*
põlastama ˈ *detest*
põletama ˈ *burn*
põlvitama ˈ *kneel*
põristama ˈ *rattle*
põrutama ˈ *jolt*
päevitama *sun-bathe*
pärandama ˈ *bequeath*
pööritama ˈ *roll*
pühendama ˈ *dedicate*
püherdama ˈ *wallow*
püştitama ˈ *erect*
ragistama ˈ *crackle*
rahuldama ˈ *satisfy*
rahustama ˈ *calm down*
rakendama ˈ *apply*
raksatama ˈ *crack (sound)*
raputama ˈ *shake*
raskendama ˈ *aggravate*
ratsutama *ride horse-back*
rauTama ˈ *shoe a horse*
reaStama ˈ *line up*
rebestama ˈ *tear*
relvastama ˈ *arm*

continued -tama -Tama - dama 349F

reoStama ˈ *pollute*
riietama ˈ *dress*
riigistama ˈ *nationalize*
rikastama ˈ *enrich*
ringutama ˈ *stretch*
rinnastama ˈ *coordinate*
riputama ˈ *hang*
rivistama ˈ *line up*
roostetama ˈ *rust*
ropendama ˈ *swear (cuss)*
rõhutama ˈ *emphasize*
rõivastama ˈ *dress*
rõngastama ˈ *ring (band)*
rõõmustama ˈ *rejoice*
röhitama ˈ *belch*
rühmitama ˈ *group*
saavutama ˈ *achieve*
sadestama ˈ *precipitate*
saduldama ˈ *saddle*
sahistama ˈ *rustle*
sajatama ˈ *curse*
salvestama ˈ *record*
samastama ˈ *identify with*
seemendama ˈ *seed*
seisatama ˈ *come to standstill*
sekeldama ˈ *fuss*
seletama ˈ *explain*
selgitama ˈ *explain*
seljatama ˈ *floor (wrestling)*
seOstama ˈ *associate*
sepistama *forge metal*
silbitama ˈ *syllabify*
silitama ˈ *stroke (pet)*
sillutama ˈ *pave*
sinatama ˈ *address familiarly*
sinetama ˈ *glow bluish*
siristama ˈ *chirp*
sirutama ˈ *stretch*
sisaldama ˈ *contain*
sisendama ˈ *instill*
sisustama ˈ *furnish house*
soeTama ˈ *procure*
solistama ˈ *splash*
soodustama ˈ *favour*
soojendama ˈ *warm*
sooritama ˈ *execute (perform)*
soovitama ˈ *recommend*
soperdama *bungle*
sosistama *whisper*

spikerdama *cheat at school*
suitsetama *smoke (cigarette)*
suitsetama ˈ *smoke*
suitsutama ˈ *cure meat*
sulatama ˈ *melt*
summutama ˈ *muffle*
suurendama ˈ *enlarge*
suusatama ˈ *ski*
suvitama ˈ *acation*
sõbrustama ˈ *be friends with*
sõidutama ˈ *give lift*
sõnastama ˈ *word*
sõrendama ˈ *emphasize*
sähvatama ˈ *flash*
säilitama ˈ *preserve*
säritama ˈ *expose (photo)*
sätendama ˈ *glisten*
söAndama ˈ *enture*
söövitama ˈ *etch*
sülitama *spit*
süŋnitama ˈ *give birth*
süţitama ˈ *kindle*
süvendama ˈ *deepen*
süüdistama ˈ *accuse*
taaStama ˈ *restore*
tagandama ˈ *fire from job*
tagastama ˈ *return (give back)*
takistama ˈ *hinder*
talitama *tend*
tallutama ˈ *sole*
taltsutama ˈ *tame*
talutama ˈ *guide*
talvitama ˈ *winter*
tarastama ˈ *fence in*
targutama ˈ *philosophize*
tarretama ˈ *congeal*
tarvitama ˈ *use*
tasakaalustama ˈ *balance*
tasandama ˈ *make level*
taţistama *befoul with snot*
teadustama ˈ *announce*
teaTama ˈ *inform*
teenindama ˈ *serve customer*
teietama ˈ *address formally*
tekitama ˈ *cause*
tembeldama ˈ *stamp*
teoStama ˈ *implement*
teoTama ˈ *abuse*
teravdama ˈ make sharper

349F -tama -Tama - dama continued **continued -tama -Tama - dama 349F**

teretama ' *greet*
teritama ' *sharpen*
tervendama ' *make healthier*
tervitama ' *greet*
tibutama [i] *drizzle*
tihendama ' *make denser*
tiivustama ' *inspire*
tilgutama ' *drip*
tinutama ' *solder*
toeStama ' *prop*
toeTama ' *support*
toimetama ' *edit*
toitlustama ' *cater*
tolmeldama ' *pollinate*
tolmutama ' *dust over*
tooŋitama ' *stress*
topistama ' *stuff*
traageldama ' *baste*
trummeldama ' *drum*
tugevdama ' *strengthen*
tuhastama ' *cremate*
tuhmistama ' *dim*
tuigerdama [i] *stagger*
tuimastama ' *make numb*
tuletama ' *derive*
tulistama ' *fire*
tunnetama ' *perceive*
tuŋnistama ' *witness*
tunnustama ' *acknowledge*
tupsutama ' *dab*
turustama ' *market*
tuţistama ' *pull by the hair*
tutvustama ' *introduce*
tuulutama ' *air*
tuututama *toot*
tõEndama ' *provide proof*
tõeStama ' *prove*
tõkestama ' *obstruct*
tõlgendama ' *interpret*
tõoTama ' *promise*
tõstatama ' *raise an issue*
tähendama ' *mean*
tähistama ' *mark occasion*
täiendama ' *complement*
täiustama ' *elaborate*
täkestama ' *notch*
täpsustama ' *specify*

tärgeldama ' *starch*
töllerdama [i] *loaf about*
tööTama [i] *work*
tühistama ' *cancel*
tühjendama ' *empty*
tükeldama ' *cut into pieces*
tülitama ' *disturb*
udutama [i] *be foggy*
uhkeldama [i] *have airs*
uhkustama [i] *pride oneself*
uimastama ' *daze*
uinutama ' *lull to sleep*
uisutama [i] *skate*
ujutama ' *flood*
ulatama ' *extend*
ummistama ' *clog*
unistama ' *day-dream*
unustama ' *forget*
uputama ' *drown*
usaldama ' *trust*
uşsitama [i] *be worm-eaten*
uudistama ' *wonder at*
uuendama ' *renew*
uuristama ' *erode*
vabandama ' *pardon*
vabastama ' *free*
vadistama [i] *prattle*
vahatama ' *wax*
vahendama ' *mediate*
vahetama ' *exchange*
vahistama ' *arrest*
vahustama ' *whip (food)*
vahutama [i] *foam*
vaigistama ' *alleviate*
vaimustama ' *enthuse*
vajutama ' *press*
valetama [i] *lie (deceive)*
valgendama ' *whiten*
valgustama ' *enlighten*
vallandama ' *dismiss (office)*
vallatama [i] *frolic*
vallutama ' *conquer*
vaļmistama ' *prepare*
valutama [i] *hurt*
vangistama ' *imprison*
vangutama ' *wag (head)*
vaŋnitama ' *bathe*

vapustama ' *shock*
varastama ' *steal*
varustama ' *supply*
vasardama ' *hammer*
vastandama ' *contrast*
vastutama [i] *be responsible*
vaterdama [i] *prattle*
vedrutama [i] *be springy*
veeretama ' *roll*
veiderdama [i] *play the fool*
vembutama [i] *play pranks*
venestama ' *Russify*
venitama ' *stretch out*
veristama ' *bloody*
vibutama ' *brandish*
vidistama *twitter*
vigastama *injure*
vigurdama *do stunts*
vihastama ' *anger*
viigistama ' *draw (game)*
viigitama ' *crease*
viisistama ' *set to music*
viiuldama [i] *fiddle*
viivitama [i] *delay*
vilistama *whistle*
viļjastama ' *fertilize*
vilksatama [i] *flash*
vingerdama [i] *squirm*
virgutama ' *rouse*
virutama ' *hurl*
virvendama [i] *ripple*
visandama ' *outline*
vispeldama ' *whisk*
volitama ' *authorize*
vooderdama ' *line (clothing)*
vormistama ' *put into form*
vuristama ' *whir*
vusserdama ' *bungle*
võimaldama ' *enable*
võimendama ' *amplify*
võngutama ' *rock*
võpatama [i] *wince*
võrdsustama ' *equalize*
võrgutama ' *seduce*
võõrandama ' *expropriate*
võõrastama [i] *be shy*

võõrustama ' *entertain guest*
võõrutama ' *estrange*
väeTama ' *fertilize*
vägistama ' *rape*
vähendama ' *lessen*
välgatama [i] *flash*
välistama ' *exclude*
väļjastama ' *issue*
väļjendama ' *express*
väristama ' *make tremble*
värskendama ' *refresh*
väsitama ' *tire*
vääratama [i] *err*
vääristama ' *dignify*
väärtustama ' *appraise*
vürtsitama ' *spice*
õgvendama ' *straighten*
õhetama [i] *be flushed*
õhutama ' *instigate*
õiendama *rectify*
õigustama ' *justify*
õilistama ' *ennoble*
õlitama ' *oil*
õŋnistama ' *bless*
õpetama ' *teach*
õõnestama ' *hollow out*
õõtsutama ' *sway*
äeStama ' *harrow*
ähvardama ' *threaten*
äiutama ' *lull to sleep*
äpardama [i] *miscarry*
äratama ' *waken*
ärritama ' *irritate*
äşsitama ' *provoke*
ääristama ' *edge*
ökitama [i] *stammer*
ühendama ' *unite*
ühtlustama ' *even out*
üļdistama ' *generalize*
ülendama ' *promote*
ületama ' *surpass*
ülistama ' *glorify*
üllatama ' *surprise*
ümardama ' *round off*
ümmardama ' *wait on*
üritama ' *attempt*

349G all verbs ending in -uma *become (reflexive)* -uma 349G

abieLLuma [i] *marry*
aEguma [i] *lapse*
aLLuma [i] *be subordinated*
aRmuma [i] *fall in love*
aUruma [i] *evaporate*
basEEruma [i] *be based on*
eHmuma [i] *be startled*
eksmatrikulEEruma [i] *drop out*
hAAvuma [i] *take offence*
haRjuma [i] *become accustomed*
hiRmuma [i] *be frightened*
huKKuma [i] *perish*
hÕÕguma [i] *glow*
iLmuma [i] *appear*
iMbuma [i] *soak in*
jaHmuma [i] *be dismayed*
jOObuma [i] *become drunk*
jäTkuma [i] *last*
kapitulEEruma [i] *capitulate*
kiHluma [i] *become engaged*
koHkuma [i] *be startled*
korTsuma [i] *become wrinkled*
kUUluma [i] *belong*
kõHnuma [i] *become thin*
küLmuma [i] *freeze*
laeKuma [i] *be paid in*
laHkuma [i] *depart*
laİuma [i] *spread out*
laSkuma [i] *lower oneself*
lOObuma [i] *renounce*
lOOjuma [i] *set (astronomic)*
lõiKuma [i] *intersect*
lõTvuma [i] *become limp*
läMbuma [i] *suffocate*
mAAbuma [i] *disembark*
mEEnuma [i] *come to mind*
niHkuma [i] *shift*
nuRjuma [i] *come to nought*
nõRguma [i] *drip-dry*
näRbuma [i] *wilt*
orientEEruma [i] *orientate*
paEluma [i] *fascinate*
paİsuma [i] *expand*
purSkuma [i] *spurt*
põİmuma [i] *twine*
põKKuma [i] *dock (rocket)*
raPPuma [i] *shake*
raSvuma [i] *become fat*
registrEEruma [i] *register*
roiSkuma [i] *putrefy*
ruinEEruma [i] *become ruined*
sAAbuma [i] *arrive*
seKKuma [i] *intervene*
seLguma [i] *become evident*
siRguma [i] *grow tall*
soLvuma [i] *take offence*
spetsialisEEruma [i] *specialize*
stabilisEEruma [i] *stabilize*
suLguma [i] *be enclosed*
sUUbuma [i] *disembogue*
toİbuma [i] *recover*
toİmuma [i] *occur*
tuHmuma [i] *become dim*
tuRsuma [i] *swell*
tuTvuma [i] *become acquainted*
tõMbuma [i] *withdraw*
uİnuma [i] *fall asleep*
vaEsuma [i] *become poor*
vaİbuma [i] *subside*
vaLguma [i] *disperse*
vaPPuma [i] *be shocked*
variEEruma [i] *ary*
veTruma [i] *be elastic*
viRguma [i] *become awake*
viSkuma [i] *throw oneself*
võRsuma [i] *sprout*
väĻjuma [i] *depart (exit)*
õHkuma [i] *radiate*

349H verbs in -tuma -Tuma -duma *(causative/reflexive)* -tuma -Tuma -duma 349H

alanduma [i] *degrade oneself*
alistuma [i] *submit (surrender)*
aNduma [i] *devote oneself*
avalduma [i] *be expressed*
avarduma [i] *broaden*
eemalduma [i] *withdraw*
eestistuma [i] *Estonianize*
elatuma [i] *subsist*
elustuma [i] *revive*
eralduma [i] *separate*
erutuma [i] *become excited*
haigestuma [i] *sicken*
haiHtuma [i] *anish*
haUduma [i] *stew*
hoİduma [i] *avoid*
huvituma [i] *become interested*
hÕÕrduma [i] *rub*
hämarduma [i] *become dusky*
hämmastuma [i] *be astonished*
jaHtuma [i] *cool off*
jOOnduma [i] *align oneself*
joovastuma [i] *intoxicate*
juHtuma [i] *happen*
jUUrduma [i] *take root*
jõuStuma [i] *come into force*
ärelduma [i] *be inferred*
jääTuma [i] *freeze over*
kahvatuma [i] *turn pale*
kainestuma [i] *sober up*
kajastuma [i] *be expressed*
kaLduma [i] *be inclined*
kaNduma [i] *be carried over*
karastuma [i] *harden*
kaTTuma [i] *coincide*
kEElduma [i] *refuse*
kehastuma [i] *be embodied*
kehtestuma [i] *come into effect*
keskenduma [i] *concentrate*
kibestuma [i] *become embittered*
kİInduma [i] *become fond of*
klaaşistuma [i] *become glassy*
kohmetuma [i] *numb slowly*
koHtuma [i] *meet*
kohustuma [i] *bind oneself*
kOOlduma [i] *curve*
kOOnduma [i] *rally*
koRduma [i] *recur*
kummarduma [i] *bend down*
kurvastuma [i] *become sad*
kUUlduma [i] *be rumoured*
kõverduma [i] *curve*
käharduma [i] *curl*
käiTuma [i] *behave*
kÄÄnduma [i] *decline (gram)*
küllastuma [i] *glut*
külmetuma [i] *catch cold*
ladestuma [i] *be deposited*
lahustuma [i] *dissolve*
laoStuma [i] *be ruined*
leİduma [i] *be found*
liiTuma [i] *join up*
linnastuma [i] *urbanize*
luiTuma [i] *fade*
lõõgastuma [i] *relax*
läHtuma [i] *originate*
mAAnduma [i] *land*
maNduma [i] *degenerate*
mOOnduma [i] *transform*
muRduma [i] *fracture*
muuTuma [i] *change*
mÄÄrduma [i] *get dirty*
mÖÖduma [i] *pass by*
naiTuma [i] *get married*
nakatuma [i] *become infected*
nõjatuma [i] *lean against*
nõuStuma [i] *agree*
osutuma [i] *turn out to be*
paİnduma [i] *bend*
peaTuma [i] *stop*
peegelduma [i] *be reflected*
pehastuma [i] *moulder*
peTTuma [i] *be disappointed*
pİIrduma [i] *be limited*
pUUduma [i] *be absent*
puuTuma [i] *concern*
päevituma [i] *become tanned*
pÖÖrduma [i] *turn*
pühenduma [i] *devote oneself*
rahulduma [i] *be satisfied*
raNduma [i] *land boat*
rasestuma [i] *become pregnant*
raugastuma [i] *become senile*
relvastuma [i] *arm oneself*
reoStuma [i] *become polluted*
riietuma [i] *dress oneself*
rikastuma [i] *become rich*
riStuma [i] *intersect*
rivistuma [i] *line up*
roİduma [i] *become weary*
rõivastuma [i] *dress oneself*
sadestuma [i] *precipitate*
sammalduma [i] *become mossy*
saTTuma [i] *happen upon*
seoStuma [i] *be associated*

349H -tuma -Tuma -duma continued **continued -tuma -Tuma -duma 349H**

sIIrduma [i] *proceed*	taRduma [i] *congeal*	ulatuma [i] *be extended*	võsastuma [i] *overgrow*
sirutuma [i] *stretch*	tarretuma [i] *congeal*	ummistuma [i] *become clogged*	vÕÕrduma [i] *become estranged*
suHtuma [i] *relate to*	teoStuma [i] *materialize*	vahelduma [i] *alternate*	väljenduma [i] *be expressed*
sukelduma [i] *dive*	toeTuma [i] *lean against*	vahetuma [i] *become exchanged*	õnnestuma [i] *succeed*
sUUnduma [i] *make one's way*	toiTuma [i] *feed on something*	valmistuma [i] *get ready*	ägestuma [i] *get worked up*
sõlTuma [i] *depend on*	tuhmistuma [i] *become dim*	vEEnduma [i] *become convinced*	äparduma [i] *miscarry*
söeStuma [i] *become charred*	tuNduma [i] *seem*	vihastuma [i] *become angry*	ärrituma [i] *become irritated*
tAAnduma [i] *retreat*	tUUlduma [i] *be aired*	viirastuma [i] *hallucinate*	ühilduma [i] *agree*
takerduma [i] *become stuck*	täiTuma [i] *become filled*	võRduma [i] *be equal*	üllatuma [i] *be surprised*

350 juLgema [t] *dare* juLgema 350

	into case	stem	partitive	indicative		participle	imperative
personal	**juLgema**	**juLge**	**juLgeda**	**juLgen**	**juLgeb**	**juLgev**	**juLgegu!**
past		**juLgesi-**		**juLgesin**	**juLges**	**juLgenud**	
						julenud	
impersonal		**juleta**		**juletakse**		**juletav**	**juletagu!**
		juLgeta		juLgetakse		juLgetav	juLgetagu!
past				**juleti**		**juletud**	
				juLgeti		juLgetud	

Also like juLgema: vaiKima [i] *be silent*

TYPE 26 - Mixed Type

351 õŋnitlema or **õŋnitelema** [t] ***congratulate*** **õŋnitlema 351**

	into case	stem	partitive	indicative		participle	imperative
personal	**õŋnitlema**	**õŋnitle**	**õŋnitleda**	**õŋnitlen**	**õŋnitleb**	**õŋnitlev**	**õŋnitlegu!**
past		**õŋnitlesi-**		**õŋnitlesin**	**õŋnitles**	**õŋnitlenud**	
impersonal		**õŋnitleta**		**õŋnitletakse**		**õŋnitletav**	**õŋnitletagu!**
past				**õŋnitleti**		**õŋnitletud**	

or

	into case	stem	partitive	indicative		participle	imperative
personal	**õŋnitelema**	**õŋnitele**	**õŋniteLLa**	**õŋnitelen**	**õŋniteleb**	**õŋnitelev**	**õŋnitelgu!**
past		**õŋniteli-**		**õŋnitelin**	**õŋniteli**	**õŋnitelnud**	
impersonal		**õŋniteLda**		**õŋnitellakse**		**õŋniteLdav**	**õŋniteLdagu!**
past				**õŋniteLdi**		**õŋniteLdud**	

Also like õŋnitlema:
ahvatlema [t] *entice*
esitlema [t] *introduce a person*
imetlema [t] *admire*
kaalutlema [t] *ponder*
keskustlema [i] *converse*
kujutlema [t] *imagine*
käsitlema [t] *deal with*
küsitlema [t] *interrogate*
loeTlema [t] *enumerate*
mõtisklema [i] *ponder*
määratlema [t] *define*
piiritlema [t] *define*
taoTlema [t] *apply for*
usutlema [t] *interview*
vallatlema [i] *frolic*
viimistlema [t] *touch up*

PART III

ESTONIAN - ENGLISH GLOSSARY

EXPLANATORY NOTES

Parts III and IV are alphabetical Estonian-English and English-Estonian glossaries. In the Estonian-English glossary, the Estonian entry is followed by a superscript letter indicating the part of speech of the Estonian word. The letters are:

^{N} for nouns
^{A} for adjectives
^{Vi} for intransitive verbs
^{Vt} for transitive verbs
^{V} for verbs that are either intransitive or transitive

Following this is the number indicating the pattern to which the Estonian word belongs in the index of Part II.

Finally each Estonian word is followed by a simple English gloss. Since this handbook is meant as a guide to forms and is not a substitute for a good dictionary the English glosses have been kept to the bare minimum.

In some instances two or three meanings are listed for one word if it is absolutely warranted. For example the verb **käİma** has all of the following meanings; go, walk, attend, frequent and visit listed in the following manner:

käİl $^{N\ 49B}$ *prow (ship)*
käİma $^{Vi\ 264B}$ *go, walk*
attend
frequent
visit
käİmla $^{N\ 227B}$ *toilet (outhouse)*
käİsed (pl) $^{N\ 254}$ *sleeves*

The English-Estonian glossary is set up in the same way. The English meaning is followed by the letter indicating the part of speech of the Estonian word. After this comes the Estonian word followed by number of its pattern.

aromatic ^{A} *aromaaTne* ^{247}
arrange ^{Vt} *kohendama* ^{349F}
^{Vt} *seAdma* ^{314}
arrangement ^{N} *järjestus* ^{260A}
arrest ^{Vt} *arretEErima* ^{291B}
^{Vt} *vahistama* ^{349F}
arrest ^{N} *vahistus* ^{260A}
arrival ^{N} *sAAbumine* ^{257E}

A head word is not repeated if it has more than one synonym in Estonian belonging to the same part of speech. For example **arrest** has two synonyms, **arretEErima** and **vahistama,** both of which are transitive verbs. These are listed one under the other. **Arrest** as a noun is listed as a separate word.

ABBREVIATIONS

This glossary also lists irregular or unusual forms that most dictionaries do not. This will allow the student to easily find the head word of these irregular forms. The following abbreviations are used:

gen.	genitive/stem form
ill.	illative (short **INTO** case form)
imper.	impersonal verb stem
part.	partitive form of nominal or verb (**-da** infinitive)
past	past tense form of verb
pl.	plural form
(pl)	usually used in plural
pres.	non-past (present) stem of verb

A

aabits N 231A *ABC-book*
aade N 177E *elevated idea*
AAdel N 240A *nobleman*
AAdreŞS N 58A *address*
aafriklane N 257C *African*
aaKer N 240A *acre*
AArde *gen. of aare*
aare N 211A *treasure*
AAria N 227A *aria*
AAs N 49A *meadow*
noose
AAsialane N 257C *Asian*
aaSta N 227B *year*
aaStane A 257B *year-old*
aaTom N 229A *atom*
abi N 13B *help*
abieLLuma Vi 349G *marry*
abiline N 257D *helper*
abistama Vt 349F *help*
abitu A 227A *helpless*
abiturieŋT N 58E *graduate*
ablas A 159D *voracious*
aboneŋT N 58E *subscriber*
aborT N 58E *abortion*
aborTima Vt 291F *abort*
absoluuTne A 247 *absolute*
abstraKtne A 247 *abstract*
absuRdne A 247 *absurd*
abu N 13B *waist*
adaptEErima Vt 291B *adapt*
adekvaaTne A 247 *adequate*
ader N 78B *plough*
administraaTor N 229A *administrator*
administratsiOOn N 58A *administration*
admiral N 245 *admiral*
adoptEErima Vt 291B *adopt*
adressaaT N 58E *addressee*
adressEErima Vt 291B *address*
adru N 152 *seaweed*
adveŋT N 58E *advent*
adventiSt N 58B *Adventist*
adveRb N 58B *adverb*
advokaaT N 58E *lawyer*
aEd N 90 *garden*
aEdniK N 62 *gardener*
aEg N 98 *time*
aEglane A 257C *slow*
aEglema Vi 335 *dawdle*
aEguma Vi 349G *lapse*
aEgumatu A 227A *ageless*
aEr N 61B *oar*
aerutama Vi 349F *row*

aeTa *imper. of ajama*
aevastama Vi 349F *sneeze*
aevastus N 260A *sneeze*
aferiSt N 58B *fortune-hunter*
afiŠŠ N 58C *placard*
afÄÄr N 58A *affair*
agar A 231A *eager*
agarus N 260A *eagerness*
ageŋT N 58E *agent*
agentUUr N 58A *agency*
agitaaTor N 229A *political agitator*
agitatsiOOn N 58A *agitation*
agitEErima Vt 291B *agitate*
aglutinatsiOOn N 58A *agglutination*
agOOnia N 227A *agony*
agressİİvne A 247 *aggressive*
agressiOOn N 58A *aggression*
agreSSor N 229A *aggressor*
agronOOm N 58A *agronomist*
agu N 31 *daybreak*
agul N 229A *slum*
ahas A 190 *narrow*
ahel N 231A *chain*
ahi N 74 *stove*
ahne A 177B *greedy*
ahnitsema V 349E *be greedy*
aHnus N 260B *greed*
aHta *gen. of ahas*
aHter N 240A *stern of ship*
aHv N 58B *monkey*
ahvatlema Vt 351 *entice*
ahvatlev A 231A *enticing*
ahven N 231A *perch (fish)*
aia *gen. of aEd*
aiand N 229A *garden farm*
aiandus N 260A *gardening*
aİm N 61B *inkling*
aİmama Vt 327B *have an inkling*
aine N 177B *substance*
aİneline A 257D *material*
aİnsus N 260B *singular*
ainus A 169 *sole*
aİs N 50 *shaft*
aiStima Vt 291C *sense*
aisting N 234A *sense (perception)*
aiT N 49E *storehouse*
aiTama V 327E *help*
aja *gen. of aEg*
ajalOOlane N 257C *historian*
ajalOOline A 257D *historic(al)*
ajama Vt 270 *drive*
ajastu N 227A *epoch*

ajelda *part. of aEglema*
ajend N 229A *inducement*
aJJu *ill. of aju*
aju N 13A *brain*
ajutine A 257A *temporary*
akaaTsia N 227A *acacia*
akadEEmia N 227A *academy*
akadeemik N 234A *academician*
akadeemiline A 257D *academic*
aken N 172 *window*
aklimatisEErima Vt 291B *acclimatize*
akoRd N 58B *musical chord*
akoRdion N 246 *accordion*
akrobaaT N 58E *acrobat*
akrobaatika N 227A *acrobatics*
akrobaatiline A 257D *acrobatic*
aksiOOm N 58A *axiom*
aKt N 58B *deed (document)*
nude (art)
aktİİvne A 247 *active*
aktİİvsus N 260B *activity*
aktivisEErima Vt 291B *activate*
aktiviSt N 58B *activist*
aKtsia N 227A *stock-market share*
aktuAAlne A 247 *topical*
aKtus N 260B *ceremony*
aku N 152 *car battery*
akumulaaTor N 229A *car battery*
akustika N 227A *acoustics*
akuuTne A 247 *acute*
akvAArium N 246 *aquarium*
akvalaNg N 58B *aqualung*
akvalangiSt N 58B *diver*
akvareĻL N 58A *water-colour*
ala N 14A *area*
alaline A 257D *permanent*
alam N 231A *subordinate*
alandama Vt 349F *humiliate*
alandamine N 257E *humiliation*
alandliK A 62 *humble*
alandliKKus N 260B *humility*
alanduma Vi 349H *degrade oneself*
alanema Vi 349D *decrease*
alaRm N 58B *alarm*
alarmEErima Vt 291B *alarm*
alaRmima Vt 291C *alarm*
alasi N 225A *anvil*
alata *part. of aLgama*
alatine A 257A *perpetual*
alatu A 227A *vile*
alatus N 260A *villainy*
albAAnlane N 257C *Albanian*

aLbum N 229A *album*
aļdis A 163B *prone to*
alev N 229A *town*
aLgama Vi 348B *begin*
algataja N 227A *instigator*
algatama Vt 349F *instigate*
algatus N 260A *initiative*
algebra N 227A *algebra*
aLgeline A 257D *rudimentary*
aLgus N 260B *beginning*
alimeŋdid (pl) N 58E *alimony*
alistama Vt 349F *subdue*
alistuma Vi 349H *submit (surrender)*
alistumine N 257E *submission*
alistuv A 231A *submissive*
alkeemik N 234A *alchemist*
alkohol N 245 *alcohol*
alkoholiSm N 58B *alcoholism*
alkohoolik N 234A *alcoholic*
alkohOOlne A 247 *alcoholic*
aLLahiNdlus N 260B *reduction in price*
aLLakirjutanu N 227A *undersigned*
allEE N 2 *avenue*
alleRgia N 227A *allergy*
aļlikas N 243A *source*
aLLuma Vi 349G *subordinate oneself*
allutama Vt 349F *subordinate*
aLLuv N 231A *subordinate*
aLLuvus N 260A *subordination*
almanaHH N 58A *almanac*
aļpiniSm N 58B *mountaineering*
aļpiniSt N 58B *mountaineer*
aļT N 58E *alto*
alTar N 229A *altar*
alu *pl. part. of ala*
alumÏInium N 246 *aluminium*
alumine A 257F *bottom-most*
alus N 253 *foundation*
alusetu A 227A *groundless*
alustama Vt 349F *commence*
amatÖÖr N 58A *amateur*
aMb N 122 *bow (archery)*
ambulaŋTs N 58B *dispensary*
ambulatOOrium N 246 *dispensary*
ambulatOOrne A 247 *dispensary*
aMbuma V 304 *shoot with bow*
ameeriklane N 257C *American*
amet N 229A *profession*
ametiühinglane N 257C *trade-unionist*
ametliK A 62 *official*
ametniK N 62 *official*
ametniKkoNd N 106 *staff (personnel)*
aMM N 63A *wet-nurse*
ammendama Vt 349F *exhaust*
ammendamatu A 227A *inexhaustible*
ammendav A 231A *exhaustive*
ammu *pres. of aMbuma*
ammu *gen. of aMb*
aMMuma Vi 291A *moo*
ammune A 251 *remote in time*
ammutama Vt 349F *deplete*
amneStia N 227A *amnesty*
amorAAlne A 247 *immoral*
ampuĻL N 58A *ampoule*
amputatsiOOn N 58A *amputation*
anakroniSm N 58B *anachronism*
analOOgia N 227A *analogy*
analoogiline A 257D *analogous*
analÜÜs N 58A *analysis*
ananaSS N 58A *pineapple*
anarHia N 227A *anarchy*
anarhiSm N 58B *anarchism*
anarhiSt N 58B *anarchist*
anastama Vt 349F *usurp*
anastamine N 257E *usurpation*
anatOOmia N 227A *anatomy*
anatoomiline A 257D *anatomical*
aŅd N 118 *yield*
aNde *gen. of anne*
aNdekas A 243A *talented*
aNdekus N 260A *aptitude*
andestama Vt 349F *forgive*
aNdetu A 227A *untalented*
aŅdja N 227B *giver*
aNdma Vt 317 *give*
aNdmed (pl) N 221 *data*
aNdmestiK N 62 *corpus of data*
aNduma Vi 349H *devote oneself*
aNdumus N 260A *devotion*
anekdooT N 58E *anecdote*
angerjas N 243A *eel*
angÏIn N 58A *tonsillitis*
anglitsiSm N 58B *Anglicism*
ankeeT N 58E *questionnaire*
anKur N 242A *anchor*
anna *pres. of aNdma*
anne N 214 *endowment (talent)*
annetaja N 227A *donor*
annetama Vt 349F *donate*
annetus N 260A *donation*
aŋni *gen. of aŅd*
annullEErima Vt 291B *cancel*
annus N 253 *dose*
anonÜÜmne A 247 *anonymous*
anorgaaniline A 257D *inorganic*
ansaMbel N 240A *ensemble*
antagoniSm N 58B *antagonism*
antagoniSt N 58B *antagonist*
antagoniStliK A 62 *antagonistic*
antarktiline A 257D *Antarctic*
anteŅN N 58A *antenna*
antibiootikum N 245 *antibiotic*
antifrÏIs N 58A *antifreeze*
antiiKne A 247 *antique*
antikvAAr N 58A *antiquary*
antikvariaaT N 58E *used bookshop*
antilooP N 58D *antelope*
antipaaTia N 227A *antipathy*
antipaaTne A 247 *antipathetic*
antolOOgia N 227A *anthology*
antreprenÖÖr N 58A *entrepreneur*
anum N 231A *receptacle*
anuma V 269 *implore*
aO *gen. of agu*
apaaTia N 227A *apathy*
apaaTne A 247 *apathetic*
aparaaT N 58E *apparatus*
aparatUUr N 58A *equipment*
apelsin N 245 *orange (fruit)*
aplaUs N 58B *applause*
aplikatsiOOn N 58A *appliqué*
aplitsEErima Vt 291B *appliqué*
aplodEErima Vi 291B *applaud*
aPlus N 260B *voracity*
apoliitiline A 257D *apolitical*
apoStel N 240A *apostle*
apostrooF N 58A *apostrophe*
aPPi *ill. of abi*
aprikOOs N 58A *apricot*
apriĻL N 58A *April*
aPteeK N 58F *drugstore*
aPteeKer N 240A *druggist*
ara *gen. of aRg*
arAAblane N 257C *Arab*
aRbuja N 227A *soothsayer*
aRbuma V 291C *soothsay*
arbUUs N 58A *water-melon*
arEEn N 58A *arena*
arendama Vt 349F *evolve*
arenema Vi 349D *evolve*
areng N 234A *evolution*
aretama Vt 349F *breed*
aretus N 260A *breeding*
aRg A 95A *cowardly*
argentÏInlane N 257C *Argentinean*
aRgliK A 62 *timid*

aRgliKKus N 260B *timidness*
argOO N 1 *slang*
argumeŋT N 58E *argument (reason)*
aRgus N 260B *cowardice*
arhaİline A 257D *archaic*
arhaiSm N 58B *archaism*
arheolOOg N 58A *archeologist*
arheolOOgia N 227A *archeology*
arhİIv N 58A *archives*
arhiteKt N 58B *architect*
arhitektUUr N 58A *architecture*
arhitektuuriline A 257D *architectural*
arhivAAr N 58A *archivist*
aristokraaT N 58E *aristocrat*
aristokraaTia N 227A *aristocracy*
aristokraaTliK A 62 *aristocratic*
aritmeetiline A 257D *arithmetical*
arktiline A 257D *Arctic*
aRm N 61B *mercy*
aRm N 58B *scar*
armanjaKK N 58C *Armagnac*
armas A 165B *beloved*
armastaja N 227A *lover*
armastama Vt 349F *love*
armastus N 260A *love*
armatUUr N 58A *fixture*
armEE N 2 *army*
armEEnlane N 257C *Armenian*
armetu A 227A *pitiful*
armetus N 260A *wretchedness*
aRmsam N 231A *sweetheart*
aRmsus N 260B *belovedness*
armuliK A 62 *merciful*
aRmuma Vi 349G *fall in love*
armutu A 227A *pitiless*
aromaaTne A 247 *aromatic*
arOOm N 58A *aroma*
arretEErima Vt 291B *arrest*
arseenik N 234A *arsenic*
arSt N 58B *doctor*
arStim N 229A *remedy*
arteĻL N 58A *artel*
arTer N 229A *artery*
artiSt N 58B *artiste*
artišoKK N 58C *artichoke*
aru N 13A *reason*
arukas A 243A *sensible*
arukus N 260A *common sense*
arutama Vt 349F *discuss*
arutelu N 13A *discussion*
arutlus N 260A *discussion*
aRv N 61B *number*
aRvama Vt 327B *suppose*
aRvamus N 260A *opinion*
arve N 177B *bill*
arvestama Vt 349F *consider*
arvestus N 260A *calculation*
arvukas A 243A *numerous*
arvustaja N 227A *critic*
arvustama Vt 349F *critique*
arvustus N 260A *criticism*
arvutama Vt 349F *calculate*
arvuti N 225A *computer*
arvutu A 227A *countless*
asa *gen. of aSk*
aSbeSt N 58B *asbestos*
ase N 157 *site*
asend N 229A *position*
asendaja N 227A *substitute*
asendama Vt 349F *substitute*
asendamatu A 227A *indispensable*
asetama Vt 349F *place*
asetsema Vi 349E *be located*
aSfalT N 58E *asphalt*
asfaltEErima Vt 291B *asphalt*
aSfalTima Vt 291F *asphalt*
asi N 69A *thing*
aşjaliK A 62 *businesslike*
aşjatu A 227A *futile*
aSk N 95B *sorcery*
askeeT N 58E *ascetic*
askeeTliK A 62 *ascetic*
askeldama Vi 349F *bustle*
askeldus N 260A *bustling*
aspiraŋT N 58E *post-graduate*
aspirantUUr N 58A *post-graduate course*
aspirİIn N 58A *aspirin*
assamblEE N 2 *assembly*
assisteŋT N 58E *assistant*
aste N 177B *step (pace)*
aste N 179C *step (stair)*
astel N 173B *sting*
aSter N 240A *aster*
asteriSk N 58B *asterisk*
aStma N 227B *asthma*
astmaatik N 234A *asthmatic*
aStmeline A 257D *gradual (by steps)*
astrolOOg N 58A *astrologer*
astrolOOgia N 227A *astrology*
astronauT N 58E *astronaut*
astronautika N 227A *astronautics*
astronOOm N 58A *astronomer*
astronOOmia N 227A *astronomy*
astronoomiline A 257D *astronomical*
aStuma Vi 291C *step*
asula N 227A *settlement*
asuma Vi 269 *settle*
asundus N 260A *colony*
asuniK N 62 *settler*
asustama Vt 349F *colonize*
asutaja N 227A *founder*
asutama Vt 349F *found*
asutamine N 257E *founding*
asutus N 260A *institution*
ateiSm N 58B *atheism*
ateiSt N 58B *atheist*
ateiStliK A 62 *atheistic*
ateljEE N 2 *studio*
aTlas N 260B *atlas*
atleeT N 58E *athlete*
atleetika N 227A *athletics*
atleeTliK A 62 *athletic*
atmosfÄÄr N 58A *atmosphere (air)*
atmosfääriline A 257D *atmospheric*
atraktsiOOn N 58A *attraction*
atributİIvne A 247 *attributive*
atribuuT N 58E *attribute*
aU N 12 *honour*
audienTs N 58B *audience*
auditOOrium N 246 *auditorium*
augustama Vt 349F *perforate*
auK N 61F *hole*
auKliK A 62 *full of holes*
aula N 152 *assembly hall*
aUr N 61B *steam*
aUrama Vi 327B *steam*
aurik N 234A *steamer*
aUruma Vi 349G *evaporate*
aurune A 251 *steamy*
aUs A 231B *honest*
auStaja N 227A *admirer*
auStama Vt 349F *respect*
auStav A 231A *respectful*
auSter N 240A *oyster*
austerlane N 257C *Austrian*
austrAAllane N 257C *Australian*
auStus N 260B *respect*
aUsus N 260B *honesty*
auto N 152 *automobile*
automaaT N 58E *automaton*
automaatika N 227A *automation*
automaaTne A 247 *automatic*
automatisEErima Vt 291B *automatize*
automatisEErimine N 257E *automating*
autonOOmia N 227A *autonomy*
autonOOmne A 247 *autonomous*

auTor N 229A *author*
autoritAArne A 247 *authoritarian*
autoriteeT N 58E *authority*
autoriteeTne A 247 *authoritative*
auTu A 227B *dishonourable*
ava N 13A *opening*
avaldama Vt 349F *make known*
avalduma Vi 349H *be expressed*
avaldus N 260A *declaration*
avaliK A 62 *public*
avaliKKus N 260B *public*
avama Vt 269 *open*
avanema Vi 349D *open*
avangaRd N 58B *vanguard*
avanŞS N 58G *advance-payment*
avantüriSt N 58B *adventurer*
avar A 231A *spacious*
avardama Vt 349F *broaden*
avarduma Vi 349H *broaden*
avarİI N 1 *accident*
avarus N 260A *expanse*
avastaja N 227A *discoverer*
avastama Vt 349F *discover*
avastus N 260A *discovery*
avaus N 260A *opening*
aVVa *ill. of ava*

B

bAAr N 58A *bar*
bAAş N 58A *base*
baKter N 229A *bacterium*
bakteriolOOg N 58A *bacteriologist*
balanssEErima Vt 291B *balance*
balerİIn N 58A *ballerina*
baĻL N 58A *ball (social)*
ballAAd N 58A *ballad*
balleŢT N 58C *ballet*
ballOOn N 58A *balloon*
baļTlane N 257C *Balt*
banAAn N 58A *banana*
bankeŢT N 58C *banquet*
baraKK N 58C *barracks*
barbAArne A 247 *barbaric*
baRbar N 229A *barbarian*
bareŢT N 58C *beret*
bariton N 245 *baritone*
barjÄÄr N 58A *barrier*
barrikAAd N 58A *barricade*
basEEruma Vi 349G *be based on*
baŞS N 58A *bass*
basseİn N 58B *swimming-pool*
batsiĻL N 58A *germ*
beebi N 152 *baby*
bEEž A 58A *beige*
beLglane N 257C *Belgian*
belletristika N 227A *belles-lettres*
bensİIn N 58A *gasoline*
betOOn N 58A *concrete*
bibliograaF N 58A *bibliographer*
bidEE N 2 *bidet*
biiFsteeK N 58F *beefsteak*
bilanSS N 58G *balance*
biĻjon N 229A *billion*
binoKKel N 240B *binoculars*
biograaF N 58A *biographer*
biograaFia N 227A *biography*
biolOOg N 58A *biologist*
biolOOgia N 227A *biology*
biskviiT N 58E *biscuit*
bisneSS N 58A *business*
blamEErima Vt 291B *disgrace*
blankeŢT N 58C *form (blank)*
blindAAž N 58A *dug-out*
blokAAd N 58A *blockade*
blokEErima Vt 291B *blockade*
bloKK N 58C *bloc*
bloKnooT N 58E *pad of paper*
bloNd A 58B *blonde*
blondİIn N 58A *blonde*
bluFF N 58C *bluff*
blUUs N 58A *blues (jazz)*
boA N 1 *boa*
bohEEmlane N 257C *Bohemian*
boikotEErima Vt 291B *boycott*
boikoTT N 58C *boycott*
bolİIvlane N 257C *Bolivian*
bOOl N 58A *punch (drink)*
bordeĻL N 58A *brothel*
borŠ N 58A *borscht*
botaanik N 234A *botanist*
botaanika N 227A *botany*
boţikud (pl) N 234A *overshoes*
brasİIllane N 257C *Brazilian*
briDž N 58B *bridge (card game)*
brigAAd N 58A *brigade*
brigadir N 245 *brigade-leader*
brikeŢT N 58C *briquette*
briljanT N 58E *diamond*
bronEErima Vt 291B *reserve tickets*
bronhiiT N 58E *bronchitis*
brošÜÜr N 58A *brochure*
brutAAlne A 247 *brutal*
brutAAlsus N 260B *brutality*
bruto N 152 *gross*
brüneŢT A 58C *brunette*
bukeŢT N 58C *bouquet*
buLdog N 229A *bulldog*
buldOOser N 229A *bulldozer*
bulgAArlane N 257C *Bulgarian*
burŠ N 58A *fraternity member*
buŞS N 58A *bus*
butafOOria N 227A *kitsch*
bädminton N 245 *badminton*
böfstrooganov N 245 *beef Stroganoff*
böRs N 58B *stock exchange*
büdžeTT N 58C *budget*
bülletÄÄn N 58A *bulletin*
bürokraaT N 58E *bureaucrat*
bürokraaTia N 227A *bureaucracy*
bürokraaTliK A 62 *bureaucratic*
bürokratiSm N 58B *bureaucracy*
bürOO N 1 *office*
büŞt N 58B *bust*

D

dAAm N 58A *lady*
daamiliK A 62 *lady-like*
daTTel N 240B *date fruit*
debütEErima Vi 291B *debut*
debüüT N 58E *debut*
deebet N 229A *debit*
dEEmon N 229A *demon*
defeKt N 58B *defect*
defektİIvne A 247 *defective*
defeKtne A 247 *faulty*
defilEErima Vi 291B *defile*
definEErima Vt 291B *define*

deformEErima Vt 291B *deform*

degeneraŋT N 58E *degenerate*

dekAAd N 58A *ten-day period*

dekAAn N 58A *dean*

dekadeŋT N 58E *decadent*

dekanaaT N 58E *dean's office*

deklamEErima Vt 291B *recite*

deklaratsiOOn N 58A *declaration*

deklarEErima Vt 291B *declare*

dekoltEE N 2 *décolletage*

dekoratİİvne A 247 *decorative*

dekoratsiOOn N 58A *stage set*

dekorEErima Vt 291B *decorate*

dekreeT N 58E *decree*

delegaaT N 58E *delegate*

delegatsiOON N 58A *delegation*

delfİİn N 58A *dolphin*

delikaaTne A 247 *delicate*

delikateŞS N 58A *delicacy*

demilitarisEErima Vt 291B *demilitarize*

demobilisatsiOOn N 58A *demobilization*

demobilisEErima Vt 291B *demobilize*

demokraaTia N 227A *democracy*

demokraaTliK A 62 *democratic*

demonstraŋT N 58E *demonstrator*

demonstratİİvne A 247 *demonstrative*

demonstratsiOOn N 58A *demonstration*

demonstrEErima Vt 291B *demonstrate*

demoralisEErima Vt 291B *demoralize*

depOO N 1 *depot*

deputaaT N 58E *deputy*

desarmEErima Vt 291B *disarm*

desarmEErimine N 257E *disarmament*

desertEErima Vi 291B *desert*

desertÖÖr N 58A *deserter*

desinfektsiOOn N 58A *disinfection*

desinfitsEErima Vt 291B *disinfect*

desodoraŋT N 58E *deodorant*

despooT N 58E *despot*

despooTliK A 62 *despotic*

desserT N 58E *dessert*

destillEErima Vt 291B *distil*

dešifrEErima Vt 291B *decipher*

detaİl N 58B *detail*

detaİlne A 247 *detailed*

detektİİv N 58A *detective*

detseMber N 240A *December*

diabeetik N 234A *diabetic*

diafragma N 152 *diaphragm*

diagnOOs N 58A *diagnosis*

diagonAAlne A 247 *diagonal*

diagraMM N 58A *diagram*

dialOOg N 58A *dialogue*

diametrAAlne A 247 *diametric(al)*

diapositİİv N 58A *photo slide*

didaktiline A 257D *didactic*

diEEs N 58A *sharp (music)*

dieeT N 58E *diet*

diftEEria N 227A *diphtheria*

diftoNg N 58B *diphthong*

dİİsel N 240A *diesel*

dİİvan N 229A *divan*

diktaaT N 58E *dictation*

diktaaTor N 229A *dictator*

diktaaTorliK A 62 *dictatorial*

diktatUUr N 58A *dictatorship*

diktEErima Vt 291B *dictate*

diKtor N 229A *radio, TV announcer*

diktsiOOn N 58A *diction*

diletaŋT N 58E *dilettante*

diletaŋTliK A 62 *dilettante*

diPlom N 229A *diploma*

diplomaaT N 58E *diplomat*

diplomaaTia N 227A *diplomacy*

diplomaatiline A 257D *diplomatic*

direktİİv N 58A *directive*

direKtor N 229A *director*

direktsiOOn N 58A *directorate*

dirigEErima Vt 291B *conduct*

dirigeŋT N 58E *conductor*

disaİn N 58B *design*

disaİner N 229A *designer*

diskreeTne A 247 *discreet*

diskreeTsus N 260B *discretion*

diskussiOOn N 58A *discussion*

dispaNser N 229A *dispensary*

dispeTšer N 229A *dispatcher*

dissertatsiOOn N 58A *dissertation*

dissidenT N 58E *dissident*

distsiplİİn N 58A *discipline*

distsiplinEErima Vt 291B *discipline*

diversaŋT N 58E *saboteur*

diversiOOn N 58A *sabotage*

divİİs N 58A *military division*

dogmaatiline A 257D *dogmatic*

doKK N 58C *dock*

doKtor N 229A *doctor*

doktoranT N 58E *doctoral candidate*

dokumeŋT N 58E *document*

doLLar N 229A *dollar*

dolomiiT N 58E *dolomite*

dominEErima Vt 291B *predominate*

dOOnor N 229A *donor*

dOOs N 58A *dose*

dotatsiOOn N 58A *subsidy*

dotseŋT N 58E *lecturer*

draama N 152 *drama*

dramaatiline A 257D *dramatic*

dramatisEErima Vt 291B *dramatize*

dramatiseering N 234A *dramatization*

dramatuRg N 58B *playwright*

dražEE N 2 *pill (placebo)*

drenAAž N 58A *drainage*

dreŞS N 58A *track-suit*

dressEErija N 227A *trainer of animals*

dressEErima Vt 291B *train an animal*

driĻL N 58A *drill*

driĻLima Vt 291A *drill*

džeMM N 58A *jam*

džemPer N 240A *jumper*

džentelmen N 245 *gentleman*

džiinid (pl) N 58A *jeans*

džiNN N 58A *gin*

džoki N 152 *jockey*

džuNgel N 240A *jungle*

džuudo N 152 *judo*

džäSS N 58A *jazz*

dublaŋT N 58E *understudy*

dublEErima Vt 291B *dub a film*

dueĻL N 58A *duel*

dueŢT N 58C *duet*

duŠŠ N 58C *shower bath*

dünaamika N 227A *dynamics*

dünaamiline A 257D *dynamic*

dünamiiT N 58E *dynamite*

düsentEEria N 227A *dysentery*

E

eA *gen. of iga*

eaKas A 243B *elderly*

ebalema Vi 349A *doubt*

ebalema Vi 349A *waver*

edasilüKKamatu A 227A *urgent*

edasine A 257A *further*

edel N 231A *south-west*

edendama Vt 349F *further*

edenema Vi 349D *progress*

edev A 231A *vain*
edevus N 260A *vanity*
edu N 13C *success*
edukas A 243A *successful*
edutama Vt 349F *promote*
edutamine N 257E *promotion*
edvistama Vi 349F *flirt*
EE *gen. of esi*
EElaRvamusetu A 227A *unprejudiced*
EEldama Vt 349F *assume*
EEldus N 260B *assumption*
eelis N 253 *advantage*
eelistama Vt 349F *prefer*
EElkoolieAline N 257D *pre-schooler*
EElmine A 257F *previous*
EElnema Vi 349D *precede*
EElnev A 231A *preceding*
eemaldama Vt 349F *remove*
eemaldamine N 257E *removal*
eemalduma Vi 349H *withdraw*
eemaldumine N 257E *withdrawal*
EEmaletõuKav A 231A *repulsive*
eepiline A 257D *epic*
eePos N 260B *epic*
EEsel N 240A *donkey*
EEskujuliK A 62 *exemplary*
EEsriNdliK A 62 *progressive*
eestindama Vt 349F *translate into Estonian*
eestindus N 260A *translation into Estonian*
eestistama Vt 349F *Estonianize*
eestistuma Vi 349H *Estonianize*
eeStlane N 257C *Estonian*
eeStlus N 260B *Estonian nationalism*
eeTer N 240A *ether*
eetika N 227A *ethics*
eetiline A 257D *ethical*
efeKt N 58B *effect*
efektİİvne A 247 *effective*
efektİİvsus N 260B *efficiency*
egiPtlane N 257C *Egyptian*
egoiSm N 58B *egoism*
egoiSt N 58B *egoist*
egoiStliK A 62 *egoistic(al)*
eha N 13A *sunset glow*
ehe N 211B *ornament*
ehi *pres. of eHtima*
ehitaja N 227A *builder*
ehitama Vt 349F *build*
ehitamine N 257E *building (action)*
ehitis N 260A *building (structure)*
ehitus N 260A *building (structure)*
ehmatama Vt 349F *startle*
ehmatus N 260A *scare*
eHmuma Vi 349G *be startled*
eHte *gen. of ehe*
eHtima Vt 308B *adorn*
eHtne A 249 *genuine*
eİlne A 247 *yesterday's*
eine N 177B *meal*
eine(s)tama Vi 349F *dine*
eiT N 63D *crone*
eiTama Vt 349F *deny*
eiTav A 231A *negative*
eiTus N 260B *negation*
ekrAAn N 58A *screen*
eKsam N 229A *examination*
eksaminaaTor N 229A *examiner*
eksaminEErima Vt 291B *examine*
eksemplar N 245 *copy of a book*
eKsima Vi 291C *lose one's way*
eKsimatu A 227A *infallible*
eKsimus N 260A *mistake*
eksistEErima Vi 291B *exist*
eksitama Vt 349F *mislead*
eksitus N 260A *error*
ekskavaaTor N 229A *excavator*
ekskremeŋT N 58E *excrement*
ekskursaŋT N 58E *excursionist*
ekskursiOOn N 58A *excursion*
eksliibris N 253 *ex libris*
eKsliK A 62 *erroneous*
eksmatrikulEErima Vt 291B *expel from*
eksmatrikulEEruma Vi 349G *drop out*
eksootiline A 257D *exotic*
ekspansiOOn N 58A *expansion*
ekspediiTor N 229A *forwarding agent*
ekspeditsiOOn N 58A *dispatch office*
eksperimeŋT N 58E *experiment*
eksperimentAAlne A 247 *experimental*
eKsperT N 58E *expert*
ekspluataaTor N 229A *exploiter*
ekspluatatsiOOn N 58A *exploitation*
ekspluatEErima Vt 291B *exploit*
eksponaaT N 58E *exhibit*
eksponEErima Vt 291B *exhibit*
eKsporT N 58E *export*
eksporTima Vt 291F *export*
ekspromPt N 58B *impromptu*
eksteRn N 58B *external student*
ekstraKt N 58B *extract*
eKstravaganTne A 247 *extravagant*
ekvaaTor N 229A *equator*
ekvatoriAAlne A 247 *equatorial*
elajaliK A 62 *beastly*
elajas N 243A *beast*
elama Vi 269 *live*
elamu N 227A *dwelling*
elamus N 260A *experience*
elaniK N 62 *inhabitant*
elaniKKoNd N 106 *population*
elaStne A 247 *elastic*
elaStsus N 260B *elasticity*
elatis N 260A *livelihood*
elatuma Vi 349H *subsist*
elav A 231A *lively*
eleganTne A 247 *elegant*
eleganTsus N 260B *elegance*
eleKter N 240A *electricity*
elektrifitsEErima Vt 291B *electrify*
elektrik N 234A *electrician*
elektron N 245 *electron*
elektroonika N 227A *electronics*
elemeŋT N 58E *element*
elementAArne A 247 *elementary*
elevaaTor N 229A *grain elevator*
elevaŋT N 58E *elephant*
elevus N 260A *excitement*
eliiT N 58E *elite*
eliksİİr N 58A *elixir*
elliptiline A 257D *elliptical*
eLLu *ill. of elu*
eLLujäänu N 186 *survivor*
elu N 13A *life*
eluline A 257D *vital*
elund N 229A *organ (anatomical)*
elus A 231A *living*
elustama Vt 349F *revive*
elustuma Vi 349H *revive*
elutu A 227A *lifeless*
ema N 13A *mother*
emaİl N 58B *enamel*
emaİlima Vt 291C *enamel*
emand N 231A *matron*
emane A 251 *female*
eMbama Vt 340 *embrace*
eMb-kuMb N 102 *either or*
emblEEm N 58A *emblem*
eMbus N 260B *embrace*
emigraŋT N 58E *emigrant*
emis N 253 *sow*
eMM N 63A *mommy*
emma-kumma *gen. of eMb-kuMb*
emmata *part. of eMbama*
emotsionAAlne A 247 *emotional*
enam N 231A *more*
enamiK N 62 *majority*

enamus N 260A *majority*
eNde *gen. of enne*
eŅdine A 257B *former*
energeetika N 227A *energetics*
energeetiline A 257D *energetic*
eneRgia N 227A *energy*
ennatliK A 62 *ill-advised*
enne N 214 *omen*
ennetama Vt 349F *forestall*
eņnistama Vt 349F *restore*
ennustaja N 227A *foreteller*
ennustama Vt 349F *foretell*
ennustus N 260A *forecast*
entsüklopEEdia N 227A *encyclopedia*
entusiaSm N 58B *enthusiasm*
entusiaSt N 58B *enthusiast*
entusiaStliK A 62 *enthusiastic*
epidEEmia N 227A *epidemic*
epideemiline A 257D *epidemic*
epileptik N 234A *epileptic*
epilOOg N 58A *epilogue*
episOOd N 58A *episode*
epiteeT N 58E *epithet*
epoHH N 58A *epoch*
eraeTTevõTlus N 260B *private enterprise*
erak N 234A *recluse*
erakliK A 62 *reclusive*
erakoNd N 106 *political party*
eraldama Vt 349F *separate*
eraldamine N 257E *separation*
eralduma Vi 349H *separate*
eramu N 227A *detached house*
erand N 229A *exception*
erandliK A 62 *irregular*
ere A 235 *bright*
ergas A 165C *alert*
ergutama Vt 349F *encourage*
ergutus N 260A *encouragement*
eriline A 257D *particular*
erinema Vi 349D *differ*
erinev A 231A *different*
erinevus N 260A *difference*
eristama Vt 349F *distinguish*
erK A 61F *brisk*
erutama Vt 349F *excite*
erutuma Vi 349H *become excited*
erutus N 260A *excitement*
ese N 157 *object*
esi N 46 *forefront*
esik N 234A *entrance-hall*
esimene A 257A *first*
esindaja N 227A *representative*
esindama Vt 349F *represent*
esindusliK A 62 *dignified*
esineja N 227A *performer*
esinema Vi 349D *perform*
esinemine N 257E *performance*
esitama Vt 349F *present*
esitlema Vt 351 *introduce a person*
esitus N 260A *presentation*
eskalaaTor N 229A *escalator*
eskaloPP N 58C *chop (meat), escalope*
eskimo N 227A *Eskimo*
essEE N 2 *essay*
esteeT N 58E *aesthete*
esteetika N 227A *aesthetics*
esteetiline A 257D *aesthetic*
estofİIl N 58A *Estophile*
etaPP N 58C *stage (level)*
etendama Vt 349F *perform*
etendus N 260A *performance*
etikeŢT N 58C *label*
eTlema Vi 326C *recite*
etnograaF N 58A *ethnographer*
etnograaFia N 227A *ethnography*
eTT *part. of esi*
eTTe *ill. of esi*
eTTevaaTamatu A 227A *careless*
eTTevaaTliK A 62 *careful*
eTTevaļmistamatu A 227A *unprepared*
eTTeüTleja N 227A *prompter*
eTTur N 229A *pawn*
eurooPlane N 257C *European*
evakuatsiOOn N 58A *evacuation*
evakuEErima Vt 291B *evacuate*
evangEElium N 246 *Gospel*
evangelisatsiOOn N 58A *evangelization*
evima Vt 269 *possess*
evitama Vt 349F *put to use*
evolutsiOOn N 58A *evolution*

F

faabula N 227A *fable*
fAAş N 58A *phase*
fAAsan N 229A *pheasant*
fagoŢT N 58C *bassoon*
faKt N 58B *fact*
faktiline A 257D *factual*
fakultatİIvne A 247 *optional*
fakulteeT N 58E *faculty*
familiAArne A 247 *familiar*
fanaatik N 234A *fanatic*
fanaatiline A 257D *fanatical*
fanaatilisus N 260A *fanaticism*
fanfAAr N 58A *fanfare*
fantAAsia N 227A *imagination*
fantasEErima V 291B *imagine*
fantastiline A 257D *fantastic*
faRm N 58B *farm*
farmaaTsia N 227A *pharmacology*
farmatseuT N 58E *pharmacist*
faRmer N 229A *farmer*
farSS N 58G *farce*
fassAAd N 58A *façade*
fašiSm N 58B *fascism*
fašiSt N 58B *fascist*
fatamorgaana N 152 *mirage*
favoriiT N 58E *favourite*
fenniSm N 58B *Fennicism*
fennougriSt N 58B *Finno-Ugricist*
fennougristika N 227A *Finno-Ugric studies*
fenomenAAlne A 247 *phenomenal*
feodAAl N 58A *feudal lord*
feodAAlne A 247 *feudal*
festival N 245 *festival*
fetiš N 229A *fetish*
figurEErima V 291B *figure (be present)*
figUUr N 58A *figure*
fiktİIvne A 247 *fictitious*
filatEElia N 227A *philately*
filateliSt N 58B *philatelist*
filharmOOnia N 227A *philharmonic*
filiAAl N 58A *branch office*
filigrAAn N 58A *filigree*
fiĻm N 58B *film*
fiĻmima Vt 291C *film*
filolOOg N 58A *philologist*
filolOOgia N 227A *philology*
filoloogiline A 257D *philological*
filosooF N 58A *philosopher*
filosooFia N 227A *philosophy*
filosoofiline A 257D *philosophical*
filTer N 240A *filter*
filtrEErima Vt 291B *filter*
filTrima Vt 291I *filter*
finAAl N 58A *finals in sport*
finantsEErima Vt 291B *finance*
finiš N 229A *finish in sport*
finišEErima Vi 291B *finish in sport*

firma N 152 *company*
flaneĻL N 58A *flannel*
flegmaatiline A 257D *phlegmatic*
flirT N 58E *flirtation*
flirTima Vi 291F *flirt*
floKs N 58B *phlox*
flötiSt N 58B *flautist*
flööŢ N 58E *flute*
folkloriSt N 58B *folklorist*
foNd N 58B *stock*
foneetika N 227A *phonetics*
foneetiline A 257D *phonetic*
fOOlium N 246 *foil*
fOOr N 58A *traffic light*
foreĻL N 58A *trout*
formAAlne A 247 *formal*
formAAlsus N 260B *formality*
formulEErima Vt 291B *formulate*
forssEErima Vt 291B *force*
forT N 58E *fort*
fosfaaT N 58E *phosphate*
fosforiiT N 58E *phosphorite*
foto N 152 *photo*
fotograaF N 58A *photographer*
fotograaFia N 227A *photography*
fotografEErima Vt 291B *photograph*
fototeeK N 58F *photo file*
frAAş N 58A *phrase*
fraaTer N 240A *fraternity brother*
fragmeŋT N 58E *fragment*
fraKK N 58C *tailed coat*
fraseolOOgia N 227A *phraseology*
frEEşima Vt 291A *mill*
froŋT N 58E *front*
frotEE N 2 *terry cloth*
fruKt N 58B *fruit*
fuajEE N 2 *foyer*
fundamentAAlne A 247 *fundamental*
funktsionEErima Vi 291B *function*
funktsiOOn N 58A *function*
furgOOn N 58A *van*
futurolOOgia N 227A *futurology*
föderAAlne A 247 *federal*
föderatİİvne A 247 *federative*
föderatsiOOn N 58A *federation*
föļjeton N 245 *feuilleton*
fÖÖn N 58A *hair-dryer*
füsiolOOgia N 227A *physiology*
füüsik N 234A *physicist*
füüsika N 227A *physics*
füüsiline A 257D *physical*

G

gAAş N 58A *gas*
gaİd N 58B *girl guide*
galerİİ N 1 *gallery*
galopEErima Vi 291B *gallop*
galoPP N 58C *gallop*
galoPPima Vi 291D *gallop*
ganGster N 229A *gangster*
garAAž N 58A *garage*
garantEErima Vt 291B *guarantee*
garantİİ N 1 *guarantee*
garderOOb N 58A *cloak-room*
garnEErima Vt 291B *garnish*
garnison N 245 *garrison*
garnitUUr N 58A *trimmings*
gasEErima Vt 291B *aerate*
gEEl N 58A *gel*
gEEŋ N 58A *gene*
gEEnius N 260A *genius*
geİm N 58B *game*
geİser N 240A *geyser*
generaaTor N 229A *generator*
generatsiOOn N 58A *generation*
geniAAlne A 247 *brilliant (genius)*
geograaF N 58A *geographer*
geograaFia N 227A *geography*
geolOOg N 58A *geologist*
geolOOgia N 227A *geology*
geomeeTria N 227A *geometry*
glasUUr N 58A *glaze*
glasUUrima Vt 291A *glaze*
glOObus N 260B *globe*
glütserİİn N 58A *glycerine*
goļF N 58A *golf*
goNdel N 240A *gondola*
gondoljEEr N 58A *gondolier*
goNg N 58B *gong*
gorilla N 152 *gorilla*
graafik N 234A *graphic artist*
time-table
graafika N 227A *graphic art*
graaTsia N 227A *grace*
graatsiline A 257D *graceful*
grafiiT N 58E *graphite*
graMM N 58A *gram(me)*
grammatika N 227A *grammar*
grammatiline A 257D *grammatical*
grammofon N 245 *gramophone*
granaaT N 58E *grenade*
graniiT N 58E *granite*
gravEErima Vt 291B *engrave*
gravitatsiOOn N 58A *gravitation*
gravÜÜr N 58A *engraving*
greiPfruuT N 58E *grapefruit*
griĻL N 58A *barbecue*
grimEErima Vt 291B *make up for stage*
griMM N 58A *stage make-up*
griPP N 58C *flu(e) (influenza)*
grupEErima Vt 291B *group*
gruPP N 58C *group*
grusİİnlane N 257C *Georgian*
grÖÖnlane N 257C *Greenlander*
guaŠŠ N 58C *gouache*
gurmAAn N 58A *gourmet*
gümnAAsium N 246 *secondary school*
günekolOOg N 58A *gynaecologist*

H

hAAb N 86A *aspen*
haaK N 58F *hook*
haaKima Vt 291G *hook*
hAAmer N 240A *hammer*
hAArama Vt 327A *seize*
haarang N 234A *raid*
hAArav A 231A *thrilling*
hAArde *gen. of haare*
haare N 211A *grasp*
hAAv N 49A *wound*
haava *gen. of hAAb*
hAAvama Vt 327A *wound*
haavand N 229A *ulcer*
hAAvel N 240A *pellet*
hAAvuma Vi 349G *take offence*
habe N 157 *beard*
habemiK N 62 *bearded man*
habras A 159D *fragile*

hageja N 227A *plaintiff*
hagema Vt 269 *sue*
hagu N 31 *brushwood*
haİ N 1 *shark*
haİge A 227B *sick*
haigestuma Vi 349H *sicken*
haİgla N 227B *hospital*
haİglane A 257C *sickly*
haİgus N 260B *disease*
haigutama Vi 349F *yawn*
haigutus N 260A *yawn*
haiHtuma Vi 349H *vanish*
haİs N 61B *stink*
haİsema Vi 291C *stink*
haİsev A 241A *stinking*
haiStma Vt 297A *smell*
hajuma Vi 269 *dissipate*
hajutama Vt 349F *dissipate*
haKK N 58C *jackdaw*
haKKama Vi 327C *start to do*
haKKima Vt 291D *mince*
halastama Vi 349F *have mercy on*
halastus N 260A *mercy*
haLb A 86B *nasty*
haLdama Vt 342 *administer*
haĻdjas N 243B *fairy*
haLdus N 260B *administrative area*
hale A 235 *sorrowful*
haletsema Vi 349E *bemoan*
haLg N 131B *log*
halisema Vi 349C *lament*
haļjas A 159B *verdant*
haļjendama Vi 349F *be verdant*
haLL N 49A *frost*
haĻL A 58A *grey*
haĻL N 58A *hall*
hallata *part. of haLdama*
hallelUUja N 227B *hallelujah*
haļlikas A 243A *greyish*
haļlitama Vi 349F *be mouldy*
haļlitus N 260A *mould*
haltuura N 152 *moonlighting*
halu *gen. of haLg*
halva *gen. of haLb*
halvAA N 1 *halvah*
halvatu N 227A *paralytic*
halvatus N 260A *paralysis*
halvem A 231A *worse*
halvendama Vt 349F *worsen*
halvenema Vi 349D *worsen*
haMba *gen. of hammas*
haMbuline A 257D *toothed*

hammas N 188 *tooth*
hammustama Vt 349F *bite*
hammustus N 260A *bite*
hane *gen. and part. of hani*
haNg N 63B *snowdrift*
hangeldama Vi 349F *deal in (traffic)*
hangeldamine N 257E *dealing (traffic)*
hani N 18 *goose*
hanKima Vt 291G *procure*
Hansa N 152 *Hanseatic League*
haŋT N 58E *Khanty*
haO *gen. of hagu*
hape N 177C *acid*
hapendama Vt 349F *make sour*
haPnema Vi 349D *become sour*
haPniK N 62 *oxygen*
hapu A 152 *sour*
harakas N 243A *magpie*
haRda *gen. of harras*
harF N 58A *harp*
harfiSt N 58B *harpist*
haRgnema Vi 349D *fork*
hari N 68A *brush*
ridge
haridus N 260A *education*
haridusliK A 62 *educational*
hariliK A 62 *ordinary*
harima Vt 269 *educate*
haritlane N 257C *intellectual*
haritlaskoNd N 106 *intelligentsia*
harjakas N 243A *Harjumaa native*
haRjuma Vi 349G *become accustomed to*
haRjumatu A 227A *unaccustomed*
haRjumus N 260A *habit*
haRjumusliK A 62 *habitual*
harjutama Vt 349F *practice*
harjutus N 260A *exercise*
harK N 58F *pitchfork*
harmonisEErima Vt 291B *harmonize*
harmooniline A 257D *harmonious*
harras A 193 *devout*
harrastama Vt 349F *engage in as hobby*
harrastus N 260A *hobby*
haRRu *ill. of haru*
haru N 13A *branch*
haru N 13A *department*
haruldane A 257A *uncommon*
haruldus N 260A *rarity*
harunema Vi 349D *branch off*
harutama Vt 349F *unravel*
haRv A 49B *rare*
harvendama Vt 349F *thin out*

harvenema Vi 349D *thin out*
hasarT N 58E *risk*
hašiš N 229A *hashish*
haU *pres. of haUduma*
haua *gen. of haUd*
haUd N 88A *grave*
haUdme *gen. of haue*
haUduma Vi 349H *stew*
haUduma Vt 306 *brood (hatch out)*
haue N 219B *brood*
haUg N 148 *pike*
hauKuma Vi 291G *bark*
hauTama Vt 349F *stew*
havi *gen. of haUg*
heA A 10 *good*
heAdus N 260B *goodness*
heegeldama Vt 349F *crochet*
heegeldus N 260A *crocheting*
heeringas N 243A *herring*
heide N 177E *casting*
heide N 179D *waste (material)*
heidutama Vt 349F *discourage*
heİn N 50 *hay*
heinaline N 257D *haymaker*
heisata *part. of heiSkama*
heiSkama Vt 348C *hoist*
heiTlema Vi 326E *struggle*
heiTlus N 260B *struggle*
heiTma Vt 297C *cast*
heKK N 58C *hedge*
heKtar N 229A *hectare*
heLbe *gen. of helves or helve*
heLde A 227B *generous*
heLdus N 260B *generosity*
hele A 235 *bright*
heledus N 260A *brightness*
heLge A 227B *radiant*
heli N 13A *sound*
helikoPter N 229A *helicopter*
heliline A 257D *sonant*
helin N 231A *sound of bell*
helisema Vi 349C *ring (bell)*
helistama Vi 349F *telephone*
helistama Vt 349F *ring (bell)*
helitu A 227A *soundless*
heļKima Vi 291G *shimmer*
heLL A 53A *tender*
heļlitama Vt 349F *pamper*
heļlitus N 260A *caress*
helmes N 161B *bead*
helve N 208B helves N 195 *flake*
herbAArium N 246 *herbarium*

herilane N 257C *wasp*
hermeetiline A 257D *hermetic*
hernes N 161B *pea*
heroİİn N 58A *heroin*
heroİline A 257D *heroic*
heroiSm N 58B *heroism*
hertsog N 229A *duke*
hertsoginna N 152 *duchess*
heTk N 63B *moment*
higi N 13D *sweat*
higine A 251 *sweaty*
higistama Vi 349F *sweat*
hİİd N 123A *giant*
hİİdlane N 257C *Hiiumaa native*
hiie *gen. of hİİs*
hİİglane N 257C *giant*
hİİglasliK A 62 *gigantic*
hiilata *part. of hİİlgama*
hiile N 217A *shining*
hİİlgama Vi 348A *shine*
hİİlgav A 231A *shining*
hİİlge *gen. of hiile*
hİİlgus N 260B *shine*
hİİlima Vi 291A *sneak*
hİİnlane N 257C *Chinese*
hİİr N 82 *mouse*
hiireke(ne) N 257G *mouse (diminutive)*
hİİs N 143B *sacred grove*
hiiT *part. of hİİs*
hiiu *gen. of hİİd*
hİİvama Vt 327A *heave anchor*
hiline A 251 *late*
hilinema Vi 349D *be late*
hiļjutine A 257A *recent*
himu N 13A *desire*
hiNd N 92 *price*
hiNdama Vt 343 *value*
hiNdamatu A 227A *priceless*
hiNdamine N 257E *appreciating*
hiNde *gen. of hinne*
hiNg N 63B *hinge*
soul
hiNgama Vi 327B *breathe*
hiNgamine N 257E *breathing*
hingeldama Vi 349F *pant*
hingeline A 257D *spiritual*
hingestama Vt 349F *animate*
hingetu A 227A *lifeless*
hiNgus N 260B *breath*
hinna *gen. of hiNd*
hinnaline A 257D *valuable*
hinnang N 234A *evaluation*

hinnata *part. of hiNdama*
hinne N 214 *marks at school*
hiRm N 61B *fear*
hiRmuma Vi 349G *be frightened*
hiRmus A 250A *horrible*
hirmutama Vt 349F *frighten*
hiRnuma Vi 291C *neigh*
hiRnumine N 257E *neighing*
hirSS N 58G *millet*
hiRv N 63B *deer*
hirveke(ne) N 257G *deer (diminutive)*
hispAAnlane N 257C *Spaniard*
hobi N 13B *hobby*
hobune N 251 *horse*
hoia *pres. of hoİdma*
hoiak N 234A *posture*
hoiatama Vt 349F *warn*
hoiatus N 260A *warning*
hoİd N 123B *storage*
hoidis N 253 *tinned food*
hoİdma Vt 316C *hold*
hoİduma Vi 349H *avoid*
hoiu *gen. of hoİd*
hoius N 253 *deposit in bank*
hoiustaja N 227A *depositor*
hoiustama Vt 349F *deposit in bank*
hoki N 152 *hockey*
hollandlane N 257C *Netherlander*
hommik N 234A *morning*
hoMne A 247 *tomorrow*
homonÜÜm N 58A *homonym*
honorar N 245 *honorarium*
hOO *gen. of hOOg*
hOOb N 101A *lever*
hOObama Vt 339A *lever*
hOOg N 133 *momentum*
hOOgne A 249 *brisk*
hOOl N 82 *care*
hoolas A 165A *diligent*
hOOldaja N 227A *guardian*
hOOldama Vt 349F *care of*
hOOldus N 260B *maintenance*
hooletu A 227A *careless*
hooletus N 260A *carelessness*
hooļikas A 243A *careful*
hOOļima Vi 291A *care for*
hOOļimatu A 227A *inconsiderate*
hooļitsema Vi 349E *attend to*
hOOļitsus N 260A *tending*
hoone N 177A *edifice*
hooP N 58D *blow (hit)*
hooPleja N 227A *braggart*

hooPlema Vi 326D *brag*
hOOr N 53A *whore*
hOOv N 58A *courtyard*
hoova *gen. of hOOb*
hOOvama Vi 327A *stream*
hoovata *part. of hOObama*
hOOvus N 260B *current in water*
horisoŋT N 58E *horizon*
horisontAAlne A 247 *horizontal*
horoskooP N 58D *horoscope*
hospitalisEErima Vt 291B *hospitalize*
hospitalisEErimine N 257E *hospitalization*
hoteĻL N 58A *hotel*
hubane A 251 *cosy*
hudi N 72B *cudgel*
hukatus N 260A *ruination*
hukatusliK A 62 *disastrous*
huKKama Vt 327C *execute*
huKKamine N 257E *execution*
huKKuma Vi 349G *perish*
huligAAn N 58A *hooligan*
hulK N 53F *quantity*
hulKuma Vi 291G *roam*
hulKur N 229A *vagabond*
huLL A 61A *crazy*
huLLama Vi 327A *frolic*
humAAnsus N 260B *humaneness*
humal N 231A *hop in beer making*
humaniSm N 58B *humanism*
humaniSt N 58B *humanist*
humanitAArne A 247 *humanitarian*
humoorikas A 243A *humorous*
huŋnik N 234A *pile*
huŋT N 58E *wolf*
huRmav A 231A *charming*
hurT N 53E *greyhound*
hurtsik N 234A *hut*
huua *gen. of hUUg*
hUUg N 108 *droning*
hUUl N 82 *lip*
hUUmor N 229A *humour*
huve *pl. part. of huvi*
huvi N 17 *interest*
huvitama Vt 349F *interest*
huvitav A 231A *interesting*
huvituma Vi 349H *become interested in*
hõbe N 235 *silver*
hõiKama V 327F *shout*
hõİm N 61B *tribe*
hõisata *part. of hõiSkama*
hõise N 217C *shout*
hõiSkama Vi 348C *cheer*

hõiSke *gen. of hõise*
hõİvama Vt 327B *occupy*
hõlbus A 168B *easy*
hõĻjuma Vi 291C *hover*
hõLm N 49B *tail of coat, dress*
hõLmama Vt 327B *comprise*
hõlPus A 250A *easy*
hõre A 235 *sparse*
hõrendama Vt 349F *make sparse*
hõrenema Vi 349D *become sparse*
hõrgutis N 260A *delicacy*
hÕÕguma Vi 349G *glow*
hÕÕgus N 260B *glow*
hÕÕguv A 231A *glowing*
hÕÕrduma Vi 349H *rub*
hÕÕruma Vt 291A *rub*
hÕÕrumine N 257E *friction*
häbe N 157 *vulva*
häbeliK A 62 *shy*
häbeliKKus N 260B *shyness*
häbematu A 227A *impudent*
häbematus N 260A *impudence*
häbemed (pl) N 157 *female genitals*
häbenema Vi 349D *be ashamed*
häbi N 13B *shame*
häbistama Vt 349F *shame*
häbistav A 231A *shameful*
häbitu A 227A *shameless*
häda N 13C *trouble*
hädaldama Vi 349F *fuss*
häİd *part. pl. of heA and hÄÄ*
häire N 177B *disturbance*
häİrima Vt 291C *disturb*
häĻbima Vi 303 *deviate*
häĻL N 58A *cradle*
häļvi *pres. of häĻbima*
hämar A 231A *dusky*
hämarduma Vi 349H *become dusky*
hämariK N 62 *dusk*
hämmastama Vt 349F *astonish*
hämmastav A 231A *astonishing*
hämmastuma Vi 349H *be astonished*
hämmastus N 260A *astonishment*
hämmeldama Vt 349F *bewilder*
hämmeldus N 260A *bewilderment*
häNd N 106 *tail*
hänna *gen. of häNd*
häRda *gen. of härras*
häRg N 112 *ox*
härja *gen. of häRg*
härra N 152 *gentleman*
härras A 193 *woeful*
härrased (pl) N 253 *gentry*
häTTa *ill. of häda*
hävima Vi 269 *perish*
häving N 234A *destruction*
hävitaja N 227A *destroyer*
hävitama Vt 349F *destroy*
hävitav A 231A *destructive*
hävitus N 260A *destruction*
hÄÄ A 10 *good*
hÄÄl N 82 *voice*
hÄÄldama Vt 349F *pronounce*
hÄÄldamine N 257E *pronunciation*
häälestaja N 227A *tuner*
häälestama Vt 349F *tune*
hääletaja N 227A *voter*
hääletama V 349F *vote*
hääletama V 349F *hitch-hike*
hääletamine N 257E *voting*
hääletus N 260A *voting*
häälik N 234A *sound (language)*
häälitsema Vi 349E *make sounds*
hÄÄrber N 229A *manor house*
hÖÖvel N 240A *plane*
hööveldama Vt 349F *plane*
hüdrauliline A 257D *hydraulic*
hügiEEn N 58A *hygiene*
hügieeniline A 257D *hygienic*
hüLgama Vt 346 *abandon*
hüĻge *gen. of hüļjes*
hüļjata *part. of hüLgama*
hüļjes N 197 *seal (animal)*
hüMn N 58B *anthem*
hüpe N 177C *jump*
hüpitama Vt 349F *dandle*
hüPlema Vi 326C *jump about*
hüpnOOs N 58A *hypnosis*
hüpnotisEErima Vt 291B *hypnotize*
hüpoteeK N 58F *mortgage*
hüPPama Vi 327C *jump*
hüsteerika N 227A *hysterics*
hüsteeriline A 257D *hysterical*
hüŢT N 58C *hut*
hüvang N 234A *well-being*
hüve N 153 *advantage*
hüvitama Vt 349F *compensate*
hüvitus N 260A *compensation*
hüÄÄn N 58A *hyena*
hüüa *pres. of hÜÜdma*
hüüatama Vi 349F *cry out*
hÜÜbima Vi 349B *coagulate*
hÜÜd N 123A *exclamation*
hÜÜde *gen. of hüüe*
hÜÜdma V 316B *call out*
hüüe N 210C *call*
hüüu *gen. of hÜÜd*

I

ida N 13C *east*
idanema Vi 349D *germinate*
idanemine N 257E *germination*
ideAAl N 58A *ideal*
ideAAlne A 247 *ideal*
idealisEErima Vt 291B *idealize*
idealiSm N 58B *idealism*
idealiSt N 58B *idealist*
idealiStliK A 62 *idealistic*
idEE N 2 *idea*
identifitsEErima Vt 291B *identify*
identifitsEErimine N 257E *identification*
ideolOOgia N 227A *ideology*
idiomaatiline A 257D *idiomatic*
idiOOm N 58A *idiom*
idiooT N 58E *idiot*
idiooTliK A 62 *idiotic*
idu N 13C *sprout*
idüĻL N 58A *idyll*
idüļliline A 257D *idyllic*
iga A 13D *every*
iga N 30 *age*
igand N 229A *relic*
iganema Vi 349D *become obsolete*
igatsema Vt 349E *yearn*
igatsus N 260A *yearning*
igav A 231A *boring*
igavene A 257A *eternal*
igaviK N 62 *eternity*
igavus N 260A *boredom*
ige N 157 *gum (teeth)*
igihali N 69A *evergreen*
ignorEErima Vt 291B *ignore*
iha N 13A *lust*
ihaldama Vt 349F *crave*
ihalema Vt 349A *covet*
iHHu *ill. of ihu*
ihne A 177B *stingy*
iHnsus N 260B *stinginess*

iHnur N 229A *miser*
ihnus A 168A *miserly*
iHnus N 260B *miserliness*
ihu N 13A *body (flesh)*
ihuma Vt 269 *whet*
İİbe *gen. of iive*
iiris N 253 *iris*
İİrlane N 257C *Irish*
iive N 208A *population growth*
iiveldama Vi 349F *be nauseous*
iiveldus N 260A *nausea*
ikaldus N 260A *crop failure*
ike N 177C *yoke*
iKKa *ill. of iga*
ikOOn N 58A *icon*
ila N 13A *saliva*
iLge A 227B *loathsome*
illegAAlne A 247 *illegal*
illuminatsiOOn N 58A *illumination*
illusiOOn N 58A *illusion*
illustratsiOOn N 58A *illustration*
illustrEErima Vt 291B *illustrate*
iLm N 49B *weather*
ilmaliK A 62 *secular*
ilmastiK N 62 *climate*
ilme N 177B *facial expression*
iLmekas A 243A *expressive*
ilmetu A 227A *expressionless*
iLmne A 247 *evident*
iLmnema Vi 349D *become evident*
iLmuma Vi 349G *appear*
iLmumine N 257E *appearing*
ilmutama Vt 349F *develop film*
ilmuti N 225A *developer for film*
ilu N 13A *beauty*
iludus N 260A *beautiful person*
ilus A 231A *beautiful*
ilustama Vt 349F *beautify*
ilutu A 227A *plain*
ilves N 253 *lynx*
imal A 231A *insipid*
imama Vt 269 *absorb*
iMb N 138 *maiden*
iMbuma Vi 349G *soak in*
ime N 153 *miracle*
imeliK A 62 *strange*
imema Vt 269 *suck*
imestama V 349F *wonder at*
imestus N 260A *wonder*
imetaja N 227A *mammal*
imetama Vt 349F *suckle*
imetlema Vt 351 *admire*
imetlus N 260A *admiration*
imik N 234A *baby*
imitatsiOOn N 58A *imitation*
imitEErima Vt 291B *imitate*
imme *gen. of iMb*
immigraŋT N 58E *immigrant*
immitsema Vi 349E *ooze*
immUUnne A 247 *immune*
impEErium N 246 *empire*
imperialiSm N 58B *imperialism*
imperialiSt N 58B *imperialist*
imperialiStliK A 62 *imperialistic*
impersonAAlne A 247 *impersonal*
imponEErima Vt 291B *impress*
imPorT N 58E *import*
imporTima Vt 291F *import*
improvisEErima Vt 291B *improvise*
impulsİİvne A 247 *impulsive*
iNd N 129 *enthusiasm*
indeks N 229A *index*
individuAAlne A 247 *individual*
indonEEslane N 257C *Indonesian*
industriAAlne A 247 *industrial*
industrialisEErima Vt 291B *industrialize*
inerTs N 58B *inertia*
inetu A 227A *ugly*
inetus N 260A *ugliness*
infarKt N 58B *heart attack*
infektsiOOn N 58A *infection*
inflatsiOOn N 58A *inflation*
influentsa N 152 *influenza*
informatsiOOn N 58A *information*
informEErima Vt 291B *inform*
iNgel N 240A *angel*
iNgerlane N 257C *Ingrian*
iNglane N 257C *English*
iNgver N 229A *ginger*
inimene N 257A *human being*
inimkoNd N 106 *humanity*
inimliK A 62 *humane*
initsiAAl N 58A *initial*
initsiaaTor N 229A *initiator*
inkvisitsiOOn N 58A *inquisition*
innu *gen. of iNd*
innukas A 243A *fervent*
innukus N 260A *fervency*
innustama Vt 349F *fill with fervour*
innustus N 260A *filling with fervour*
insener N 245 *engineer*
inspeKtor N 229A *inspector*
inspektsiOOn N 58A *inspection*
inspiratsiOOn N 58A *inspiration*
inspirEErima Vt 291B *inspire*
inspitsieŋT N 58E *stage manager*
instanTs N 58B *instance*
instinKt N 58B *instinct*
instinktİİvne A 247 *instinctive*
instituuT N 58E *institute*
instruEErima Vt 291B *instruct*
instruKtor N 229A *instructor*
instruktsiOOn N 58A *instruction*
instrumeŋT N 58E *instrument*
insulİİn N 58A *insulin*
insuļT N 58E *stroke (brain)*
intelleKt N 58B *intellect*
intellektuAAlne A 247 *intellectual*
inteļligenTne A 247 *intelligent*
inteļligenTs N 58B *intelligentsia*
inteļligenTsus N 260B *intelligence*
intensİİvne A 247 *intensive*
intensİİvsus N 260B *intensity*
internaaT N 58E *hostel*
internEErima Vt 291B *intern*
internEErimine N 257E *internment*
interneeritu N 227A *internee*
intervjuEErija N 227A *interviewer*
intervjuEErima Vt 291B *interview*
intervjUU N 1 *interview*
intİİmne A 247 *intimate*
intİİmsus N 260B *intimacy*
intonatsiOOn N 58A *intonation*
intrigEErima Vi 291B *intrigue*
intrİİg N 58A *intrigue*
invalİİd N 58A *invalid*
invalİİdsus N 260B *invalidism*
invasiOOn N 58A *invasion*
inventar N 245 *inventory*
inventUUr N 58A *make inventory*
inversiOOn N 58A *inversion*
irAAnlane N 257C *Iranian*
ironisEErima Vi 291B *be sarcastic*
irOOnia N 227A *irony*
irooniline A 257D *ironic(al)*
irvitama Vi 349F *sneer*
irvitus N 260A *sneer*
isa N 13A *father*
isaliK A 62 *fatherly*
isamAAliK A 62 *patriotic*
isand N 231A *lord (master)*
isane A 251 *male*
isekas A 243A *selfish*
isekus N 260A *selfishness*
iseloomustus N 260A *characterization*
isemajandav A 231A *self-supporting*

iseseİsvus [N 260B] *independence*
iseteAdev [A 241A] *self-confident*
iseärasus [N 260A] *peculiarity*
isik [N 234A] *person*
isikliK [A 62] *personal*
isiksus [N 260A] *personality*
iSlandlane [N 257C] *İcelander*
isolaaTor [N 229A] *insulator*
isolatsiOOn [N 58A] *insulation*
isolEErima [Vt 291B] *insulate*
İSSand [N 231A] *Lord (God)*
istandus [N 260A] *plantation*
iste [N 179C] *seat*
iStuma [Vi 291C] *sit down*
be sitting
istung [N 229A] *session*
istutama [Vt 349F] *plant*
isu [N 13A] *appetite*
isur [N 229A] *Izhorian*
itAAllane [N 257C] *Italian*
iTk [N 61B] *lamentation*
iţsitama [Vi 349F] *giggle*
iTTa *ill. of ida*
iva [N 13A] *grain*

J

jaaguar [N 246] *jaguar*
jAAm [N 49A] *station*
jaanuar [N 246] *January*
jaaPanlane [N 257C] *Japanese*
jaaTama [V 349F] *affirm*
jaaTav [A 231A] *affirmative*
jaaTus [N 260B] *affirmation*
jagama [Vt 269] *divide*
jagamatu [A 227A] *indivisible*
jagamine [N 257E] *division*
jagatav [A 231A] *divisible*
jagatis [N 260A] *quotient*
jagu [N 31] *share*
jaguma [Vi 269] *be divisible*
jagunema [Vi 349D] *be divided*
jahe [A 235] *cool*
jahedus [N 260A] *coolness*
jahenema [Vi 349D] *become cool*
jahi *gen. of jaHt*
jahmatama [Vt 349F] *dismay*
jahmatus [N 260A] *dismay*
jaHmuma [Vi 349G] *be dismayed*
jaHt [N 116] *hunt*
yacht
jaHtuma [Vi 349H] *cool off*
jahu [N 13A] *flour*
jahune [A 251] *floury*
jahutama [Vt 349F] *cool off*
jahvatama [Vt 349F] *grind*
jaKK [N 58C] *jacket*
jala *gen. of jaLg*
jalakas [N 243A] *elm*
jalas [N 253] *runner (sled)*
jalatsid (pl) [N 229A] *footwear*
jaLg [N 100] *foot*
leg
jalus [N 253] *stirrup*
jalutama [Vi 349F] *stroll*
jaluts [N 229A] *foot of bed*
jama [N 13A] *nonsense*
janu [N 13A] *thirst*
janunema [Vi 349D] *be thirsty*
jaO *gen. of jagu*
jaOskoNd [N 106] *district*
jaoTama [Vt 349F] *distribute*
jaoTus [N 260B] *distribution*
jasmİİn [N 58A] *jasmine*
jaUram [N 229A] *twaddler*
joA *gen. of juga*
joN̦N [N 58A] *stubbornness*
joņnakas [A 243A] *stubborn*
joN̦Nima [Vi 291A] *sulk*
jOObnu [N 227B] *drunk*
joobnustama [Vt 349F] *intoxicate*
jOObuma [Vi 349G] *become drunk*
jOObunu [N 227A] *drunk*
jOOḑ [N 58A] *iodine*
jOOdav [A 231A] *drinkable*
jooḑik [N 234A] *drunkard*
jooK [N 58F] *drink*
jooKs [N 61B] *run*
jooKsev [A 241A] *running*
jooksik [N 234A] *fugitive*
jooKsma [Vi 302] *run*
jooKsva [N 227B] *rheumatism*
jOOma [Vt 267] *drink*
jOOmar [N 229A] *drunkard*
jooming [N 234A] *drinking party*
jOOn [N 82] *line*
jOOnduma [Vi 349H] *align oneself*
jooneline [A 257D] *lined*
joonestaja [N 227A] *draftsperson*
joonestama [Vt 349F] *draw (draft)*
joonestamine [N 257E] *drafting*
jooniline [A 257D] *lined*
joonis [N 253] *drawing (result)*
joonistaja [N 227A] *drawer (person)*
joonistama [Vt 349F] *draw a picture*
joonistamine [N 257E] *drawing (action)*
joonistus [N 260A] *drawing (result)*
jooSta *part. of jooKsma*
jooTma [Vt 297C] *water animal*
joovastama [Vt 349F] *intoxicate*
joovastav [A 231A] *intoxicating*
joovastuma [Vi 349H] *become intoxicated*
joovastus [N 260A] *intoxication*
jope [N 152] *jacket*
joRjen [N 229A] *dahlia*
jorutama [Vi 349F] *loll while droning*
jube [A 235] *ghastly*
judin [N 231A] *shudder*
juga [N 39] *cascade*
juge *pl. part. of juga*
juhataja [N 227A] *manager*
juhatama [Vt 349F] *direct*
lead
juhatus [N 260A] *management*
juhe [N 220] *conducting wire*
juhend [N 229A] *instruction*
juhendaja [N 227A] *adviser*
juhendama [Vt 349F] *advise*
juhi *gen. of juHt [N 116]*
juhi *pres. of juHtima*
juhis [N 253] *instruction*
juHm [A 58B] *doltish*
juHt [N 124B] *instance*
juHt [N 116] *leader*
juHtima [Vt 308B] *lead*
juHtimine [N 257E] *leadership*
juHtkoNd [N 106] *management*
juHtme *gen. of juhe*
juHtum [N 229A] *incident*
juHtuma [Vi 349H] *happen*
juHtumus [N 260A] *occurrence*
juhu *gen. of juHt [N 124B]*
juhus [N 253] *opportunity*
juhusliK [A 62] *incidental*
juLge [A 227B] *bold*
juLgema [Vt 350] *dare*
juLgus [N 260B] *boldness*
julgustama [Vt 349F] *encourage*
julgustus [N 260A] *encouragement*
julK [N 53F] *turd*

juLm A 53B *cruel*
juLmus N 260B *cruelty*
julTumus N 260A *insolence*
Jumal N 231A *God*
jumaldama Vt 349F *adore*
jumaliK A 62 *divine*
jume N 153 *complexion*
juŅN N 58A *turd*
juPP N 58C *stub*
juriidiline A 257D *juridical*
juriSt N 58B *jurist*
juTlus N 260B *sermon*
jutlustaja N 227A *preacher*
jutlustama Vi 349F *preach*
juTT N 61C *story*
juŢT N 58C *streak*
jutukas A 243A *talkative*
jutustaja N 227A *narrator*
jutustama Vt 349F *narrate a story*
jutustav A 231A *narrative*
jutustus N 260A *narrative*
jUUa *part. of jOOma*
jUUbel N 229A *jubilee anniversary*
juubeldama Vi 349F *rejoice*
juubeldus N 260A *rejoicing*
juubilar N 245 *jubilarian*
juuKsed (pl) N 256 *hair (human head)*
juuKsur N 229A *hairdresser*
juuli N 152 *July*
juuni N 152 *June*
jUUr N 82 *root*
juura N 152 *jurisprudence*
jUUrdlema Vt 331A *investigate*
jUUrdlus N 260B *investigation*
jUUrduma Vi 349H *take root*
juurelda *part. of jUUrdlema*
juuretis N 260A *leaven*
jUUrima Vt 291A *uproot*
juurutama Vt 349F *inculcate*
juuSt N 61B *cheese*
juuŢ N 58E *Jew*
juvEEl N 58A *jewel*
juvelİİr N 58A *jeweller*
jõE *gen. of jõgi*
jõge *part. of jõgi*
jõgi N 42 *river*
jõgikoNd N 106 *river system*
jõHker A 241A *brutal*
jõHkrus N 260B *brutality*
jõHv N 58B *horsehair*
jõhvikas N 243A *cranberry*
jõİ *past of jOOma*
jõKKe *ill. of jõgi*
jõļlitama Vt 349F *goggle*
jõmpsikas N 243A *urchin*
jõU *gen. of jõUd*
jõua *pres. of jõUdma*
jõUd N 127 *strength*
jõUdma V 316A *manage to do*
jõuetu A 227A *powerless*
jõuK N 61F *gang*
jõuKas A 243B *prosperous*
jõuKus N 260B *prosperity*
jõUline A 257D *robust*
jõulud (pl) N 61B *Christmas*
jõuStuma Vi 349H *come into force*
jäeTa *imper. of jäTma*
jähe *ill. of jÄÄ*
jäİ *past of jÄÄma*
jäiK A 49F *stark*
jäiKus N 260B *starkness*
jäİne A 252 *icy*
jäle A 235 *disgusting*
jäĻg N 141 *track*
jäĻgima Vt 349B *follow*
jälitama Vt 349F *pursue*
jäļje *gen. of jäĻg*
jäļjendama Vt 349F *copy*
jäļjetu A 227A *traceless*
jäļK A 58F *repulsive*
jäme A 235 *thick*
jämedus N 260A *thickness*
jänes N 253 *hare*
jänki N 152 *Yankee*
jäņku N 152 *bunny*
järeldama Vt 349F *conclude*
järelduma Vi 349H *be inferred*
järeldus N 260A *conclusion*
järelejäTmatu A 227A *incessant*
jäRg N 120A *footstool*
jäRg N 141 *sequel*
jäRgima Vt 349B *conform to*
jäRglane N 257C *successor*
jäRgmine A 257F *next*
jäRgnema Vi 349D *ensue*
jäRgnev A 231A *subsequent*
järguline A 257D *phasic*
järi *gen. of jäRg N 120A*
järje *gen. of jäRg N 141*
järjestama Vt 349F *arrange in order*
järjestiK N 62 *succession of order*
järjestus N 260A *arrangement*
järK N 61F *phase*
järSk A 131C *steep*
järSkus N 260B *steepness*
järsu *gen. of järSk*
jäRv N 63B *lake*
järvakas N 243A *Järvamaa native*
järvalane N 257C *Järvamaa native*
järvestiK N 62 *lake system*
jäse N 157 *limb*
jäTk N 61B *extension*
jäTkama Vt 327B *continue*
jäTkuma Vi 349G *last*
jäTma Vt 300 *leave behind*
jÄÄ N 4 *ice*
jÄÄdav A 231A *permanent*
jäädvustama Vt 349F *record*
jääK N 58F *residue*
jÄÄma Vi 266 *remain*
become
jäänu N 186 *survivor*
jäänus N 253 *remains*
jÄÄpurikas N 243A *icicle*
jÄÄr N 53A *ram*
jääTis N 260B *ice-cream*
jääTmed (pl) N 179D *refuse*
jääTuma Vi 349H *freeze over*
jÄÄv A 231B *constant*
jüNger N 240A *disciple*

K

kaabakas N 243A *scoundrel*
kAAbel N 240A *cable*
kaabu (man's) N 152 *hat*
kAAder N 240A *personnel*
kaagutama Vi 349F *cackle*
kAAl N 61A *weight*
kaaļikas N 243A *turnip*
kaalud (pl) N 61A *scales (weight)*
kaalukas A 243A *weighty*
kAAluma Vt 291A *weigh*
kaalutlema Vt 351 *ponder*
kaalutlus N 260A *consideration*
kaalutu A 227A *weightless*
kAAluv A 231A *weighty*
kAAmel N 229A *camel*

kaamera N 227A *movie camera*
kAAŋ N 58A *leech*
kaane *gen. of kAAş*
kaanT *part. of kAAş*
kaaPima Vt 291E *scrape*
kAAr N 82 *arc*
kaardistama Vt 349F *map*
kAAren N 241A *raven*
kaarik N 234A *cart*
kaarT N 58E *card*
kaarutama Vt 349F *turn over*
kAAş N 146 *lid*
kaasa N 152 *companion*
kaasik N 234A *birch grove*
kaasitaja N 227A *singer at wedding*
kAAslane N 257C *companion*
satellite
kAAsnema Vi 349D *be concurrent*
kaaTer N 240A *hangover*
launch
kabarEE N 2 *cabaret*
kabe N 153 *checkers*
kabel N 229A *chapel*
kabi N 68B *hoof*
kabİIn N 58A *cabin*
kabineŢ N 58H *study*
kabli N 152 *hoe*
kablima Vt 269 *hoe*
kadakas N 243A *juniper*
kade A 235 *envious*
kadedus N 260A *envy*
kadestama Vt 349F *envy*
kadeŢT N 58C *cadet*
kadu N 27 *loss*
kaduma Vi 280 *get lost*
kadunu N 227A *deceased*
kaE N 1 *cataract (eye)*
kaEbaja N 227A *complainant*
kaEbama V 339B *complain*
kaEblema Vi 328 *bewail*
kaEbliK A 62 *plaintive*
kaEbus N 260B *grievance*
kaEl N 49B *neck*
kaElkirjak N 234A *giraffe*
kaelus N 253 *collar*
kaelustama Vt 349F *hug*
kaEma Vt 262 *behold*
kaenal N 170B *underarm*
kaEr N 50 *oat*
kaeTa *imper. of kaTma*
kaEv N 61B *well*
kaEvama Vt 327B *dig*
kaevandama Vt 349F *mine*
kaevandus N 260A *mine*
kaevata *part. of kaEbama*
kaevelda *part. of kaEblema*
kaevik N 234A *trench*
kaEvur N 229A *miner*
kagu N 13D *south-east*
kahandama Vt 349F *diminish*
kahandus N 260A *diminution*
kahanema Vi 349D *diminish*
kahe *gen. of kaKs*
kaheksa N 227A *eight*
kaheksandiK N 62 *eighth*
kaheksas A 237B *eighth*
kahelda *part. of kaHtlema*
kahemõTTeline A 257D *ambiguous*
kahemõTTelisus N 260A *ambiguity*
kahetsema Vt 349E *regret*
kahetsus N 260A *regret*
kaHHel N 240B *glazed tile*
kahi N 74 *damage*
kahin N 231A *rustle*
kahisema Vi 349C *rustle*
kahistama Vt 349F *rustle*
kahju N 152 *harm*
kahjuliK A 62 *harmful*
kaHjum N 229A *loss*
kaHjur N 229A *pest*
kahjustama Vt 349F *harm*
kahjustus N 260A *injury*
kahjutu A 227A *harmless*
kaHlama Vi 327B *wade*
kaHmama Vt 327B *grab*
kaHt(e) *part. of kaKs*
kaHtlane A 257C *dubious*
kaHtleja N 227A *sceptic*
kaHtlema Vt 331B *doubt*
kaHtlus N 260B *doubt*
kahtlustama Vt 349F *suspect*
kahtlustus N 260A *suspicion*
kahur N 229A *cannon*
kahvatu A 227A *pale*
kahvatuma Vi 349H *turn pale*
kahvatus N 260A *pallor*
kaHvel N 240A *fork*
kaİ N 1 *quay*
kaigas N 159E *stick*
kaine A 177B *sober*
kainestuma Vi 349H *sober up*
kaiSS N 61G *bosom*
kaisutama Vt 349F *embrace*
kaisutus N 260A *embrace*
kaitse N 177B *defence (shelter)*
kaitse N 179C *defence (device)*
kaiTsema Vt 295 *defend*
kaiTsetu A 227A *defenceless*
kaiTsja N 227B *defender*
kaiTsma Vt 295 *defend*
kaja N 13A *echo*
kajakas N 243A *sea-gull*
kajama Vi 269 *resound*
kajastama Vt 349F *express*
kajastuma Vi 349H *be expressed*
kajut N 229A *cabin in ship*
kakadUU N 1 *cockatoo*
kakaO N 1 *cocoa*
kaker N 174 *present from guest*
kaKKu *ill. of kagu*
kaKlema Vi 326C *fight*
kaKlus N 260B *fight*
kaKs N 149 *two*
kaksik N 234A *twin*
kaKtus N 260B *cactus*
kala N 14A *fish*
kalandus N 260A *fishing industry*
kalastama V 349F *fish*
kalastus N 260A *fishing*
kalavinSkid (pl) N 225B *waterproof boots*
kaLda *gen. of kallas*
kaLduma Vi 349H *be inclined*
kaLduvus N 260A *inclination*
kaleNder N 240A *calendar*
kalev N 229A *broadcloth*
kali N 69A *light ale*
kalİIber N 240A *calibre*
kaļju N 152 *cliff*
kaļjune A 251 *craggy*
kaļK A 58F *hard-hearted*
kaļka N 152 *tracing paper*
kalkulaaTor N 229A *calculator*
kalkulatsiOON N 58A *calculation*
kalkulEErima Vt 291B *calculate*
kalKun N 229A *turkey*
kalla N 152 *calla lily*
kallak N 234A *slope*
kaLLama Vt 327A *pour*
kallas N 191 *shore*
kalligraaFia N 227A *calligraphy*
kaĻLim A 231A *darling*
kaļlinema Vi 349D *become expensive*
kaļlis A 164A *dear*
kaļlistama Vt 349F *caress*
kaLLur N 229A *dumper*
kallutama Vt 349F *tilt*

kaLm N 61B *grave*
kalmAAr N 58A *squid*
kaļmistu N 227A *graveyard*
kalor N 229A *calorie*
kalTs N 61B *rag*
kaļTsium N 246 *calcium*
kalu *pl. part. of kala*
kalur N 229A *fisherman*
kama N 13A *sour milk grain mix*
kamar N 231A *rind of meat*
kaMber N 240A *chamber*
kamin N 231A *fireplace*
kaMM N 58A *comb*
kaMMima Vt 291A *comb*
kammits N 231A *fetter*
kammitsema Vt 349E *fetter*
kamP N 49D *gang*
kampAAnia N 227A *campaign*
kamPer N 240A *camphor*
kamPsun N 229A *cardigan*
kana N 14A *hen*
kanadalane N 257C *Canadian*
kanal N 229A *canal*
kanala N 227A *hen-house*
kanalisatsiOOn N 58A *sewerage*
kanalisEErima Vt 291B *sewer*
kanarbiK N 62 *heather*
kaNd N 92 *heel*
kaNde *gen. of kanne*
kaŋdidatUUr N 58A *candidacy*
kaŋdidEErima Vi 291B *be a candidate*
kaŋdik N 234A *tray*
kaŋditaaT N 58E *candidate*
kaN̦dja N 227B *carrier*
kaNdle *gen. of kannel*
kaNdma Vt 317 *carry*
kaNduma Vi 349H *be carried over*
kanEEl N 58A *cinnamon*
kanep N 229A *hemp*
kaNg N 58B *archway*
crow-bar
kangas N 159B *woven material*
kaNge A 227B *stiff*
kaNgekaElne A 247 *obstinate*
kaNgekaElsus N 260B *obstinacy*
kaNgelane N 257C *hero*
kaNgelasliK A 62 *heroic*
kaNgelasliKKus N 260B *heroism*
kaNgur N 242A *weaver*
kaNgus N 260B *stiffness*
kangutama Vt 349F *wrench*
kaNN N 61A *jug*

kaN̦N N 58A *toy*
kanna *gen. of kaNd*
kanna *pres. of kaNdma*
kannataja N 227A *sufferer*
kannatama V 349F *suffer*
kannatamatu A 227A *impatient*
kannatamatus N 260A *impatience*
kannatliK A 62 *patient*
kannatliKKus N 260B *patience*
kannatus N 260A *patience*
kanne N 214 *carrying*
kannel N 205 *zither*
kaŋnikad (pl) N 243A *buttocks*
kaŋnike(ne) N 257G *violet (flower)*
kannus N 253 *spur*
kaŋT N 58E *region*
kantaaT N 58E *cantata*
kanTav A 231A *portable*
kaŋTs N 58B *stronghold*
kanTsel N 240A *pulpit*
kantseleİ N 1 *office*
kanTsler N 229A *chancellor*
kanu *pl. part. of kana*
kanUU N 1 *canoe*
kanvAA N 1 *canvas*
kaO *pres. of kaduma*
kaO *gen. of kadu*
kAos N 253 *chaos*
kaoTaja N 227A *loser*
kaoTama Vt 349F *lose*
kaoTus N 260B *loss*
kapitAAlne A 247 *capital*
kapital N 245 *capital*
kapitulatsiOOn N 58A *capitulation*
kapitulEEruma Vi 349G *capitulate*
kaPP N 58C *cupboard*
kaPP N 49C *wooden drinking mug*
kaPral N 229A *corporal*
kaprİİs N 58A *caprice*
kaprİİsne A 248 *capricious*
kaPron N 229A *kapron*
kapsas N 159B *cabbage*
kaPten N 229A *captain*
kapuuTs N 58B *hood*
karahvin N 245 *carafe*
karaKter N 229A *character*
karameL̦L N 58A *candy*
karantİİn N 58A *quarantine*
karastama Vt 349F *refresh*
karastav A 231A *refreshing*
karastuma Vi 349H *harden*
karata *part. of kaRgama*

karavan N 245 *caravan*
kaRbol N 229A *carbolic*
karbonAAd N 58A *chop (meat)*
karburaaTor N 229A *carburettor*
kardemon N 245 *cardamom*
kardetav A 231A *dangerous*
kardin N 231A *curtain*
kare A 235 *rough*
karedus N 260A *roughness*
kaRgama Vi 348B *leap*
kaRge A 227B *fresh*
kari N 68A *herd*
kari N 13A *reef*
karikakar N 171C *daisy*
karikas N 243A *goblet*
karikaturiSt N 58B *caricaturist*
karikatUUr N 58A *caricature*
karistama Vt 349F *punish*
karistatav A 231A *punishable*
karistus N 260A *punishment*
karjalane N 257C *Karelian*
karjandus N 260A *livestock breeding*
karjane N 251 *herder*
karjatama Vi 349F *cry out*
pasture
karjatus N 260A *shout*
karjeriSt N 58B *careerist*
kaRjuma Vi 291C *scream*
karjÄÄr N 58A *career*
quarry
karK N 61F *crutch*
kaRm A 58B *harsh*
kaRmus N 260B *harshness*
karneval N 245 *carnival*
karP N 58D *box*
karSklane N 257C *abstainer*
karSkus N 260B *abstinence*
karTliK A 62 *timid*
karTliKKus N 260B *timidity*
karTma Vt 297C *fear*
karTmatu A 227A *fearless*
kartoNg N 58B *cardboard box*
kartoteeK N 58F *card file*
karTul N 229A *potato*
karTus N 260B *fear*
karu N 13A *bear*
karusseL̦L N 58A *merry-go-round*
kaRv N 49B *hair*
karvane A 251 *hairy*
kasarm N 234A *barracks*
kase *gen. of kaõk*
kasiino N 152 *casino*

kaŞk N 142B *birch*
kaŞS N 58A *cat*
kassa N 152 *cash desk*
kassEErima Vt 291B *cash in*
kasseŢT N 58C *cassette*
kassİİr N 58A *cashier*
kaŞt N 58B *crate*
kaStan N 229A *chestnut*
kaste N 177B *dew*
kaste N 179C *sauce*
kaStene A 257B *dewy*
kaStma Vt 297A *water plants*
kastraaT N 58E *eunuch*
kaStrul N 229A *saucepan*
kasu N 13A *use (benefit)*
kasukas N 243A *fur coat*
kasuliK A 62 *useful*
kasuliKKus N 260B *usefulness*
kasutama Vt 349F *use*
kasutu A 227A *useless*
kaSv N 61B *growth*
kaSvaja N 227A *tumour*
kaSvama Vi 291C *grow*
kasvandiK N 62 *ward (child)*
kasvataja N 227A *educator*
kasvatama Vt 349F *raise (grow)*
kasvatamatu A 227A *ill-bred*
kasvatus N 260A *upbringing*
kasvatusliK A 62 *educational*
katalOOg N 58A *catalogue*
katastrooF N 58A *catastrophe*
katastroofiline A 257D *catastrophic*
kate N 177C *covering*
katedrAAl N 58A *cathedral*
katEEder N 240A *department (university)*
kategOOria N 227A *category*
kategooriline A 257D *categorical*
katel N 173A *kettle*
kaTk N 61B *plague*
kaTkema Vi 349B *break off*
katkend N 229A *extract*
katkendliK A 62 *fragmentary*
katkestama Vt 349F *interrupt*
katkestus N 260A *interruption*
kaŢkine A 257B *broken*
kaTma Vt 300 *cover*
katoliiKlane N 257C *Catholic*
katse N 177B *attempt*
kaTseline A 257D *experimental*
katsetama Vt 349F *experiment*
katsetus N 260A *experimenting*
kaTsuma Vt 291C *touch*
kaTsumus N 260A *ordeal*
kaTTuma Vi 349H *coincide*
katus N 253 *roof*
kaubandus N 260A *commerce*
kaubandusliK A 62 *commercial*
kaubastama Vt 349F *market*
kaUdne A 247 *indirect*
kaUge A 227B *distant*
kaugenema Vi 349D *recede*
kaUgus N 260B *distance*
kaukAAslane N 257C *Caucasian*
kaUn N 50 *pod*
kaUnidus N 260A *beauty*
kaunis A 164B *beautiful*
kaunistama Vt 349F *adorn*
kaunistus N 260A *adornment*
kaunitar N 245 *female beauty*
kauP N 49D *commodity*
wares
kauPlema V 326D *barter*
kauPlus N 260B *shop*
kaUr N 58B *loon*
kauSS N 58G *bowl*
kauSt N 49B *folder*
kaustik N 234A *notebook*
kauTsjon N 229A *bail*
kava N 14A *programme*
kaval A 231A *sly*
kavaler N 245 *beau*
kavalus N 260A *slyness*
kavand N 229A *outline*
kavandama Vt 349F *outline*
kavatsema Vt 349E *intend*
kavatsus N 260A *intention*
kavu *pl. part. of kava*
kaVVa *ill. of kava*
kEE N 1 *necklace*
keedis N 253 *preserves*
keeFir N 229A *kefir*
kEEgel N 240A *bowling*
keeKs N 58B *pound cake*
kEEl N 82 *tongue*
kEElama Vt 327A *forbid*
kEEld N 124A *prohibition*
kEElduma Vi 349H *refuse*
kEEldumine N 257E *refusal*
keeleline A 257D *linguistic*
keelend N 229A *expression*
keeletu A 227A *speechless*
kEElkoNd N 106 *language family*
keelu *gen. of kEEld*
keelustama Vt 349F *ban*
kEEma Vi 261A *boil*
keemik N 234A *chemist.*
keemiline A 257D *chemical*
keeP N 58D *cloak*
kEErama Vt 327A *wind*
kEErd N 124A *twist*
keeris N 253 *eddy*
kEErlema Vi 326A *revolve*
keeru *gen. of kEErd*
keerukas A 243A *intricate*
keeruline A 257D *complicated*
keerutama Vt 349F *twist*
keeTma Vt 297C *boil*
kEEv A 231B *boiling*
keevitaja N 227A *welder*
keevitama Vt 349F *weld*
keha N 15 *body*
kehakas A 243A *stout*
kehaline A 257D *physical*
kehastama Vt 349F *embody*
kehastuma Vi 349H *be embodied*
kehastus N 260A *embodiment*
keHHa *ill. of keha*
kehi *pl. part. of keha*
kehitama Vt 349F *shrug shoulders*
kehtestama Vt 349F *enact*
kehtestuma Vi 349H *come into effect*
keHtetu A 227A *invalid*
keHtima Vi 349B *be valid*
keHtiv A 231A *valid*
keHtivus N 260A *validity*
keHv A 53B *poor*
keHvus N 260B *poverty*
keİgar N 229A *dandy*
keİgarliK A 62 *dandyish*
keİser N 240A *emperor*
keKs N 61B *hopscotch*
keKs N 58B *show-off*
keKsima Vi 291C *skip (hop about)*
keLder N 240A *cellar*
kelgutama Vi 349F *sled*
kelK N 61F *sled*
keļKima Vi 291G *brag*
keLL N 53A *clock*
kellu N 152 *trowel*
kellukas N 243A *bell-flower*
keĻm N 58B *rogue*
keļmikas A 243A *roguish*
keĻmus N 260B *roguery*
keLner N 229A *waiter*
kemikAAl N 58A *chemical*
kemmerg N 234A *outhouse*

kemPs N 61B *outhouse*
kena A 15 *nice*
keni *pl. part. of kena*
kePP N 58C *stick*
kePslema Vi 326B *gambol*
kepsutama Vi 349F *gambol*
kera N 13A *sphere*
keraamiline A 257D *ceramic*
kere N 154 *body*
keRge A 227B *easy*
light (weight)
kergendama Vt 349F *lighten (weight)*
kergendus N 260A *relief*
kergenema Vi 349D *lighten (weight)*
kergitama Vt 349F *raise (lift)*
keRgus N 260B *lightness (weight)*
kerima Vt 269 *wind*
keRjama Vt 327B *beg*
kerjus N 253 *beggar*
keRjus N 260B *beggary*
kerKima Vi 349B *rise*
keRRa *ill. of kera*
kesa N 13A *fallow*
keskendama Vt 349F *concentrate*
keskenduma Vi 349H *concentrate*
keSkkoNd N 106 *environment*
keSkmiK N 62 *central part*
keSkmine A 257F *average*
keSkne A 257B *central*
keSkus N 260B *centre*
keskustelu N 13A *conversation*
keskustlema Vi 351 *converse*
keSt N 53B *husk*
kestendama Vi 349F *be chapped*
keStev A 241A *durable*
keStma Vi 297A *endure*
keStus N 260B *duration*
keStvus N 260B *durability*
ketas N 159C *disk*
keTraja N 227A *spinner*
keTrama Vt 327E *spin*
keţsid (pl) N 58B *sneakers*
ketšup N 229A *ketchup*
keŢT N 58C *chain*
kevad N 233A *spring season*
kevadine A 257A *spring*
kibe A 235 *bitter*
kibedus N 260A *bitterness*
kibelema Vi 325 *fidget*
kibestama Vt 349F *embitter*
kibestuma Vi 349H *become embittered*
kibrutama Vt 349F *pucker*
kihama Vi 269 *swarm*
kihar N 231A *curl*
kihelema Vi 325 *tingle*
kihelkoNd N 106 *parish*
kihi *gen. of kiHt*
kihiline A 257D *layered*
kihisema Vi 349C *seethe*
kihistama Vi 349F *snigger*
kihlad (pl) N 49B *engagement (action)*
kiHluma Vi 349G *become engaged*
kiHlus N 260B *engagement (result)*
kiHnlane N 257C *Kihnu native*
kiHt N 116 *layer*
kihulane N 257C *midge*
kihutama Vt 349F *incite*
kiHv N 49B *fang*
kiHvt A 58B *terrific*
kiigutama V 349F *rock*
kiiK N 63E *swing*
kiiKer N 240A *telescope*
kiiKuma Vi 291G *rock*
swing
kİİl N 58A *dragon-fly*
kİİl N 61A *keel*
kİİl N 61A *wedge*
kiilakas A 243A *bald-headed*
kİİluma Vt 291A *wedge*
kİİn N 58A *chopper*
gadfly
kİİnduma Vi 349H *become fond of*
kİİndumus N 260A *affection*
kİİr N 61A *haste*
kİİr N 82 *ray*
kiirata *part. of kİİrgama*
kiire A 177A *fast*
kiirendama Vt 349F *speed up*
kiirenema Vi 349D *speed up*
kİİrgama Vi 348A *radiate*
kİİrgus N 260B *radiation*
kiiritama Vt 349F *irradiate*
kiiritus N 260A *irradiation*
kİİrus N 260B *speed*
kiirustama V 349F *hurry*
kiisa *gen. of kiiSk*
kiiSk N 95B *ruff (fish)*
kiisu N 152 *pussy-cat*
kiiTleja N 227A *boaster*
kiiTlema Vi 326E *boast*
kiiTma Vt 297C *praise*
kiiTus N 260B *praise*
kiivas A 159A *jealous*
kİİver N 240A *helmet*
kikas N 159C *cock (bird)*
kiLd N 128 *splinter of glass*
kile A 235 *piercing*
kile N 153 *membrane*
kiļjatama Vi 349F *give a shriek*
kiļjatus N 260A *shriek*
kiĻjuma Vi 291C *shriek*
kiļK N 58F *tipsiness*
kilKama Vi 327F *shout for joy*
killu *gen. of kiLd*
killunema Vi 349D *become splintered*
killustama Vt 349F *break into splinters*
killustiK N 62 *broken stones*
kilo N 13A *kilo*
kiļP N 58D *shield*
kilPlane N 257C *foolish person*
kilPlasliK A 62 *foolish*
kilu N 13A *sprat*
kimbatus N 260A *perplexity*
kimbutama Vt 349F *harass*
kimP N 61D *bouquet*
kiNda *gen. of kinnas*
kiNdel A 241A *sure*
kiNdlus N 260B *fortress*
kiNdlusetus N 260A *uncertainty*
kindlustama Vt 349F *insure*
kindlustus N 260A *insurance*
kiNdra *gen. of kinner*
kiNdral N 229A *general*
kiNg N 53B *shoe*
kingitus N 260A *gift*
kinK N 58F *gift*
kinK N 61F *mound*
kinKima Vt 291G *give as present*
kinnas N 192 *glove*
kinner N 204 *hollow behind knee*
kiŅNine A 257B *closed*
kiņnistama Vt 349F *fasten*
kiņnitama Vt 349F *certify*
kiņniti N 225A *fastener*
kiņnitus N 260A *assurance*
kiNNo *ill. of kino*
kino N 13A *cinema*
kinTs N 61B *haunch*
kiosK N 229B *kiosk*
kipitama Vi 349F *prickle*
kiPPuma Vi 291D *be anxious to do*
kiPs N 58B *gypsum*
kiRde *gen. of kirre*
kire *gen. of kiRg*
kirema Vi 269 *crow*
kirev A 231A *dazzling*

kiRg N 140A *passion*
kiRgliK A 62 *passionate*
kiri N 68A *letter*
kirik N 234A *church*
kirikliK A 62 *ecclesiastical*
kiristama Vt 349F *gnash*
kirjaliK A 62 *written*
kirjand N 229A *essay*
kirjandus N 260A *literature*
kirjandusliK A 62 *literary*
kirjaniK N 62 *writer (author)*
kirjastama Vt 349F *publish*
kirjastus N 260A *publishing house*
kirjeldama Vt 349F *describe*
kirjeldus N 260A *description*
kirju A 152 *multi-coloured*
kiRju A 227B *multi-coloured*
kirjutaja N 227A *writer*
kirjutama Vt 349F *write*
kirjutus N 260A *writing*
kirka N 152 *pick(axe)*
kiRn N 61B *churn*
kirP N 61D *flea*
kirre N 215 *north-east*
kirSS N 58G *cherry*
kirSt N 61B *coffin*
kirtsutama Vt 349F *wrinkle*
kiruma Vt 269 *cuss*
kiruRg N 58B *surgeon*
kiruRgia N 227A *surgery*
kirurgiline A 257D *surgical*
kisa N 13A *clamour*
kisama Vi 269 *bawl*
kiselda *part. of kiSklema*
kisendama Vi 349F *yell*
kiŞkjaliK A 62 *rapacious*
kiSklema Vi 336 *fight*
kiSkuma Vt 313B *tear at*
kisseĻL N 58A *cold berry soup*
kisu *pres. of kiSkuma*
kitaRR N 58A *guitar*
kitarriSt N 58B *guitarist*
kiTkuma Vt 291C *pluck*
kiTs N 63B *goat*
kitsas A 159B *narrow*
kitsendama Vt 349F *restrict*
kitsendus N 260A *restriction*
kitsenema Vi 349D *become narrower*
kiţsi A 152 *stingy*
kiţsidus N 260A *stinginess*
kiţsikus N 260A *difficulty*
kiTsus N 260B *narrowness*

kiTš N 58B *kitsch*
kiŢT N 58C *putty*
kiTTel N 240B *smock*
kiŢTima Vt 291D *putty*
kiU *gen. of kiUd*
kiUd N 127 *fibre*
kiUnuma Vi 291C *whimper*
kiUsama Vt 327B *tease*
kiusatus N 260A *temptation*
kiusatusliK A 62 *tempting*
kive *pl. part. of kivi*
kivi N 17 *stone*
kivine A 251 *stony*
kivinema Vi 349D *petrify*
kiVVi *ill. of kivi*
klAArima Vt 291A *clarify*
klAAş N 58A *glass*
klAAşima Vt 291A *glaze (glass)*
klaaşistuma Vi 349H *become glassy*
klaHv N 58B *piano key*
klahvistiK N 62 *piano keyboard*
klaMber N 240A *clip*
klaPP N 58C *valve*
klarnet N 229A *clarinet*
klaŞS N 58A *class*
klaşsifitsEErima Vt 291B *classify*
klaşsik N 234A *classic*
klaşsikaline A 257D *classical*
klaTš N 58B *gossip*
klaTšima Vt 291C *gossip*
klaver N 229A *piano*
kleebis N 253 *sticker*
kleePima Vt 291E *stick (glue)*
kleiT N 58E *dress*
klibu N13B *stone, shingle*
klieņT N 58E *client*
klİİd (pl) N 1 *bran*
kliima N 152 *climate*
kliinik N 234A *clinic*
kliiSter N 240A *paste (glue)*
kliisterdama Vt 349F *paste*
klimP N 58D *dumpling*
klirin N 231A *clatter*
klirisema Vi 349C *clatter*
klišEE N 2 *cliché*
kloaaK N 58F *cesspool*
klobisema Vi 349C *rattle*
klobistama Vt 349F *rattle*
klomP N 58D *lump*
klooSter N 240A *cloister*
klooSter N 240A *monastery*
klopits N 231A *beater*

kloPPima Vt 291D *beat*
kloseŢT N 58C *toilet*
kloŢs N 58B *block (toy)*
kloUn N 58B *clown*
klubi N 13B *club*
kluPPi *ill. of klubi*
klõbin N 231A *clatter*
klõPs N 61B *click*
klõpsatus N 260A *click*
kläHvima Vi 291C *yelp*
kniKs N 61B *curtsey*
knopka N 152 *thumbtack*
koba N 13B *clamp*
kobama Vi 269 *grope*
kobar N 231A *cluster*
kobestama Vt 349F *loosen soil*
kobras N 159D *beaver*
koda N 29 *chamber*
corridor
kodakoNdsus N 260B *citizenship*
kodaniK N 62 *citizen*
kodar N 231A *spoke*
kodeİİn N 58A *codeine*
kodu N 13C *home*
kodundus N 260A *home economics*
kodune A 251 *homy*
kodunema Vi 349D *get used to*
kodustama Vt 349F *domesticate*
kodutu A 227A *homeless*
koE *gen. of kude*
koE *pres. of kudema*
koEr N 54 *dog*
koErus N 260B *mischief*
kofeİİn N 58A *caffeine*
kogelema Vi 325 *stammer*
kogema Vt 269 *experience*
kogemus N 260A *experience*
kogenematu A 227A *inexperienced*
koger N 81B *Yellow fish*
kogu A 13D *whole*
kogu N 13D *bulk*
collection
kogudus N 260A *congregation*
koguja N 227A *collector*
kogukas A 243A *bulky*
kogukoNd N 106 *community*
koguma Vt 269 *collect*
kogunema Vi 349D *gather together*
kogunemine N 257E *gathering (action)*
kogus A 231A *massive*
kogus N 253 *amount*
koha *gen. of koHt*

koha N 13A *pike-perch*
kohaliK A 62 *local*
kohandama Vt 349F *adapt*
kohanema Vi 349D *adapt oneself*
kohata *part. of koHtama*
kohelda *part. of koHtlema*
kohendama Vt 349F *arrange*
kohene A 251 *instantaneous*
kohev A 231A *fluffy*
kohin N 231A *murmur*
kohisema Vi 349C *murmur*
koHkuma Vi 349G *be startled*
koHkumatu A 227A *dauntless*
kohmakas A 243A *clumsy*
kohmakus N 260A *clumsiness*
kohmetama Vi 349F *numb fast*
kohmetu A 227A *numbed*
kohmetuma Vi 349H *numb slowly*
kohmetus N 260A *numbness*
koHt N 104B *place*
koHtama Vt 341B *meet*
koHtamine N 257E *encounter*
koHtlema Vt 331B *treat*
koHtu *gen. of kohus*
koHtuliK A 62 *judicial*
koHtuma Vi 349H *meet*
koHtumine N 257E *rendezvous*
koHtuniK N 62 *judge*
kohus N 198 *court of law*
kohus N 253 *duty*
kohustama Vt 349F *oblige*
kohustuma Vi 349H *bind oneself*
kohustus N 260A *obligation*
kohustusliK A 62 *obligatory*
kohutama Vt 349F *terrify*
kohutav A 231A *dreadful*
koHv N 58B *coffee*
koHver N 240A *suitcase*
kohvik N 234A *café*
koİ N 1 *berth*
moth
koİb N 101B *shank*
koidik N 234A *dawn*
koiT N 61E *dawn*
koiTma Vi 297C *dawn*
koiva *gen. of koİb*
koja *gen. of koda*
kokaİIn N 58A *cocaine*
koKK N 53C *cook*
koKKu *ill. of kogu*
koKs N 58B *coke (coal)*
koKsima Vt 291C *tap*

koKteİl N 58B *cocktail*
kokutama Vi 349F *stutter*
kolama Vi 269 *knock about*
koĻb N 114 *flask*
koLde *gen. of kolle*
kole A 235 *horrible*
koledus N 260A *horror*
koletis N 260A *monster*
kolgas N 159E *backwoods*
koli N 13A *junk*
kolima Vi 269 *move household*
kolimine N 257E *moving household*
kolin N 231A *clatter*
kolisema Vi 349C *clatter*
kolistama Vt 349F *clatter*
koļju N 152 *skull*
koļK N 58F *thrashing*
koļKima Vt 291G *thrash*
koĻL N 58A *bogy*
kollAAž N 58A *collage*
kollakas A 243A *yellowish*
kollane A 251 *yellow*
kolle N 213 *hearth*
kolledž N 229A *college*
kollEEg N 58A *colleague*
kollektİIv N 58A *collective*
kollektİIvne A 247 *collective*
kollektİIvsus N 260B *collectivity*
kollektsionÄÄr N 58A *collector*
kollektsiOOn N 58A *collection*
kolletama V 349F *turn yellow*
koLm N 63B *three*
koLmainus N 169 *holy trinity*
kolmandiK N 62 *third*
kolmas A 238A *third*
koļmik N 234A *triplet*
kolonel N 245 *colonel*
koloniAAlne A 247 *colonial*
kolonisaaTor N 229A *colonizer*
kolonisEErima Vt 291B *colonize*
kolonisEErimine N 257E *colonization*
koloniSt N 58B *colonist*
koloŅN N 58A *column*
kolOOnia N 227A *colony*
koloriiT N 58E *colouring*
kolossAAlne A 247 *colossal*
kolP N 53D *skull*
koļvi *gen. of koĻb*
koma N 13A *comma*
komandaŋT N 58E *superintendent*
komandEErima Vt 291B *send on mission*
komandeering N 234A *business trip*

komandör N 245 *commander*
kombaİn N 58B *combine*
kombaİner N 229A *combine operator*
koMbe *gen. of komme*
komberdama Vi 349F *hobble*
koMbestiK N 62 *body of customs*
kombinaaT N 58E *plant (factory)*
kombinatsiOOn N 58A *combination*
kombinEE N 2 *camiknickers*
kombinEErima Vt 291B *contrive*
komisjon N 245 *commission*
komissariaaT N 58E *commissariat*
komistama Vi 349F *stumble*
komistus N 260A *stumble*
komitEE N 2 *committee*
koMM N 58A *candy*
komme N 209 *custom*
kommentAAr N 58A *commentary*
kommentaaTor N 229A *commentator*
kommerSS N 58G *fraternity party*
kommerTs N 58B *commerce*
kommunAAlne A 247 *communal*
kommutaaTor N 229A *switchboard*
kommünikEE N 2 *communiqué*
kompaKtne A 247 *compact*
komPama Vi 327D *grope*
kompanİI N 1 *company*
komparEErima Vt 291B *compare*
komPaŞS N 58A *compass*
kompensatsiOOn N 58A *compensation*
kompensEErima Vt 291B *compensate*
kompetenTne A 247 *competent*
kompetenTs N 58B *competence*
komPima Vi 291E *grope*
komPleKs N 58B *complex*
kompleKsne A 247 *complex*
kompleKt N 58B *set*
komplektEErima Vt 291B *complement*
komplikatsiOOn N 58A *complication*
komplimeŋT N 58E *compliment*
komplitsEErima Vt 291B *complicate*
komponEErima Vt 291B *compose (music)*
komponiSt N 58B *composer*
kompositsiOOn N 58A *composition*
kompoŞt N 58B *compost*
kompostEErima Vt 291B *validate a ticket*
kompoSter N 240A *ticket punch*
kompoŢT N 58C *stewed fruit*
komPreŞS N 58A *compress*
kompromiŞS N 58A *compromise*
kompromitEErima Vt 291B *compromise*
komPs N 61B *bundle*

kompu N 152 *candy*
komPveK N 58H *candy*
komteSS N 58A *countess*
komÖÖdia N 227A *comedy*
konarliK A 62 *uneven*
kondiiTer N 240A *confectioner*
koŋdine A 251 *bony*
kondOOm N 58A *condom*
konduKtor N 229A *conductor*
konferansjEE N 2 *M.C.*
konferEErima Vi 291B *act as MC*
konfiskEErima Vt 291B *confiscate*
konfiskEErimine N 257E *confiscation*
konfliKt N 58B *conflict*
koNg N 58B *cell (prison)*
kongreŞS N 58A *congress*
koni N 13A *cigarette stub*
konkreeTne A 247 *concrete (real)*
konKs N 61B *hook*
konkurEErima Vi 291B *compete*
konkureŋT N 58E *competitor*
konkurenTs N 58B *competition*
konKurSS N 58G *contest*
koNN N 53A *frog*
-konna *gen. of -koNd*
konseRv N 58B *canned food*
konservatİİv N 58A *conservative*
konservatİİvne A 247 *conservative*
konservatOOrium N 246 *conservatory*
konservEErima Vt 291B *preserve*
konseRvima Vt 291C *preserve*
konsistOOrium N 246 *consistory*
konsonaŋT N 58E *consonant*
konspeKt N 58B *précis*
konspektEErima Vt 291B *take notes*
konspeKtima Vt 291C *take notes*
konspiratİİvne A 247 *conspiratorial*
konstatEErima Vt 291B *state*
konstitutsiOOn N 58A *constitution*
konstruEErima Vt 291B *construct*
konstruKtor N 229A *constructor*
konstruktsiOOn N 58A *construction*
koNsul N 229A *consul*
konsulaaT N 58E *consulate*
konsultaŋT N 58E *consultant*
konsultatsiOOn N 58A *consultation*
konsultEErima Vt 291B *consult*
koŋT N 58E *bone*
kontaKt N 58B *contact*
konteİner N 229A *container*
konteKst N 58B *context*
kontinentAAlne A 247 *continental*
kontingeŋT N 58E *contingent*
konTor N 229A *office*
konTrahi *gen. of konTraHt*
konTraHt N 116 *contract*
kontraŞt N 58B *contrast*
kontraStne A 247 *contrastive*
kontroĻL N 58A *inspection*
kontroĻLima Vt 291A *inspect*
kontroĻLimine N 257E *inspecting*
kontrolör N 245 *inspector*
konTs N 53B *heel (shoe)*
konTs N 61B *stub*
konTserT N 58E *concert*
konveİer N 229A *conveyer*
koNveŋT N 58E *fraternity house*
konventsionAAlne A 247 *conventional*
konverenTs N 58B *conference*
kOO *pres. of kuduma*
kOO *gen. of kubu*
koobas N 159D *cave*
kOOḑ N 58A *code*
kooK N 58F *cake*
kooK N 61F *hook*
kOOļ N 58A *school*
kOOlduma Vi 349H *curve*
koole N 179A *ford*
kooļitama Vt 349F *school*
kOOļkoNd N 106 *school (disciples)*
kOOlon N 229A *colon*
koolutama Vt 349F *curve*
koomik N 234A *comedian*
koomiline A 257D *comic*
kOOn N 61A *snout*
kOOndama Vt 349F *rally*
kOOndis N 260B *association*
kOOnduma Vi 349H *rally*
kOOndus N 260B *gathering (result)*
koonerdama Vi 349F *be stingy*
koonus N 253 *cone*
kOOnus N 260B *cone*
kooperatİİv N 58A *co-operative*
kooPia N 227A *copy*
kOOr N 58A *choir*
kOOr N 82 *cream (dairy)*
peel
koordinaaT N 58E *co-ordinates*
koordinEErima Vt 291B *co-ordinate*
koorik N 234A *crust*
kOOrima Vt 291A *peel*
kOOrmama Vt 327A *burden*
kOOrmus N 260B *burden*
kooruke(ne) N 257G *crust*
kOOskõlastama Vt 349F *co-ordinate*
kOOsnema Vi 349D *consist of*
kooStama Vt 349F *compose*
kopEErima Vt 291B *copy*
koPP N 53C *scoop*
koPPel N 240B *enclosure*
koPs N 61B *lung*
kopsik N 234A *dipper*
koPter N 229A *helicopter*
kopulatsiOOn N 58A *copulation*
koputama Vi 349F *knock*
koputus N 260A *knock*
korAAl N 58A *hymn*
korAAn N 58A *Koran*
koraĻL N 58A *coral*
koRd N 107 *order*
koRdama Vt 344 *repeat*
koRdamine N 257E *repetition*
koRduma Vi 349H *recur*
koRdumine N 257E *recurrence*
koRduv A 231A *recurrent*
korEalane N 257C *Korean*
koreograaFia N 227A *choreography*
koreograafiline A 257D *choreographic*
korgits N 231A *corkscrew*
koriaNder N 240A *coriander*
koridor N 245 *corridor*
koristaja N 227A *cleaner (person)*
koristama Vt 349F *tidy up*
koRjama Vt 327B *gather*
korjandus N 260A *collection*
korjus N 253 *carcass*
korK N 58F *cork*
kornet N 229A *cornet*
korP N 58D *curd cake*
korporaŋT N 58E *fraternity member*
korporaŋTliK A 62 *fraternity-like*
korporatsiOOn N 58A *fraternity*
sorority
korPus N 260B *corps*
korra *gen. of koRd*
korraldama Vt 349F *organize*
korraldus N 260A *order (directive)*
korraliK A 62 *orderly*
korraliKKus N 260B *orderliness*
korrastama Vt 349F *put into order*
korrata *part. of koRdama*
korratu A 227A *disorderly*
korratus N 260A *disorder*
korreKtor N 229A *proof-reader*
korrektUUr N 58A *proof-reading*
korrespondeŋT N 58E *correspondent*

korrigEErima Vt 291B *correct*
korruptsiOOn N 58A *corruption*
korrus N 253 *storey in building*
korrutama Vt 349F *multiply*
korrutamine N 257E *multiplication*
korSten N 241A *chimney*
korTer N 229A *apartment*
korTs N 61B *wrinkle*
korTsuma Vi 349G *become wrinkled*
korTsumatu A 227A *crease-proof*
kortsutama Vt 349F *wrinkle*
koRv N 58B *basket*
koRvama Vt 327B *compensate*
kose *gen. of koŞk*
kosilane N 257C *wooer*
kosima Vt 269 *woo*
koŞk N 142B *waterfall*
kosmeetik N 234A *beautician*
kosmeetika N 227A *cosmetics*
kosmeetiline A 257D *cosmetic*
kosmiline A 257D *cosmic*
kosmonauT N 58E *astronaut*
koştitama Vt 349F *entertain guest*
koştitus N 260A *treat*
koStma Vi 297A *be heard*
kostÜÜm N 58A *suit*
kosuma Vi 269 *recover from illness*
kosutama Vt 349F *refresh*
kosutav A 231A *refreshing*
kotkas N 159B *eagle*
koTleŢ N 58H *meat-ball*
koŢT N 58C *bag*
koTTa *ill. of koda*
krAAḑ N 58A *degree*
krAAḑima Vt 291A *measure temperature*
kraaKsuma Vi 291C *croak*
krAAm N 58A *stuff*
krAAmima Vt 291A *clean up*
krAAŋ N 58A *tap*
kraana N 152 *crane (machine)*
kraaPima Vt 291E *scrape*
krAAş N 58A *card (wool)*
kraaTer N 240A *crater*
krAAv N 58A *ditch*
kraavitama Vt 349F *drain with ditches*
krabi N 13B *crab*
krabin N 231A *rustle*
krabisema Vi 349C *rustle*
krabistama Vt 349F *rustle*
kraE N 1 *collar*
kraHH N 58A *crash*
kraHv N 58B *count (person)*
kraHvinna N 152 *countess*
kraHvkoNd N 106 *county*
kramP N 58D *cramp*
staple for paper
kramPliK A 62 *convulsive*
kraŢsima Vt 291C *scratch*
kraŢT N 58C *hob-goblin*
krediiT N 58E *credit*
kreeK N 58F *bullace*
kreeKlane N 257C *Greek*
krEEm N 58A *cream*
krematOOrium N 246 *crematorium*
krePP N 58C *crêpe*
kreŞS N 58A *cress*
kreveŢT N 58C *shrimp*
krigin N 231A *crunch*
krigisema Vi 349C *crunch*
krigistama Vt 349F *crunch*
kriiKsuma Vi 291C *creak*
kriimustama Vt 349F *scratch*
kriimustus N 260A *scratch (graze)*
kriiPs N 61B *line*
kriipsutama Vt 349F *draw lines*
krİİs N 58A *crisis*
kriisata *part. of kriiSkama*
kriiSkama Vi 348C *screech*
kriiSkav A 231A *shrill*
kriiT N 58E *chalk*
kriitik N 234A *critic*
kriitika N 227A *criticism*
kriitiline A 257D *critical*
kriminAAlne A 247 *criminal*
kriNgel N 240A *knot-shaped pastry*
kristaĻL N 58A *crystal*
kriStlane N 257C *Christian*
kriStliK A 62 *Christian*
kritisEErima Vt 291B *criticize*
kritseldama Vt 349F *scribble*
kritseldus N 260A *scribble*
kriuKsuma Vi 291C *squeak*
krobe A 235 *rough*
krobeline A 257D *rough*
kroHv N 58B *plaster*
kroHvija N 227A *plasterer*
kroHvima Vt 291C *plaster*
kroket N 229A *croquet*
krokodiĻL N 58A *crocodile*
krooKima Vt 291G *gather into ruff*
krooKsuma Vi 291C *croak*
krooKus N 260B *crocus*
krOOļ N 58A *crawl (swimming)*
krOOļima Vi 291A *crawl (swimming)*
krOOŋ N 58A *crown*
kroonika N 227A *chronicle*
krooniline A 257D *chronic*
krOOŋima Vt 291A *crown*
krOOŋimine N 257E *coronation*
kroŞS N 58A *cross-country race*
kruŋT N 58E *plot of land*
kruŋTima Vt 291F *prime*
kruubid (pl) N 58D *pearl-barley*
krUUs N 53A *gravel*
krUUş N 58A *mug*
kruve *pl. part. of kruvi*
kruvi N 17 *screw*
kruvima Vt 269 *screw*
kruvits N 231A *screw-driver*
krõbe A 235 *crisp*
krõhva N 152 *hag*
krõõT N 49E *hag*
kräUnuma Vi 291C *caterwaul*
krüsantEEm N 58A *chrysanthemum*
ksülofon N 245 *xylophone*
kube N 157 *groin*
kubel N 79A *bubble*
kuberner N 245 *governor*
kubisema Vi 349C *teem*
kubjas N 159D *overseer*
kubu N 13B or 24 *truss*
kude N 26 *tissue*
kudema Vi 278 *spawn*
kudrutama Vi 349F *coo*
kudu N 13C *spawn*
kuduja N 227A *weaver*
kuduma Vt 283 *weave*
kudumine N 257E *weaving*
kugistama Vt 349F *gulp down*
kuhi N 71A *heap*
kuHjama Vt 327B *heap up*
kuİv A 53B *dry*
kuİvama Vi 291C *dry*
kuivatama Vt 349F *dry*
kuivendama Vt 349F *drain land*
kuivenema Vi 349D *dry up*
kuivik N 234A *rusk*
kuİvus N 260B *dryness*
kuju *pres. of kuduma*
kuju N 13A *shape*
kujundama Vt 349F *shape*
kujunema Vi 349D *take shape*
kujur N 229A *sculptor*
kujustama Vt 349F *depict*
kujustus N 260A *depiction*
kujutama Vt 349F *depict*

kujuteLm N 53B *imagination*
kujutlema Vt 351 *imagine*
kujutletav A 231A *imaginary*
kujutlus N 260A *mental picture*
kukal N 170C *back of head*
kuKK N 63C *cock (bird)*
kuKKel N 240B *bun*
kuKKuma Vi 291D *cuckoo*
kuKKuma Vi 291D *fall*
kuKKur N 242B *pouch*
kukutama Vt 349F *overthrow*
kuLd N 105 *gold*
kuLdama Vt 342 *gild*
kuLdne A 247 *golden*
kuLg N 131B *course (progress)*
kuLgema Vi 349B *proceed*
kulinAAria N 227A *cookery*
kulişsid (pl) N 58A *stage-setting*
kuļjus N 253 *sleigh-bell*
kuĻL N 58A *hawk*
kulla *gen. of kuLd*
kullake(ne) N 257G *darling*
kullata *part. of kuLdama*
kuLLer N 229A *courier*
kuLm N 61B *brow*
kuļP N 58D *ladle*
kuļtivEErima Vt 291B *cultivate*
kulTus N 260B *cult*
kultUUr N 58A *culture*
kultuuriline A 257D *cultural*
kultUUrne A 247 *cultured*
kulu *gen. of kuLg*
kulu N 13A *expense*
kuluaarid (pl) N 58A *lobby*
kulukas A 243A *costly*
kuluma Vi 269 *wear out*
kulutama Vt 349F *spend (use up)*
kulutus N 260A *expenditure*
kuma N 13A *glow*
kuMb N 102 *which of two*
kuMbki N 102 *either of two*
kuMM N 58A *tire*
rubber
kumma *gen. of kuMb*
kummagi *gen. of kuMbki*
kummaline A 257D *strange*
kummardama V 349F *bow*
kummarduma Vi 349H *bend down*
kummardus N 260A *bow (motion)*
kummEErima Vt 291B *rubberize*
kummel N 229A *camomile*
kummi N 152 *rubber*
kummitama Vt 349F *haunt*
kummut N 229A *chest of drawers*
kunde N 152 *client*
kuninganna N 152 *queen*
kuningas N 243A *king*
kuningliK A 62 *regal*
kuŋSt N 58B *art*
kuŋstiline A 257D *artistic*
kuŋStliK A 62 *artificial*
kuŋStniK N 62 *artist*
kupatama Vt 349F *parboil*
kupEE N 2 *compartment (train)*
kupoNg N 58B *coupon*
kuPPel N 240B *dome*
kuPPu *ill. of kubu*
kuramEErima Vi 291B *court*
kuramEErimine N 257E *courtship*
kurat N 230 *devil*
kuratliK A 62 *devilish*
kuRb A 101B *sad*
kuRbliK A 62 *melancholy*
kuRbus N 260B *sorrow*
kure *gen. of kuRg*
kuRg N 140A *crane (bird)*
kuri A 71A *angry*
mean
kuristama V 349F *gargle*
kuristiK N 62 *precipice*
kuRjakuulutav A 231A *ominous*
kuRjus N 260B *evil*
kurK N 58F *cucumber*
kurK N 61F *throat*
kuRn N 53B *strainer*
kuRnaja N 227A *oppressor*
kuRnama Vt 327B *oppress*
kuRnav A 231A *gruelling*
kursaŋT N 58E *cadet*
kursEErima Vi 291B *ply*
kursİİv N 58A *italics*
kurSS N 58G *exchange rate*
kuRsus N 260B *course*
kurT A 58E *deaf*
kurTma V 297C *complain*
kuRv N 58B *curve*
kurva *gen. of kuRb*
kurvastama V 349F *grieve*
kurvastuma Vi 349H *become sad*
kurvastus N 260A *grief*
kuse *gen. of kusi*
kusema Vi 272 *urinate*
kusi *past of kusema*
kusi N 19 *urine*
kuSt *part. of kusi*
kuSta *part. of kusema*
kuStuma Vi 291C *become extinguished*
kustutama Vt 349F *extinguish*
kustuti N 225A *fire extinguisher*
kušeŢT N 58C *couch*
kutse N 177B *invitation*
kuTseline A 257D *professional*
kuţsikas N 243A *puppy*
kuţsu N 152 *puppy*
kuTsuma Vt 291C *invite*
kuTsumus N 260A *vocation*
kUU N 3 *month*
moon
kuuas N 189 *axe handle*
kUUb N 136 *coat*
kuubik N 234A *cube*
kUUda *gen. of kuuas*
kuue *gen. of kUUb*
kuue *gen. of kUUs*
kuuendiK N 62 *sixth*
kuues A 238A *sixth*
kUUļ N 58A *bullet*
kUUlaja N 227A *listener*
kUUlajaskoNd N 106 *audience (listeners)*
kUUlama Vt 327A *listen to*
kuulatama V 349F *eavesdrop*
kUUldav A 231A *audible*
kUUldavus N 260A *audibility*
kUUlduma Vi 349H *be rumoured*
kUUldus N 260B *rumour*
kuulekas A 243A *obedient*
kuulekus N 260A *obedience*
kuuļike(ne) N 257G *pellet*
kUUlma Vt 294 *hear*
kUUlsus N 260B *fame*
kUUluma Vi 349G *belong*
kUUlus A 250A *famous*
kuulutama Vt 349F *advertise*
kuulutus N 260A *advertisement*
kUUluvus N 260A *membership*
kUUm A 53A *hot*
kuumendama Vt 349F *heat*
kuumenema Vi 349D *heat up*
kUUmus N 260B *heat*
kuumutama Vt 349F *make hot*
kUUne A 252 *month-old*
kuuP N 58D *cube*
kUUr N 58A *shed*
course of treatment
kUUrorT N 58E *resort*
kUUs N 143A *six*

kuuse *gen. of kuuSk*
kuusik N 234A *fir grove*
kuuSk N 140B *fir*
kuuT *part. of kUUs*
kuvar N 229A *video monitor*
kvalifikatsiOOn N 58A *qualification*
kvalifitsEErima Vt 291B *qualify*
kvalitatİIvne A 247 *qualitative*
kvaliteeT N 58E *quality*
kvaliteeTne A 247 *good-quality*
kvantiteeT N 58E *quantity*
kvarTal N 229A *city block*
kvarteŢT N 58C *quartette*
kvarTs N 58B *quartz*
kviiTung N 229A *receipt*
kvinteŢT N 58C *quintet*
kvOOrum N 229A *quorum*
kõbin N 231A *rustle*
kõblas N 159D *hoe*
kõbus A 231A *hale and hearty*
kõdi N 13C *tickle*
kõdistama Vt 349F *tickle*
kõdisti N 225A *clitoris*
kõditama Vt 349F *tickle*
kõdunema Vi 349D *decay*
kõhe A 235 *uneasy*
kõhelda *part. of kõHklema*
kõHklema Vi 336 *hesitate*
kõHklus N 260B *hesitation*
kõHn A 49B *thin*
kõhnuke(ne) A 257G *slender*
kõHnuma Vi 349G *become thin*
kõHt N 124B *belly*
kõhu *gen. of kõHt*
kõigutama Vt 349F *sway*
kõiK N 64 *all*
kõiKuma Vi 291G *sway*
kõiKumatu A 227A *unwavering*
kõiKuv A 231A *unsteady*
kõİv N 61B *birch*
kõla N 13A *sound*
kõlakas N 243A *grapevine (gossip)*
kõlama Vi 269 *resound*
kõlatu A 227A *soundless*
kõlav A 231A *sonorous*
kõlavus N 260A *sonority*
kõLbama Vi 339B *be good for*
kõLbeline A 257D *moral*
kõLbliK A 62 *morally suitable*
kõLblus N 260B *morality*
kõLbmatu A 227A *useless*
kõle A 235 *bleak*
kõlgutama Vt 349F *dangle*
kõlin N 231A *tinkle*
kõlisema Vi 349C *tinkle*
kõlistama Vt 349F *tinkle*
kõLLa *ill. of kõla*
kõlvata *part. of kõLbama*
kõlvatu A 227A *immoral*
kõlvatus N 260A *moral impropriety*
kõmin N 231A *rumble*
kõmisema Vi 349C *rumble*
kõmPima Vi 291E *plod*
kõmPsima Vi 291C *plod*
kõmu N 13A *sensation*
kõmuline A 257D *sensational*
kõṆdima Vi 310 *walk*
kõne N 153 *speech*
kõneleja N 227A *speaker*
kõnelema Vi 325 *speak*
kõnelus N 260A *talk*
kõnetama Vt 349F *address someone*
kõnnak N 234A *gait*
kõṇni *pres. of kõṆdima*
kõnTs N 49B *sludge*
kõPlama Vt 327D *hoe*
kõRb N 137 or 233B *desert*
kõRbema Vi 349B *scorch*
kõRge A 227B *high*
kõrgendama Vt 349F *elevate*
kõrgendiK N 62 *plateau*
kõrgenema Vi 349D *become elevated*
kõRgus N 260B *height*
kõRgustiK N 62 *uplands*
kõri N 13A *throat*
kõristi N 225A *rattle*
kõrKjas N 243B *bulrush*
kõrKus N 260B *haughtiness*
kõrre *gen. of kõRs*
kõRRi *ill. of kõri*
kõRs N 144 *straw*
kõrT *part. of kõRs*
kõrTs N 58B *tavern*
kõrTsmiK N 62 *tavern keeper*
kõRv N 49B *ear*
kõrvaldama Vt 349F *remove*
kõrvaldamine N 257E *removal*
kõrvaline A 257D *secondary*
kõrve *gen. of kõRb*
kõrvetama Vt 349F *scorch*
kõrvits N 231A *pumpkin*
kõRvulukustav A 231A *ear-splitting*
kõrvutama Vt 349F *compare*
kõU N 63B *thunder*
kõva A 14A *hard*
kõvendama Vt 349F *intensify*
kõvenema Vi 349D *intensify*
kõver A 231A *crooked*
kõverdama Vt 349F *curve*
kõverduma Vi 349H *curve*
kõvu *pl. part. of kõva*
kõõlus N 253 *sinew*
kÕÕm N 49A *dandruff*
käba N 13B *float*
käbi N 13B *cone (pine, fir etc)*
käblik N 234A *wren*
käE *gen. of käsi*
käEndama Vt 349F *bail*
käEndus N 260B *bail*
kägistama Vt 349F *strangle*
kägu N 31 *cuckoo*
kähar A 231A *curly*
kähardama Vt 349F *curl*
käharduma Vi 349H *curl*
kähisema Vi 349C *speak hoarsely*
käİ N 49B *grindstone*
käİa *part. of käİma*
käİbe *gen. of käive*
käİbima Vi 349B *circulate*
käİdav A 231A *practicable*
käiK N 61F *walkway*
käİl N 49B *prow (ship)*
käİma Vi 264B *go, walk*
attend
frequent
visit
käİmla N 227B *toilet (outhouse)*
käİsed (pl) N 254 *sleeves*
käiTis N 260B *enterprise*
käiTuma Vi 349H *behave*
käiTumine N 257E *behaviour*
käive N 208B *circulation*
käivitama Vt 349F *start up*
käiviti N 225A *ignition switch*
käKK N 58C *blood pudding*
käli N 13A *wife's sister*
kämping N 234A *camp grounds*
käNd N 129 *stump of tree*
kännu *gen. of käNd*
käO *gen. of kägu*
käpard N 229A *bungler*
käpik N 234A *mitten*
käPP N 53C *paw*
kära N 13A *uproar*
käratsema Vi 349E *be rowdy*
käratu A 227A *noiseless*

kärbe N 177D *omission in text*
kärbes N 162 *fly*
käre A 235 *severe*
kärestiK N 62 *rapids*
käRg N 141 *honeycomb*
kärisema Vi 349C *tear*
käristama Vt 349F *tear*
kärje *gen. of käRg*
kärmas A 159B *nimble*
kärme A 177B *nimble*
käRn N 53B *scab*
kärnane A 251 *scabby*
kärPima Vt 291E *prune*
käRRu *ill. of käru*
kärsitu A 227A *impatient*
kärsitus N 260A *impatience*
kärSS N 53G *snout*
käru N 13A *wheel-barrow*
käse *pres. of käSkma*
käsi N 45 *hand*
käşi *pres. of käŞkima*
käsitama Vt 349F *comprehend*
käsitlema Vt 351 *deal with*
käsitlus N 260A *treatment*
käsitsema Vt 349E *handle*
käsitsus N 260A *handling*
käsitus N 260A *interpretation*
käSk N 131C *command*
käŞkima Vt 321 or 313B *command*
käSklus N 260B *command*
käSkma Vt 321 *command*
käSn N 53B *sponge*
käSta *part. of käSkma*
käsu *gen. of käSk*
käsutama Vt 349F *order about*
käsutus N 260A *beck and call*
käţis N 253 *cuff*
käTT *part. of käsi*
käTTe *ill. of käsi*
kääbus N 253 *dwarf*
käänak N 234A *bend in road*
kÄÄnama Vt 327A *turn*
kÄÄnde *gen. of kääne*
kÄÄnduma Vi 349H *decline (grammar)*
kääne N 211A *case (grammatical)*
käänis N 253 *lapel*
kÄÄr N 61A *bend of river*
käärid (pl) N 58A *scissors*
kÄÄrima Vi 291A *ferment*
köE *pres. of küdema*
köeTa *imper. of küTma*
köeTav A 231A *heatable*
köha N 13A *cough*
köhima Vi 269 *cough*
köide N 179D *fetter*
köide N 177E *volume (book)*
köie *gen. of köİs*
köİs N 143C *rope*
köiT *part. of köİs*
köiTma Vt 297C *fascinate*
körT N 58E *gruel*
köSter N 240A *parish clerk*
kööK N 58F *kitchen*
kööme N 185 *caraway-seed*
köömen N 185 *caraway-seed*
köömes N 161A *triviality*
kÖÖsner N 229A *furrier*
kübar N 231A *hat*
küberneetika N 227A *cybernetics*
küdema Vi 279 *be burning*
küdi N 13C *husband's brother*
küHm N 61B *hump*
küHvel N 240A *shovel*
kühveldama Vt 349F *shovel*
kükitama Vi 349F *squat*
küla N 13A *village*
külakoNd N 106 *rural community*
külastaja N 227A *visitor*
külastama Vt 349F *visit*
küĻg N 141 *side*
küĻgnema Vi 349D *be adjacent*
küļje *gen. of küĻg*
küLLa *ill. of küla*
küllastuma Vi 349H *glut*
küllastus N 260A *satiation*
küLLus N 260B *abundance*
küLm A 53B *cold*
külmenema Vi 349D *become colder*
külmetama Vt 349F *freeze*
külmetuma Vi 349H *catch cold*
külmik N 234A *refrigerator*
küLmuma Vi 349G *freeze*
küLmus N 260B *coldness*
külmutama Vt 349F *refrigerate*
külmutus N 260A *refrigeration*
küĻv N 58B *sowing*
küLvama Vt 327B *sow*
küMblema Vi 329 *bathe*
küMblus N 260B *bathing*
kümme N 183B *ten*
kümmekoNd N 106 *ten or so*
kümmelda *part. of küMblema*
-kümmend N 184 *tens (20, 30, etc.)*
küMnendiK N 62 *tenth*
küMnes A 237C *tenth*
küna N 13A *trough*
küNdma Vt 317 *plough*
küngas N 159E *hillock*
küniSm N 58B *cynicism*
künKliK A 62 *hilly*
künna *pres. of küNdma*
küņnis N 253 *threshold*
küpreŞS N 58A *cypress*
küPs A 233B *ripe*
küPsema Vi 291C *bake*
ripen
küpsetama Vt 349F *bake*
küpsis N 253 *cookie*
küPsus N 260B *ripeness*
küRb N 101B *penis*
kürva *gen. of küRb*
küsima Vt 269 *ask*
küsimus N 260A *question*
küsitav A 231A *questionable*
küsitlema Vt 351 *interrogate*
küsitlus N 260A *quiz*
küsiv A 231A *interrogative*
küte N 177C *heating of house*
kütkestama Vt 349F *captivate*
kütkestav A 231A *captivating*
küTma Vt 301 *heat house*
küŢT N 58C *hunter*
kütus N 253 *fuel*
küüditama Vt 349F *deport*
küülik N 234A *domestic rabbit*
kÜÜn N 58A *hay shed*
küünal N 170A *candle*
küünar N 171A *elbow*
kÜÜndima Vi 308A *extend*
küüne *gen. of kÜÜş*
küüni *pres. of kÜÜndima*
küünik N 234A *cynic*
küüniline A 257D *cynical*
küünis N 253 *claw*
küünistama Vt 349F *claw*
küünT *part. of kÜÜş*
kÜÜr N 61A *stoop*
küürakas A 243A *hunchback*
kÜÜrima Vt 291A *scrub*
küürutama Vi 349F *stoop*
kÜÜş N 146 *nail (finger, toe)*
kÜÜslauK N 61F *garlic*

L

laaberdama Vi 349F *be rowdy*
lAAḑ N 58A *manner*
lAAḑija N 227A *stevedore*
lAAḑima Vt 291A or 305 *load*
laadung N 229A *load*
lAAger N 240A *camp*
laamendama Vi 349F *bluster*
laane *gen. of lAAş*
laanT *part. of lAAş*
lAAş N 146 *virgin forest*
laaSt N 61B *chip*
laaStama Vt 327B *ravage*
laaT N 49E *fair*
labane A 251 *vulgar*
labastama Vt 349F *vulgarize*
labasus N 260A *vulgarity*
labidas N 243A *shovel*
laboraŋT N 58E *laboratory assistant*
laboratOOrium N 246 *laboratory*
laboratOOrne A 247 *laboratory*
labüriŋT N 58E *labyrinth*
lade N 157 *layer*
ladestuma Vi 349H *be deposited*
ladu N 27 *warehouse*
laduma Vt 280 *pile up*
ladus A 231A *fluent*
ladusus N 260A *fluency*
laE *gen. of lagi*
laE *pres. of lAAḑima*
laegas N 159E *chest (box)*
laeKuma Vi 349G *be paid in*
laeKur N 229A *treasurer*
laEn N 61B *loan*
laEnaja N 227A *borrower*
laEnama Vt 327B *borrow*
laEng N 234B *charge*
laenutaja N 227A *lender*
laenutama Vt 349F *hire out*
laEv N 49B *ship*
laevandus N 260A *shipping*
laevastiK N 62 *fleet*
laevatama Vi 349F *navigate*
laevatamatu A 227A *unnavigable*
laevatatav A 231A *navigable*
laEvniK N 62 *shipowner*
lage *part. of lagi*
lage A 235 *bare (empty)*
lagendiK N 62 *plain*
lagi N 42 *ceiling*
lagle N 152 *brant goose*
lagrits N 231A *liquorice*
lagunema Vi 349D *fall to pieces*
lagUUn N 58A *lagoon*
lahas N 253 *splint*
lahata *part. of laHkama*
lahe *gen. of laHt*
lahe A 235 *affable*
lahendama Vt 349F *solve*
lahendamatu A 227A *unsolvable*
lahendus N 260A *solution*
lahing N 234A *battle*
lahja A 152 *meagre*
lahjendama Vt 349F *dilute*
laHk N 131C *parting*
laHkama Vt 348C *dissect*
laHke A 227B *kind*
laHkuma Vi 349G *depart*
laHkunu N 227A *the departed*
laHkus N 260B *kindness*
laHt N 139 *bay*
laHtine A 257B *open*
lahu *gen. of laHk*
lahus N 253 *solution*
lahustama Vt 349F *dissolve*
lahustuma Vi 349H *dissolve*
lahustumatu A 227A *insoluble*
lahustuv A 231A *soluble*
lahutama Vt 349F *divorce*
lahutamatu A 227A *inseparable*
lahutus N 260A *divorce*
laİ A 49B *wide*
laialdane A 257A *extensive*
laialivaLguv A 231A *diffuse*
laİd N 123B *islet*
laiendama Vt 349F *widen*
laiendus N 260A *widening*
laienema Vi 349D *widen*
laienemine N 257E *widening*
laiK N 61F *stain*
laİm N 61B *slander*
laİmama Vt 327B *slander*
laine N 177B *wave*
lainetama Vi 349F *undulate*
lainetus N 260A *waves*
laiP N 49D *corpse*
laisa *gen. of laiSk*
laiselda *part. of laiSklema*
laiSk A 95B *lazy*
laiSkleja N 227A *idler*
laiSklema Vi 336 *laze about*
laiSkur N 229A *sluggard*
laiSkus N 260B *laziness*
laiTma Vt 297C *find fault with*
laiTmatu A 227A *irreproachable*
laiTus N 260B *reproof*
laiu *gen. of laİd*
laİuma Vi 349G *spread out*
laİus N 260B *width*
laKK N 49C *loft*
laKK N 49C *mane*
laKK N 58C *varnish*
laKKama Vi 327C *cease*
laKKamatu A 227A *ceaseless*
laKKe *ill. of lagi*
laKKima Vt 291D *varnish*
laKKuma Vt 291D *lick*
lakooniline A 257D *laconic*
laKs N 61B *smack*
laksak N 234A *smack*
laKsuma Vi 291C *flap*
laksutama Vt 349F *click*
lamama Vi 269 *lie about (recline)*
laMba *gen. of lammas*
lame A 235 *flat*
lammas N 188 *sheep*
lammutama Vt 349F *tear down*
lamP N 58D *lamp*
laNgema Vi 349B *fall*
langetama Vt 349F *lower*
laNgevaRjur N 229A *parachutist*
laNgus N 260B *decline*
laO *gen. of ladu*
laO *pres. of laduma*
laoStama Vt 349F *ruin*
laoStuma Vi 349H *be ruined*
laoTama Vt 349F *spread out*
laPlane N 257C *Laplander*
laPP N 58C *patch*
laPPima Vt 291D *patch*
laPs N 85 *child*
lapseliK A 62 *childlike*
lapsendama Vt 349F *adopt*
lapsik A 234A *childish*
larüngiiT N 58E *laryngitis*
lase *pres. of laSkma*
laser N 229A *laser*
lasi *past of laSkma*
laSk N 131C *shot*
laSkma Vt 323 *shoot*
laSkuma Vi 349G *lower oneself*
laSkur N 229A *marksman*
lasT *part. of laPs*
laSta *part. of laSkma*
lasu *gen. of laSk*
lasuma Vi 269 *lie on (recline)*
latern N 231A *lantern*

laţikas N 243A *bream (fish)*
latrİIn N 58A *latrine*
laŢT N 58C *lath*
laTTu *ill. of ladu*
laTv N 49E *top of tree*
laU *gen. of laUg*
laua *gen. of laUd*
laUd N 88A *table*
laUdkoNd N 106 *table guests*
laUg N 134 *eyelid*
laUl N 61B *song*
laulik N 234A *songster*
laUlja N 227B *singer*
laUlma V 292B *sing*
lauP N 49D *forehead*
laureaaT N 58E *laureate*
lause N 177B *sentence*
lausik N 234A *flat*
laUsuma Vt 291C *utter*
lauT N 49E *barn*
lava N 14A *stage*
lavastaja N 227A *producer*
lavastama Vt 349F *stage*
lavastus N 260A *stage production*
laveNdel N 240A *lavender*
lavİIn N 58A *avalanche*
lebama Vi 269 *rest*
lEE N 1 *hearth*
lEEbe A 227B *mild*
leedi N 152 *lady*
leedulane N 257C *Lithuanian*
leegitsema Vi 349E *blaze*
leeK N 58F *flame*
leelutaja N 227A *leelu singer*
lEEm N 83 *broth*
lEEņ N 58A *back of chair*
lEEr N 58A *camp*
confirmation class
leeritama Vt 349F *confirm (church)*
leeTrid (pl) N 240A *measles*
leevendama Vt 349F *soothe*
leevike(ne) N 257G *bullfinch*
legeNd N 58B *legend*
legendAArne A 247 *legendary*
leha *gen. of leHk*
lehe *gen. of leHt*
lehestiK N 62 *foliage*
lehis N 253 *larch*
lehitsema Vt 349E *leaf*
leHk N 109 *stink*
leHkav A 231A *stinking*
leHm N 53B *cow*

leHt N 139 *leaf*
leHter N 240A *funnel*
leHtla N 227B *arbour*
leHv N 58B *bow (ribbon)*
lehvik N 234A *fan (paper)*
leHvima Vi 291C *flutter*
lehvitama Vt 349F *wave*
lehvitus N 260A *wave of hand*
leia *pres. of leİdma*
leİb N 86B *rye bread*
leİbkoNd N 106 *household*
leİbur N 229A *baker*
leİd N 123B *find*
leİdliK A 62 *resourceful*
leİdma Vt 316C *find*
leİduma Vi 349H *be found*
leİdur N 229A *inventor*
leİge A 227B *lukewarm*
leİl N 58B *steam in sauna*
leİn N 49B *mourning*
leİnaja N 227A *mourner*
leİnama Vt 327B *mourn*
leiTnanT N 58E *lieutenant*
leitsak N 234A *overwhelming heat*
leiu *gen. of leİd*
leiutaja N 227A *inventor*
leiutama Vt 349F *invent*
leiutis N 260A *invention*
leiva *gen. of leİb*
leKKima Vi 291D *leak*
lektOOrium N 246 *lecture-hall*
leKtor N 229A *lecturer*
lektÜÜr N 58A *reading matter*
leLL N 63A *father's brother*
lelu N 13A *toy*
leMbe *gen. of lemmes*
lemmel N 175 *duckweed*
lemmes N 196 *shred*
lemmik N 234A *favourite*
leNd N 129 *flight*
leNdama Vi 343 *fly*
leNdlema Vi 332 *flutter*
leNdur N 229A *flier*
lennata *part. of leNdama*
lennelda *part. of leNdlema*
lennu *gen. of leNd*
lennuk N 229A *airplane*
lennundus N 260A *aviation*
leO *pres. of liguma*
leO *gen. of ligu*
leoPaRd N 58B *leopard*
leoTama Vt 349F *soak*

lepatriinu N 152 *ladybug*
lepik N 234A *alder grove*
leping N 234A *treaty*
lepistiK N 62 *alder grove*
lepitama Vt 349F *reconcile*
lepitamatu A 227A *irreconcilable*
lepitus N 260A *reconciliation*
lePliK A 62 *tolerant*
lePliKKus N 260B *tolerance*
lePP N 53C *alder*
lePPima Vi 291D *be content with*
lePPimatu A 227A *implacable*
lese *gen. of leSk*
leSk N 140B *widow(er)*
leSt N 53B *flounder*
leŢT N 58C *counter (table)*
leukEEmia N 227A *leukemia*
levik N 234A *distribution*
levima Vi 269 *be disseminated*
levitama Vt 349F *disseminate*
levkoİ N 1 *gillyflower*
libe A 235 *slippery*
liberAAlne A 247 *liberal*
libisema Vi 349C *slip*
libistama Vt 349F *slide*
lible N 152 *blade (grass)*
liblikas N 243A *butterfly*
libreto N 152 *libretto*
libu N 13B *harlot*
liFt N 58A *elevator*
ligida N 236 *cf. ligidane*
ligidane A 257A *close*
liginema Vi 349D *approach*
ligu N 32 *soak*
liguma Vi 287 *soak*
ligunema Vi 349D *soak*
liha N 13A *meat*
lihas N 253 *muscle*
lihaseline A 257D *muscular*
lihav A 231A *plump*
liHtne A 249 *simple*
liHtsus N 260B *simplicity*
lihtsustama Vt 349F *simplify*
lihtsustamine N 257E *simplification*
lihuniK N 62 *butcher*
liHv N 58B *elegance*
liHvima Vt 291C *polish*
liia *gen. of lİİg*
liialdama Vt 349F *exaggerate*
liialdus N 260A *exaggeration*
liiderliK A 62 *licentious*
lİİg N 94B *excess*

liiga [N 152] *league*
liige [N 179E] *member*
liiges [N 253] *joint*
liigitama [Vt 349F] *classify*
liigitus [N 260A] *classification*
lİİgne [A 247] *excessive*
liigutama [Vt 349F] *move*
liigutav [A 231A] *touching*
liigutus [N 260A] *gesture*
liiK [N 58F] *species*
liiKlus [N 260B] *traffic*
liiKuma [Vi 291G] *move*
liiKumatu [A 227A] *motionless*
liiKumine [N 257E] *movement*
liiKuv [A 231A] *mobile*
lİİlia [N 227A] *lily*
lİİm [N 58A] *glue*
lİİmima [Vt 291A] *glue*
lİİn [N 58A] *line*
liiPer [N 240A] *tie (railway)*
liiSk [N 131C] *lot*
liisu *gen. of liiSk*
liiT [N 61E] *alliance*
liiTer [N 240A] *litre*
liiTlane [N 257C] *ally*
liiTma [Vt 297C] *join*
liiTmine [N 257E] *adding*
liiTuma [Vi 349H] *join up*
lİİv [N 49A] *sand*
liivane [A 251] *sandy*
liivatama [Vt 349F] *sand*
lİİvlane [N 257C] *Livonian*
liKKu *ill. of ligu*
likvidEErima [Vt 291B] *liquidate*
likÖÖr [N 58A] *liqueur*
lilipuŢ [N 58H] *midget*
liLL [N 63A] *flower*
lilla [A 152] *purple*
lilla [N 152] *faggot (gay)*
lillakas [A 243A] *purplish*
lilleline [A 257D] *flowery*
lima [N 13A] *slime*
limane [A 251] *slimy*
limiiT [N 58E] *limit*
limonAAd [N 58A] *soft drink*
lina [N 14A] *linen*
linane [A 251] *linen*
linastama [Vt 349F] *screen a film*
liNd [N 129] *bird*
liŋdistama [Vt 349F] *tape*
liNdla [N 227B] *poultry house*
linEErima [Vt 291B] *rule (draw lines)*
liNg [N 61B] *sling*
linik [N 234A] *place-mat*
linK [N 58F] *latch*
liNlane [N 257C] *city dweller*
liNN [N 49A] *city*
linnased (pl) [N 253] *malt*
linnastama [Vt 349F] *urbanize*
linnastuma [Vi 349H] *urbanize*
linnu *gen. of liNd*
linnuke(ne) [N 257G] *birdie*
linnus [N 253] *stronghold*
linolEum [N 58B] *linoleum*
liŋT [N 58E] *tape*
liŋTšima [Vt 291C] *lynch*
linu *pl. part. of lina*
lipik [N 234A] *tag*
lipitsema [Vi 349E] *fawn*
liPkoNd [N 106] *troop of horsemen*
liPP [N 61C] *flag*
liPs [N 61B] *tie*
liputama [Vt 349F] *wag (tail)*
lisa [N 13A] *addition*
lisama [Vt 269] *add*
lisand [N 229A] *addition*
lita [N 152] *bitch*
liŢs [N 58B] *prostitute*
liTTer [N 240B] *sequin*
lituRgia [N 227A] *liturgy*
liuelda *part. of liUglema*
liUglema [Vi 334] *glide*
liuStiK [N 62] *glacier*
loA *gen. of luba*
loba [N 13B] *gibberish*
lobisema [Vi 349C] *prattle*
lodev [A 231A] *slack*
loE *pres. of lugema*
loE [N 212] *north-west*
loEnd [N 229B] *enumeration*
loEndama [Vt 349F] *enumerate*
loEndus [N 260B] *enumeration*
loEng [N 234B] *lecture*
loeTav [A 231A] *readable*
loeTavus [N 260A] *readability*
loeTelu [N 13A] *enumeration*
loeTlema [Vt 351] *enumerate*
logard [N 229A] *loafer*
logelema [Vi 325] *loaf*
logisema [Vi 349C] *wobble*
logu [N 13D] *rattletrap*
lohakas [A 243A] *sloppy*
lohakus [N 260A] *sloppiness*
lohe [N 153] *dragon*
lohe [N 153] *kite*
lohisema [Vi 349C] *drag*
lohistama [Vt 349F] *drag*
loHk [N 131C] *hollow*
lohu *gen. of loHk*
lohuke(ne) [N 257G] *dimple*
lohutama [Vt 349F] *console*
lohutus [N 260A] *consolation*
loi̇d [A 123B] *apathetic*
loi̇dus [N 260B] *apathy*
loiK [N 61F] *puddle*
loiTma [Vi 297C] *flare*
loiu *gen. of loi̇d*
lokAAl [N 58A] *pub*
lokauT [N 58E] *lockout*
loKK [N 58C] *curl*
loKKima [Vt 291D] *curl*
loKsuma [Vi 291C] *shake (liquid)*
loksutama [Vt 349F] *shake (liquid)*
loĻL [A 58A] *stupid*
loļlakas [A 243A] *simpleton*
loĻLus [N 260B] *stupidity*
lombak [N 234A] *cripple*
lombakas [A 243A] *crippled*
lomP [N 58D] *puddle*
lonKama [Vi 327F] *limp*
lonKima [Vi 291G] *saunter*
lonKs [N 61B] *gulp*
loŋT [N 58E] *trunk (animal)*
lonTrus [N 260B] *hooligan*
lOO *gen. of lugu*
lOObuma [Vi 349G] *renounce*
lOOde *gen. of loE*
loode [N 177E] *embryo*
lOOdus [N 260B] *nature*
lOOdusliK [A 62] *natural*
loogika [N 227A] *logic*
loogiline [A 257D] *logical*
lOOja [N 227B] *Creator*
loojang [N 234A] *sunset*
lOOjuma [Vi 349G] *set astronomically*
looKlema [Vi 326F] *meander*
looKlev [A 231A] *meandering*
lOOm [N 53A] *animal*
lOOm [N 61A] *characteristic*
lOOma [Vt 267] *create*
lOOmine [N 257E] *creation*
looming [N 234A] *creative work*
loomuliK [A 62] *natural*
lOOmus [N 260B] *disposition*
loomus [N 253] *knitting beginning*
looPima [Vt 291E] *hurl*

lOOr [N 58A] *veil*
lOOrber [N 229A] *laurel*
lOOrima [Vt 291A] *veil*
looritama [Vt 349F] *veil*
lOOş [N 58A] *lottery ticket*
lOOşima [Vt 291A] *raffle*
lOOşimine [N 257E] *lottery*
loosung [N 229A] *slogan*
lOOž [N 58A] *box in theatre*
looTma [V 297C] *hope*
looŢs [N 58B] *pilot boat*
looţsik [N 234A] *boat*
looTus [N 260B] *hope*
looTusetu [A 227A] *hopeless*
looTusetus [N 260A] *hopelessness*
lOOv [A 231B] *creative*
loovutama [Vt 349F] *relinquish*
lopsakas [A 243A] *lush*
loputama [Vt 349F] *rinse*
loRd [N 58B] *lord (aristocrat)*
lornjeŢT [N 58C] *lorgnette*
loru [N 13A] *lout*
loŞS [N 58A] *castle*
lotendama [Vi 349F] *droop*
loterİI [N 1] *lottery*
loto [N 152] *lotto*
loŢT [N 58C] *double chin*
luba [N 38] *permission*
lubadus [N 260A] *promise*
lubama [Vt 269] *allow*
promise
lubamatu [A 227A] *improper*
lubatav [A 231A] *permissible*
lube *pl. part. of luba*
lubi [N 71B] *lime (mineral)*
lugeja [N 227A] *reader*
lugejaskoNd [N 106] *readership*
lugema [V 284] *count*
read
lugematu [A 227A] *countless*
lugemiK [N 62] *reader (book)*
lugemine [N 257E] *reading*
lugu [N 33] *tale*
luha *gen. of luHt*
luHt [N 104B] *wetland*
luide [N 177E] *dune*
luiK [N 63E] *swan*
luİne [A 252] *bony*
luisata *part. of luiSkama*
luiSk [N 131C] *whetstone*
luiSkama [Vi 348C] *fib*
luiSkama [Vt 348C] *whet*

luisu *gen. of luiSk*
luiTuma [Vi 349H] *fade*
luka [N 180] *projection*
luKK [N 61C] *lock*
luKKu *ill. of lugu*
luKsuma [Vi 291C] *hiccough*
luKsus [N 260B] *luxury*
luKsusliK [A 62] *luxurious*
lukustama [Vt 349F] *lock*
lume *gen. of lumi*
lumi [N 21] *snow*
lumine [A 251] *snowy*
luMMe *ill. of lumi*
lunastaja [N 227A] *Saviour*
lunastama [Vt 349F] *redeem*
luNd *part. of lumi*
luPjama [Vt 327D] *whitewash*
lurjus [N 253] *scoundrel*
lusikas [N 243A] *spoon*
luŞt [N 58B] *pleasure*
luştakas [A 243A] *pleasurable*
luŞtliK [A 62] *jolly*
luţikas [N 243A] *bedbug*
luTs [N 61B] *burbot*
luŢT [N 58C] *artificial nipple*
lUU [N 7] *bone*
luua *gen. of lUUd*
lUUa *part. of lOOma*
lUUd [N 103] *broom*
luuK [N 58F] *shutter*
luule [N 177A] *poetry*
lUUleline [A 257D] *poetic*
luuletaja [N 227A] *poet*
luuletama [Vt 349F] *write poetry*
luuletus [N 260A] *poem*
luuP [N 58D] *magnifying glass*
lUUraja [N 227A] *scout*
lUUrama [Vt 327A] *spy*
luure [N 177A] *espionage*
luuStiK [N 62] *skeleton*
lõA *gen. of lÕÕg*
lõbu [N 13B] *fun*
lõbus [A 231A] *fun*
lõbustama [Vt 349F] *entertain*
lõbustus [N 260A] *entertainment*
lõbusus [N 260A] *gaiety*
lõbutsema [Vi 349E] *enjoy oneself*
lõdisema [Vi 349C] *shiver*
lõdistama [Vt 349F] *make shiver*
lõdvendama [Vt 349F] *slacken*
lõdvenema [Vi 349D] *slacken*
lõhata *part. of lõHkama*

lõhe [N 153] *fissure*
salmon
lõhenema [Vi 349D] *split apart*
lõhestama [Vt 349F] *split apart*
lõhi [N 18] *salmon*
lõHk [N 131C] *split*
lõHkama [Vt 348C] *explode*
lõHkema [Vi 349B] *explode*
lõHkev [A 231A] *explosive*
lõHkuma [Vt 313B] *break*
lõhmus [N 253] *linden tree*
lõHn [N 49B] *aroma*
lõHnama [Vi 327B] *smell*
lõhnastama [Vt 349F] *scent*
lõHnav [A 231A] *fragrant*
lõhu *gen. of lõHk*
lõhu *pres. of lõHkuma*
lõİ *past of lÖÖma*
lõİ *past of lOOma*
lõige [N 177F] *pattern*
lõiK [N 61F] *slice*
lõiKama [Vt 327F] *cut*
lõiKav [A 231A] *cutting*
lõiKuma [Vi 349G] *intersect*
lõiKus [N 260B] *operation (surgical)*
lõİm [N 63B] *warp*
lõke [N 177C] *bonfire*
lõKs [N 61B] *trap*
lõNg [N 49B] *yarn*
lõngus [N 253] *gang member*
lõoKe(ne) [N 257G] *lark (bird)*
lõpetaja [N 227A] *graduate*
lõpetama [Vt 349F] *finish*
lõPliK [A 62] *final*
lõPma [Vi 299] *end*
lõPmatu [A 227A] *endless*
lõPP [N 61C] *end*
lõPPema [Vi 291D] *end*
lõpus [N 253] *gill*
lõputu [A 227A] *endless*
lõTv [A 49E] *limp*
lõTvuma [Vi 349G] *become limp*
lõua *gen. of lõUg*
lõuata *part. of lõUgama*
lõuend [N 229A] *canvas*
lõUg [N 94A] *chin*
lõUgama [Vi 345A] *bawl*
lõuna [N 178B] *noon*
south
lõunastama [Vi 349F] *dine (noon)*
lõunatama [Vt 349F] *dine (noon)*
lõuSt [N 49B] *ugly face*

lõvi N 13A *lion*
lÕÕg N 97 *leash*
lõõgastuma Vi 349H *relax*
lõõgastus N 260A *relaxation*
lÕÕm N 49A *blaze*
lÕÕmama Vi 327A *blaze*
lÕÕr N 58A *flue*
lõõritama Vi 349F *warble*
lõõTs N 49B *bellows*
läbima Vt 269 *pass through*
läbituNgimatu A 227A *impenetrable*
lähe *pres. of minema*
läheda N 236 *cf. lähedane*
lähedane A 257A *near*
lähedus N 260A *nearness*
lähem A 231A *nearer*
lähendama Vt 349F *bring closer*
lähenema Vi 349D *come closer*
lähenemine N 257E *approaching*
lähim A 231A *nearest*
lähised (pl) N 253 *approaches*
läHtuma Vi 349H *originate*
läige N 177F *gloss*
läiKima Vi 291G *sparkle*
läiKiv A 231A *glossy*
läila A 152 *insipid*
läinu N 186 *departed*
läkastama Vi 349F *have coughing fit*
läkitama Vt 349F *dispatch*
läkitus N 260A *summons*
läks *past of minema*
läMbuma Vi 349G *suffocate*
läMbus N 260B *suffocation*
lämmastiK N 62 *nitrogen*
lämmatama Vt 349F *suffocate*
lämmatav A 231A *suffocating*
läRm N 58B *noise*
lärmakas A 243A *noisy*
läRmama Vi 327B *be noisy*
läte N 177C *spring of water*
läTlane N 257C *Latvian*
läve *gen. and part. of lävi*
lävi N 18 *doorsill*
lävima Vi 269 *associate with*
lÄÄge A 227B *insipid*
lääne *gen. of lÄÄş*
lÄÄnlane N 257C *native of Läänemaa*
läänT *part. of lÄÄş*
lÄÄş N 146 *west*
lääTs N 63B *lens*
lömastama Vt 349F *squash*
lömitama Vi 349F *grovel*
lörTs N 58B *slush*
lÖÖbe *gen. of lööve*
lööK N 58F *blow (hit)*
lÖÖma Vt 268 *hit*
lööming N 234A *fight*
lööve N 208A *rash*
lüheldane A 257A *shortish*
lühem A 231A *shorter*
lühend N 229A *abbreviation*
lühendama Vt 349F *shorten*
lühenema Vi 349D *shorten*
lühidus N 260A *brevity*
lühike(ne) A 257G *short*
lühinägeliK A 62 *near-sighted*
lükati N 225A *slide rule*
lüKKama Vt 327C *push*
lüKKima Vt 291D *string*
lüli N 13A *link*
lülitama Vt 349F *switch*
lüliti N 225A *switch*
lünK N 53F *gap*
lünKliK A 62 *having gaps*
lüpsik N 234A *milk pail*
lüPsja N 227B *milker*
lüPsma Vt 293A *milk*
lüPsmine N 257E *milking*
lüTseum N 246 *lyceum*
lÜÜa *part. of lÖÖma*
lüürika N 227A *lyrics*
lüüriline A 257D *lyrical*
lÜÜs N 58A *sluice*

M

mAA N 9 *land*
mAAbuma Vi 349G *disembark*
mAAbumine N 257E *disembarkation*
mAAdleja N 227A *wrestler*
mAAdlema Vi 326A *wrestle*
mAAdlus N 260B *wrestling*
maagiline A 257D *magical*
maaK N 58F *ore*
mAAkoNd N 106 *province*
mAAkoNdliK A 62 *provincial*
mAAļ N 58A *painting (art)*
mAAler N 240A *painter (artist)*
maaļiline A 257D *picturesque*
mAAļima V 291A *paint (art)*
mAAndama Vt 349F *ground electrically*
mAAndama Vt 349F *land airplane*
mAAnduma Vi 349H *land*
mAAnia N 227A *mania*
mAArde *gen. of maare*
mAArdla N 227B *mineral deposit*
maare N 211A *mineral resource*
maasikas N 243A *strawberry*
maaStiK N 62 *landscape*
madal A 231A *low*
madaldama Vt 349F *lower*
madaliK N 62 *shallow*
madar N 231A *bedstraw (plant)*
maḑjar N 229A *Hungarian*
madrats N 229A *mattress*
madrus N 253 *sailor*
madu N 27 *viper*
maeTa *imper. of maTma*
maFFia N 227A *Mafia*
magama Vi 269 *sleep*
mage A 235 *unsalted*
magiSter N 240A *master (university)*
magistrAAl N 58A *main line*
magneeTima Vt 291F *magnetize*
magnet N 229A *magnet*
magnetiline A 257D *magnetic*
magnetisEErima Vt 291B *magnetize*
magnetofon N 245 *tape-recorder*
magnetofOOnima Vt 291A *tape-record*
magu N 31 *stomach*
magus A 231A *sweet*
magustama Vt 349F *sweeten*
maha *ill. of mAA*
mahe A 235 *mild*
mahedus N 260A *mildness*
mahhinatsiOOn N 58A *machination*
maHl N 49B *juice*
mahlakas A 243A *juicy*
mahlane A 251 *juicy*
maHt N 124B *capacity*
maHtuma Vi 308B *fit*
maHtuvus N 260A *capacity*
mahu *gen. of maHt*
mahu *pres. of maHtuma*
mahukas A 243A *roomy*
mahutama Vt 349F *fit*
maHv N 58B *puff*
maİ N 1 *May*
maias A 159B *fond of sweets*

maika [N 152] *sleeveless undershirt*
maİne [A 252] *earthly*
maine [N 177B] *reputation*
maİnima [Vt 291C] *mention*
maİs [N 58B] *corn*
maitse [N 177B] *taste*
maiTsekas [A 243A] *tasteful*
maiTsema [V 295] *taste*
maitsestama [Vt 349F] *season with spices*
maiTsetu [A 227A] *tasteless*
maiTsev [A 241A] *tasty*
maiTsma [V 295] *taste*
maja [N 14A] *house*
majakas [N 243A] *lighthouse*
majand [N 229A] *farm*
majandama [Vt 349F] *finance*
majandus [N 260A] *economics*
majanduslİK [A 62] *economic*
majesteeT [N 58E] *majesty*
majesteeTliK [A 62] *majestic*
maJJa *ill. of maja*
majonEEs [N 58A] *mayonnaise*
major [N 229A] *major*
majorAAn [N 58A] *marjoram*
maju *pl. part. of maja*
majutama [Vt 349F] *house*
majutus [N 260A] *housing*
makaron [N 245] *macaroni*
makeŢT [N 58C] *model*
maKK [N 58C] *blood sausage*
maKK [N 58C] *tape-recorder*
maKKu *ill. of magu*
makreĻL [N 58A] *mackerel*
maKs [N 49B] *liver*
maKs [N 61B] *payment*
maksimAAlne [A 247] *maximum*
maksimum [N 245] *maximum*
maKsma [Vi 293A] *cost*
maKsma [Vt 293A] *pay*
maksuline [A 257D] *liable to a fee*
maKsumus [N 260A] *cost*
maksustama [Vt 349F] *tax*
maksustamine [N 257E] *taxation*
maKsvus [N 260B] *validity*
male [N 153] *chess*
malend [N 229A] *chess-man*
maletaja [N 227A] *chess-player*
maletama [Vi 349F] *play chess*
malev [N 231A] *brigade*
maĻL [N 58A] *protractor*
maĻm [N 58B] *cast-iron*
malTs [N 49B] *orache*

mamma [N 152] *mommy*
mammi [N 152] *mommy*
maMMon [N 231A] *Mammon*
mammut [N 229A] *mammoth*
manala [N 227A] *land of the dead*
mandaaT [N 58E] *mandate*
mandarİİn [N 58A] *tangerine*
maNdel [N 240A] *almond*
tonsil
maNder [N 240A] *continent*
mandolİİn [N 58A] *mandolin*
maNdri *gen. of manner*
maNduma [Vi 349H] *degenerate*
maNdumine [N 257E] *degeneration*
maNdunu [N 227A] *degenerate*
manEEž [N 58A] *riding-school*
manifeSt [N 58B] *manifesto*
manikÜÜr [N 58A] *manicure*
manitsema [Vt 349E] *admonish*
manitsus [N 260A] *admonition*
manna [N 152] *semolina*
mannekEEn [N 58A] *fashion model*
manner [N 207] *continent*
mannerg [N 234A] *can*
mannetu [A 227A] *helpless*
mansaRd [N 58B] *attic*
mansi [N 152] *Mansi*
manTel [N 240A] *coat*
manufaktUUr [N 58A] *textile factory*
manus [N 253] *accessory*
manÖÖver [N 240A] *manoeuvre*
manööverdama [Vt 349F] *manoeuvre*
maO *gen. of magu*
maO *gen. of madu*
maPP [N 58C] *folder*
mardikas [N 243A] *beetle*
margarİİn [N 58A] *margarine*
margistama [Vt 349F] *affix stamp*
mari [N 68A] *berry*
marinAAd [N 58A] *marinade*
marinEErima [Vt 291B] *marinade*
marjuline [N 257D] *berry-picker*
marK [N 49F] *mark (currency)*
marK [N 58F] *postage stamp*
trade-mark
marli [N 152] *gauze*
marmelAAd [N 58A] *marmalade*
maRmor [N 229A] *marble*
maRRi *ill. of mari*
maRRu *ill. of maru*
marSruuT [N 58E] *route*
marSS [N 58G] *march*

marSSal [N 229A] *marshal*
marSSima [Vi 291H] *march*
martsipan [N 245] *marzipan*
maru [N 13A] *tempest*
masendama [Vt 349F] *depress*
masendav [A 231A] *depressing*
masendus [N 260A] *depression*
masin [N 231A] *machine*
maŞk [N 58B] *mask*
maskEErima [Vt 291B] *disguise*
masohhiSt [N 58B] *masochist*
maŞS [N 58A] *mass*
massAAž [N 58A] *massage*
massEErima [Vt 291B] *massage*
massİİvne [A 247] *massive*
maşsiline [A 257D] *mass*
maŞt [N 58B] *mast*
maStaaP [N 58D] *scale*
masturbatsiOOn [N 58A] *masturbation*
masuuT [N 58E] *fuel oil*
matEEria [N 227A] *substance*
matemaatik [N 234A] *mathematician*
matemaatika [N 227A] *mathematics*
matemaatiline [A 257D] *mathematical*
materiAAlne [A 247] *material*
materialiStliK [A 62] *materialistic*
materjal [N 245] *material*
maTk [N 49B] *hike*
maTkaja [N 227A] *hiker*
maTkama [Vi 327B] *hike*
maTkima [Vt 291C] *imitate*
maTma [Vt 300] *bury*
maTmine [N 257E] *burial*
maŢs [N 58B] *peasant*
maŢsliK [A 62] *peasant-like*
matsutama [Vt 349F] *smack (lips)*
maTš [N 58B] *match (sport)*
maŢT [A 58C] *mat (dull colour)*
maŢT [N 58C] *checkmate*
mat (floor)
maTTu *ill. of madu*
matus [N 253] *funeral*
mausolEum [N 58B] *mausoleum*
medal [N 229A] *medal*
medikameŋT [N 58E] *medicine*
meditsİİn [N 58A] *medicine*
meditsiiniline [A 257D] *medicinal*
mEE *gen. of mesi*
meedik [N 234A] *medic*
mEEl [N 82] *mind*
mEEldima [Vi 349B] *be pleasing*
mEEldiv [A 231A] *pleasing*

meelemärKusetu A 227A *unconscious*
meeletu A 227A *frantic*
meeletus N 260A *frenzy*
meelitama Vt 349F *coax*
meelitav A 231A *flattering*
mEElsus N 260B *mentality*
meelTlahutav A 231A *amusing*
meene N 177A *souvenir*
mEEnuma Vi 349G *come to mind*
meenutama Vt 349F *call to mind*
mEEs N 147 *man*
mEEskoNd N 106 *men's team*
meesT *part. of mEEs*
meeTer N 229A *metre*
meeTmed (pl) N 179D *measure*
meetod N 229A *method*
mehaanik N 234A *mechanic*
mehaanika N 227A *mechanics*
mehaaniline A 257D *mechanical*
mehe *gen. of mEEs*
meheliK A 62 *manly*
mehhanisaaTor N 229A *mechanizer*
mehhanisEErima Vt 291B *mechanize*
mehhanisEErimine N 257E *mechanization*
mehhaniSm N 58B *mechanism*
mehhiklane N 257C *Mexican*
meHHu *ill. of mehu*
mehine A 251 *manly*
mehisus N 260A *manliness*
mehitama Vt 349F *man*
mehu N 13A *juice*
meiereİ N 1 *dairy*
meiSter N 240A *master (expert)*
meiSterliK A 62 *masterful*
meiSterliKKus N 260B *mastery*
melanhOOlia N 227A *melancholy*
melanhOOlne A 247 *melancholic*
melioratsiOOn N 58A *amelioration*
meLLu *ill. of melu*
melon N 229A *melon*
melOOdia N 227A *melody*
meloodiline A 257D *melodious*
melu N 13A *din*
membrAAn N 58A *membrane*
meMM N 63A *mommy*
memuaarid N 58A *memoirs*
meNNu *ill. of menu*
menstruatsiOOn N 58A *menstruation*
menu N 13A *success*
menukas A 243A *successful*
menÜÜ N 1 *menu*
meri N 20 *sea*
meridiAAn N 58A *meridian*
meRRe *ill. of meri*
mesi N 46 *honey*
mesila N 227A *apiary*
mesilane N 257C *honey bee*
mesindus N 260A *apiculture*
mesiniK N 62 *bee-keeper*
meŞS N 58A *fair*
meŞS N 58A *Catholic mass*
meSSias N 243A *Messiah*
metaĻL N 58A *metal*
metaļliline A 257D *metallic*
metalluRgia N 227A *metallurgy*
metallurgiline A 257D *metallurgical*
meteOOr N 58A *meteor*
meteoriiT N 58E *meteorite*
meteorolOOg N 58A *meteorologist*
meteorolOOgia N 227A *meteorology*
metodiSt N 58B *methodist*
metoodika N 227A *methodology*
metoodiline A 257D *methodical*
metrOO N 1 *subway*
metropol N 245 *metropolis*
metropoliiT N 58E *metropolitan (church)*
meTs N 53B *forest*
metsandus N 260A *forestry*
metsane A 251 *forested*
meţsik A 234A *wild*
meTskoNd N 106 *forest district*
meTslane N 257C *savage*
meTsniK N 62 *forester*
meTT *part. of mesi*
meTTe *ill. of mesi*
migratsiOOn N 58A *migration*
mİİl N 58A *mile*
miimika N 227A *facial expression*
mİİn N 58A *mine (explosive)*
miinimum N 245 *minimum*
miinus N 253 *minus*
miiting N 234A *political rally*
mikrofon N 245 *microphone*
mikrOOb N 58A *microbe*
mikroskooP N 58D *microscope*
mikroskoopiline A 257D *microscopic*
miKser N 229A *mixer*
militariSm N 58B *militarism*
militsionÄÄr N 58A *militiaman*
miļjard N 229A *billion*
miļjardes A 237B *billionth*
miļjardär N 245 *multi-millionaire*
miĻjon N 229A *million*
miĻjones A 237C *millionth*
miļjonär N 245 *millionaire*
miljÖÖ N 1 *milieu*
miļlimaļlikas N 243A *jelly-fish*
miļline A 251 *what kind of*
minareŢT N 58C *minaret*
minEErima Vt 291B *undermine*
minek N 234A *departure*
minema Vi 274 *go*
minerAAl N 58A *mineral*
minerAAlne A 247 *mineral*
mineralOOgia N 227A *mineralogy*
minestama Vi 349F *faint*
minestus N 260A *faint*
mineviK N 62 *past*
miNgi A 225B *some (a certain)*
minia N 227A *daughter-in-law*
miniatUUr N 58A *miniature*
minimAAlne A 247 *minimal*
ministEErium N 246 *ministry*
miniSter N 240A *minister*
minK N 58F *make-up (cosmetic)*
minKima Vt 291G *make up*
miNNa *part. of minema*
minut N 229A *minute*
mirT N 58E *myrtle*
misjonär N 245 *missionary*
miSS N 58A *beauty-queen*
missiOOn N 58A *mission*
miTmekesistama Vt 349F *diversify*
miTmekesisus N 260A *diversification*
miTmes A 238B *which (ordinal)*
miTmus N 260B *plural*
mitu N 182 *many*
mobilisEErima Vt 291B *mobilize*
modellEErima Vt 291B *model*
modernisEErima Vt 291B *modernize*
modeRnne A 247 *modern*
moE *gen. of mOOḑ*
moeKas A 243B *stylish*
moKK N 53C *lip*
moĻd N 117 *trough*
moldAAvlane N 257C *Moldavian*
molekul N 245 *molecule*
moļli *gen. of moĻd*
momeņT N 58E *moment*
momentAAnne A 247 *instantaneous*
monarH N 58B *monarch*
monarHia N 227A *monarchy*
monolOOg N 58A *monologue*
monopol N 245 *monopoly*
monotOOnne A 247 *monotonous*
montAAž N 58A *fitting*

montEErima Vt 291B *mount*
montÖÖr N 58A *fitter*
monumeŋT N 58E *monument*
monumentAAlne A 247 *monumental*
mOOḑ N 115 *fashion*
mOOdne A 249 *fashionable*
moodustama Vt 349F *form*
moodustis N 260A *formation*
mOOn N 53A *provisions*
mOOŋ N 58A *poppy*
mOOndama Vt 349F *transform*
mOOnduma Vi 349H *transform*
moonutama Vt 349F *distort*
moonutus N 260A *distortion*
mOOş N 58A *jam*
moosekaŋT N 58E *musician*
mooTor N 229A *motor*
morAAl N 58A *moral*
morAAlne A 247 *moral*
moRdvalane N 257C *Mordvin*
morfolOOgia N 227A *morphology*
morfoloogiline A 257D *morphological*
moRn N 58B *sullen*
morsa *gen. of morSk*
morse N 152 *Morse*
morSk N 109 *walrus*
morSS N 58G *berry drink*
mosaiiK N 58F *mosaic*
moşsitama V 349F *pout*
mošEE N 2 *mosque*
moteĻL N 58A *motel*
motİİv N 58A *motive*
motivEErima Vt 291B *motivate*
moto N 152 *motto*
muda N 13C *mud*
mudane A 251 *muddy*
mudel N 229A *model*
mudilane N 257C *toddler*
mugav A 231A *comfortable*
mugavus N 260A *comfort*
mugul N 231A *tuber*
muhamEEdlane N 257C *Muslim*
muhelema Vi 325 *smile smugly*
muHk N 131C *bump on skin*
muhu *gen. of muHk*
muHv N 58B *muff*
muiata *part. of muİgama*
muie N 216 *smirk*
muİgama Vi 345B *smirk*
muİge *gen. of muie*
muİnsus N 260B *antiquity*
muistend N 229A *folk-tale*
muiStne A 247 *ancient*
muLd N 105 *soil*
muLdama Vt 342 *earth*
mulgustama Vt 349F *perforate*
mulgusti N 225A *perforator*
muļje N 177B *impression*
muĻjuma Vt 291C *bruise*
muļjutus N 260A *contusion*
muļK N 58F *native of Mulgimaa*
muĻL N 58A *bubble*
mulla *gen. of muLd*
mullata *part. of muLdama*
muļlikas N 243A *heifer*
mumPs N 58B *mumps*
muna N 16 *egg*
munand N 229A *testicle*
muNder N 240A *uniform*
munema V 269 *lay eggs*
munK N 53F *monk*
muNNa *ill. of muna*
muŋnid (pl) N 58A *balls (testicles)*
murakas N 243A *cloudberry*
muRd N 130 *fracture*
muRde *gen. of murre N 215*
muRdeline A 257D *dialectal*
muRdma Vt 318 *fracture*
muRdmed (pl) N 222 *fractured pieces*
muRduma Vi 349H *fracture*
muRdumatu A 227A *unbreakable*
mure N 153 *worry*
mureliK A 62 *worried*
muretsema Vi 349E *worry*
muretsema Vt 349E *procure*
muretu A 227A *carefree*
murra *pres. of muRdma*
murrak N 234A *minor dialect*
murre *nom. of muRdmed*
murre N 215 *major dialect*
murre N 215 *fracture*
murru *gen. of muRd*
muRRu *ill. of muru*
muru N 13A *lawn*
murulauK N 61F *chive*
musi N 13A *kiss*
musikAAlne A 247 *musical*
muskaaT N 58E *nutmeg*
muSkel N 240A *muscle*
muSkliline A 257D *muscular*
muSSi *ill. of musi*
muŞSu *ill. of muşu*
muSt A 53B *black*
dirty
muStama Vt 327B *blacken*
mustand N 229A *draft copy*
muSter N 240A *pattern*
muştikas N 243A *blueberry*
muStlane N 257C *Gipsy*
muStriline A 257D *patterned*
muStus N 260B *dirt*
muşu N 13A *kiss*
muşutama Vt 349F *kiss*
muŢT N 58C *mole*
muTTa *ill. of muda*
muTTer N 240B *nut (bolt)*
mUU N 7 *other (different)*
muudatus N 260A *change*
mUUļ N 58A *jetty*
mUUlane N 257C *foreigner*
mUUmia N 227A *mummy*
mUUseum N 246 *museum*
muusik N 234A *musician*
muusika N 227A *music*
muusikal N 245 *musical*
muusikaline A 257D *musical*
muuTliK A 62 *changeable*
muuTma Vt 297C *change*
muuTuma Vi 349H *change*
muuTumatu A 227A *unchangeable*
muuTus N 260B *change*
mõdu N 13C *mead*
mõElda *part. of mõTlema*
mõİs N 231B *estate*
mõİsniK N 62 *squire*
mõistatama Vt 349F *guess*
mõistatus N 260A *riddle*
mõistatusliK A 62 *puzzling*
mõiste N 177B *notion*
mõistetav A 231A *understandable*
mõiStliK A 62 *reasonable*
mõiStma Vt 297A *understand*
mõiStmatu A 227A *irrational*
mõiStmine N 257E *comprehension*
mõiStus N 260B *reason (intelligence)*
mõJJu *ill. of mõju*
mõju N 13A *influence*
mõjukas A 243A *influential*
mõjuma Vi 269 *influence*
mõjustama Vt 349F *influence*
mõjutama Vt 349F *influence*
mõjutu A 227A *ineffective*
mõjuv A 231A *effective*
mõla N 13A *paddle*
mõlema(no nominative A 232 *both*
mõlgutama Vt 349F *meditate*

mõLLa *ill. of mõla*
mõMM N 58A *teddy bear*
mõNd(a) *part. of mõni*
mõNda *ill. of mõni*
mõni A 22 *some*
mõningane A 257A *some*
mõnitama Vt 349F *mock*
mõnitamine N 257E *mocking*
mõnitus N 260A *mockery*
mõNNu *ill. of mõnu*
mõnu N 13A *enjoyment*
mõnulema Vi 349A *luxuriate*
mõnus A 231A *cosy*
mõra N 13A *flaw*
mõranema Vi 349D *crack*
mõRd N 93 *weir*
mõRRa *ill. of mõra*
mõrra *gen. of mõRd*
mõRRu *ill. of mõru*
mõRsja N 227B *bride*
mõrtsukas N 243A *murderer*
mõru A 13A *bitter*
mõRv N 49B *murder*
mõRvama Vt 327B *murder*
mõRvar N 229A *murderer*
mõse *pres. of mõSkma*
mõSkma Vt 322 *wash*
mõSta *part. of mõSkma*
mõte N 177C *thought*
mõtestama Vt 349F *give meaning to*
mõtiskelu N 13A *meditation*
mõtisklema Vi 351 *ponder*
mõTlema Vt 337 *think*
mõTlematu A 227A *thoughtless*
mõTlematus N 260A *thoughtlessness*
mõTliK A 62 *pensive*
mõTTetu A 227A *senseless*
mõTTetus N 260A *senselessness*
mõTTu *ill. of mõdu*
mõõde N 179D *dimension*
mõõdukas A 243A *moderate*
mõõdukus N 260A *moderation*
mõõK N 49F *sword*
mÕÕn N 49A *ebb*
mÕÕnama Vi 327A *ebb*
mõõT N 61E *measure*
mõõTma Vt 297C *measure*
mõõTmatu A 227A *immeasurable*
mõõTmine N 257E *measuring*
mäda N 13C *pus*
mädane A 251 *festering*
mädanema Vi 349D *fester*
mädaniK N 62 *abscess*
mädarõigas N 159E *horse-radish*
mäE *gen. of mägi*
mäEndus N 260B *mining*
mäeStiK N 62 *mountain range*
mäger N 79C *badger*
mägi N 42 *hill*
mägilane N 257C *highlander*
mägine A 251 *hilly*
mähe N 224 *diaper*
mähi *pres. of mäHkima*
mähis N 253 *wrapping*
mäHkima Vt 313B *wrap*
mäHkme *gen. of mähe*
mäKKe *ill. of mägi*
mälestama Vt 349F *commemorate*
mälestis N 260A *memorial*
mälestus N 260A *memory*
mäletama Vt 349F *remember*
mäletseja N 227A *ruminant*
mäletsema Vi 349E *ruminate*
mäLLu *ill. of mälu*
mälu N 13A *memory*
mäLv N 53B *skin for tanning*
mäLv N 63B *sternum*
mäMM N 58A *mush*
mäNd N 106 *whisk*
mäŅd N 118 *pine*
mänedžer N 245 *manager*
mäNg N 61B *game*
mäNgima V 291C *play*
männa *gen. of mäNd N 106*
mäŋni *gen. of mäŅd N 118*
mäŋnik N 234A *pine grove*
mära N 13A *mare*
märatsema Vi 349E *rage*
mäRg A 112 *wet*
märgatav A 231A *noticeable*
märge N 179E *note*
märgis N 253 *imprint*
märgistama Vt 349F *imprint*
märja *gen. of mäRg*
märK N 58F *mark*
märK N 61F *signal*
märKama Vt 327F *notice*
märKima Vt 291G *make a note*
märKmiK N 62 *notebook*
märKus N 260B *remark*
märTer N 240A *martyr*
märTerliK A 62 *martyr-like*
märTs N 58B *March*
mäSlema Vi 326G *rave*
mäSS N 61A *rebellion*
mäSSaja N 227A *rebel*
mäSSama Vi 327A *rebel*
mäŞSima Vt 291A *wrap*
mässuline A 257D *rebellious*
mässuline N 257D *insurgent*
mätas N 159C *sod*
mäŢsima Vt 291C *hush up*
mÄÄgima Vi 291A *bleat*
mÄÄr N 53A *extent*
mÄÄrama Vt 327A *determine*
mÄÄramatu A 227A *indefinite*
mÄÄramine N 257E *determining*
mааratlema Vt 351 *define*
määratlus N 260A *definition*
määratu A 227A *immense*
mÄÄrav A 231A *decisive*
mÄÄrde *gen. of määre*
mÄÄrduma Vi 349H *get dirty*
määre N 211A *lubricant*
mÄÄrima Vt 291A *lubricate*
mÄÄrus N 260B *regulation*
mÄÄrustiK N 62 *regulations*
möblEErima Vt 291B *furnish*
möga N 13D *nonsense*
möirata *part. of mölrgama*
mölrgama Vi 345B *roar*
möla N 13A *nonsense*
mölakas N 243A *oaf*
möLder N 240A *miller*
möLL N 61A *uproar*
möLLama Vi 327A *be in an uproar*
mÖÖbel N 240A *furniture*
mÖÖduma Vi 349H *pass by*
mÖÖnma V 292A *concede*
mühin N 231A *rumbling*
mühisema Vi 349C *rumble*
müKs N 61B *nudge*
müKsama Vt 327B *nudge*
müŋT N 58E *coin*
müra N 13A *fracas*
mürama Vi 269 *romp*
müRgel N 240A *boisterousness*
mürgeldama Vi 349F *kick up a ruckus*
mürgitama Vt 349F *poison*
mürgitus N 260A *poisoning*
mürin N 231A *rumble*
mürisema Vi 349C *rumble*
müristama Vi 349F *thunder*
müristamine N 257E *thundering*
mürK N 58F *poison*
müRR N 58A *myrrh*

mürSk N 131C *artillery shell*
mürsu *gen. of mürSk*
müstiline A 257D *mysterious*
mütolOOg N 58A *mythologist*
mütolOOgia N 227A *mythology*

müŢs N 58B *hat*
mÜÜa *part. of mÜÜma*
mÜÜdav A 231A *saleable*
mÜÜja N 227B *seller*
müüK N 58F *sale*

mÜÜma Vt 264A *sell*
mÜÜr N 58A *wall*
müüT N 58E *myth*
müütiline A 257D *mythical*

N

nAAber N 240A *neighbour*
nAAbrus N 260B *neighbourhood*
naarits N 231A *mink*
naaSkel N 240A *awl*
nAAsma Vi 296A *return*
naaTrium N 246 *sodium*
naba N 13B *navel*
pole (geographic)
nadu N 27 *husband's sister*
naEl N 50 *nail (metal)*
pound
naelutama Vt 349F *nail*
naEr N 61B *laugh*
naeratama Vi 349F *smile*
naeratus N 260A *smile*
naeris N 164B *turnip*
naErma V 292B *laugh*
nafta N 152 *oil (crude)*
naftalİİn N 58A *naphthalene*
nagi N 13D *coat rack*
nagisema Vi 349C *creak*
naha *gen. of naHk*
naHk N 95B *skin*
naİvne A 247 *naive*
naİlon N 229A *nylon*
naİma Vt 261B *marry*
naine N 258A *woman*
naiseliK A 62 *womanly*
naİskoNd N 106 *women's team*
naiTuma Vi 349H *get married*
nakatama Vt 349F *infect*
nakatuma Vi 349H *become infected*
naKKav A 231A *infectious*
naKKus N 260B *infection*
nali N 69A *joke*
naļjakas A 243A *funny*
naļjatama Vi 349F *joke*
naO *gen. of nadu*
napaĻm N 58B *napalm*
naPP A 58C *scarce*
naPPa *ill. of naba*
naPPus N 260B *scarcity*
naPs N 58B *shot of liquor*
naPsama Vt 327B *grab at*

nari N 13A *plank-bed*
narkomAAn N 58A *drug addict*
narkootikum N 245 *narcotics*
narmas N 159B *fringe*
narmendama Vi 349F *fray*
naRR N 58A *fool*
naRRima Vt 291A *tease*
naRRus N 260B *foolishness*
narTs N 61B *rag*
nartsiŞS N 58A *narcissus*
narvakas N 243A *native of Narva*
naştik N 234A *ringed snake*
naSv N 49B *sandbank*
natsionalisEErima Vt 291B *nationalize*
natsionaliStliK A 62 *nationalistic*
natuke(ne) A 257G *little (a bit)*
naturAAlne A 247 *natural*
naturaliSm N 58B *naturalism*
naturaliSt N 58B *naturalist*
naturaliStliK A 62 *naturalistic*
natÜÜrmorT N 58E *still life*
nauding N 234A *delight*
nauTima Vt 291F *enjoy*
navigatsiOOn N 58A *navigation*
neA *pres. of nEEdma*
nEEdma Vt 315 *curse*
nEEdus N 260B *curse*
nEElama Vt 327A *swallow*
nEEm N 63A *cape*
neenets N 229A *Nenets*
nEEr N 61A *kidney*
neeŢ N 58E *rivet*
neeŢima Vt 291F *rivet*
neİd N 123B *maiden*
neiTsi N 225B *virgin*
neiu *gen. of neİd*
neiu N 152 *maiden*
nekrolOOg N 58A *obituary*
nekrut N 229A *conscript*
neli N 69A *four*
neļjandiK N 62 *fourth*
neļjas A 238A *fourth*
neļK N 58F *carnation*
clove

neŋTima Vt 291F *state*
neutrAAlne A 247 *neutral*
neutraliteeT N 58E *neutrality*
nigel A 231A *puny*
nihe N 217C *shift*
nihestama Vt 349F *dislocate*
nihestus N 260A *dislocation*
niHke *gen. of nihe*
niHkuma Vi 349G *shift*
nihutama Vt 349F *shift*
niiduk N 229A *mower*
niie *gen. of nİİs*
nİİs N 143B *heddle*
niiSke A 227B *moist*
niiSkus N 260B *moisture*
niisutama Vt 349F *irrigate*
niiT *part. of nİİs*
niiT N 58E *thread*
niiT N 61E *meadow*
niiTja N 227B *mower*
niiTma Vt 297C *mow*
nikastama Vt 349F *sprain*
nikastus N 260A *sprain*
niKKel N 240B *nickel*
niKKuma Vt 291D *fuck*
nikotİİn N 58A *nicotine*
niKs N 61B *curtsey*
nime *gen. and part. of nimi*
nimekas A 243A *renowned*
nimestiK N 62 *list of names*
nimetama Vt 349F *name*
nimetav N 231A *nominative*
nimetu A 227A *nameless*
nimetus N 260A *name*
nimi N 18 *name*
nimistu N 227A *list of names*
niMMe *ill. of nimi*
nina N 13A *nose*
ninakas A 243A *snooty*
niNNa *ill. of nina*
niPP N 58C *trick*
niPs N 58B *flick*
nirisema Vi 349C *trickle*
nirK N 58F *weasel*

nisa N 13A *teat*
nisu N 13A *wheat*
niŠŠ N 58C *niche*
nitraaT N 58E *nitrate*
nivOO N 1 *level*
noA *gen. of nuga*
nobe A 235 *nimble*
nohu N 13A *cold (illness)*
nokauT N 58E *knockout*
noKK N 53C *beak*
noKKima Vt 291D *peck*
noku N 152 *little boy's penis*
noǰK N 58F *callow youth*
nOObel A 240A *grand*
nooḑistama Vt 349F *set to music*
noogutama Vt 349F *nod*
noogutus N 260A *nod*
nOOl N 82 *arrow*
nOOmima Vt 291A *reprimand*
noomitus N 260A *reprimand*
nOOr A 82 *young*
noorendama Vt 349F *rejuvenate*
noorik N 234A *newly-wed woman*
nooruk N 229A *young man*
nOOrus N 260B *youth*
nOOrusliK A 62 *youthful*
nOOrusliKKus N 260B *youthfulness*
nooT N 53E *seine*
nooŢ N 58E *note*
sheet of music
noPPima Vt 291D *pick*
norima V 269 *pick a quarrel*
norin N 231A *snore*
norisema Vi 349C *snore*
noRm N 58B *norm*
normAAlne A 247 *normal*
normEErima Vt 291B *standardize*
noRmima Vt 291C *standardize*
norsata *part. of norSkama*
norSkama Vi 348C *snore*
norutama Vi 349F *mope*
noşu N 13A *mug (nose)*
notar N 229A *notary*
noţsu N 152 *piggy*
novaaTor N 229A *innovator*
noveĻL N 58A *short story*
noveMber N 240A *November*
nudiSt N 58B *nudist*
nuga N 39 *knife*
nuge *pl. part. of nuga*
nuhelda *part. of nuHtlema*
nuhi *gen. of nuHk*
nuhi *pres. of nuHkima*
nuHk N 120B *spy*
nuHkima Vt 313B *spy*
nuHtlema Vt 331B *punish*
nuHtlus N 260B *nuisance*
nuİ N 57 *cudgel*
nukits N 231A *small horn*
nuKK N 53C *corner*
nuKK N 58C *knob*
nuKK N 61C *doll*
nuKKer A 241B *melancholy*
nuKrus N 260B *melancholy*
nukrutsema Vi 349E *be melancholy*
nuĻL N 58A *zero*
nuMber N 240A *number*
numerEErima Vt 291B *number*
numismaatik N 234A *numismatist*
numismaatika N 227A *numismatics*
nummerdama Vt 349F *number*
nuNN N 53A *nun*
nuPP N 61C *knob*
nupukas A 243A *quick-witted*
nuputama Vt 349F *devise*
nurgeline A 257D *angular*
nurin N 231A *grumbling*
nurisema Vi 349C *grumble*
nuRjama Vt 327B *bring to nought*
nuRjuma Vi 349G *come to nought*
nurK N 53F *corner*
nuRm N 63B *meadow*
nuŞSima Vt 291A *fuck*
nuTma V 297B *cry*
nuTT N 61C *crying*
nUUdel N 240A *noodle*
nuuKsuma Vi 291C *sob*
nUUm N 53A *fattening of animals*
nUUmama Vt 327A *fatten animals*
nuusata *part. of nuuSkama*
nuuSkama Vt 348C *blow nose*
nuuştik N 234A *wash-cloth*
nuusutama Vt 349F *smell (sniff)*
nuuT N 58E *whip*
nõbu N 23 *cousin*
nõder A 78B *feeble*
nõE *gen. of nõgi*
nõEl N 50 *needle*
nõElama Vt 327B *sting of snake*
nõEluma Vt 291C *darn*
nõge *part. of nõgi*
nõgi N 42 *soot*
nõgu N 31 *hollow*
nõgus A 231A *concave*
nõia *gen. of nõİd*
nõİd N 88B *witch (shaman)*
nõİduma Vt 307 *conjure*
nõİdus N 260B *witchcraft*
nõİdusliK A 62 *bewitching*
nõiu *pres. of nõİduma*
nõjatuma Vi 349H *lean against*
nõKS N 61B *jerk*
nõksatama Vi 349F *jerk*
nõLv N 49B *slope*
nõme A 235 *ignorant (stupid)*
nõmedus N 260A *ignorance (stupidity)*
nõMM N 63A *heath*
nõO *gen. of nõgu*
nõO *gen. of nõbu*
nõOs N 256 *cousin*
nõrgendama Vt 349F *weaken*
nõrgenema Vi 349D *weaken*
nõRguma Vi 349G *drip-dry*
nõrK A 49F *weak*
nõrKema Vi 349B *weaken*
nõrKus N 260B *weakness*
nõTke A 227B *supple (pliant)*
nõtke N 177B *bending*
nõTkuma Vi 291C *bend*
nõTrus N 260B *infirmity*
nõU N 12 *advice*
counsel
dish
vessel
nõua *pres. of nõUdma*
nõUaNdla N 227B *consultation office*
nõUde *gen. of nõue*
nõUdliK A 62 *demanding*
nõUdliKKus N 260B *strictness*
nõUdma Vt 316A *demand*
nõUdmine N 257E *demand*
nõue N 210B *requirement*
nõuKus N 260B *ingenuity*
nõUniK N 62 *councillor*
nõuStuma Vi 349H *agree*
nõuTav A 231A *required*
nõuTu A 227B *perplexed*
nädal N 231A *week*
näE *pres. of nägema*
nägelema Vi 325 *wrangle*
nägema V 289 *see*
nägemine N 257E *sight*
nägemus N 260A *vision*
nägu N 31 *face*
nägus A 231A *pretty*
nähe N 211B *phenomenon*

näHtamatu [A 227A] *invisible*
näHtav [A 231A] *visible*
näHtavus [N 260A] *visibility*
näHte *gen. of nähe*
näHtus [N 260B] *phenomenon*
näide [N 177E] *example*
näidend [N 229A] *play*
näidis [N 253] *sample*
näiliK [A 62] *seeming*
näima [Vi 261B] *seem*
näiTaja [N 227A] *indicator*
näiTama [Vt 327E] *show*
näiTav [A 231A] *demonstrative*
näiTleja [N 227A] *actor*
näiTlema [Vi 326E] *act in theatre*
näiTliK [A 62] *visual*
näiTlikustama [Vt 349F] *make graphic*
näiTus [N 260B] *exhibition*
näiv [A 231B] *apparent*
näKK [N 58C] *mermaid*
näKKu *ill. of nägu*
näĻg [N 112] *famine*
näĻgima [Vi 349B] *starve*

nälja *gen. of näĻg*
näljane [A 251] *hungry*
näljutama [Vt 349F] *starve*
nälKjas [N 243B] *slug*
näO *gen. of nägu*
näoTu [A 227B] *unseemly*
näpistama [Vt 349F] *pinch*
näpits [N 231A] *tweezers*
näPP [N 61C] *finger*
näPPama [Vt 327C] *pilfer*
närakas [N 243A] *rag*
näRbuma [Vi 349G] *wilt*
närima [Vt 269] *chew*
närTsima [Vi 349B] *wither*
näru [N 13A] *tatter*
närune [A 251] *lousy*
näRv [N 58B] *nerve*
närvEErima [Vi 291B] *be nervous*
näRvesÖÖv [A 231B] *nerve-racking*
närviline [A 257D] *nervous*
närvilisus [N 260A] *nervousness*
närvitsema [Vi 349E] *be nervous*
näTs [N 61B] *chewing gum*

näTske [A 227B] *chewy*
näU *pres. of näUguma*
näUguma [Vi 312] *mew*
näägutama [Vt 349F] *nag*
nÄÄl [N 61B] *wife's brother*
näärе [N 179A] *gland*
näärid (pl) [N 58A] *New-Year holidays*
nöPs [N 58B] *button*
nöRdimus [N 260A] *indignation*
nööKima [Vt 291G] *chaff*
nööP [N 58D] *button*
nööPima [Vt 291E] *button*
nÖÖr [N 58A] *string*
nüanSS [N 58G] *nuance*
nühi *pres. of nüHkima*
nüHkima [Vt 313B] *scrub*
nüĻgima [Vt 313A] *skin*
nüli *pres. of nüĻgima*
nümF [N 58A] *nymph*
nüri [A 13A] *blunt*
nürinema [Vi 349D] *become blunt*
nÜÜdne [A 247] *present*

O

oA *gen. of uba*
oAAş [N 58A] *oasis*
objeKt [N 58B] *object*
objektIIv [N 58A] *lens (camera)*
objektIIvne [A 247] *objective*
objektIIvsus [N 260B] *objectivity*
obligatOOrne [A 247] *compulsory*
oblikas [N 243A] *sorrel*
oboE [N 1] *oboe*
observatOOrium [N 246] *observatory*
oda [N 13C] *spear*
odav [A 231A] *cheap*
odavus [N 260A] *cheapness*
odekoloŅN [N 58A] *eau-de-Cologne*
oder [N 79B] *barley*
ofitsiAAlne [A 247] *official*
ohakas [N 243A] *thistle*
ohata *part. of oHkama*
ohatis [N 260A] *rash*
ohe [N 217C] *sigh*
ohi [N 71A] *rein*
ohjeldama [Vt 349F] *restrain*
ohjeldamatu [A 227A] *unrestrained*
oHkama [Vi 348C] *sigh*
oHke *gen. of ohe*
oHt [N 124B] *danger*

oHter [A 241A] *abundant*
oHtliK [A 62] *dangerous*
ohu *gen. of oHt*
ohustama [Vt 349F] *endanger*
ohutu [A 227A] *safe*
ohutus [N 260A] *safety*
oHver [N 240A] *sacrifice*
victim
ohverdama [Vt 349F] *sacrifice*
ohvitser [N 245] *officer*
oiata *part. of oigama*
oie [N 216] *groan*
oigama [Vi 345B] *groan*
oige *gen. of oie*
oim [N 61B] *temple (head)*
oinas [N 159B] *ram*
oivaline [A 257D] *marvellous*
oja [N 13A] *brook*
oJJa *ill. of oja*
okas [N 159C] *thorn*
oKKaline [A 257D] *thorny*
oKs [N 55] *branch*
okse [N 177B] *vomit*
oksendama [V 349F] *vomit*
oKsjon [N 229A] *auction*
oKsliK [A 62] *branchy*

oktAAv [N 58A] *octave*
oKtav [N 229A] *octave*
okteŢT [N 58C] *octet*
oktOOber [N 240A] *October*
okupaŋT [N 58E] *invader*
okupatsiOOn [N 58A] *occupation (political)*
okupEErima [Vt 291B] *invade*
olek [N 234A] *state of being*
olema [Vi 273] *be*
olematu [A 227A] *non-existent*
olemus [N 260A] *essence*
olend [N 229A] *creature*
olenema [Vi 349D] *depend on*
oletama [Vt 349F] *suppose*
oletus [N 260A] *supposition*
oleviK [N 62] *present*
oli *past of olema*
olIIv [N 58A] *olive*
olija [N 227A] *one who is present*
oLLa *part. of olema*
ollus [N 253] *substance*
olme [N 177B] *living conditions*
olud (pl) [N 13A] *circumstances*
oluline [A 257D] *essential*
olümpiAAd [N 58A] *Olympiad*
oma [A 15] *own*

omadus N 260A *characteristics*
omama Vt 269 *possess*
omand N 229A *property*
omandama Vt 349F *acquire*
omandamine N 257E *acquisition*
omandus N 260A *possession*
omane A 251 *characteristic*
omaniK N 62 *owner*
omas N 255 *near and dear*
omastama Vt 349F *appropriate*
omastamine N 257E *appropriation*
omastav N 231A *genitive*
omi *pl. part. of oma*
omistama Vt 349F *attribute*
omleŢT N 58C *omelette*
omnibuŞS N 58A *bus*
onanEErima Vi 291B *masturbate*
onanEErimine N 257E *masturbating*
onaniSm N 58B *masturbation*
onaniSt N 58B *masturbator*
oŅN N 58A *hut*
onu N 13A *uncle*
OOd N 58A *ode*
ooKean N 246 *ocean*
ooPer N 229A *opera*
ooPium N 246 *opium*
ooTama Vt 327E *wait*
ooTamatu A 227A *unexpected*
ooTamine N 257E *waiting*
ooTus N 260B *expectation*
operatİİvne A 247 *operative*
operEErima V 291B *operate*
opereŢT N 58C *operetta*
oponeņT N 58E *opponent*
optik N 234A *optician*
optika N 227A *optics*
optiline A 257D *optic*
optimAAlne A 247 *optimum*
optimiSm N 58B *optimism*
optimiSt N 58B *optimist*
optimiStliK A 62 *optimistic*

ora N 13A *spike*
oraaTor N 229A *orator*
oraNž A 58B *orange (colour)*
orav N 231A *squirrel*
oRb N 121 *orphan*
orbiiT N 58E *orbit*
oRden N 229A *award*
oRder N 229A *order*
ordu N 152 *Teutonic Order*
orel N 229A *organ*
oRg N 131B *valley*
orgaaniline A 257D *organic*
oRgan N 229A *organ*
organisaaTor N 229A *organizer*
organisatsiOOn N 58A *organization*
organisEErima Vt 291B *organize*
organisEErimine N 257E *organizing*
orgaSm N 58B *orgasm*
oRgia N 227A *orgy*
orhidEE N 2 *orchid*
ori N 71A *slave*
orientatsiOOn N 58A *orientation*
orientEErima Vt 291B *orientate*
orientEEruma Vi 349G *orientate oneself*
originAAl N 58A *original*
originAAlne A 247 *original*
originAAlsus N 260B *originality*
orikas N 243A *barrow (pig)*
orjaliK A 62 *slavish*
oRjama V 327B *slave*
orjastama Vt 349F *enslave*
oRjus N 260B *slavery*
orK N 58F *spike*
orkAAn N 58A *hurricane*
orkeSter N 240A *orchestra*
ornameņT N 58E *ornament*
ortograaFia N 227A *orthography*
oru *gen. of oRg*
orvu *gen. of oRb*
osa N 15 *part*

osake(ne) N 257G *particle*
osakoNd N 106 *department*
osalema Vi 349A *participate*
osaline A 257D *partial*
osaline N 257D *participant*
osaniK N 62 *share holder*
osastav N 231A *partitive*
osata *part. of oSkama*
osatama Vt 349F *mimic*
osav A 231A *skilful*
osavus N 260A *skill*
osi *pl. part. of osa*
osi N 72A *horsetail (plant)*
oSkama Vt 348C *know how to*
oSkamatu A 227A *unskilled*
oSkamatus N 260A *incompetence*
oSkus N 260B *skill*
oSkusliK A 62 *skilled*
osOOn N 58A *ozone*
oSSa *ill. of osa*
oSt N 61B *purchase*
oŞtja N 227B *buyer*
oŞtjaskoNd N 106 *clientele*
oStma Vt 297A *buy*
osutama Vt 349F *indicate*
osuti N 225A *pointer*
osutuma Vi 349H *turn out to be*
oTs N 55 *tip*
otsekohesus N 260A *frankness*
otsene A 251 *frank*
oŢsima Vt 291C *seek*
oTsmiK N 62 *forehead*
oTstaRbekas A 243A *expedient*
otsus N 253 *decision*
otsustama Vt 349F *decide*
otsustav A 231A *decisive*
oŢT N 58C *bear*
ovAAlne A 247 *oval*
ovatsiOOn N 58A *ovation*
ovulatsiOOn N 58A *ovulation*

P

paaK N 58F *tank*
paanika N 227A *panic*
paaniline A 257D *panic-stricken*
pAAr N 58A *pair*
paaritu A 227A *odd (number)*
pAAş N 145 *limestone*
paaSt N 61B *fasting*
paaStuma Vi 291C *fast*

paaT *part. of pAAş*
paaŢ N 58E *boat*
paaTer N 240A *necklace (ethnic)*
paavSt N 58B *pope*
paber N 229A *paper*
pabul N 231A *droppings (animal)*
pada N 36 *pot*
pada N 13C *spades (cards)*

padi N 69B *pillow*
padin N 231A *babble*
padrik N 234A *thicket*
padrun N 229A *cartridge*
padu *pl. part. of pada*
paE *gen. of pAAş*
paEl N 50 *ribbon*
paEluma Vt 349G *fascinate*

paEne [A 252] *limestone*
pagan [N 231A] *pagan*
pagar [N 229A] *baker*
pagas [N 229A] *baggage*
pagendama [Vt 349F] *banish*
pagendus [N 260A] *banishment*
pagulane [N 257C] *exile*
pagulus [N 260A] *state of exile*
paha [A 14A] *bad*
pahandama [Vt 349F] *annoy*
pahandus [N 260A] *mischief*
pahane [A 251] *annoyed*
pahareŢ [N 58H] *demon*
pahe [N 153] *evil*
pahem [A 231A] *worse*
paHn [N 49B] *litter*
paHtel [N 240A] *palette-knife*
pahteldama [Vt 349F] *putty*
pahu *pl. part. of paha*
pahur [A 231A] *sulky*
paHvama [Vi 327B] *blurt out*
pahvatama [Vi 349F] *blurt out*
pahvatus [N 260A] *outburst*
paigutama [Vt 349F] *place*
paiK [N 49F] *place*
paiKnema [Vi 349D] *be situated*
paİnduma [Vi 349H] *bend*
paİndumatu [A 227A] *inflexible*
paİndumatus [N 260A] *inflexibility*
paİnduv [A 231A] *flexible*
paİnduvus [N 260A] *flexibility*
painutama [Vt 349F] *bend*
paİs [N 61B] *dam*
paisata *part. of paiSkama*
paise [N 177B] *boil*
paiSkama [Vt 348C] *fling*
paistetama [Vi 349F] *swell*
paistetus [N 260A] *swelling*
paiStma [Vi 297A] *be visible*
paİsuma [Vi 349G] *expand*
paİsumine [N 257E] *expansion*
paisutama [Vt 349F] *dam up*
paiTama [Vt 349F] *stroke (pet)*
paja *gen. of pada*
paju [N 13A] *willow*
pakane [A 251] *severely cold*
pakatama [Vi 349F] *burst into bloom*
pakend [N 229A] *packing*
pakiline [A 257D] *urgent*
paKK [N 58C] *package*
paKK [N 61C] *chopping block*
paKKima [Vt 291D] *pack*

paKKuma [Vt 291D] *offer*
paKKumine [N 257E] *offer*
paKs [A 61B] *fat*
paksenema [Vi 349D] *fatten*
paKsus [N 260B] *fatness*
paKt [N 58B] *pact*
pala [N 14A] *morsel*
palav [A 231A] *hot*
palaviK [N 62] *fever*
palavus [N 260A] *heat*
palderjan [N 245] *valerian*
pale [N 217B] *countenance*
palEE [N 2] *palace*
paleus [N 260A] *ideal*
palgaline [N 257D] *employee*
paLge *gen. of pale*
palistama [Vt 349F] *hem*
palistus [N 260A] *hemming*
palitu [N 227A] *coat*
paļjas [A 159B] *bare (naked)*
paļjastama [Vt 349F] *bare*
paļjundama [Vt 349F] *duplicate*
paļjunema [Vi 349D] *increase*
palK [N 49F] *pay*
paļK [N 58F] *log*
palKama [Vt 327F] *employ*
palKon [N 229A] *balcony*
paĻL [N 58A] *ball (toy)*
paĻLima [Vt 291A] *serve in sport*
paļling [N 234A] *serve (sport)*
paĻm [N 58B] *palm tree*
paļmik [N 234A] *plait*
paĻmima [Vt 291B] *plait*
paļmitsema [Vt 349E] *plait*
paluja [N 227A] *applicant*
paluma [Vt 269] *request*
palve [N 177B] *prayer*
palvetama [Vi 349F] *pray*
palvetus [N 260A] *praying*
pamP [N 61D] *bundle*
panderoĻL [N 58A] *printed matter*
paNdla *gen. of pannal*
panEEl [N 58A] *panel*
panEErima [Vt 291B] *bread*
panema [Vt 271] *put*
paNg [N 63B] *bucket*
pangandus [N 260A] *banking*
pani *past of panema*
panK [N 49F] *financial bank*
coastal cliff
lump of earth
panKur [N 229A] *banker*

paŅN [N 58A] *pan*
paNNa *part. of panema*
pannal [N 202] *buckle*
paNsion [N 246] *boarding-house*
paŋT [N 58E] *hostage*
panTer [N 240A] *panther*
paŋTima [Vt 291F] *pawn*
pantomİİm [N 58A] *pantomime*
panus [N 253] *contribution*
papa [N 152] *daddy*
papagoİ [N 1] *parrot*
paPP [N 58C] *cardboard*
paPP [N 58C] *priest*
paPPel [N 240B] *poplar*
paprika [N 227A] *paprika*
parAAd [N 58A] *parade*
parAAdna [N 227B] *main entrance*
paradİİs [N 58A] *paradise*
paradoKs [N 58B] *paradox*
parafrAAşima [Vt 291A] *paraphrase*
paragraHv [N 58B] *paragraph*
parallEEl [N 58A] *parallel*
parallEElne [A 247] *parallel*
parandaja [N 227A] *repairer*
parandama [Vt 349F] *repair*
parandamatu [A 227A] *incorrigible*
parandus [N 260A] *repair*
paranema [Vi 349D] *heal*
paranemine [N 257E] *healing*
paras [A 156] *suitable*
parašütiSt [N 58B] *parachutist*
parašüTT [N 58C] *parachute*
paratamatu [A 227A] *inevitable*
paratamatus [N 260A] *inevitability*
paRda *gen. of parras*
paRdel [N 240A] *shaver*
parem [A 231A] *better*
paremus [N 260A] *superiority*
parfÜÜm [N 58A] *perfume*
parim [A 231A] *best*
parK [N 58F] *park*
tanning of hide
parkeŢT [N 58C] *parquet*
parKima [Vt 291G] *park*
tan hide
parKimine [N 257E] *parking*
parKla [N 227B] *parking-lot*
parlameŋT [N 58E] *parliament*
parlamentAArne [A 247] *parliamentary*
paRm [N 61B] *horsefly*
parOOdia [N 227A] *parody*
parOOl [N 58A] *password*

parras N 193 *board of ship*
parT N 58E *duck*
partİİ N 1 *consignment*
round in game
partiKKel N 240B *particle*
partisan N 245 *partisan*
partitUUr N 58A *score in music*
parTner N 229A *partner*
parukas N 243A *wig*
parun N 229A *baron*
paRv N 63B *raft*
parvetama Vt 349F *raft*
pasa *gen. of paSk*
pasandama V 349F *have diarrhoea*
pasaTski N 225B *crook*
paSk N 95B *shit*
paŞliK A 62 *appropriate*
paŞS N 58A *passport*
paŞSima Vt 291A *try on*
pasta N 152 *paste (food)*
pasteeŢ N 58E *paté*
pastel N 173B *moccasin*
pastiĻL N 58A *pastille*
paStor N 229A *pastor*
pastoraaT N 58E *parsonage*
pasun N 231A *trumpet*
pasundama V 349F *blare*
pataljon N 245 *battalion*
patareİ N 1 *battery*
pateņT N 58E *patent*
patriarH N 58B *patriarch of church*
patriooT N 58E *patriot*
patriootiline A 257D *patriotic*
patriotiSm N 58B *patriotism*
patrOOn N 58A *patron*
patruĻL N 58A *patrol*
patruĻLima V 291A *patrol*
paŢs N 58B *plait*
patsienT N 58E *patient*
patsifiSt N 58B *pacifist*
patsutama Vt 349F *pat*
paTT N 61C *sin*
paTTa *ill. of pada*
patune A 251 *sinful*
patustama Vi 349F *sin*
paU N 52 *bead*
paugutama Vt 349F *bang*
pauK N 61F *bang*
paùKuma Vi 291G *bang*
paUn N 49B *knapsack*
paUs N 58B *pause*
paviljon N 245 *pavilion*
peA *pres. of pidama*
peA N 11 *head*
peAdpööritav A 231A *dizzying*
peAletiKKuv A 231A *intrusive*
peAletüKKiv A 231A *intrusive*
peAlsed (pl) N 247 *greens (plant)*
peAmine A 257F *main*
peaTama Vt 349F *stop*
peaTs N 229B *head of bed*
peaTuma Vi 349H *stop*
peaTus N 260B *stop*
pedAAl N 58A *pedal*
pedagOOg N 58A *pedagogue*
pedagoogika N 227A *pedagogy*
pedagoogiline A 257D *pedagogical*
pedajas N 243A *pine*
pederaSt N 58B *pederast*
pedikÜÜr N 58A *pedicure*
pedomeeTer N 240A *pedometer*
pEE N 1 *ass (buttocks)*
pEEgel N 240A *mirror*
peegeldama Vt 349F *reflect*
peegelduma Vi 349H *be reflected*
peegeldus N 260A *reflection*
peeKer N 240A *goblet*
peeKon N 229A *bacon*
pEEn A 82 *fine*
peenar N 171A *flower bed*
peenendama Vt 349F *make finer*
peenike(ne) A 257G *slender*
pEEnsus N 260B *subtlety*
pEEnus N 260B *finesse*
peenutsema Vi 349E *be over-refined*
pEEr N 61A *fart*
peeretama Vi 349F *fart*
pEErg N 131A *torch*
peeru *gen. of pEErg*
peesitama Vt 349F *sunbathe*
peeŢ N 58E *beet*
peeTa *imper. of pidama*
pehastuma Vi 349H *moulder*
peHkima Vi 349B *moulder*
peHme A 227B *soft*
pehmendama Vt 349F *soften*
pehmendi N 225A *softener*
pehmenema Vi 349D *soften*
peHmus N 260B *softness*
peibutama Vt 349F *decoy*
peİed (pl) N 177B *funereal wake*
peİg N 131B *fiancé*
peiTel N 240A *chisel*
peiTma Vt 297C *hide*
peiTmine N 257E *hiding*
peiTus N 260B *hide-and-go-seek*
peiu *gen. of peİg*
peiu N 152 *fiancé*
peKK N 58C *fat*
peKsma Vt 293A *beat*
pelargOOn N 58A *geranium*
peļdik N 234A *outhouse*
peletama Vt 349F *frighten*
peLg N 135 *fear*
peLgama Vt 346 *be afraid*
peLgliK A 62 *timid*
peļjata *part. of peLgama*
peļju *gen. of peLg*
pelK A 53F *mere*
peNdel N 240A *pendulum*
penitsillİİn N 58A *penicillin*
peŅN N 58A *penny*
peNsion N 246 *pension*
peNsionär N 245 *pensioner*
peņtsik A 234A *queer*
peO *gen. of pidu*
pepu N 152 *bum (rear end)*
pere N 154 *family*
perekoNd N 106 *family*
perekoNdliK A 62 *family*
perfeKtne A 247 *perfect*
perforaaTor N 229A *perforator*
perforEErima Vt 291B *perforate*
periOOd N 58A *period*
perioodiline A 257D *periodic*
perpendikulAArne A 247 *perpendicular*
perrOOn N 58A *platform*
perse N 177B *ass (buttocks)*
persik N 234A *peach*
personal N 245 *personnel*
personifikatsiOOn N 58A *personification*
personifitsEErima Vt 291B *personify*
perspektİİv N 58A *perspective*
perUUlane N 257C *Peruvian*
pesa N 15 *nest*
pesema Vt 272 *wash*
pesi *pl. part. of pesa*
pesi *past of pesema*
pesitama Vi 349F *nest*
pesitsema Vi 349E *nest*
peSSa *ill. of pesa*
pessimiStliK A 62 *pessimistic*
peSta *part. of pesema*
pesu N 13A *wash*
pesula N 227A *laundry house*
peterseĻL N 58A *parsley*

peţis [N 253] *swindler*
peţisliK [A 62] *deceitful*
peTliK [A 62] *deceptive*
peTma [Vt 297B] *deceive*
petrOOleum [N 246] *kerosene*
peŢT [N 58C] *buttermilk*
peTTuma [Vi 349H] *be disappointed*
peTTumus [N 260A] *disappointment*
peTTur [N 229A] *cheat*
peTTurliK [A 62] *deceitful*
peTTus [N 260B] *deception*
pianiSt [N 58B] *pianist*
pidama [V 288] *must*
pidama [Vt 277] *hold*
keep
maintain
pidev [A 231A] *continual*
pidžaama [N 152] *pyjamas*
pidu [N 13C or 28] *party (social event)*
piduliK [A 62] *festive*
pidur [N 229A] *brake*
pidurdama [Vt 349F] *brake*
pidustus [N 260A] *festivity*
pidutsema [Vi 349E] *party*
pigi [N 13D] *pitch*
pigistama [Vt 349F] *squeeze*
piha *gen. of piHt* [N 89B]
pihi *gen. of piHt* [N 116]
pihi *pres. of piHtima*
pihik [N 234A] *bodice*
piHk [N 131C] *palm (hand)*
piHl [N 49B] *mountain ash*
pihlakas [N 243A] *mountain ash*
piHt [N 89B] *waist*
piHt [N 116] *confession*
piHtima [Vt 308B] *confess*
pihu *gen. of piHk*
pihustama [Vt 349F] *pulverize*
pihusti [N 225A] *pulverizer*
pİİ [N 1] *tooth*
pİİbel [N 240A] *Bible*
pİİber [N 240A] *beaver*
piiK [N 58F] *lance*
piiksatama [Vi 349F] *squeak*
piiKsuma [Vi 291C] *cheep*
pİİluma [Vt 291A] *peer*
pİİm [N 58A] *beam*
pİİm [N 49A] *milk*
pİİn [N 49A] *torment*
pİİnaja [N 227A] *tormentor*
pİİnama [Vt 327A] *torment*
pİİnliK [A 62] *embarrassing*
pİİnliKKus [N 260B] *embarrassment*
piiP [N 61D] *pipe for smoking*
pİİr [N 58A] *border*
piira *gen. of pİİrd*
pİİrama [Vt 327A] *limit*
pİİramatu [A 227A] *unlimited*
pİİrd [N 89A] *sley*
pİİrduma [Vi 349H] *be limited*
piiritlema [Vt 351] *define*
piiritu [A 227A] *boundless*
piiritus [N 260A] *spirit alcohol*
pİİrkoNd [N 106] *district*
pİİrkoNdliK [A 62] *district*
pİİrnema [Vi 349D] *border*
piisa *gen. of piiSk*
pİİsama [Vi 327A] *suffice*
pİİsav [A 231A] *sufficient*
piiSk [N 95B] *droplet*
piiSkoP [N 58H] *bishop*
pİİson [N 229A] *bison*
piiT [N 49E] *jamb*
piiTs [N 49B] *whip*
piitsutama [Vt 349F] *whip (punish)*
pikaldane [A 257A] *sluggish*
pikem [A 231A] *longer*
pikendama [Vt 349F] *prolong*
pikendus [N 260A] *extension*
pikenema [Vi 349D] *lengthen*
pikergune [A 257A] *oblong*
piKK [A 53C] *long*
piKKus [N 260B] *length*
piKliK [A 62] *oblong*
piKne [N 247] *lightning*
pilbas [N 159D] *splinter*
piļdistama [Vt 349F] *photograph*
piLduma [Vt 309] *toss*
pilet [N 229A] *ticket*
pilge [N 177F] *ridicule*
pilgutama [Vt 349F] *blink*
pilgutus [N 260A] *wink*
piļjard [N 229A] *billiards*
pilK [N 61F] *glance*
pilKama [Vt 327F] *mock*
pilKav [A 231A] *mocking*
piĻL [N 58A] *instrument*
pill
piLLama [Vt 327A] *drop*
pillu *pres. of piLduma*
pilooT [N 58E] *pilot*
piļT [N 58E] *picture*
piļTliK [A 62] *figurative*
piļTniK [N 62] *photographer*
pilu [N 13A] *hem-stitch*
pilutama [Vt 349F] *hem-stitch*
piLv [N 63B] *cloud*
pilvik [N 234A] *russula (mushroom)*
pilvine [A 251] *cloudy*
pilvitu [A 227A] *cloudless*
pime [A 235] *blind*
dark
pime [N 235] *blind person*
pimedus [N 260A] *darkness*
pimendama [Vt 349F] *darken*
pimendus [N 260A] *darkening*
pimenema [Vi 349D] *darken*
pimestama [Vt 349F] *blind*
pimestav [A 231A] *blinding*
pimik [N 234A] *dark-room*
pinal [N 229A] *pencil-case*
piNd [N 92] *surface*
piNd [N 129] *sliver*
pinev [A 231A] *tense*
pinevus [N 260A] *tenseness*
pinge [N 177B] *tension*
piNgeline [A 257D] *strenuous*
piNgne [A 249] *strenuous*
pingutama [Vt 349F] *strain*
pingutus [N 260A] *exertion*
pingvİİn [N 58A] *penguin*
pinK [N 58F] *bench*
pinna *gen. of piNd* [N 92]
pinnaline [A 257D] *superficial*
pinnas [N 253] *ground cover*
pinnu *gen. of piNd* [N 129]
pintsak [N 234A] *blazer*
pinTsel [N 240A] *paintbrush*
pintseŢT [N 58C] *tweezers*
pionEEr [N 58A] *pioneer*
pipar [N 171C] *pepper*
pipeŢT [N 58C] *pipette*
piPrane [A 257B] *spicy*
piRn [N 58B] *pear*
pirtsakas [A 243A] *petulant*
pirukas [N 243A] *patty (pie)*
pisar [N 231A] *tear (crying)*
pisem [A 231A] *smaller*
piserdama [Vt 349F] *sprinkle*
piserdi [N 225A] *sprinkler*
pisik [N 234A] *germ*
pisike(ne) [A 257G] *tiny*
pisim [A 231A] *tiniest*
pişşima [V 324] *piss*
pişşitama [Vt 349F] *take child to pee*
pissuAAr [N 58A] *urinal*

piste N 177B *stitch*
pistik N 234A *plug*
pistis N 253 *bribe*
piStma Vt 297A *stick (put)*
piŢs N 58B *cigarette holder*
lace
shot of liquor
pitsat N 229A *seal*
pitsEErima Vt 291B *seal*
piTser N 229A *seal*
piTTu *ill. of pidu*
piuKsuma Vi 291C *squeak*
plAAŋ N 58A *plan*
plAAner N 229A *glider*
plAAŋima Vt 291A *plan*
plaaŋitsema Vt 349E *plan*
plaaSter N 240A *plaster (surgical)*
plAAž N 58A *beach*
plaaŢ N 58E *record (sound)*
plaatina N 227A *platinum*
pladin N 231A *splash*
pladisema Vi 349C *splash*
plagiaaT N 58E *plagiarism*
plagiEErima Vt 291B *plagiarize*
plagin N 231A *clatter*
plagisema Vi 349C *clatter*
plahvatama Vi 349F *explode*
plahvatus N 260A *explosion*
plakat N 229A *poster*
plaksutama V 349F *clap*
planEErima Vt 291B *plan*
planeeT N 58E *planet*
planetAArium N 246 *planetarium*
planK N 58F *application form*
planK N 61F *plank*
plaşku N 152 *flask*
plaştikaaT N 58E *plastic*
plaştilİİn N 58A *plasticine*
plaştiline A 257D *plastic*
plaştilisus N 260A *plasticity*
platOO N 1 *plateau*
plaŢs N 58B *square*
plaTvoRm N 58B *platform*
pleegitama Vt 349F *bleach*
pleeKima Vi 291G *bleach*
plEEnum N 229A *plenum*
plekiline A 257D *stained*
pleKK N 58C *stain*
tin
plİİ N 1 *lead*
pliiats N 229A *pencil*
pliiT N 58E *stove*

plika N 152 *girl*
plissEErima Vt 291B *pleat*
ploKK N 58C *pulley block*
plombEErima Vt 291B *fill a tooth*
ploMM N 58A *filling in tooth*
ploMMima Vt 291A *fill a tooth*
plOOm N 58A *plum*
pluSS N 58A *plus*
plUUs N 58A *blouse*
plõKs N 61B *click*
plära N 13A *gibberish*
pneumaatiline A 257D *pneumatic*
podisema Vi 349C *simmer*
poE *gen. of pOOḑ*
poE *pres. of pugema*
poeeT N 58E *poet*
poeetiline A 257D *poetic*
poEg N 113 *son*
poEgima V 349B *give birth (animal)*
poeTama Vt 349F *slip through*
poeteSS N 58A *poetess*
poHl N 53B *whortleberry*
poİ N 1 *buoy*
poisike(ne) N 257G *boy*
poisiliK A 62 *boyish*
poiSS N 59 *boy*
poja *gen. of poEg*
pojeNg N 58B *peony*
poju N 13A *sonny*
poKs N 58B *boxing*
poKsija N 227A *boxer*
poKsima Vi 291C *box*
polAArne A 247 *polar*
poleemika N 227A *polemics*
polEErima Vt 291B *polish*
poliitik N 234A *politician*
poliitika N 227A *politics*
polikliinik N 234A *polyclinic*
politseİ N 1 *police*
politseİniK N 62 *police officer*
polK N 61F *regiment*
polsterdama Vt 349F *upholster*
poļT N 58E *bolt*
poluvernik N 234A *half-breed*
polügOOn N 58A *artillery range*
polümEEr N 58A *polymer*
pomin N 231A *mutter*
pomisema Vi 349C *mutter*
poMM N 58A *bomb*
pommitama Vt 349F *bomb*
pommitus N 260A *bombing*
poni N 13A *pony*

pOOḑ N 115 *store*
pOOḑniK N 62 *storekeeper*
pOOgen N 241A *bow (violin, cello)*
sheet (book printing)
pooKima Vt 291G *graft*
pOOl N 82 *half*
pOOl N 58A *spool*
poolakas N 243A *Pole*
pOOldaja N 227A *supporter*
pOOldama Vt 349F *favour*
pooļik A 234A *half-finished*
pooļitama Vt 349F *halve*
pOOlteiSt N 258B *one and half*
pOOlus N 260B *pole (geographic)*
poolus N 253 *pole (geographic)*
pOOma Vt 265 *hang a person*
pOOnima Vt 291A *wax*
poonu N 186 *hanged person*
pOOr N 58A *pore*
pOOrne A 247 *porous*
pOOş N 58A *pose*
poPs N 58B *cotter*
poPsniK N 62 *cotter*
populAArne A 247 *popular*
populAArsus N 260B *popularity*
popularisEErima Vt 291B *popularize*
poputama Vt 349F *pamper*
porgand N 229A *carrot*
pori N 13A *mud*
porine A 251 *muddy*
pornograaFia N 227A *pornography*
poRRi *ill. of pori*
portatİİvne A 247 *portable*
porTfeĻL N 58A *briefcase*
portjEE N 2 *doorkeeper*
portrEE N 2 *portrait*
portselan N 245 *porcelain*
portsigar N 245 *cigarette-case*
porTsjon N 229A *helping*
posEErima Vi 291B *pose*
positİİvne A 247 *positive*
positsiOOn N 58A *position*
poŞt N 58B *mail*
post
sentry
postameŋT N 58E *pedestal*
poştiljon N 245 *mailman*
poStskriPtum N 229A *postscript*
postUUmne A 247 *posthumous*
potentsiAAlne A 247 *potential*
poŢT N 58C *pot*
prAAḑ N 115 *roast*

prAAḑima Vt 305 *fry*
praaK N 58F *reject*
praaKima Vt 291G *cull*
prAAļima Vi 291A *boast*
prAAm N 58A *ferry*
praE *pres. of prAAḑima*
praE *gen. of prAAḑ*
praEgune A 257B *present-day*
pragama Vi 269 *scold*
pragu N 31 *crack*
pragunema Vi 349D *become cracked*
prahi *gen. of praHt*
praHt N 116 *rubbish*
praKKu *ill. of pragu*
praktika N 227A *practise*
praktikaŋT N 58E *trainee*
praktikum N 245 *training*
praktiline A 257D *practical*
praktisEErima Vt 291B *practice*
pranTslane N 257C *French*
praO *gen. of pragu*
praoSt N 58B *provost*
praoTama Vt 349F *open slightly*
prEEmia N 227A *bonus*
prEEria N 227A *prairie*
prEEş N 58A *brooch*
preeSter N 240A *priest*
preili N 152 *miss*
premEErima Vt 291B *award with bonus*
preparaaT N 58E *preparation*
presbüter N 245 *presbyter*
preseŋT N 58E *tarpaulin*
preservatİİv N 58A *condom*
presidEErima Vt 291B *preside*
presideŋT N 58E *president*
presİİdium N 246 *presidium*
preŞSima Vt 291A *press*
prestİİž N 58A *prestige*
pretendEErima Vi 291B *lay claim*
pretensioonikas A 243A *pretentious*
prİİ A 1 *free of charge*
priimula N 227A *primrose*
prİİus N 260B *freedom*
priļlid (pl) N 58A *eye glasses*
primadonna N 152 *prima donna*
primitİİvne A 247 *primitive*
prinK A 58F *firm*
prinTer N 229A *printer (computer)*
priŋTima Vt 291F *print computer file*
prinTs N 58B *prince*
printseŞS N 58A *princess*
printsiiP N 58D *principle*
printsipAAlne A 247 *principle*
priSke A 227B *vigorous*
prisma N 152 *prism*
priŢs N 58B *syringe*
pritse N 179C *spatter*
priŢsima Vt 291C *spray*
problEEm N 58A *problem*
problemaatiline A 257D *problematic*
produKt N 58B *product*
produktİİvne A 247 *productive*
produktİİvsus N 260B *productivity*
produktsiOOn N 58A *production*
produtsEErima Vt 291B *produce*
profeSSor N 229A *professor*
profİİl N 58A *profile*
profiiT N 58E *profit*
profülaktika N 227A *prophylaxis*
profülaktiline A 257D *prophylactic*
prognOOs N 58A *prognosis*
prognOOsima Vt 291A *prognosticate*
prograMM N 58A *computer program*
prograMM N 58A *programme*
progreŞS N 58A *progress*
progressİİvne A 247 *progressive*
prohvet N 229A *prophet*
projeKt N 58B *project*
projektEErima Vt 291B *project*
projeKtor N 229A *projector*
projektsiOOn N 58A *projection*
prokurör N 245 *prosecutor*
prolOOg N 58A *prologue*
pronKs N 58B *bronze*
proosa N 152 *prose*
proosaline A 257D *prosaic*
prOOv N 58A *rehearsal*
prOOvima Vt 291A *try*
propaganda N 152 *propaganda*
propagEErima Vt 291B *advocate*
propeLLer N 229A *propeller*
proportsionAAlne A 247 *proportional*
proŞS N 58A *brooch*
prostitutsiOOn N 58A *prostitution*
prostituuT N 58E *prostitute*
prožeKtor N 229A *spotlight*
protEEs N 58A *denture*
prosthesis
proteİİn N 58A *protein*
proteŞt N 58B *protest*
protestaŋT N 58E *protestant*
protestEErima Vt 291B *protest*
proteŞtima Vt 291C *protest*
protokoĻL N 58A *minutes of meeting*
protokoĻLima Vt 291A *take minutes*
protsedUUr N 58A *procedure*
proTseŋT N 58E *per cent*
protseŞS N 58A *lawsuit*
protseŞSima V 291A *litigate*
proua N 152 *Mrs.*
prouaIiK A 62 *lady-like*
proviŋTs N 58B *province*
proviŋTslane N 257C *provincial*
provokatsiOOn N 58A *provocation*
provokatsiooniline A 257D *provocative*
provotsEErima Vt 291B *provoke*
pruŋT N 58E *plug*
prussakas N 243A *cockroach*
pruuK N 58F *usage*
pruuKima Vt 291G *use*
prUUkoŞt N 58B *breakfast*
prUUļima Vt 291A *brew*
prUUŋ A 58A *brown*
pruuŋikas A 243A *brownish*
pruuŋistama Vt 349F *brown*
pruuŢ N 58E *fiancée*
prügi N 13D *garbage*
pseudonÜÜm N 58A *pseudonym*
psühhiaaTer N 240A *psychiatrist*
psühhiaaTria N 227A *psychiatry*
psühholOOg N 58A *psychologist*
psühholOOgia N 227A *psychology*
psühhOOs N 58A *psychosis*
psüühiline A 257D *psychic*
ptruuTama V 349F *whoa*
puberteeT N 58E *puberty*
publik N 234A *audience*
publitsistika N 227A *essayistics*
publitsiStliK A 62 *essayistic*
pudel N 229A *bottle*
pudendama Vt 349F *crumble*
pudenema Vi 349D *crumble*
puder N 80 *porridge*
puding N 229A or 234A *pudding*
pudistama Vi 349F *lisp*
crumble
pugeja N 227A *bootlicker*
pugema Vi 284 *creep*
suck up to
pugu N 13D *gizzard*
puhang N 234A *gust*
puhas A 190 *clean*
puhastama Vt 349F *clean*
puhastus N 260A *cleaning*
puhata *part. of puHkama*
puHk N 131C *occasion*

puHkaja [N 227A] *one who rests*
puHkama [Vi 348C] *rest*
puHkema [Vi 349B] *burst out*
puHkus [N 260B] *vacation*
puHta *gen. of puhas*
puhtand [N 229A] *clean copy*
puHtus [N 260B] *cleanliness*
puhu *gen. of puHk*
puhuma [V 269] *blow*
puhvet [N 229A] *canteen*
puiKlema [Vi 326F] *prevaricate*
puİne [A 252] *wooden*
puiStama [Vt 327B] *strew*
puiT [N 61E] *timber*
pujeNg [N 58B] *peony*
puKK [N 58C] *ram*
puKKu *ill. of pugu*
puLber [N 240A] *powder*
puļbitsema [Vi 349E] *seethe*
puLdan [N 229A] *sailcloth*
puļjong [N 229A] *bouillon*
pulK [N 53F] *stick*
puĻL [N 58A] *bull*
pullover [N 245] *pullover*
pulmad (pl) [N 53B] *wedding*
pulsEErima [Vi 291B] *pulsate*
puļSS [N 58G] *pulse*
puļT [N 58E] *lectern*
pulverisaaTor [N 229A] *pulverizer*
pumP [N 53D] *pump*
pumPama [Vt 327D] *pump*
puna [N 13A] *redness*
punakas [A 243A] *reddish*
punane [A 251] *red*
punastama [Vi 349F] *blush*
pundar [N 171D] *bundle*
punetama [Vi 349F] *glow red*
puNg [N 53B] *bud*
punKer [N 240A] *bunker*
punKt [N 58B] *point*
puŅN [N 58A] *pustule*
punuma [Vt 269] *weave*
puraviK [N 62] *boletus (mushroom)*
puRde *gen. of purre*
purelema [Vi 325] *squabble*
purema [Vt 269] *bite*
puri [N 76] *sail*
puritAAn [N 58A] *puritan*
purjekas [N 243A] *sailboat*
purjetama [Vi 349F] *sail*
purjutama [Vi 349F] *booze up*
purK [N 58F] *jar*

purPur [N 229A] *purple dye*
purPurne [A 247] *purple*
purre [N 215] *foot-bridge*
pursata *part. of purSkama*
purse [N 217C] *spurt*
purSkama [Vt 348C] *spurt*
purSke *gen. of purse*
purSkuma [Vi 349G] *spurt*
purSSima [Vt 291H] *speak language badly*
puru [N 13A] *crumb*
purunema [Vi 349D] *shatter*
purustama [Vt 349F] *shatter*
puselda *part. of puSklema*
puSkar [N 229A] *moonshine*
puSklema [Vi 336] *butt*
puŞS [N 58A] *sheath-knife*
puşsitama [Vt 349F] *knife*
puţka [N 152] *booth*
puŢs [N 58B] *cunt*
putukas [N 243A] *insect*
pUU [N 7] *tree*
pUUa *part. of pOOma*
pUUde *gen. of puue*
pUUdel [N 240A] *poodle*
pUUder [N 240A] *face powder*
puuderdama [Vt 349F] *facial powder*
pUUduja [N 227A] *absentee*
puuduliK [A 62] *deficient*
pUUduma [Vi 349H] *be absent*
pUUdumine [N 257E] *absence*
pUUdus [N 260B] *shortage*
puudutama [Vt 349F] *touch*
puudutus [N 260A] *touch*
puue [N 210A] *defect*
puuK [N 58F] *tick (insect)*
pUUr [N 58A] *cage*
drill
pUUrima [Vt 291A] *drill*
pUUs [N 53A] *hip*
puuTuma [Vi 349H] *concern*
puuTumatu [A 227A] *intact*
põdema [Vi 275] *be ill*
põder [N 78B] *elk*
põdur [A 231A] *sickly*
põE *pres. of põdema*
põeTaja [N 227A] *nurse*
põeTama [Vt 349F] *nurse*
põgenema [Vi 349D] *escape*
põgenemine [N 257E] *escape*
põgeniK [N 62] *refugee*
põgus [A 231A] *brief*
põhi [N 68A] *bottom*

põhi [N 68A] *north*
põhiline [A 257D] *fundamental*
põhinema [Vi 349D] *be based on*
põhjala [N 227A] *Northland*
põhjaliK [A 62] *thorough*
põhjaliKKus [N 260B] *thoroughness*
põhjatu [A 227A] *bottomless*
põhjendama [Vt 349F] *justify*
põhjendamatu [A 227A] *unjustified*
põhjendus [N 260A] *justification*
põhjenema [Vi 349D] *be based on*
põHjus [N 260B] *cause*
põhjustama [Vt 349F] *cause*
põHk [N 131C] *litter*
põhu *gen. of põHk*
põie *gen. of põİs*
põiKama [Vi 327F] *swerve*
põiKlema [Vi 326F] *evade*
põiKlev [A 231A] *evasive*
põİmima [Vt 291C] *twine*
põİmuma [Vi 349G] *twine*
põİs [N 143C] *bladder*
põiT *part. of põİs*
põKKama [Vt 327C] *dock (rocket)*
põKKuma [Vi 349G] *dock (rocket)*
põKsuma [Vi 291C] *throb*
põlastama [Vt 349F] *detest*
põlastav [A 231A] *disdainful*
põlastus [N 260A] *disdain*
põlata *part. of põLgama*
põLd [N 128] *field*
põlema [Vi 269] *burn*
põletama [Vt 349F] *burn*
põletamine [N 257E] *burning*
põletav [A 231A] *burning*
põleti [N 225A] *burner*
põletiK [N 62] *inflammation*
põLg [N 131B] *banishment*
põLgama [Vt 348B] *despise*
põLgliK [A 62] *contemptuous*
põLgus [N 260B] *contempt*
põli [N 66] *generation*
knee
põline [A 251] *ancient*
põLL [N 63A] *apron*
põllu *gen. of põLd*
põllundus [N 260A] *agriculture*
põlu *gen. of põLg*
põĻv [N 66] *generation*
knee
põļvitama [Vi 349F] *kneel*
põĻvkoNd [N 106] *generation*

põLvnema [Vi 349D] *originate*
põLvnemine [N 257E] *origin*
põnev [A 231A] *exciting*
põnevus [N 260A] *excitement*
põngerjas [N 243A] *brat*
põnTs [N 49B] *thud*
põrand [N 231A] *floor*
põRgu [N 228] *hell*
põrin [N 231A] *buzz*
põrisema [Vi 349C] *buzz*
põristama [Vt 349F] *rattle*
põrKama [Vi 327F] *collide*
põRm [N 61B] *earthly remains*
põRn [N 49B] *spleen*
põrnikas [N 243A] *beetle*
põrnitsema [Vi 349E] *scowl*
põrsas [N 159F] *piglet*
põruma [Vi 269] *jolt*
põrutama [Vt 349F] *jolt*
põrutus [N 260A] *contusion*
põse *gen. of põŞk*
põŞk [N 142B] *cheek*
põTk [N 49B] *shank*
põU [N 63B] *bosom*
põua *gen. of põUd*
põuane [A 251] *droughty*
põUd [N 88A] *drought*
põõsas [N 159A] *bush*
põõsastiK [N 62] *shrubbery*
pädev [A 231A] *competent*
päEv [N 53B] *day*
päevane [A 251] *daily*
päevik [N 234A] *diary*
päevitama [V 349F] *sun-bathe*
päevituma [Vi 349H] *become tanned*
päevitus [N 260A] *suntan*
pähe *ill. of peA and pÄÄ*
päHkel [N 240A] *nut*
päİd *part. pl. of peA and pÄÄ*
päiKe(ne) [N 259] *sun*
päiKesepaiste [N 177B] *sunshine*
päiTsed (pl) [N 177B] *bridle*
päkapiKK [N 61C] *elf*
päKK [N 53C] *ball of thumb or foot*
päĻvima [Vt 291C] *deserve*
pärand [N 229A] *heritage*
pärandama [Vt 349F] *bequeath*
pärandus [N 260A] *legacy*
päRg [N 112] *wreath*
päRgama [Vt 347] *wreathe*

pärgameŋT [N 58E] *parchment*
pärija [N 227A] *heir*
päriliK [A 62] *hereditary*
pärima [Vt 269] *inherit*
inquire
pärimus [N 260A] *tradition*
pärimusliK [A 62] *traditional*
pärinema [Vi 349D] *derive*
päritav [A 231A] *hereditary*
pärja *gen. of päRg*
pärjata *part. of päRgama*
päRl [N 229B] *pearl*
päRm [N 58B] *yeast*
päRn [N 53B] *linden tree*
pärnakas [N 243A] *native of Pärnumaa*
päŢs [N 58B] *loaf*
päŢT [N 58C] *slipper*
tramp
pÄÄ [N 11] *head*
pÄÄs [N 61A] *escape*
pääse [N 179A] *admission ticket*
pÄÄsema [Vi 291A] *escape*
pÄÄsemine [N 257E] *escape*
pääsik [N 234A] *pass*
pÄÄsmiK [N 62] *pass*
päästik [N 234A] *trigger*
pääStja [N 227B] *rescuer*
pääStma [Vt 297A] *rescue*
pääsuke(ne) [N 257G] *swallow*
pöA *pres. of pügama*
pöE *gen. of pügi*
pöia *gen. of pöİd*
pöial [N 201] *thumb*
pöİd [N 111] *instep*
pöİdla *gen. of pöial*
pööning [N 234A] *attic*
pÖÖrama [Vt 327A] *turn*
pÖÖramine [N 257E] *turning*
pöörane [A 251] *frantic*
pöörang [N 234A] *turn*
pÖÖrde *gen. of pööre*
pÖÖrdeline [A 257D] *decisive*
pÖÖrduma [Vi 349H] *turn*
pööre [N 179A] *switch (change)*
pööre [N 211A] *upheaval*
pööris [N 253] *whirl*
pööritama [Vt 349F] *roll*
pööritus [N 260A] *dizziness*
pÖÖrlema [Vi 326A] *revolve*

pügal [N 231A] *notch*
pügama [Vt 269 or 286] *crop*
pügi [N 34] *shearing*
püha [A 15] *holy*
püha [N 15] *holiday*
pühak [N 234A] *saint*
pühaliK [A 62] *solemn*
pühaliKKus [N 260B] *solemnity*
pühe *gen. of püHkmed*
pühendama [Vt 349F] *dedicate*
pühenduma [Vi 349H] *devote oneself*
pühendus [N 260A] *dedication*
püherdama [Vi 349F] *wallow*
pühi *pl. part. of püha*
pühi *pres. of püHkima*
pühitsema [Vt 349E] *celebrate*
pühitsemine [N 257E] *celebration*
püHkima [Vt 313B] *sweep*
püHkmed (pl) [N 224] *sweepings*
püHvel [N 240A] *buffalo*
püksid (pl) [N 60] *pants*
püksikud (pl) [N 234A] *shorts*
püramİId [N 58A] *pyramid*
pürEE [N 2] *purée*
püsima [Vi 269] *endure*
püsimatu [A 227A] *restless*
püsimatus [N 260A] *restlessness*
püsiv [A 231A] *persistent*
püsivus [N 260A] *persistence*
püŞS [N 58A] *gun*
püŞtine [A 257B] *upright*
püştitama [Vt 349F] *erect*
püStol [N 229A] *pistol*
püŢT [N 58C] *grebe*
tub
püüa *pres. of pÜÜdma*
pÜÜde *gen. of püüe*
pÜÜdlema [Vi 330A] *aspire*
pÜÜdliK [A 62] *diligent*
pÜÜdliKKus [N 260B] *diligence*
pÜÜdlus [N 260B] *aspiration*
pÜÜdma [Vt 316B] *catch*
try
püüe [N 210C] *attempt*
püüelda *part. of pÜÜdlema*
püüK [N 58F] *catch*
püünis [N 253] *trap*
pÜÜr [N 58A] *pillowcase*
pÜÜs [N 254] *trap*

R

rAAḑ N 115 *town council*
rAAdio N 227A *radio*
rAAdium N 246 *radium*
rAAdius N 260A *radius*
rAAg N 132 *twig*
rAAļ N 58A *computer*
rAAm N 58A *frame*
raamat N 234A *book*
rAAmima Vt 291A *frame*
raamistiK N 62 *framework*
raasuke(ne) N 257G *morsel*
raaŢsima Vt 291C *have the heart to*
raba N 14B *moor*
rabaRber N 229A or 240A *rhubarb*
rabav A 231A *striking*
rabelema Vi 325 *struggle*
rabi N 13B *rabbi*
rabu *pl. part. of raba*
rada N 36 *path*
radar N 229A *radar*
radiaaTor N 229A *radiator*
radikAAlne A 247 *radical*
radu *pl. part. of rada*
raE *gen. of rAAḑ*
raEv N 61B *rage*
raevukas A 243A *enraged*
raevutsema Vi 349E *rage*
ragin N 231A *crackle*
ragisema Vi 349C *crackle*
ragistama Vt 349F *crackle*
raha N 13A *money*
rahandus N 260A *finance*
rahandusliK A 62 *financial*
rahatu A 227A *penniless*
rahe N 153 *hail*
rahhiiT N 58E *rickets*
rahhiitiline A 257D *rachitic*
rahu N 13A *peace*
reef
rahuarmastav A 231A *peace-loving*
rahula N 227A *cemetery*
rahuldama Vt 349F *satisfy*
rahuldamatu A 227A *insatiable*
rahuldav A 231A *satisfactory*
rahulduma Vi 349H *be satisfied*
rahuldus N 260A *satisfaction*
rahuliK A 62 *peaceful*
rahunema Vi 349D *calm down*
rahustama Vt 349F *calm down*
rahusti N 225A *sedative*
rahutu A 227A *restless*
rahutus N 260A *restlessness*
raHvaliK A 62 *folksy*
rahvas N 159B *people*
rahvastiK N 62 *population*
raHvus N 260B *nationality*
raHvusliK A 62 *national*
raibe N 177D *carcass*
raİdmed (pl) N 219C *offal*
raie *gen. of raİdmed*
raiesmiK N 62 *clearing*
raiestiK N 62 *clearing*
raisa *gen. of raiSk*
raisata *part. of raiSkama*
raiSk N 95B *carrion*
raiSkama Vt 348C *waste*
raiSkamine N 257E *wasting*
raİuma Vt 291C *chop*
raja *gen. of rada*
raja N 13A *frontier*
rajama Vt 269 *establish*
rajanema Vi 349D *be founded*
rajatis N 260A *construction*
rajOOn N 58A *district*
raju N 13A *tempest*
rakend N 229A *team (horses)*
rakendama Vt 349F *apply*
rakeŢT N 58C *rocket*
raKK N 61C *cell*
raKmed (pl) N 179B *harness*
raksatama Vt 349F *crack (sound)*
raksatus N 260A *crack (sound)*
raļli N 152 *sports rally*
raMb A 87 *feeble*
ramma *gen. of raMb*
rammus A 231A *robust*
raNd N 92 *beach*
randAAl N 58A *disc harrow*
raNdlane N 257C *native of shore*
raNdme *gen. of ranne*
raNduma Vi 349H *land boat*
raNge A 227B *strict*
rangid (pl) N 58B *hames*
raNgus N 260B *strictness*
ranits N 231A *satchel*
ranna *gen. of raNd*
ranne N 221 *wrist*
raŋnik N 234A *coast*
raŋT N 58E *brim*
raO *gen. of rAAg*
rapİİr N 58A *rapier*
raport N 229A *report*
raportEErima Vt 291B *report*
raporTima Vt 291F *report*
raPPa *ill. of raba*
raPPuma Vi 349G *shake*
raputama Vt 349F *shake*
raputus N 260A *shake*
rase A 235 *pregnant*
rasedus N 260A *pregnancy*
rasEErima Vt 291B *shave*
rasestuma Vi 349H *become pregnant*
raSke A 227B *difficult*
heavy
raskendama Vt 349F *aggravate*
raskenema Vi 349D *become difficult*
raSkus N 260B *difficulty*
raSkus N 260B *weight*
raŞS N 58A *race (genetic)*
raşsiline A 257D *racial*
raSv N 49B *lard*
rasvane A 251 *greasy*
raSvuma Vi 349G *become fat*
ratas N 159C *wheel*
raTsaniK N 62 *horse rider*
ratsionalisEErima Vt 291B *rationalize*
ratsu N 152 *horse (mount)*
ratsutama V 349F *ride horse-back*
raua *gen. of raUd*
raUd N 88A *iron*
raUdne A 247 *iron*
raugaliK A 62 *senile*
raugastuma Vi 349H *become senile*
rauK N 49F *old decrepit person*
raUn N 49B *stony spot*
rauTama Vt 349F *shoe a horse*
ravi N 13A *treatment (cure)*
ravim N 229A *remedy*
ravima Vt 269 *treat (medicine)*
ravimatu A 227A *incurable*
ravitav A 231A *curable*
reA *gen. of rida*
reAAlne A 247 *practicable*
reagEErima Vi 291B *react*
reaktsionÄÄr N 58A *reactionary*
reaktsiOOn N 58A *reaction*
reaktsiooniline A 257D *reactionary*
realisEErima Vt 291B *cash in*
realiSm N 58B *realism*
realiSt N 58B *realist*
realiStliK A 62 *realistic*
reanimatsiOOn N 58A *resuscitation unit*
reaStama Vt 349F *line up*
reba N 13B *haunch*
rebane N 251 *fox*
rebenema Vi 349D *tear*

rebestama Vt 349F *tear*
rebestus N 260A *tear*
rebima Vt 269 *tear*
rebitav A 231A *tearable*
rebu N 13B *yolk*
redaktsiOOn N 58A *edition*
redel N 229A *ladder*
redigEErima Vt 291B *revise*
redis N 253 *radish*
redu N13C *hiding place*
rEE *gen. of regi*
rEEde N 227B *Friday*
rEEgel N 240A *rule*
reeKviem N 246 *requiem*
reeling N 234A *railing*
reeTliK A 62 *treacherous*
reeTma Vt 297C *betray*
reeTmine N 257E *betrayal*
reeTur N 229A *traitor*
referaaT N 58E *talk*
referEErima Vt 291B *make a report*
refereŋT N 58E *reviewer*
refoRm N 58B *reform*
reformaaTor N 229A *reformer*
reformatsiOOn N 58A *reformation*
reformEErima Vt 291B *reform*
refoRmima Vt 291C *reform*
refrÄÄn N 58A *refrain*
regaŢT N 58C *regatta*
regi N 41 *sleigh*
regiSter N 240A *register*
registraaTor N 229A *registrar*
registratsiOOn N 58A *registration*
registratUUr N 58A *registry*
registrEErima Vt 291B *register*
registrEErimine N 257E *registration*
registrEEruma Vi 349G *register*
regulAArne A 247 *regular*
regulAArsus N 260B *regularity*
regulaaTor N 229A *regulator*
regulEErima Vt 291B *adjust*
reha N 13A *rake*
rehabilitEErima Vt 291B *rehabilitate*
rehabilitEErimine N 257E *rehabilitation*
rehe *gen. of rehi*
rehi N 150 *drying barn*
rehitsema Vt 349E *rake*
reht(e) *part. of rehi*
reHv N 58B *tire*
reibas A 159D *lively*
reie *gen. of reİs*
reİnleNder N 240A *schottische*

reİs N 58B *trip*
reİs N 143C *thigh*
reİsija N 227A *traveller*
reİsima Vi 291C *travel*
reİsimine N 257E *travelling*
reiT *part. of reİs* N 143C
reket N 229A *racket (sport)*
reKKe *ill. of regi*
reklAAm N 58A *advertisement*
reklAAmima Vt 291A *advertise*
rekonstruEErima Vt 291B *reconstruct*
rekonstruEErimine N 257E *reconstruction*
rekord N 229A *record*
rekordiline A 257D *record*
reKtor N 229A *rector*
rekvisiidid (pl) N 58E *props (theatre)*
relatİİvne A 247 *relative*
relatİİvsus N 260B *relativity*
relEE N 2 *relay*
religiOOn N 58A *religion*
reliiKvia N 227A *relic*
reljeeF N 58A *embossment*
reLv N 53B *weapon*
relvastama Vt 349F *arm*
relvastuma Vi 349H *arm oneself*
relvastumine N 257E *arming*
relvastus N 260A *armament*
remmelgas N 243A *willow*
remoŋT N 58E *redecorating*
repairs
remoŋTima Vt 291F *redecorate*
remoŋTima Vt 291F *repair*
renessanSS N 58G *Renaissance*
reŋT N 58E *rent*
reŋTima Vt 291F *rent*
reŋTniK N 62 *tenant*
renTsel N 240A *gutter*
reorganisEErima Vt 291B *reorganize*
reoStama Vt 349F *pollute*
reoStuma Vi 349H *become polluted*
repatriEErima Vt 291B *repatriate*
repertuAAr N 58A *repertoire*
reportAAž N 58A *reporting*
reporTer N 229A *reporter*
repressEErima Vt 291B *repress*
repressiOOn N 58A *repression*
reproduKtor N 229A *loudspeaker*
reproduktsiOOn N 58A *reproduction*
reprodutsEErima Vt 291B *reproduce*
reputatsiOOn N 58A *reputation*
reseRv N 58B *reserve*
reservatsiOOn N 58A *reservation*

reservEErima Vt 291B *reserve*
residenTs N 58B *residence*
resolutsiOOn N 58A *resolution*
resoluuTne A 247 *resolute*
reŞt N 58B *grate*
remnant
restauraaTor N 229A *restorer*
restauratsiOOn N 58A *restoration*
restaurEErima Vt 291B *restore*
restoran N 245 *restaurant*
resultaaT N 58E *result*
resümEE N 2 *summary*
režİİm N 58A *regime*
režissÖÖr N 58A *film director*
retentsiOOn N 58A *retention*
reTk N 63B *journey*
retsensEErima Vt 291B *review*
retsensiOOn N 58A *review*
retsePt N 58B *prescription*
recipe
retušEErima Vt 291B *retouch*
retuŠŠima Vt 291D *retouch*
reuma N 152 *rheumatism*
reumatiSm N 58B *rheumatism*
revanŠ N 58B *revenge*
reveranSS N 58G *curtsey*
revidEErima Vt 291B *revise*
revidEErimine N 257E *revision*
revideŋT N 58E *inspector*
revisjon N 245 *audit*
revoļT N 58E *revolt*
revolutsionÄÄr N 58A *revolutionary*
revolutsiOOn N 58A *revolution*
revoLver N 240A *revolver*
revÄÄr N 58A *lapel*
riba N 13B *strip*
ribi N 13B *rib*
ribu N13B *trash*
rida N 35 *row*
ridikül N 245 *reticule*
ridu *pl. part. of rida*
riHm N 49B *belt*
rihmikud (pl) N 234A *sandals*
riHv N 49B *flute (groove)*
shingle (grit)
riiakas A 243A *quarrelsome*
rİİd N 123A *quarrel*
rİİde *gen. of riie*
rİİdlema Vi 330A *scold*
riie N 210C *cloth*
riielda *part. of rİİdlema*
riietama Vt 349F *dress*

riietuma Vi 349H *dress oneself*
riietus N 260A *clothing*
riigistama Vt 349F *nationalize*
riiK N 58F *state*
riiKliK A 62 *state*
rİİm N 58A *rhyme*
rİİmima V 291A *rhyme*
rİİs N 58A *rice*
riise N 179A *debris*
riisikas N 243A *milk mushroom*
riisling N 229A *Riesling*
riiSt N 49B *tool*
rİİsuma Vt 291A *plunder*
riiT N 49E *pyre*
riiu *gen. of rİİd*
riiul N 229A *shelf*
rİİv N 58A *bolt*
grater
rİİvama Vt 327A *graze*
rİİvima Vt 291A *grate*
rikas A 159C *rich*
rikastama Vt 349F *enrich*
rikastuma Vi 349H *become rich*
riKKaliK A 62 *abundant*
riKKuma Vt 291D *spoil*
riKKus N 260B *wealth*
riKnema Vi 349D *spoil*
riNd N 99 *breast*
chest
riNde *gen. of rinne*
riNg N 58B *circle*
riNghääling N 234A *broadcasting*
riNgkoNd N 106 *set of people*
riNglema Vi 326B *circulate*
ringutama Vi 349F *stretch*
rinna *gen. of riNd*
rinnakas A 243A *broad-chested*
full-breasted
rinnastama Vt 349F *coordinate*
rinne N 214 *front*
ripats N 229A *pendant*
riPnema Vi 349D *dangle*
riPPuma Vi 291D *hang*
ripse N 179C *eyelash*
riputama Vt 349F *hang*
riSk N 58B *risk*
riskanTne A 247 *risky*
riskEErima Vt 291B *risk*
riSkima Vt 291C *risk*
riŞt N 58B *cross*
riStama Vt 327B *cross*
rişti N 152 *clubs (cards)*
riştik N 234A *clover*
riŞtima Vt 291C *christen*
riStleja N 227A *cruiser*
riStlema Vi 326B *cruise*
riStuma Vi 349H *intersect*
risu N 13A *litter*
riTTa *ill. of rida*
rituAAl N 58A *ritual*
riTv N 49E *pole*
rivAAl N 58A *rival*
rivi N 13A *line*
row
rivistama Vt 349F *line up*
rivistuma Vi 349H *line up*
rivistus N 260A *line-up*
riVVi *ill. of rivi*
roA *gen. of rOOg N 110*
robot N 229A *robot*
rodu N13C *line, row*
rohe *gen. of rohi*
rohekas A 243A *greenish*
roheline A 257D *green*
rohelus N 260A *greenery*
rohi N 151 *grass*
medicine
rohima Vt 269 *weed*
roHke A 227B *plentiful*
roHkus N 260B *plenty*
roHtla N 227B *grass-land*
roHtu *part. of rohi*
roİde *gen. of roie*
roİduma Vi 349H *become weary*
roİdumus N 260A *weariness*
roie N 210D *rib*
roİm N 53B *crime*
roİmar N 229A *criminal*
roiSkuma Vi 349G *putrefy*
roju N 13A *cur*
scrag
romAAn N 58A *novel*
romanSS N 58G *romance*
romaņtik N 234A *romantic*
romaņtika N 227A *romance*
romaņtiline A 257D *romantic*
romantiSm N 58B *romanticism*
roNg N 58B *train*
ronima Vi 269 *climb*
ronK N 53F *raven*
rOO *gen. of rOOd N 126*
rOO *gen. of rOOg N 133*
roobas N 159D *track (railway)*
rOOd N 61A *company (army)*
rOOd N 126 *fish-bone*
rOOg N 110 *food*
rOOg N 133 *reed*
roojane A 251 *filthy*
rOOļ N 58A *steering-wheel*
rOOļima Vt 291A *steer*
rOOmaja N 227A *reptile*
rOOmama Vi 327A *crawl*
rooP N 58D *poker*
rOOş N 58A *rose*
roosa A 152 *pink*
roosakas A 243A *pinkish*
rooste N 177B *rust*
roostetama Vi 349F *rust*
rooTslane N 257C *Swede*
ropendama Vi 349F *swear (cuss)*
roPP A 61C *dirty*
rosin N 231A *raisin*
rosmarİİn N 58A *rosemary*
rosoļje N 152 *beet salad*
rotapriņT N 58E *offset printing*
roŢT N 58C *rat*
rubİİn N 58A *ruby*
rubriiK N 58F *newspaper column*
ruHnlane N 257C *native of Ruhnu*
ruiata *part. of ruİgama*
ruİgama Vi 345B *grunt*
ruinEErima Vt 291B *ruin*
ruinEEruma Vi 349G *become ruined*
rukis N 163A *rye*
rulAAd N 58A *roulade*
ruleŢT N 58C *roulette*
ruĻL N 58A *roll*
ruĻLima Vt 291A *roll*
rumal A 231A *stupid*
rumalus N 260A *stupidity*
rumEEnlane N 257C *Romanian*
ruMM N 58A *rum*
ruMM N 61A *hub*
runo N 13A *runic song*
ruPskid (pl) N 225B *tripe*
rusikas N 243A *fist*
rusuma Vt 269 *oppress*
ruTT N 61C *haste*
ruTTama Vi 327C *hurry*
rutuline A 257D *hurried*
ruuduline A 257D *checked*
rUUm N 58A *room*
ruumikas A 243A *roomy*
rUUn N 53A *gelding*
ruunid (pl) N 58A *runes*
ruuPor N 229A *megaphone*

ruuT N 61E *square (geometry)*
ruutu N 152 *diamonds (cards)*
rõdu N 13C *balcony*
rõHk N 131C *pressure*
rõhu *gen. of rõHk*
rõhud (pl) N 131C *copper chains (ethnic)*
rõhuja N 227A *oppressor*
rõhuline A 257D *stressed*
rõhuma Vt 269 *oppress*
rõhumine N 257E *oppression*
rõhutama Vt 349F *emphasize*
rõhutu A 227A *unstressed*
rõhuv A 231A *oppressive*
rõivas N 159B *clothing*
rõivastama Vt 349F *dress*
rõivastuma Vi 349H *dress oneself*
rõivastus N 260A *clothing*
rõngas N 159B *ring (circle)*
rõngastama Vt 349F *ring (band)*
rõSke A 227B *damp*
rõSkus N 260B *dampness*
rõUged (pl) N 227B *smallpox*
rõve A 235 *obscene*
rõvedus N 260A *obscenity*
rÕÕm N 61A *joy*
rÕÕmus A 250A *joyful*
rõõmustama Vi 349F *rejoice*
rõõmutu A 227A *cheerless*
rõõsa *gen. of rõõSk*
rõõSk A 95B *fresh*
räbal N 231A *tatter*
rägastiK N 62 *thicket*
räİm N 63B *herring*
rämPs N 61B *trash*
räNdama Vi 343 *wander*
räNde *gen. of ränne*
räNdur N 229A *wanderer*
räni N 13A *silicone*
ränK A 53F *grave*
rännak N 234A *wanderings*
rännata *part. of räNdama*
ränne N 214 *migration*
räpane A 251 *slovenly*
rästas N 159B *thrush*
räştik N 234A *viper*
räţik N 234A *towel*
rätsep N 231A *tailor*
räŢT N 58C *kerchief*
rääKima V 291G *speak*
räästas N 159B *eaves*
röhi *pres. of röHkima*
röhitama Vi 349F *belch*
röHkima Vi 313B *grunt*
rönTgen N 229A *X-ray*
röŞtima Vt 291C *toast*
rööbas N 159D *track (railway)*
rööKima Vi 291G *bawl*
rÖÖv N 58A *robbery*
rÖÖvel N 240A *robber*
röövik N 234A *caterpillar*
rÖÖvima Vt 291A *rob*
rügemeŋT N 58E *regiment*
rühi *gen. of rüHt*
rüHm N 53B *group*
rühmitama Vt 349F *group*
rüHt N 116 *carriage of person*
rüNdama Vt 343 *attack*
rüngas N 159E *crag*
rünK N 53F *rock*
rünnak N 234A *attack*
rünnata *part. of rüNdama*
rüPP N 63C *lap*
rüselema Vi 325 *romp*
rüTm N 58B *rhythm*
rütmiline A 257D *rhythmic*
rüve A 235 *impure*
rÜÜ N 1 *robe*
rüüPama Vt 327D *sip*
rüüStama Vt 327B *ravage*
rüüTel N 240A *knight*
rüüTelliK A 62 *chivalrous*

S

saabas N 159D *boot*
sAAbuma Vi 349G *arrive*
sAAbumine N 257E *arrival*
sAAd N 125 *haycock*
sAAdan N 231A *Satan*
saade N 177E *broadcast*
saadetis N 260A *missive*
saadik N 234A *ambassador*
sAAdus N 260B *product (agricultural)*
sAAg N 119 *saw*
saagikus N 260A *yield*
sAAgima Vt 311 *saw*
sAAja N 227B *recipient*
saajad (pl) N 70 *bridegroom's family*
saaK N 58F *crop*
sAAļ N 58A *hall*
sAAma Vi 266 *be able*
become
sAAma Vt 266 *get*
receive
saamatu A 227A *clumsy*
sAAŋ N 58A *sleigh*
saanu N 186 *recipient*
sAAr N 82 *ash-tree*
island
saarestiK N 62 *archipelago*
sAArlane N 257C *native of Saaremaa*
saarmas N 159A *otter*
saaSt N 49B *pollution*
saaStama Vt 327B *pollute*
saaTan N 231A *Satan*
saaTja N 227B *sender*
saaTkoNd N 106 *embassy*
saaTma Vt 297C *send*
saaTmine N 257E *sending*
saaTus N 260B *fate*
saaTusliK A 62 *fateful*
saavutama Vt 349F *achieve*
saavutus N 260A *achievement*
saba N 14B *tail*
sabotAAž N 58A *sabotage*
sabotEErima Vt 291B *sabotage*
sabu *pl. part. of saba*
sada N 36 *hundred*
sadam N 231A *harbour*
sadama Vi 282 *rain*
sademed (pl) N 157 *precipitation*
sadestama Vt 349F *precipitate*
sadestuma Vi 349H *precipitate*
sadiSt N 58B *sadist*
sadiStliK A 62 *sadistic*
sadu *pl. part. of sada*
sadu N 29 *rainfall*
sadul N 231A *saddle*
saduldama Vt 349F *saddle*
saE *pres. of sAAgima*
saE *gen. of sAAg*
safÏÏr N 58A *sapphire*
saFran N 229A *saffron*
sage A 235 *frequent*
sagedane A 257A *frequent*
sagedus N 260A *frequency*
sagenema Vi 349D *become frequent*
saha *gen. of saHk*
sah(h)arÏIn N 58A *saccharin*
sahin N 231A *rustle*

sahisema [Vi 349C] *rustle*
sahistama [Vt 349F] *rustle*
saHk [N 95B] *plough*
saHtel [N 240A] *drawer*
saHver [N 240A] *pantry*
saHvt [N 58B] *juice*
saİ *past of sAAma*
saİ [N 49B] *white bread*
saja *gen. of sada*
saja *pres. of sadama*
sajand [N 229A] *century*
sajandiK [N 62] *hundredth*
sajas [A 237A] *hundredth*
sajatama [Vt 349F] *curse*
saju *gen. of sadu*
sajune [A 251] *rainy*
sakiline [A 257D] *jagged*
saKK [N 58C] *jag*
sakrameņT [N 58E] *sacrament*
saKs [N 51] *gentleman*
saKslane [N 257C] *German*
saksofon [N 245] *saxophone*
sakusmeņT [N 58E] *snack*
saladus [N 260A] *secret*
saladusliK [A 62] *mysterious*
salajane [A 257A] *secret*
salaliK [A 62] *secretive*
salat [N 229A] *salad*
salata *part. of saLgama*
sale [A 235] *slim*
saledus [N 260A] *slimness*
saLgama [Vt 348B] *disown*
saLgamatu [A 227A] *undeniable*
salK [N 49F] *lock of hair*
salK [N 61F] *squad*
saĻL [N 58A] *scarf*
saĻLima [Vt 291A] *tolerate*
saĻLimatu [A 227A] *intolerant*
saĻLimatus [N 260A] *intolerance*
saLm [N 63B] *strait*
saĻm [N 58B] *verse*
saļmike(ne) [N 257G] *verse*
saloNg [N 58B] *parlour*
salto [N 152] *somersault*
salu [N 13A] *grove*
salutEErima [Vt 291B] *salute*
saluuT [N 58E] *salute*
saĻv [N 58B] *ointment*
saĻv [N 65] *corn-bin*
salvestama [Vt 349F] *record*
salvestamine [N 257E] *recording*
sama [A 14A] *same*
samane [A 251] *identical*
samastama [Vt 349F] *identify with*
samastamine [N 257E] *identification with*
samasus [N 260A] *sameness*
saMb [N 87] *sturgeon*
saMba *gen. of sammas*
saMbla *gen. of sammal*
saMblane [A 257C] *mossy*
saMbliK [N 62] *lichen*
samet [N 229A] *velvet*
sametine [A 257A] *velvety*
saMM [N 61A] *step (footstep)*
samma *gen. of saMb*
sammal [N 200] *moss*
sammas [N 188] *column (pillar)*
saMMuma [Vi 291A] *pace*
samu *pl. part. of sama*
sanatOOrium [N 246] *sanatorium*
sanatOOrne [A 247] *sanatorium*
sandAAl [N 58A] *sandal*
sandaleŢT [N 58C] *sandal*
saNg [N 49B] *handle*
saNgar [N 229A] *hero*
saNgarliK [A 62] *heroic*
saNgarlus [N 260A] *heroism*
sanitAArne [A 247] *sanitary*
sanitar [N 245] *orderly*
sanktsionEErima [Vt 291B] *sanction*
sanktsiOOn [N 58A] *sanction*
saņT [A 58E] *cripple*
saO *gen. of sAAd*
sapine [A 251] *crabby*
saPP [N 58C] *bile*
saPPa *ill. of saba*
sapÖÖr [N 58A] *sapper*
sarapiK [N 62] *hazel tree grove*
sardeĻL [N 58A] *wiener*
sardİİn [N 58A] *sardine*
sari [N 68A] *series*
sarikas [N 243A] *rafter*
sarkastiline [A 257D] *sarcastic*
sarlakid (pl) [N 229A] *scarlet fever*
saRm [N 58B] *charm*
sarmikas [A 243A] *charming*
sarnanema [Vi 349D] *resemble*
sarnasus [N 260A] *resemblance*
saRž [N 58B] *serge*
saRv [N 63B] *horn*
sarvik [N 234A] *demon*
sasima [Vt 269] *tousle*
sataniSm [N 58B] *Satanism*
satelliiT [N 58E] *satellite*
satİİr [N 58A] *satire*
saţikas [N 243A] *crab-louse*
saŢs [N 58B] *lot of goods*
saTTuma [Vi 349H] *happen upon*
saTTuma [Vi 291D] *happen upon*
satÄÄn [N 58A] *satin*
saU [N 52] *shepherd's crook*
saUn [N 49B] *sauna*
savi [N 13A] *clay*
savine [A 251] *clayey*
saVVi *ill. of savi*
seA *pres. of seAdma*
seA *gen. of siga*
seade [N 179C] *fixture*
seadis [N 253] *device*
seAdlus [N 260B] *decree*
seAdma [Vt 314] *arrange*
seAdus [N 260B] *law*
seAdusliK [A 62] *lawful*
seAlne [A 247] *there*
seanSS [N 58G] *sitting*
sebra [N 152] *zebra*
sedel [N 229A] *label*
seebine [A 251] *soapy*
seede [N 177A] *digestion*
sEEder [N 240A] *cedar*
sEEdimatu [A 227A] *indigestible*
sEEdimine [N 257E] *digestion*
seeditav [A 231A] *digestible*
seelik [N 234A] *skirt*
seeme [N 183A] *seed*
seemendama [Vt 349F] *seed*
sEEn [N 82] *mushroom (generic)*
seeneline [N 257D] *mushroom-picker*
seeP [N 58D] *soap*
sEEria [N 227A] *series*
sEErsanT [N 58E] *sergeant*
sEEsam [N 229A] *sesame*
sEEsmine [A 257F] *internal*
segadus [N 260A] *confusion*
segama [Vt 269] *mix*
segane [A 251] *confused*
segu [N 13D] *mixture*
segunema [Vi 349D] *mingle*
seİb [N 58B] *sheave*
seiF [N 58A] *safe (for valuables)*
seiK [N 49F] *circumstance*
seiKleja [N 227A] *adventurer*
seiKlema [Vi 326F] *seek adventures*
seiKlus [N 260B] *adventure*
seİn [N 50] *wall*
seİs [N 61B] *standing*

seisak N 234A *standstill*
seisatama Vi 349F *come to standstill*
seİsma Vi 293B *stand*
seİsnema Vi 349D *consist of*
seisund N 229A *status*
seİsus N 260B *social position*
seitse N 179C *seven*
seiTsmendiK N 62 *seventh*
seiTsmes A 237C *seventh*
sekeldama Vi 349F *fuss*
sekeldus N 260A *fuss*
seKK N 58C *sack*
seKKu *ill. of segu*
seKKuma Vi 349G *intervene*
seKKumine N 257E *intervention*
sekretariaaT N 58E *secretariat*
sekretär N 245 *secretary*
seKs N 58B *sex*
seksapİİl N 58A *sex appeal*
seKser N 229A *plate of cold cuts*
seksteŢT N 58C *sextet*
seksuAAlne A 247 *sexual*
seksuolOOg N 58A *sexologist*
seKtor N 229A *sector*
sektsiOOn N 58A *section*
sekuNd N 58B *second of time*
sekund N 229A *second of time*
sekundAArne A 247 *secondary*
seletama Vt 349F *explain*
seletamatu A 227A *inexplicable*
seletus N 260A *explanation*
seĻg N 112 *back*
seLge A 227B *clear*
seĻgima Vi 349B *brighten*
seļgitama Vt 349F *explain*
seļgitus N 260A *explanation*
seLguma Vi 349G *become evident*
seLgus N 260B *clarity*
seLgusetu A 227A *obscure*
seļja *gen. of seĻg*
seļjak N 234A *ridge*
seļjatama Vt 349F *floor in wrestling*
seĻL N 58A *journeyman*
seLLer N 229A *celery*
seļTs N 58B *society (organization)*
seļtsiline N 257D *companion*
seļTsiv A 231A *sociable*
seļTskoNd N 106 *coterie*
seļTskoNdliK A 62 *social*
selve N 177B *self-service*
semafor N 245 *semaphore*
semantika N 227A *semantics*
semeSter N 240A *semester*
seminar N 245 *seminar*
semu N 13A *pal*
senaaTor N 229A *senator*
senat N 229A *senate*
seniiT N 58E *zenith*
senine A 251 *hitherto existing*
sensatsiOOn N 58A *sensation*
seŋT N 58E *cent*
sentimentAAlne A 247 *sentimental*
sentimentAAlsus N 260B *sentimentality*
seO *pres. of siduma*
seOs N 254 *connection*
seOsetu A 227A *disjointed*
seOstama Vt 349F *associate*
seoStuma Vi 349H *be associated*
sepik N 234A *whole wheat bread*
sepistama V 349F *forge metal*
sepitsema Vt 349E *scheme*
sepitsus N 260A *scheme*
sePP N 53C *smith*
septeMber N 240A *September*
septeŢT N 58C *septet*
serenAAd N 58A *serenade*
seRv N 53B *edge*
seRv N 58B *serve in sport*
servEErima Vt 291B *serve*
servİİs N 58A *set of dishes*
seRvima Vt 291C *serve in sport*
sesOOn N 58A *season of year*
seŞS N 58A *session*
sessiOOn N 58A *session*
sete N 177C *sediment*
seŢT N 58C *set*
seŢTima Vi 291D *be deposited*
setu N 152 *Setu (SE Estonian)*
setukas N 243A *nag (horse)*
sfÄÄr N 58A *sphere*
siberlane N 257C *Siberian*
siblima Vi 269 *scratch*
sibul N 231A *onion*
side N 157 *bandage*
side N 153 *communication*
sidrun N 229A *lemon*
siduma Vt 281 *tie*
sidur N 229A *clutch (car)*
siduv A 231A *binding*
siga N 37 *pig*
sigadus N 260A *dirty trick*
sigala N 227A *pigsty*
sigar N 229A *cigar*
sigareŢ N 58H *cigarette*
siginema Vi 349D *breed*
signAAl N 58A *signal*
signalisatsiOOn N 58A *burglar alarm*
signalisEErima Vt 291B *signal*
sigu *pl. part. of siga*
sigur N 229A *chicory*
sihi *gen. of siHt*
sihi *pres. of siHtima*
sihiliK A 62 *intentional*
sihitu A 227A *aimless*
siHt N 116 *aim*
siHtima Vt 308B *aim*
sihvakas A 243A *slender*
sihvakus N 260A *slenderness*
sihvka N 152 *sunflower seed*
siia *gen. of sİİg*
sİİber N 240A *damper*
sİİd N 58A *silk*
siidine A 251 *silky*
sİİg N 94B *white fish*
sİİl N 58A *hedgehog*
sİİnne A 247 *local*
siiras A 159A *sincere*
siirata *part. of sİİrdama*
sİİrdama Vt 341A *transplant*
sİİrduma Vi 349H *proceed*
siirup N 229A *syrup*
sİİrus N 260B *sincerity*
siKK N 61C *billy-goat*
siKsaK N 58H *zigzag*
siKsakiline A 257D *zigzag*
siļbitama Vt 349F *syllabify*
siLd N 91 *bridge*
quay
sile A 235 *smooth*
siledus N 260A *smoothness*
silikaaT N 58E *silica*
siliNder N 240A *top-hat*
silitama Vt 349F *stroke (pet)*
silK N 61F *herring*
silla *gen. of siLd*
sillutama Vt 349F *pave*
sillutis N 260A *pavement*
siLm N 56 *eye*
siLm N 61B *lamprey*
silmakirjatseja N 227A *hypocrite*
silmakirjatsema Vi 349E *be hypocritical*
siLmama Vt 327B *sight*
silmitsema Vt 349E *eye*
silmus N 253 *noose*
silo N 13A *silage*
siļP N 58D *syllable*

siļT N 58E *signboard*
silueŢT N 58C *silhouette*
siluma Vt 269 *smooth*
siMMan N 229A *village hop*
simulEErima Vt 291B *simulate*
simultAAn N 58A *simultaneous game*
sinakas A 243A *bluish*
sinatama Vt 349F *address familiarly*
siNdel N 240A *shingle (roof)*
sine N 153 *ultramarine*
sinel N 229A *overcoat*
sinep N 229A *mustard*
sinetama Vi 349F *glow bluish*
sinikas N 243A *whortleberry*
sinine A 251 *blue*
sinirAA *gen. of sinirAAg*
sinirAAg N 96 *roller (bird)*
sinK N 58F *ham*
sinod N 229A *synod*
sipelgas N 243A *ant*
sirel N 229A *lilac*
siRge A 227B *straight*
siRguma Vi 349G *grow tall*
siristama Vi 349F *chirp*
sirKel N 240A *compasses*
siRm N 58B *screen*
sirP N 58D *sickle*
sirTsuma Vi 291C *chirp*
sirutama Vt 349F *stretch*
siruTuma Vi 349H *stretch*
sirutus N 260A *stretch*
sisaldama Vt 349F *contain*
sisaliK N 62 *lizard*
sisemine A 257F *inner*
sisemus N 260A *interior*
sisendama Vt 349F *instill*
sisendus N 260A *power of suggestion*
sisenema Vi 349D *enter*
sisin N 231A *sizzle*
sisisema Vi 349C *sizzle*
siSSejuhatav A 231A *introductory*
sisu N 13A *contents*
sisukas A 243A *substantial*
sisustama Vt 349F *furnish house*
sisustus N 260A *furnishings*
sisutu A 227A *pointless*
sitane A 251 *shitty*
siţikas N 243A *beetle*
siTke A 227B *tough*
siTkus N 260B *toughness*
siŢs N 58B *cotton print*
siTT N 49C *shit*
siTTuma V 291D *shit*
situatsiOOn N 58A *situation*
siU *gen. of siUg*
siUg N 134 *snake*
siUnama Vt 327B *curse*
skaala N 152 *scale*
skandAAl N 58A *scandal*
skandaalitsema Vi 349E *kick up a fuss*
skandAAlne A 247 *scandalous*
skandinAAvlane N 257C *Scandinavian*
skauT N 58E *boy scout*
skauTlus N 260B *scouting*
skEEm N 58A *diagram*
skeleŢT N 58C *skeleton*
skemaatiline A 257D *schematic*
skeptiline A 257D *sceptical*
skiTs N 58B *sketch*
skitsEErima Vt 291B *sketch*
skOOr N 58A *score*
skorPion N 246 *scorpion*
skulPtor N 229A *sculptor*
skulptUUr N 58A *sculpture*
skuMbria N 227A *mackerel*
slAAlom N 229A *skiing downhill*
slAAvlane N 257C *Slav*
släNg N 58B *slang*
smaraGd N 58B *emerald*
smoking N 229A or 234A *tuxedo*
snePPer N 240B *Yale lock*
soA *gen. of suga*
sobima Vi 269 *suit*
sobimatu A 227A *unsuitable*
sobiv A 231A *suitable*
sodiaaK N 58F *zodiac*
sodomiiT N 58E *sodomite*
soE *gen. of susi*
soE A 73 *warm*
soEnd N 229B *werewolf*
soEng N 234B *hairdo*
soeTama Vt 349F *procure*
soga N 13D *mud*
sogane A 251 *muddy*
sohi *gen. of soHk*
soHk N 120B *fraud*
sohu *ill. of sOO*
sohva N 152 *sofa*
soİne A 252 *swampy*
soKK N 58C *sock*
soKK N 61C *buck*
soldat N 229A *soldier*
solidAArne A 247 *unanimous*
solidAArsus N 260B *solidarity*
solİİdne A 247 *respectable*
solİİdsus N 260B *respectability*
solin N 231A *splash*
solisema Vi 349C *splash*
soliSt N 58B *soloist*
solistama Vi 349F *splash*
soļK N 58F *slop*
soļKima Vt 291G *soil*
soLvama Vt 327B *insult*
solvang N 234A *insult*
soLvav A 231A *insulting*
soLvuma Vi 349G *take offence*
sondEErima Vt 291B *probe*
soneŢT N 58C *sonnet*
soNg N 53B *hernia*
sonima Vi 269 *be delirious*
sonimine N 257E *delirium*
sOO *gen. of sugu*
sOO N 5 *swamp*
sOObel N 240A *sable*
sooda N 152 *soda*
sOOdne A 249 *favourable*
sOOdus A 250A *opportune*
soodustama Vt 349F *favour*
soodustus N 260A *advantages*
soojendama Vt 349F *warm*
soojendus N 260A *warming*
soojenema Vi 349D *become warmer*
sOOjus N 260B *warmth*
sOOl N 53A *salt*
sOOl N 82 *intestine*
sOOlama Vt 327A *salt*
soolane A 251 *salty*
soolikas N 243A *intestine*
soolo N 152 *solo*
soome-ugriline A 257D *Finno-Ugric*
sOOmlane N 257C *Finn*
soomus N 253 *fish scale*
sOOn N 82 *vein*
sOOnima Vt 291A *groove*
sooritama Vt 349F *execute (perform)*
soosik N 234A *favourite*
sOOsima Vt 291A *favour*
soosing N 234A *patronage*
sOOv N 58A *wish*
sOOvima Vt 291A *wish*
soovitama Vt 349F *recommend*
soovitav A 231A *desirable*
soovitus N 260A *recommendation*
soperdama V 349F *bungle*
soPP N 58C *nook*
soPran N 229A *soprano*

sorav [A 231A] *fluent*
soravus [N 260A] *fluency*
sorima [V 269] *rummage*
sorT [N 58E] *sort*
sortEErima [Vt 291B] *sort*
sorTima [Vt 291F] *sort*
sortimeŋT [N 58E] *assortment*
sorTs [N 58B] *sorcerer*
sosin [N 231A] *whisper*
sosistama [V 349F] *whisper*
sotsiAAlne [A 247] *social*
sotsiolOOg [N 58A] *sociologist*
sotsiolOOgia [N 227A] *sociology*
souSt [N 58B] *gravy*
spaaTel [N 240A] *spatula*
spaRgel [N 240A] *asparagus*
speKter [N 240A] *spectrum*
spekulaŋT [N 58E] *speculator*
spekulatsiOOn [N 58A] *speculation*
spekulEErima [Vt 291B] *speculate*
sperma [N 152] *sperm*
speŢs [N 58B] *specialist*
spetsiAAlne [A 247] *special*
spetsialisEEruma [Vi 349G] *specialize*
spetsialisEErumine [N 257E] *specialization*
spetsiifiline [A 257D] *specific*
spiiker [N 229A] *speaker in parliament*
spikerdama [V 349F] *cheat at school*
spiKKer [N 240B] *cheat-sheet*
spinat [N 229A] *spinach*
spinnaker [N 245] *spinnaker*
spinning [N 234A] *spinning-rod*
spionAAž [N 58A] *espionage*
spionEErima [V 291B] *spy*
spiOOn [N 58A] *spy*
spirAAl [N 58A] *spiral*
spirAAlne [A 247] *spiral*
spiritualiSm [N 58B] *spiritualism*
spontAAnne [A 247] *spontaneous*
sporT [N 58E] *sport*
sporTima [Vi 291F] *engage in sports*
sporTlane [N 257C] *sportsperson*
sporTlasliK [A 62] *sporting*
sporTliK [A 62] *sports*
sprinTer [N 229A] *sprinter*
sproŢT [N 58C] *sprat*
stAAdion [N 246] *stadium*
stAAdium [N 246] *phase*
staaP [N 58D] *headquarters*
stAAr [N 58A] *star (actor)*
stAAž [N 58A] *seniority*
staaTus [N 260B] *status*

stabİİlne [A 247] *stable*
stabİİlsus [N 260B] *stability*
stabilisEEruma [Vi 349G] *stabilize*
stagnatsiOOn [N 58A] *stagnation*
standard [N 229A] *standard*
standardisEErima [Vt 291B] *standardize*
standaRdne [A 247] *standard*
staNNiol [N 246] *tin-foil*
staŋTs [N 58B] *punch (metal)*
starT [N 58E] *start in sport*
starTer [N 229A] *starter*
starTima [Vi 291F] *start*
stažEErima [Vi 291B] *be in apprenticeship*
stažÖÖr [N 58A] *apprentice*
statistika [N 227A] *statistics*
statistiline [A 257D] *statistical*
steNd [N 58B] *stand*
stenografEErima [Vt 291B] *write shorthand*
stePP [N 58C] *steppe*
stePPima [Vi 291D] *tap-dance*
stereofooniline [A 257D] *stereophonic*
stereomeeTria [N 227A] *stereometry*
stereoskoopiline [A 257D] *stereoscopic*
sterİİlne [A 247] *sterile*
sterİİlsus [N 260B] *sterility*
sterilisEErima [Vt 291B] *sterilize*
stiihiline [A 257D] *elemental*
stİİl [N 58A] *style*
stiililine [A 257D] *stylistic*
stİİlne [A 247] *stylish*
stİİmul [N 229A] *stimulus*
stilistika [N 227A] *stylistics*
stimulEErima [Vt 291B] *stimulate*
stipendiaaT [N 58E] *scholarship holder*
stipeŅdium [N 246] *scholarship*
stiPP [N 58C] *scholarship*
stjuardeSS [N 58A] *stewardess*
stjuuard [N 229A] *steward*
stoPPer [N 229A] *stop-watch*
stratEEgia [N 227A] *strategy*
streiK [N 58F] *strike*
streiKija [N 227A] *striker*
streiKima [Vi 291G] *strike*
streŞS [N 58A] *stress*
striptİİs [N 58A] *strip-tease*
striTsel [N 240A] *coffee cake*
strooF [N 58A] *stanza*
struktUUr [N 58A] *structure*
struktuuriline [A 257D] *structural*
stsEEn [N 58A] *scene*
stsenAArium [N 246] *scenario*
stsenariSt [N 58B] *script writer*

stUUdio [N 227A] *studio*
subjektİİvne [A 247] *subjective*
sudu [N 13C] *smog*
suflÖÖr [N 58A] *prompter*
suga [N 39] *sley*
suge *pl. part. of suga*
sugu [N 33] *gender*
sex (gender)
sugulane [N 257C] *relative (blood)*
sugulus [N 260A] *relationship (blood)*
suguühe [N 211B] *sexual intercourse*
suguüHte *gen. of suguühe*
suhe [N 211B] *relationship*
suhelda *part. of suHtlema*
suHkur [N 242A] *sugar*
suHte *gen. of suhe*
suHteline [A 257D] *relative*
suHtlema [Vi 331B] *associate with*
suHtlemine [N 257E] *associating with*
suHtuma [Vi 349H] *relate to*
suHtumine [N 257E] *attitude*
suhu *ill. of sUU*
suiTs [N 61B] *smoke*
suiTsema [Vi 291C] *smoke*
suitsetaja [N 227A] *smoker*
suitsetama [V 349F] *smoke (cigarette)*
smoke (meats)
suitsetamine [N 257E] *smoking*
suitsune [A 251] *smoky*
suitsutama [Vt 349F] *cure meat*
sujuma [Vi 269] *progress smoothly*
sujuv [A 231A] *fluent*
sukAAd [N 58A] *candied peel*
sukelduma [Vi 349H] *dive*
sukeldus [N 260A] *diving*
suKK [N 53C] *stocking*
sula [N 13A] *thaw*
sulam [N 229A] *alloy*
sulama [Vi 269] *melt*
sulane [N 251] *farm-hand*
sulatama [Vt 349F] *melt*
sule *pres. of suLgema*
sule *gen. of suĻg*
sulestiK [N 62] *plumage*
suLg [N 131B] *parenthesis*
suĻg [N 142A] *feather*
suLgema [Vt 313A] *enclose*
suLguma [Vi 349G] *be enclosed*
suLgur [N 229A] *stopper*
suli [N 13A] *crook*
sulisema [Vi 349C] *babble (brook)*
sulPsama [Vi 327B] *splash*

sulpsatus [N 260A] *splash*
sulu *gen. of suLg*
sumadan [N 245] *suitcase*
sumama [Vi 269] *wade*
sumin [N 231A] *drone*
sumisema [Vi 349C] *drone*
summa [N 152] *sum*
summAArne [A 247] *summary*
summutama [Vt 349F] *muffle*
sumu [N 13A] *mist*
suŅdima [Vt 310] *compel*
suŅdimatu [A 227A] *unconstrained*
suŅdus [N 260B] *compulsion*
suŅdusliK [A 62] *compulsory*
suŋni *pres. of suŅdima*
suPleja [N 227A] *bather*
suPlema [Vi 326C] *bathe*
suPlus [N 260B] *bathing*
suPP [N 58C] *soup*
sureliK [A 62] *mortal*
surema [Vi 271] *die*
surematu [A 227A] *immortal*
surematus [N 260A] *immortality*
suremus [N 260A] *mortality*
suri *past of surema*
surija [N 227A] *dying person*
suRm [N 53B] *death*
suRmama [Vt 327B] *execute*
suRmasaanu [N 186] *fatality*
suRmav [A 231A] *deadly*
suRnu [N 227B] *dead person*
suRRa *part. of surema*
suruma [Vt 269] *press*
surumine [N 257E] *pressing*
surutis [N 260A] *press*
surve [N 177B] *pressure*
susi [N 47] *wolf*
susisema [Vi 349C] *hiss*
suŞS [N 58A] *slipper*
suTT *part. of susi*
sUU [N 6] *mouth*
sUUbuma [Vi 349G] *disembogue*
sUUdlema [Vt 326A] *kiss*
sUUdlus [N 260B] *kiss*
sUUdme *gen. of suue*
suue [N 219A] *river mouth*
sUUline [A 257D] *oral*
suuna *gen. of sUUnd*
sUUnama [Vt 327A] *aim*
direct
sUUnd [N 104A] *direction*
sUUnduma [Vi 349H] *make one's way*

sUUr [A 82] *big*
suureline [A 257D] *haughty*
suurendama [Vt 349F] *enlarge*
suurendus [N 260A] *enlargement*
suurenema [Vi 349D] *become larger*
sUUrus [N 260B] *size*
suusa *gen. of suuSk*
suusataja [N 227A] *skier*
suusatama [Vi 349F] *ski*
suusatamine [N 257E] *skiing*
suuSk [N 109] *ski*
suuTeline [A 257D] *able*
suuTma [Vt 297C] *be able*
suvatsema [V 349E] *deign*
suve *gen. and part. of suvi*
suvenİİr [N 58A] *souvenir*
suverÄÄnne [A 247] *sovereign*
suvi [N 18] *summer*
suvila [N 227A] *summer cottage*
suvine [A 251] *summery*
suvitaja [N 227A] *vacationer*
suvitama [Vi 349F] *vacation*
sviiTer [N 240A] *sweater*
sõba [N 13B] *blanket*
sõber [N 78A] *friend*
sõbraliK [A 62] *friendly*
sõbrustama [Vi 349F] *be friends with*
sõbrutsema [Vi 349E] *be friends with*
sõda [N 36] *war*
sõdima [Vi 269] *wage war*
sõdu *pl. part. of sõda*
sõdur [N 229A] *soldier*
sõEl [N 49B] *sieve*
sõEluma [Vt 291C] *sieve*
sõİ *past of sÕÕma*
sõiduk [N 229A] *vehicle*
sõidutama [Vt 349F] *give lift*
sõİm [N 61B] *invective*
sõİm [N 63B] *manger*
sõİmama [V 327B] *revile*
sõİr [N 49B] *a type of cheese*
sõiT [N 61E] *ride*
sõiTja [N 227B] *passenger*
sõiTma [Vi 297C] *ride*
sõja *gen. of sõda*
sõjakas [A 243A] *warlike*
sõjaline [A 257D] *military*
sõle *gen. of sõĻg*
sõĻg [N 142A] *Estonian brooch*
sõĻm [N 65] *knot*
sõĻmima [Vt 291C] *knot*
sõlTuma [Vi 349H] *depend on*

sõlTumatu [A 227A] *independent*
sõlTumatus [N 260A] *independence*
sõlTuv [A 231A] *dependent*
sõna [N 14A] *word*
sõnakuuleliK [A 62] *obedient*
sõnaline [A 257D] *verbal*
sõnastama [Vt 349F] *word*
sõnastiK [N 62] *glossary*
sõnastus [N 260A] *wording*
sõŅN [N 58A] *bull*
sõŋnik [N 234A] *manure*
sõnu *pl. part. of sõna*
sõnum [N 229A] *message*
sõPrus [N 260B] *friendship*
sõra *gen. of sõRg*
sõrendama [Vt 349F] *emphasize (italicize)*
sõrendus [N 260A] *emphasis (italics)*
sõRg [N 95A] *hoof (cloven)*
sõRm [N 63B] *finger*
sõrmitsema [V 349E] *finger*
sõrmus [N 253] *ring (finger)*
sõsar [N 231A] *sister*
sõstar [N 171B] *currant*
sõTkuma [Vt 291C] *knead*
sõtse [N 152] *father's sister*
sõTTa *ill. of sõda*
sõua *pres. of sõUdma*
sõUdja [N 227B] *rower*
sõUdma [V 316A] *row*
sÕÕm [N 61A] *gulp*
sÕÕr [N 58A] *circle*
sõõre [N 179A] *nostril*
säde [N 157] *spark*
sädelema [Vi 325] *sparkle*
säga [N 13D] *sheatfish*
sähvatama [Vi 349F] *flash*
säie [N 223] *strand of yarn or rope*
säİgme *gen. of säie*
säİlima [Vi 291C] *preserve*
säilitama [Vt 349F] *preserve*
säilitus [N 260A] *preservation*
säinas [N 159B] *ide (fish)*
sälK [N 61F] *notch*
sälKima [Vt 291G] *notch*
säNg [N 58B] *bed*
sära [N 13A] *radiance*
särama [Vi 269] *sparkle*
särav [A 231A] *sparkling*
säRg [N 141] *roach (fish)*
särgik [N 234A] *singlet*
särisema [Vi 349C] *sizzle*
säritama [Vt 349F] *expose (photo)*

säritus N 260A *exposure (photo)*
särje *gen. of säRg*
särK N 58F *shirt*
särTs N 61B *pep*
särtsakas A 243A *peppy*
sätendama Vi 349F *glisten*
sätendus N 260A *glisten*
sÄÄr N 82 *shank*
säärane A 251 *such*
säärik N 234A *boot*
sääse *gen. of sääSk*
sääSk N 140B *mosquito*
sääSt N 61B *savings*
sääStliK A 62 *economical*
sääStma Vt 297A *save money*
söAndama Vt 349F *venture*
söE *gen. of süsi*
söeStuma Vi 349H *become charred*
sörK N 58F *trot*
sörKima Vi 291G *trot*
sÖÖdav A 231A *edible*
sööK N 58F *food*
sööKla N 227B *cafeteria*
sÖÖma Vt 268 *eat*
sööming N 234A *feasting*
sÖÖr N 58A *sir*
sööStma Vi 297A *dash*
sööT N 53E *fodder*
sööT N 61E *pass (sport)*
sööŢ N 58E *fallow*
sööTma Vt 297C *feed*
söövitama Vt 349F *etch*
söövitus N 260A *etching*
süda N 158 *heart*
südametu A 227A *heartless*
südamiK N 62 *core*
südamliK A 62 *cordial*
südamliKKus N 260B *cordiality*
sügama Vt 269 *scratch*
sügav A 231A *deep*
sügavus N 260A *depth*
sügelema Vi 325 *itch*
sügelus N 260A *itch*
sügis N 253 *autumn*
sügisene A 257A *autumnal*
süiT N 58E *suite*
süLd N 105 *fathom*
süle *gen. and part. of süli*
sülelema Vt 325 *cuddle*
süĻg N 141 *spittle*
süli N 18 *lap*
sülitama V 349F *spit*
süļje *gen. of süĻg*
sülla *gen. of süLd*
süLLe *ill. of süli*
süļT N 58E *head cheese*
süMbol N 229A *symbol*
sümbolisEErima Vt 291B *symbolize*
sümbOOlne A 247 *symbolic*
sümfOOnia N 227A *symphony*
sümmeeTria N 227A *symmetry*
sümmeetriline A 257D *symmetrical*
sümpaaTia N 227A *sympathy*
sümpaaTne A 247 *sympathetic*
sümpOOsion N 246 *symposium*
sümPtom N 229A *symptom*
süŊd N 118 *birth*
süŊdima Vi 310 *be born*
süNdmus N 260B *event*
sündmustiK N 62 *plot*
süŊdsa *gen. of süŋnis*
süŊdsusetu A 227A *indecent*
süNge A 227B *gloomy*
süNgus N 260B *gloom*
süŋni *gen. of süŊd*
süŋni *pres. of süŊdima*
süŋnis A 199 *decent*
süŋnitama Vt 349F *give birth*
sünonÜÜm N 58A *synonym*
süntaks N 229A *syntax*
süntEEs N 58A *synthesis*
sünteetiline A 257D *synthetic*
süsi N 48 *coal*
süsiniK N 62 *carbon*
süSt N 53B *canoe*
süŞt N 58B *injection*
süstal N 170B *syringe*
süstEEm N 58A *system*
süstemaatiline A 257D *systematic*
süstematisEErima Vt 291B *systematize*
süştik N 234A *shuttle*
süŞtima Vt 291C *inject*
süŞtimine N 257E *injecting*
süžEE N 2 *subject matter*
süţitama Vt 349F *kindle*
sütitav A 231A *inspiring*
süTT *part. of süsi*
süŢTima Vi 349B *ignite*
süŢTiv A 231A *inflammable*
süvendama Vt 349F *deepen*
süvenema Vi 349D *concentrate on*
sÜÜ N 1 *blame*
sÜÜa *part. of sÖÖma*
süüdistama Vt 349F *accuse*
süüdistus N 260A *accusation*
sÜÜdlane N 257C *culprit*
süüTama Vt 327E *ignite*
süüTu A 227B *innocent*
süüTus N 260B *innocence*

Š

šaaKal N 229A *jackal*
šablOOn N 58A *stencil*
šablooniline A 257D *trite*
šaHt N 58B *mine shaft*
šamAAn N 58A *shaman*
šampanja N 152 *champagne*
šampinjon N 245 *mushroom (common)*
šampOOn N 58A *shampoo*
šamPus N 260B *champagne*
šanSS N 58G *chance*
šantAAž N 58A *blackmail*
šantažEErima Vt 291B *blackmail*
šaRž N 58B *caricature*
šašlõKK N 58C *shishkebab*
šeFF N 58C *boss*
šeFlus N 260B *patronage*
šerri N 152 *sherry*
šiFFer N 240B *cipher*
šifrEErima Vt 291B *cipher*
šiiiT N 58E *Shiite*
šiKK A 58C *chic*
šimpaNs N 58B *chimpanzee*
šniTsel N 240A *cutlet*
šoKK N 58C *shock*
šokolAAd N 58A *chocolate*
šoTlane N 257C *Scot*
šoviniSt N 58B *chauvinist*
šoviniStliK A 62 *chauvinistic*
šveiTser N 229A *doorkeeper*
šveiTslane N 257C *Swiss*

Z

zoolOOg N 58A *zoologist*
zoolOOgia N 227A *zoology*

Ž

žaNr N 58B or 229B *genre*
žargOOn N 58A *jargon*
želatİİn N 58A *gelatine*
želEE N 2 *jelly*
žeŞt N 58B *gesture*
žestikulatsiOOn N 58A *gesticulation*
žestikulEErima Vi 291B *gesticulate*
žestikulEErimine N 257E *gesticulating*
žileŢT N 58C *safety razor*
žonglEErima Vi 291B *juggle*
žonglÖÖr N 58A *juggler*
žurnAAl N 58A *magazine*
žurnaliSt N 58B *journalist*
žurnalistika N 227A *journalism*
žürİİ N 1 *jury*

T

tAAnduma Vi 349H *retreat*
tAAndumine N 257E *retreat*
tAAnlane N 257C *Dane*
taara N 152 *packing material*
tAAruma Vi 291A *stagger*
taaStama Vt 349F *restore*
taaStamine N 257E *restoration*
taaŢ N 58E *old man*
taba N 13B *padlock*
tabama Vt 269 *catch*
tabamus N 260A *hit*
tabav A 231A *striking*
tabel N 229A *table (chart)*
tableŢT N 58C *tablet*
tabureŢ N 58H *stool*
taEl N 49B *tinder*
taEvaliK A 62 *heavenly*
taevas N 160 *heaven*
tagajärjekas A 243A *effective*
tagala N 227A *home front*
tagama Vt 269 *guarantee*
tagandama Vt 349F *fire from employment*
taganema Vi 349D *retreat*
tagasihoİdliK A 62 *modest*
tagastama Vt 349F *return (give back)*
tagatis N 260A *guarantee*
taguma Vt 285 *pound*
tagumiK N 62 *buttocks*
tagumine A 257F *hindmost*
tagumine N 257E *pounding*
tagurlane N 257C *reactionary*
tagurliK A 62 *reactionary*
taha *pres. of taHtma*
tahe A 235 *dry*
tahe N 211B *will (desire)*
tahenema Vi 349D *become dry*
tahi *gen. of taHt*
taHke A 227B *solid*
taHm N 49B *soot*
tahmane A 251 *sooty*
taHt N 116 *wick*
taHte *gen. of tahe*
taHtliK A 62 *intentional*
taHtma Vt 320 *want*
taHtmatu A 227A *involuntary*
taHtmine N 257E *want*
tahuma Vt 269 *hew*
tahumatu A 227A *uncouth*
taHvel N 240A *black-board*
taİ N 1 *lean meat*
taibukas A 243A *intelligent*
taibukus N 260A *intelligence*
taİde *gen. of taie*
taİdlus N 260B *amateur activities*
taİdur N 229A *artist*
taie N 210D *art*
taies N 253 *work of art*
taİgen N 241A *dough*
taİm N 63B *plant*
taimestiK N 62 *vegetation*
taİmne A 247 *vegetable*
tainas N 159B *dough*
taİne A 252 *lean of meat*
taiP N 61D *wit*
taiPama Vt 327D *realize*
taiPamatu A 227A *dim-witted*
taiPliK A 62 *quick-witted*
taju N 13A *perception*
tajuma Vt 269 *perceive*
tajutav A 231A *perceptible*
takerduma Vi 349H *become stuck*
takistama Vt 349F *hinder*
takistamatu A 227A *unhindered*
takistus N 260A *hindrance*
taKjas N 243B *burdock*
taksEErima Vt 291B *appraise*
takso N 152 *taxi*
taKt N 58B *tact*
taktika N 227A *tactics*
taktikaline A 257D *tactical*
taktiline A 257D *tactful*
taktitu A 227A *tactless*
tala N 13A *girder*
talAAr N 58A *robe of office*
taLd N 91 *sole*
taldrik N 234A *plate*
taleŋT N 58E *talent*
taLgud (pl) N 227B *bee(communal work)*
tali N 66 *winter*
talisman N 245 *talisman*
talitaja N 227A *tender (person)*
talitama V 349F *tend*
talitus N 260A *tending*
taļK N 58F *talc*
taLL N 63A *lamb*
taĻL N 58A *stall*
talla *gen. of taLd*
taLLama V 327A *tread*
taĻLinlane N 257C *native of Tallinn*
taLLu *ill. of talu*
tallutama Vt 349F *sole*
taloNg N 58B *voucher*
taltsas A 159B *tame*
taltsutaja N 227A *tamer*
taltsutama Vt 349F *tame*
talu N 13A *farm*
taluma Vt 269 *bear*
talumatu A 227A *unbearable*
taluniK N 62 *farmer*
talupoEgliK A 62 *peasant-like*
talutama Vt 349F *guide*
talutav A 231A *tolerable*
taĻv N 66 *winter*
taļvine A 251 *wintry*
taļvitama Vi 349F *winter*
taMM N 58A *dam*
taMM N 63A *oak*

tammik N 234A *oak grove*
tamPima Vt 291E *pack down*
tampOOn N 58A *tampon*
tangid (pl) N 58B *pliers*
tangud (pl) N 61B *barley*
tanKima Vt 291G *fill up (car)*
tanKla N 227B *filling station*
tanTs N 61B *dance*
taŋTsija N 227A *dancer*
taŋTsima Vi 291C *dance*
tanu N 13A *cap (woman's)*
taO *pres. of taguma*
taOline A 257D *such*
taoTlema Vt 351 *apply for*
taoTlus N 260B *application*
tapeeŢ N 58E *wall-paper*
tapeeŢima Vt 291F *wall-paper*
taPlema Vi 326C *battle*
taPma Vt 298 *kill*
taPmine N 257E *killing*
taPP N 49C *slaughter*
taPPer N 240B *battle-axe*
tara N 13A *fence*
tarandiK N 62 *enclosure*
tarastama Vt 349F *fence in*
taRbe *gen. of tarve*
taRbetu A 227A *useless*
taRbija N 227A *consumer*
taRbima Vt 349B *consume*
taRbimine N 257E *consumption*
taRde *gen. of tarre*
taRduma Vi 349H *congeal*
tare N 154 *cabin*
targutama Vi 349F *philosophize*
tariiF N 58A *tariff*
tarind N 229A *construction*
tarK A 49F *wise*
tarKus N 260B *wisdom*
taRn N 49B *sedge*
taRnima Vt 291C *supply*
tarre N 215 *jelly*
tarretama Vt 349F *congeal*
tarretis N 260A *jelly*
tarretuma Vi 349H *congeal*
taRRu *ill. of taru*
tarTlane N 257C *native of Tartu*
taru N 13A *bee hive*
tarvas N 159B *aurochs*
tarve N 208B *need*
tarvidus N 260A *need*
tarviliK A 62 *necessary*
tarviliKKus N 260B *necessity*
tarvitama Vt 349F *use*
tarvitsema Vi 349E *need*
tarvitus N 260A *use*
tasakaalustama Vt 349F *balance*
tasand N 229A *level*
tasandama Vt 349F *make level*
tasandiK N 62 *plain*
tasane A 251 *even*
tase N 157 *level*
taSku N 227B *pocket*
taŞS N 58A *cup*
taŞSima Vt 291A *haul*
tasu N 13A *payment*
tasuja N 227A *avenger*
tasuline A 257D *done for pay*
tasuma Vt 269 *repay*
tasuv A 231A *profitable*
tatar N 171C *buckwheat*
tatarlane N 257C *Tatar*
taţine A 251 *snotty*
taţistama V 349F *befoul with snot*
taŢT N 58C *snot*
taUd N 58B *epidemic*
taUnima Vt 291C *condemn*
tauSt N 49B *background*
tava N 13A *custom*
tavaline A 257D *usual*
tavatsema Vi 349E *be in the habit*
teA *pres. of teAdma*
teAbe *gen. of teave*
teade N 177E *message*
teAdlane N 257C *scientist*
teAdliK A 62 *aware*
teAdliKKus N 260B *awareness*
teAdma Vt 314 *know a fact*
teAdmatu A 227A *unknown*
teAdmatus N 260A *ignorance(uncertainty)*
teAdmine N 257E *knowledge*
teAdur N 229A *researcher*
teAdus N 260B *science*
teAduskoNd N 106 *faculty*
teAdusliK A 62 *scientific*
teadustaja N 227A *announcer*
teadustama Vt 349F *announce*
teAdvus N 260B *consciousness*
teAdvusetu A 227A *unconscious*
teAdvusetus N 260A *unconsciousness*
teaTama Vt 349F *inform*
teaTav A 231A *certain (a certain)*
teaTer N 240A *theatre*
teaTmed (pl) N 179D *data*
teaTmiK N 62 *reference book*
teatrAAlne A 247 *theatrical*
teave N 208B *information*
teder N 81A *grouse*
tEE *pres. of tegema*
tEE N 1 *tea*
tEE N 2 *road*
tEEkoNd N 106 *way*
teema N 152 *theme*
tEEmaŋT N 58E *diamond*
teene N 177A *service*
tEEneline A 257D *merited*
tEEner N 240A *servant*
tEEnija N 227A *servant*
tEEnima Vt 291A *serve*
tEEnimatu A 227A *unwarranted*
teenindaja N 227A *attendant*
teenindama Vt 349F *serve a customer*
teenistuja N 227A *employee*
teenistus N 260A *employ*
teenus N 253 *service*
tEEs N 58A *thesis*
teeselda *part. of teeSklema*
teeSkleja N 227A *pretender*
teeSklema V 336 *pretend*
teeSklus N 260B *pretence*
teFlon N 229A *teflon*
tegelane N 257C *public figure*
tegelaskoNd N 106 *characters*
tegelema Vi 325 *be engaged in*
tegeliK A 62 *actual*
tegeliKKus N 260B *reality*
tegelinSki N 225B *go-getter*
tegema Vt 290 *do*
make
tegemine N 257E *doing*
making
tegev A 231A *active*
tegevus N 260A *activity*
tegevusetu A 227A *idle*
tegevustiK N 62 *action*
tegu N 31 *act*
deed
tegur N 229A *factor*
tegutsema Vi 349E *act (do)*
tehas N 253 *factory*
tehing N 234A *transaction*
tehnik N 234A *technician*
tehnika N 227A *technology*
tehnikum N 245 *technical college*
tehniline A 257D *technical*
tehnolOOg N 58A *technologist*
tehnolOOgia N 227A *technology*

tehnoloogiline A 257D *technological*
teİb N 114 *dace*
teİba *gen. of teivas*
teietama Vt 349F *address formally*
teine A 258A *another*
second
teine N 258A *other (another)*
teisend N 229A *version*
teisik N 234A *double*
teİsmeline A 257D *teenaged*
teivas N 187 *stake*
teivi *gen. of teİb*
teke N 177C *origin*
tekitama Vt 349F *cause*
teKK N 58C *blanket*
deck on ship
teKKel N 240B *student's cap*
teKKima Vi 291D *arise (come about)*
teKKima Vi 349B *arise*
teksased (pl) N 253 *blue jeans*
teKst N 58B *text*
tekstİİl N 58A *textile*
telefon N 245 *telephone*
telefonEErima Vi 291B *telephone*
telefoniSt N 58B *operator*
telefOOnima Vi 291A *telephone*
telegraaF N 58A *telegraph*
telegrafEErima Vi 291B *telegraph*
telegrafiSt N 58B *telegraphist*
telegraMM N 58A *telegram*
teleks N 229A *telex*
teler N 229A *television set*
teleskooP N 58D *telescope*
televİİsor N 229A *television set*
televisiOOn N 58A *television*
teĻg N 141 *axis*
axle
teļje *gen. of teĻg*
teļjed (pl) N 141 *loom*
teļK N 58F *tent*
teĻLija N 227A *subscriber*
teĻLima Vt 291A *adjust*
order (restaurant)
subscribe
teĻLimine N 257E *subscription*
teĻLimus N 260A *subscription*
teļling N 234A *scaffold*
teļlis N 253 *brick*
temaatika N 227A *subject matter*
temaatiline A 257D *topical*
tembeldama Vt 349F *stamp*
temP N 61D *prank*
temPel N 240A *stamp*
temple (worship)
temperameŋT N 58E *temperament*
temperamenTne A 247 *temperamental*
temperatUUr N 58A *temperature*
tempo N 152 *tempo*
tendenTs N 58B *tendency*
tendenTsliK A 62 *tendentious*
teŋnis N 253 *tennis*
tenor N 229A *tenor*
teO *gen. of tigu*
teO *gen. of tegu*
teolOOg N 58A *theologist*
teOOria N 227A *theory*
teoreetiline A 257D *theoretic*
teOs N 254 *work of art, literature*
teoStama Vt 349F *implement*
teoStatav A 231A *feasible*
teoStuma Vi 349H *materialize*
teoTama Vt 349F *abuse*
teoTus N 260B *abuse*
tera N 15 *blade (knife)*
grain
teraline A 257D *granular*
teras N 253 *steel*
terav A 231A *sharp*
teravdama Vt 349F *make sharper*
teraviK N 62 *point*
teravnema Vi 349D *become sharper*
teravus N 260A *sharpness*
teretama Vt 349F *greet*
teri *pl. part. of tera*
teritama Vt 349F *sharpen*
teRmin N 229A *term*
terminolOOgia N 227A *terminology*
termos N 253 *thermos*
terrakota N 152 *terra cotta*
terraŞS N 58A *terrace*
territOOrium N 246 *territory*
territoriAAlne A 247 *territorial*
teRRor N 229A *terror*
terrorisEErima Vt 291B *terrorize*
terroriSt N 58B *terrorist*
tertseŢT N 58C *tercet*
terve A 177B *healthy*
whole
tervendama Vt 349F *make healthier*
tervenema Vi 349D *become healthier*
tervik N 234A *whole*
terviklik A 62 *integral*
tervis N 253 *health*
teRvis N 260B *health*
tervisliK A 62 *wholesome*
tervitama Vt 349F *greet*
tervitus N 260A *greeting*
teŞt N 58B *test*
testameŋT N 58E *will (testament)*
tiba N 13B *droplet*
tibama Vi 269 *drizzle*
tibu N 13B *chick*
tibutama Vi 349F *drizzle*
tige A 235 *angry*
tigedus N 260A *anger*
tigu N 32 *snail*
tihane N 251 *titmouse*
tihe A 235 *dense*
tihedus N 260A *density*
tihendama Vt 349F *make denser*
tihenema Vi 349D *become denser*
tihnik N 234A *thicket*
tİİb N 86A *wing*
tiibetlane N 257C *Tibetan*
tİİblema Vi 328 *flit*
tİİger N 240A *tiger*
tiiK N 58F *pond*
tiine A 177A *pregnant of animals*
tİİr N 61A *round (turn)*
shooting-range
tiirane A 251 *horny (sexual)*
tİİrlema Vi 326A *spin*
tiisikus N 260A *tuberculosis*
tiiTel N 240A *title*
tiiva *gen. of tİİb*
tiivelda *part. of tİİblema*
tiivustama Vt 349F *inspire*
tikand N 229A *embroidery*
tikerber N 245 *gooseberry*
tiKK N 61C *match (fire)*
tiKKima Vt 291D *embroider*
tiKKuma Vi 291D *intrude*
tiKsuma Vi 291C *tick*
tila N 13A *spout*
tilgutama Vt 349F *drip*
tilK N 49F *drop*
tiĻL N 58A *cock (penis)*
dill
timukas N 243A *executioner*
tina N 13A *tin*
tiŋdine A 251 *inky*
tiNgima V 291C *bargain*
tiNgimus N 260A *condition*
tiŋT N 58E *ink*
smelt (fish)
tinutama Vt 349F *solder*

tiPmine A 257F *topmost*
tiPP N 61C *tip*
tiPPima Vt 291D *type*
tirAAž N 58A *tirage*
tirima Vt 269 *tug*
tiSler N 229A *cabinet-maker*
tiŞS N 58A *tit*
tita N 152 *baby*
titake(ne) N 257G *baby*
tiTT N 63C *baby*
toA *gen. of tuba*
tobe A 235 *dumb*
tobu N 13B *dunce*
toE *gen. of tugi*
toeKas A 243B *sturdy*
toeStama Vt 349F *prop*
toeStiK N 62 *props*
toeTaja N 227A *supporter*
toeTama Vt 349F *support*
toeTuma Vi 349H *lean against*
toeTus N 260B *support*
tohi *pres. of toHtima*
toHman N 229A *dupe*
toHt N 124B *birch-bark*
toHtima Vt 308B *be allowed*
tohu *gen. of toHt*
tohutu A 227A *enormous*
toİbuma Vi 349G *recover*
toİm N 63B *texture*
toime N 177B *effect*
toimetaja N 227A *editor*
toimetama Vt 349F *edit*
toimetus N 260A *editorial office*
toimik N 234A *file (document)*
toİmima Vi 291C *operate*
toiming N 234A *operation*
toİmkoNd N 106 *committee*
toİmuma Vi 349G *occur*
toiT N 61E *food*
toiTev A 241A *nourishing*
toiTja N 227B *feeder*
toitlustama Vt 349F *cater*
toitlustus N 260A *catering*
toiTma Vt 297C *feed*
toiTuma Vi 349H *feed on something*
toKK N 58C *skein*
tola N 13A *dolt*
toĻL N 58A *customs*
inch
toĻLima Vt 291A *impose duty*
toLm N 61B *dust*
toLmama Vi 327B *be dusty*
tolmeldama Vt 349F *pollinate*
toLmlema Vi 326B *release pollen*
tolmune A 251 *dusty*
tolmutama Vt 349F *dust over*
tomat N 229A *tomato*
tomP N 61D *lump*
toŅN N 58A *tonne*
toŋT N 58E *ghost*
toodang N 234A *production*
toode N 177E *product (manufacture)*
tOOļ N 58A *chair*
tOOma Vt 267 *bring*
toomingas N 243A *bird-cherry tree*
tOOŋ N 58A *tone*
toonela N 227A *underworld of dead*
tooŋitama Vt 349F *stress*
toores A 161A *raw*
toorik N 234A *blank*
tOOrus N 260B *brutality*
tOOş N 58A *box*
tooTev A 241A *productive*
tooTja N 227B *producer*
tooTliK A 62 *productive*
tooTliKKus N 260B *productivity*
tooTma Vt 297C *produce*
tooTmine N 257E *production*
topAAs N 58A *topaz*
topend N 229A *wad*
topistama Vt 349F *stuff*
toPPima Vt 291D *cram*
toPs N 58B *mug*
tore A 235 *splendid*
toredus N 260A *splendour*
torge N 177F *prick of needle*
torin N 231A *grumble*
toriseja N 227A *grumbler*
torisema Vi 349C *grumble*
torKama Vt 327F *stab*
torKima Vt 291G *prick*
toRm N 58B *storm*
toRmaja N 227A *forward (sport)*
tormakas A 243A *impetuous*
toRmama Vi 327B *storm*
tormiline A 257D *stormy*
tormine A 251 *stormy*
toRn N 58B *tower*
torT N 58E *torte*
toru N 13A *pipe*
tube (pipe)
torustiK N 62 *plumbing*
tosin N 231A *dozen*
totAAlne A 247 *total*
totakas A 243A *brainless*
toTrus N 260B *idiocy*
toŢs N 58B *girl*
toTTer A 241B *idiotic*
traageldama Vt 349F *baste*
traagika N 227A *tragedy*
traagiline A 257D *tragic*
trAAler N 229A *trawler*
trAAļima Vt 291A *trawl*
traaŢ N 58E *wire*
traditsiOOn N 58A *tradition*
traditsiooniline A 257D *traditional*
trafareTne A 247 *stereotypical*
tragi A 13D *spry*
tragÖÖdia N 227A *tragedy*
traHv N 58B *penalty*
traHvima Vt 291C *fine*
traksid (pl) N 58B *suspenders*
traKtor N 229A *tractor*
traktoriSt N 58B *tractor driver*
traMM N 58A *tram*
tramPima Vi 291E *stamp feet*
tramplİİn N 58A *trampoline*
transformaaTor N 229A *transformer*
transkribEErima Vt 291B *transcribe*
translEErima Vt 291B *transmit*
tranSporT N 58E *transport*
transporTima Vt 291F *transport*
trapets N 229A *trapeze*
trauma N 152 *trauma*
trEEner N 229A *trainer*
trEEnima Vi 291A *train*
treening N 234A *training*
treeningud (pl) N 234A *training suit*
treİal N 229A *lathe operator*
treİma Vt 262 *turn on lathe*
treļlid (pl) N 58A *grating*
treŅN N 58A *training*
trePP N 58C *stairs*
tribÜÜn N 58A *tribune*
triibuline A 257D *striped*
triiKima Vt 291G *iron*
triiP N 61D *stripe*
trİİvima Vi 291A *drift*
triKK N 58C *trick*
trikolOOr N 58A *tricolour*
trikOO N 1 *bathing suit*
trikotAAž N 58A *knitted goods*
triĻjon N 229A *trillion*
trİo N 1 *trio*
triPP N 58C *fastener (clothes)*
triumF N 58A *triumph*

triumfEErima Vi 291B *triumph*
trofEE N 2 *trophy*
troĻL N 58A *troll (goblin)*
trolley bus
troļli N 152 *trolley bus*
troļlibuŞS N 58A *trolley bus*
trombOOn N 58A *trombone*
trompet N 229A *trumpet*
trOOŋ N 58A *throne*
troopika N 227A *tropics*
troopiline A 257D *tropical*
troŞS N 58A *cable*
troŢs N 58B *defiance*
troŢsima V 291C *defy*
troŢsliK A 62 *defiant*
truMM N 58A *drum*
trummeldama Vt 349F *drum*
trumP N 58D *trump*
trumPama V 327D *trump*
truPP N 58C *troupe*
truşsikud (pl) N 234A *underpants*
trUU A 7 *faithful*
trUUalamliK A 62 *loyal*
trUUdus N 260B *faithfulness*
trUUdusetu A 227A *unfaithful*
trööŞt N 58B *consolation*
trööŞtima Vt 291C *console*
trügima Vi 269 *elbow one's way*
trükis N 253 *printed matter*
trüKK N 58C *print*
trüKKal N 229A *printer*
trüKKima Vt 291D *print*
tsAAr N 58A *czar*
tseHH N 58A *department (factory)*
tselluloİd N 58B *celluloid*
tsellulOOS N 58A *cellulose*
tsemeŋT N 58E *cement*
tsementEErima Vt 291B *cement*
tsemeŋTima Vt 291F *cement*
tsensEErima Vt 291B *censor*
tseNsor N 229A *censor*
tsensUUr N 58A *censorship*
tsentrAAlne A 247 *central*
tsentralisatsiOOn N 58A *centralization*
tsentralisEErima Vt 291B *centralize*
tsentrifUUg N 58A *centrifuge*
tsenTrum N 229A *centre*
tsepelİİn N 58A *Zeppelin*
tseremoniAAlne A 247 *ceremonial*
tseremOOnia N 227A *ceremony*
tsinK N 58F *zinc*
tsirKus N 260B *circus*

tsisteRn N 58B *cistern*
tsitaaT N 58E *quotation*
tsitadeĻL N 58A *citadel*
tsitEErima Vt 291B *quote*
tsivilisatsiOOn N 58A *civilization*
tsivilisEErima Vt 291B *civilize*
tsOOn N 58A *zone*
tsüKKel N 240B *cycle*
tsüKlon N 229A *cyclone*
tšeHH N 58A *Czech*
tšeKK N 58C *cheque*
tšelliSt N 58B *cellist*
tšello N 152 *cello*
tšemPion N 246 *champion*
tšİİllane N 257C *Chilean*
tšUUd N 58A *Chude*
tualeŢT N 58C *toilet*
tuba N 38 *room*
tubakas N 243A *tobacco*
tube *pl. part. of tuba*
tuberkulOOS N 58A *tuberculosis*
tuberkulOOsne A 248 *tubercular*
tubli A 152 *good*
tudeng N 229A *student*
tudi N 13C *doddering fool*
tuge *part. of tugi*
tugev A 231A *strong*
tugevdama Vt 349F *strengthen*
tugevnema Vi 349D *strengthen*
tugevus N 260A *strength*
tugi N 43 *support*
tuginema Vi 349D *rely on*
tuha *gen. of tuHk*
tuhandes A 237B *thousandth*
tuhandiK N 62 *thousandth*
tuharad (pl) N 231A *buttocks*
tuhastama Vt 349F *cremate*
tuhat N 239 *thousand*
tuHk N 109 *ash*
tuhkatriinu N 152 *Cinderella*
tuHkur A 242A *ashen*
tuHkur N 242A *polecat*
tuHm A 58B *dim*
tuhmistama Vt 349F *dim*
tuhmistuma Vi 349H *become dim*
tuHmuma Vi 349G *become dim*
tuHnima Vi 291C *rummage*
tuHvel N 240A *slipper*
tuigerdama Vi 349F *stagger*
tuiKuma Vi 291G *stagger*
tuİm A 53B *numb*
tuimastama Vt 349F *make numb*

tuimasti N 225A *anaesthetics*
tuİmus N 260B *numbness*
tuisata *part. of tuiSkama*
tuiSk N 131C *blizzard*
tuiSkama Vi 348C *drift snow*
tuisu *gen. of tuiSk*
tuJJu *ill. of tuju*
tuju N 13A *mood*
tujukas A 243A *moody*
tujutu A 227A *spiritless*
tuKK N 53C *tuft of hair*
tuKK N 58C *firebrand*
tuKKuma Vi 291D *doze*
tuKsuma Vi 291C *throb*
tuLd *part. of tuli*
tule *gen. of tuli*
tulek N 234A *arrival*
tulema Vi 271 *come*
tulemine N 257E *coming*
tulemus N 260A *result*
tulenema Vi 349D *result from*
tulestiK N 62 *lighting*
tuletama Vt 349F *derive*
tuletamine N 257E *derivation*
tuletis N 260A *derivative*
tuletus N 260A *derivation*
tulev A 231A *coming (next)*
tulevane A 257A *future*
tuleviK N 62 *future*
tuli *past of tulema*
tuli N 20 *fire*
tulikas N 243A *buttercup*
tuline A 251 *hot*
tulistama Vt 349F *fire*
tuLLa *part. of tulema*
tuLLe *ill. of tuli*
tulP N 53D *post*
tuļP N 58D *tulip*
tulu N 13A *profit*
tulus A 231A *profitable*
tume A 235 *dark of colour*
tumenema Vi 349D *darken colour*
tuMM N 53A *mute*
tuŅd N 118 *hour*
tuNde *gen. of tunne*
tuNdel N 241A *feeler*
tuNdeline A 257D *emotional*
tuNdetu A 227A *unfeeling*
tuNdliK A 62 *sensitive*
tuNdliKKus N 260B *sensitivity*
tuNdma Vt 319 *know a person*
tuNdmatu A 227A *unknown*

tuNdmus N 260B *feeling*
tuNdra N 227B *tundra*
tuNduma Vi 349H *seem*
tungal N 170B *torch*
tuNgima Vi 291C *force one's way*
tuNgiv A 231A *urgent*
tuNglema Vi 326B *crowd*
tunne *pres. of tuNdma*
tunne N 214 *feeling*
tuNNel N 229A *tunnel*
tunnetama Vt 349F *perceive*
tunnetus N 260A *perception*
tuņni *gen. of tuŅd*
tuņnistaja N 227A *witness*
tuņnistama Vt 349F *witness*
tuņnistus N 260A *testimony*
tunnus N 253 *feature*
tunnustama Vt 349F *acknowledge*
tunnustav A 231A *approving*
tunnustus N 260A *acknowledgement*
tupik N 234A *dead end*
tuPP N 63C *sheath*
tuPPa *ill. of tuba*
tuPs N 61B *tassel*
tupsuline A 257D *tasselled*
tupsutama Vt 349F *dab*
turakas N 243A *blockhead*
tuRba *gen. of turvas*
tuRg N 131B *market*
turi N 71A *upper back*
turiSt N 58B *tourist*
turnEE N 2 *tour*
turnİİr N 58A *tournament*
tursa *gen. of turSk*
turSk N 109 *cod*
tuRsuma Vi 349G *swell*
turtsakas A 243A *peevish*
turTsuma Vi 291C *fume*
turu *gen. of tuRg*
turustama Vt 349F *market*
turustus N 260A *marketing*
turvas N 187 *peat*
tusane A 251 *sulky*
tusatsema Vi 349E *sulk*
tuŞS N 58A *fart*
tuŠŠ N 58C *flourish*
Indian ink
tuŠŠima Vt 291D *ink Indian ink*
tuţistama Vt 349F *pull by the hair*
tuŢT N 58C *tuft*
tuTvuma Vi 349G *become acquainted*
tuTvus N 260B *acquaintance*
tuTvuskoNd N 106 *circle of acquaintances*
tutvustama Vt 349F *introduce*
tUUa *part. of tOOma*
tUUb N 58A *tube*
tuuba N 152 *tuba*
tuuKer N 240A *diver*
tUUl N 82 *wind*
tUUlduma Vi 349H *be aired*
tuulik N 234A *windmill*
tuuline A 251 *windy*
tuulutama Vt 349F *air*
tuulutus N 260A *airing*
tUUm N 53A *nucleus*
tuuPija N 227A *crammer*
tuuPima Vt 291E *cram*
tuuPur N 229A *crammer*
tUUr N 58A *round*
tuuŞt N 58B *wisp*
tuututama V 349F *toot*
tuvi N 13A *pigeon*
tõbi N 40 *disease*
tõbine A 251 *sickly*
tõbras N 159D *brute*
tõde N 25 *truth*
tõdema Vt 269 *arrive at truth*
tõE *gen. of tõsi*
tõE *gen. of tõde*
tõEline A 257D *true*
tõElisus N 260A *reality*
tõEnd N 229B *proof*
tõEndama Vt 349F *provide proof*
tõEndus N 260B *proof*
tõEnäOlisus N 260A *probability*
tõEnäOsus N 260B *probability*
tõeStama Vt 349F *prove*
tõeStus N 260B *proof*
tõHk N 131C *polecat*
tõhu *gen. of tõHk*
tõhus A 231A *efficient*
tõİ *past of tOOma*
tõiK N 49F *fact*
tõke N 177C *obstacle*
tõkestama Vt 349F *obstruct*
tõLd N 91 *coach*
tõlge N 177F *translation*
tõlgendama Vt 349F *interpret*
tõlgendus N 260A *interpretation*
tõļgitsema Vt 349E *interpret*
tõļgitsus N 260A *interpretation*
tõĻK N 58F *interpreter*
tõĻKija N 227A *translator*
tõĻKima Vt 291G *translate*
tõlla *gen. of tõLd*
tõLv N 49B *battledore*
tõMbama Vt 340 *pull*
tõMbe *gen. of tõmme*
tõMblema Vi 329 *twitch*
tõMbuma Vi 349G *withdraw oneself*
tõMbus N 260B *draft*
tõmmata *part. of tõMbama*
tõmme N 209 *jerk*
tõmmelda *part. of tõMblema*
tõmmis N 253 *galley proof*
tõmmu A 152 *swarthy*
tõoTama Vt 349F *promise*
tõoTus N 260B *promise*
tõPPe *ill. of tõbi*
tõrelema Vi 325 *chide*
tõrelus N 260A *chiding*
tõrges A 166B *stubborn*
tõri N 67 *horn*
tõrje N 177B *pest control*
tõRjuma Vt 291C *repel*
tõrKuma Vi 291G *resist*
tõrre *gen. of tõRs*
tõRs N 144 *vat*
tõrT *part. of tõRs*
tõru N 13A *acorn*
tõRv N 49B *tar*
tõRvama Vt 327B *tar*
tõrvane A 251 *tarry*
tõrvik N 234A *torch*
tõsi N 44 *earnestness*
tõsidus N 260A *seriousness*
tõsine A 251 *serious*
tõstatama Vt 349F *raise an issue*
tõStma Vt 297A *lift*
tõstuk N 229A *hoist*
tõTT *part. of tõsi*
tõTTama Vi 327C *hurry*
tõU *gen. of tõUg*
tõUg N 134 *breed*
tõuge N 177F *push*
tõuK N 61F *larva*
tõuKama Vt 327F *push*
tõuKlema Vi 326F *jostle*
tõUs N 61B *ascent*
tõusik N 234A *upstart*
tõUsma Vi 296B *rise*
tõve *gen. of tõbi*
täbar A 231A *awkward*
tädi N 13C *aunt*
tähe *gen. of täHt*
täheke(ne) N 257G *starlet (sky)*

tähelepaneliK [A 62] *attentive*
tähelepanematu [A 227A] *inattentive*
tähendama [Vt 349F] *mean*
tähendus [N 260A] *meaning*
tähestiK [N 62] *alphabet*
tähestikuline [A 257D] *alphabetical*
tähi *pres. of täHtima*
tähik [N 234A] *receipt*
tähis [N 253] *sign*
tähistama [Vt 349F] *mark an occasion*
tähniline [A 257D] *speckled*
täHt [N 139] *star*
täHtima [Vt 308B] *register a letter*
täHtis [A 250A] *important*
täHtsus [N 260B] *importance*
täHtsusetu [A 227A] *unimportant*
täİ [N 1] *louse*
täidis [N 253] *filling*
täİdlane [A 257C] *plump*
täİdlus [N 260B] *plumpness*
täie *gen. of täİs*
täieliK [A 62] *complete*
täiend [N 229A] *complement*
täiendama [Vt 349F] *complement*
täiendav [A 231A] *supplementary*
täiendus [N 260A] *addition*
täienema [Vi 349D] *become complete*
täİs [A 143C] *full*
täİskaSvanu [N 227A] *adult*
täiT *part. of täİs*
täiTma [Vt 297C] *fill*
täiTmine [N 257E] *filling*
täiTuma [Vi 349H] *become filled*
täİusliK [A 62] *complete*
täİusliKKus [N 260B] *completeness*
täiustama [Vt 349F] *elaborate*
täiustus [N 260A] *elaboration*
täke [N 177C] *notch*
täkestama [Vt 349F] *notch*
täkiline [A 257D] *notched*
täKK [N 61C] *stallion*
tänama [Vt 269] *thank*
tänamatu [A 227A] *ungrateful*
tänamatus [N 260A] *ingratitude*
tänane [A 251] *today's*

tänav [N 231A] *street*
tänavastiK [N 62] *street network*
tänavune [A 257A] *this year's*
tänu [N 13A] *thanks*
tänuliK [A 62] *thankful*
tänuliKKus [N 260B] *gratitude*
täpe [N 177C] *speck*
täpes [N 161C] *speck*
täpiline [A 257D] *spotted*
täPne [A 247] *precise*
täPP [N 58C] *spot*
täPPis [A 250B] *precise*
täPsus [N 260B] *precision*
täpsustama [Vt 349F] *specify*
täpsustus [N 260A] *specification*
tärgeldama [Vt 349F] *starch*
täring [N 234A] *die*
tärKama [Vi 327F] *sprout*
täRn [N 58B] *asterisk*
tärpentin [N 245] *turpentine*
tätovEErima [Vt 291B] *tattoo*
tääK [N 58F] *bayonet*
tõgama [Vt 269] *chaff*
tõhe *ill. of tÖÖ*
töllerdama [Vi 349F] *loaf about*
töŋTs [A 58B] *blunt*
tÖÖ [N 8] *work*
tööKas [A 243B] *industrious*
tööKus [N 260B] *diligence*
tÖÖline [N 257D] *worker*
tÖÖliskoNd [N 106] *workers*
tööStur [N 229A] *industrialist*
tööStus [N 260B] *industry*
tööStusliK [A 62] *industrial*
tööTaja [N 227A] *employee*
tööTama [Vi 349F] *work*
tööTlema [Vt 326E] *process*
tööTu [A 227B] *unemployed*
tüdimatu [A 227A] *untiring*
tüdimus [N 260A] *weariness*
tüdinema [Vi 349D] *become bored*
tüdruk [N 234A] *girl*
tühi [A 71A] *empty*
tühik [N 234A] *void*

tühimiK [N 62] *void*
tühine [A 251] *trivial*
tühistama [Vt 349F] *cancel*
tühisus [N 260A] *triviality*
tühi-tähi [N 71A] *trifle*
tühjendama [Vt 349F] *empty*
tühjenema [Vi 349D] *become empty*
tüHjus [N 260B] *emptiness*
tükeldama [Vt 349F] *cut into pieces*
tükike(ne) [N 257G] *morsel*
tüKK [N 58C] *piece*
tülgastus [N 260A] *disgust*
tüli [N 13A] *quarrel*
tülikas [A 243A] *troublesome*
tülin [N 231A] *trouble*
tülitama [Vt 349F] *disturb*
tülitsema [Vi 349E] *quarrel*
tüĻL [N 58A] *tulle*
tüLLi *ill. of tüli*
tüļPimus [N 260A] *boredom*
tüŅN [N 58A] *barrel*
türa [N 13A] *cock (penis)*
türaŅN [N 58A] *tyrant*
türaŅNia [N 227A] *tyranny*
türannisEErima [Vt 291B] *tyrannize*
türkİİs [N 58A] *turquoise*
türKlane [N 257C] *Turk*
tüse [A 235] *stout*
tüsedus [N 260A] *stoutness*
tüsenema [Vi 349D] *become stout*
tütar [N 176] *daughter*
tüve *gen. and part. of tüvi*
tüvi [N 18] *trunk (tree)*
stem (grammar)
tüVVe *ill. of tüvi*
tüüFus [N 260B] *typhus*
tüügas [N 159E] *stump*
tÜÜmian [N 246] *thyme*
tüüP [N 58D] *type*
tüüpiline [A 257D] *typical*
tÜÜr [N 58A] *rudder*
tÜÜrima [Vt 291A] *steer*
tüüTama [Vt 327E] *pester*
tüüTu [A 227B] *tiresome*

U

uba [N 38] *bean*
ube *pl. part. of uba*
udar [N 231A] *udder*
udmurT [N 58E] *Udmurt*

udu [N 13C] *fog*
udune [A 251] *foggy*
udutama [Vi 349F] *be foggy*
uha *pres. of uHtma*

uHke [A 227B] *proud*
uhkeldama [Vi 349F] *have airs*
uHkus [N 260B] *pride*
uhkustama [Vi 349F] *pride oneself*

uHmer [N 240A] *mortar*
uHtma [Vi 320] *wash ashore*
uHtuma [Vi 308B] *wash ashore*
uhu *pres. of uHtuma*
uİm [N 63B] *fin*
uimane [A 251] *dazed*
uimastama [Vt 349F] *daze*
uinak [N 234A] *nap*
uİnuma [Vi 349G] *fall asleep*
uinutama [Vt 349F] *lull to sleep*
uinuti [N 225A] *soporific*
uiSk [N 131C] *skate*
uisu *gen. of uiSk*
uisutaja [N 227A] *skater*
uisutama [Vi 349F] *skate*
uiTama [Vi 327E] *roam*
uiTma [Vi 297C] *roam*
ujuja [N 227A] *swimmer*
ujula [N 227A] *swimming-pool*
ujuma [Vi 269] *swim*
ujutama [Vt 349F] *flood*
ukraİnlane [N 257C] *Ukrainian*
uKs [N 84] *door*
ulakas [A 243A] *hooligan-like*
ulakus [N 260A] *hooliganism*
ulatama [Vt 349F] *extend*
ulatuma [Vi 349H] *be extended*
ulatus [N 260A] *extent*
ulatusliK [A 62] *extensive*
uLguma [Vi 313A] *howl*
uļjas [A 159B] *daring*
uĻjus [N 260B] *daring*
ulme [N 177B] *fantasy*
ultimaaTum [N 229A] *ultimatum*
ultramarİİn [A 58A] *ultramarine*
ulu *pres. of uLguma*
uluk [N 229A] *wild animal*
uluma [Vi 269] *howl*
uMbe *gen. of umme*
uMbne [A 247] *stuffy*
umme [N 209] *whitlow*
ummik [N 234A] *deadlock*
ummistama [Vt 349F] *clog*
ummistuma [Vi 349H] *become clogged*

uNd *part. of uni*
uNdama [Vi 343] *hum*
une *gen. of uni*
unelm [N 231A] *day-dream*
unetu [A 227A] *sleepless*
unetus [N 260A] *sleeplessness*
uni [N 20] *sleep*
unine [A 251] *sleepy*
unistaja [N 227A] *dreamer*
unistama [Vt 349F] *day-dream*
unistus [N 260A] *dream (wish)*
unisus [N 260A] *sleepiness*
universAAlne [A 247] *universal*
univeRsum [N 229A] *universe*
unnata *part. of uNdama*
uNNe *ill. of uni*
uŋTs [N 58B] *ounce*
unuma [Vi 269] *become forgotten*
ununema [Vi 349D] *become forgotten*
unustama [Vt 349F] *forget*
unustamatu [A 227A] *unforgettable*
uPPuja [N 227A] *drowning person*
uPPuma [Vi 291D] *drown*
upsakas [A 243A] *arrogant*
upsakus [N 260A] *arrogance*
uputama [Vt 349F] *drown*
uputus [N 260A] *flood*
urAAn [N 58A] *uranium*
uralistika [N 227A] *Uralic studies*
uRb [N 101B] *catkin*
uRbne [A 247] *porous*
uRg [N 131B] *burrow*
urgitsema [Vi 349E] *poke*
urİİn [N 58A] *urine*
urin [N 231A] *growl*
urinEErima [Vi 291B] *urinate*
urisema [Vi 349C] *growl*
uRn [N 58B] *urn*
uru *gen. of uRg*
urva *gen. of uRb*
usaldama [Vt 349F] *trust*
usaldatav [A 231A] *trustworthy*
usaldus [N 260A] *trust*
usaldusliK [A 62] *confidential*

usin [A 231A] *diligent*
usinus [N 260A] *diligence*
uSk [N 131C] *belief*
uSkliK [A 62] *religious*
uSkmatu [A 227A] *incredulous*
uSkuma [Vt 313B] *believe*
uSkumatu [A 227A] *incredible*
uSkumus [N 260A] *belief*
uŞS [N 58A] *snake*
uşsitama [Vi 349F] *be worm-eaten*
usT *part. of uKs*
uStav [A 231A] *faithful*
uStavus [N 260A] *faithfulness*
usu *gen. of uSk*
usu *pres. of uSkuma*
usuline [A 257D] *religious*
usund [N 229A] *religion*
usutav [A 231A] *plausible*
usutelu [N 13A] *interview*
usutlema [Vt 351] *interview*
usutlus [N 260A] *interview*
utİİl [N 58A] *scrap*
utooPia [N 227A] *Utopia*
utoopiline [A 257D] *Utopian*
uTT [N 63C] *ewe*
uTTu *ill. of udu*
uudis [N 253] *news*
uudishimuliK [A 62] *curious*
uudistama [Vt 349F] *wonder at*
UUdne [A 247] *novel*
UUdsus [N 260B] *novelty*
UUdus [N 260B] *newness*
uue *gen. of UUs*
uuendaja [N 227A] *innovator*
uuendama [Vt 349F] *renew*
uuendus [N 260A] *renewal*
uuenema [Vi 349D] *become renewed*
UUr [N 58A] *watch (clock)*
UUrija [N 227A] *investigator*
UUrima [Vt 291A] *investigate*
UUrimus [N 260A] *research*
uuristama [Vt 349F] *erode*
UUs [A 143A] *new*
uuT *part. of UUs*

V

vaade [N 177E] *view*
vaaderpaŞS [N 58A] *level (tool)*
vAAgen [N 241A] *platter*
vaaKum [N 229A] *vacuum*
vaaKuum [N 246] *vacuum*

vAAl [N 49A] *whale*
vAAr [N 58A] *grandfather*
vaarikas [N 243A] *raspberry*
vAAş [N 58A] *vase*
vaaŢ [N 58E] *barrel*

vaaTajaskoNd [N 106] *audience (viewers)*
vaaTama [Vt 327E] *look at*
vaaTlema [Vt 326E] *observe*
vaaTlus [N 260B] *observation*
vaaTus [N 260B] *act of play*

vaba A 14B *free*
vabadiK N 62 *cotter*
vabadus N 260A *freedom*
vabandama Vt 349F *pardon*
vabandatav A 231A *excusable*
vabandus N 260A *apology*
vabanema Vi 349D *become free*
vabastama Vt 349F *free*
vabisema Vi 349C *tremble*
vabrik N 234A *factory*
vabu *pl. part. of vaba*
vadak N 234A *whey*
vader N 229A *godparent*
vadin N 231A *prattle*
vadistama Vi 349F *prattle*
vaḑjalane N 257C *Vote*
vaEgus N 260B *deficiency*
vaEn N 61B *enmity*
vaEne A 252 *poor*
vaEnlane N 257C *enemy*
vaenuliK A 62 *hostile*
vaEseke(ne) N 257G *poor thing*
vaEsuma Vi 349G *become poor*
vaEsus N 260B *poverty*
vaEv N 49B *hardship*
vaevaline A 257D *arduous*
vaEvama Vt 327B *trouble*
vaEvlema Vi 326B *be tormented*
vaga A 14D *pious*
vagel N 78C *maggot*
vagiina N 152 *vagina*
vagu *pl. part. of vaga*
vagu N 31 *furrow*
vagun N 229A *carriage*
vaha N 13A *wax*
vahatama Vt 349F *wax*
vahe N 153 *difference*
vahelduma Vi 349H *alternate*
vaheldus N 260A *change*
vahelduv A 231A *alternating*
vahemiK N 62 *interval*
vahend N 229A *means*
vahendaja N 227A *intermediary*
vahendama Vt 349F *mediate*
vaher N 206 *maple*
vahetama Vt 349F *exchange*
vahetamine N 257E *exchange*
vahetu A 227A *immediate*
vahetuma Vi 349H *become exchanged*
vahetus N 260A *exchange*
vahi *gen. of vaHt*
vahi *pres. of vaHtima*

vahistama Vt 349F *arrest*
vahistus N 260A *arrest*
vaHt N 116 *guard*
vaHt N 124B *foam*
vaHtima Vt 308B *stare at*
vaHtra *gen. of vaher*
vaHtriK N 62 *maple grove*
vahu *gen. of vaHt*
vahune A 251 *foamy*
vahustama Vt 349F *whip (food)*
vahutama Vi 349F *foam*
vaHva A 227B *outstanding*
vaHvel N 240A *wafer*
vaHvus N 260B *bravery*
vaİ N 49B *peg*
vaİbuma Vi 349G *subside*
vaİdlema Vi 330B *argue*
vaİdlematu A 227A *indisputable*
vaİdlus N 260B *argument (dispute)*
vaielda *part. of vaİdlema*
vaieldav A 231A *debatable*
vaigistama Vt 349F *alleviate*
vaigune A 251 *resinous*
vaiK N 61F *resin*
vaiKima Vi 350 *be silent*
vaiKiv A 231A *silent*
vaiKne A 247 *quiet*
vaiKus N 260B *silence*
vaİm N 61B *spirit*
vaİmne A 247 *spiritual*
vaimukas A 243A *witty*
vaimukus N 260A *wit*
vaimuliK A 62 *ecclesiastical*
vaimustama Vt 349F *enthuse*
vaimustav A 231A *inspiring*
vaimustuma Vi 349H *become enthused*
vaimustus N 260A *enthusiasm*
vaiP N 49D *rug*
vaiSt N 61B *instinct*
vaiStliK A 62 *instinctive*
vajadus N 260A *need*
vajaliK A 62 *necessary*
vajama Vt 269 *need*
vajuma Vi 269 *sink*
vajutama Vt 349F *press*
vakanTne A 247 *vacant*
vaKK N 49C *bushel*
vaKKu *ill. of vagu*
vaKsal N 229A *train station*
vaktsİİn N 58A *vaccine*
vaktsinatsiOOn N 58A *vaccination*
vaktsinEErima Vt 291B *vaccinate*

valaja N 227A *caster (moulder)*
valama Vt 269 *pour*
valamu N 227A *sink*
valang N 234A *downpour*
vaLd N 91 *township*
vaLdaja N 227A *proprietor*
vaLdama Vt 342 *possess*
vaLdav A 231A *predominant*
vaLdkoNd N 106 *sphere of activity*
vaLdus N 260B *possession*
vale A 153 *wrong (false)*
vale N 153 *lie (deception)*
valeliK A 62 *deceitful*
valem N 229A *formula*
valetaja N 227A *liar*
valetama Vi 349F *lie (deceive)*
vaLge A 227B *white*
valgendama Vt 349F *whiten*
valgendi N 225A *whitener*
valgenema Vi 349D *become lighter*
vaLguma Vi 349G *disperse*
vaLgus N 260B *light*
valgustaja N 227A *enlightener*
valgustama Vt 349F *enlighten*
vali A 75 *loud*
valija N 227A *voter*
valijaskoNd N 106 *electorate*
valik N 234A *choice*
valima Vt 269 *choose*
valimiK N 62 *selection*
valimine N 257E *elections*
valitseja N 227A *ruler*
valitsema Vt 349E *rule*
valitsus N 260A *government*
vaĻjad (pl) N 159B *bridle*
vaĻjus N 260B *loudness*
valK N 61F *protein*
vaĻL N 58A *rampart*
valla *gen. of vaLd*
vallaline A 257D *unmarried*
vallandama Vt 349F *dismiss from office*
vallandus N 260A *dismissal*
vallata *part. of vaLdama*
vallatama Vi 349F *frolic*
vallatlema Vi 351 *frolic*
vallatu A 227A *mischievous*
vallatus N 260A *mischief*
vallutaja N 227A *conqueror*
vallutama Vt 349F *conquer*
vallutus N 260A *conquest*
vaĻm N 58B *fable*
vaĻmima Vi 349B *become finished*

vaĻmima Vi 349B *ripen*
vaĻmis A 244 *finished*
ripe
vaļmistama Vt 349F *prepare*
vaļmistuma Vi 349H *get ready*
vaļsi *gen. of vaļSk*
vaļSk A 120B *spurious*
vaļSS N 58G *waltz*
vaļSSima Vi 291H *waltz*
vaļTs N 58B *roller*
vaļTsima Vt 291C *mill*
valu N 13A *die (metal)*
valu N 13A *pain*
valuliK A 62 *painful*
valuline A 257D *painful*
valus A 231A *painful*
valutama Vi 349F *hurt*
valutu A 227A *painless*
valuuta N 152 *currency*
valvakas A 243A *watchful*
vaLvama Vt 327B *guard*
valvas A 165B *vigilant*
valve N 177B *watch (guard)*
vaLvsus N 260B *vigilance*
vaLvur N 229A *guard*
vampİIr N 58A *vampire*
vana A 14A *old*
vanadus N 260A *old age*
vanake(ne) N 257G *old person*
vanaldane A 257A *elderly*
vananema Vi 349D *age*
vandAAl N 58A *vandal*
vandaliSm N 58B *vandalism*
vaNde *gen. of vanne*
vaNduma Vi 310 *swear*
vanem N 231A *parent*
vaNg N 58B *prisoner*
vangistama Vt 349F *imprison*
vangistus N 260A *imprisonment*
vaNgla N 227B *prison*
vangutama Vt 349F *wag (head)*
vanik N 234A *garland*
vaniļje N 152 *vanilla*
vanKer N 240A *wagon*
vanKuma Vi 291G *totter*
vanKumatu A 227A *unshakable*
vaŅN N 58A *bath*
vanne N 214 *oath*
vaņnitama Vt 349F *bathe*
vannu *pres. of vaNduma*
vaņTsima Vi 291C *trudge*
vanu *pl. part. of vana*

vanuma Vi 269 *become matted*
vanur N 229A *old person*
vanus N 253 *age*
vaO *gen. of vagu*
vaPP N 58C *coat of arms*
vaPPer A 241B *brave*
vaPPuma Vi 349G *be shocked*
vaPrus N 260B *bravery*
vapustama Vt 349F *shock*
vapustav A 231A *shocking*
vapustus N 260A *shock*
vara N 13A *wealth*
varajane A 257A *early*
varandus N 260A *possessions*
varandusliK A 62 *property*
varane A 251 *early*
varas N 194 *thief*
varastama Vt 349F *steal*
vaRba *gen. of varvas*
vaRblane N 257C *sparrow*
vaRda *gen. of varras*
varem A 231A *earlier*
varemed (pl) N 157 *ruins*
vares N 253 *crow*
vaRga *gen. of varas*
vaRgus N 260B *theft*
vari N 74 *shadow*
variaņT N 58E *version*
variEErima Vt 291B *vary*
variEEruma Vi 349G *vary*
varietEE N 2 *variety show*
varisema Vi 349C *collapse*
variser N 245 *Pharisee*
varitsema Vt 349E *lie in wait for*
vaRjama Vt 327B *conceal*
vaRjamatu A 227A *unconcealed*
varjend N 229A *shelter*
varjukas A 243A *shady*
varjuline A 257D *shady*
varjund N 229A *tinge*
varjutus N 260A *eclipse*
vaRn N 49B *clothes-rack*
varras N 193 *skewer*
varre *gen. of vaRs*
varrukas N 243A *sleeve*
vaRs N 144 *stem*
varSS N 49G *foal*
varT *part. of vaRs*
varu N 13A *supply*
varuma Vt 269 *supply*
varustaja N 227A *supplier*
varustama Vt 349F *supply someone*

varustus N 260A *outfit*
varvas N 187 *toe*
vasak A 234A *left*
vasar N 231A *hammer*
vasardama Vt 349F *hammer*
vase *gen. of vaŞk*
vaselİIn N 58A *vaseline*
vasem A 231A *left*
vasikas N 243A *calf*
vaŞk N 142B *copper*
vaŞkne A 247 *copper*
vaŞSima Vt 291A *muddle*
vaStama V 327B *answer*
vastand N 229A *opposite*
vastandama Vt 349F *contrast*
vastandliK A 62 *opposite*
vastane A 251 *contrary*
vastane N 251 *opponent*
vastastikune A 251 *mutual*
vaStav A 231A *corresponding*
vaste N 177B *equivalent*
vaştik A 234A *repugnant*
vaştikus N 260A *repugnance*
vaStlad (pl) N 241A *Shrove-tide*
vaStne A 247 *new*
vaStne N 247 *larva*
vastus N 253 *answer*
vastutama Vi 349F *be responsible for*
vastutav A 231A *responsible*
vastutus N 260A *responsibility*
vatEErima Vt 291B *quilt*
vaterdaja N 227A *prattler*
vaterdama Vi 349F *prattle*
vaTs N 49B *belly*
vaŢT N 58C *cotton-wool*
vaŢT N 58C *watt*
veA *pres. of vedama*
veA *gen. of viga*
veaTu A 227B *faultless*
vedama Vt 276 *haul*
vedel A 231A *liquid*
vedelema Vi 325 *idle about*
vedeliK N 62 *fluid*
vedru N 152 *spring*
vedrutama Vi 349F *be springy*
vedu N 27 *haulage*
vedur N 229A *locomotive*
vEE *gen. of vesi*
vEEbruar N 246 *February*
vEEnduma Vi 349H *become convinced*
vEEndumus N 260A *conviction*
vEEnma Vt 292A *convince*

vEEnmine N 257E *convincing*
vEEr N 61A *slope*
vEEr N 82 *edge*
veerand N 229A *quarter*
vEErema Vi 291A *roll*
veeretama Vt 349F *roll*
vEErg N 131A *newspaper column*
vEErima Vt 291B *spell*
veeris N 253 *margin*
veeru *gen. of vEErg*
veeTlema Vt 326E *charm*
veeTlev A 231A *charming*
veeTlus N 260B *charm*
veeTma Vt 297C *spend time*
vehelda *part. of veHklema*
vehi *pres. of veHkima*
veHkima Vi 313B *gesticulate*
veHkleja N 227A *fencer*
veHklema Vi 336 *fence*
veHklemine N 257E *fencing*
veİder A 241A *odd (strange)*
veiderdaja N 227A *buffoon*
veiderdama Vi 349F *play the fool*
veİdriK N 62 *eccentric*
veİdrus N 260B *eccentricity*
veimed (pl) N 63B *presents from bride*
veİn N 58B *wine*
veİs N 254 *ox*
veKKima Vt 291D *preserve (can)*
veli N 77 *brother*
velvet N 229A *velvet*
veMbla *gen. of vemmal*
vembutama Vi 349F *play pranks*
vemmal N 200 *scamp*
vemP N 61D *prank*
veNd N 106 *brother*
veNdlus N 260B *brotherhood*
vene N 153 *boat*
venelane N 257C *Russian*
venestama Vt 349F *Russify*
venima Vi 269 *be drawn out*
venitama Vt 349F *stretch out*
venitatav A 231A *elastic*
venna *gen. of veNd*
vennaliK A 62 *brotherly*
ventİIl N 58A *valve*
ventilaaTor N 229A *fan*
ventilatsiOOn N 58A *ventilation*
ventilEErima Vt 291B *ventilate*
veO *gen. of vedu*
veoK N 229B *vehicle*
veOndus N 260B *transport*
vePslane N 257C *Vepsian*
veranda N 152 *verandah*
verbAAlne A 247 *verbal*
veRd *part. of veri*
vere *gen. of veri*
veretu A 227A *bloodless*
veri N 20 *blood*
verine A 251 *bloody*
veristama Vt 349F *bloody*
verme N 177B *gash*
vermut N 229A *vermouth*
veRRe *ill. of veri*
versiOOn N 58A *version*
verSt N 53B *mile*
vertikAAlne A 247 *vertical*
vesi N 46 *water*
vesine A 251 *watery*
vesiniK N 62 *hydrogen*
veŞki N 225B *mill*
veŞt N 58B *vest*
veStlema Vi 326B *chat*
veStlus N 260B *chat*
veStma Vt 297A *tell a story*
veStma Vt 297A *whittle*
veStmiK N 62 *phrase-book*
veteran N 245 *veteran*
veţikad (pl) N 243A *algae*
veto N 152 *veto*
veTruma Vi 349G *be elastic*
veTruv A 231A *springy*
veTruvus N 260A *elasticity*
veTT *part. of vesi*
veTTe *ill. of vesi*
veŢTima Vi 349B *become waterlogged*
viaduKt N 58B *viaduct*
vibratsiOOn N 58A *vibration*
vibrEErima V 291B *vibrate*
vibu N 13B *bow (archery)*
vibutama Vt 349F *brandish*
videviK N 62 *dusk*
vidistama V 349F *twitter*
vidu N13C *mistiness*
viga N 37 *mistake*
vigane A 251 *defective*
vigastama V 349F *injure*
vigastus N 260A *injury*
vigur N 229A *stunt*
vigurdama V 349F *do stunts*
viha *gen. of viHt* N 89B
viha N 13A *anger*
vihane A 251 *angry*
vihastama Vt 349F *anger*
vihastuma Vi 349H *become angry*
vihata *part. of viHkama*
vihatav A 231A *hateful*
vihelda *part. of viHtlema*
vihi *gen. of viHt* N 116
vihik N 234A *exercise book*
vihisema Vi 349C *swish*
viHjama V 327B *hint at*
vihje N 177B *hint*
viHk N 131C *sheaf*
viHkama Vt 348C *hate*
viHm N 49B *rain*
vihmane A 251 *rainy*
viHt N 89B *whisk in sauna*
viHt N 116 *skein*
weight (scales)
viHtlema V 331B *whisk in sauna*
vihu *gen. of viHk*
vİIa *part. of vİIma*
vİIbima Vi 349B *stay for a time*
viide N 177E *allusion*
viie *gen. of vİIs* N 143B
viiendiK N 62 *fifth*
viies A 238A *fifth*
viigistama Vt 349F *draw (game)*
viigitama Vt 349F *crease*
viiK N 58F *crease*
draw (game)
viiking N 229A *Viking*
vİIl N 58A *file (tool)*
vİIl N 61A *slice*
vİIlima Vi 291A *shirk*
viilukas N 243A *slice*
vİIma Vt 264A *take (carry off)*
viimane A 251 *final*
viimistlema Vt 351 *touch up*
viimistlus N 260A *finishing touches*
vİImne A 247 *final*
vİIn N 49A *liquor*
vodka
vİIner N 229A *wiener*
viiPama Vi 327D *beckon*
viirastuma Vi 349H *hallucinate*
viirastus N 260A *hallucination*
viirastusliK A 62 *hallucinatory*
vİIrg N 131A *line*
viiru *gen. of vİIrg*
viiruk N 229A *incense*
viiruline A 257D *lined*
vİIrus N 260B *virus*
vİIs N 58A *manner*
melody

vİİs N 143B *five*
viisa N 152 *visa*
viisakas A 243A *polite*
viisakus N 260A *politeness*
viisik N 234A *quintuplet*
viisistama Vt 349F *set to music*
viiSk N 131C *bast shoe*
viisu *gen. of viiSk*
viiT *part. of vİİs N 143B*
viiTama Vt 327E *refer*
viiTma Vt 297C *idle away*
viiTsima V 291C *feel like doing*
viiul N 229A *violin*
viiuldaja N 227A *fiddler*
viiuldama Vi 349F *fiddle*
vİİv N 61A *moment*
viivitama Vi 349F *delay*
viivitus N 260A *delay*
vikAAr N 58A *vicar*
vikat N 229A *scythe*
vikonteSS N 58A *viscountess*
viKs A 58B *alert*
viKs N 58B *shoe polish*
viKsima Vt 291C *polish*
vildak A 234A *slanting*
vildakas A 243A *slanting*
vile N 153 *whistle*
vilets A 231A *shabby*
viletsus N 260A *poverty*
vilgas A 159E *quick*
vili N 69A *crop*
vilistama V 349F *whistle*
vilistlane N 257C *alumnus / alumna*
vilistlaskoNd N 106 *alumni*
viļjakas A 243A *fertile*
viļjakus N 260A *fertility*
viļjastama Vt 349F *fertilize*
viļjatu A 227A *barren*
viļjelema Vt 325 *cultivate*
viļjelus N 260A *cultivation*
vilksatama Vi 349F *flash*
vilKuma Vi 291G *blink*
viLL N 49A *wool*
viĻL N 58A *blister*
villa N 152 *villa*
villane A 251 *woollen*
viļlis N 253 *jeep*
viļT N 58E *felt*
vilTune A 257B *slanting*
vilu A 13A *cool*
viluma Vi 269 *become experienced*
vilumatu A 227A *inexperienced*
vilumatus N 260A *inexperience*
vilumus N 260A *experience*
viMb N 87 *bream (fish)*
viMM N 49A *grudge*
vimma *gen. of viMb*
vimPel N 240A *pennant*
vine N 153 *haze*
vinEEr N 58A *plywood*
viNg N 61B *carbon monoxide*
viNge A 227B *piercing*
vingerdama Vi 349F *squirm*
viNguma Vi 291C *whine*
vinKel N 240A *right angel*
viŅN N 58A *pimple*
viNNama Vt 327A *draw*
viņT N 58E *finch*
thread (screw)
vinTske A 227B *tough of meat*
violeTne A 247 *violet (colour)*
viperus N 260A *mishap*
virelema Vi 325 *be in poor health*
virgats N 229A *express messenger*
viRge A 227B *wide-awake*
viRguma Vi 349G *become awake*
virgutama Vt 349F *rouse*
viril N 231A *whimpering*
virin N 231A *whimper*
virisema Vi 349C *whimper*
virK A 49F *diligent*
virKus N 260B *diligence*
virmalised (pl) N 257A *northern lights*
viRn N 49B *pile*
virsik N 234A *peach*
virTs N 49B *manure (liquid)*
virtuOOsliKKus N 260B *virtuosity*
virtuOOsne A 248 *masterly*
virulane N 257C *native of Virumaa*
virutama Vt 349F *hurl*
virvendama Vi 349F *ripple*
virvendus N 260A *rippling*
visa A 13A *persistent*
visadus N 260A *persistence*
visand N 229A *outline*
visandama Vt 349F *outline*
visandliK A 62 *sketchy*
visata *part. of viSkama*
vise N 217C *throw*
viselda *part. of viSklema*
viSkama Vt 348C *throw*
viSke *gen. of vise*
viski N 152 *whisky*
viSklema Vi 336 *toss and turn*
viSkuma Vi 349G *throw oneself*
viSpel N 240A *whisk*
vispeldama Vt 349F *whisk*
viStriK N 62 *pimple*
visuAAlne A 247 *visual*
vitamİİn N 58A *vitamin*
vitrAAž N 58A *stained glass*
vitrİİn N 58A *display-case*
viTs N 51 *switch (rod)*
viTT N 61C *cunt*
vohama Vi 269 *thrive*
vokAAl N 58A *vowel*
voKK N 58C *spinning-wheel*
volaNg N 58B *flounce*
voļdik N 234A *pamphlet*
voliniK N 62 *trustee*
volitama Vt 349F *authorize*
volitus N 260A *authorization*
voļT N 58E *fold*
volt
voļTima Vt 291F *fold*
vOO *gen. of vOOg*
vOOder N 240A *lining*
vooderdama Vt 349F *line (clothing)*
vooderdis N 260A *lining*
vOOḑi N 226 *bed*
vOOg N 133 *billow*
vOOl N 61A *current*
vOOlama Vi 327A *flow*
vOOlav A 231A *flowing*
vooļik N 234A *hose*
vOOļima Vt 291A *carve*
vOOlus N 260B *stream*
vOOr N58A *transport train*
vOOr N 61A *turn (in game)*
vOOr N 82 *drumlin*
vOOrima Vi 291A *move in crowd*
vOOrus N 260B *virtue*
vOOrusliK A 62 *virtuous*
vOOrusliKKus N 260B *virtuousness*
voRm N 58B *uniform*
voRmel N 229A *formula*
vormiline A 257D *pertaining to form*
vormilisus N 260A *formality*
voRmima Vt 291C *shape*
vormistama Vt 349F *put into proper form*
vormitu A 227A *shapeless*
vorP N 58D *weal from beating*
vorSt N 58B *sausage*
vraKK N 58C *wreck*
vuhin N 231A *whiz*
vuhisema Vi 349C *whiz*

vulgAArne A 247 *vulgar*
vulgAArsus N 260B *vulgarity*
vulin N 231A *gurgle*
vulisema Vi 349C *gurgle*
vulkAAn N 58A *volcano*
vulkaaniline A 257D *volcanic*
vulkanisEErima Vt 291B *vulcanize*
vundameŋT N 58E *foundation*
vuŋTs N 58B *moustache*
vurin N 231A *whir*
vurisema Vi 349C *whir*
vuristama Vt 349F *whir*
vuRR N 58A *top (toy)*
vuRR N 61A *moustache*
vurTs N 61B *carbonated drink*
vuSSer N 229A *bungler*
vusserdama Vt 349F *bungle*
vusserdis N 260A *bungler*
vuŞSima Vt 291A *bungle*
vuTlar N 229A *case for eye glasses*
vuŢT N 58C *quail*
võbin N 231A *quiver*
võbisema Vi 349C *quiver*
võeTa *imper. of võTma*
võhik N 234A *ignoramus*
võhikliK A 62 *ignorant (inexpert)*
võhiklus N 260A *ignorance (inexpert)*
võHm N49B *energy (strength)*
võİ N 1 *butter*
võİa *part. of võİma*
võİde *gen. of võie*
võidukas A 243A *victorious*
võidutsema Vi 349E *exult in triumph*
võie N 210D *ointment*
võigas A 159E *hideous*
võİm N 61B *power*
võİma V 263 *can*
võimaldama Vt 349F *enable*
võimaliK A 62 *possible*
võimaliKKus N 260B *possibility*
võimalus N 260A *opportunity*
võimas A 165B *powerful*
võimatu A 227A *impossible*
võimatus N 260A *impossibility*
võime N 177B *ability*
võimeline A 257D *able*
võimelisus N 260A *ability*
võimendama Vt 349F *amplify*
võimendi N 225A *amplifier*
võİmetu A 227A *incapable*
võİmetus N 260A *inability*
võİmla N 227B *gymnasium*
võİmleja N 227A *gymnast*
võİmlema Vi 326B *do gymnastics*
võİmlemine N 257E *gymnastics*
võİmsus N 260B *potency*
võimus N 253 *authority*
võimutsema Vi 349E *exult in power*
võiStkoNd N 106 *mixed team*
võiStlema Vi 326B *compete*
võiStlus N 260B *competition*
võiT N 61E *victory*
võiTja N 227B *winner*
võiTleja N 227A *champion (hero)*
võiTlema Vi 326E *fight*
võiTlus N 260B *fight*
võiTma V 297C *win*
võiTmatu A 227A *invincible*
võiTmatus N 260A *invincibility*
võla *gen. of võLg*
võLg N 95A *debt*
võLglane N 257C *debtor*
võLgnema Vi 349D *owe*
võLgnevus N 260A *indebtedness*
võLgniK N 62 *debtor*
võĻL N 58A *shaft*
võllas N 159A *gallows*
võļTs A 58B *counterfeit*
võļTsija N 227A *forger*
võļTsima Vt 291C *forge*
võļtsing N 234A *forgery*
võlu N 13A *charm*
võluma Vt 269 *charm*
võlur N 229A *wizard*
võluv A 231A *charming*
võĻv N 58B *vault*
võļvistiK N 62 *vaulting*
võMM N 61A *cop*
võnge N 177F *vibration*
võngutama Vt 349F *rock*
võnKuma Vi 291G *rock*
võnKumine N 257E *vibration*
võpatama Vi 349F *wince*
võpatus N 260A *wince*
võra N 13A *crown of tree*
võRde *gen. of võrre*
võRdeline A 257D *proportional*
võRdlema Vt 333 *compare*
võRdlematu A 227A *incomparable*
võRdlemine N 257E *comparing*
võRdlev A 231A *comparative*
võRdlus N 260B *comparison*
võRdne A 247 *equal*
võRdsus N 260B *equality*
võrdsustama Vt 349F *equalize*
võRduma Vi 349H *be equal*
võre N 153 *grate*
võrestiK N 62 *trellis*
võrgutama Vt 349F *seduce*
võrK N 61F *net*
võrrand N 229A *equation*
võrratu A 227A *incomparable*
võrre N 215 *proportion*
võrrelda *part. of võRdlema*
võrreldamatu A 227A *incomparable*
võrreldav A 231A *comparable*
võRRu *ill. of võru*
võrse N 177B *sprout*
võRsuma Vi 349G *sprout*
võru N 13A *hoop*
võrulane N 257C *native of Võrumaa*
võsa N 13A *undergrowth*
võsastiK N 62 *undergrowth*
võsastuma Vi 349H *overgrow*
võsaviLLem N 229A *wolf*
võSSa *ill. of võsa*
võsu N 13A *shoot (plant)*
võsund N 229A *runner (plant)*
võte N 177C *method*
võţi N 181 *key*
võTma Vt 300 *take (pick up)*
vööPama Vt 327D *paint*
võõrandama Vt 349F *expropriate*
võõras A 159A *strange*
võõras N 159A *guest*
stranger
võõrastama Vi 349F *be shy of strangers*
vÕÕrduma Vi 349H *become estranged*
võõrustaja N 227A *host*
võõrustama Vt 349F *entertain guest*
võõrutama Vt 349F *estrange*
väE *gen. of vägi*
väeTama Vt 349F *fertilize*
väeTi A 225B *feeble*
väeTis N 260B *fertilizer*
väeTus N 260B *fertilizing*
väge *part. of vägi*
vägev A 231A *mighty*
vägevus N 260A *might*
vägi N 42 *army*
vägilane N 257C *hero*
vägistama Vt 349F *rape*
vähem A 231A *lesser*
vähemus N 260A *minority*
vähendama Vt 349F *lessen*
vähene A 251 *scanty*

vähenema [Vi 349D] *lessen*
vähesus [N 260A] *shortage*
vähi *gen. of väHk*
vähim [A 231A] *least*
väHk [N 120B] *cancer*
crab
väİ [N 1] *son-in-law*
väide [N 177E] *statement*
väiKe(ne) [A 259] *small*
väiKlane [A 257C] *petty*
väiKlus [N 260B] *pettiness*
väİn [N 49B] *strait*
väiTma [Vt 297C] *state*
väiTs [N 63B] *knife*
väKKe *ill. of vägi*
välde [N 177E] *duration*
väļditav [A 231A] *avoidable*
väle [A 235] *nimble*
väledus [N 260A] *nimbleness*
välgatama [Vi 349F] *flash*
välgatus [N 260A] *flash*
välge [N 177F] *flashing*
välguti [N 225A] *camera flash*
väli [N 69A] *field*
välimiK [N 62] *exterior*
välimus [N 260A] *appearance*
väline [A 251] *external*
välistama [Vt 349F] *exclude*
välistus [N 260A] *exclusion*
väļjak [N 234A] *square*
väļjastama [Vt 349F] *issue*
väļjastus [N 260A] *issuing*
väļjend [N 229A] *expression*
väļjendama [Vt 349F] *express*
väļjendamatu [A 227A] *inexpressible*
väļjenduma [Vi 349H] *be expressed*
väļjendus [N 260A] *expression*
väĻjuma [Vi 349G] *depart (exit)*
välK [N 61F] *lightning*
välKuma [Vi 291G] *flash*
väļTima [Vt 291F] *avoid*
väļTimatu [A 227A] *unavoidable*
väļTimatus [N 260A] *inevitability*
välTus [N 260B] *duration*
välu [N 13A] *glade*
väNge [A 227B] *rank*
vänT [N 53E] *crank*
vänTama [Vt 327E] *crank*
värav [N 231A] *gate*
väRbama [Vt 339B] *enlist*
väRdjas [N 243B] *freak*
värin [N 231A] *tremble*
värisema [Vi 349C] *tremble*
väristama [Vt 349F] *make tremble*
värnits [N 231A] *varnish*
värSke [A 227B] *fresh*
värskendama [Vt 349F] *refresh*
värSkus [N 260B] *freshness*
värSS [N 58G] *verse*
värTen [N 241A] *bobbin*
väRv [N 58B] *colour*
väRval [N 229A] *dyer*
värvata *part. of väRbama*
väRvel [N 240A] *waistband*
värvikas [A 243A] *colourful*
värviline [A 257D] *coloured*
väRvima [Vt 291C] *paint*
värvine [A 251] *paint-covered*
värving [N 234A] *hue (colour)*
värvitu [A 227A] *colourless*
väRvus [N 260B] *colour*
väsima [Vi 269] *become tired*
väsimatu [A 227A] *untiring*
väsimus [N 260A] *fatigue*
väsitama [Vt 349F] *tire*
väsitav [A 231A] *tiring*
väStriK [N 62] *wagtail*
vÄÄnama [Vt 327A] *sprain*
vÄÄnlema [Vi 326A] *writhe*
vÄÄr [A 53A] *incorrect*
vääratama [Vi 349F] *err*
vääratus [N 260A] *error*
väärikas [A 243A] *dignified*
väärikus [N 260A] *dignity*
vääriline [A 257D] *worthy*
vÄÄrima [Vt 291A] *deserve*
vääristama [Vt 349F] *dignify*
vääristus [N 260A] *refinement*
vääritu [A 227A] *undignified*
väärTus [N 260B] *value*
väärTusetu [A 227A] *worthless*
väärTusliK [A 62] *valuable*
väärtustama [Vt 349F] *appraise*
vääŢ [N 58E] *vine*
vÄÄvel [N 240A] *sulphur*
vÖÖ [N 3] *belt*
vööḑiline [A 257D] *striped*
vÖÖnd [N 229B] *zone*
vööŢ [N 58E] *stripe*
vürSt [N 58B] *prince*
vürStinna [N 152] *princess*
vürstitar [N 245] *princess*
vürStliK [A 62] *princely*
vürTs [N 58B] *spice*
vürtsine [A 251] *spicy*
vürtsitama [Vt 349F] *spice*

Õ

õde [N 25] *sister*
õdu [N13C] *comfort*
õdus [A 231A] *cosy*
õE *gen. of õde*
õEl [A 231B] *wicked*
õEliK [A 62] *sisterly*
õElus [N 260B] *wickedness*
õEs [N 256] *sister*
õgima [Vt 269] *devour*
õgvendama [Vt 349F] *straighten*
õgvenema [Vi 349D] *straighten*
õhem [A 231A] *thinner*
õhetama [Vi 349F] *be flushed*
õhetus [N 260A] *flush in face*
õhin [N 231A] *zeal*
õHk [N 131C] *air*
õHkkoNd [N 106] *atmosphere (feeling)*
õHkuma [Vi 349G] *radiate*
õHtu [N 227B] *evening*
õHtune [A 257B] *evening*
õhu *gen. of õHk*
õhuke(ne) [A 257G] *thin*
õhuline [A 257D] *airy*
õhutaja [N 227A] *instigator*
õhutama [Vt 349F] *instigate*
õhutus [N 260A] *instigation*
õie *gen. of õİs*
õiendama [V 349F] *rectify*
õiendamine [N 257E] *rectification*
õİge [A 227B] *right*
õİglane [A 257C] *just*
õİglus [N 260B] *justice*
õİglusetus [N 260A] *injustice*
õİgsus [N 260B] *correctness*
õİgus [N 260B] *right*
õİgusliK [A 62] *legal*
õigustama [Vt 349F] *justify*
õigustamatu [A 227A] *unjustified*
õigustus [N 260A] *justification*

õilis [A 167] *noble*
õilistama [Vt 349F] *ennoble*
õİlsus [N 260B] *noble-mindedness*
õİs [N 143C] *blossom*
õiT *part. of õİs*
õiTsema [Vi 291C] *bloom*
õitseng [N 234A] *blossoming*
õiTsev [A 231A] *blossoming*
õla *gen. of õLg*
õle *gen. of õL̦g*
õLg [N 95A] *shoulder*
õL̦g [N 142A] *straw*
õli [N 13A] *oil*
õline [A 251] *oily*
õlitama [Vt 349F] *oil*
õlitus [N 260A] *oiling*
õlle *gen. of õlu(t)*
õlu(t) [N 155] *beer*
õMbleja [N 227A] *seamstress*
õMblema [Vt 329] *sew*
õMblus [N 260B] *seam*
õmmelda *part. of õMblema*
õnar [N 231A] *groove*
õnarus [N 260A] *groove*
õNdra *gen. of õnnar*
õN̦dsa *gen. of õņnis*
õN̦dsus [N 260B] *bliss*
õNg [N 63B] *fishing hook*
õngitseja [N 227A] *angler*
õngitsema [V 349E] *fish*
õN̦N [N 65] *happiness*
õnnar [N 203] *coccyx*
õnneliK [A 62] *happy*
õnnestuma [Vi 349H] *succeed*
õnnestumine [N 257E] *success*
õnnetu [A 227A] *unhappy*
õnnetus [N 260A] *misfortune*
õņnis [A 199] *blessed*
õņnistama [Vt 349F] *bless*
õņnistamine [N 257E] *blessing (action)*
õņnistus [N 260A] *blessing (result)*
õņnitelu [N 13A] *congratulations*
õņnitlema [Vt 351] *congratulate*
õņnitlus [N 260A] *congratulations*
õpetaja [N 227A] *teacher*
õpetajaskoNd [N 106] *teaching staff*
õpetama [Vt 349F] *teach*
õpetlane [N 257C] *scholar*
õpetliK [A 62] *instructive*
õpetus [N 260A] *instruction*
õpik [N 234A] *textbook*
õpilane [N 257C] *student*
õpilaskoNd [N 106] *student body*
õpingud (pl) [N 234A] *studies*
õPPija [N 227A] *learner*
õPPima [Vt 291D] *learn*
õPPima [Vt 291D] *study*
õPPus [N 260B] *training*
õRn [A 49B] *tender*
õRnus [N 260B] *tenderness*
õrre *gen. of õRs*
õRs [N 144] *perch*
õrT *part. of õRs*
õU [N 63B] *yard*
õUdne [A 247] *ghastly*
õUdus [N 260B] *horror*
õUkoNd [N 106] *royal court*
õUn [N 50] *apple*
õõne *gen. of ÕÕş*
õõnes [A 166A] *hollow*
õõnestama [Vt 349F] *hollow out*
ÕÕnsus [N 260B] *cavity*
õõnT *part. of ÕÕş*
ÕÕş [N 146] *cavity*
õõTsuma [Vi 291C] *sway*
õõtsutama [Vt 349F] *sway*
õõtsutus [N 260A] *swaying*

Ä

äeStama [Vt 349F] *harrow*
ägama [Vi 269] *groan*
äge [A 235] *impetuous*
ägedus [N 260A] *impetuosity*
ägenema [Vi 349D] *become violent*
ägestuma [Vi 349H] *get worked up*
ähi *pres. of äHkima*
äHkima [Vi 313B] *pant*
äHm [N 58B] *excitement*
ähmane [A 251] *faint*
ähvardama [Vt 349F] *threaten*
ähvardus [N 260A] *threat*
äİ [N 49B] *father-in-law*
äiKe(ne) [N 259] *thunder-storm*
äiutama [Vt 349F] *lull to sleep*
äke [N 177C] *harrow*
äkiline [A 257D] *abrupt*
äkilisus [N 260A] *abruptness*
äMber [N 240A] *pail*
äMbliK [N 62] *spider*
äMM [N 53A] *mother-in-law*
äpardama [Vi 349F] *miscarry*
äparduma [Vi 349H] *miscarry*
äpardus [N 260A] *failure*
äratama [Vt 349F] *waken*
äratus [N 260A] *getting wakened*
ärev [A 231A] *agitated*
ärevus [N 260A] *agitation*
äri [N 13A] *business*
shop
äritseja [N 227A] *dealer (trafficker)*
äritsema [Vi 349E] *deal in (traffic)*
ärKama [Vi 327F] *waken*
ärKamine [N 257E] *waking up*
äRRi *ill. of äri*
ärritama [Vt 349F] *irritate*
ärrituma [Vi 349H] *become irritated*
ärritus [N 260A] *irritation*
ärrituv [A 231A] *irritable*
ärtu [N 152] *heart (cards)*
äşjane [A 251] *recent*
äSS [N 53A] *ace in cards*
äşsitaja [N 227A] *provoker*
äşsitama [Vt 349F] *provoke*
ääḑikas [N 243A] *vinegar*
ÄÄr [N 82] *edge*
ääretu [A 227A] *boundless*
ääris [N 253] *edging*
ääristama [Vt 349F] *edge*
ÄÄrmine [A 257F] *outermost*
ÄÄrmus [N 260B] *extremity*
ÄÄrmuslane [N 257C] *extremist*
ÄÄrmusliK [A 62] *extreme*

öElda *part. of üTlema*
öhe *ill. of ÖÖ*
öİne [A 252] *night*

ökitama [Vi 349F] *stammer*
ökolOOg [N 58A] *ecologist*
ökolOOgia [N 227A] *ecology*
ökoloogiline [A 257D] *ecological*
ökonomiSt [N 58B] *economist*
ökonOOmia [N 227A] *economy*
ökonoomika [N 227A] *economics*
ökonOOmsus [N 260B] *economy (result)*
ÖÖ [N 8] *night*
ööbik [N 234A] *nightingale*
ÖÖbima [Vi 349B] *spend the night*
ööKima [Vi 291G] *retch*

üdi [N 13C] *marrow*
ühe *gen. of üKs*
üheksa [N 227A] *nine*
üheksandiK [N 62] *ninth*
üheksas [A 237B] *ninth*
ühend [N 229A] *compound*
ühendama [Vt 349F] *unite*
ühendus [N 260A] *union*
ühik [N 234A] *unit*
ühilduma [Vi 349H] *agree*
ühine [A 251] *common*
ühinema [Vi 349D] *unite*
ühing [N 234A] *workers' union*
ühiskoNd [N 106] *society*
ühiskoNdliK [A 62] *social*
ühistu [N 227A] *co-operative*
üHt(e) *part. of üKs*
üHtlane [A 257C] *uniform*
ühtlustama [Vt 349F] *even out*
üHtne [A 247] *united*
üHtsus [N 260B] *unity*
üKs [N 149] *one*
üksik [A 234A] *single*
üksiklane [N 257C] *hermit*
üksildane [A 257A] *lonely*
üksildus [N 260A] *loneliness*
üksindus [N 260A] *solitude*
üKsköiKne [A 247] *indifferent*
üKsluİsus [N 260B] *monotony*
üKsus [N 260B] *unit*
ülane [N 251] *wood anemone*
ülang [N 234A] *horst*
üLbe [A 227B] *arrogant*
üLbus [N 260B] *arrogance*
üĻdine [A 257B] *general*
üļdistama [Vt 349F] *generalize*
üļdistus [N 260A] *generalization*
üĻdsus [N 260B] *general public*
üleannetu [A 227A] *naughty*
üleannetus [N 260A] *naughtiness*
ülearune [A 251] *superfluous*
ülekoHtune [A 257B] *unfair*
ülem [N 231A] *superior*
ülemine [A 257F] *uppermost*
ülemus [N 260A] *authorities*
ülendama [Vt 349F] *promote*
ülendus [N 260A] *promotion*
ületama [Vt 349F] *surpass*
ületamatu [A 227A] *unsurpassable*
ülev [A 231A] *elated*
ülikkoNd [N 106] *elite*
ülikoNd [N 106] *suit*
ülim [A 231A] *supreme*
ülistama [Vt 349F] *glorify*
ülistus [N 260A] *glorification*
üllas [A 159A] *noble*
üllatama [Vt 349F] *surprise*
üllatuma [Vi 349H] *be surprised*
üllatus [N 260A] *surprise*
üllatusliK [A 62] *surprising*
üLLus [N 260B] *high-mindedness*
ümar [A 231A] *rounded*
ümardama [Vt 349F] *round off*
ümarus [N 260A] *roundness*
üMbriK [N 62] *envelope*
ümbrik [N 234A] *envelope*
ümbris [N 253] *wrapper*
ümbritsema [Vt 349E] *surround*
üMbrus [N 260B] *surroundings*
üMbruskoNd [N 106] *neighbourhood*
ümin [N 231A] *hum*
ümisema [Vi 349C] *hum*
ümmardaja [N 227A] *handmaiden*
ümmardama [Vt 349F] *wait on*
ümmargune [A 257A] *round*
üRge *gen. of ürje*
üRgne [A 247] *primeval*
ürik [N 234A] *historical document*
üritama [Vt 349F] *attempt*
üritus [N 260A] *event*
ürje [N 218] *beginning*
üsa *gen. of üSk*
üSk [N 109] *womb*
üTlema [Vt 338] *say*
üTlus [N 260B] *saying*
ÜÜr [N 58A] *rent*
üürike(ne) [A 257G] *fleeting*
üüriline [N 257D] *tenant*
ÜÜrima [Vt 291A] *rent*

PART IV

ENGLISH - ESTONIAN GLOSSARY

A

abandon [Vt] *hüLgama* [346]
abbreviation [N] *lühend* [229A]
ABC-book [N] *aabits* [231A]
ability [N] *võime* [177B]
[N] *võimelisus* [260A]
able [A] *suuTeline* [257D]
[A] *võimeline* [257D]
able (be) [Vi] *sAAma* [266]
[Vt] *suuTma* [297C]
abort [Vt] *aborTima* [291F]
abortion [N] *aborT* [58E]
abrupt [A] *äkiline* [257D]
abruptness [N] *äkilisus* [260A]
abscess [N] *mädaniK* [62]
absence [N] *pUUdumine* [257E]
absent (be) [Vi] *pUUduma* [349H]
absentee [N] *pUUduja* [227A]
absolute [A] *absoluuTne* [247]
absorb [Vt] *imama* [269]
abstainer [N] *karSklane* [257C]
abstinence [N] *karSkus* [260B]
abstract [A] *abstraKtne* [247]
absurd [A] *absuRdne* [247]
abundance [N] *küLLus* [260B]
abundant [A] *oHter* [241A]
[A] *riKKaliK* [62]
abuse [Vt] *teoTama* [349F]
abuse [N] *teoTus* [260B]
acacia [N] *akaaTsia* [227A]
academic [A] *akadeemiline* [257D]
academician [N] *akadeemik* [234A]
academy [N] *akadEEmia* [227A]
accessory [N] *manus* [253]
accident [N] *avarİİ* [1]
acclimatize [Vt] *aklimatisEErima* [291B]
accordion [N] *akoRdion* [246]
accusation [N] *süüdistus* [260A]
accuse [Vt] *süüdistama* [349F]
accustomed to (become) [Vi] *haRjuma* [349G]
ace (cards) [N] *äSS* [53A]
achieve [Vt] *saavutama* [349F]
achievement [N] *saavutus* [260A]
acid [N] *hape* [177C]
acknowledge [Vt] *tunnustama* [349F]
acknowledgement [N] *tunnustus* [260A]
acorn [N] *tõru* [13A]
acoustics [N] *akustika* [227A]
acquaintance [N] *tuTvus* [260B]
acquainted (become) [Vi] *tuTvuma* [349G]
acquaintances [N] *tuTvuskoNd* [106]
acquire [Vt] *omandama* [349F]
acquisition [N] *omandamine* [257E]

acre [N] *aaKer* [240A]
acrobat [N] *akrobaaT* [58E]
acrobatic [A] *akrobaatiline* [257D]
acrobatics [N] *akrobaatika* [227A]
act [N] *tegu* [31]
act (do) [Vi] *tegutsema* [349E]
act (in play) [N] *vaaTus* [260B]
act (theatre, film) [Vi] *näiTlema* [326E]
act as MC [Vi] *konferEErima* [291B]
action [N] *tegevustiK* [62]
activate [Vt] *aktivisEErima* [291B]
active [A] *aktİivne* [247]
[A] *tegev* [231A]
activist [N] *aktiviSt* [58B]
activities [N] *vaLdkoNd* [106]
activity [N] *aktİivsus* [260B]
[N] *tegevus* [260A]
actor [N] *näiTleja* [227A]
actual [A] *tegeliK* [62]
acute [A] *akuuTne* [247]
adapt [Vt] *adaptEErima* [291B]
[Vt] *kohandama* [349F]
adapt oneself [Vi] *kohanema* [349D]
add (mix) [Vt] *lisama* [269]
adding [N] *liiTmine* [257E]
addition [N] *lisa* [13A]
[N] *lisand* [229A]
[N] *täiendus* [260A]
address [N] *AAdreŞS* [58A]
address [Vt] *adressEErima* [291B]
address familiarly [Vt] *sinatama* [349F]
address formally [Vt] *teietama* [349F]
address someone [Vt] *kõnetama* [349F]
addressee [N] *adressaaT* [58E]
adequate [A] *adekvaaTne* [247]
adjacent (be) [Vi] *küĻgnema* [349D]
adjust [Vt] *regulEErima* [291B]
[Vt] *teĻLima* [291A]
administer [Vt] *haLdama* [342]
administration [N] *administratsiOOn* [58A]
administrative area [N] *haLdus* [260B]
administrator [N] *administraaTor* [229A]
admiral [N] *admiral* [245]
admiration [N] *imetlus* [260A]
admire [Vt] *imetlema* [351]
admirer [N] *auStaja* [227A]
admission ticket [N] *pääse* [179A]
admonish [Vt] *manitsema* [349E]
admonition [N] *manitsus* [260A]
adopt [Vt] *adoptEErima* [291B]
[Vt] *lapsendama* [349F]
adore [Vt] *jumaldama* [349F]

adorn [Vt] *eHtima* [308B]
[Vt] *kaunistama* [349F]
adornment [N] *kaunistus* [260A]
adult [N] *täİskaSvanu* [227A]
advance-payment [N] *avanŞS* [58G]
advantage [N] *eelis* [253]
[N] *hüve* [153]
advantages [N] *soodustus* [260A]
advent [N] *adveņT* [58E]
Adventist [N] *adventiSt* [58B]
adventure [N] *seiKlus* [260B]
adventurer [N] *avantüriSt* [58B]
[N] *seiKleja* [227A]
adventuring (go) [Vi] *seiKlema* [326F]
adverb [N] *adveRb* [58B]
advertise [Vt] *kuulutama* [349F]
[Vt] *reklAAmima* [291A]
advertisement [N] *kuulutus* [260A]
[N] *reklAAm* [58A]
advice [N] *nõU* [12]
advise [Vt] *juhendama* [349F]
adviser [N] *juhendaja* [227A]
advocate [Vt] *propagEErima* [291B]
aerate [Vt] *gasEErima* [291B]
aesthete [N] *esteeT* [58E]
aesthetic [A] *esteetiline* [257D]
aesthetics [N] *esteetika* [227A]
affable [A] *lahe* [235]
affair [N] *afÄÄr* [58A]
affection [N] *kİİndumus* [260A]
affirm [V] *jaaTama* [349F]
affirmation [N] *jaaTus* [260B]
affirmative [A] *jaaTav* [231A]
affix stamp [Vt] *margistama* [349F]
afraid (be) [Vt] *peLgama* [346]
African [N] *aafriklane* [257C]
age [N] *iga* [30]
[N] *vanus* [253]
age [Vi] *vananema* [349D]
ageless [A] *aEgumatu* [227A]
agency [N] *agentUUr* [58A]
agent [N] *ageņT* [58E]
agglutination [N] *aglutinatsiOOn* [58A]
aggravate [Vt] *raskendama* [349F]
aggression [N] *agressiOOn* [58A]
aggressive [A] *agressİivne* [247]
aggressor [N] *agreSSor* [229A]
agitate [Vt] *agitEErima* [291B]
agitated [A] *ärev* [231A]
agitation [N] *agitatsiOOn* [58A]
[N] *ärevus* [260A]
agitator (political) [N] *agitaaTor* [229A]

agony N agOOnia 227A
agree Vi nõuStuma 349H
Vi ühilduma 349H
agriculture N põllundus 260A
agronomist N agronOOm 58A
aim N siHt 116
aim Vt siHtima 308B
Vt sUUnama 327A
aimless A sihitu 227A
air Vt tuulutama 349F
air N õHk 131C
aired (be) Vi tUUlduma 349H
airing N tuulutus 260A
airplane N lennuk 229A
airs (have) Vi uhkeldama 349F
airy A õhuline 257D
alarm N alaRm 58B
alarm Vt alarmEErima 291B
Vt alaRmima 291C
Albanian N albAAnlane 257C
album N aLbum 229A
alchemist N alkeemik 234A
alcohol N alkohol 245
alcoholic N alkohoolik 234A
alcoholic A alkohOOlne 247
alcoholism N alkoholiSm 58B
alder N lePP 53C
alder grove N lepik 234A
N lepistiK 62
alert A ergas 165C
A viKs 58B
algae N veţikad (pl) 243A
algebra N algebra 227A
align oneself Vi jOOnduma 349H
alimony N alimeņdid (pl) 58E
all N kõiK 64
allergy N alleRgia 227A
alleviate Vt vaigistama 349F
alliance N liiT 61E
allow Vt lubama 269
allowed (be) Vt toHtima 308B
alloy N sulam 229A
allusion N viide 177E
ally N liiTlane 257C
almanac N almanaHH 58A
almond N maNdel 240A
alphabet N tähestiK 62
alphabetical A tähestikuline 257D
altar N alTar 229A
alternate Vi vahelduma 349H
alternating A vahelduv 231A
alto N aļT 58E

aluminium N alumİinium 246
alumni N vilistlaskoNd 106
alumnus, alumna N vilistlane 257C
amateur N amatÖÖr 58A
amateur activities N taİdlus 260B
ambassador N saadik 234A
ambiguity N kahemõTTelisus 260A
ambiguous A kahemõTTeline 257D
amelioration N melioratsiOOn 58A
American N ameeriklane 257C
amnesty N amneStia 227A
amount N kogus 253
amplifier N võimendi 225A
amplify Vt võimendama 349F
ampoule N ampuĻL 58A
amputation N amputatsiOOn 58A
amusing A meelTlahutav 231A
anachronism N anakroniSm 58B
anaesthetics N tuimasti 225A
analogous A analoogiline 257D
analogy N analOOgia 227A
analysis N analÜÜs 58A
anarchism N anarhiSm 58B
anarchist N anarhiSt 58B
anarchy N anarHia 227A
anatomical A anatoomiline 257D
anatomy N anatOOmia 227A
anchor N anKur 242A
ancient A muiStne 247
A põline 251
anecdote N anekdooT 58E
angel N iNgel 240A
anger N tigedus 260A
N viha 13A
anger Vt vihastama 349F
angler N õngitseja 227A
Anglicism N anglitsiSm 58B
angry A kuri 71A
A tige 235
A vihane 251
angry (become) Vi vihastuma 349H
angular A nurgeline 257D
animal N lOOm 53A
animal tamer N taltsutaja 227A
animate Vt hingestama 349F
announce Vt teadustama 349F
announcer N teadustaja 227A
announcer (radio, TV) N diKtor 229A
annoy Vt pahandama 349F
annoyed A pahane 251
anonymous A anonÜÜmne 247
another A teine 258A

answer V vaStama 327B
answer N vastus 253
ant N sipelgas 243A
antagonism N antagoniSm 58B
antagonist N antagoniSt 58B
antagonistic A antagoniStliK 62
Antarctic A antarktiline 257D
antelope N antilooP 58D
antenna N anteŅN 58A
anthem N hüMn 58B
anthology N antolOOgia 227A
antibiotic N antibiootikum 245
antifreeze N antifrİİs 58A
antipathetic A antipaaTne 247
antipathy N antipaaTia 227A
antiquary N antikvAAr 58A
antique A antiiKne 247
antiquity N muİnsus 260B
anvil N alasi 225A
anxious to do (be) Vi kiPPuma 291D
apartment N korTer 229A
apathetic A apaaTne 247
A loİd 123B
apathy N apaaTia 227A
N loİdus 260B
apiary N mesila 227A
apiculture N mesindus 260A
apolitical A apoliitiline 257D
apology N vabandus 260A
apostle N apoStel 240A
apostrophe N apostrooF 58A
apparatus N aparaaT 58E
apparent A näİv 231B
appear Vi iLmuma 349G
appearance N välimus 260A
appearing N iLmumine 257E
appetite N isu 13A
applaud Vi aplodEErima 291B
applause N aplaUs 58B
apple N õUn 50
applicant N paluja 227A
application N taoTlus 260B
application form N planK 58F
appliqué N aplikatsiOOn 58A
appliqué Vt aplitsEErima 291B
apply Vt rakendama 349F
apply for Vt taoTlema 351
appraise Vt taksEErima 291B
Vt väärtustama 349F
appreciating N hiNdamine 257E
apprentice N stažÖÖr 58A
apprenticeship (be in) Vi stažEErima 291B

approach [Vi] *liginema* [349D]
approaches [N] *lähised (pl)* [253]
approaching [N] *lähenemine* [257E]
appropriate [Vt] *omastama* [349F]
appropriate [A] *paŞliK* [62]
appropriation [N] *omastamine* [257E]
approving [A] *tunnustav* [231A]
apricot [N] *aprikOOs* [58A]
April [N] *apriĻL* [58A]
apron [N] *põLL* [63A]
aptitude [N] *aNdekus* [260A]
aqualung [N] *akvalaNg* [58B]
aquarium [N] *akvAArium* [246]
Arab [N] *arAAblane* [257C]
arbour [N] *leHtla* [227B]
arc [N] *kAAr* [82]
archaic [A] *arhaİline* [257D]
archaism [N] *arhaiSm* [58B]
archeologist [N] *arheolOOg* [58A]
archeology [N] *arheolOOgia* [227A]
archipelago [N] *saarestiK* [62]
architect [N] *arhiteKt* [58B]
architectural [A] *arhitektuuriline* [257D]
architecture [N] *arhitektUUr* [58A]
archives [N] *arhİİv* [58A]
archivist [N] *arhivAAr* [58A]
archway [N] *kaNg* [58B]
Arctic [A] *arktiline* [257D]
arduous [A] *vaevaline* [257D]
area [N] *ala* [14A]
arena [N] *arEEn* [58A]
Argentinean [N] *argentİInlane* [257C]
argue [Vi] *vaİdlema* [330B]
argument (reason) [N] *argumeņT* [58E]
argument (dispute) [N] *vaİdlus* [260B]
aria [N] *AAria* [227A]
arise [Vi] *teKKima* [349B]
arise (come about) [Vi] *teKKima* [291D]
aristocracy [N] *aristokraaTia* [227A]
aristocrat [N] *aristokraaT* [58E]
aristocratic [A] *aristokraaTliK* [62]
arithmetical [A] *aritmeetiline* [257D]
arm [Vt] *relvastama* [349F]
arm oneself [Vi] *relvastuma* [349H]
Armagnac [N] *armanjaKK* [58C]
armament [N] *relvastus* [260A]
Armenian [N] *armEEnlane* [257C]
arming [N] *relvastumine* [257E]
army [N] *armEE* [2]
[N] *vägi* [42]
aroma [N] *arOOm* [58A]
[N] *lõHn* [49B]

aromatic [A] *aromaaTne* [247]
arrange [Vt] *kohendama* [349F]
[Vt] *seAdma* [314]
arrangement [N] *järjestus* [260A]
arrest [Vt] *arretEErima* [291B]
[Vt] *vahistama* [349F]
arrest [N] *vahistus* [260A]
arrival [N] *sAAbumine* [257E]
[N] *tulek* [234A]
arrive [Vi] *sAAbuma* [349G]
arrogance [N] *upsakus* [260A]
[N] *üLbus* [260B]
arrogant [A] *upsakas* [243A]
[A] *üLbe* [227B]
arrow [N] *nOOl* [82]
arsenic [N] *arseenik* [234A]
art [N] *kuņSt* [58B]
[N] *taie* [210D]
artel [N] *arteĻL* [58A]
artery [N] *arTer* [229A]
artichoke [N] *artišoKK* [58C]
artificial [A] *kuņStliK* [62]
artificial nipple [N] *luŢT* [58C]
artillery range [N] *polügOOn* [58A]
artillery shell [N] *mürSk* [131C]
artist [N] *kuņStniK* [62]
[N] *taİdur* [229A]
artiste [N] *artiSt* [58B]
artistic [A] *kuņstiline* [257D]
asbestos [N] *aSbeSt* [58B]
ascent [N] *tõUs* [61B]
ascetic [N] *askeeT* [58E]
ascetic [A] *askeeTliK* [62]
ash [N] *tuHk* [109]
ash-tree [N] *sAAr* [82]
ashamed (be) [Vi] *häbenema* [349D]
ashen [A] *tuHkur* [242A]
Asian [N] *AAsialane* [257C]
ask [Vt] *küsima* [269]
asparagus [N] *spaRgel* [240A]
aspen [N] *hAAb* [86A]
asphalt [N] *aSfalT* [58E]
asphalt [Vt] *asfaltEErima* [291B]
[Vt] *aSfalTima* [291F]
aspiration [N] *pÜÜdlus* [260B]
aspire [Vi] *pÜÜdlema* [330A]
aspirin [N] *aspirİIn* [58A]
ass (buttocks) [N] *pEE* [1]
[N] *perse* [177B]
assembly [N] *assamblEE* [2]
assembly hall [N] *aula* [152]
assistant [N] *assisteņT* [58E]

associate [Vt] *seOstama* [349F]
associate with [Vi] *lävima* [269]
associate with [Vi] *suHtlema* [331B]
associated (be) [Vi] *seoStuma* [349H]
associating with [N] *suHtlemine* [257E]
association [N] *kOOndis* [260B]
assortment [N] *sortimeņT* [58E]
assume [Vt] *EEldama* [349F]
assumption [N] *EEldus* [260B]
assurance [N] *kiņnitus* [260A]
aster [N] *aSter* [240A]
asterisk [N] *asteriSk* [58B]
[N] *täRn* [58B]
asthma [N] *aStma* [227B]
asthmatic [N] *astmaatik* [234A]
astonish [Vt] *hämmastama* [349F]
astonished (be) [Vi] *hämmastuma* [349H]
astonishing [A] *hämmastav* [231A]
astonishment [N] *hämmastus* [260A]
astrologer [N] *astrolOOg* [58A]
astrology [N] *astrolOOgia* [227A]
astronaut [N] *astronauT* [58E]
[N] *kosmonauT* [58E]
astronautics [N] *astronautika* [227A]
astronomer [N] *astronOOm* [58A]
astronomical [A] *astronoomiline* [257D]
astronomy [N] *astronOOmia* [227A]
atheism [N] *ateiSm* [58B]
atheist [N] *ateiSt* [58B]
atheistic [A] *ateiStliK* [62]
athlete [N] *atleeT* [58E]
athletic [A] *atleeTliK* [62]
athletics [N] *atleetika* [227A]
atlas [N] *aTlas* [260B]
atmosphere (air) [N] *atmosfÄÄr* [58A]
atmosphere (feeling) [N] *õHkkoNd* [106]
atmospheric [A] *atmosfääriline* [257D]
atom [N] *aaTom* [229A]
attack [Vt] *rüNdama* [343]
attack [N] *rünnak* [234A]
attempt [N] *katse* [177B]
[N] *püüe* [210C]
attempt [Vt] *üritama* [349F]
attend [Vi] *käİma* [264B]
attend to [Vi] *hooļitsema* [349E]
attendant [N] *teenindaja* [227A]
attentive [A] *tähelepaneliK* [62]
attic [N] *mansaRd* [58B]
[N] *pööning* [234A]
attitude [N] *suHtumine* [257E]
attraction [N] *atraktsiOOn* [58A]
attribute [N] *atribuuT* [58E]

attribute Vt *omistama* [349F]
attributive A *atributİİvne* [247]
auction N *oKsjon* [229A]
audibility N *kUUldavus* [260A]
audible A *kUUldav* [231A]
audience N *audienTs* [58B]
N *publik* [234A]
audience (listeners) N *kUUlajaskoNd* [106]
audience (viewers) N *vaaTajaskoNd* [106]
audit N *revisjon* [245]
auditorium N *auditOOrium* [246]
aunt N *tädi* [13C]
aunt (father's sister) N *sõtse* [152]
aurochs N *tarvas* [159B]
Australian N *austrAAllane* [257C]
Austrian N *austerlane* [257C]
author N *auTor* [229A]
authoritarian A *autoritAArne* [247]
authoritative A *autoriteeTne* [247]
authorities N *ülemus* [260A]
authority N *autoriteeT* [58E]
N *võimus* [253]
authorization N *volitus* [260A]
authorize Vt *volitama* [349F]
automatic A *automaaTne* [247]
automating N *automatisEErimine* [257E]
automation N *automaatika* [227A]
automatize Vt *automatisEErima* [291B]
automaton N *automaaT* [58E]
automobile N *auto* [152]
autonomous A *autonOOmne* [247]
autonomy N *autonOOmia* [227A]
autumn N *sügis* [253]
autumnal A *sügisene* [257A]
avalanche N *lavİİn* [58A]
avenger N *tasuja* [227A]
avenue N *allEE* [2]
average A *keSkmine* [257F]
aviation N *lennundus* [260A]
avoid Vi *hoİduma* [349H]
avoid Vt *väĻTima* [291F]
avoidable A *väĻditav* [231A]
awake (become) Vi *viRguma* [349G]
award N *oRden* [229A]
aware A *teAdliK* [62]
awareness N *teAdliKKus* [260B]
awkward A *täbar* [231A]
awl N *naaSkel* [240A]
axe handle N *kuuas* [189]
axiom N *aksiOOm* [58A]
axis N *teĻg* [141]
axle N *teĻg* [141]

B

babble N *padin* [231A]
babble (brook) Vi *sulisema* [349C]
baby N *beebi* [152]
N *imik* [234A]
N *tita* [152]
N *titake(ne)* [257G]
N *tiTT* [63C]
back N *seĻg* [112]
back of chair N *lEEņ* [58A]
back of head N *kukal* [170C]
background N *tauSt* [49B]
backwoods N *kolgas* [159E]
bacon N *peeKon* [229A]
bacteriologist N *bakteriolOOg* [58A]
bacterium N *baKter* [229A]
bad A *paha* [14A]
badger N *mäger* [79C]
badminton N *bädminton* [245]
bag N *koŢT* [58C]
baggage N *pagas* [229A]
bail N *kauTsjon* [229A]
bail Vt *käEndama* [349F]
bail N *käEndus* [260B]
bake Vi *küPsema* [291C]
bake Vt *küpsetama* [349F]
baker N *leİbur* [229A]
N *pagar* [229A]
balance Vt *balanssEErima* [291B]
Vt *tasakaalustama* [349F]
balance N *bilanSS* [58G]
balcony N *palKon* [229A]
balcony N *rõdu* [13C]
bald-headed A *kiilakas* [243A]
ball (social) N *baĻL* [58A]
ball (toy) N *paĻL* [58A]
ball of thumb or foot N *päKK* [53C]
ballad N *ballAAd* [58A]
ballerina N *balerİİn* [58A]
ballet N *balleŢT* [58C]
balloon N *ballOOn* [58A]
balls (testicles) N *muņnid (pl)* [58A]
Balt N *baĻTlane* [257C]
ban Vt *keelustama* [349F]
banana N *banAAn* [58A]
bandage N *side* [157]
bang Vt *paugutama* [349F]
bang N *pauK* [61F]
bang Vi *pauKuma* [291G]
banish Vt *pagendama* [349F]
banishment N *pagendus* [260A]
N *põLg* [131B]
bank (financial) N *panK* [49F]
banker N *panKur* [229A]
banking N *pangandus* [260A]
banquet N *bankeŢT* [58C]
bar N *bAAr* [58A]
barbarian N *baRbar* [229A]
barbaric A *barbAArne* [247]
barbecue N *griĻL* [58A]
bare (empty) A *lage* [235]
bare (naked) A *paĻjas* [159B]
bare Vt *paĻjastama* [349F]
bargain V *tiNgima* [291C]
baritone N *bariton* [245]
bark Vi *hauKuma* [291G]
barley N *oder* [79B]
N *tangud (pl)* [61B]
barn N *lauT* [49E]
barn (for drying) N *rehi* [150]
baron N *parun* [229A]
barracks N *baraKK* [58C]
N *kasarm* [234A]
barrel N *tüŅN* [58A]
N *vaaŢ* [58E]
barren A *viĻjatu* [227A]
barricade N *barrikAAd* [58A]
barrier N *barjÄÄr* [58A]
barrow (pig) N *orikas* [243A]
barter V *kauPlema* [326D]
base N *bAAş* [58A]
based on (be) Vi *basEEruma* [349G]
Vi *põhinema* [349D]
Vi *põhjenema* [349D]
basket N *koRv* [58B]
bass N *baŞS* [58A]
bassoon N *fagoŢT* [58C]
bast shoe N *viiSk* [131C]
baste (sew) Vt *traageldama* [349F]
bath N *vaŅN* [58A]
bathe Vi *küMblema* [329]
Vi *suPlema* [326C]
bathe Vt *vaņnitama* [349F]
bather N *suPleja* [227A]

bathing [N] *küMblus* [260B]
[N] *suPlus* [260B]
bathing suit [N] *trikOO* [1]
battalion [N] *pataljon* [245]
battery [N] *patareİ* [1]
battery (car) [N] *aku* [152]
[N] *akumulaaTor* [229A]
battle [N] *lahing* [234A]
battle [Vi] *taPlema* [326C]
battle-axe [N] *taPPer* [240B]
battledore [N] *tõLv* [49B]
bawl [Vi] *kisama* [269]
[Vi] *lõUgama* [345A]
[Vi] *rööKima* [291G]
bay [N] *laHt* [139]
bayonet [N] *tääK* [58F]
be [Vi] *olema* [273]
beach [N] *plAAž* [58A]
[N] *raNd* [92]
bead [N] *helmes* [161B]
[N] *paU* [52]
beak [N] *noKK* [53C]
beam [N] *pİİm* [58A]
bean [N] *uba* [38]
bear [N] *karu* [13A]
[N] *oŢT* [58C]
bear (endure) [Vt] *taluma* [269]
beard [N] *habe* [157]
bearded man [N] *habemiK* [62]
beast [N] *elajas* [243A]
beastly [A] *elajaliK* [62]
beat [Vt] *peKsma* [293A]
[Vt] *kloPPima* [291D]
beater [N] *klopits* [231A]
beau [N] *kavaler* [245]
beautician [N] *kosmeetik* [234A]
beautiful [A] *ilus* [231A]
[A] *kaunis* [164B]
beautiful person [N] *iludus* [260A]
beautify [Vt] *ilustama* [349F]
beauty [N] *ilu* [13A]
beauty [N] *kaUnidus* [260A]
beauty (female) [N] *kaunitar* [245]
beauty-queen [N] *miSS* [58A]
beaver [N] *kobras* [159D]
[N] *pİİber* [240A]
beck and call [N] *käsutus* [260A]
beckon [Vi] *viiPama* [327D]
become [Vi] *jÄÄma* [266]
[Vi] *sAAma* [266]
bed [N] *säNg* [58B]
[N] *vOOḑi* [226]

bedbug [N] *luţikas* [243A]
bedstraw (plant) [N] *madar* [231A]
bee (communal work) [N] *taLgud (pl)* [227B]
bee (honey) [N] *mesilane* [257C]
bee-keeper [N] *mesiniK* [62]
beef Stroganoff [N] *böfstrooganov* [245]
beefsteak [N] *biiFsteeK* [58F]
beer [N] *õlu(t)* [155]
beet [N] *peeŢ* [58E]
beet salad [N] *rosoļje* [152]
beetle [N] *mardikas* [243A]
[N] *põrnikas* [243A]
[N] *siţikas* [243A]
beg [Vt] *keRjama* [327B]
beggar [N] *kerjus* [253]
beggary [N] *keRjus* [260B]
begin [Vi] *aLgama* [348B]
beginning [N] *aLgus* [260B]
[N] *ürje* [218]
behave [Vi] *käiTuma* [349H]
behaviour [N] *käiTumine* [257E]
behold [Vt] *kaEma* [262]
beige [A] *bEEž* [58A]
belch [Vi] *röhitama* [349F]
Belgian [N] *beLglane* [257C]
belief [N] *uSk* [131C]
[N] *uSkumus* [260A]
believe [Vt] *uSkuma* [313B]
bell-flower [N] *kellukas* [243A]
belles-lettres [N] *belletristika* [227A]
bellows [N] *lõõTs* [49B]
belly [N] *kõHt* [124B]
[N] *vaTs* [49B]
belong [Vi] *kUUluma* [349G]
beloved [A] *armas* [165B]
belovedness [N] *aRmsus* [260B]
belt [N] *riHm* [49B]
[N] *vÖÖ* [3]
bemoan [Vi] *haletsema* [349E]
bench [N] *pinK* [58F]
bend [Vi] *nõTkuma* [291C]
[Vi] *paİnduma* [349H]
bend [Vt] *painutama* [349F]
bend down [Vi] *kummarduma* [349H]
bend in road [N] *käänak* [234A]
bend of river [N] *kÄÄr* [61A]
bending [N] *nõtke* [177B]
bequeath [Vt] *pärandama* [349F]
beret [N] *bareŢT* [58C]
berry [N] *mari* [68A]
berry drink [N] *morSS* [58G]
berry soup (cold) [N] *kisseĻL* [58A]

berry-picker [N] *marjuline* [257D]
berth [N] *koİ* [1]
best [A] *parim* [231A]
betray [Vt] *reeTma* [297C]
betrayal [N] *reeTmine* [257E]
better [A] *parem* [231A]
bewail [Vi] *kaEblema* [328]
bewilder [Vt] *hämmeldama* [349F]
bewilderment [N] *hämmeldus* [260A]
bewitching [A] *nõİdusliK* [62]
Bible [N] *pİİbel* [240A]
bibliographer [N] *bibliograaF* [58A]
bidet [N] *bidEE* [2]
big [A] *sUUr* [82]
bile [N] *saPP* [58C]
bill [N] *arve* [177B]
billiards [N] *piļjard* [229A]
billion [N] *biĻjon* [229A]
[N] *miļjard* [229A]
billionth [A] *miļjardes* [237B]
billow [N] *vOOg* [133]
billy-goat [N] *siKK* [61C]
bind oneself [Vi] *kohustuma* [349H]
binding [A] *siduv* [231A]
binoculars [N] *binoKKel* [240B]
biographer [N] *biograaF* [58A]
biography [N] *biograaFia* [227A]
biologist [N] *biolOOg* [58A]
biology [N] *biolOOgia* [227A]
birch [N] *kaŞk* [142B]
[N] *kõİv* [61B]
birch grove [N] *kaasik* [234A]
birch-bark [N] *toHt* [124B]
bird [N] *liNd* [129]
bird-cherry tree [N] *toomingas* [243A]
birdie [N] *linnuke(ne)* [257G]
birth [N] *süŅd* [118]
birth (give of animal) [V] *poEgima* [349B]
birth (give) [Vt] *süņnitama* [349F]
birthday bread [N] *kriNgel* [240A]
biscuit [N] *biskviiT* [58E]
bishop [N] *piiSkoP* [58H]
bison [N] *pİİson* [229A]
bitch [N] *lita* [152]
bite [Vt] *hammustama* [349F]
[Vt] *purema* [269]
bite [N] *hammustus* [260A]
bitter [A] *kibe* [235]
[A] *mõru* [13A]
bitterness [N] *kibedus* [260A]
black [A] *muSt* [53B]
black-board [N] *taHvel* [240A]

blacken [Vt] *muStama* [327B]
blackmail [N] *šantAAž* [58A]
blackmail [Vt] *šantažEErima* [291B]
bladder [N] *põİs* [143C]
blade (knife) [N] *tera* [15]
blade (grass) [N] *lible* [152]
blame [N] *sÜÜ* [1]
blank [N] *toorik* [234A]
blanket [N] *sõba* [13B]
[N] *teKK* [58C]
blare [V] *pasundama* [349F]
blaze [Vi] *leegitsema* [349E]
[Vi] *lÕÕmama* [327A]
blaze [N] *lÕÕm* [49A]
blazer [N] *pintsak* [234A]
bleach [Vt] *pleegitama* [349F]
bleach [Vi] *pleeKima* [291G]
bleak [A] *kõle* [235]
bleat [Vi] *mÄÄgima* [291A]
bless [Vt] *õņnistama* [349F]
blessed [A] *õņnis* [199]
blessing (action) [N] *õņnistamine* [257E]
blessing (result) [N] *õņnistus* [260A]
blind [A] *pime* [235]
blind [Vt] *pimestama* [349F]
blind person [N] *pime* [235]
blinding [A] *pimestav* [231A]
blink [Vt] *pilgutama* [349F]
blink [Vi] *vilKuma* [291G]
bliss [N] *õŅdsus* [260B]
blister [N] *viĻL* [58A]
blizzard [N] *tuiSk* [131C]
bloc [N] *bloKK* [58C]
block (toy) [N] *kloŢs* [58B]
blockade [N] *blokAAd* [58A]
blockade [Vt] *blokEErima* [291B]
blockhead [N] *turakas* [243A]
blonde [A] *bloNd* [58B]
blonde [N] *blondİİn* [58A]
blood [N] *veri* [20]
blood pudding [N] *käKK* [58C]
blood sausage [N] *maKK* [58C]
bloodless [A] *veretu* [227A]
bloody [A] *verine* [251]
bloody [Vt] *veristama* [349F]
bloom [Vi] *õiTsema* [291C]
bloom suddenly [Vi] *pakatama* [349F]
blossom [N] *õİs* [143C]
blossoming [N] *õitseng* [234A]
blossoming [A] *õiTsev* [231A]
blouse [N] *plUUs* [58A]
blow [V] *puhuma* [269]
blow (hit) [N] *lööK* [58F]
[N] *hooP* [58D]
blow nose [Vt] *nuuSkama* [348C]
blue [A] *sinine* [251]
blue jeans [N] *teksased (pl)* [253]
blueberry [N] *muştikas* [243A]
blues (jazz) [N] *blUUs* [58A]
bluff [N] *bluFF* [58C]
bluish [A] *sinakas* [243A]
blunt [A] *nüri* [13A]
[A] *töņTs* [58B]
blunt (become) [Vi] *nürinema* [349D]
blurt out [Vi] *paHvama* [327B]
[Vi] *pahvatama* [349F]
blush [Vi] *punastama* [349F]
bluster [Vi] *laamendama* [349F]
boa [N] *boA* [1]
board of ship [N] *parras* [193]
boarding-house [N] *paNsion* [246]
boast [Vi] *kiiTlema* [326E]
[Vi] *prAAļima* [291A]
boaster [N] *kiiTleja* [227A]
boat [N] *ļooţsik* [234A]
[N] *paaŢ* [58E]
[N] *vene* [153]
bobbin [N] *värTen* [241A]
bodice [N] *pihik* [234A]
body [N] *keha* [15]
[N] *kere* [154]
body (flesh) [N] *ihu* [13A]
bogy [N] *koĻL* [58A]
Bohemian [N] *bohEEmlane* [257C]
boil [Vi] *kEEma* [261A]
boil [Vt] *keeTma* [297C]
boil [N] *paise* [177B]
boiling [A] *kEEv* [231B]
boisterousness [N] *müRgel* [240A]
bold [A] *juLge* [227B]
boldness [N] *juLgus* [260B]
boletus (mushroom) [N] *puraviK* [62]
Bolivian [N] *bolİİvlane* [257C]
bolt [N] *poļT* [58E]
[N] *rİİv* [58A]
bomb [N] *poMM* [58A]
bomb [Vt] *pommitama* [349F]
bombing [N] *pommitus* [260A]
bone [N] *koņT* [58E]
[N] *lUU* [7]
bonfire [N] *lõke* [177C]
bonus [N] *prEEmia* [227A]
bonus (give) [Vt] *premEErima* [291B]
bony [A] *koņdine* [251]
bony [A] *luİne* [252]
book [N] *raamat* [234A]
boot [N] *saabas* [159D]
[N] *säärik* [234A]
booth [N] *puţka* [152]
bootlicker [N] *pugeja* [227A]
booze up [Vi] *purjutama* [349F]
border [N] *pİİr* [58A]
border [Vi] *pİİrnema* [349D]
bored (become) [Vi] *tüdinema* [349D]
boredom [N] *igavus* [260A]
[N] *tüļPimus* [260A]
boring [A] *igav* [231A]
born (be) [Vi] *süŅdima* [310]
borrow [Vt] *laEnama* [327B]
borrower [N] *laEnaja* [227A]
borscht [N] *borŠ* [58A]
bosom [N] *kaiSS* [61G]
[N] *põU* [63B]
boss [N] *šeFF* [58C]
botanist [N] *botaanik* [234A]
botany [N] *botaanika* [227A]
both [A] *mõlema(no nominative* [232]
bottle [N] *pudel* [229A]
bottom [N] *põhi* [68A]
bottom-most [A] *alumine* [257F]
bottomless [A] *põhjatu* [227A]
bouillon [N] *puļjong* [229A]
boundless [A] *piiritu* [227A]
[A] *ääretu* [227A]
bouquet [N] *bukeŢT* [58C]
[N] *kimP* [61D]
bow [V] *kummardama* [349F]
bow (archery) [N] *aMb* [122]
[N] *vibu* [13B]
bow (motion) [N] *kummardus* [260A]
bow (ribbon) [N] *leHv* [58B]
bow (violin, cello) [N] *pOOgen* [241A]
bowl [N] *kauSS* [58G]
bowling [N] *kEEgel* [240A]
box [N] *karP* [58D]
[N] *tOOş* [58A]
box (sport) [Vi] *poKsima* [291C]
box seat (theatre) [N] *lOOž* [58A]
boxer [N] *poKsija* [227A]
boxing [N] *poKs* [58B]
boy [N] *poiSS* [59]
[N] *poisike(ne)* [257G]
boy scout [N] *skauT* [58E]
boycott [Vt] *boikotEErima* [291B]
boycott [N] *boikoTT* [58C]
boyish [A] *poisiliK* [62]

brag [Vi] *hooPlema* [326D]
[Vi] *keļKima* [291G]
braggart [N] *hooPleja* [227A]
brain [N] *aju* [13A]
brainless [A] *totakas* [243A]
brake [N] *pidur* [229A]
brake [Vt] *pidurdama* [349F]
bran [N] *klİİd (pl)* [1]
branch [N] *haru* [13A]
[N] *oKs* [55]
branch off [Vi] *harunema* [349D]
branch office [N] *filiAAl* [58A]
branchy [A] *oKsliK* [62]
brandish [Vt] *vibutama* [349F]
brant goose [N] *lagle* [152]
brat [N] *põngerjas* [243A]
brave [A] *vaPPer* [241B]
bravery [N] *vaHvus* [260B]
[N] *vaPrus* [260B]
Brazilian [N] *brasİİllane* [257C]
bread [Vt] *panEErima* [291B]
bread (rye) [N] *leİb* [86B]
bread (white) [N] *saİ* [49B]
break [Vt] *lõHkuma* [313B]
break off [Vi] *kaTkema* [349B]
breakfast [N] *prUUkoŞt* [58B]
bream (fish) [N] *laţikas* [243A]
[N] *viMb* [87]
breast [N] *riNd* [99]
breath [N] *hiNgus* [260B]
breathe [Vi] *hiNgama* [327B]
breathing [N] *hiNgamine* [257E]
breed [Vt] *aretama* [349F]
breed [Vi] *siginema* [349D]
breed [N] *tõUg* [134]
breeding [N] *aretus* [260A]
brevity [N] *lühidus* [260A]
brew [Vt] *prUUļima* [291A]
bribe [N] *pistis* [253]
brick [N] *teļlis* [253]
bride [N] *mõRsja* [227B]
bridge [N] *siLd* [91]
bridge (card game) [N] *briDž* [58B]
bridle [N] *päiTsed (pl)* [177B]
[N] *vaĻjad (pl)* [159B]
brief [A] *põgus* [231A]
briefcase [N] *porTfeĻL* [58A]
brigade [N] *brigAAd* [58A]
[N] *malev* [231A]
brigade-leader [N] *brigadir* [245]
bright [A] *ere* [235]
[A] *hele* [235]

brighten [Vi] *seĻgima* [349B]
brightness [N] *heledus* [260A]
brilliant (genius) [A] *geniAAlne* [247]
brim [N] *raņT* [58E]
bring [Vt] *tOOma* [267]
briquette [N] *brikeŢT* [58C]
brisk [A] *erK* [61F]
[A] *hOOgne* [249]
broad-chested [A] *rinnakas* [243A]
broadcast [N] *saade* [177E]
broadcasting [N] *riNghääling* [234A]
broadcloth [N] *kalev* [229A]
broaden [Vt] *avardama* [349F]
broaden [Vi] *avarduma* [349H]
brochure [N] *brošÜÜr* [58A]
broken [A] *kaŢkine* [257B]
bronchitis [N] *bronhiiT* [58E]
bronze [N] *pronKs* [58B]
brooch [N] *prEEş* [58A]
[N] *proŞS* [58A]
[N] *sõĻg* [142A]
brood [N] *haue* [219B]
brood (hatch out) [Vt] *haUduma* [306]
brook [N] *oja* [13A]
broom [N] *lUUd* [103]
broth [N] *lEEm* [83]
brothel [N] *bordeĻL* [58A]
brother [N] *veli* [77]
brother [N] *veNd* [106]
brother-in-law (husb's brother) [N] *küdi* [13C]
brother-in-law (wife's brother) [N] *nÄÄl* [61B]
brotherhood [N] *veNdlus* [260B]
brotherly [A] *vennaliK* [62]
brow [N] *kuLm* [61B]
brown [A] *prUUņ* [58A]
brown [Vt] *pruuņistama* [349F]
brownish [A] *pruuņikas* [243A]
bruise [Vt] *muĻjuma* [291C]
brunette [A] *brüneŢT* [58C]
brush [N] *hari* [68A]
brushwood [N] *hagu* [31]
brutal [A] *brutAAlne* [247]
[A] *jõHker* [241A]
brutality [N] *brutAAlsus* [260B]
[N] *jõHkrus* [260B]
[N] *tOOrus* [260B]
brute [N] *tõbras* [159D]
bubble [N] *kubel* [79A]
[N] *muĻL* [58A]
buck [N] *soKK* [61C]
bucket [N] *paNg* [63B]
buckle [N] *pannal* [202]

buckwheat [N] *tatar* [171C]
bud [N] *puNg* [53B]
budget [N] *büdžeTT* [58C]
buffalo [N] *püHvel* [240A]
buffoon [N] *veiderdaja* [227A]
build [Vt] *ehitama* [349F]
builder [N] *ehitaja* [227A]
building (action) [N] *ehitamine* [257E]
building (structure) [N] *ehitis* [260A]
[N] *ehitus* [260A]
Bulgarian [N] *bulgAArlane* [257C]
bulk [N] *kogu* [13D]
bulky [A] *kogukas* [243A]
bull [N] *puĻL* [58A]
[N] *sõŅN* [58A]
bullace [N] *kreeK* [58F]
bulldog [N] *buLdog* [229A]
bulldozer [N] *buldOOser* [229A]
bullet [N] *kUUļ* [58A]
bulletin [N] *bülletÄÄn* [58A]
bullfinch [N] *leevike(ne)* [257G]
bulrush [N] *kõrKjas* [243B]
bum(rear end) [N] *pepu* [152]
bump on skin [N] *muHk* [131C]
bun [N] *kuKKel* [240B]
bundle [N] *komPs* [61B]
[N] *pamP* [61D]
[N] *pundar* [171D]
bungle [V] *soperdama* [349F]
[Vt] *vusserdama* [349F]
[Vt] *vuŞSima* [291A]
bungler [N] *käpard* [229A]
[N] *vuSSer* [229A]
bungler [N] *vusserdis* [260A]
bunker [N] *punKer* [240A]
bunny [N] *jäņku* [152]
buoy [N] *poİ* [1]
burbot [N] *luTs* [61B]
burden [Vt] *kOOrmama* [327A]
burden [N] *kOOrmus* [260B]
burdock [N] *taKjas* [243B]
bureaucracy [N] *bürokraaTia* [227A]
bureaucracy [N] *bürokratiSm* [58B]
bureaucrat [N] *bürokraaT* [58E]
bureaucratic [A] *bürokraaTliK* [62]
burglar alarm [N] *signalisatsiOOn* [58A]
burial [N] *maTmine* [257E]
burn [Vi] *põlema* [269]
burn [Vt] *põletama* [349F]
burner [N] *põleti* [225A]
burning [N] *põletamine* [257E]
burning [A] *põletav* [231A]

burning (be) [Vi] *küdema* [279]
burrow [N] *uRg* [131B]
burst out [Vi] *puHkema* [349B]
bury [Vt] *maTma* [300]
bus [N] *buŞS* [58A]
[N] *omnibuŞS* [58A]
bush [N] *põõsas* [159A]
bushel [N] *vaKK* [49C]
business [N] *bisneSS* [58A]
[N] *äri* [13A]
business trip [N] *komandeering* [234A]
businesslike [A] *aşjaliK* [62]
bust [N] *büŞt* [58B]
bustle [Vi] *askeldama* [349F]
bustling [N] *askeldus* [260A]
butcher [N] *lihuniK* [62]
butt [Vi] *puSklema* [336]
butter [N] *võİ* [1]
buttercup [N] *tulikas* [243A]
butterfly [N] *liblikas* [243A]
buttermilk [N] *peŢT* [58C]
buttocks [N] *kaŋnikad (pl)* [243A]
buttocks [N] *tagumiK* [62]
[N] *tuharad (pl)* [231A]
button [N] *nöPs* [58B]
[N] *nööP* [58D]
button [Vt] *nööPima* [291E]
buy [Vt] *oStma* [297A]
buyer [N] *oŞtja* [227B]
buzz [N] *põrin* [231A]
buzz [Vi] *põrisema* [349C]

C

cabaret [N] *kabarEE* [2]
cabbage [N] *kapsas* [159B]
cabin [N] *kabİİn* [58A]
[N] *tare* [154]
cabin in ship [N] *kajut* [229A]
cabinet-maker [N] *tiSler* [229A]
cable [N] *kAAbel* [240A]
[N] *troŞS* [58A]
cackle [Vi] *kaagutama* [349F]
cactus [N] *kaKtus* [260B]
cadet [N] *kadeŢT* [58C]
[N] *kursaŋT* [58E]
café [N] *kohvik* [234A]
cafeteria [N] *sööKla* [227B]
caffeine [N] *kofeİİn* [58A]
cage [N] *pUUr* [58A]
cake [N] *kooK* [58F]
calcium [N] *kaļTsium* [246]
calculate [Vt] *arvutama* [349F]
[Vt] *kalkulEErima* [291B]
calculation [N] *arvestus* [260A]
[N] *kalkulatsiOON* [58A]
calculator [N] *kalkulaaTor* [229A]
calendar [N] *kaleNder* [240A]
calf [N] *vasikas* [243A]
calibre [N] *kalİİber* [240A]
call [N] *hüüe* [210C]
call out [V] *hÜÜdma* [316B]
calla lily [N] *kalla* [152]
calligraphy [N] *kalligraaFia* [227A]
calm down [Vi] *rahunema* [349D]
calm down [Vt] *rahustama* [349F]
calorie [N] *kalor* [229A]
camel [N] *kAAmel* [229A]
camera flash [N] *välguti* [225A]
camiknickers [N] *kombinEE* [2]
camomile [N] *kummel* [229A]
camp [N] *lAAger* [240A]
camp [N] *lEEr* [58A]
camp grounds [N] *kämping* [234A]
campaign [N] *kampAAnia* [227A]
camphor [N] *kamPer* [240A]
can [N] *mannerg* [234A]
can [V] *võİma* [263]
Canadian [N] *kanadalane* [257C]
canal [N] *kanal* [229A]
cancel [Vt] *annullEErima* [291B]
[Vt] *tühistama* [349F]
cancer [N] *väHk* [120B]
candidacy [N] *kaŋdidatUUr* [58A]
candidate [N] *kaŋditaaT* [58E]
candidate (be) [Vi] *kaŋdidEErima* [291B]
candied peel [N] *sukAAd* [58A]
candle [N] *küünal* [170A]
candy [N] *karameĻL* [58A]
[N] *koMM* [58A]
[N] *kompu* [152]
[N] *komPveK* [58H]
canned food [N] *konseRv* [58B]
cannon [N] *kahur* [229A]
canoe [N] *kanUU* [1]
[N] *süSt* [53B]
cantata [N] *kantaaT* [58E]
canteen [N] *puhvet* [229A]
canvas [N] *kanvAA* [1]
[N] *lõuend* [229A]
cap (woman's) [N] *tanu* [13A]
capacity [N] *maHt* [124B]
[N] *maHtuvus* [260A]
cape [N] *nEEm* [63A]
capital [A] *kapitAAlne* [247]
capital [N] *kapital* [245]
capitulate [Vi] *kapitulEEruma* [349G]
capitulation [N] *kapitulatsiOOn* [58A]
caprice [N] *kaprİİs* [58A]
capricious [A] *kaprİİsne* [248]
captain [N] *kaPten* [229A]
captivate [Vt] *kütkestama* [349F]
captivating [A] *kütkestav* [231A]
carafe [N] *karahvin* [245]
caravan [N] *karavan* [245]
caraway-seed [N] *kööme* [185]
[N] *köömen* [185]
carbolic [N] *kaRbol* [229A]
carbon [N] *süsiniK* [62]
carbon monoxide [N] *viNg* [61B]
carbonated drink [N] *vurTs* [61B]
carburettor [N] *karburaaTor* [229A]
carcass [N] *korjus* [253]
[N] *raibe* [177D]
card [N] *kaarT* [58E]
card (wool) [N] *krAAş* [58A]
card file [N] *kartoteeK* [58F]
cardamom [N] *kardemon* [245]
cardboard [N] *paPP* [58C]
cardboard box [N] *kartoNg* [58B]
cardigan [N] *kamPsun* [229A]
care [N] *hOOl* [82]
care for [Vt] *hOOldama* [349F]
care for [Vi] *hOOļima* [291A]
career [N] *karjÄÄr* [58A]
careerist [N] *karjeriSt* [58B]
carefree [A] *muretu* [227A]
careful [A] *eTTevaaTliK* [62]
[A] *hooļikas* [243A]
careless [A] *eTTevaaTamatu* [227A]
[A] *hooletu* [227A]
carelessness [N] *hooletus* [260A]
caress [N] *heļlitus* [260A]
caress [Vt] *kaļlistama* [349F]
caricature [N] *karikatUUr* [58A]
[N] *šaRž* [58B]
caricaturist [N] *karikaturiSt* [58B]
carnation [N] *neļK* [58F]

carnival [N] *karneval* [245]
carriage [N] *vagun* [229A]
carriage (of person) [N] *rüHt* [116]
carried over (be) [Vi] *kaNduma* [349H]
carrier [N] *kaŅdja* [227B]
carrion [N] *raiSk* [95B]
carrot [N] *porgand* [229A]
carry [Vt] *kaNdma* [317]
carrying [N] *kanne* [214]
cart [N] *kaarik* [234A]
cartridge [N] *padrun* [229A]
carve [Vt] *vOOļima* [291A]
cascade [N] *juga* [39]
case (grammatical) [N] *kääne* [211A]
case (small box) [N] *vuTlar* [229A]
cash desk [N] *kassa* [152]
cash in [Vt] *kassEErima* [291B]
[Vt] *realisEErima* [291B]
cashier [N] *kassİİr* [58A]
casino [N] *kasiino* [152]
cassette [N] *kasseŢT* [58C]
cast [Vt] *heiTma* [297C]
cast-iron [N] *maĻm* [58B]
caster (moulder) [N] *valaja* [227A]
casting [N] *heide* [177E]
castle [N] *loŞS* [58A]
cat [N] *kaŞS* [58A]
catalogue [N] *katalOOg* [58A]
cataract (eye) [N] *kaE* [1]
catastrophe [N] *katastrooF* [58A]
catastrophic [A] *katastroofiline* [257D]
catch [Vt] *pÜÜdma* [316B]
[Vt] *tabama* [269]
catch [N] *püüK* [58F]
catch cold [Vi] *külmetuma* [349H]
categorical [A] *kategooriline* [257D]
category [N] *kategOOria* [227A]
cater [Vt] *toitlustama* [349F]
catering [N] *toitlustus* [260A]
caterpillar [N] *röövik* [234A]
caterwaul [Vi] *kräUnuma* [291C]
cathedral [N] *katedrAAl* [58A]
Catholic [N] *katoliiKlane* [257C]
catkin [N] *uRb* [101B]
Caucasian [N] *kaukAAslane* [257C]
cause [N] *põHjus* [260B]
cause [Vt] *põhjustama* [349F]
[Vt] *tekitama* [349F]
cave [N] *koobas* [159D]
cavity [N] *ÕÕnsus* [260B]
[N] *ÕÕş* [146]
cease [Vi] *laKKama* [327C]

ceaseless [A] *laKKamatu* [227A]
cedar [N] *sEEder* [240A]
ceiling [N] *lagi* [42]
celebrate [Vt] *pühitsema* [349E]
celebration [N] *pühitsemine* [257E]
celery [N] *seLLer* [229A]
cell [N] *raKK* [61C]
cell (prison) [N] *koNg* [58B]
cellar [N] *keLder* [240A]
cellist [N] *tšelliSt* [58B]
cello [N] *tšello* [152]
celluloid [N] *tselluloİd* [58B]
cellulose [N] *tsellulOOS* [58A]
cement [N] *tsemeņT* [58E]
cement [Vt] *tsementEErima* [291B]
[Vt] *tsemeņTima* [291F]
cemetery [N] *rahula* [227A]
censor [Vt] *tsensEErima* [291B]
censor [N] *tseNsor* [229A]
censorship [N] *tsensUUr* [58A]
cent [N] *seņT* [58E]
central [A] *keSkne* [257B]
[A] *tsentrAAlne* [247]
central part [N] *keSkmiK* [62]
centralization [N] *tsentralisatsiOOn* [58A]
centralize [Vt] *tsentralisEErima* [291B]
centre [N] *keSkus* [260B]
[N] *tsenTrum* [229A]
centrifuge [N] *tsentrifUUg* [58A]
century [N] *sajand* [229A]
ceramic [A] *keraamiline* [257D]
ceremonial [A] *tseremoniAAlne* [247]
ceremony [N] *aKtus* [260B]
[N] *tseremOOnia* [227A]
certain (a certain) [A] *teaTav* [231A]
certify [Vt] *kiņnitama* [349F]
cesspool [N] *kloaaK* [58F]
chaff [Vt] *nööKima* [291G]
[Vt] *tögama* [269]
chain [N] *ahel* [231A]
[N] *keŢT* [58C]
chair [N] *tOOļ* [58A]
chalk [N] *kriiT* [58E]
chamber [N] *kaMber* [240A]
[N] *koda* [29]
champagne [N] *šampanja* [152]
[N] *šamPus* [260B]
champion [N] *tšemPion* [246]
champion (hero) [N] *võiTleja* [227A]
chance [N] *šanSS* [58G]
chancellor [N] *kanTsler* [229A]
change [N] *muudatus* [260A]

change [N] *muuTus* [260B]
[N] *vaheldus* [260A]
change [Vt] *muuTma* [297C]
change [Vi] *muuTuma* [349H]
changeable [A] *muuTliK* [62]
chaos [N] *kAos* [253]
chapel [N] *kabel* [229A]
chapped (be) [Vi] *kestendama* [349F]
character [N] *karaKter* [229A]
characteristic [N] *lOOm* [61A]
characteristic [A] *omane* [251]
characteristics [N] *omadus* [260A]
characterization [N] *iseloomustus* [260A]
characters [N] *tegelaskoNd* [106]
charge [N] *laEng* [234B]
charm [N] *saRm* [58B]
[N] *veeTlus* [260B]
[N] *võlu* [13A]
charm [Vt] *veeTlema* [326E]
[Vt] *võluma* [269]
charming [A] *huRmav* [231A]
[A] *sarmikas* [243A]
[A] *veeTlev* [231A]
[A] *võluv* [231A]
charred (become) [Vi] *söeStuma* [349H]
chat [Vi] *veStlema* [326B]
chat [N] *veStlus* [260B]
chauvinist [N] *šoviniSt* [58B]
chauvinistic [A] *šoviniStliK* [62]
cheap [A] *odav* [231A]
cheapness [N] *odavus* [260A]
cheat [N] *peTTur* [229A]
cheat at school [V] *spikerdama* [349F]
cheat-sheet [N] *spiKKer* [240B]
checked [A] *ruuduline* [257D]
checkers [N] *kabe* [153]
checkmate [N] *maŢT* [58C]
cheek [N] *põŞk* [142B]
cheep [Vi] *piiKsuma* [291C]
cheer [Vi] *hõiSkama* [348C]
cheerless [A] *rõõmutu* [227A]
cheese [N] *juuSt* [61B]
chemical [A] *keemiline* [257D]
chemical [N] *kemikAAl* [58A]
chemist [N] *keemik* [234A]
cheque [N] *tšeKK* [58C]
cherry [N] *kirSS* [58G]
chess [N] *male* [153]
chess (play) [Vi] *maletama* [349F]
chess-piece [N] *malend* [229A]
chess-player [N] *maletaja* [227A]
chest [N] *riNd* [99]

chest (box) [N] *laegas* [159E]
chest of drawers [N] *kummut* [229A]
chestnut [N] *kaStan* [229A]
chew [Vt] *närima* [269]
chewy [A] *näTske* [227B]
chic [A] *šiKK* [58C]
chick [N] *tibu* [13B]
chicory [N] *sigur* [229A]
chide [Vi] *tõrelema* [325]
chiding [N] *tõrelus* [260A]
child [N] *laPs* [85]
childish [A] *lapsik* [234A]
childlike [A] *lapseliK* [62]
Chilean [N] *tšİİllane* [257C]
chimney [N] *korSten* [241A]
chimpanzee [N] *šimpaNs* [58B]
chin [N] *lõUg* [94A]
Chinese [N] *hİİnlane* [257C]
chip [N] *laaSt* [61B]
chirp [Vi] *siristama* [349F]
[Vi] *sirTsuma* [291C]
chisel [N] *peiTel* [240A]
chivalrous [A] *rüüTelliK* [62]
chive [N] *murulauK* [61F]
chocolate [N] *šokolAAd* [58A]
choice [N] *valik* [234A]
choir [N] *kOOr* [58A]
choose [Vt] *valima* [269]
chop [Vt] *raİuma* [291C]
chop (meat) [N] *eskaloPP* [58C]
[N] *karbonAAd* [58A]
chopper [N] *kİİn* [58A]
chopping block [N] *paKK* [61C]
chord (music) [N] *akoRd* [58B]
choreographic [A] *koreograafiline* [257D]
choreography [N] *koreograaFia* [227A]
Christen [Vt] *riŞtima* [291C]
Christian [N] *kriStlane* [257C]
Christian [A] *kriStliK* [62]
Christmas [N] *jõulud (pl)* [61B]
chronic [A] *krooniline* [257D]
chronicle [N] *kroonika* [227A]
chrysanthemum [N] *krüsantEEm* [58A]
Chude [N] *tšUUd* [58A]
church [N] *kirik* [234A]
churn [N] *kiRn* [61B]
cigar [N] *sigar* [229A]
cigarette [N] *sigareŢ* [58H]
cigarette holder [N] *piŢs* [58B]
cigarette stub [N] *koni* [13A]
cigarette-case [N] *portsigar* [245]
Cinderella [N] *tuhkatriinu* [152]

cinema [N] *kino* [13A]
cinnamon [N] *kanEEl* [58A]
cipher [N] *šiFFer* [240B]
cipher [Vt] *šifrEErima* [291B]
circle [N] *riNg* [58B]
[N] *sÕÕr* [58A]
circulate [Vi] *käİbima* [349B]
[Vi] *riNglema* [326B]
circulation [N] *käive* [208B]
circumstance [N] *seiK* [49F]
circumstances [N] *olud (pl)* [13A]
circus [N] *tsirKus* [260B]
cistern [N] *tsisteRn* [58B]
citadel [N] *tsitadeĻL* [58A]
citizen [N] *kodaniK* [62]
citizenship [N] *kodakoNdsus* [260B]
city [N] *liNN* [49A]
city block [N] *kvarTal* [229A]
city dweller [N] *liNlane* [257C]
civilization [N] *tsivilisatsiOOn* [58A]
civilize [Vt] *tsivilisEErima* [291B]
clamour [N] *kisa* [13A]
clamp [N] *koba* [13B]
clap [V] *plaksutama* [349F]
clarify [Vt] *klAArima* [291A]
clarinet [N] *klarnet* [229A]
clarity [N] *seLgus* [260B]
class [N] *klaŞS* [58A]
classic [N] *klaşsik* [234A]
classical [A] *klaşsikaline* [257D]
classification [N] *liigitus* [260A]
classify [Vt] *klaşsifitsEErima* [291B]
[Vt] *liigitama* [349F]
clatter [N] *klirin* [231A]
[N] *klõbin* [231A]
[N] *kolin* [231A]
[N] *plagin* [231A]
clatter [Vi] *klirisema* [349C]
[Vi] *kolisema* [349C]
[Vi] *plagisema* [349C]
clatter [Vt] *kolistama* [349F]
claw [N] *küünis* [253]
claw [Vt] *küünistama* [349F]
clay [N] *savi* [13A]
clayey [A] *savine* [251]
clean [A] *puhas* [190]
clean [Vt] *puhastama* [349F]
clean copy [N] *puhtand* [229A]
clean up [Vt] *krAAmima* [291A]
cleaner (person) [N] *koristaja* [227A]
cleaning [N] *puhastus* [260A]
cleanliness [N] *puHtus* [260B]

clear [A] *seLge* [227B]
clearing [N] *raiesmiK* [62]
[N] *raiestiK* [62]
cliché [N] *klišEE* [2]
click [N] *klõPs* [61B]
[N] *klõpsatus* [260A]
[N] *plõKs* [61B]
click [Vt] *laksutama* [349F]
client [N] *klieņT* [58E]
[N] *kunde* [152]
clientele [N] *oŞtjaskoNd* [106]
cliff [N] *kaļju* [152]
climate [N] *ilmastiK* [62]
[N] *kliima* [152]
climb [Vi] *ronima* [269]
clinic [N] *kliinik* [234A]
clip [N] *klaMber* [240A]
clitoris [N] *kõdisti* [225A]
cloak [N] *keeP* [58D]
cloak-room [N] *garderOOb* [58A]
clock [N] *keLL* [53A]
clog [Vt] *ummistama* [349F]
clogged (become) [Vi] *ummistuma* [349H]
cloister [N] *klooSter* [240A]
close [A] *ligidane* [257A]
[A] *lähedane* [257A]
closed [A] *kiŅNine* [257B]
closer (bring) [Vt] *lähendama* [349F]
closer (come) [Vi] *lähenema* [349D]
cloth [N] *riie* [210C]
clothes-rack [N] *vaRn* [49B]
clothing [N] *riietus* [260A]
[N] *rõivas* [159B]
[N] *rõivastus* [260A]
cloud [N] *piLv* [63B]
cloudberry [N] *murakas* [243A]
cloudless [A] *pilvitu* [227A]
cloudy [A] *pilvine* [251]
clove [N] *neļK* [58F]
clover [N] *riştik* [234A]
clown [N] *kloUn* [58B]
club [N] *klubi* [13B]
clubs (cards) [N] *rişti* [152]
clumsiness [N] *kohmakus* [260A]
clumsy [A] *kohmakas* [243A]
[A] *saamatu* [227A]
cluster [N] *kobar* [231A]
clutch (car) [N] *sidur* [229A]
co-operative [N] *kooperatİİv* [58A]
[N] *ühistu* [227A]
co-ordinate [Vt] *koordinEErima* [291B]
[Vt] *kOOskõlastama* [349F]

co-ordinates [N] *koordinaaT* [58E]
coach [N] *tõLd* [91]
coagulate [Vi] *hÜÜbima* [349B]
coal [N] *süsi* [48]
coast [N] *raņnik* [234A]
coastal cliff [N] *panK* [49F]
coat [N] *kUUb* [136]
[N] *manTel* [240A]
[N] *palitu* [227A]
coat of arms [N] *vaPP* [58C]
coat rack [N] *nagi* [13D]
coax [Vt] *meelitama* [349F]
cocaine [N] *kokaİİn* [58A]
coccyx [N] *õnnar* [203]
cock (bird) [N] *kikas* [159C]
[N] *kuKK* [63C]
cock (penis) [N] *tiĻL* [58A]
[N] *türa* [13A]
cockatoo [N] *kakadUU* [1]
cockroach [N] *prussakas* [243A]
cocktail [N] *koKteİl* [58B]
cocoa [N] *kakaO* [1]
cod [N] *turSk* [109]
code [N] *kOOḑ* [58A]
codeine [N] *kodeİİn* [58A]
coffee [N] *koHv* [58B]
coffee cake [N] *striTsel* [240A]
coffin [N] *kirSt* [61B]
coin [N] *müņT* [58E]
coincide [Vi] *kaTTuma* [349H]
coke (coal) [N] *koKs* [58B]
cold [A] *küLm* [53B]
cold (illness) [N] *nohu* [13A]
cold (severely) [A] *pakane* [251]
cold cut plate [N] *seKser* [229A]
colder (become) [Vi] *külmenema* [349D]
coldness [N] *küLmus* [260B]
collage [N] *kollAAž* [58A]
collapse [Vi] *varisema* [349C]
collar [N] *kaelus* [253]
[N] *kraE* [1]
colleague [N] *kollEEg* [58A]
collect [Vt] *koguma* [269]
collection [N] *kogu* [13D]
[N] *kollektsiOOn* [58A]
[N] *korjandus* [260A]
collective [N] *kollektİİv* [58A]
collective [A] *kollektİİvne* [247]
collectivity [N] *kollektİİvsus* [260B]
collector [N] *koguja* [227A]
[N] *kollektsionÄÄr* [58A]
college [N] *kolledž* [229A]

collide [Vi] *põrKama* [327F]
colon [N] *kOOlon* [229A]
colonel [N] *kolonel* [245]
colonial [A] *koloniAAlne* [247]
colonist [N] *koloniSt* [58B]
colonization [N] *kolonisEErimine* [257E]
colonize [Vt] *asustama* [349F]
[Vt] *kolonisEErima* [291B]
colonizer [N] *kolonisaaTor* [229A]
colony [N] *asundus* [260A]
[N] *kolOOnia* [227A]
colossal [A] *kolossAAlne* [247]
colour [N] *väRv* [58B]
[N] *väRvus* [260B]
coloured [A] *värviline* [257D]
colourful [A] *värvikas* [243A]
colouring [N] *koloriiT* [58E]
colourless [A] *värvitu* [227A]
column [N] *koloŅN* [58A]
column (newspaper) [N] *vEErg* [131A]
column (pillar) [N] *sammas* [188]
comb [N] *kaMM* [58A]
comb [Vt] *kaMMima* [291A]
combination [N] *kombinatsiOOn* [58A]
combine [N] *kombaİn* [58B]
combine operator [N] *kombaİner* [229A]
come [Vi] *tulema* [271]
come into effect [Vi] *kehtestuma* [349H]
come into force [Vi] *jõuStuma* [349H]
comedian [N] *koomik* [234A]
comedy [N] *komÖÖdia* [227A]
comfort [N] *mugavus* [260A]
comfortable [A] *mugav* [231A]
comic [A] *koomiline* [257D]
coming [N] *tulemine* [257E]
coming (next) [A] *tulev* [231A]
comma [N] *koma* [13A]
command [N] *käSk* [131C]
[N] *käSklus* [260B]
command [Vt] *käŞkima* [321 or 313B]
[Vt] *käSkma* [321]
commander [N] *komandör* [245]
commemorate [Vt] *mälestama* [349F]
commence [Vt] *alustama* [349F]
commentary [N] *kommentAAr* [58A]
commentator [N] *kommentaaTor* [229A]
commerce [N] *kaubandus* [260A]
[N] *kommerTs* [58B]
commercial [A] *kaubandusliK* [62]
commissariat [N] *komissariaaT* [58E]
commission [N] *komisjon* [245]
committee [N] *komitEE* [2]

committee [N] *toİmkoNd* [106]
commodity [N] *kauP* [49D]
common [A] *ühine* [251]
common sense [N] *arukus* [260A]
communal [A] *kommunAAlne* [247]
communication [N] *side* [153]
communiqué [N] *kommünikEE* [2]
community [N] *kogukoNd* [106]
compact [A] *kompaKtne* [247]
companion [N] *kaasa* [152]
[N] *kAAslane* [257C]
[N] *seļtsiline* [257D]
company [N] *firma* [152]
[N] *kompanİİ* [1]
company (army) [N] *rOOd* [61A]
comparable [A] *võrreldav* [231A]
comparative [A] *võRdlev* [231A]
compare [Vt] *komparEErima* [291B]
[Vt] *kõrvutama* [349F]
[Vt] *võRdlema* [333]
comparing [N] *võRdlemine* [257E]
comparison [N] *võRdlus* [260B]
compartment (train) [N] *kupEE* [2]
compass [N] *komPaŞS* [58A]
compasses [N] *sirKel* [240A]
compel [Vt] *suŅdima* [310]
compensate [Vt] *hüvitama* [349F]
[Vt] *kompensEErima* [291B]
[Vt] *koRvama* [327B]
compensation [N] *hüvitus* [260A]
[N] *kompensatsiOOn* [58A]
compete [Vi] *konkurEErima* [291B]
[Vi] *võiStlema* [326B]
competence [N] *kompetenTs* [58B]
competent [A] *kompetenTne* [247]
[A] *pädev* [231A]
competition [N] *konkurenTs* [58B]
[N] *võiStlus* [260B]
competitor [N] *konkureņT* [58E]
complain [V] *kaEbama* [339B]
[V] *kurTma* [297C]
complainant [N] *kaEbaja* [227A]
complement [Vt] *komplektEErima* [291B]
[Vt] *täiendama* [349F]
complement [N] *täiend* [229A]
complete [A] *täieliK* [62]
[A] *täİusliK* [62]
complete (become) [Vi] *täienema* [349D]
completeness [N] *täİusliKKus* [260B]
complex [N] *komPleKs* [58B]
complex [A] *kompleKsne* [247]
complexion [N] *jume* [153]

complicate Vt *komplitsEErima* 291B
complicated A *keeruline* 257D
complication N *komplikatsiOOn* 58A
compliment N *komplimeņT* 58E
compose Vt *kooStama* 349F
compose (music) Vt *komponEErima* 291B
composer N *komponiSt* 58B
composition N *kompositsiOOn* 58A
compost N *kompoŞt* 58B
compound N *ühend* 229A
comprehend Vt *käsitama* 349F
comprehension N *mõiStmine* 257E
compress N *komPreŞS* 58A
comprise Vt *hõLmama* 327B
compromise N *kompromiŞS* 58A
compromise Vt *kompromitEErima* 291B
compulsion N *suŅdus* 260B
compulsory A *obligatOOrne* 247
A *suŅdusliK* 62
computer N *arvuti* 225A
N *rAAļ* 58A
concave A *nõgus* 231A
conceal Vt *vaŖjama* 327B
concede V *mÖÖnma* 292A
concentrate Vt *keskendama* 349F
concentrate Vi *keskenduma* 349H
concentrate on Vi *süvenema* 349D
concentrate(make) Vt *kontsentrEErima* 291B
concern Vi *puuTuma* 349H
concert N *konTserT* 58E
conclude Vt *järeldama* 349F
conclusion N *järeldus* 260A
concrete N *betOOn* 58A
concrete (real) A *konkreeTne* 247
concurrent (be) Vi *kAAsnema* 349D
condemn Vt *taUnima* 291C
condition N *tiNgimus* 260A
condom N *kondOOm* 58A
N *preservatİİv* 58A
conduct Vt *dirigEErima* 291B
conducting wire N *juhe* 220
conductor N *dirigeņT* 58E
N *konduKtor* 229A
cone N *koonus* 253
N *kOOnus* 260B
cone (pine, fir etc) N *käbi* 13B
confectioner N *kondiiTer* 240A
conference N *konverenTs* 58B
confess Vt *piHtima* 308B
confession N *piHt* 116
confidential A *usaldusliK* 62
confirm (church) Vt *leeritama* 349F
confirmation class N *lEEr* 58A
confiscate Vt *konfiskEErima* 291B
confiscation N *konfiskEErimine* 257E
conflict N *konfliKt* 58B
conform to Vt *jäRgima* 349B
confused A *segane* 251
confusion N *segadus* 260A
congeal Vi *taRduma* 349H
Vi *tarretuma* 349H
congeal Vt *tarretama* 349F
congratulate Vt *õņnitlema* 351
congratulations N *õņnitelu* 13A
N *õņnitlus* 260A
congregation N *kogudus* 260A
congress N *kongreŞS* 58A
conjure Vt *nõİduma* 307
connection N *seOs* 254
conquer Vt *vallutama* 349F
conqueror N *vallutaja* 227A
conquest N *vallutus* 260A
consciousness N *teAdvus* 260B
conscript N *nekrut* 229A
conservative N *konservatİİv* 58A
conservative A *konservatİİvne* 247
conservatory N *konservatOOrium* 246
consider Vt *arvestama* 349F
consideration N *kaalutlus* 260A
consignment N *partİİ* 1
consist of Vi *kOOsnema* 349D
Vi *seİsnema* 349D
consistory N *konsistOOrium* 246
consolation N *lohutus* 260A
N *trööŞt* 58B
console Vt *lohutama* 349F
Vt *trööŞtima* 291C
consonant N *konsonaņT* 58E
conspiratorial A *konspiratİİvne* 247
constant A *jÄÄv* 231B
constitution N *konstitutsiOOn* 58A
construct Vt *konstruEErima* 291B
construction N *konstruktsiOOn* 58A
N *rajatis* 260A
N *tarind* 229A
constructor N *konstruKtor* 229A
consul N *koNsul* 229A
consulate N *konsulaaT* 58E
consult Vt *konsultEErima* 291B
consultant N *konsultaņT* 58E
consultation N *konsultatsiOOn* 58A
consultation office N *nõUaNdla* 227B
consume Vt *taRbima* 349B
consumer N *taRbija* 227A
consumption N *taRbimine* 257E
contact N *kontaKt* 58B
contain Vt *sisaldama* 349F
container N *kontejner* 229A
contempt N *põLgus* 260B
contemptuous A *põLgliK* 62
content with (be) Vi *lePPima* 291D
contents N *sisu* 13A
contest N *konKurSS* 58G
context N *konteKst* 58B
continent N *maNder* 240A
N *manner* 207
continental A *kontinentAAlne* 247
contingent N *kontingeņT* 58E
continual A *pidev* 231A
continue Vt *jäTkama* 327B
contract N *konTraHt* 116
contrary A *vastane* 251
contrast N *kontraŞt* 58B
contrast Vt *vastandama* 349F
contrastive A *kontraStne* 247
contribution N *panus* 253
contrive Vt *kombinEErima* 291B
contusion N *muļjutus* 260A
N *põrutus* 260A
conventional A *konventsionAAlne* 247
conversation N *keskustelu* 13A
converse Vi *keskustlema* 351
conveyer N *konveİer* 229A
conviction N *vEEndumus* 260A
convince Vt *vEEnma* 292A
convinced (become) Vi *vEEnduma* 349H
convincing N *vEEnmine* 257E
convulsive A *kramPliK* 62
coo Vi *kudrutama* 349F
cook N *koKK* 53C
cookery N *kulinAAria* 227A
cookie N *küpsis* 253
cool A *jahe* 235
A *vilu* 13A
cool (become) Vi *jahenema* 349D
cool off Vi *jaHtuma* 349H
cool off Vt *jahutama* 349F
coolness N *jahedus* 260A
coordinate Vt *rinnastama* 349F
cop N *võMM* 61A
copper N *vaŞk* 142B
copper A *vaŞkne* 247
copulation N *kopulatsiOOn* 58A
copy N *kooPia* 227A
copy Vt *jäļjendama* 349F
Vt *kopEErima* 291B

copy of a book N *eksemplar* 245
coral N *koraĻL* 58A
cordial A *südamliK* 62
cordiality N *südamliKKus* 260B
core N *südamiK* 62
coriander N *koriaNder* 240A
cork N *korK* 58F
corkscrew N *korgits* 231A
corn N *maİs* 58B
corn-bin N *saĻv* 65
corner N *nuKK* 53C
 N *nurK* 53F
cornet N *kornet* 229A
coronation N *krOOņimine* 257E
corporal N *kaPral* 229A
corps N *korPus* 260B
corpse N *laiP* 49D
corpus of data N *aNdmestiK* 62
correct Vt *korrigEErima* 291B
correctness N *õİgsus* 260B
correspondent N *korrespondeņT* 58E
corresponding A *vaStav* 231A
corridor N *koda* 29
 N *koridor* 245
corruption N *korruptsiOOn* 58A
cosmetic A *kosmeetiline* 257D
cosmetics N *kosmeetika* 227A
cosmic A *kosmiline* 257D
cost Vi *maKsma* 293A
cost N *maKsumus* 260A
costly A *kulukas* 243A
cosy A *hubane* 251
 A *mõnus* 231A
 A *õdus* 231A
coterie N *seļTskoNd* 106
cotter N *poPs* 58B
 N *poPsniK* 62
 N *vabadiK* 62
cotton print N *siŢs* 58B
cotton-wool N *vaŢT* 58C
couch N *kušeŢT* 58C
cough N *köha* 13A
cough Vi *köhima* 269
cough badly Vi *läkastama* 349F
councillor N *nõUniK* 62
counsel N *nõU* 12
count V *lugema* 284
count (person) N *kraHv* 58B
countenance N *pale* 217B
counterfeit A *võļTs* 58B
counter (table) N *leŢT* 58C
countess N *komteSS* 58A
countess N *kraHvinna* 152
countless A *arvutu* 227A
countless A *lugematu* 227A
county N *kraHvkoNd* 106
coupon N *kupoNg* 58B
courier N *kuLLer* 229A
course N *kuRsus* 260B
course (progress) N *kuLg* 131B
court Vi *kuramEErima* 291B
court (royal) N *õUkoNd* 106
court of law N *kohus* 198
courtship N *kuramEErimine* 257E
courtyard N *hOOv* 58A
cousin N *nõbu* 23
 N *nõOs* 256
cover Vt *kaTma* 300
covering N *kate* 177C
covet Vt *ihalema* 349A
cow N *leHm* 53B
cowardice N *aRgus* 260B
cowardly A *aRg* 95A
crab N *krabi* 13B
 N *väHk* 120B
crab-louse N *saţikas* 243A
crabby A *sapine* 251
crack Vi *mõranema* 349D
crack N *pragu* 31
crack (sound) Vt *raksatama* 349F
crack (sound) N *raksatus* 260A
cracked (become) Vi *pragunema* 349D
crackle N *ragin* 231A
crackle Vi *ragisema* 349C
crackle Vt *ragistama* 349F
cradle N *häĻL* 58A
crag N *rüngas* 159E
craggy A *kaļjune* 251
cram Vt *toPPima* 291D
cram (study) Vt *tuuPima* 291E
crammer N *tuuPija* 227A
 N *tuuPur* 229A
cramp N *kramP* 58D
cranberry N *jõhvikas* 243A
crane (bird) N *kuRg* 140A
crane (machine) N *kraana* 152
crank N *vänT* 53E
crank Vt *vänTama* 327E
crash N *kraHH* 58A
crate N *kaŞt* 58B
crater N *kraaTer* 240A
crave Vt *ihaldama* 349F
crawl Vi *rOOmama* 327A
crawl (swimming) N *krOOļ* 58A
crawl (swimming) Vi *krOOļima* 291A
crazy A *huLL* 61A
creak Vi *kriiKsuma* 291C
creak Vi *nagisema* 349C
cream N *krEEm* 58A
cream (dairy) N *kOOr* 82
crease Vt *viigitama* 349F
crease N *viiK* 58F
crease-proof A *korTsumatu* 227A
create Vt *lOOma* 267
creation N *lOOmine* 257E
creative A *lOOv* 231B
creative work N *looming* 234A
Creator N *lOOja* 227B
creature N *olend* 229A
credit N *krediiT* 58E
creep Vi *pugema* 284
cremate Vt *tuhastama* 349F
crematorium N *krematOOrium* 246
crêpe N *krePP* 58C
cress N *kreŞS* 58A
crime N *roİm* 53B
criminal A *kriminAAlne* 247
criminal N *roİmar* 229A
cripple N *lombak* 234A
cripple A *saņT* 58E
crippled A *lombakas* 243A
crisis N *krİİs* 58A
crisp A *krõbe* 235
critic N *arvustaja* 227A
 N *kriitik* 234A
critical A *kriitiline* 257D
criticism N *arvustus* 260A
 N *kriitika* 227A
criticize Vt *kritisEErima* 291B
critique Vt *arvustama* 349F
croak Vi *kraaKsuma* 291C
 Vi *krooKsuma* 291C
crochet Vt *heegeldama* 349F
crocheting N *heegeldus* 260A
crocodile N *krokodiĻL* 58A
crocus N *krooKus* 260B
crone N *eiT* 63D
crook N *pasaTski* 225B
 N *suli* 13A
crook (shepherd's) N *saU* 52
crooked A *kõver* 231A
crop Vt *pügama* 269 or 286
crop N *saaK* 58F
 N *vili* 69A
crop failure N *ikaldus* 260A
croquet N *kroket* 229A

cross [N] *riŞt* [58B]
cross (breed) [Vt] *riStama* [327B]
crow [Vi] *kirema* [269]
crow [N] *vares* [253]
crow-bar [N] *kaNg* [58B]
crowd [Vi] *tuNglema* [326B]
crown [N] *krOOņ* [58A]
crown [Vt] *krOOņima* [291A]
crown of tree [N] *võra* [13A]
cruel [A] *juLm* [53B]
cruelty [N] *juLmus* [260B]
cruise [Vi] *riStlema* [326B]
cruiser [N] *riStleja* [227A]
crumb [N] *puru* [13A]
crumble [Vt] *pudendama* [349F]
[Vt] *pudistama* [349F]
crumble [Vi] *pudenema* [349D]
crunch [N] *krigin* [231A]
crunch [Vi] *krigisema* [349C]
crunch [Vt] *krigistama* [349F]
crust [N] *koorik* [234A]
[N] *kooruke(ne)* [257G]
crutch [N] *karK* [61F]
cry [V] *nuTma* [297B]
cry out [Vi] *hüüatama* [349F]
[Vi] *karjatama* [349F]
crying [N] *nuTT* [61C]
crystal [N] *kristaĻL* [58A]
cube [N] *kuubik* [234A]
[N] *kuuP* [58D]
cuckoo [Vi] *kuKKuma* [291D]
cuckoo [N] *kägu* [31]
cucumber [N] *kurK* [58F]

cuddle [Vt] *sülelema* [325]
cudgel [N] *hudi* [72B]
cudgel [N] *nuİ* [57]
cuff [N] *käţis* [253]
cull [Vt] *praaKima* [291G]
culprit [N] *sÜÜdlane* [257C]
cult [N] *kulTus* [260B]
cultivate [Vt] *kuļtivEErima* [291B]
[Vt] *viļjelema* [325]
cultivation [N] *viļjelus* [260A]
cultural [A] *kultuuriline* [257D]
culture [N] *kultUUr* [58A]
cultured [A] *kultUUrne* [247]
cunt [N] *puŢs* [58B]
[N] *viTT* [61C]
cup [N] *taŞS* [58A]
cupboard [N] *kaPP* [58C]
cur [N] *roju* [13A]
curable [A] *ravitav* [231A]
curd cake [N] *korP* [58D]
curd cheese [N] *sõİr* [49B]
cure meat [Vt] *suitsutama* [349F]
curious [A] *uudishimuliK* [62]
curl [N] *kihar* [231A]
[N] *loKK* [58C]
curl [Vt] *kähardama* [349F]
curl [Vi] *käharduma* [349H]
curl (hair) [Vt] *loKKima* [291D]
curly [A] *kähar* [231A]
currant [N] *sõstar* [171B]
currency [N] *valuuta* [152]
current [N] *vOOl* [61A]

current in water [N] *hOOvus* [260B]
curse [N] *nEEdus* [260B]
curse [Vt] *nEEdma* [315]
[Vt] *sajatama* [349F]
[Vt] *siUnama* [327B]
curtain [N] *kardin* [231A]
curtsey [N] *kniKs* [61B]
[N] *niKs* [61B]
[N] *reveranSS* [58G]
curve [N] *kuRv* [58B]
curve [Vi] *kOOlduma* [349H]
[Vi] *kõverduma* [349H]
curve [Vt] *koolutama* [349F]
[Vt] *kõverdama* [349F]
cuss [Vt] *kiruma* [269]
custom [N] *komme* [209]
[N] *tava* [13A]
customs [N] *toĻL* [58A]
customs (social) [N] *koMbestiK* [62]
cut [Vt] *lõiKama* [327F]
cut into pieces [Vt] *tükeldama* [349F]
cutlet [N] *šniTsel* [240A]
cutting [A] *lõiKav* [231A]
cybernetics [N] *küberneetika* [227A]
cycle [N] *tsüKKel* [240B]
cyclone [N] *tsüKlon* [229A]
cynic [N] *küünik* [234A]
cynical [A] *küüniline* [257D]
cynicism [N] *küniSm* [58B]
cypress [N] *küpreŞS* [58A]
czar [N] *tsAAr* [58A]
Czech [N] *tšeHH* [58A]

D

dab [Vt] *tupsutama* [349F]
dace [N] *teİb* [114]
daddy [N] *papa* [152]
dahlia [N] *joRjen* [229A]
daily [A] *päevane* [251]
dairy [N] *meiereİ* [1]
daisy [N] *karikakar* [171C]
dam [N] *paİs* [61B]
[N] *taMM* [58A]
dam up [Vt] *paisutama* [349F]
damage [N] *kahi* [74]
damp [A] *rõSke* [227B]
damper [N] *sİİber* [240A]
dampness [N] *rõSkus* [260B]
dance [N] *tanTs* [61B]
dance [Vi] *taņTsima* [291C]

dancer [N] *taņTsija* [227A]
dandle [Vt] *hüpitama* [349F]
dandruff [N] *kÕÕm* [49A]
dandy [N] *keİgar* [229A]
dandyish [A] *keİgarliK* [62]
Dane [N] *tAAnlane* [257C]
danger [N] *oHt* [124B]
dangerous [A] *kardetav* [231A]
[A] *oHtliK* [62]
dangle [Vi] *riPnema* [349D]
dangle [Vt] *kõlgutama* [349F]
dare [Vt] *juLgema* [350]
daring [A] *uļjas* [159B]
daring [N] *uĻjus* [260B]
dark [A] *pime* [235]
dark (of colour) [A] *tume* [235]

dark-room [N] *pimik* [234A]
darken [Vi] *pimenema* [349D]
darken [Vt] *pimendama* [349F]
darken colour [Vi] *tumenema* [349D]
darkening [N] *pimendus* [260A]
darkness [N] *pimedus* [260A]
darling [A] *kaĻLim* [231A]
[N] *kullake(ne)* [257G]
darn [Vt] *nõEluma* [291C]
dash [Vi] *sööStma* [297A]
data [N] *aNdmed (pl)* [221]
[N] *teaTmed (pl)* [179D]
date fruit [N] *daTTel* [240B]
daughter [N] *tütar* [176]
daughter-in-law [N] *minia* [227A]
dauntless [A] *koHkumatu* [227A]

dawdle [Vi] *aEglema* [335]
dawn [N] *koidik* [234A]
dawn [N] *koiT* [61E]
dawn [Vi] *koiTma* [297C]
day [N] *päEv* [53B]
day-dream [N] *unelm* [231A]
day-dream [Vt] *unistama* [349F]
daybreak [N] *agu* [31]
daze [Vt] *uimastama* [349F]
dazed [A] *uimane* [251]
dazzling [A] *kirev* [231A]
dead end [N] *tupik* [234A]
dead person [N] *suRnu* [227B]
deadlock [N] *ummik* [234A]
deadly [A] *suRmav* [231A]
deaf [A] *kurT* [58E]
deal in (traffic) [Vi] *hangeldama* [349F]
[Vi] *äritsema* [349E]
deal with [Vt] *käsitlema* [351]
dealer (trafficker) [N] *äritseja* [227A]
dealing (traffic) [N] *hangeldamine* [257E]
dean [N] *dekAAn* [58A]
dean's office [N] *dekanaaT* [58E]
dear [A] *kaļlis* [164A]
death [N] *suRm* [53B]
debatable [A] *vaieldav* [231A]
debit [N] *deebet* [229A]
debris [N] *riise* [179A]
debt [N] *võLg* [95A]
debtor [N] *võLglane* [257C]
[N] *võLgniK* [62]
debut [Vi] *debütEErima* [291B]
debut [N] *debüüT* [58E]
decadent [N] *dekadeņT* [58E]
decay [Vi] *kõdunema* [349D]
deceased [N] *kadunu* [227A]
deceitful [A] *peţisliK* [62]
[A] *peTTurliK* [62]
[A] *valeliK* [62]
deceive [Vt] *peTma* [297B]
December [N] *detseMber* [240A]
decent [A] *süņnis* [199]
deception [N] *peTTus* [260B]
deceptive [A] *peTliK* [62]
decide [Vt] *otsustama* [349F]
decipher [Vt] *dešifrEErima* [291B]
decision [N] *otsus* [253]
decisive [A] *mÄÄrav* [231A]
[A] *otsustav* [231A]
[A] *pÖÖrdeline* [257D]
deck (ship) [N] *teKK* [58C]
declaration [N] *avaldus* [260A]
declaration [N] *deklaratsiOOn* [58A]
declare [Vt] *deklarEErima* [291B]
decline (grammar) [Vt] *kÄÄnduma* [349H]
decline [N] *laNgus* [260B]
décolletage [N] *dekoltEE* [2]
decorate [Vt] *dekorEErima* [291B]
decorative [A] *dekoratİİvne* [247]
decoy [Vt] *peibutama* [349F]
decrease [Vi] *alanema* [349D]
decree [N] *dekreeT* [58E]
[N] *seAdlus* [260B]
dedicate [Vt] *pühendama* [349F]
dedication [N] *pühendus* [260A]
deed [N] *tegu* [31]
deed (document) [N] *aKt* [58B]
deep [A] *sügav* [231A]
deepen [Vt] *süvendama* [349F]
deer [N] *hiRv* [63B]
deer (diminutive) [N] *hirveke(ne)* [257G]
defect [N] *defeKt* [58B]
[N] *puue* [210A]
defective [A] *defektİİvne* [247]
[A] *vigane* [251]
defence (shelter) [N] *kaitse* [177B]
defence (device) [N] *kaitse* [179C]
defenceless [A] *kaiTsetu* [227A]
defend [Vt] *kaiTsema* [295]
[Vt] *kaiTsma* [295]
defender [N] *kaiTsja* [227B]
defiance [N] *troŢs* [58B]
defiant [A] *troŢsliK* [62]
deficiency [N] *vaEgus* [260B]
deficient [A] *puuduliK* [62]
defile [Vi] *defilEErima* [291B]
define [Vt] *definEErima* [291B]
[Vt] *määratlema* [351]
[Vt] *piiritlema* [351]
definition [N] *määratlus* [260A]
deform [Vt] *deformEErima* [291B]
defy [V] *troŢsima* [291C]
degenerate [N] *degeneraņT* [58E]
[N] *maNdunu* [227A]
degenerate [Vi] *maNduma* [349H]
degeneration [N] *maNdumine* [257E]
degrade oneself [Vi] *alanduma* [349H]
degree [N] *krAAḑ* [58A]
deign [V] *suvatsema* [349E]
delay [N] *viivitus* [260A]
delay [Vi] *viivitama* [349F]
delegate [N] *delegaaT* [58E]
delegation [N] *delegatsiOON* [58A]
delicacy [N] *delikateŞS* [58A]
delicacy [N] *hõrgutis* [260A]
delicate [A] *delikaaTne* [247]
delight [N] *nauding* [234A]
delirious (be) [Vi] *sonima* [269]
delirium [N] *sonimine* [257E]
demand [N] *nõUdmine* [257E]
demand [Vt] *nõUdma* [316A]
demanding [A] *nõUdliK* [62]
demilitarize [Vt] *demilitarisEErima* [291B]
demobilization [N] *demobilisatsiOOn* [58A]
demobilize [Vt] *demobilisEErima* [291B]
democracy [N] *demokraaTia* [227A]
democratic [A] *demokraaTliK* [62]
demon [N] *dEEmon* [229A]
[N] *pahareŢ* [58H]
[N] *sarvik* [234A]
demonstrate [Vt] *demonstrEErima* [291B]
demonstration [N] *demonstratsiOOn* [58A]
demonstrative [A] *demonstratİİvne* [247]
[A] *näiTav* [231A]
demonstrator [N] *demonstraņT* [58E]
demoralize [Vt] *demoralisEErima* [291B]
dense [A] *tihe* [235]
denser (become) [Vi] *tihenema* [349D]
denser (make) [Vt] *tihendama* [349F]
density [N] *tihedus* [260A]
denture [N] *protEEs* [58A]
deny [Vt] *eiTama* [349F]
deodorant [N] *desodoraņT* [58E]
depart [Vi] *laHkuma* [349G]
depart (exit) [Vi] *väĻjuma* [349G]
departed [N] *läinu* [186]
departed (dead) [N] *laHkunu* [227A]
department [N] *haru* [13A]
[N] *osakoNd* [106]
department (university) [N] *katEEder* [240A]
department (factory) [N] *tseHH* [58A]
departure [N] *minek* [234A]
depend on [Vi] *olenema* [349D]
[Vi] *sõlTuma* [349H]
dependent [A] *sõlTuv* [231A]
depict [Vt] *kujustama* [349F]
[Vt] *kujutama* [349F]
depiction [N] *kujustus* [260A]
deplete [Vt] *ammutama* [349F]
deport [Vt] *küüditama* [349F]
deposit in bank [N] *hoius* [253]
deposit in bank [Vt] *hoiustama* [349F]
deposited (be) [Vi] *ladestuma* [349H]
[Vi] *seŢTima* [291D]
depositor [N] *hoiustaja* [227A]
depot [N] *depOO* [1]

depress Vt *masendama* 349F
depressing A *masendav* 231A
depression N *masendus* 260A
depth N *sügavus* 260A
deputy N *deputaaT* 58E
derivation N *tuletamine* 257E
N *tuletus* 260A
derivative N *tuletis* 260A
derive Vi *pärinema* 349D
derive Vt *tuletama* 349F
describe Vt *kirjeldama* 349F
description N *kirjeldus* 260A
desert N *kõRb* 137 or 233B
desert Vi *desertEErima* 291B
deserter N *desertÖÖr* 58A
deserve Vt *päĻvima* 291C
Vt *vÄÄrima* 291A
design N *disaİn* 58B
designer N *disaİner* 229A
desirable A *soovitav* 231A
desire N *himu* 13A
despise Vt *põLgama* 348B
despot N *despooT* 58E
despotic A *despooTliK* 62
dessert N *desserT* 58E
destroy Vt *hävitama* 349F
destroyer N *hävitaja* 227A
destruction N *häving* 234A
N *hävitus* 260A
destructive A *hävitav* 231A
detached house N *eramu* 227A
detail N *detaİl* 58B
detailed A *detaİlne* 247
detective N *detektİİv* 58A
determine Vt *mÄÄrama* 327A
determining N *mÄÄramine* 257E
detest Vt *põlastama* 349F
develop film Vt *ilmutama* 349F
developer for film N *ilmuti* 225A
deviate Vi *häĻbima* 303
device N *seadis* 253
devil N *kurat* 230
devilish A *kuratliK* 62
devise Vt *nuputama* 349F
devote oneself Vi *aNduma* 349H
Vi *pühenduma* 349H
devotion N *aNdumus* 260A
devour Vt *õgima* 269
devout A *harras* 193
dew N *kaste* 177B
dewy A *kaStene* 257B
diabetic N *diabeetik* 234A

diagnosis N *diagnOOs* 58A
diagonal A *diagonAAlne* 247
diagram N *diagraMM* 58A
N *skEEm* 58A
dialect (major) N *murre* 215
dialect (minor) N *murrak* 234A
dialectal A *muRdeline* 257D
dialogue N *dialOOg* 58A
diametric(al) A *diametrAAlne* 247
diamond N *briljanT* 58E
N *tEEmaņT* 58E
diamonds (cards) N *ruutu* 152
diaper N *mähe* 224
diaphragm N *diafragma* 152
diarrhoea (have) V *pasandama* 349F
diary N *päevik* 234A
dice N *täring* 234A
dictate Vt *diktEErima* 291B
dictation N *diktaaT* 58E
dictator N *diktaaTor* 229A
dictatorial A *diktaaTorliK* 62
dictatorship N *diktatUUr* 58A
diction N *diktsiOOn* 58A
didactic A *didaktiline* 257D
die Vi *surema* 271
die (metal) N *valu* 13A
diesel N *dİİsel* 240A
diet N *dieeT* 58E
differ Vi *erinema* 349D
difference N *erinevus* 260A
N *vahe* 153
different A *erinev* 231A
difficult A *raSke* 227B
difficult (become) Vi *raskenema* 349D
difficulty N *kiţsikus* 260A
N *raSkus* 260B
diffuse A *laialivaLguv* 231A
dig Vt *kaEvama* 327B
digestible A *seeditav* 231A
digestion N *seede* 177A
N *sEEdimine* 257E
dignified A *esindusliK* 62
A *väärikas* 243A
dignify Vt *vääristama* 349F
dignity N *väärikus* 260A
dilettante N *diletaņT* 58E
dilettante A *diletaņTliK* 62
diligence N *pÜÜdliKKus* 260B
N *tööKus* 260B
N *usinus* 260A
N *virKus* 260B
diligent A *hoolas* 165A

diligent A *pÜÜdliK* 62
diligent A *usin* 231A
A *virK* 49F
dill N *tiĻL* 58A
dilute Vt *lahjendama* 349F
dim A *tuHm* 58B
dim Vt *tuhmistama* 349F
dim (become) Vi *tuhmistuma* 349H
Vi *tuHmuma* 349G
dim-witted A *taiPamatu* 227A
dimension N *mõõde* 179D
diminish Vi *kahanema* 349D
diminish Vt *kahandama* 349F
diminution N *kahandus* 260A
dimple N *lohuke(ne)* 257G
din N *melu* 13A
dine Vi *eine(s)tama* 349F
dine (noon) Vi *lõunastama* 349F
dine (noon) Vt *lõunatama* 349F
diphtheria N *diftEEria* 227A
diphthong N *diftoNg* 58B
diploma N *diPlom* 229A
diplomacy N *diplomaaTia* 227A
diplomat N *diplomaaT* 58E
diplomatic A *diplomaatiline* 257D
dipper N *kopsik* 234A
direct Vt *juhatama* 349F
direct Vt *sUUnama* 327A
direction N *sUUnd* 104A
directive N *direktİİv* 58A
director N *direKtor* 229A
director (film) N *režissÖÖr* 58A
directorate N *direktsiOOn* 58A
dirt N *muStus* 260B
dirty A *muSt* 53B
A *roPP* 61C
dirty (get) Vi *mÄÄrduma* 349H
dirty trick N *sigadus* 260A
disappointed (be) Vi *peTTuma* 349H
disappointment N *peTTumus* 260A
disarm Vt *desarmEErima* 291B
disarmament N *desarmEErimine* 257E
disastrous A *hukatusliK* 62
disc harrow N *randAAl* 58A
disciple N *jüNger* 240A
discipline N *distsiplİİn* 58A
discipline Vt *distsiplinEErima* 291B
discourage Vt *heidutama* 349F
discover Vt *avastama* 349F
discoverer N *avastaja* 227A
discovery N *avastus* 260A
discreet A *diskreeTne* 247

discretion [N] *diskreeTsus* [260B]
discuss [Vt] *arutama* [349F]
discussion [N] *arutelu* [13A]
[N] *arutlus* [260A]
discussion [N] *diskussiOOn* [58A]
disdain [N] *põlastus* [260A]
disdainful [A] *põlastav* [231A]
disease [N] *haİgus* [260B]
[N] *tõbi* [40]
disembark [Vi] *mAAbuma* [349G]
disembarkation [N] *mAAbumine* [257E]
disembogue [Vi] *sUUbuma* [349G]
disgrace [Vt] *blamEErima* [291B]
disguise [Vt] *maskEErima* [291B]
disgust [N] *tülgastus* [260A]
disgusting [A] *jäle* [235]
dish [N] *nõU* [12]
dishes (set) [N] *servİis* [58A]
dishonourable [A] *auTu* [227B]
disinfect [Vt] *desinfitsEErima* [291B]
disinfection [N] *desinfektsiOOn* [58A]
disjointed [A] *seOsetu* [227A]
disk [N] *ketas* [159C]
dislocate [Vt] *nihestama* [349F]
dislocation [N] *nihestus* [260A]
dismay [N] *jahmatus* [260A]
dismay [Vt] *jahmatama* [349F]
dismayed (be) [Vi] *jaHmuma* [349G]
dismiss (fire) [Vt] *tagandama* [349F]
dismiss from office [Vt] *vallandama* [349F]
dismissal [N] *vallandus* [260A]
disorder [N] *korratus* [260A]
disorderly [A] *korratu* [227A]
disown [Vt] *saLgama* [348B]
dispatch [Vt] *läkitama* [349F]
dispatch office [N] *ekspeditsiOOn* [58A]
dispatcher [N] *dispeTšer* [229A]
dispensary [N] *ambulaņTs* [58B]
[N] *ambulatOOrium* [246]
[N] *dispaNser* [229A]
dispensary [A] *ambulatOOrne* [247]
disperse [Vi] *vaLguma* [349G]
display-case [N] *vitrİin* [58A]
disposition [N] *lOOmus* [260B]
dissect [Vt] *laHkama* [348C]
disseminate [Vt] *levitama* [349F]
disseminated (be) [Vi] *levima* [269]
dissertation [N] *dissertatsiOOn* [58A]
dissident [N] *dissidenT* [58E]
dissipate [Vi] *hajuma* [269]
dissipate [Vt] *hajutama* [349F]
dissolve [Vi] *lahustuma* [349H]
dissolve [Vt] *lahustama* [349F]
distance [N] *kaUgus* [260B]
distant [A] *kaUge* [227B]
distil [Vt] *destillEErima* [291B]
distinguish [Vt] *eristama* [349F]
distort [Vt] *moonutama* [349F]
distortion [N] *moonutus* [260A]
distribute [Vt] *jaoTama* [349F]
distribution [N] *jaoTus* [260B]
[N] *levik* [234A]
district [N] *jaOskoNd* [106]
[N] *pİİrkoNd* [106]
[N] *rajOOn* [58A]
district [A] *pİİrkoNdliK* [62]
disturb [Vt] *häİrima* [291C]
[Vt] *tülitama* [349F]
disturbance [N] *häire* [177B]
ditch [N] *krAAv* [58A]
divan [N] *dİİvan* [229A]
dive [Vi] *sukelduma* [349H]
diver [N] *akvalangiSt* [58B]
[N] *tuuKer* [240A]
diversification [N] *miTmekesisus* [260A]
diversify [Vt] *miTmekesistama* [349F]
divide [Vt] *jagama* [269]
divided (be) [Vi] *jagunema* [349D]
divine [A] *jumaliK* [62]
diving [N] *sukeldus* [260A]
divisible [A] *jagatav* [231A]
divisible (be) [Vi] *jaguma* [269]
division [N] *jagamine* [257E]
division (military) [N] *divİis* [58A]
divorce [N] *lahutus* [260A]
divorce [Vt] *lahutama* [349F]
dizziness [N] *pööritus* [260A]
dizzying [A] *peAdpööritav* [231A]
do [Vt] *tegema* [290]
dock [N] *doKK* [58C]
dock (rocket) [Vi] *põKKuma* [349G]
dock (rocket) [Vt] *põKKama* [327C]
doctor [N] *arSt* [58B]
[N] *doKtor* [229A]
doctoral candidate [N] *doktoranT* [58E]
document [N] *dokumeņT* [58E]
document (historical) [N] *ürik* [234A]
doddering fool [N] *tudi* [13C]
dog [N] *koEr* [54]
dogmatic [A] *dogmaatiline* [257D]
doing [N] *tegemine* [257E]
doll [N] *nuKK* [61C]
dollar [N] *doLLar* [229A]
dolomite [N] *dolomiiT* [58E]
dolphin [N] *delfİin* [58A]
dolt [N] *tola* [13A]
doltish [A] *juHm* [58B]
dome [N] *kuPPel* [240B]
domesticate [Vt] *kodustama* [349F]
donate [Vt] *annetama* [349F]
donation [N] *annetus* [260A]
done for pay [A] *tasuline* [257D]
donkey [N] *EEsel* [240A]
donor [N] *annetaja* [227A]
[N] *dOOnor* [229A]
door [N] *uKs* [84]
doorkeeper [N] *portjEE* [2]
[N] *šveiTser* [229A]
doorsill [N] *lävi* [18]
dose [N] *annus* [253]
[N] *dOOs* [58A]
double [N] *teisik* [234A]
double chin [N] *loŢT* [58C]
doubt [N] *kaHtlus* [260B]
doubt [Vi] *ebalema* [349A]
doubt [Vt] *kaHtlema* [331B]
dough [N] *taİgen* [241A]
[N] *tainas* [159B]
downpour [N] *valang* [234A]
doze [Vi] *tuKKuma* [291D]
dozen [N] *tosin* [231A]
draft [N] *tõMbus* [260B]
draft copy [N] *mustand* [229A]
drafting [N] *joonestamine* [257E]
draftsperson [N] *joonestaja* [227A]
drag [Vi] *lohisema* [349C]
drag [Vt] *lohistama* [349F]
dragon [N] *lohe* [153]
dragon-fly [N] *kİİl* [58A]
drain land [Vt] *kuivendama* [349F]
drain with ditches [Vt] *kraavitama* [349F]
drainage [N] *drenAAž* [58A]
drama [N] *draama* [152]
dramatic [A] *dramaatiline* [257D]
dramatization [N] *dramatiseering* [234A]
dramatize [Vt] *dramatisEErima* [291B]
draw [N] *viiK* [58F]
draw [Vt] *viNNama* [327A]
draw (draft) [Vt] *joonestama* [349F]
draw (in game) [Vt] *viigistama* [349F]
draw (picture) [Vt] *joonistama* [349F]
draw (lines) [Vt] *kriipsutama* [349F]
drawer [N] *saHtel* [240A]
drawer (person) [N] *joonistaja* [227A]
drawing [N] *joonis* [253]
drawing [N] *joonistus* [260A]

drawing (action) [N] *joonistamine* [257E]
drawn out (be) [Vi] *venima* [269]
dreadful [A] *kohutav* [231A]
dream (wish) [N] *unistus* [260A]
dreamer [N] *unistaja* [227A]
dress [N] *kleiT* [58E]
dress [Vt] *riietama* [349F]
[Vt] *rõivastama* [349F]
dress oneself [Vi] *riietuma* [349H]
[Vi] *rõivastuma* [349H]
drift [Vi] *trİivima* [291A]
drift (snow) [Vi] *tuiSkama* [348C]
drill [N] *driĻL* [58A]
[N] *pUUr* [58A]
drill [Vt] *driĻLima* [291A]
[Vt] *pUUrima* [291A]
drink [N] *jooK* [58F]
drink [Vt] *jOOma* [267]
drinkable [A] *jOOdav* [231A]
drinking party [N] *jooming* [234A]
drip [Vt] *tilgutama* [349F]
drip-dry [Vi] *nõRguma* [349G]
drive [Vt] *ajama* [270]
drizzle [Vi] *tibama* [269]
[Vi] *tibutama* [349F]
drone [N] *sumin* [231A]
drone [Vi] *sumisema* [349C]
droning [N] *hUUg* [108]
droop [Vi] *lotendama* [349F]
drop [N] *tilK* [49F]
drop [Vt] *piLLama* [327A]
drop out [Vi] *eksmatrikulEEruma* [349G]
droplet [N] *piiSk* [95B]
droplet [N] *tiba* [13B]
droppings (animal) [N] *pabul* [231A]
drought [N] *põUd* [88A]
droughty [A] *põuane* [251]
drown [Vi] *uPPuma* [291D]
drown [Vt] *uputama* [349F]
drowning person [N] *uPPuja* [227A]
drug addict [N] *narkomAAn* [58A]
druggist [N] *aPteeKer* [240A]
drugstore [N] *aPteeK* [58F]
drum [N] *truMM* [58A]
drum [Vi] *trummeldama* [349F]
drumlin [N] *vOOr* [82]
drunk [N] *jOObnu* [227B]
[N] *jOObunu* [227A]
drunk (become) [Vi] *jOObuma* [349G]
drunkard [N] *jooḑik* [234A]
[N] *jOOmar* [229A]
dry [A] *kuİv* [53B]
[A] *tahe* [235]
dry [Vi] *kuİvama* [291C]
dry [Vt] *kuivatama* [349F]
dry (become) [Vi] *tahenema* [349D]
dry up [Vi] *kuivenema* [349D]
dryness [N] *kuİvus* [260B]
dub (film) [Vt] *dublEErima* [291B]
dubious [A] *kaHtlane* [257C]
duchess [N] *hertsoginna* [152]
duck [N] *parT* [58E]
duckweed [N] *lemmel* [175]
duel [N] *dueĻL* [58A]
duet [N] *dueȚT* [58C]
dug-out [N] *blindAAž* [58A]
duke [N] *hertsog* [229A]
dumb [A] *tobe* [235]
dumper [N] *kaLLur* [229A]
dumpling [N] *klimP* [58D]
dunce [N] *tobu* [13B]
dune [N] *luide* [177E]
dupe [N] *toHman* [229A]
duplicate [Vt] *paļjundama* [349F]
durability [N] *keStvus* [260B]
durable [A] *keStev* [241A]
duration [N] *keStus* [260B]
[N] *välde* [177E]
[N] *välTus* [260B]
dusk [N] *hämariK* [62]
[N] *videviK* [62]
dusky [A] *hämar* [231A]
dusky (become) [Vi] *hämarduma* [349H]
dust [N] *toLm* [61B]
dust over [Vt] *tolmutama* [349F]
dusty [A] *tolmune* [251]
dusty (be) [Vi] *toLmama* [327B]
duty [N] *kohus* [253]
dwarf [N] *kääbus* [253]
dwelling [N] *elamu* [227A]
dyer [N] *väRval* [229A]
dying person [N] *surija* [227A]
dynamic [A] *dünaamiline* [257D]
dynamics [N] *dünaamika* [227A]
dynamite [N] *dünamiiT* [58E]
dysentery [N] *düsentEEria* [227A]

E

eager [A] *agar* [231A]
eagerness [N] *agarus* [260A]
eagle [N] *kotkas* [159B]
ear [N] *kõRv* [49B]
ear-splitting [A] *kõRvulukustav* [231A]
earlier [A] *varem* [231A]
early [A] *varajane* [257A]
[A] *varane* [251]
earth [Vt] *muLdama* [342]
earthly [A] *maİne* [252]
earthly remains [N] *põRm* [61B]
east [N] *ida* [13C]
easy [A] *hõlbus* [168B]
[A] *hõlPus* [250A]
[A] *keRge* [227B]
eat [Vt] *sÖÖma* [268]
eau-de-Cologne [N] *odekoloŅN* [58A]
eaves [N] *räästas* [159B]
eavesdrop [V] *kuulatama* [349F]
ebb [N] *mÕÕn* [49A]
ebb [Vi] *mÕÕnama* [327A]
eccentric [N] *veİdriK* [62]
eccentricity [N] *veİdrus* [260B]
ecclesiastical [A] *kirikliK* [62]
[A] *vaimuliK* [62]
echo [N] *kaja* [13A]
eclipse [N] *varjutus* [260A]
ecological [A] *ökoloogiline* [257D]
ecologist [N] *ökolOOg* [58A]
ecology [N] *ökolOOgia* [227A]
economic [A] *majandusliK* [62]
economical [A] *sääStliK* [62]
economics [N] *majandus* [260A]
[N] *ökonoomika* [227A]
economist [N] *ökonomiSt* [58B]
economy [N] *ökonOOmia* [227A]
economy (result) [N] *ökonOOmsus* [260B]
eddy [N] *keeris* [253]
edge [N] *seRv* [53B]
[N] *vEEr* [82]
[N] *ÄÄr* [82]
edge [Vt] *ääristama* [349F]
edging [N] *ääris* [253]
edible [A] *sÖÖdav* [231A]
edifice [N] *hoone* [177A]
edit [Vt] *toimetama* [349F]
edition [N] *redaktsiOOn* [58A]
editor [N] *toimetaja* [227A]

editorial office [N] *toimetus* [260A]
educate [Vt] *harima* [269]
education [N] *haridus* [260A]
educational [A] *haridusliK* [62]
[A] *kasvatusliK* [62]
educator [N] *kasvataja* [227A]
eel [N] *angerjas* [243A]
effect [N] *efeKt* [58B]
[N] *toime* [177B]
effective [A] *efektİİvne* [247]
[A] *mõjuv* [231A]
[A] *tagajärjekas* [243A]
efficiency [N] *efektİİvsus* [260B]
efficient [A] *tõhus* [231A]
egg [N] *muna* [16]
egoism [N] *egoiSm* [58B]
egoist [N] *egoiSt* [58B]
egoistic(al) [A] *egoiStliK* [62]
Egyptian [N] *egiPtlane* [257C]
eight [N] *kaheksa* [227A]
eighth [N] *kaheksandiK* [62]
eighth [A] *kaheksas* [237B]
either of two [N] *kuMbki* [102]
either or [N] *eMb-kuMb* [102]
elaborate [Vt] *täiustama* [349F]
elaboration [N] *täiustus* [260A]
elastic [A] *elaStne* [247]
[A] *venitatav* [231A]
elastic (be) [Vi] *veTruma* [349G]
elasticity [N] *elaStsus* [260B]
[N] *veTruvus* [260A]
elated [A] *ülev* [231A]
elbow [N] *küünar* [171A]
elbow one's way [Vi] *trügima* [269]
elderly [A] *eaKas* [243B]
[A] *vanaldane* [257A]
elections [N] *valimine* [257E]
electorate [N] *valijaskoNd* [106]
electrician [N] *elektrik* [234A]
electricity [N] *eleKter* [240A]
electrify [Vt] *elektrifitsEErima* [291B]
electron [N] *elektron* [245]
electronics [N] *elektroonika* [227A]
elegance [N] *eleganTsus* [260B]
[N] *liHv* [58B]
elegant [A] *eleganTne* [247]
element [N] *elemeņT* [58E]
elemental [A] *stiihiline* [257D]
elementary [A] *elementAArne* [247]
elephant [N] *elevaņT* [58E]
elevate [Vt] *kõrgendama* [349F]
elevated (become) [Vi] *kõrgenema* [349D]

elevator [N] *liFt* [58A]
elf [N] *päkapiKK* [61C]
elite [N] *eliiT* [58E]
elite [N] *ülikkoNd* [106]
elixir [N] *eliksİİr* [58A]
elk [N] *põder* [78B]
elliptical [A] *elliptiline* [257D]
elm [N] *jalakas* [243A]
embarrassing [A] *pİİnliK* [62]
embarrassment [N] *pİİnliKKus* [260B]
embassy [N] *saaTkoNd* [106]
embitter [Vt] *kibestama* [349F]
embittered (become) [Vi] *kibestuma* [349H]
emblem [N] *emblEEm* [58A]
embodied (be) [Vi] *kehastuma* [349H]
embodiment [N] *kehastus* [260A]
embody [Vt] *kehastama* [349F]
embossment [N] *reljeeF* [58A]
embrace [N] *eMbus* [260B]
[N] *kaisutus* [260A]
embrace [Vt] *eMbama* [340]
[Vt] *kaisutama* [349F]
embroider [Vt] *tiKKima* [291D]
embroidery [N] *tikand* [229A]
embryo [N] *loode* [177E]
emerald [N] *smaraGd* [58B]
emigrant [N] *emigraņT* [58E]
emotional [A] *emotsionAAlne* [247]
[A] *tuNdeline* [257D]
emperor [N] *keİser* [240A]
emphasis (italics) [N] *sõrendus* [260A]
emphasize [Vt] *rõhutama* [349F]
emphasize (italicize) [Vt] *sõrendama* [349F]
empire [N] *impEErium* [246]
employ [N] *teenistus* [260A]
employ [Vt] *palKama* [327F]
employee [N] *palgaline* [257D]
[N] *teenistuja* [227A]
[N] *tööTaja* [227A]
emptiness [N] *tüHjus* [260B]
empty [A] *tühi* [71A]
empty [Vi] *tühjenema* [349D]
empty [Vt] *tühjendama* [349F]
enable [Vt] *võimaldama* [349F]
enact [Vt] *kehtestama* [349F]
enamel [N] *emaİl* [58B]
enamel [Vt] *emaİlima* [291C]
enclose [Vt] *suLgema* [313A]
enclosed (be) [Vi] *suLguma* [349G]
enclosure [N] *koPPel* [240B]
[N] *tarandiK* [62]
encounter [N] *koHtamine* [257E]

encourage [Vt] *ergutama* [349F]
[Vt] *julgustama* [349F]
encouragement [N] *ergutus* [260A]
encouragement [N] *julgustus* [260A]
encyclopedia [N] *entsüklopEEdia* [227A]
end [N] *lõPP* [61C]
end [Vi] *lõPma* [299]
[Vi] *lõPPema* [291D]
endanger [Vt] *ohustama* [349F]
endless [A] *lõPmatu* [227A]
[A] *lõputu* [227A]
endowment (talent) [N] *anne* [214]
endure [Vi] *püsima* [269]
enemy [N] *vaEnlane* [257C]
energetic [A] *energeetiline* [257D]
energetics [N] *energeetika* [227A]
energy [N] *eneRgia* [227A]
engage in [Vi] *tegelema* [325]
engaged (become) [Vi] *kiHluma* [349G]
engagement (action) [N] *kihlad (pl)* [49B]
engagement (result) [N] *kiHlus* [260B]
engineer [N] *insener* [245]
English [N] *iNglane* [257C]
engrave [Vt] *gravEErima* [291B]
engraving [N] *gravÜÜr* [58A]
enjoy [Vt] *nauTima* [291F]
enjoy oneself [Vi] *lõbutsema* [349E]
enjoyment [N] *mõnu* [13A]
enlarge [Vt] *suurendama* [349F]
enlarged (become) [Vi] *suurenema* [349D]
enlargement [N] *suurendus* [260A]
enlighten [Vt] *valgustama* [349F]
enlightener [N] *valgustaja* [227A]
enlist [Vt] *väRbama* [339B]
enmity [N] *vaEn* [61B]
ennoble [Vt] *õilistama* [349F]
enormous [A] *tohutu* [227A]
enraged [A] *raevukas* [243A]
enrich [Vt] *rikastama* [349F]
ensemble [N] *ansaMbel* [240A]
enslave [Vt] *orjastama* [349F]
ensue [Vi] *jäRgnema* [349D]
enter [Vi] *sisenema* [349D]
enterprise [N] *käiTis* [260B]
entertain [Vt] *lõbustama* [349F]
entertain guest [Vt] *koştitama* [349F]
[Vt] *võõrustama* [349F]
entertainment [N] *lõbustus* [260A]
enthuse [Vt] *vaimustama* [349F]
enthused (become) [Vi] *vaimustuma* [349H]
enthusiasm [N] *entusiaSm* [58B]
[N] *iNd* [129]

enthusiasm [N] *vaimustus* [260A]
enthusiast [N] *entusiaSt* [58B]
enthusiastic [A] *entusiaStliK* [62]
entice [Vt] *ahvatlema* [351]
enticing [A] *ahvatlev* [231A]
entrance-hall [N] *esik* [234A]
entrepreneur [N] *antreprenÖÖr* [58A]
enumerate [Vt] *loEndama* [349F]
[Vt] *loeTlema* [351]
enumeration [N] *loEnd* [229B]
[N] *loEndus* [260B]
[N] *loeTelu* [13A]
envelope [N] *üMbriK* [62]
[N] *ümbrik* [234A]
envious [A] *kade* [235]
environment [N] *keSkkoNd* [106]
envy [N] *kadedus* [260A]
envy [Vt] *kadestama* [349F]
epic [N] *eePos* [260B]
epic [A] *eepiline* [257D]
epidemic [N] *epidEEmia* [227A]
[N] *taUd* [58B]
epidemic [A] *epideemiline* [257D]
epileptic [N] *epileptik* [234A]
epilogue [N] *epilOOg* [58A]
episode [N] *episOOd* [58A]
epithet [N] *epiteeT* [58E]
epoch [N] *ajastu* [227A]
[N] *epoHH* [58A]
equal [A] *võRdne* [247]
equal (be) [Vi] *võRduma* [349H]
equality [N] *võRdsus* [260B]
equalize [Vt] *võrdsustama* [349F]
equation [N] *võrrand* [229A]
equator [N] *ekvaaTor* [229A]
equatorial [A] *ekvatoriAAlne* [247]
equipment [N] *aparatUUr* [58A]
equivalent [N] *vaste* [177B]
erect [Vt] *püştitama* [349F]
erode [Vt] *uuristama* [349F]
err [Vi] *vääratama* [349F]
erroneous [A] *eKsliK* [62]
error [N] *eksitus* [260A]
[N] *vääratus* [260A]
escalator [N] *eskalaaTor* [229A]
escalope [N] *eskaloPP* [58C]
escape [N] *pÄÄs* [61A]
escape [Vi] *põgenema* [349D]
[Vi] *pÄÄsema* [291A]
escaping [N] *põgenemine* [257E]
[N] *pÄÄsemine* [257E]
Eskimo [N] *eskimo* [227A]
espionage [N] *luure* [177A]
[N] *spionAAž* [58A]
essay [N] *essEE* [2]
essay [N] *kirjand* [229A]
essayistic [A] *publitsiStliK* [62]
essayistics [N] *publitsistika* [227A]
essence [N] *olemus* [260A]
essential [A] *oluline* [257D]
establish [Vt] *rajama* [269]
estate [N] *mõİs* [231B]
Estonian [N] *eeStlane* [257C]
Estonian nationalism [N] *eeStlus* [260B]
Estonianize [Vi] *eestistuma* [349H]
Estonianize [Vt] *eestistama* [349F]
Estophile [N] *estofİİl* [58A]
estrange [Vt] *võõrutama* [349F]
estranged (become) [Vi] *vÕÕrduma* [349H]
etch [Vt] *söövitama* [349F]
etching [N] *söövitus* [260A]
eternal [A] *igavene* [257A]
eternity [N] *igaviK* [62]
ether [N] *eeTer* [240A]
ethical [A] *eetiline* [257D]
ethics [N] *eetika* [227A]
ethnographer [N] *etnograaF* [58A]
ethnography [N] *etnograaFia* [227A]
eunuch [N] *kastraaT* [58E]
European [N] *eurooPlane* [257C]
evacuate [Vt] *evakuEErima* [291B]
evacuation [N] *evakuatsiOOn* [58A]
evade [Vi] *põiKlema* [326F]
evaluation [N] *hinnang* [234A]
evangelization [N] *evangelisatsiOOn* [58A]
evaporate [Vi] *aUruma* [349G]
evasive [A] *põiKlev* [231A]
even [A] *tasane* [251]
even out [Vt] *ühtlustama* [349F]
evening [N] *õHtu* [227B]
evening [A] *õHtune* [257B]
event [N] *süNdmus* [260B]
[N] *üritus* [260A]
evergreen [N] *igihali* [69A]
every [A] *iga* [13D]
evident [A] *iLmne* [247]
evident [Vi] *iLmnema* [349D]
evident (become) [Vi] *seLguma* [349G]
evil [N] *kuRjus* [260B]
[N] *pahe* [153]
evolution [N] *areng* [234A]
[N] *evolutsiOOn* [58A]
evolve [Vi] *arenema* [349D]
evolve [Vt] *arendama* [349F]
ewe [N] *uTT* [63C]
ex libris [N] *eksliibris* [253]
exaggerate [Vt] *liialdama* [349F]
exaggeration [N] *liialdus* [260A]
examination [N] *eKsam* [229A]
examine [Vt] *eksaminEErima* [291B]
examiner [N] *eksaminaaTor* [229A]
example [N] *näide* [177E]
excavator [N] *ekskavaaTor* [229A]
exception [N] *erand* [229A]
excess [N] *lİİg* [94B]
excessive [A] *lİİgne* [247]
exchange [N] *vahetus* [260A]
exchange [Vt] *vahetama* [349F]
exchange rate [N] *kurSS* [58G]
exchanged (become) [Vi] *vahetuma* [349H]
exchanging [N] *vahetamine* [257E]
excite [Vt] *erutama* [349F]
excited (become) [Vi] *erutuma* [349H]
excitement [N] *elevus* [260A]
[N] *erutus* [260A]
[N] *põnevus* [260A]
[N] *äHm* [58B]
exciting [A] *põnev* [231A]
exclamation [N] *hÜÜd* [123A]
exclude [Vt] *välistama* [349F]
exclusion [N] *välistus* [260A]
excrement [N] *ekskremeņT* [58E]
excursion [N] *ekskursiOOn* [58A]
excursionist [N] *ekskursaņT* [58E]
excusable [A] *vabandatav* [231A]
execute (kill) [Vt] *huKKama* [327C]
[Vt] *suRmama* [327B]
execute (perform) [Vt] *sooritama* [349F]
execution [N] *huKKamine* [257E]
executioner [N] *timukas* [243A]
exemplary [A] *EEskujuliK* [62]
exercise [N] *harjutus* [260A]
exercise book [N] *vihik* [234A]
exertion [N] *pingutus* [260A]
exhaust [Vt] *ammendama* [349F]
exhaustive [A] *ammendav* [231A]
exhibit [N] *eksponaaT* [58E]
exhibit [Vt] *eksponEErima* [291B]
exhibition [N] *näiTus* [260B]
exile [N] *pagulane* [257C]
exile (state) [N] *pagulus* [260A]
exist [Vi] *eksistEErima* [291B]
exotic [A] *eksootiline* [257D]
expand [Vi] *paİsuma* [349G]
expanse [N] *avarus* [260A]
expansion [N] *ekspansiOOn* [58A]

expansion [N] *paĺsumine* [257E]
expectation [N] *ooTus* [260B]
expedient [A] *oTstaRbekas* [243A]
expel (school) [Vt] *eksmatrikulEErima* [291B]
expenditure [N] *kulutus* [260A]
expense [N] *kulu* [13A]
expensive (become) [Vi] *kaļlinema* [349D]
experience [N] *elamus* [260A]
[N] *kogemus* [260A]
[N] *vilumus* [260A]
experience [Vt] *kogema* [269]
experienced (become) [Vi] *viluma* [269]
experiment [N] *eksperimeņT* [58E]
experiment [Vt] *katsetama* [349F]
experimental [A] *eksperimentAAlne* [247]
[A] *kaTseline* [257D]
experimenting [N] *katsetus* [260A]
expert [N] *eKsperT* [58E]
explain [Vt] *seletama* [349F]
[Vt] *seļgitama* [349F]
explanation [N] *seletus* [260A]
[N] *seļgitus* [260A]
explode [Vi] *lõHkema* [349B]
[Vi] *plahvatama* [349F]
explode [Vt] *lõHkama* [348C]
exploit [Vt] *ekspluatEErima* [291B]
exploitation [N] *ekspluatatsiOOn* [58A]
exploiter [N] *ekspluataaTor* [229A]
explosion [N] *plahvatus* [260A]
explosive [A] *lõHkev* [231A]
export [N] *eKsporT* [58E]
export [Vt] *eksporTima* [291F]
expose (photo) [Vt] *säritama* [349F]
exposure (photo) [N] *säritus* [260A]
express [Vt] *kajastama* [349F]
[Vt] *väļjendama* [349F]
express messenger [N] *virgats* [229A]
expressed (be) [Vi] *avalduma* [349H]
[Vi] *kajastuma* [349H]
[Vi] *väļjenduma* [349H]
expression [N] *keelend* [229A]
[N] *väļjend* [229A]
[N] *väļjendus* [260A]
expression (facial) [N] *ilme* [177B]
[N] *miimika* [227A]
expressionless [A] *ilmetu* [227A]
expressive [A] *iLmekas* [243A]
expropriate [Vt] *võõrandama* [349F]
extend [Vi] *kÜÜndima* [308A]
extend [Vt] *ulatama* [349F]
extended (be) [Vi] *ulatuma* [349H]
extension [N] *jäTk* [61B]
[N] *pikendus* [260A]
extensive [A] *laialdane* [257A]
[A] *ulatusliK* [62]
extent [N] *mÄÄr* [53A]
[N] *ulatus* [260A]
exterior [N] *välimiK* [62]
external [A] *väline* [251]
external student [N] *eksteRn* [58B]
extinguish [Vt] *kustutama* [349F]
extinguished (become) [Vi] *kuStuma* [291C]
extract [N] *ekstraKt* [58B]
[N] *katkend* [229A]
extravagant [A] *eKstravaganTne* [247]
extreme [A] *ÄÄrmusliK* [62]
extremist [N] *ÄÄrmuslane* [257C]
extremity [N] *ÄÄrmus* [260B]
exult in power [Vi] *võimutsema* [349E]
exult in triumph [Vi] *võidutsema* [349E]
eye [N] *siLm* [56]
eye [Vt] *silmitsema* [349E]
eyelash [N] *ripse* [179C]
eyelid [N] *laUg* [134]

F

fable [N] *faabula* [227A]
[N] *vaļm* [58B]
façade [N] *fassAAd* [58A]
face [N] *nägu* [31]
face powder [N] *pUUder* [240A]
fact [N] *faKt* [58B]
[N] *tõiK* [49F]
factor [N] *tegur* [229A]
factory [N] *tehas* [253]
[N] *vabrik* [234A]
factory (textile mill) [N] *manufaktUUr* [58A]
factual [A] *faktiline* [257D]
faculty [N] *fakulteeT* [58E]
[N] *teAduskoNd* [106]
fade [Vi] *luiTuma* [349H]
faggot (gay) [N] *lilla* [152]
failure [N] *äpardus* [260A]
faint [N] *minestus* [260A]
faint [A] *ähmane* [251]
faint [Vi] *minestama* [349F]
fair [N] *laaT* [49E]
[N] *meŞS* [58A]
fairy [N] *haļdjas* [243B]
faithful [A] *trUU* [7]
faithful [A] *uStav* [231A]
faithfulness [N] *trUUdus* [260B]
[N] *uStavus* [260A]
fall [Vi] *kuKKuma* [291D]
[Vi] *laNgema* [349B]
fall asleep [Vi] *uĺnuma* [349G]
fall in love [Vi] *aRmuma* [349G]
fall to pieces [Vi] *lagunema* [349D]
false [A] *vale* [153]
fallow [N] *kesa* [13A]
[N] *söö Ţ* [58E]
fame [N] *kUUlsus* [260B]
familiar [A] *familiAArne* [247]
family [N] *pere* [154]
[N] *perekoNd* [106]
family [A] *perekoNdliK* [62]
family of bridegroom [N] *saajad (pl)* [70]
famine [N] *näļg* [112]
famous [A] *kUUlus* [250A]
fan [N] *ventilaaTor* [229A]
fan (paper) [N] *lehvik* [234A]
fanatic [N] *fanaatik* [234A]
fanatical [A] *fanaatiline* [257D]
fanaticism [N] *fanaatilisus* [260A]
fanfare [N] *fanfAAr* [58A]
fang [N] *kiHv* [49B]
fantastic [A] *fantastiline* [257D]
fantasy [N] *ulme* [177B]
farce [N] *farSS* [58G]
farm [N] *faRm* [58B]
[N] *majand* [229A]
[N] *talu* [13A]
farm-hand [N] *sulane* [251]
farmer [N] *faRmer* [229A]
[N] *taluniK* [62]
fart [N] *pEEr* [61A]
[N] *tuŞS* [58A]
fart [Vi] *peeretama* [349F]
fascinate [Vt] *köiTma* [297C]
[Vt] *paEluma* [349G]
fascism [N] *fašiSm* [58B]
fascist [N] *fašiSt* [58B]
fashion [N] *mOOḑ* [115]
fashionable [A] *mOOdne* [249]
fast [A] *kiire* [177A]
fast [Vi] *paaStuma* [291C]
fasten [Vt] *kiņnistama* [349F]
fastener [N] *kiņniti* [225A]

fastener (clothes) N *triPP* 58C
fasting N *paaSt* 61B
fat N *peKK* 58C
fat A *paKs* 61B
fat (become) Vi *raSvuma* 349G
fatality N *suRmasaanu* 186
fate N *saaTus* 260B
fateful A *saaTusliK* 62
father N *isa* 13A
father-in-law N *äİ* 49B
fatherly A *isaliK* 62
fathom N *süLd* 105
fatigue N *väsimus* 260A
fatness N *paKsus* 260B
fatten Vi *paksenema* 349D
fatten animals Vt *nUUmama* 327A
fattening of animals N *nUUm* 53A
faultless A *veaTu* 227B
faulty A *defeKtne* 247
favour Vt *pOOldama* 349F
Vt *soodustama* 349F
Vt *sOOsima* 291A
favourable A *sOOdne* 249
favourite N *favoriiT* 58E
N *lemmik* 234A
N *soosik* 234A
fawn Vi *lipitsema* 349E
fear N *hiRm* 61B
N *karTus* 260B
N *peLg* 135
fear Vt *karTma* 297C
fearless A *karTmatu* 227A
feasible A *teoStatav* 231A
feasting N *sööming* 234A
feather N *suĻg* 142A
feature N *tunnus* 253
February N *vEEbruar* 246
federal A *föderAAlne* 247
federation N *föderatsiOOn* 58A
federative A *föderatİİvne* 247
feeble A *nõder* 78B
A *raMb* 87
A *väeTi* 225B
feed Vt *sööTma* 297C
Vt *toiTma* 297C
feed on something Vi *toiTuma* 349H
feeder N *toiTja* 227B
feel like doing V *viiTsima* 291C
feeler N *tuNdel* 241A
feeling N *tuNdmus* 260B
N *tunne* 214
felt N *viļT* 58E

female A *emane* 251
fence N *tara* 13A
fence (sport) Vi *veHklema* 336
fence in Vt *tarastama* 349F
fencer N *veHkleja* 227A
fencing N *veHklemine* 257E
Fennicism N *fenniSm* 58B
ferment Vi *kÄÄrima* 291A
ferry N *prAAm* 58A
fertile A *viļjakas* 243A
fertility N *viļjakus* 260A
fertilize Vt *viļjastama* 349F
Vt *väeTama* 349F
fertilizer N *väeTis* 260B
fertilizing N *väeTus* 260B
fervency N *innukus* 260A
fervent A *innukas* 243A
fervour (fill with) Vt *innustama* 349F
fester Vi *mädanema* 349D
festering A *mädane* 251
festival N *festival* 245
festive A *piduliK* 62
festivity N *pidustus* 260A
fetish N *fetiš* 229A
fetter N *kammits* 231A
N *köide* 179D
fetter Vt *kammitsema* 349E
feudal A *feodAAlne* 247
feudal lord N *feodAAl* 58A
feuilleton N *föļjeton* 245
fever N *palaviK* 62
fiancé N *peİg* 131B
N *peiu* 152
fiancée N *pruuŢ* 58E
fib Vi *luiSkama* 348C
fibre N *kiUd* 127
fictitious A *fiktİİvne* 247
fiddle Vi *viiuldama* 349F
fiddler N *viiuldaja* 227A
fidget Vi *kibelema* 325
field N *põLd* 128
N *väli* 69A
fifth N *viiendiK* 62
fifth A *viies* 238A
fight N *kaKlus* 260B
N *lööming* 234A
N *võiTlus* 260B
fight Vi *kaKlema* 326C
Vi *kiSklema* 336
Vi *võiTlema* 326E
figurative A *piļTliK* 62
figure N *figUUr* 58A

figure (be present) V *figurEErima* 291B
file (document) N *toimik* 234A
file (tool) N *vİİl* 58A
filigree N *filigrAAn* 58A
fill Vt *täiTma* 297C
fill (tooth) Vt *plombEErima* 291B
Vt *ploMMima* 291A
fill up (car) Vt *tanKima* 291G
filled (become) Vi *täiTuma* 349H
filling (action) N *täiTmine* 257E
filling (substance) N *täidis* 253
filling in tooth N *ploMM* 58A
filling station N *tanKla* 227B
filling with fervour N *innustus* 260A
film N *fiĻm* 58B
film Vt *fiĻmima* 291C
filter N *filTer* 240A
filter Vt *filtrEErima* 291B
Vt *filTrima* 291I
filthy A *roojane* 251
fin N *uİm* 63B
final A *lõPliK* 62
A *viimane* 251
A *vİİmne* 247
finals (sport) N *finAAl* 58A
finance N *rahandus* 260A
finance Vt *finantsEErima* 291B
Vt *majandama* 349F
financial A *rahandusliK* 62
finch N *viņT* 58E
find N *leİd* 123B
find Vt *leİdma* 316C
find fault with Vt *laiTma* 297C
fine A *pEEn* 82
fine Vt *traHvima* 291C
finer (make) Vt *peenendama* 349F
finesse N *pEEnus* 260B
finger N *näPP* 61C
N *sõRm* 63B
finger V *sõrmitsema* 349E
finish Vt *lõpetama* 349F
finish (sport) N *finiš* 229A
finish (sport) Vi *finišEErima* 291B
finished A *vaĻmis* 244
finished (become) Vi *vaĻmima* 349B
finishing touches N *viimistlus* 260A
Finn N *sOOmlane* 257C
Finno-Ugric A *soome-ugriline* 257D
Finno-Ugric studies N *fennougristika* 227A
Finno-Ugricist N *fennougriSt* 58B
fir N *kuuSk* 140B
fir grove N *kuusik* 234A

fire [N] *tuli* [20]
fire (guns) [Vt] *tulistama* [349F]
fire extinguisher [N] *kustuti* [225A]
firebrand [N] *tuKK* [58C]
fireplace [N] *kamin* [231A]
firm [A] *prinK* [58F]
first [A] *esimene* [257A]
fish [N] *kala* [14A]
fish [V] *kalastama* [349F]
fish [V] *õngitsema* [349E]
fish-bone [N] *rOOd* [126]
fisherman [N] *kalur* [229A]
fishing [N] *kalastus* [260A]
fishing industry [N] *kalandus* [260A]
fissure [N] *lõhe* [153]
fist [N] *rusikas* [243A]
fit [Vi] *maHtuma* [308B]
fit [Vt] *mahutama* [349F]
fitter [N] *montÖÖr* [58A]
fitting [N] *montAAž* [58A]
five [N] *vİİs* [143B]
fixture [N] *armatUUr* [58A]
[N] *seade* [179C]
flag [N] *liPP* [61C]
flake [N] *helve* [208B]
[N] *helves* [195]
flame [N] *leeK* [58F]
flannel [N] *flaneĻL* [58A]
flap [Vi] *laKsuma* [291C]
flare [Vi] *loiTma* [297C]
flash [N] *välgatus* [260A]
flash [Vi] *sähvatama* [349F]
[Vi] *vilksatama* [349F]
[Vi] *välgatama* [349F]
[Vi] *välKuma* [291G]
flashing [N] *välge* [177F]
flask [N] *koĻb* [114]
[N] *plaşku* [152]
flat [N] *lausik* [234A]
flat [A] *lame* [235]
flattering [A] *meelitav* [231A]
flautist [N] *flötiSt* [58B]
flaw [N] *mõra* [13A]
flea [N] *kirP* [61D]
fleet [N] *laevastiK* [62]
fleeting [A] *üürike(ne)* [257G]
flexibility [N] *paİnduvus* [260A]
flexible [A] *paİnduv* [231A]
flick [N] *niPs* [58B]
flier [N] *leNdur* [229A]
flight [N] *leNd* [129]
fling [Vt] *paiSkama* [348C]
flirt [Vi] *edvistama* [349F]
[Vi] *flirTima* [291F]
flirtation [N] *flirT* [58E]
flit [Vi] *tİİblema* [328]
float [N] *käba* [13B]
flood [N] *uputus* [260A]
flood [Vt] *ujutama* [349F]
floor [N] *põrand* [231A]
floor (wrestling) [Vt] *seļjatama* [349F]
flounce [N] *volaNg* [58B]
flounder [N] *leSt* [53B]
flour [N] *jahu* [13A]
flourish [N] *tuŠŠ* [58C]
floury [A] *jahune* [251]
flow [Vi] *vOOlama* [327A]
flower [N] *liLL* [63A]
flower bed [N] *peenar* [171A]
flowery [A] *lilleline* [257D]
flowing [A] *vOOlav* [231A]
flue [N] *lÕÕr* [58A]
flu(e) (influenza) [N] *griPP* [58C]
fluency [N] *ladusus* [260A]
[N] *soravus* [260A]
fluent [A] *ladus* [231A]
[A] *sorav* [231A]
[A] *sujuv* [231A]
fluffy [A] *kohev* [231A]
fluid [N] *vedeliK* [62]
flush (facial) [N] *õhetus* [260A]
flushed (be) [Vi] *õhetama* [349F]
flute [N] *flööŢ* [58E]
flutter [Vi] *leHvima* [291C]
[Vi] *leNdlema* [332]
fly [N] *kärbes* [162]
fly [Vi] *leNdama* [343]
foal [N] *varSS* [49G]
foam [N] *vaHt* [124B]
foam [Vi] *vahutama* [349F]
foamy [A] *vahune* [251]
fodder [N] *söö̃T* [53E]
fog [N] *udu* [13C]
foggy [A] *udune* [251]
foggy (be) [Vi] *udutama* [349F]
fold [N] *voļT* [58E]
fold [Vt] *voļTima* [291F]
folder [N] *kauSt* [49B]
[N] *maPP* [58C]
foliage [N] *lehestiK* [62]
folk-tale [N] *muistend* [229A]
folklorist [N] *folkloriSt* [58B]
folksy [A] *raHvaliK* [62]
follow [Vt] *jäĻgima* [349B]
fond of (become) [Vi] *kİİnduma* [349H]
food [N] *rOOg* [110]
[N] *sööK* [58F]
[N] *toiT* [61E]
fool [N] *naRR* [58A]
fool (play the) [Vi] *veiderdama* [349F]
foolish [A] *kilPlasliK* [62]
foolish person [N] *kilPlane* [257C]
foolishness [N] *naRRus* [260B]
foot [N] *jaLg* [100]
foot of bed [N] *jaluts* [229A]
foot-bridge [N] *purre* [215]
footstool [N] *jäRg* [120A]
footwear [N] *jalatsid (pl)* [229A]
forbid [Vt] *kEElama* [327A]
force [Vt] *forssEErima* [291B]
force one's way [Vi] *tuNgima* [291C]
ford [N] *koole* [179A]
forecast [N] *ennustus* [260A]
forefront [N] *esi* [46]
forehead [N] *lauP* [49D]
[N] *oTsmiK* [62]
foreigner [N] *mUUlane* [257C]
forest [N] *meTs* [53B]
forest (virgin) [N] *lAAş* [146]
forest district [N] *meTskoNd* [106]
forestall [Vt] *ennetama* [349F]
forested [A] *metsane* [251]
forester [N] *meTsniK* [62]
forestry [N] *metsandus* [260A]
foretell [Vt] *ennustama* [349F]
foreteller [N] *ennustaja* [227A]
forge [Vt] *võļTsima* [291C]
forge (metal) [V] *sepistama* [349F]
forger [N] *võļTsija* [227A]
forgery [N] *võļtsing* [234A]
forget [Vt] *unustama* [349F]
forgive [Vt] *andestama* [349F]
forgotten (become) [Vi] *unuma* [269]
forgotten (become) [Vi] *ununema* [349D]
fork [N] *kaHvel* [240A]
fork [Vi] *haRgnema* [349D]
form [Vt] *moodustama* [349F]
form (blank) [N] *blankeŢT* [58C]
formal [A] *formAAlne* [247]
formality [N] *formAAlsus* [260B]
[N] *vormilisus* [260A]
formality [A] *vormiline* [257D]
formation [N] *moodustis* [260A]
former [A] *eŅdine* [257B]
formula [N] *valem* [229A]
[N] *voRmel* [229A]

formulate [Vt] *formulEErima* [291B]
[Vt] *vormistama* [349F]
fort [N] *forT* [58E]
fortress [N] *kiNdlus* [260B]
fortune-hunter [N] *aferiSt* [58B]
forward [N] *toRmaja (sport)* [227A]
forwarding agent [N] *ekspediiTor* [229A]
found [Vt] *asutama* [349F]
found (be) [Vi] *leİduma* [349H]
foundation [N] *alus* [253]
[N] *vundameņT* [58E]
founded (be) [Vi] *rajanema* [349D]
founder [N] *asutaja* [227A]
founding [N] *asutamine* [257E]
four [N] *neli* [69A]
fourth [N] *neļjandiK* [62]
fourth [A] *neļjas* [238A]
fox [N] *rebane* [251]
foyer [N] *fuajEE* [2]
fracas [N] *müra* [13A]
fracture [N] *muRd* [130]
[N] *murre* [215]
fracture [Vi] *muRduma* [349H]
fracture [Vt] *muRdma* [318]
fractured pieces [N] *muRdmed (pl)* [222]
fragile [A] *habras* [159D]
fragment [N] *fragmeņT* [58E]
fragmentary [A] *katkendliK* [62]
fragrant [A] *lõHnav* [231A]
frame [N] *rAAm* [58A]
frame [Vt] *rAAmima* [291A]
framework [N] *raamistiK* [62]
frank [A] *otsene* [251]
frankness [N] *otsekohesus* [260A]
frantic [A] *meeletu* [227A]
[A] *pöörane* [251]
fraternity [N] *korporatsiOOn* [58A]
fraternity brother [N] *fraaTer* [240A]
fraternity house [N] *koNveņT* [58E]
fraternity member [N] *burŠ* [58A]
[N] *korporaņT* [58E]
fraternity party [N] *kommerSS* [58G]
fraternity-like [A] *korporaņTliK* [62]
fraud [N] *soHk* [120B]
fray [Vi] *narmendama* [349F]
freak [N] *väRdjas* [243B]
free [A] *vaba* [14B]
free [Vt] *vabastama* [349F]
free (become) [Vi] *vabanema* [349D]
free of charge [A] *prİİ* [1]
freedom [N] *prİİus* [260B]
[N] *vabadus* [260A]
freeze [Vi] *küLmuma* [349G]
freeze [Vt] *külmetama* [349F]
freeze over [Vi] *jääTuma* [349H]
French [N] *pranTslane* [257C]
frenzy [N] *meeletus* [260A]
frequency [N] *sagedus* [260A]
frequent [A] *sage* [235]
[A] *sagedane* [257A]
frequent [Vi] *käİma* [264B]
frequent (become) [Vi] *sagenema* [349D]
fresh [A] *kaRge* [227B]
[A] *rõõSk* [95B]
[A] *värSke* [227B]
freshness [N] *värSkus* [260B]
friction [N] *hÕÕrumine* [257E]
Friday [N] *rEEde* [227B]
friend [N] *sõber* [78A]
friendly [A] *sõbraliK* [62]
friends with (be) [Vi] *sõbrustama* [349F]
[Vi] *sõbrutsema* [349E]
friendship [N] *sõPrus* [260B]
frighten [Vt] *hirmutama* [349F]
[Vt] *peletama* [349F]
frightened (be) [Vi] *hiRmuma* [349G]
fringe [N] *narmas* [159B]
frog [N] *koNN* [53A]
frolic [Vi] *huLLama* [327A]
[Vi] *vallatama* [349F]
[Vi] *vallatlema* [351]
front [N] *froņT* [58E]
front [N] *rinne* [214]
frontier [N] *raja* [13A]
frost [N] *haLL* [49A]
fruit [N] *fruKt* [58B]
fry [Vt] *prAAḑima* [305]
fuck [Vt] *niKKuma* [291D]
[Vt] *nuŞSima* [291A]
fuel [N] *kütus* [253]
fuel oil [N] *masuuT* [58E]
fugitive [N] *jooksik* [234A]
full [A] *täİs* [143C]
full of holes [A] *auKliK* [62]
full-breasted [A] *rinnakas* [243A]
fume [Vi] *turTsuma* [291C]
fun [N] *lõbu* [13B]
fun [A] *lõbus* [231A]
function [N] *funktsiOOn* [58A]
function [Vi] *funktsionEErima* [291B]
fundamental [A] *fundamentAAlne* [247]
[A] *põhiline* [257D]
funeral [N] *matus* [253]
funnel [N] *leHter* [240A]
funny [A] *naļjakas* [243A]
fur coat [N] *kasukas* [243A]
furnish (space) [Vt] *möblEErima* [291B]
[Vt] *sisustama* [349F]
furnishings [N] *sisustus* [260A]
furniture [N] *mÖÖbel* [240A]
furrier [N] *kÖÖsner* [229A]
furrow [N] *vagu* [31]
further [A] *edasine* [257A]
further [Vt] *edendama* [349F]
fuss [N] *sekeldus* [260A]
fuss [Vi] *hädaldama* [349F]
[Vi] *sekeldama* [349F]
futile [A] *aşjatu* [227A]
future [N] *tuleviK* [62]
future [A] *tulevane* [257A]
futurology [N] *futurolOOgia* [227A]

G

gadfly [N] *kİİn* [58A]
gaiety [N] *lõbusus* [260A]
gait [N] *kõnnak* [234A]
gallery [N] *galerİİ* [1]
galley proof [N] *tõmmis* [253]
gallop [N] *galoPP* [58C]
gallop [Vi] *galopEErima* [291B]
[Vi] *galoPPima* [291D]
gallows [N] *võllas* [159A]
gambol [Vi] *kePslema* [326B]
gambol [Vi] *kepsutama* [349F]
game [N] *geİm* [58B]
[N] *mäNg* [61B]
gang [N] *jõuK* [61F]
[N] *kamP* [49D]
gang member [N] *lõngus* [253]
gangster [N] *ganGster* [229A]
gap [N] *lünK* [53F]
garage [N] *garAAž* [58A]
garbage [N] *prügi* [13D]
garden [N] *aEd* [90]
garden farm [N] *aiand* [229A]
gardener [N] *aEdniK* [62]
gardening [N] *aiandus* [260A]

gargle V *kuristama* 349F
garland N *vanik* 234A
garlic N *kÜÜslauK* 61F
garnish Vt *garnEErima* 291B
garrison N *garnison* 245
gas N *gAAş* 58A
gash N *verme* 177B
gasoline N *bensİİn* 58A
gate N *värav* 231A
gather Vt *koRjama* 327B
gather together Vi *kogunema* 349D
gathering (action) N *kogunemine* 257E
gathering (result) N *kOOndus* 260B
gauze N *marli* 152
gel N *gEEl* 58A
gelatine N *želatİİn* 58A
gelding N *rUUn* 53A
gender N *sugu* 33
gene N *gEEņ* 58A
general N *kiNdral* 229A
general A *üĻdine* 257B
general public N *üĻdsus* 260B
generalization N *üļdistus* 260A
generalize Vt *üļdistama* 349F
generation N *generatsiOOn* 58A
N *põli* 66
N *põĻv* 66
N *põĻvkoNd* 106
generator N *generaaTor* 229A
generosity N *heLdus* 260B
generous A *heLde* 227B
genitals (female) N *häbemed (pl)* 157
genitive N *omastav* 231A
genius N *gEEnius* 260A
genre N *žaNr* 58B or 229B
gentleman N *džentelmen* 245
N *härra* 152
N *saKs* 51
gentry N *härrased (pl)* 253
genuine A *eHtne* 249
geographer N *geograaF* 58A
geography N *geograaFia* 227A
geologist N *geolOOg* 58A
geology N *geolOOgia* 227A
geometry N *geomeeTria* 227A
Georgian N *grusİİnlane* 257C
geranium N *pelargOOn* 58A
germ N *batsiĻL* 58A
N *pisik* 234A
German N *saKslane* 257C
germinate Vi *idanema* 349D
germination N *idanemine* 257E
gesticulate Vi *žestikulEErima* 291B
Vi *veHkima* 313B
gesticulating N *žestikulEErimine* 257E
gesticulation N *žestikulatsiOOn* 58A
gesture N *liigutus* 260A
gesture N *žeŞt* 58B
get Vt *sAAma* 266
get used to Vi *kodunema* 349D
geyser N *geİser* 240A
ghastly A *jube* 235
A *õUdne* 247
ghost N *toņT* 58E
giant N *hİİd* 123A
N *hİİglane* 257C
gibberish N *loba* 13B
N *plära* 13A
gift N *kingitus* 260A
N *kinK* 58F
gigantic A *hİİglasliK* 62
giggle Vi *iţsitama* 349F
gild Vt *kuLdama* 342
gill N *lõpus* 253
gillyflower N *levkoİ* 1
gin N *džiNN* 58A
ginger N *iNgver* 229A
Gipsy N *muStlane* 257C
giraffe N *kaElkirjak* 234A
girder N *tala* 13A
girl N *plika* 152
N *toŢs* 58B
N *tüdruk* 234A
girl guide N *gaİd* 58B
give Vt *aNdma* 317
giver N *aŅdja* 227B
gizzard N *pugu* 13D
glacier N *liuStiK* 62
glade N *välu* 13A
glance N *pilK* 61F
gland N *nääre* 179A
glass N *klAAş* 58A
glasses (eye) N *priļlid (pl)* 58A
glassy (become) Vi *klaaşistuma* 349H
glaze N *glasUUr* 58A
glaze Vt *glasUUrima* 291A
glaze (glass) Vt *klAAşima* 291A
glazed tile N *kaHHel* 240B
glide Vi *liUglema* 334
glider N *plAAner* 229A
glisten N *sätendus* 260A
glisten Vi *sätendama* 349F
globe N *glOObus* 260B
gloom N *süNgus* 260B
gloomy A *süNge* 227B
glorification N *ülistus* 260A
glorify Vt *ülistama* 349F
gloss N *läige* 177F
glossary N *sõnastiK* 62
glossy A *läiKiv* 231A
glove N *kinnas* 192
glow N *hÕÕgus* 260B
N *kuma* 13A
glow Vi *hÕÕguma* 349G
glow bluish Vi *sinetama* 349F
glow red Vi *punetama* 349F
glowing A *hÕÕguv* 231A
glue N *lİİm* 58A
glue Vt *lİİmima* 291A
glut Vi *küllastuma* 349H
glycerine N *glütserİİn* 58A
gnash Vt *kiristama* 349F
go Vi *käİma* 264B
Vi *minema* 274
go-getter N *tegelinSki* 225B
goat N *kiTs* 63B
goblet N *karikas* 243A
N *peeKer* 240A
God N *Jumal* 231A
godparent N *vader* 229A
goggle Vt *jõļlitama* 349F
gold N *kuLd* 105
golden A *kuLdne* 247
golf N *goļF* 58A
gondola N *goNdel* 240A
gondolier N *gondoljEEr* 58A
gong N *goNg* 58B
good A *heA* 10
A *hÄÄ* 10
A *tubli* 152
good for (be) Vi *kõLbama* 339B
good-quality A *kvaliteeTne* 247
goodness N *heAdus* 260B
goose N *hani* 18
gooseberry N *tikerber* 245
gorilla N *gorilla* 152
Gospel N *evangEElium* 246
gossip N *klaTš* 58B
gossip Vt *klaTšima* 291C
gouache N *guaŠŠ* 58C
gourmet N *gurmAAn* 58A
government N *valitsus* 260A
governor N *kuberner* 245
grab Vt *kaHmama* 327B
grab at Vt *naPsama* 327B
grace N *graaTsia* 227A

graceful [A] *graatsiline* [257D]
gradual (by steps) [A] *aStmeline* [257D]
graduate [N] *abiturieņT* [58E]
  [N] *lõpetaja* [227A]
graft [Vt] *pooKima* [291G]
grain [N] *iva* [13A]
  [N] *tera* [15]
grain elevator [N] *elevaaTor* [229A]
grain flour [N] *kama* [13A]
gram(me) [N] *graMM* [58A]
grammar [N] *grammatika* [227A]
grammatical [A] *grammatiline* [257D]
gramophone [N] *grammofon* [245]
grand [A] *nOObel* [240A]
grandfather [N] *vAAr* [58A]
granite [N] *graniiT* [58E]
granular [A] *teraline* [257D]
grapefruit [N] *greiPfruuT* [58E]
grapevine (gossip) [N] *kõlakas* [243A]
graphic (make) [Vt] *näiTlikustama* [349F]
graphic art [N] *graafika* [227A]
graphic artist [N] *graafik* [234A]
graphite [N] *grafiiT* [58E]
grasp [N] *haare* [211A]
grass [N] *rohi* [151]
grass-land [N] *roHtla* [227B]
grate [N] *reŞt* [58B]
  [N] *võre* [153]
grate [Vt] *rİİvima* [291A]
grater [N] *rİİv* [58A]
grating [N] *treļlid (pl)* [58A]
gratitude [N] *tänuliKKus* [260B]
grave [N] *haUd* [88A]
  [N] *kaLm* [61B]
grave [A] *ränK* [53F]
gravel [N] *krUUs* [53A]
graveyard [N] *kaļmistu* [227A]
gravitation [N] *gravitatsiOOn* [58A]
gravy [N] *souSt* [58B]
graze (wound) [Vt] *rİİvama* [327A]
greasy [A] *rasvane* [251]
grebe [N] *püŢT* [58C]
greed [N] *aHnus* [260B]
greedy [A] *ahne* [177B]
greedy (be) [V] *ahnitsema* [349E]
Greek [N] *kreeKlane* [257C]
green [A] *roheline* [257D]
greenery [N] *rohelus* [260A]
greenish [A] *rohekas* [243A]
Greenlander [N] *grÖÖnlane* [257C]
greens (plant) [N] *peAlsed (pl)* [247]
greet [Vt] *teretama* [349F]
  [Vt] *tervitama* [349F]
greeting [N] *tervitus* [260A]
grenade [N] *granaaT* [58E]
grey [A] *haĻL* [58A]
greyhound [N] *hurT* [53E]
greyish [A] *haļlikas* [243A]
grief [N] *kurvastus* [260A]
grievance [N] *kaEbus* [260B]
grieve [V] *kurvastama* [349F]
grind [Vt] *jahvatama* [349F]
grindstone [N] *käİ* [49B]
grit [N] *riHv* [49B]
groan [N] *oie* [216]
groan [Vi] *oİgama* [345B]
  [Vi] *ägama* [269]
groin [N] *kube* [157]
groove [N] *riHv* [49B]
  [N] *õnar* [231A]
  [N] *õnarus* [260A]
groove [Vt] *sOOnima* [291A]
grope [Vi] *kobama* [269]
  [Vi] *komPama* [327D]
  [Vi] *komPima* [291E]
gross [N] *bruto* [152]
ground cover [N] *pinnas* [253]
ground electrically [Vt] *mAAndama* [349F]
groundless [A] *alusetu* [227A]
group [N] *gruPP* [58C]
  [N] *rüHm* [53B]
group [Vt] *grupEErima* [291B]
  [Vt] *rühmitama* [349F]
grouse [N] *teder* [81A]
grove [N] *salu* [13A]
grovel [Vi] *lömitama* [349F]
grow [Vi] *kaSvama* [291C]
growl [N] *urin* [231A]
growl [Vi] *urisema* [349C]
growth [N] *kaSv* [61B]
grudge [N] *viMM* [49A]
gruel [N] *körT* [58E]
gruelling [A] *kuRnav* [231A]
grumble [N] *torin* [231A]
grumble [Vi] *nurisema* [349C]
  [Vi] *torisema* [349C]
grumbler [N] *toriseja* [227A]
grumbling [N] *nurin* [231A]
grunt [Vi] *ruİgama* [345B]
  [Vi] *röHkima* [313B]
guarantee [N] *garantİİ* [1]
  [N] *tagatis* [260A]
guarantee [Vt] *garantEErima* [291B]
  [Vt] *tagama* [269]
guard [N] *vaHt* [116]
  [N] *vaLvur* [229A]
guard [Vt] *vaLvama* [327B]
guardian [N] *hOOldaja* [227A]
guess [Vt] *mõistatama* [349F]
guest [N] *võõras* [159A]
guide [Vt] *talutama* [349F]
guitar [N] *kitaRR* [58A]
guitarist [N] *kitarriSt* [58B]
gulp [N] *lonKs* [61B]
  [N] *sÕÕm* [61A]
gulp down [Vt] *kugistama* [349F]
gum (chewing) [N] *näTs* [61B]
gum (teeth) [N] *ige* [157]
gun [N] *püŞS* [58A]
gurgle [N] *vulin* [231A]
gurgle [Vi] *vulisema* [349C]
gust [N] *puhang* [234A]
gutter [N] *renTsel* [240A]
gymnasium [N] *võİmla* [227B]
gymnast [N] *võİmleja* [227A]
gymnastics [N] *võİmlemine* [257E]
gymnastics (do) [Vi] *võİmlema* [326B]
gynaecologist [N] *günekolOOg* [58A]
gypsum [N] *kiPs* [58B]

H

habit [N] *haRjumus* [260A]
habit (be in) [Vi] *tavatsema* [349E]
habitual [A] *haRjumusliK* [62]
hag [N] *kröhva* [152]
  [N] *krööT* [49E]
hail [N] *rahe* [153]
hair [N] *kaRv* [49B]
hair (human) [N] *juuKsed (pl)* [256]
hair-dryer [N] *fÖÖn* [58A]
hairdo [N] *soEng* [234B]
hairdresser [N] *juuKsur* [229A]
hairy [A] *karvane* [251]
hale and hearty [A] *kõbus* [231A]
half [N] *pOOl* [82]
half-breed [N] *poluvernik* [234A]
half-finished [A] *pooļik* [234A]
hall [N] *haĻL* [58A]
  [N] *sAAļ* [58A]

hallelujah [N] *hallelUUja* [227B]
hallucinate [Vi] *viirastuma* [349H]
hallucination [N] *viirastus* [260A]
hallucinatory [A] *viirastusliK* [62]
halvah [N] *halvAA* [1]
halve [Vt] *pooļitama* [349F]
ham [N] *sinK* [58F]
hames [N] *rangid (pl)* [58B]
hammer [N] *hAAmer* [240A]
[N] *vasar* [231A]
hammer [Vt] *vasardama* [349F]
hand [N] *käsi* [45]
handle [N] *saNg* [49B]
handle [Vt] *käsitsema* [349E]
handling [N] *käsitsus* [260A]
handmaiden [N] *ümmardaja* [227A]
hang [Vi] *riPPuma* [291D]
hang [Vt] *riputama* [349F]
hang (person) [Vt] *pOOma* [265]
hanged person [N] *poonu* [186]
hangover [N] *kaaTer* [240A]
Hanseatic League [N] *Hansa* [152]
happen [Vi] *juHtuma* [349H]
happen upon [Vi] *saTTuma* [291D]
[Vi] *saTTuma* [349H]
happiness [N] *õŅN* [65]
happy [A] *õnneliK* [62]
harass [Vt] *kimbutama* [349F]
harbour [N] *sadam* [231A]
hard [A] *kõva* [14A]
hard-hearted [A] *kaļK* [58F]
harden [Vi] *karastuma* [349H]
hardship [N] *vaEv* [49B]
hare [N] *jänes* [253]
Harjumaa native [N] *harjakas* [243A]
harlot [N] *libu* [13B]
harm [N] *kahju* [152]
harm [Vt] *kahjustama* [349F]
harmful [A] *kahjuliK* [62]
harmless [A] *kahjutu* [227A]
harmonious [A] *harmooniline* [257D]
harmonize [Vt] *harmonisEErima* [291B]
harness [N] *raKmed (pl)* [179B]
harp [N] *harF* [58A]
harpist [N] *harfiSt* [58B]
harrow [N] *äke* [177C]
harrow [Vt] *äeStama* [349F]
harsh [A] *kaRm* [58B]
harshness [N] *kaRmus* [260B]
hashish [N] *hašiš* [229A]
haste [N] *kİİr* [61A]
[N] *ruTT* [61C]

hat [N] *kaabu (man's)* [152]
[N] *kübar* [231A]
[N] *müŢs* [58B]
hate [Vt] *viHkama* [348C]
hateful [A] *vihatav* [231A]
haughtiness [N] *kõrKus* [260B]
haughty [A] *suureline* [257D]
haul [Vt] *taŞSima* [291A]
[Vt] *vedama* [276]
haulage [N] *vedu* [27]
haunch [N] *kinTs* [61B]
[N] *reba* [13B]
haunt [Vt] *kummitama* [349F]
having gaps [A] *lünKliK* [62]
hawk [N] *kuĻL* [58A]
hay [N] *heİn* [50]
hay shed [N] *kÜÜn* [58A]
haycock [N] *sAAd* [125]
haymaker [N] *heinaline* [257D]
haze [N] *vine* [153]
hazel tree grove [N] *sarapiK* [62]
head [N] *peA* [11]
[N] *pÄÄ* [11]
head cheese [N] *süļT* [58E]
head of bed [N] *peaTs* [229B]
headquarters [N] *staaP* [58D]
heal [Vi] *paranema* [349D]
healing [N] *paranemine* [257E]
health [N] *tervis* [253]
[N] *teRvis* [260B]
healthier (become) [Vi] *tervenema* [349D]
healthier (make) [Vt] *tervendama* [349F]
healthy [A] *terve* [177B]
heap [N] *kuhi* [71A]
heap up [Vt] *kuHjama* [327B]
hear [Vt] *kUUlma* [294]
heard (be) [Vi] *koStma* [297A]
heart [N] *süda* [158]
heart (cards) [N] *ärtu* [152]
heart (have a) [Vt] *raaŢsima* [291C]
heart attack [N] *infarKt* [58B]
hearth [N] *kolle* [213]
[N] *lEE* [1]
heartless [A] *südametu* [227A]
heat [N] *kUUmus* [260B]
[N] *palavus* [260A]
heat (overwhelming) [N] *leitsak* [234A]
heat [Vt] *kuumendama* [349F]
heat (space) [Vt] *küTma* [301]
heat up [Vi] *kuumenema* [349D]
heatable [A] *köeTav* [231A]
heath [N] *nõMM* [63A]

heather [N] *kanarbiK* [62]
heating (house) [N] *küte* [177C]
heave anchor [Vt] *hİİvama* [327A]
heaven [N] *taevas* [160]
heavenly [A] *taEvaliK* [62]
heavy [A] *raSke* [227B]
hectare [N] *heKtar* [229A]
heddle [N] *nİİs* [143B]
hedge [N] *heKK* [58C]
hedgehog [N] *sİİl* [58A]
heel [N] *kaNd* [92]
heel (shoe) [N] *konTs* [53B]
heifer [N] *muļlikas* [243A]
height [N] *kõRgus* [260B]
heir [N] *pärija* [227A]
helicopter [N] *helikoPter* [229A]
[N] *koPter* [229A]
hell [N] *põRgu* [228]
helmet [N] *kİİver* [240A]
help [N] *abi* [13B]
help [V] *aiTama* [327E]
help [Vt] *abistama* [349F]
helper [N] *abiline* [257D]
helping [N] *porTsjon* [229A]
helpless [A] *abitu* [227A]
[A] *mannetu* [227A]
hem [Vt] *palistama* [349F]
hem-stitch [N] *pilu* [13A]
hem-stitch [Vt] *pilutama* [349F]
hemming [N] *palistus* [260A]
hemp [N] *kanep* [229A]
hen [N] *kana* [14A]
hen-house [N] *kanala* [227A]
herbarium [N] *herbAArium* [246]
herd [N] *kari* [68A]
herder [N] *karjane* [251]
hereditary [A] *päriliK* [62]
[A] *päritav* [231A]
heritage [N] *pärand* [229A]
hermetic [A] *hermeetiline* [257D]
hermit [N] *üksiklane* [257C]
hernia [N] *soNg* [53B]
hero [N] *kaNgelane* [257C]
[N] *saNgar* [229A]
[N] *vägilane* [257C]
heroic [A] *heroİline* [257D]
[A] *kaNgelasliK* [62]
[A] *saNgarliK* [62]
heroin [N] *heroİİn* [58A]
heroism [N] *heroiSm* [58B]
[N] *kaNgelasliKKus* [260B]
[N] *saNgarlus* [260A]

herring [N] *heeringas* [243A]
[N] *räl̇m* [63B]
[N] *silK* [61F]
hesitate [Vi] *kõHklema* [336]
hesitation [N] *kõHklus* [260B]
hew [Vt] *tahuma* [269]
hiccough [Vi] *luKsuma* [291C]
hide [Vt] *peiTma* [297C]
hide-and-go-seek [N] *peiTus* [260B]
hideous [A] *võigas* [159E]
hiding [N] *peiTmine* [257E]
high [A] *kõRge* [227B]
high-mindedness [N] *üLLus* [260B]
highlander [N] *mägilane* [257C]
Hiiumaa native [N] *hl̇idlane* [257C]
hike [N] *maTk* [49B]
hike [Vi] *maTkama* [327B]
hiker [N] *maTkaja* [227A]
hill [N] *mägi* [42]
hillock [N] *küngas* [159E]
hilly [A] *künKliK* [62]
[A] *mägine* [251]
hinder [Vt] *takistama* [349F]
hindmost [A] *tagumine* [257F]
hindrance [N] *takistus* [260A]
hinge [N] *hiNg* [63B]
hint [N] *vihje* [177B]
hint at [V] *viHjama* [327B]
hip [N] *pUUs* [53A]
hire out [Vt] *laenutama* [349F]
hiss [Vi] *susisema* [349C]
historian [N] *ajalOOlane* [257C]
historic(al) [A] *ajalOOline* [257D]
hit [N] *tabamus* [260A]
hit [Vt] *lÖÖma* [268]
hitch-hike [Vi] *hääletama* [349F]
hitherto existing [A] *senine* [251]
hive (bee) [N] *taru* [13A]
hob-goblin [N] *kraŢT* [58C]
hobble [Vi] *komberdama* [349F]
hobby [N] *harrastus* [260A]
[N] *hobi* [13B]
hobby (have) [Vt] *harrastama* [349F]
hockey [N] *hoki* [152]
hoe [N] *kabli* [152]
[N] *kõblas* [159D]
hoe [Vt] *kablima* [269]
[Vt] *kõPlama* [327D]
hoist [N] *tõstuk* [229A]
hoist [Vt] *heiSkama* [348C]
hold [Vt] *hol̇dma* [316C]
[Vt] *pidama* [277]

hole [N] *auK* [61F]
holiday [N] *püha* [15]
hollow [N] *loHk* [131C]
hollow [N] *nõgu* [31]
hollow [A] *õõnes* [166A]
hollow behind knee [N] *kinner* [204]
hollow out [Vt] *õõnestama* [349F]
holy [A] *püha* [15]
holy trinity [N] *koLmainus* [169]
home [N] *kodu* [13C]
home economics [N] *kodundus* [260A]
home front [N] *tagala* [227A]
homeless [A] *kodutu* [227A]
homonym [N] *homonÜÜm* [58A]
homy [A] *kodune* [251]
honest [A] *aUs* [231B]
honesty [N] *aUsus* [260B]
honey [N] *mesi* [46]
honeycomb [N] *käRg* [141]
honorarium [N] *honorar* [245]
honour [N] *aU* [12]
hood [N] *kapuuTs* [58B]
hoof [N] *kabi* [68B]
hoof (cloven) [N] *sõRg* [95A]
hook [N] *haaK* [58F]
[N] *konKs* [61B]
[N] *kooK* [61F]
hook (fishing) [N] *õNg* [63B]
hook [Vt] *haaKima* [291G]
hooligan [N] *huligAAn* [58A]
[N] *lonTrus* [260B]
hooligan-like [A] *ulakas* [243A]
hooliganism [N] *ulakus* [260A]
hoop [N] *võru* [13A]
hop (beer) [N] *humal* [231A]
hope [N] *looTus* [260B]
hope [V] *looTma* [297C]
hopeless [A] *looTusetu* [227A]
hopelessness [N] *looTusetus* [260A]
hopscotch [N] *keKs* [61B]
horizon [N] *horisoņT* [58E]
horizontal [A] *horisontAAlne* [247]
horn [N] *saRv* [63B]
[N] *tõri* [67]
horny (sexual) [A] *tiirane* [251]
horoscope [N] *horoskooP* [58D]
horrible [A] *hiRmus* [250A]
[A] *kole* [235]
horror [N] *koledus* [260A]
[N] *õUdus* [260B]
horse [N] *hobune* [251]
horse (mount) [N] *ratsu* [152]

horse-radish [N] *mädarõigas* [159E]
horsefly [N] *paRm* [61B]
horsehair [N] *jõHv* [58B]
horse rider [N] *raTsaniK* [62]
horsetail (plant) [N] *osi* [72A]
horst [N] *ülang* [234A]
hose [N] *vooļik* [234A]
hospital [N] *hal̇gla* [227B]
hospitalization [N] *hospitalisEErimine* [257E]
hospitalize [Vt] *hospitalisEErima* [291B]
host [N] *võõrustaja* [227A]
hostage [N] *paņT* [58E]
hostel [N] *internaaT* [58E]
hostile [A] *vaenuliK* [62]
hot [A] *kUUm* [53A]
[A] *palav* [231A]
[A] *tuline* [251]
hot (make) [Vt] *kuumutama* [349F]
hotel [N] *hoteĻL* [58A]
hour [N] *tuŅd* [118]
house [N] *maja* [14A]
house [Vt] *majutama* [349F]
household [N] *leİbkoNd* [106]
housing [N] *majutus* [260A]
hover [Vi] *hõĻjuma* [291C]
howl [Vi] *uLguma* [313A]
[Vi] *uluma* [269]
hub [N] *ruMM* [61A]
hue (colour) [N] *värving* [234A]
hug [Vt] *kaelustama* [349F]
hum [N] *ümin* [231A]
hum [Vi] *uNdama* [343]
[Vi] *ümisema* [349C]
human being [N] *inimene* [257A]
humane [A] *inimliK* [62]
humaneness [N] *humAAnsus* [260B]
humanism [N] *humaniSm* [58B]
humanist [N] *humaniSt* [58B]
humanitarian [A] *humanitAArne* [247]
humanity [N] *inimkoNd* [106]
humble [A] *alandliK* [62]
humiliate [Vt] *alandama* [349F]
humiliation [N] *alandamine* [257E]
humility [N] *alandliKKus* [260B]
humorous [A] *humoorikas* [243A]
humour [N] *hUUmor* [229A]
hump [N] *küHm* [61B]
hunchback [N] *küürakas* [243A]
hunchback [A] *küürakas* [243A]
hundred [N] *sada* [36]
hundredth [N] *sajandiK* [62]
hundredth [A] *sajas* [237A]

Hungarian [N] *maḑjar* [229A]
hungry [A] *näļjane* [251]
hunt [N] *jaHt* [116]
hunter [N] *küŢT* [58C]
hurl [Vt] *looPima* [291E]
hurl [Vt] *virutama* [349F]
hurricane [N] *orkAAn* [58A]
hurried [A] *rutuline* [257D]
hurry [V] *kiirustama* [349F]
hurry [Vi] *ruTTama* [327C]
hurry [Vi] *tõTTama* [327C]
hurt [Vi] *valutama* [349F]
husk [N] *keSt* [53B]
hut [N] *hurtsik* [234A]
[N] *hüŢT* [58C]
[N] *oŅN* [58A]
hydraulic [A] *hüdrauliline* [257D]
hydrogen [N] *vesiniK* [62]
hyena [N] *hüÄÄn* [58A]
hygiene [N] *hügiEEn* [58A]
hygienic [A] *hügieeniline* [257D]
hymn [N] *korAAl* [58A]
hypnosis [N] *hüpnOOs* [58A]
hypnotize [Vt] *hüpnotisEErima* [291B]
hypocrite [N] *silmakirjatseja* [227A]
hypocritical (be) [Vi] *silmakirjatsema* [349E]
hysterical [A] *hüsteeriline* [257D]
hysterics [N] *hüsteerika* [227A]

I

ice [N] *jÄÄ* [4]
ice-cream [N] *jääTis* [260B]
Icelander [N] *iSlandlane* [257C]
icicle [N] *jÄÄpurikas* [243A]
icon [N] *ikOOn* [58A]
icy [A] *jäl̇ne* [252]
ide (fish) [N] *säinas* [159B]
idea [N] *aade* [177E]
[N] *idEE* [2]
ideal [N] *ideAAl* [58A]
ideal [N] *paleus* [260A]
ideal [A] *ideAAlne* [247]
idealism [N] *idealiSm* [58B]
idealist [N] *idealiSt* [58B]
idealistic [A] *idealiStliK* [62]
idealize [Vt] *idealisEErima* [291B]
identical [A] *samane* [251]
identification [N] *identifitsEErimine* [257E]
identification with [N] *samastamine* [257E]
identify [Vt] *identifitsEErima* [291B]
identify with [Vt] *samastama* [349F]
ideology [N] *ideolOOgia* [227A]
idiocy [N] *toTrus* [260B]
idiom [N] *idiOOm* [58A]
idiomatic [A] *idiomaatiline* [257D]
idiot [N] *idiooT* [58E]
idiotic [A] *idiooTliK* [62]
[A] *toTTer* [241B]
idle [A] *tegevusetu* [227A]
idle about [Vi] *vedelema* [325]
idle away [Vt] *viiTma* [297C]
idler [N] *laiSkleja* [227A]
idyll [N] *idüĻL* [58A]
idyllic [A] *idüļliline* [257D]
ignite [Vi] *süŢTima* [349B]
ignite [Vt] *süüTama* [327E]
ignition switch [N] *käiviti* [225A]
ignoramus [N] *võhik* [234A]
ignorance (inexpert) [N] *võhiklus* [260A]
ignorance (stupidity) [N] *nõmedus* [260A]
ignorance (uncertainty) [N] *teAdmatus* [260A]
ignorant (inexpert) [A] *võhikliK* [62]
ignorant (stupid) [A] *nõme* [235]
ignore [Vt] *ignorEErima* [291B]
ill (be) [Vi] *põdema* [275]
ill-advised [A] *ennatliK* [62]
ill-bred [A] *kasvatamatu* [227A]
illegal [A] *illegAAlne* [247]
illumination [N] *illuminatsiOOn* [58A]
illusion [N] *illusiOOn* [58A]
illustrate [Vt] *illustrEErima* [291B]
illustration [N] *illustratsiOOn* [58A]
imaginary [A] *kujutletav* [231A]
imagination [N] *fantAAsia* [227A]
[N] *kujuteLm* [53B]
imagine [V] *fantasEErima* [291B]
imagine [Vt] *kujutlema* [351]
imitate [Vt] *imitEErima* [291B]
[Vt] *maTkima* [291C]
imitation [N] *imitatsiOOn* [58A]
immeasurable [A] *mõõTmatu* [227A]
immediate [A] *vahetu* [227A]
immense [A] *määratu* [227A]
immigrant [N] *immigraņT* [58E]
immoral [A] *amorAAlne* [247]
[A] *kõlvatu* [227A]
immortal [A] *surematu* [227A]
immortality [N] *surematus* [260A]
immune [A] *immUUnne* [247]
impatience [N] *kannatamatus* [260A]
[N] *kärsitus* [260A]
impatient [A] *kannatamatu* [227A]
[A] *kärsitu* [227A]
impenetrable [A] *läbituNgimatu* [227A]
imperialism [N] *imperialiSm* [58B]
imperialist [N] *imperialiSt* [58B]
imperialistic [A] *imperialiStliK* [62]
impersonal [A] *impersonAAlne* [247]
impetuosity [N] *ägedus* [260A]
impetuous [A] *tormakas* [243A]
[A] *äge* [235]
implacable [A] *lePPimatu* [227A]
implement [Vt] *teoStama* [349F]
implore [V] *anuma* [269]
import [N] *imPorT* [58E]
import [Vt] *imporTima* [291F]
importance [N] *täHtsus* [260B]
important [A] *täHtis* [250A]
impose duty [Vt] *toĻLima* [291A]
impossibility [N] *võimatus* [260A]
impossible [A] *võimatu* [227A]
impress [Vt] *imponEErima* [291B]
impression [N] *muļje* [177B]
imprint [N] *märgis* [253]
imprint [Vt] *märgistama* [349F]
imprison [Vt] *vangistama* [349F]
imprisonment [N] *vangistus* [260A]
impromptu [N] *ekspromPt* [58B]
improper [A] *lubamatu* [227A]
improvise [Vt] *improvisEErima* [291B]
impudence [N] *häbematus* [260A]
impudent [A] *häbematu* [227A]
impulsive [A] *impulsİİvne* [247]
impure [A] *rüve* [235]
inability [N] *võl̇metus* [260A]
inattentive [A] *tähelepanematu* [227A]
incapable [A] *võl̇metu* [227A]
incense [N] *viiruk* [229A]
incessant [A] *järelejäTmatu* [227A]
inch [N] *toĻL* [58A]
incident [N] *juHtum* [229A]
incidental [A] *juhusliK* [62]
incite [Vt] *kihutama* [349F]
inclination [N] *kaLduvus* [260A]
inclined (be) [Vi] *kaLduma* [349H]
incomparable [A] *võRdlematu* [227A]
[A] *võrratu* [227A]

incomparable [A] *võrreldamatu* [227A]
incompetence [N] *oSkamatus* [260A]
inconsiderate [A] *hOOļimatu* [227A]
incorrect [A] *vÄÄr* [53A]
incorrigible [A] *parandamatu* [227A]
increase [Vi] *paļjunema* [349D]
incredible [A] *uSkumatu* [227A]
incredulous [A] *uSkmatu* [227A]
inculcate [Vt] *juurutama* [349F]
incurable [A] *ravimatu* [227A]
indebtedness [N] *võLgnevus* [260A]
indecent [A] *süŅdsusetu* [227A]
indefinite [A] *mÄÄramatu* [227A]
independence [N] *iseseİsvus* [260B]
[N] *sõlTumatus* [260A]
independent [A] *sõlTumatu* [227A]
index [N] *indeks* [229A]
indian ink [N] *tuŠŠ* [58C]
indicate [Vt] *osutama* [349F]
indicator [N] *näiTaja* [227A]
indifferent [A] *üKsköiKne* [247]
indigestible [A] *sEEdimatu* [227A]
indignation [N] *nöRdimus* [260A]
indirect [A] *kaUdne* [247]
indispensable [A] *asendamatu* [227A]
indisputable [A] *vaİdlematu* [227A]
individual [A] *individuAAlne* [247]
indivisible [A] *jagamatu* [227A]
İndonesian [N] *indonEEslane* [257C]
inducement [N] *ajend* [229A]
industrial [A] *industriAAlne* [247]
[A] *tööStusliK* [62]
industrialist [N] *tööStur* [229A]
industrialize [Vt] *industrialisEErima* [291B]
industrious [A] *tööKas* [243B]
industry [N] *tööStus* [260B]
ineffective [A] *mõjutu* [227A]
inertia [N] *inerTs* [58B]
inevitability [N] *paratamatus* [260A]
[N] *väļTimatus* [260A]
inevitable [A] *paratamatu* [227A]
inexhaustible [A] *ammendamatu* [227A]
inexperience [N] *vilumatus* [260A]
inexperienced [A] *kogenematu* [227A]
[A] *vilumatu* [227A]
inexplicable [A] *seletamatu* [227A]
inexpressible [A] *väljendamatu* [227A]
infallible [A] *eKsimatu* [227A]
infect [Vt] *nakatama* [349F]
infected (become) [Vi] *nakatuma* [349H]
infection [N] *infektsiOOn* [58A]
[N] *naKKus* [260B]

infectious [A] *naKKav* [231A]
inferred (be) [Vi] *järelduma* [349H]
infirmity [N] *nõTrus* [260B]
inflammable [A] *süŢTiv* [231A]
inflammation [N] *põletiK* [62]
inflation [N] *inflatsiOOn* [58A]
inflexibility [N] *paİndumatus* [260A]
inflexible [A] *paİndumatu* [227A]
influence [N] *mõju* [13A]
influence [Vi] *mõjuma* [269]
influence [Vt] *mõjustama* [349F]
[Vt] *mõjutama* [349F]
influential [A] *mõjukas* [243A]
influenza [N] *influentsa* [152]
inform [Vt] *informEErima* [291B]
[Vt] *teaTama* [349F]
information [N] *informatsiOOn* [58A]
[N] *teave* [208B]
ingenuity [N] *nõuKus* [260B]
ingratitude [N] *tänamatus* [260A]
Ingrian [N] *iNgerlane* [257C]
inhabitant [N] *elaniK* [62]
inherit [Vt] *pärima* [269]
initial [N] *initsiAAl* [58A]
initiative [N] *algatus* [260A]
initiator [N] *initsiaaTor* [229A]
inject [Vt] *süŞtima* [291C]
injecting [N] *süŞtimine* [257E]
injection [N] *süŞt* [58B]
injure [V] *vigastama* [349F]
injury [N] *kahjustus* [260A]
[N] *vigastus* [260A]
injustice [N] *õİglusetus* [260A]
ink [N] *tiņT* [58E]
ink with indian ink [Vt] *tuŠŠima* [291D]
inkling [N] *aİm* [61B]
inkling (have) [Vt] *aİmama* [327B]
inky [A] *tiņdine* [251]
inner [A] *sisemine* [257F]
innocence [N] *süüTus* [260B]
innocent [A] *süüTu* [227B]
innovator [N] *novaaTor* [229A]
[N] *uuendaja* [227A]
inorganic [A] *anorgaaniline* [257D]
inquire [Vt] *pärima* [269]
inquisition [N] *inkvisitsiOOn* [58A]
insatiable [A] *rahuldamatu* [227A]
insect [N] *putukas* [243A]
inseparable [A] *lahutamatu* [227A]
insipid [A] *imal* [231A]
[A] *läila* [152]
[A] *lÄÄge* [227B]

insolence [N] *julTumus* [260A]
insoluble [A] *lahustumatu* [227A]
inspect [Vt] *kontroĻLima* [291A]
inspecting [N] *kontroĻLimine* [257E]
inspection [N] *inspektsiOOn* [58A]
[N] *kontroĻL* [58A]
inspector [N] *inspeKtor* [229A]
inspector [N] *kontrolör* [245]
[N] *revideņT* [58E]
inspiration [N] *inspiratsiOOn* [58A]
inspire [Vt] *inspirEErima* [291B]
[Vt] *tiivustama* [349F]
inspiring [A] *sütitav* [231A]
[A] *vaimustav* [231A]
instance [N] *instanTs* [58B]
[N] *juHt* [124B]
instantaneous [A] *kohene* [251]
[A] *momentAAnne* [247]
instep [N] *pöİd* [111]
instigate [Vt] *algatama* [349F]
[Vt] *õhutama* [349F]
instigation [N] *õhutus* [260A]
instigator [N] *algataja* [227A]
[N] *õhutaja* [227A]
instill [Vt] *sisendama* [349F]
instinct [N] *instinKt* [58B]
[N] *vaiSt* [61B]
instinctive [A] *instinktİİvne* [247]
[A] *vaiStliK* [62]
institute [N] *instituuT* [58E]
institution [N] *asutus* [260A]
instruct [Vt] *instruEErima* [291B]
instruction [N] *instruktsiOOn* [58A]
[N] *juhend* [229A]
[N] *juhis* [253]
[N] *õpetus* [260A]
instructive [A] *õpetliK* [62]
instructor [N] *instruKtor* [229A]
instrument [N] *instrumeņT* [58E]
[N] *piĻL* [58A]
insulate [Vt] *isolEErima* [291B]
insulation [N] *isolatsiOOn* [58A]
insulator [N] *isolaaTor* [229A]
insulin [N] *insulİİn* [58A]
insult [N] *solvang* [234A]
insult [Vt] *soLvama* [327B]
insulting [A] *soLvav* [231A]
insurance [N] *kindlustus* [260A]
insure [Vt] *kindlustama* [349F]
insurgent [N] *mässuline* [257D]
intact [A] *puuTumatu* [227A]
integral [A] *terviklíK* [62]

intellect N *intelleKt* 58B
intellectual N *haritlane* 257C
intellectual A *intellektuAAlne* 247
intelligence N *inteļligenTsus* 260B
intelligence N *taibukus* 260A
intelligent A *inteļligenTne* 247
A *taibukas* 243A
intelligentsia N *haritlaskoNd* 106
intelligentsia N *inteļligenTs* 58B
intend Vt *kavatsema* 349E
intensify Vi *kõvenema* 349D
intensify Vt *kõvendama* 349F
intensity N *intensİİvsus* 260B
intensive A *intensİİvne* 247
intention N *kavatsus* 260A
intentional A *sihiliK* 62
A *taHtliK* 62
interest N *huvi* 17
interest Vt *huvitama* 349F
interested (become) Vi *huvituma* 349H
interesting A *huvitav* 231A
interior N *sisemus* 260A
intermediary N *vahendaja* 227A
intern Vt *internEErima* 291B
internal A *sEEsmine* 257F
internee N *interneeritu* 227A
internment N *internEErimine* 257E
interpret Vt *tõlgendama* 349F
Vt *tõļgitsema* 349E
interpretation N *käsitus* 260A
N *tõlgendus* 260A
N *tõļgitsus* 260A
interpreter N *tõļK* 58F
interrogate Vt *küsitlema* 351
interrogative A *küsiv* 231A
interrupt Vt *katkestama* 349F
interruption N *katkestus* 260A
intersect Vi *lõiKuma* 349G
Vi *riStuma* 349H
interval N *vahemiK* 62
intervene Vi *seKKuma* 349G
intervention N *seKKumine* 257E
interview N *intervjUU* 1
interview N *usutelu* 13A
N *usutlus* 260A
interview Vt *intervjuEErima* 291B
Vt *usutlema* 351
interviewer N *intervjuEErija* 227A
intestine N *sOOl* 82
N *soolikas* 243A
intimacy N *intİİmsus* 260B
intimate A *intİİmne* 247
intolerance N *saļLimatus* 260A
intolerant A *saļLimatu* 227A
intonation N *intonatsiOOn* 58A
intoxicate Vt *joobnustama* 349F
Vt *joovastama* 349F
intoxicated (become) Vi *joovastuma* 349H
intoxicating A *joovastav* 231A
intoxication N *joovastus* 260A
intricate A *keerukas* 243A
intrigue N *intrİİg* 58A
intrigue Vi *intrigEErima* 291B
introduce Vt *tutvustama* 349F
introduce a person Vt *esitlema* 351
introductory A *siSSejuhatav* 231A
intrude Vi *tiKKuma* 291D
intrusive A *peAletiKKuv* 231A
A *peAletüKKiv* 231A
invade Vt *okupEErima* 291B
invader N *okupaņT* 58E
invalid N *invalİİd* 58A
invalid A *keHtetu* 227A
invalidism N *invalİİdsus* 260B
invasion N *invasiOOn* 58A
invective N *sõİm* 61B
invent Vt *leiutama* 349F
invention N *leiutis* 260A
inventor N *leİdur* 229A
inventor N *leiutaja* 227A
inventory N *inventar* 245
inventory N *inventUUr* 58A
inversion N *inversiOOn* 58A
investigate Vt *jUUrdlema* 331A
Vt *UUrima* 291A
investigation N *jUUrdlus* 260B
investigator N *UUrija* 227A
invincibility N *võiTmatus* 260A
invincible A *võiTmatu* 227A
invisible A *näHtamatu* 227A
invitation N *kutse* 177B
invite Vt *kuTsuma* 291C
involuntary A *taHtmatu* 227A
iodine N *jOOḑ* 58A
iris N *iiris* 253
Irish N *İİrlane* 257C
iron N *raUd* 88A
iron A *raUdne* 247
iron Vt *triiKima* 291G
ironic(al) A *irooniline* 257D
irony N *irOOnia* 227A
irradiate Vt *kiiritama* 349F
irradiation N *kiiritus* 260A
irrational A *mõiStmatu* 227A
irreconcilable A *lepitamatu* 227A
irregular A *erandliK* 62
irreproachable A *laiTmatu* 227A
irrigate Vt *niisutama* 349F
irritable A *ärrituv* 231A
irritate Vt *ärritama* 349F
irritated (become) Vi *ärrituma* 349H
irritation N *ärritus* 260A
island N *sAAr* 82
islet N *laİd* 123B
issue Vt *väļjastama* 349F
issuing N *väļjastus* 260A
Italian N *itAAllane* 257C
italics N *kursİİv* 58A
itch N *sügelus* 260A
itch Vi *sügelema* 325
Izhorian N *isur* 229A

J

jackal N *šaaKal* 229A
jackdaw N *haKK* 58C
jacket N *jaKK* 58C
N *jope* 152
jag N *saKK* 58C
jagged A *sakiline* 257D
jaguar N *jaaguar* 246
jam N *džeMM* 58A
jam N *mOOş* 58A
jamb N *piiT* 49E
January N *jaanuar* 246
Japanese N *jaaPanlane* 257C
jar N *purK* 58F
jargon N *žargOOn* 58A
Järvamaa native N *järvakas* 243A
N *järvalane* 257C
jasmine N *jasmİİn* 58A
jazz N *džäSS* 58A
jealous A *kiivas* 159A
jeans N *džiinid (pl)* 58A
jeep N *viļlis* 253
jelly N *želEE* 2
N *tarre* 215
N *tarretis* 260A

jelly-fish N *miļlimaļlikas* 243A
jerk N *nõKS* 61B
jerk N *tõmme* 209
jerk Vi *nõksatama* 349F
jetty N *mUUļ* 58A
Jew N *juuŢ* 58E
jewel N *juvEEl* 58A
jeweller N *juvelİİr* 58A
jockey N *džoki* 152
join Vt *liiTma* 297C
join up Vi *liiTuma* 349H
joint N *liiges* 253
joke N *nali* 69A
joke Vi *naļjatama* 349F
jolly A *luŞtliK* 62
jolt Vi *põruma* 269
jolt Vt *põrutama* 349F
jostle Vi *tõuKlema* 326F
journalism N *žurnalistika* 227A
journalist N *žurnaliSt* 58B
journey N *reTk* 63B
journeyman N *seĻL* 58A
joy N *rÕÕm* 61A
joyful A *rÕÕmus* 250A
jubilarian N *juubilar* 245
jubilee anniversary N *jUUbel* 229A
judge N *koHtuniK* 62
judicial A *koHtuliK* 62
judo N *džuudo* 152
jug N *kaNN* 61A
juggle Vi *žonglEErima* 291B
juggler N *žonglÖÖr* 58A
juice N *maHl* 49B
N *mehu* 13A
N *saHvt* 58B
juicy A *mahlakas* 243A
A *mahlane* 251
July N *juuli* 152
jump N *hüpe* 177C
jump Vi *hüPPama* 327C
jump about Vi *hüPlema* 326C
jumper N *džemPer* 240A
June N *juuni* 152
jungle N *džuNgel* 240A
juniper N *kadakas* 243A
junk N *koli* 13A
juridical A *juriidiline* 257D
jurisprudence N *juura* 152
jurist N *juriSt* 58B
jury N *žürİİ* 1
just A *õİglane* 257C
justice N *õİglus* 260B
justification N *põhjendus* 260A
justification N *õigustus* 260A
justify Vt *põhjendama* 349F
Vt *õigustama* 349F

K

kapron N *kaPron* 229A
Karelian N *karjalane* 257C
keel N *kİİl* 61A
keep Vt *pidama* 277
kefir N *keeFir* 229A
kerchief N *räŢT* 58C
kerosene N *petrOOleum* 246
ketchup N *ketšup* 229A
kettle N *katel* 173A
key N *võţi* 181
keyboard (piano) N *klahvistiK* 62
Khanty N *haņT* 58E
kick up fuss Vi *skandaalitsema* 349E
kick up ruckus Vi *mürgeldama* 349F
kidney N *nEEr* 61A
Kihnu native N *kiHnlane* 257C
kill Vt *taPma* 298
killing N *taPmine* 257E
kilo N *kilo* 13A
kind A *laHke* 227B
kindle Vt *süţitama* 349F
kindness N *laHkus* 260B
king N *kuningas* 243A
kiosk N *kiosK* 229B
kiss N *musi* 13A
N *muşu* 13A
N *sUUdlus* 260B
kiss Vt *muşutama* 349F
Vt *sUUdlema* 326A
kitchen N *kööK* 58F
kite N *lohe* 153
kitsch N *butafOOria* 227A
kitsch N *kiTš* 58B
knapsack N *paUn* 49B
knead Vt *sõTkuma* 291C
knee N *põli* 66
N *põĻv* 66
kneel Vi *põļvitama* 349F
knife N *nuga* 39
N *väiTs* 63B
knife Vt *pusşitama* 349F
knight N *rüüTel* 240A
knitted goods N *trikotAAž* 58A
knitting beginning N *loomus* 253
knob N *nuKK* 58C
N *nuPP* 61C
knock N *koputus* 260A
knock Vi *koputama* 349F
knock about Vi *kolama* 269
knockout N *nokauT* 58E
knot N *sõĻm* 65
knot Vt *sõĻmima* 291C
know (fact) Vt *teAdma* 314
know (person) Vt *tuNdma* 319
know how to Vt *oSkama* 348C
knowledge N *teAdmine* 257E
known (make) Vt *avaldama* 349F
Koran N *korAAn* 58A
Korean N *korEalane* 257C

L

label N *etikeŢT* 58C
N *sedel* 229A
laboratory N *laboratOOrium* 246
laboratory A *laboratOOrne* 247
laboratory assistant N *laboraņT* 58E
labyrinth N *labüriņT* 58E
lace N *piŢs* 58B
laconic A *lakooniline* 257D
ladder N *redel* 229A
ladle N *kuļP* 58D
lady N *dAAm* 58A
N *leedi* 152
lady-like A *proualiK* 62
A *daamiliK* 62
ladybug N *lepatriinu* 152
lagoon N *lagUUn* 58A
lake N *jäRv* 63B
lake system N *järvestiK* 62
lamb N *taLL* 63A
lament Vi *halisema* 349C
lamentation N *iTk* 61B

lamp N *lamP* 58D
lamprey N *siLm* 61B
lance N *piiK* 58F
land N *mAA* 9
land Vi *mAAnduma* 349H
land airplane Vt *mAAndama* 349F
land boat Vi *raNduma* 349H
land of the dead N *manala* 227A
landscape N *maaStiK* 62
language family N *kEElkoNd* 106
lantern N *latern* 231A
lap N *rüPP* 63C
N *süli* 18
lapel N *käänis* 253
N *revÄÄr* 58A
Laplander N *laPlane* 257C
lapse Vi *aEguma* 349G
larch N *lehis* 253
lard N *raSv* 49B
lark (bird) N *lõoKe(ne)* 257G
larva N *tõuK* 61F
N *vaStne* 247
laryngitis N *larüngiiT* 58E
laser N *laser* 229A
last Vi *jäTkuma* 349G
Vi *keStma* 297A
latch N *linK* 58F
late A *hiline* 251
late (be) Vi *hilinema* 349D
lath N *laŢT* 58C
lathe (turn on) Vt *treİma* 262
lathe operator N *treİal* 229A
latrine N *latrİİn* 58A
Latvian N *läTlane* 257C
laugh N *naEr* 61B
laugh V *naErma* 292B
launch N *kaaTer* 240A
laundry house N *pesula* 227A
laureate N *laureaaT* 58E
laurel N *lOOrber* 229A
lavender N *laveNdel* 240A
law N *seAdus* 260B
lawful A *seAdusliK* 62
lawn N *muru* 13A
lawsuit N *protseŞS* 58A
lawyer N *advokaaT* 58E
lay claim Vi *pretendEErima* 291B
lay eggs V *munema* 269
layer N *kiHt* 116
N *lade* 157
layered A *kihiline* 257D
laze about Vi *laiSklema* 336

laziness N *laiSkus* 260B
lazy A *laiSk* 95B
lead Vt *juhatama* 349F
Vt *juHtima* 308B
lead N *plİİ* 1
leader N *juHt* 116
leadership N *juHtimine* 257E
leaf N *leHt* 139
leaf Vt *lehitsema* 349E
league N *liiga* 152
leak Vi *leKKima* 291D
lean against Vi *nõjatuma* 349H
Vi *toeTuma* 349H
lean meat N *taİ* 1
lean of meat A *taİne* 252
leap Vi *kaRgama* 348B
learn Vt *õPPima* 291D
learner N *õPPija* 227A
leash N *lÕÕg* 97
least A *vähim* 231A
leave behind Vt *jäTma* 300
leaven N *juuretis* 260A
lectern N *puļT* 58E
lecture N *loEng* 234B
lecture-hall N *lektOOrium* 246
lecturer N *dotseņT* 58E
N *leKtor* 229A
leech N *kAAņ* 58A
leelu singer N *leelutaja* 227A
left A *vasak* 234A
A *vasem* 231A
leg N *jaLg* 100
legacy N *pärandus* 260A
legal A *õİgusliK* 62
legend N *legeNd* 58B
legendary A *legendAArne* 247
lemon N *sidrun* 229A
lender N *laenutaja* 227A
length N *piKKus* 260B
lengthen Vi *pikenema* 349D
lens N *lääTs* 63B
lens (camera) N *objektİİv* 58A
leopard N *leoPaRd* 58B
lessen Vi *vähenema* 349D
lessen Vt *vähendama* 349F
lesser A *vähem* 231A
letter N *kiri* 68A
leukemia N *leukEEmia* 227A
level N *nivOO* 1
N *tasand* 229A
N *tase* 157
level (make) Vt *tasandama* 349F

level (tool) N *vaaderpaŞS* 58A
lever N *hOOb* 101A
lever Vt *hOObama* 339A
liable to a fee A *maksuline* 257D
liar N *valetaja* 227A
liberal A *liberAAlne* 247
libretto N *libreto* 152
licentious A *liiderliK* 62
lichen N *saMbliK* 62
lick Vt *laKKuma* 291D
lid N *kAAş* 146
lie (deceive) Vi *valetama* 349F
lie (deception) N *vale* 153
lie about (recline) Vi *lamama* 269
lie in wait for Vt *varitsema* 349E
lie on (recline) Vi *lasuma* 269
lieutenant N *leiTnanT* 58E
life N *elu* 13A
lifeless A *elutu* 227A
lifeless A *hingetu* 227A
lift Vt *tõStma* 297A
lift (give) Vt *sõidutama* 349F
light N *vaLgus* 260B
light (weight) A *keRge* 227B
light ale N *kali* 69A
lighten Vi *valgenema* 349D
lighten (weight) Vi *kergenema* 349D
lighten (weight) Vt *kergendama* 349F
lighthouse N *majakas* 243A
lighting N *tulestiK* 62
lightness (weight) N *keRgus* 260B
lightning N *piKne* 247
N *välK* 61F
lilac N *sirel* 229A
lily N *lİİlia* 227A
limb N *jäse* 157
lime (mineral) N *lubi* 71B
limestone N *pAAş* 145
limestone A *paEne* 252
limit N *limiiT* 58E
limit Vt *pİİrama* 327A
limited (be) Vi *pİİrduma* 349H
limp A *lõTv* 49E
limp Vi *lonKama* 327F
limp (become) Vi *lõTvuma* 349G
linden tree N *lõhmus* 253
N *päRn* 53B
line N *jOOn* 82
line N *kriiPs* 61B
N *lİİn* 58A
N *rivi* 13A
N *vİİrg* 131A

line (clothing) [Vt] *vooderdama* [349F]
line-up [N] *rivistus* [260A]
line up [Vi] *rivistuma* [349H]
line up [Vt] *reaStama* [349F]
[Vt] *rivistama* [349F]
lined [A] *jooneline* [257D]
[A] *jooniline* [257D]
[A] *viiruline* [257D]
linen [N] *lina* [14A]
linen [A] *linane* [251]
linguistic [A] *keeleline* [257D]
lining [N] *vOOder* [240A]
[N] *vooderdis* [260A]
link [N] *lüli* [13A]
linoleum [N] *linolEum* [58B]
lion [N] *lõvi* [13A]
lip [N] *hUUl* [82]
[N] *moKK* [53C]
liqueur [N] *likÖÖr* [58A]
liquid [A] *vedel* [231A]
liquidate [Vt] *likvidEErima* [291B]
liquor [N] *vİİn* [49A]
liquorice [N] *lagrits* [231A]
lisp [Vi] *pudistama* [349F]
list of names [N] *nimestiK* [62]
[N] *nimistu* [227A]
listen to [Vt] *kUUlama* [327A]
listener [N] *kUUlaja* [227A]
literary [A] *kirjandusliK* [62]
literature [N] *kirjandus* [260A]
Lithuanian [N] *leedulane* [257C]
litigate [V] *protseŞSima* [291A]
litre [N] *liiTer* [240A]
litter [N] *paHn* [49B]
[N] *põHk* [131C]
[N] *risu* [13A]
little (a bit) [A] *natuke(ne)* [257G]
liturgy [N] *lituRgia* [227A]
live [Vi] *elama* [269]
livelihood [N] *elatis* [260A]
lively [A] *elav* [231A]
[A] *reibas* [159D]
liver [N] *maKs* [49B]
livestock breeding [N] *karjandus* [260A]
living [A] *elus* [231A]
living conditions [N] *olme* [177B]
Livonian [N] *lİİvlane* [257C]
lizard [N] *sisaliK* [62]
load [N] *laadung* [229A]
load [Vt] *lAAḑima* [291A or 305]
loaf [N] *päŢs* [58B]
loaf [Vi] *logelema* [325]
loaf about [Vi] *töllerdama* [349F]
loafer [N] *logard* [229A]
loan [N] *laEn* [61B]
loathsome [A] *iLge* [227B]
lobby [N] *kuluaarid (pl)* [58A]
local [A] *kohaliK* [62]
[A] *sİİnne* [247]
located (be) [Vi] *asetsema* [349E]
lock [N] *luKK* [61C]
lock [Vt] *lukustama* [349F]
lock of hair [N] *salK* [49F]
lockout [N] *lokauT* [58E]
locomotive [N] *vedur* [229A]
loft [N] *laKK* [49C]
log [N] *haLg* [131B]
[N] *paļK* [58F]
logic [N] *loogika* [227A]
logical [A] *loogiline* [257D]
loll while droning [Vi] *jorutama* [349F]
loneliness [N] *üksildus* [260A]
lonely [A] *üksildane* [257A]
long [A] *piKK* [53C]
longer [A] *pikem* [231A]
look at [Vt] *vaaTama* [327E]
loom [N] *teļjed (pl)* [141]
loon [N] *kaUr* [58B]
loosen soil [Vt] *kobestama* [349F]
lord (aristocrat) [N] *loRd* [58B]
Lord (God) [N] *İSSand* [231A]
lorgnette [N] *lornjeŢT* [58C]
lose [Vt] *kaoTama* [349F]
lose one's way [Vi] *eKsima* [291C]
loser [N] *kaoTaja* [227A]
loss [N] *kadu* [27]
loss [N] *kaHjum* [229A]
[N] *kaoTus* [260B]
lost (become) [Vi] *kaduma* [280]
lot [N] *liiSk* [131C]
lot of goods [N] *saŢs* [58B]
lottery [N] *lOOşimine* [257E]
[N] *loterİİ* [1]
lottery ticket [N] *lOOş* [58A]
lotto [N] *loto* [152]
loud [A] *vali* [75]
loudness [N] *vaĻjus* [260B]
loudspeaker [N] *reproduKtor* [229A]
louse [N] *täİ* [1]
lousy [A] *närune* [251]
lout [N] *loru* [13A]
love [N] *armastus* [260A]
love [Vt] *armastama* [349F]
lover [N] *armastaja* [227A]
low [A] *madal* [231A]
lower [Vi] *laSkuma* [349G]
lower [Vt] *langetama* [349F]
lower [Vt] *madaldama* [349F]
loyal [A] *trUUalamliK* [62]
lubricant [N] *määre* [211A]
lubricate [Vt] *mÄÄrima* [291A]
lukewarm [A] *leİge* [227B]
lull to sleep [Vt] *uinutama* [349F]
[Vt] *äiutama* [349F]
lump [N] *klomP* [58D]
[N] *tomP* [61D]
lump of earth [N] *panK* [49F]
lung [N] *koPs* [61B]
lush [A] *lopsakas* [243A]
lust [N] *iha* [13A]
luxuriate [Vi] *mõnulema* [349A]
luxurious [A] *luKsusliK* [62]
luxury [N] *luKsus* [260B]
lyceum [N] *lüTseum* [246]
lynch [Vt] *liņTšima* [291C]
lynx [N] *ilves* [253]
lyrical [A] *lüüriline* [257D]
lyrics [N] *lüürika* [227A]
Läänemaa native [N] *lÄÄnlane* [257C]

M

M.C. [N] *konferansjEE* [2]
macaroni [N] *makaron* [245]
machination [N] *mahhinatsiOOn* [58A]
machine [N] *masin* [231A]
mackerel [N] *makreĻL* [58A]
[N] *skuMbria* [227A]
Mafia [N] *maFFia* [227A]
magazine [N] *žurnAAl* [58A]
maggot [N] *vagel* [78C]
magical [A] *maagiline* [257D]
magnet [N] *magnet* [229A]
magnetic [A] *magnetiline* [257D]
magnetize [Vt] *magneeTima* [291F]
[Vt] *magnetisEErima* [291B]
magnifying glass [N] *luuP* [58D]
magpie [N] *harakas* [243A]
maiden [N] *iMb* [138]
[N] *neİd* [123B]

maiden [N] *neiu* [152]
mail [N] *poŞt* [58B]
mailman [N] *poştiljon* [245]
main [A] *peAmine* [257F]
main entrance [N] *parAAdna* [227B]
main line [N] *magistrAAl* [58A]
maintain [Vt] *pidama* [277]
maintenance [N] *hOOldus* [260B]
majestic [A] *majesteeTliK* [62]
majesty [N] *majesteeT* [58E]
major [N] *major* [229A]
majority [N] *enamiK* [62]
[N] *enamus* [260A]
make [Vt] *tegema* [290]
make a note [Vt] *märKima* [291G]
make one's way to [Vi] *sUUnduma* [349H]
make up (cosmetic) [Vt] *minKima* [291G]
make up (stage) [Vt] *grimEErima* [291B]
make-up [N] *minK* [58F]
make-up (stage) [N] *griMM* [58A]
making [N] *tegemine* [257E]
male [A] *isane* [251]
malt [N] *linnased (pl)* [253]
mammal [N] *imetaja* [227A]
Mammon [N] *maMMon* [231A]
mammoth [N] *mammut* [229A]
man [N] *mEEs* [147]
man [Vt] *mehitama* [349F]
manage to do [V] *jõUdma* [316A]
management [N] *juhatus* [260A]
[N] *juHtkoNd* [106]
manager [N] *juhataja* [227A]
[N] *mänedžer* [245]
mandate [N] *mandaaT* [58E]
mandolin [N] *mandolİIn* [58A]
mane [N] *laKK* [49C]
manger [N] *sõİm* [63B]
mania [N] *mAAnia* [227A]
manicure [N] *manikÜÜr* [58A]
manifesto [N] *manifeSt* [58B]
manliness [N] *mehisus* [260A]
manly [A] *meheliK* [62]
[A] *mehine* [251]
manner [N] *lAAd* [58A]
[N] *vİIs* [58A]
manoeuvre [N] *manÖÖver* [240A]
manoeuvre [Vt] *manööverdama* [349F]
manor house [N] *hÄÄrber* [229A]
Mansi [N] *mansi* [152]
manure [N] *sõņnik* [234A]
manure (liquid) [N] *virTs* [49B]
many [N] *mitu* [182]

map [Vt] *kaardistama* [349F]
maple [N] *vaher* [206]
maple grove [N] *vaHtriK* [62]
marble [N] *maRmor* [229A]
march [N] *marSS* [58G]
march [Vi] *marSSima* [291H]
March [N] *märTs* [58B]
mare [N] *mära* [13A]
margarine [N] *margarİIn* [58A]

margin [N] *veeris* [253]
marinade [N] *marinAAd* [58A]
marinade [Vt] *marinEErima* [291B]
marjoram [N] *majorAAn* [58A]
mark [N] *märK* [58F]
mark (currency) [N] *marK* [49F]
mark an occasion [Vt] *tähistama* [349F]
market [N] *tuRg* [131B]
market [Vt] *kaubastama* [349F]
[Vt] *turustama* [349F]
marketing [N] *turustus* [260A]
marks (school) [N] *hinne* [214]
marksman [N] *laSkur* [229A]
marmalade [N] *marmelAAd* [58A]
marrow [N] *üdi* [13C]
marry [Vi] *abieLLuma* [349G]
[Vi] *naiTuma* [349H]
marry [Vt] *naİma* [261B]
marshal [N] *marSSal* [229A]
martyr [N] *märTer* [240A]
martyr-like [A] *märTerliK* [62]
marvellous [A] *oivaline* [257D]
marzipan [N] *martsipan* [245]
mask [N] *maŞk* [58B]
masochist [N] *masohhiSt* [58B]
mass [N] *maŞS* [58A]
mass [A] *maşsiline* [257D]
mass (Catholic) [N] *meŞS* [58A]
massage [N] *massAAž* [58A]
massage [Vt] *massEErima* [291B]
massive [A] *kogus* [231A]
[A] *massİIvne* [247]
mast [N] *maŞt* [58B]
master (expert) [N] *meiSter* [240A]
master (lord) [N] *isand* [231A]
master (university) [N] *magiSter* [240A]
masterful [A] *meiSterliK* [62]
masterly [A] *virtuOOsne* [248]
mastery [N] *meiSterliKKus* [260B]
masturbate [Vi] *onanEErima* [291B]
masturbating [N] *onanEErimine* [257E]
masturbation [N] *masturbatsiOOn* [58A]

masturbation [N] *onaniSm* [58B]
masturbator [N] *onaniSt* [58B]
mat (dull colour) [A] *maŢT* [58C]
mat (floor) [N] *maŢT* [58C]
match (fire) [N] *tiKK* [61C]
match (sport) [N] *maTš* [58B]
material [A] *aİneline* [257D]
[A] *materiAAlne* [247]
material [N] *materjal* [245]
material (cloth) [N] *kangas* [159B]
materialistic [A] *materialiStliK* [62]
materialize [Vi] *teoStuma* [349H]
mathematical [A] *matemaatiline* [257D]
mathematician [N] *matemaatik* [234A]
mathematics [N] *matemaatika* [227A]
matron [N] *emand* [231A]
matted (become) [Vi] *vanuma* [269]
mattress [N] *madrats* [229A]
mausoleum [N] *mausolEum* [58B]
maximum [A] *maksimAAlne* [247]
maximum [N] *maksimum* [245]
May [N] *maİ* [1]
mayonnaise [N] *majonEEs* [58A]
mead [N] *mõdu* [13C]
meadow [N] *AAs* [49A]
[N] *niiT* [61E]
[N] *nuRm* [63B]
meagre [A] *lahja* [152]
meal [N] *eine* [177B]
mean [A] *kuri* [71A]
mean [Vt] *tähendama* [349F]
meander [Vi] *looKlema* [326F]
meandering [A] *looKlev* [231A]
meaning [N] *tähendus* [260A]
meaning (give) [Vt] *mõtestama* [349F]
means [N] *vahend* [229A]
measles [N] *leeTrid (pl)* [240A]
measure [N] *meeTmed (pl)* [179D]
[N] *mõõT* [61E]
measure [Vt] *mõõTma* [297C]
measuring [N] *mõõTmine* [257E]
meat [N] *liha* [13A]
meat-ball [N] *koTleŢ* [58H]
mechanic [N] *mehaanik* [234A]
mechanical [A] *mehaaniline* [257D]
mechanics [N] *mehaanika* [227A]
mechanism [N] *mehhaniSm* [58B]
mechanization [N] *mehhanisEErimine* [257E]
mechanize [Vt] *mehhanisEErima* [291B]
mechanizer [N] *mehhanisaaTor* [229A]
medal [N] *medal* [229A]
mediate [Vt] *vahendama* [349F]

medic [N] *meedik* [234A]
medicinal [A] *meditsiiniline* [257D]
medicine [N] *medikameņT* [58E]
[N] *meditsİİn* [58A]
[N] *rohi* [151]
meditate [Vt] *mõlgutama* [349F]
meditation [N] *mõtiskelu* [13A]
meet [Vi] *koHtuma* [349H]
meet [Vt] *koHtama* [341B]
megaphone [N] *ruuPor* [229A]
melancholic [A] *melanhOOlne* [247]
melancholy [N] *melanhOOlia* [227A]
[N] *nuKrus* [260B]
melancholy [A] *kuRbliK* [62]
[A] *nuKKer* [241B]
melancholy (be) [Vi] *nukrutsema* [349E]
melodious [A] *meloodiline* [257D]
melody [N] *melOOdia* [227A]
[N] *vİİs* [58A]
melon [N] *melon* [229A]
melt [Vi] *sulama* [269]
melt [Vt] *sulatama* [349F]
member [N] *liige* [179E]
membership [N] *kUUluvus* [260A]
membrane [N] *kile* [153]
[N] *membrAAn* [58A]
memoirs [N] *memuaarid* [58A]
memorial [N] *mälestis* [260A]
memory [N] *mälestus* [260A]
[N] *mälu* [13A]
menstruation [N] *menstruatsiOOn* [58A]
mentality [N] *mEElsus* [260B]
mention [Vt] *maİnima* [291C]
menu [N] *menÜÜ* [1]
merciful [A] *armuliK* [62]
mercy [N] *aRm* [61B]
[N] *halastus* [260A]
mercy (have) [Vi] *halastama* [349F]
mere [A] *pelK* [53F]
meridian [N] *meridiAAn* [58A]
merited [A] *tEEneline* [257D]
mermaid [N] *näKK* [58C]
merry-go-round [N] *karusseĻL* [58A]
message [N] *sõnum* [229A]
[N] *teade* [177E]
Messiah [N] *meSSias* [243A]
metal [N] *metaĻL* [58A]
metallic [A] *metaļliline* [257D]
metallurgical [A] *metallurgiline* [257D]
metallurgy [N] *metalluŖgia* [227A]
meteor [N] *meteOOr* [58A]
meteorite [N] *meteoriiT* [58E]
meteorologist [N] *meteorolOOg* [58A]
meteorology [N] *meteorolOOgia* [227A]
method [N] *meetod* [229A]
[N] *võte* [177C]
methodical [A] *metoodiline* [257D]
methodist [N] *metodiSt* [58B]
methodology [N] *metoodika* [227A]
metre [N] *meeTer* [229A]
metropolis [N] *metropol* [245]
metropolitan (church) [N] *metropoliiT* [58E]
mew [Vi] *näUguma* [312]
Mexican [N] *mehhiklane* [257C]
microbe [N] *mikrOOb* [58A]
microphone [N] *mikrofon* [245]
microscope [N] *mikroskooP* [58D]
microscopic [A] *mikroskoopiline* [257D]
midge [N] *kihulane* [257C]
midget [N] *lilipuŢ* [58H]
might [N] *vägevus* [260A]
mighty [A] *vägev* [231A]
migration [N] *migratsiOOn* [58A]
migration [N] *ränne* [214]
mild [A] *lEEbe* [227B]
[A] *mahe* [235]
mildness [N] *mahedus* [260A]
mile [N] *mİİl* [58A]
[N] *verSt* [53B]
milieu [N] *miljÖÖ* [1]
militarism [N] *militariSm* [58B]
military [A] *sõjaline* [257D]
militiaman [N] *militsionÄÄr* [58A]
milk [N] *pİİm* [49A]
milk [Vt] *lüPsma* [293A]
milk mushroom [N] *riisikas* [243A]
milk pail [N] *lüpsik* [234A]
milker [N] *lüPsja* [227B]
milking [N] *lüPsmine* [257E]
mill [N] *veŞki* [225B]
mill [Vt] *frEEşima* [291A]
mill (metal) [Vt] *vaļTsima* [291C]
miller [N] *möLder* [240A]
millet [N] *hirSS* [58G]
million [N] *miĻjon* [229A]
millionaire [N] *miļjonär* [245]
millionth [A] *miĻjones* [237C]
mimic [Vt] *osatama* [349F]
minaret [N] *minareŢT* [58C]
mince [Vt] *haKKima* [291D]
mind [N] *mEEl* [82]
mine [N] *kaevandus* [260A]
mine [Vt] *kaevandama* [349F]
mine (explosive) [N] *mİİn* [58A]
mine shaft [N] *šaHt* [58B]
miner [N] *kaEvur* [229A]
mineral [N] *minerAAl* [58A]
mineral [A] *minerAAlne* [247]
mineral deposit [N] *mAArdla* [227B]
mineral resource [N] *maare* [211A]
mineralogy [N] *mineralOOgia* [227A]
mingle [Vi] *segunema* [349D]
miniature [N] *miniatUUr* [58A]
minimal [A] *minimAAlne* [247]
minimum [N] *miinimum* [245]
mining [N] *mäEndus* [260B]
minister [N] *miniSter* [240A]
ministry [N] *ministEErium* [246]
mink [N] *naarits* [231A]
minority [N] *vähemus* [260A]
minus [N] *miinus* [253]
minute [N] *minut* [229A]
minutes (take) [Vt] *protokoĻLima* [291A]
minutes of meeting [N] *protokoĻL* [58A]
miracle [N] *ime* [153]
mirage [N] *fatamorgaana* [152]
mirror [N] *pEEgel* [240A]
miscarry [Vi] *äpardama* [349F]
[Vi] *äparduma* [349H]
mischief [N] *koErus* [260B]
[N] *pahandus* [260A]
[N] *vallatus* [260A]
mischievous [A] *vallatu* [227A]
miser [N] *iHnur* [229A]
miserliness [N] *iHnus* [260B]
miserly [A] *ihnus* [168A]
misfortune [N] *õnnetus* [260A]
mishap [N] *viperus* [260A]
mislead [Vt] *eksitama* [349F]
miss [N] *preili* [152]
mission [N] *missiOOn* [58A]
mission (send on) [Vt] *komandEErima* [291B]
missionary [N] *misjonär* [245]
missive [N] *saadetis* [260A]
mist [N] *sumu* [13A]
mistake [N] *eKsimus* [260A]
[N] *viga* [37]
mitten [N] *käpik* [234A]
mix [Vt] *segama* [269]
mixer [N] *miKser* [229A]
mixture [N] *segu* [13D]
mobile [A] *liiKuv* [231A]
mobilize [Vt] *mobilisEErima* [291B]
moccasin [N] *pastel* [173B]
mock [Vt] *mõnitama* [349F]
[Vt] *pilKama* [327F]

mockery N *mõnitus* 260A
mocking N *mõnitamine* 257E
mocking A *pilKav* 231A
model N *makeŢT* 58C
N *mudel* 229A
model Vt *modellEErima* 291B
model (fashion) N *mannekEEn* 58A
moderate A *mõõdukas* 243A
moderation N *mõõdukus* 260A
modern A *modeRnne* 247
modernize Vt *modernisEErima* 291B
modest A *tagasihoİdliK* 62
moist A *niiSke* 227B
moisture N *niiSkus* 260B
Moldavian N *moldAAvlane* 257C
mole N *muŢT* 58C
molecule N *molekul* 245
moment N *heTk* 63B
N *momeņT* 58E
N *vİİv* 61A
momentum N *hOOg* 133
mommy N *eMM* 63A
N *mamma* 152
N *mammi* 152
N *meMM* 63A
monarch N *monarH* 58B
monarchy N *monarHia* 227A
monastery N *klooSter* 240A
money N *raha* 13A
monk N *munK* 53F
monkey N *aHv* 58B
monologue N *monolOOg* 58A
monopoly N *monopol* 245
monotonous A *monotOOnne* 247
monotony N *üKsluİsus* 260B
monster N *koletis* 260A
month N *kUU* 3
month-old A *kUUne* 252
monument N *monumeņT* 58E
monumental A *monumentAAlne* 247
moo Vi *aMMuma* 291A
mood N *tuju* 13A
moody A *tujukas* 243A
moon N *kUU* 3
moonlighting N *haltuura* 152
moonshine N *puSkar* 229A
moor N *raba* 14B
mope Vi *norutama* 349F
moral N *morAAl* 58A
moral A *kõLbeline* 257D
A *morAAlne* 247
moral impropriety N *kõlvatus* 260A
morality N *kõLblus* 260B
morally suitable A *kõLbliK* 62
Mordvin N *moRdvalane* 257C
more N *enam* 231A
morning N *hommik* 234A
morphological A *morfoloogiline* 257D
morphology N *morfolOOgia* 227A
Morse N *morse* 152
morsel N *pala* 14A
N *raasuke(ne)* 257G
N *tükike(ne)* 257G
mortal A *sureliK* 62
mortality N *suremus* 260A
mortar N *uHmer* 240A
mortgage N *hüpoteeK* 58F
mosaic N *mosaiiK* 58F
mosque N *mošEE* 2
mosquito N *sääSk* 140B
moss N *sammal* 200
moss-covered (get) Vi *sammalduma* 349H
mossy A *saMblane* 257C
motel N *moteĻL* 58A
moth N *koİ* 1
mother N *ema* 13A
mother-in-law N *äMM* 53A
motionless A *liiKumatu* 227A
motivate Vt *motivEErima* 291B
motive N *motİİv* 58A
motor N *mooTor* 229A
motto N *moto* 152
mould N *haļlitus* 260A
moulder Vi *pehastuma* 349H
Vi *peHkima* 349B
mouldy (be) Vi *haļlitama* 349F
mound N *kinK* 61F
mount Vt *montEErima* 291B
mountain ash N *piHl* 49B
N *pihlakas* 243A
mountain range N *mäeStiK* 62
mountaineer N *aļpiniSt* 58B
mountaineering N *aļpiniSm* 58B
mourn Vt *leİnama* 327B
mourner N *leİnaja* 227A
mourning N *leİn* 49B
mouse N *hİİr* 82
moustache N *vuņTs* 58B
N *vuRR* 61A
mouth N *sUU* 6
mouth of river N *suue* 219A
move Vi *liiKuma* 291G
move Vt *liigutama* 349F
move household Vi *kolima* 269
move in crowd Vi *vOOrima* 291A
movement N *liiKumine* 257E
movie camera N *kaamera* 227A
moving household N *kolimine* 257E
mow Vt *niiTma* 297C
mower N *niiduk* 229A
N *niiTja* 227B
Mrs. N *proua* 152
mud N *muda* 13C
N *pori* 13A
N *soga* 13D
muddle Vt *vaŞSima* 291A
muddy A *mudane* 251
A *porine* 251
muddy A *sogane* 251
muff N *muHv* 58B
muffle Vt *summutama* 349F
mug N *krUUş* 58A
N *toPs* 58B
mug (nose) N *noşu* 13A
mug (wooden) N *kaPP* 49C
Mulgimaa native N *muļK* 58F
multi-coloured A *kirju* 152
A *kiRju* 227B
multi-millionaire N *miļjardär* 245
multiplication N *korrutamine* 257E
multiply Vt *korrutama* 349F
mummy N *mUUmia* 227A
mumps N *mumPs* 58B
murder N *mõRv* 49B
murder Vt *mõRvama* 327B
murderer N *mõrtsukas* 243A
N *mõRvar* 229A
murmur N *kohin* 231A
murmur Vi *kohisema* 349C
muscle N *lihas* 253
N *muSkel* 240A
muscular A *lihaseline* 257D
A *muSkliline* 257D
museum N *mUUseum* 246
mush N *mäMM* 58A
mushroom (common) N *šampinjon* 245
mushroom (generic) N *sEEn* 82
mushroom-picker N *seeneline* 257D
music N *muusika* 227A
music (set to) Vt *nooḑistama* 349F
music (sheet) N *nooŢ* 58E
musical N *muusikal* 245
musical A *musikAAlne* 247
A *muusikaline* 257D
musician N *moosekaņT* 58E
N *muusik* 234A

Muslim [N] *muhamEEdlane* [257C]
must [V] *pidama* [288]
mustard [N] *sinep* [229A]
mute [N] *tuMM* [53A]
mutter [N] *pomin* [231A]
mutter [Vi] *pomisema* [349C]
mutual [A] *vastastikune* [251]
myrrh [N] *müRR* [58A]
myrtle [N] *mirT* [58E]
mysterious [A] *müstiline* [257D]
mysterious [A] *saladusliK* [62]
myth [N] *müüT* [58E]
mythical [A] *müütiline* [257D]
mythologist [N] *mütolOOg* [58A]
mythology [N] *mütolOOgia* [227A]

N

nag [Vt] *näägutama* [349F]
nag (horse) [N] *setukas* [243A]
nail [Vt] *naelutama* [349F]
nail (finger, toe) [N] *kÜÜş* [146]
nail (metal) [N] *naEl* [50]
naive [A] *naİİvne* [247]
name [N] *nimetus* [260A]
[N] *nimi* [18]
name [Vt] *nimetama* [349F]
nameless [A] *nimetu* [227A]
nap [N] *uinak* [234A]
napalm [N] *napaĻm* [58B]
naphthalene [N] *naftalİİn* [58A]
narcissus [N] *nartsiŞS* [58A]
narcotics [N] *narkootikum* [245]
narrate story [Vt] *jutustama* [349F]
narrative [N] *jutustus* [260A]
narrative [A] *jutustav* [231A]
narrator [N] *jutustaja* [227A]
narrow [A] *ahas* [190]
[A] *kitsas* [159B]
narrower (become) [Vi] *kitsenema* [349D]
narrowness [N] *kiTsus* [260B]
Narva native [N] *narvakas* [243A]
nasty [A] *haLb* [86B]
national [A] *raHvusliK* [62]
nationalistic [A] *natsionaliStliK* [62]
nationality [N] *raHvus* [260B]
nationalize [Vt] *natsionalisEErima* [291B]
[Vt] *riigistama* [349F]
natural [A] *lOOdusliK* [62]
[A] *loomuliK* [62]
[A] *naturAAlne* [247]
naturalism [N] *naturaliSm* [58B]
naturalist [N] *naturaliSt* [58B]
naturalistic [A] *naturaliStliK* [62]
nature [N] *lOOdus* [260B]
naughtiness [N] *üleannetus* [260A]
naughty [A] *üleannetu* [227A]
nausea [N] *iiveldus* [260A]
nauseous (be) [Vi] *iiveldama* [349F]
navel [N] *naba* [13B]
navigable [A] *laevatatav* [231A]
navigate [Vi] *laevatama* [349F]
navigation [N] *navigatsiOOn* [58A]
near [A] *lähedane* [257A]
near and dear [N] *omas* [255]
near-sighted [A] *lühinägeliK* [62]
nearer [A] *lähem* [231A]
nearest [A] *lähim* [231A]
nearness [N] *lähedus* [260A]
necessary [A] *tarviliK* [62]
necessary [A] *vajaliK* [62]
necessity [N] *tarviliKKus* [260B]
neck [N] *kaEl* [49B]
necklace [N] *kEE* [1]
necklace (ethnic) [N] *paaTer* [240A]
need [N] *tarve* [208B]
[N] *tarvidus* [260A]
[N] *vajadus* [260A]
need [Vi] *tarvitsema* [349E]
need [Vt] *vajama* [269]
needle [N] *nõEl* [50]
negation [N] *eiTus* [260B]
negative [A] *eiTav* [231A]
neigh [Vi] *hiRnuma* [291C]
neighbour [N] *nAAber* [240A]
neighbourhood [N] *nAAbrus* [260B]
[N] *üMbruskoNd* [106]
neighing [N] *hiRnumine* [257E]
Nenets [N] *neenets* [229A]
nerve [N] *näRv* [58B]
nerve-racking [A] *näRvesÖÖv* [231B]
nervous [A] *närviline* [257D]
nervous (be) [Vi] *närvEErima* [291B]
[Vi] *närvitsema* [349E]
nervousness [N] *närvilisus* [260A]
nest [N] *pesa* [15]
nest [Vi] *pesitama* [349F]
[Vi] *pesitsema* [349E]
net [N] *võrK* [61F]
Netherlander [N] *hollandlane* [257C]
neutral [A] *neutrAAlne* [247]
neutrality [N] *neutraliteeT* [58E]
new [A] *UUs* [143A]
[A] *vaStne* [247]
New-Year holidays [N] *näärid (pl)* [58A]
newly-wed (woman) [N] *noorik* [234A]
newness [N] *UUdus* [260B]
news [N] *uudis* [253]
newspaper column [N] *rubriiK* [58F]
next [A] *jäRgmine* [257F]
nice [A] *kena* [15]
niche [N] *niŠŠ* [58C]
nickel [N] *niKKel* [240B]
nicotine [N] *nikotİİn* [58A]
night [N] *ÖÖ* [8]
night [A] *öİne* [252]
night (spend) [Vi] *ÖÖbima* [349B]
nightingale [N] *ööbik* [234A]
nimble [A] *kärmas* [159B]
[A] *kärme* [177B]
[A] *nobe* [235]
[A] *väle* [235]
nimbleness [N] *väledus* [260A]
nine [N] *üheksa* [227A]
ninth [N] *üheksandiK* [62]
ninth [A] *üheksas* [237B]
nitrate [N] *nitraaT* [58E]
nitrogen [N] *lämmastiK* [62]
noble [A] *õilis* [167]
[A] *üllas* [159A]
noble-mindedness [N] *õİlsus* [260B]
nobleman [N] *AAdel* [240A]
nod [N] *noogutus* [260A]
nod [Vt] *noogutama* [349F]
noise [N] *läRm* [58B]
noiseless [A] *kärатu* [227A]
noisy [A] *lärmakas* [243A]
noisy (be) [Vi] *läRmama* [327B]
nominative [N] *nimetav* [231A]
non-existent [A] *olematu* [227A]
nonsense [N] *jama* [13A]
[N] *möga* [13D]
[N] *möla* [13A]
noodle [N] *nUUdel* [240A]
nook [N] *soPP* [58C]
noon [N] *lõuna* [178B]
noose [N] *AAs* [49A]
[N] *silmus* [253]
norm [N] *noRm* [58B]
normal [A] *normAAlne* [247]

north [N] *põhi* [68A]
north-east [N] *kirre* [215]
north-west [N] *loE* [212]
northern lights [N] *virmalised (pl)* [257A]
Northland [N] *põhjala* [227A]
nose [N] *nina* [13A]
nostril [N] *sõõre* [179A]
notary [N] *notar* [229A]
notch [N] *pügal* [231A]
[N] *sälK* [61F]
[N] *täke* [177C]
notch [Vt] *sälKima* [291G]
[Vt] *täkestama* [349F]
notched [A] *täkiline* [257D]
note [N] *märge* [179E]
[N] *nooŢ* [58E]
notebook [N] *kaustik* [234A]
[N] *märKmiK* [62]
notes (take) [Vt] *konspektEErima* [291B]
[Vt] *konspeKtima* [291C]

notice [Vt] *märKama* [327F]
noticeable [A] *märgatav* [231A]
notion [N] *mõiste* [177B]
nought (bring to) [Vt] *nuRjama* [327B]
nought (come to) [Vi] *nuRjuma* [349G]
nourishing [A] *toiTev* [241A]
novel [N] *romAAn* [58A]
novel [A] *UUdne* [247]
novelty [N] *UUdsus* [260B]
November [N] *noveMber* [240A]
nuance [N] *nüanSS* [58G]
nucleus [N] *tUUm* [53A]
nude (art) [N] *aKt* [58B]
nudge [N] *müKs* [61B]
nudge [Vt] *müKsama* [327B]
nudist [N] *nudiSt* [58B]
nuisance [N] *nuHtlus* [260B]
numb [A] *tuİm* [53B]
numb (make) [Vt] *tuimastama* [349F]
numbed [A] *kohmetu* [227A]

numbed (become) [Vi] *kohmetuma* [349H]
[Vi] *kohmetama* [349F]
number [N] *aRv* [61B]
[N] *nuMber* [240A]
number [Vt] *numerEErima* [291B]
[Vt] *nummerdama* [349F]
numbness [N] *kohmetus* [260A]
[N] *tuİmus* [260B]
numerous [A] *arvukas* [243A]
numismatics [N] *numismaatika* [227A]
numismatist [N] *numismaatik* [234A]
nun [N] *nuNN* [53A]
nurse [N] *põeTaja* [227A]
nurse [Vt] *põeTama* [349F]
nut [N] *päHkel* [240A]
nut (bolt) [N] *muTTer* [240B]
nutmeg [N] *muskaaT* [58E]
nylon [N] *naİlon* [229A]
nymph [N] *nümF* [58]

A

O

oaf [N] *mölakas* [243A]
oak [N] *taMM* [63A]
oak grove [N] *tammik* [234A]
oar [N] *aEr* [61B]
oasis [N] *oAAş* [58A]
oat [N] *kaEr* [50]
oath [N] *vanne* [214]
obedience [N] *kuulekus* [260A]
obedient [A] *kuulekas* [243A]
[A] *sõnakuuleliK* [62]
obituary [N] *nekrolOOg* [58A]
object [N] *ese* [157]
[N] *objeKt* [58B]
objective [A] *objektİİvne* [247]
objectivity [N] *objektİİvsus* [260B]
obligation [N] *kohustus* [260A]
obligatory [A] *kohustusliK* [62]
oblige [Vt] *kohustama* [349F]
oblong [A] *pikergune* [257A]
[A] *piKliK* [62]
oboe [N] *oboE* [1]
obscene [A] *rõve* [235]
obscenity [N] *rõvedus* [260A]
obscure [A] *seLgusetu* [227A]
observation [N] *vaaTlus* [260B]
observatory [N] *observatOOrium* [246]
observe [Vt] *vaaTlema* [326E]

obsolete [Vi] *iganema* [349D]
obstacle [N] *tõke* [177C]
obstinacy [N] *kaNgekaElsus* [260B]
obstinate [A] *kaNgekaElne* [247]
obstruct [Vt] *tõkestama* [349F]
occasion [N] *puHk* [131C]
occupation (political) [N] *okupatsiOOn* [58A]
occupy [Vt] *hõİvama* [327B]
occur [Vi] *toİmuma* [349G]
occurrence [N] *juHtumus* [260A]
ocean [N] *ooKean* [246]
octave [N] *oktAAv* [58A]
[N] *oKtav* [229A]
octet [N] *okteŢT* [58C]
October [N] *oktOOber* [240A]
odd (number) [A] *paaritu* [227A]
odd (strange) [A] *veİder* [241A]
ode [N] *OOd* [58A]
offal [N] *raİdmed (pl)* [219C]
offence (take) [Vi] *hAAvuma* [349G]
[Vi] *soLvuma* [349G]
offer [N] *paKKumine* [257E]
offer [Vt] *paKKuma* [291D]
office [N] *bürOO* [1]
[N] *kantseleİ* [1]
[N] *konTor* [229A]
officer [N] *ohvitser* [245]

official [N] *ametniK* [62]
official [A] *ametliK* [62]
[A] *ofitsiAAlne* [247]
offset printing [N] *rotapriņT* [58E]
oil [N] *õli* [13A]
oil [Vt] *õlitama* [349F]
oil (crude) [N] *nafta* [152]
oiling [N] *õlitus* [260A]
oily [A] *õline* [251]
ointment [N] *saĻv* [58B]
[N] *võie* [210D]
old [A] *vana* [14A]
old age [N] *vanadus* [260A]
old decrepit person [N] *rauK* [49F]
old man [N] *taaŢ* [58E]
old person [N] *vanake(ne)* [257G]
[N] *vanur* [229A]
olive [N] *olİİv* [58A]
Olympiad [N] *olümpiAAd* [58A]
omelette [N] *omleŢT* [58C]
omen [N] *enne* [214]
ominous [A] *kuRjakuulutav* [231A]
omission (in text) [N] *kärbe* [177D]
one [N] *üKs* [149]
one and half [N] *pOOlteiSt* [258B]
onion [N] *sibul* [231A]
ooze [Vi] *immitsema* [349E]

open [A] *laHtine* [257B]
open [Vi] *avanema* [349D]
open [Vt] *avama* [269]
open slightly [Vt] *praoTama* [349F]
opening [N] *ava* [13A]
[N] *avaus* [260A]
opera [N] *ooPer* [229A]
operate [V] *operEErima* [291B]
operate [Vi] *toi̇mima* [291C]
operation [N] *toiming* [234A]
operation (surgical) [N] *lõiKus* [260B]
operative [A] *operati̇i̇vne* [247]
operator [N] *telefoniSt* [58B]
operetta [N] *opereṬT* [58C]
opinion [N] *aRvamus* [260A]
opium [N] *ooPium* [246]
opponent [N] *oponeṇT* [58E]
[N] *vastane* [251]
opportune [A] *sOOdus* [250A]
opportunity [N] *juhuṣ* [253]
[N] *võimalus* [260A]
opposite [N] *vastand* [229A]
opposite [A] *vastandliK* [62]
oppress [Vt] *kuRnama* [327B]
[Vt] *rusuma* [269]
[Vt] *rõhuma* [269]
oppression [N] *rõhumine* [257E]
oppressive [A] *rõhuv* [231A]
oppressor [N] *kuRnaja* [227A]
[N] *rõhuja* [227A]
optic [A] *optiline* [257D]
optician [N] *optik* [234A]
optics [N] *optika* [227A]
optimism [N] *optimiSm* [58B]
optimist [N] *optimiSt* [58B]
optimistic [A] *optimiStliK* [62]
optimum [A] *optimAAlne* [247]
optional [A] *fakultati̇i̇vne* [247]
orache [N] *malTs* [49B]
oral [A] *sUUline* [257D]
orange (colour) [A] *oraNž* [58B]
orange (fruit) [N] *apelsin* [245]
orator [N] *oraaTor* [229A]
orbit [N] *orbiiT* [58E]
orchestra [N] *orkeSter* [240A]
orchid [N] *orhidEE* [2]
ordeal [N] *kaTsumus* [260A]
order [N] *koRd* [107]
[N] *oRder* [229A]
order (arrange in) [Vt] *järjestama* [349F]
order (directive) [N] *korraldus* [260A]
order (put into) [Vt] *korrastama* [349F]
order (restaurant) [Vt] *teḶLima* [291A]
order (succession) [N] *järjestiK* [62]
order about [Vt] *käsutama* [349F]
orderliness [N] *korraliKKus* [260B]
orderly [N] *sanitar* [245]
orderly [A] *korraliK* [62]
ordinary [A] *hariliK* [62]
ore [N] *maaK* [58F]
organ [N] *orel* [229A]
[N] *oRgan* [229A]
organ (anatomical) [N] *elund* [229A]
organic [A] *orgaaniline* [257D]
organization [N] *organisatsiOOn* [58A]
organize [Vt] *korraldama* [349F]
[Vt] *organisEErima* [291B]
organizer [N] *organisaaTor* [229A]
organizing [N] *organisEErimine* [257E]
orgasm [N] *orgaSm* [58B]
orgy [N] *oRgia* [227A]
orientate [Vt] *orientEErima* [291B]
orientate oneself [Vi] *orientEEruma* [349G]
orientation [N] *orientatsiOOn* [58A]
origin [N] *põLvnemine* [257E]
[N] *teke* [177C]
original [N] *originAAl* [58A]
original [A] *originAAlne* [247]
originality [N] *originAAlsus* [260B]
originate [Vi] *läHtuma* [349H]
originate [Vi] *põLvnema* [349D]
ornament [N] *ehe* [211B]
ornament [N] *ornameṇT* [58E]
orphan [N] *oRb* [121]
orthography [N] *ortograaFia* [227A]
other (different) [A] *mUU* [7]
other (another) [A] *teine* [258A]
otter [N] *saarmas* [159A]
ounce [N] *uṇTs* [58B]
outburst [N] *pahvatus* [260A]
outermost [A] *ÄÄrmine* [257F]
outfit [N] *varustus* [260A]
outhouse [N] *kemmerg* [234A]
[N] *kemPs* [61B]
[N] *peḷdik* [234A]
outline [N] *kavand* [229A]
[N] *visand* [229A]
outline [Vt] *kavandama* [349F]
[Vt] *visandama* [349F]
outstanding [A] *vaHva* [227B]
oval [A] *ovAAlne* [247]
ovation [N] *ovatsiOOn* [58A]
over-refined (be) [Vi] *peenutsema* [349E]
overcoat [N] *sinel* [229A]
overgrow [Vi] *võsastuma* [349H]
overseer [N] *kubjas* [159D]
overshoes [N] *boṭikud (pl)* [234A]
overthrow [Vt] *kukutama* [349F]
ovulation [N] *ovulatsiOOn* [58A]
owe [Vi] *võLgnema* [349D]
own [A] *oma* [15]
owner [N] *omaniK* [62]
ox [N] *häRg* [112]
[N] *vei̇s* [254]
oxygen [N] *haPniK* [62]
oyster [N] *auSter* [240A]
ozone [N] *osOOn* [58A]

P

pace [Vi] *saMMuma* [291A]
pacifist [N] *patsifiSt* [58B]
pack [Vt] *paKKima* [291D]
pack down [Vt] *tamPima* [291E]
package [N] *paKK* [58C]
packing [N] *pakend* [229A]
packing material [N] *taara* [152]
pact [N] *paKt* [58B]
pad of paper [N] *bloKnooT* [58E]
paddle [N] *mõla* [13A]
padlock [N] *taba* [13B]
pagan [N] *pagan* [231A]
paid in (be) [Vi] *laeKuma* [349G]
pail [N] *äMber* [240A]
pain [N] *valu* [13A]
painful [A] *valuliK* [62]
[A] *valuline* [257D]
[A] *valus* [231A]
painless [A] *valutu* [227A]
paint [Vt] *võõPama* [327D]
paint [Vt] *väRvima* [291C]
paint (art) [V] *mAAḶima* [291A]
paint-covered [A] *värvine* [251]
paintbrush [N] *pinTsel* [240A]
painter (artist) [N] *mAAler* [240A]
painting (art) [N] *mAAḶ* [58A]
pair [N] *pAAr* [58A]
pal [N] *semu* [13A]
palace [N] *palEE* [2]
pale [A] *kahvatu* [227A]

pale [Vi] *kahvatuma* [349H]
palette-knife [N] *paHtel* [240A]
pallor [N] *kahvatus* [260A]
palm (hand) [N] *piHk* [131C]
palm tree [N] *paĻm* [58B]
pamper [Vt] *heļlitama* [349F]
pamper [Vt] *poputama* [349F]
pamphlet [N] *voļdik* [234A]
pan [N] *paŅN* [58A]
panel [N] *panEEl* [58A]
panic [N] *paanika* [227A]
panic-stricken [A] *paaniline* [257D]
pant [Vi] *hingeldama* [349F]
[Vi] *äHkima* [313B]
panther [N] *panTer* [240A]
pantomime [N] *pantomİİm* [58A]
pantry [N] *saHver* [240A]
pants [N] *püksid (pl)* [60]
paper [N] *paber* [229A]
paprika [N] *paprika* [227A]
parachute [N] *parašüTT* [58C]
parachutist [N] *laNgevaRjur* [229A]
[N] *parašütiSt* [58B]
parade [N] *parAAd* [58A]
paradise [N] *paradİİs* [58A]
paradox [N] *paradoKs* [58B]
paragraph [N] *paragraHv* [58B]
parallel [N] *parallEEl* [58A]
parallel [A] *parallEElne* [247]
paralysis [N] *halvatus* [260A]
paralytic [N] *halvatu* [227A]
paraphrase [Vt] *parafrAAşima* [291A]
parboil [Vt] *kupatama* [349F]
parchment [N] *pärgameņT* [58E]
pardon [Vt] *vabandama* [349F]
parent [N] *vanem* [231A]
parenthesis [N] *suLg* [131B]
parish [N] *kihelkoNd* [106]
parish clerk [N] *köSter* [240A]
park [N] *parK* [58F]
park [Vt] *parKima* [291G]
parking [N] *parKimine* [257E]
parking-lot [N] *parKla* [227B]
parliament [N] *parlameņT* [58E]
parliamentary [A] *parlamentAArne* [247]
parlour [N] *saloNg* [58B]
Pärnumaa native [N] *pärnakas* [243A]
parody [N] *parOOdia* [227A]
parquet [N] *parkeŢT* [58C]
parrot [N] *papagoİ* [1]
parsley [N] *peterseĻL* [58A]
parsonage [N] *pastoraaT* [58E]

part [N] *osa* [15]
partial [A] *osaline* [257D]
participant [N] *osaline* [257D]
participate [Vi] *osalema* [349A]
particle [N] *osake(ne)* [257G]
[N] *partiKKel* [240B]
particular [A] *eriline* [257D]
parting [N] *laHk* [131C]
partisan [N] *partisan* [245]
partitive [N] *osastav* [231A]
partner [N] *parTner* [229A]
party [Vi] *pidutsema* [349E]
party (political) [N] *erakoNd* [106]
party (social event) [N] *pidu* [13C *or* 28]
pass [N] *pääsik* [234A]
[N] *pÄÄsmiK* [62]
pass (sport) [N] *sööT* [61E]
pass by [Vi] *mÖÖduma* [349H]
pass through [Vt] *läbima* [269]
passenger [N] *sõiTja* [227B]
passion [N] *kiRg* [140A]
passionate [A] *kiRgliK* [62]
passport [N] *paŞS* [58A]
password [N] *parOOl* [58A]
past [N] *mineviK* [62]
paste (glue) [N] *kliiSter* [240A]
paste (food) [N] *pasta* [152]
paste [Vt] *kliisterdama* [349F]
pastille [N] *pastiĻL* [58A]
pastor [N] *paŚtor* [229A]
pasture [Vt] *karjatama* [349F]
pat [Vt] *patsutama* [349F]
patch [N] *laPP* [58C]
patch [Vt] *laPPima* [291D]
paté [N] *pasteeŢ* [58E]
patent [N] *pateņT* [58E]
path [N] *rada* [36]
patience [N] *kannatliKKus* [260B]
[N] *kannatus* [260A]
patient [N] *patsienT* [58E]
patient [A] *kannatliK* [62]
patriarch (church) [N] *patriarH* [58B]
patriot [N] *patriooT* [58E]
patriotic [A] *isamAAliK* [62]
[A] *patriootiline* [257D]
patriotism [N] *patriotiSm* [58B]
patrol [N] *patruĻL* [58A]
patrol [V] *patruĻLima* [291A]
patron [N] *patrOOn* [58A]
patronage [N] *soosing* [234A]
[N] *šeFlus* [260B]
pattern [N] *lõige* [177F]

[N] *muSter* [240A]
patterned [A] *muStriline* [257D]
patty (pie) [N] *pirukas* [243A]
pause [N] *paUs* [58B]
pave [Vt] *sillutama* [349F]
pavement [N] *sillutis* [260A]
pavilion [N] *paviljon* [245]
paw [N] *käPP* [53C]
pawn [N] *eTTur* [229A]
pawn [Vt] *paņTima* [291F]
pay [N] *palK* [49F]
pay [Vt] *maKsma* [293A]
payment [N] *maKs* [61B]
[N] *tasu* [13A]
pea [N] *hernes* [161B]
peace [N] *rahu* [13A]
peace-loving [A] *rahuarmastav* [231A]
peaceful [A] *rahuliK* [62]
peach [N] *persik* [234A]
[N] *virsik* [234A]
pear [N] *piRn* [58B]
pearl [N] *päRl* [229B]
pearl-barley [N] *kruubid (pl)* [58D]
peasant [N] *maŢs* [58B]
peasant-like [A] *maŢsliK* [62]
[A] *talupoEgliK* [62]
peat [N] *turvas* [187]
peck [Vt] *noKKima* [291D]
peculiarity [N] *iseärasus* [260A]
pedagogical [A] *pedagoogiline* [257D]
pedagogue [N] *pedagOOg* [58A]
pedagogy [N] *pedagoogika* [227A]
pedal [N] *pedAAl* [58A]
pederast [N] *pederaSt* [58B]
pedestal [N] *postameņT* [58E]
pedicure [N] *pedikÜÜr* [58A]
pedometer [N] *pedomeeTer* [240A]
pee (take child) [Vt] *pişsitama* [349F]
peel [N] *kOOr* [82]
peel [Vt] *kOOrima* [291A]
peer [Vi] *pİİluma* [291A]
peevish [A] *turtsakas* [243A]
peg [N] *vaİ* [49B]
pellet [N] *hAAvel* [240A]
[N] *kuuļike(ne)* [257G]
penalty [N] *traHv* [58B]
pencil [N] *pliiats* [229A]
pencil-case [N] *pinal* [229A]
pendant [N] *ripats* [229A]
pendulum [N] *peNdel* [240A]
penguin [N] *pingvİİn* [58A]
penicillin [N] *penitsillİİn* [58A]

penis [N] *küRb* [101B]
penis (little boy's) [N] *noku* [152]
pennant [N] *vimPel* [240A]
penniless [A] *rahatu* [227A]
penny [N] *peŅN* [58A]
pension [N] *peNsion* [246]
pensioner [N] *peNsionär* [245]
pensive [A] *mõTliK* [62]
peony [N] *pojeNg* [58B]
[N] *pujeNg* [58B]
people [N] *rahvas* [159B]
people (coterie) [N] *riNgkoNd* [106]
pep [N] *särTs* [61B]
pepper [N] *pipar* [171C]
peppy [A] *särtsakas* [243A]
per cent [N] *proTseņT* [58E]
perceive [Vt] *tajuma* [269]
[Vt] *tunnetama* [349F]
perceptible [A] *tajutav* [231A]
perception [N] *taju* [13A]
[N] *tunnetus* [260A]
perch [N] *õRs* [144]
perch (fish) [N] *ahven* [231A]
perfect [A] *perfeKtne* [247]
perforate [Vt] *augustama* [349F]
[Vt] *mulgustama* [349F]
[Vt] *perforEErima* [291B]
perforator [N] *mulgusti* [225A]
perforator [N] *perforaaTor* [229A]
perform [Vi] *esinema* [349D]
perform [Vt] *etendama* [349F]
performance [N] *esinemine* [257E]
[N] *etendus* [260A]
performer [N] *esineja* [227A]
perfume [N] *parfÜÜm* [58A]
period [N] *periOOd* [58A]
periodic [A] *perioodiline* [257D]
perish [Vi] *huKKuma* [349G]
[Vi] *hävima* [269]
permanent [A] *alaline* [257D]
[A] *jÄÄdav* [231A]
permissible [A] *lubatav* [231A]
permission [N] *luba* [38]
perpendicular [A] *perpendikulAArne* [247]
perpetual [A] *alatine* [257A]
perplexed [A] *nõuTu* [227B]
perplexity [N] *kimbatus* [260A]
persistence [N] *püsivus* [260A]
[N] *visadus* [260A]
persistent [A] *püsiv* [231A]
[A] *visa* [13A]
person [N] *isik* [234A]
personal [A] *isikliK* [62]
personality [N] *isiksus* [260A]
personification [N] *personifikatsiOOn* [58A]
personify [Vt] *personifitsEErima* [291B]
personnel [N] *kAAder* [240A]
[N] *personal* [245]
perspective [N] *perspektİİv* [58A]
Peruvian [N] *perUUlane* [257C]
pessimistic [A] *pessimiStliK* [62]
pest [N] *kaHjur* [229A]
pest control [N] *tõrje* [177B]
pester [Vt] *tüüTama* [327E]
petrify [Vi] *kivinema* [349D]
pettiness [N] *väiKlus* [260B]
petty [A] *väiKlane* [257C]
petulant [A] *pirtsakas* [243A]
Pharisee [N] *variser* [245]
pharmacist [N] *farmatseuT* [58E]
pharmacology [N] *farmaaTsia* [227A]
phase [N] *fAAş* [58A]
[N] *järK* [61F]
[N] *stAAdium* [246]
phasic [A] *järguline* [257D]
pheasant [N] *fAAsan* [229A]
phenomenal [A] *fenomenAAlne* [247]
phenomenon [N] *nähe* [211B]
[N] *näHtus* [260B]
philatelist [N] *filateliSt* [58B]
philately [N] *filatEElia* [227A]
philharmonic [N] *filharmOOnia* [227A]
philological [A] *filoloogiline* [257D]
philologist [N] *filolOOg* [58A]
philology [N] *filolOOgia* [227A]
philosopher [N] *filosooF* [58A]
philosophical [A] *filosoofiline* [257D]
philosophize [Vi] *targutama* [349F]
philosophy [N] *filosooFia* [227A]
phlegmatic [A] *flegmaatiline* [257D]
phlox [N] *floKs* [58B]
phonetic [A] *foneetiline* [257D]
phonetics [N] *foneetika* [227A]
phosphate [N] *fosfaaT* [58E]
phosphorite [N] *fosforiiT* [58E]
photo [N] *foto* [152]
photo file [N] *fototeeK* [58F]
photo slide [N] *diapositİİv* [58A]
photograph [Vt] *fotografEErima* [291B]
[Vt] *piļdistama* [349F]
photographer [N] *fotograaF* [58A]
[N] *piļTniK* [62]
photography [N] *fotograaFia* [227A]
phrase [N] *frAAş* [58A]
phrase-book [N] *veStmiK* [62]
phraseology [N] *fraseolOOgia* [227A]
physical [A] *füüsiline* [257D]
[A] *kehaline* [257D]
physicist [N] *füüsik* [234A]
physics [N] *füüsika* [227A]
physiology [N] *füsiolOOgia* [227A]
pianist [N] *pianiSt* [58B]
piano [N] *klaver* [229A]
piano key [N] *klaHv* [58B]
pick [Vt] *noPPima* [291D]
pick a quarrel [V] *norima* [269]
pick(axe) [N] *kirka* [152]
picture [N] *piļT* [58E]
picture (mental) [N] *kujutlus* [260A]
picturesque [A] *maaļiline* [257D]
piece [N] *tüKK* [58C]
piercing [A] *kile* [235]
[A] *viNge* [227B]
pig [N] *siga* [37]
pigeon [N] *tuvi* [13A]
piggy [N] *noțsu* [152]
piglet [N] *põrsas* [159F]
pigsty [N] *sigala* [227A]
pike [N] *haUg* [148]
pike-perch [N] *koha* [13A]
pile [N] *huņnik* [234A]
[N] *viRn* [49B]
pile up [Vt] *laduma* [280]
pilfer [Vt] *näPPama* [327C]
pill [N] *piĻL* [58A]
pill (placebo) [N] *dražEE* [2]
pillow [N] *padi* [69B]
pillowcase [N] *pÜÜr* [58A]
pilot [N] *pilooT* [58E]
pilot boat [N] *looŢs* [58B]
pimple [N] *viŅN* [58A]
[N] *viStriK* [62]
pinch [Vt] *näpistama* [349F]
pine [N] *mäŅd* [118]
[N] *pedajas* [243A]
pine grove [N] *mäņnik* [234A]
pineapple [N] *ananaSS* [58A]
pink [A] *roosa* [152]
pinkish [A] *roosakas* [243A]
pioneer [N] *pionEEr* [58A]
pious [A] *vaga* [14D]
pipe [N] *toru* [13A]
pipe (tobacco) [N] *piiP* [61D]
pipette [N] *pipeŢT* [58C]
piss [V] *pişsima* [324]
pistol [N] *püStol* [229A]

pitch [N] *pigi* [13D]
pitchfork [N] *harK* [58F]
pitiful [A] *armetu* [227A]
pitiless [A] *armutu* [227A]
placard [N] *afiŠŠ* [58C]
place [N] *koHt* [104B]
place [N] *paiK* [49F]
place [Vt] *asetama* [349F]
[Vt] *paigutama* [349F]
place-mat [N] *linik* [234A]
plagiarism [N] *plagiaaT* [58E]
plagiarize [Vt] *plagiEErima* [291B]
plague [N] *kaTk* [61B]
plain [N] *lagendiK* [62]
[N] *tasandiK* [62]
plain [A] *ilutu* [227A]
plaintiff [N] *hageja* [227A]
plaintive [A] *kaEbliK* [62]
plait [N] *paļmik* [234A]
[N] *paŢs* [58B]
plait [Vt] *paĻmima* [291B]
[Vt] *paļmitsema* [349E]
plan [N] *plAAņ* [58A]
plan [Vt] *plAAņima* [291A]
[Vt] *plaaņitsema* [349E]
[Vt] *planEErima* [291B]
plane [N] *hÖÖvel* [240A]
plane [Vt] *hööveldama* [349F]
planet [N] *planeeT* [58E]
planetarium [N] *planetAArium* [246]
plank [N] *planK* [61F]
plank-bed [N] *nari* [13A]
plant [N] *taİm* [63B]
plant [Vt] *istutama* [349F]
plant (factory) [N] *kombinaaT* [58E]
plantation [N] *istandus* [260A]
plaster [N] *kroHv* [58B]
plaster [Vt] *kroHvima* [291C]
plaster (surgical) [N] *plaaSter* [240A]
plasterer [N] *kroHvija* [227A]
plastic [N] *plaştikaaT* [58E]
plastic [A] *plaştiline* [257D]
plasticine [N] *plaştilİİn* [58A]
plasticity [N] *plaştilisus* [260A]
plate [N] *taldrik* [234A]
plateau [N] *kõrgendiK* [62]
[N] *platOO* [1]
platform [N] *perrOOn* [58A]
[N] *plaTvoRm* [58B]
platinum [N] *plaatina* [227A]
platter [N] *vAAgen* [241A]
plausible [A] *usutav* [231A]

play [N] *näidend* [229A]
play [V] *mäNgima* [291C]
playwright [N] *dramatuRg* [58B]
pleasing [A] *mEEldiv* [231A]
pleasing (be) [Vi] *mEEldima* [349B]
pleasurable [A] *luştakas* [243A]
pleasure [N] *luŞt* [58B]
pleat [Vt] *plissEErima* [291B]
plentiful [A] *roHke* [227B]
plenty [N] *roHkus* [260B]
plenum [N] *plEEnum* [229A]
pliers [N] *tangid (pl)* [58B]
plod [Vi] *kõmPima* [291E]
[Vi] *kõmPsima* [291C]
plot [N] *sündmustiK* [62]
plot of land [N] *kruņT* [58E]
plough [N] *ader* [78B]
[N] *saHk* [95B]
plough [Vt] *küNdma* [317]
pluck [Vt] *kiTkuma* [291C]
plug [N] *pistik* [234A]
[N] *pruņT* [58E]
plum [N] *plOOm* [58A]
plumage [N] *sulestiK* [62]
plumbing [N] *torustiK* [62]
plump [A] *lihav* [231A]
[A] *täİdlane* [257C]
plumpness [N] *täİdlus* [260B]
plunder [Vt] *rİİsuma* [291A]
plural [N] *miTmus* [260B]
plus [N] *pluSS* [58A]
ply [Vi] *kursEErima* [291B]
plywood [N] *vinEEr* [58A]
pneumatic [A] *pneumaatiline* [257D]
pocket [N] *taSku* [227B]
pod [N] *kaUn* [50]
poem [N] *luuletus* [260A]
poet [N] *luuletaja* [227A]
[N] *poeeT* [58E]
poetess [N] *poeteSS* [58A]
poetic [A] *lUUleline* [257D]
[A] *poeetiline* [257D]
poetry [N] *luule* [177A]
poetry (make) [Vt] *luuletama* [349F]
point [N] *punKt* [58B]
[N] *teraviK* [62]
pointer [N] *osuti* [225A]
pointless [A] *sisutu* [227A]
poison [N] *mürK* [58F]
poison [Vt] *mürgitama* [349F]
poisoning [N] *mürgitus* [260A]
poke [Vi] *urgitsema* [349E]

poker [N] *rooP* [58D]
polar [A] *polAArne* [247]
Pole [N] *poolakas* [243A]
pole [N] *riTv* [49E]
pole (geographic) [N] *naba* [13B]
[N] *poolus* [253]
pole (geographic) [N] *pOOlus* [260B]
polecat [N] *tuHkur* [242A]
[N] *tõHk* [131C]
polemics [N] *poleemika* [227A]
police [N] *politseİ* [1]
police officer [N] *politseİniK* [62]
polish [Vt] *liHvima* [291C]
[Vt] *polEErima* [291B]
[Vt] *viKsima* [291C]
polite [A] *viisakas* [243A]
politeness [N] *viisakus* [260A]
politician [N] *poliitik* [234A]
politics [N] *poliitika* [227A]
pollinate [Vt] *tolmeldama* [349F]
pollute [Vt] *reoStama* [349F]
[Vt] *saaStama* [327B]
polluted (become) [Vi] *reoStuma* [349H]
pollution [N] *saaSt* [49B]
polyclinic [N] *polikliinik* [234A]
polymer [N] *polümEEr* [58A]
pond [N] *tiiK* [58F]
ponder [Vi] *mõtisklema* [351]
ponder [Vt] *kaalutlema* [351]
pony [N] *poni* [13A]
poodle [N] *pUUdel* [240A]
poor [A] *keHv* [53B]
[A] *vaEne* [252]
poor (become) [Vi] *vaEsuma* [349G]
poor thing [N] *vaEseke(ne)* [257G]
pope [N] *paavSt* [58B]
poplar [N] *paPPel* [240B]
poppy [N] *mOOņ* [58A]
popular [A] *populAArne* [247]
popularity [N] *populAArsus* [260B]
popularize [Vt] *popularisEErima* [291B]
population [N] *elaniKKoNd* [106]
[N] *rahvastiK* [62]
population growth [N] *iive* [208A]
porcelain [N] *portselan* [245]
pore [N] *pOOr* [58A]
pornography [N] *pornograaFia* [227A]
porous [A] *pOOrne* [247]
[A] *uRbne* [247]
porridge [N] *puder* [80]
portable [A] *kanTav* [231A]
[A] *portatİİvne* [247]

portrait [N] *portrEE* [2]
pose [N] *pOOş* [58A]
pose [Vt] *posEErima* [291B]
position [N] *asend* [229A]
[N] *positsiOOn* [58A]
position (social) [N] *seİsus* [260B]
positive [A] *positİİvne* [247]
possess [Vt] *evima* [269]
[Vt] *omama* [269]
[Vt] *vaLdama* [342]
possession [N] *omandus* [260A]
[N] *vaLdus* [260B]
possessions [N] *varandus* [260A]
possibility [N] *võimaliKKus* [260B]
possible [A] *võimaliK* [62]
post [N] *poŞt* [58B]
[N] *tulP* [53D]
post-graduate [N] *aspiraņT* [58E]
post-graduate course [N] *aspirantUUr* [58A]
poster [N] *plakat* [229A]
posthumous [A] *postUUmne* [247]
postscript [N] *poStskriPtum* [229A]
posture [N] *hoiak* [234A]
pot [N] *pada* [36]
[N] *poŢT* [58C]
potato [N] *karTul* [229A]
potency [N] *võİmsus* [260B]
potential [A] *potentsiAAlne* [247]
pouch [N] *kuKKur* [242B]
poultry house [N] *liNdla* [227B]
pound [N] *naEl* [50]
pound [Vt] *taguma* [285]
pound cake [N] *keeKs* [58B]
pounding [N] *tagumine* [257E]
pour [Vt] *kaLLama* [327A]
[Vt] *valama* [269]
pout [V] *moşsitama* [349F]
poverty [N] *keHvus* [260B]
[N] *vaEsus* [260B]
[N] *viletsus* [260A]
powder [N] *puLber* [240A]
powder (face) [Vt] *puuderdama* [349F]
power [N] *võİm* [61B]
power of suggestion [N] *sisendus* [260A]
powerful [A] *võimas* [165B]
powerless [A] *jõuetu* [227A]
practicable [A] *käİdav* [231A]
[A] *reAAlne* [247]
practical [A] *praktiline* [257D]
practice [Vt] *harjutama* [349F]
[Vt] *praktisEErima* [291B]
practise [N] *praktika* [227A]

prairie [N] *prEEria* [227A]
praise [Vt] *kiiTma* [297C]
[N] *kiiTus* [260B]
prank [N] *temP* [61D]
[N] *vemP* [61D]
pranks (play) [Vi] *vembutama* [349F]
prattle [N] *vadin* [231A]
prattle [Vi] *lobisema* [349C]
[Vi] *vadistama* [349F]
[Vi] *vaterdama* [349F]
prattler [N] *vaterdaja* [227A]
pray [Vi] *palvetama* [349F]
prayer [N] *palve* [177B]
praying [N] *palvetus* [260A]
pre-schooler [N] *EElkoolieAline* [257D]
preach [Vi] *jutlustama* [349F]
preacher [N] *jutlustaja* [227A]
precede [Vi] *EElnema* [349D]
preceding [A] *EElnev* [231A]
precipice [N] *kuristiK* [62]
precipitate [Vt] *sadestama* [349F]
precipitate [Vi] *sadestuma* [349H]
precipitation [N] *sademed (pl)* [157]
précis [N] *konspeKt* [58B]
precise [A] *täPne* [247]
[A] *täPPis* [250B]
precision [N] *täPsus* [260B]
predominant [A] *vaLdav* [231A]
predominate [Vt] *dominEErima* [291B]
prefer [Vt] *eelistama* [349F]
pregnancy [N] *rasedus* [260A]
pregnant [A] *rase* [235]
pregnant (animals) [A] *tiine* [177A]
pregnant (become) [Vi] *rasestuma* [349H]
preparation [N] *preparaaT* [58E]
prepare [Vt] *vaļmistama* [349F]
presbyter [N] *presbüter* [245]
prescription [N] *retsePt* [58B]
present [N] *oleviK* [62]
present [A] *nÜÜdne* [247]
present [Vt] *esitama* [349F]
present (from guest) [N] *kaker* [174]
present (give) [Vt] *kinKima* [291G]
present (one who is) [N] *olija* [227A]
present-day [A] *praEgune* [257B]
presentation [N] *esitus* [260A]
presents (from bride) [N] *veimed (pl)* [63B]
preservation [N] *säilitus* [260A]
preserve [Vi] *säİlima* [291C]
preserve [Vt] *konservEErima* [291B]
[Vt] *konseRvima* [291C]
[Vt] *säilitama* [349F]

preserve (can) [Vt] *veKKima* [291D]
preserves [N] *keedis* [253]
preside [Vt] *presidEErima* [291B]
president [N] *presideņT* [58E]
presidium [N] *presİİdium* [246]
press [N] *surutis* [260A]
press [Vt] *preŞSima* [291A]
[Vt] *suruma* [269]
[Vt] *vajutama* [349F]
pressing [N] *surumine* [257E]
pressure [N] *rõHk* [131C]
[N] *surve* [177B]
prestige [N] *prestİİž* [58A]
pretence [N] *teeSklus* [260B]
pretend [V] *teeSklema* [336]
pretender [N] *teeSkleja* [227A]
pretentious [A] *pretensioonikas* [243A]
pretty [A] *nägus* [231A]
prevaricate [Vi] *puiKlema* [326F]
previous [A] *EElmine* [257F]
price [N] *hiNd* [92]
priceless [A] *hiNdamatu* [227A]
prick [Vt] *torKima* [291G]
prick (needle) [N] *torge* [177F]
prickle [Vi] *kipitama* [349F]
pride [N] *uHkus* [260B]
pride oneself [Vi] *uhkustama* [349F]
priest [N] *paPP* [58C]
priest [N] *preeSter* [240A]
prima donna [N] *primadonna* [152]
prime (paint) [Vt] *kruņTima* [291F]
primeval [A] *üŖgne* [247]
primitive [A] *primitİİvne* [247]
primrose [N] *priimula* [227A]
prince [N] *prinTs* [58B]
[N] *vürSt* [58B]
princely [A] *vürStliK* [62]
princess [N] *printseŞS* [58A]
[N] *vürStinna* [152]
[N] *vürstitar* [245]
principle [N] *printsiiP* [58D]
principle [A] *printsipAAlne* [247]
print [N] *trüKK* [58C]
print [Vt] *trüKKima* [291D]
print (computer) [Vt] *priņTima* [291F]
printed matter [N] *panderoĻL* [58A]
[N] *trükis* [253]
printer [N] *trüKKal* [229A]
printer (computer) [N] *prinTer* [229A]
prism [N] *prisma* [152]
prison [N] *vaNgla* [227B]
prisoner [N] *vaNg* [58B]

private enterprise [N] *eraeTTevõTlus* [260B]
probability [N] *tõEnäOlisus* [260A]
[N] *tõEnäOsus* [260B]
probe [Vt] *sondEErima* [291B]
problem [N] *problEEm* [58A]
problematic [A] *problemaatiline* [257D]
procedure [N] *protsedUUr* [58A]
proceed [Vi] *kuLgema* [349B]
[Vi] *sİIrduma* [349H]
process [Vt] *tööTlema* [326E]
procure [Vt] *hanKima* [291G]
[Vt] *muretsema* [349E]
[Vt] *soeTama* [349F]
produce [Vt] *produtsEErima* [291B]
[Vt] *tooTma* [297C]
producer [N] *lavastaja* [227A]
[N] *tooTja* [227B]
product [N] *produKt* [58B]
product (agricultural) [N] *sAAdus* [260B]
product (manufacture) [N] *toode* [177E]
production [N] *produktsiOOn* [58A]
[N] *toodang* [234A]
[N] *tooTmine* [257E]
productive [A] *produktİIvne* [247]
[A] *tooTev* [241A]
[A] *tooTliK* [62]
productivity [N] *produktİIvsus* [260B]
[N] *tooTliKKus* [260B]
profession [N] *amet* [229A]
professional [A] *kuTseline* [257D]
professor [N] *profeSSor* [229A]
profile [N] *profİIl* [58A]
profit [N] *profiiT* [58E]
[N] *tulu* [13A]
profitable [A] *tasuv* [231A]
[A] *tulus* [231A]
prognosis [N] *prognOOs* [58A]
prognosticate [Vt] *prognOOsima* [291A]
program (computer) [N] *prograMM* [58A]
programme [N] *kava* [14A]
[N] *prograMM* [58A]
progress [N] *progreŞS* [58A]
progress [Vi] *edenema* [349D]
progress smoothly [Vi] *sujuma* [269]
progressive [A] *EEsriNdliK* [62]
[A] *progressİIvne* [247]
prohibition [N] *kEEld* [124A]
project [N] *projeKt* [58B]
project [Vt] *projektEErima* [291B]
projection [N] *luka* [180]
[N] *projektsiOOn* [58A]
projector [N] *projeKtor* [229A]

prologue [N] *prolOOg* [58A]
prolong [Vt] *pikendama* [349F]
promise [N] *lubadus* [260A]
[N] *tõoTus* [260B]
promise [Vt] *lubama* [269]
[Vt] *tõoTama* [349F]
promote [Vt] *edutama* [349F]
[Vt] *ülendama* [349F]
promotion [N] *edutamine* [257E]
[N] *ülendus* [260A]
prompter [N] *eTTeüTleja* [227A]
[N] *suflÖÖr* [58A]
prone to [A] *aļdis* [163B]
pronounce [Vt] *hÄÄldama* [349F]
pronunciation [N] *hÄÄldamine* [257E]
proof [N] *tõEnd* [229B]
[N] *tõEndus* [260B]
[N] *tõeStus* [260B]
proof (provide) [Vt] *tõEndama* [349F]
proof-reader [N] *korreKtor* [229A]
proof-reading [N] *korrektUUr* [58A]
prop [Vt] *toeStama* [349F]
propaganda [N] *propaganda* [152]
propeller [N] *propeLLer* [229A]
property [N] *omand* [229A]
property [A] *varandusliK* [62]
prophet [N] *prohvet* [229A]
prophylactic [A] *profülaktiline* [257D]
prophylaxis [N] *profülaktika* [227A]
proportion [N] *võrre* [215]
proportional [A] *proportsionAAlne* [247]
[A] *võRdeline* [257D]
proprietor [N] *vaLdaja* [227A]
props [N] *toeStiK* [62]
props (theatre) [N] *rekvisiidid (pl)* [58E]
prosaic [A] *proosaline* [257D]
prose [N] *proosa* [152]
prosecutor [N] *prokurör* [245]
prosperity [N] *jõuKus* [260B]
prosperous [A] *jõuKas* [243B]
prosthesis [N] *protEEs* [58A]
prostitute [N] *liŢs* [58B]
[N] *prostituuT* [58E]
prostitution [N] *prostitutsiOOn* [58A]
protein [N] *proteİIn* [58A]
[N] *valK* [61F]
protest [N] *proteŞt* [58B]
protest [Vt] *protestEErima* [291B]
[Vt] *proteŞtima* [291C]
protestant [N] *protestaņT* [58E]
protractor [N] *maĻL* [58A]
proud [A] *uHke* [227B]

prove [Vt] *tõeStama* [349F]
province [N] *mAAkoNd* [106]
[N] *proviņTs* [58B]
provincial [N] *proviņTslane* [257C]
provincial [A] *mAAkoNdliK* [62]
provisions [N] *mOOn* [53A]
provocation [N] *provokatsiOOn* [58A]
provocative [A] *provokatsiooniline* [257D]
provoke [Vt] *provotsEErima* [291B]
[Vt] *äşsitama* [349F]
provoker [N] *äşsitaja* [227A]
provost [N] *praoSt* [58B]
prow (ship) [N] *käİl* [49B]
prune [Vt] *kärPima* [291E]
pseudonym [N] *pseudonÜÜm* [58A]
psychiatrist [N] *psühhiaaTer* [240A]
psychiatry [N] *psühhiaaTria* [227A]
psychic [A] *psüühiline* [257D]
psychologist [N] *psühholOOg* [58A]
psychology [N] *psühholOOgia* [227A]
psychosis [N] *psühhOOs* [58A]
pub [N] *lokAAl* [58A]
puberty [N] *puberteeT* [58E]
public [N] *avaliKKus* [260B]
public [A] *avaliK* [62]
public figure [N] *tegelane* [257C]
publish [Vt] *kirjastama* [349F]
publishing house [N] *kirjastus* [260A]
pucker [Vt] *kibrutama* [349F]
pudding [N] *puding* [229A or 234A]
puddle [N] *loiK* [61F]
[N] *lomP* [58D]
puff [N] *maHv* [58B]
pull [Vt] *tõMbama* [340]
pull by the hair [Vt] *tuţistama* [349F]
pulley block [N] *ploKK* [58C]
pullover [N] *pullover* [245]
pulpit [N] *kanTsel* [240A]
pulsate [Vi] *pulsEErima* [291B]
pulse [N] *puļSS* [58G]
pulverize [Vt] *pihustama* [349F]
pulverizer [N] *pihusti* [225A]
[N] *pulverisaaTor* [229A]
pump [N] *pumP* [53D]
pump [Vt] *pumPama* [327D]
pumpkin [N] *kõrvits* [231A]
punch (drink) [N] *bOOl* [58A]
punch (metal) [N] *staņTs* [58B]
punish [Vt] *karistama* [349F]
[Vt] *nuHtlema* [331B]
punishable [A] *karistatav* [231A]
punishment [N] *karistus* [260A]

puny [A] *nigel* [231A]
puppy [N] *kuţsikas* [243A]
[N] *kuţsu* [152]
purchase [N] *oSt* [61B]
purée [N] *pürEE* [2]
puritan [N] *puritAAn* [58A]
purple [A] *lilla* [152]
[A] *purPurne* [247]
purple dye [N] *purPur* [229A]
purplish [A] *lillakas* [243A]
pursue [Vt] *jälitama* [349F]
pus [N] *mäda* [13C]
push [N] *tõuge* [177F]
push [Vt] *lüKKama* [327C]
[Vi] *tõuKama* [327F]
pussy-cat [N] *kiisu* [152]
pustule [N] *puŅN* [58A]
put [Vt] *panema* [271]
put to use [Vt] *evitama* [349F]
putrefy [Vi] *roiSkuma* [349G]
putty [N] *kiŢT* [58C]
putty [Vt] *kiŢTima* [291D]
[Vt] *pahteldama* [349F]
puzzling [A] *mõistatusliK* [62]
pyjamas [N] *pidžaama* [152]
pyramid [N] *püramİİd* [58A]
pyre [N] *riiT* [49E]

Q

quail [N] *vuŢT* [58C]
qualification [N] *kvalifikatsiOOn* [58A]
qualify [Vt] *kvalifitsEErima* [291B]
qualitative [A] *kvalitatİİvne* [247]
quality [N] *kvaliteeT* [58E]
quantity [N] *hulK* [53F]
[N] *kvantiteeT* [58E]
quarantine [N] *karantİİn* [58A]
quarrel [N] *rİİd* [123A]
[N] *tüli* [13A]
quarrel [Vi] *tülitsema* [349E]
quarrelsome [A] *riiakas* [243A]
quarry [N] *karjÄÄr* [58A]
quarter [N] *veerand* [229A]
quartette [N] *kvarteŢT* [58C]
quartz [N] *kvarTs* [58B]
quay [N] *kaİ* [1]
[N] *siLd* [91]
queen [N] *kuninganna* [152]
queer [A] *peņtsik* [234A]
question [N] *küsimus* [260A]
questionable [A] *küsitav* [231A]
questionnaire [N] *ankeeT* [58E]
quick [A] *vilgas* [159E]
quick-witted [A] *nupukas* [243A]
quick-witted [A] *taiPliK* [62]
quiet [A] *vaiKne* [247]
quilt [Vt] *vatEErima* [291B]
quintet [N] *kvinteŢT* [58C]
quintuplet [N] *viisik* [234A]
quiver [N] *võbin* [231A]
quiver [Vi] *võbisema* [349C]
quiz [N] *küsitlus* [260A]
quorum [N] *kvOOrum* [229A]
quotation [N] *tsitaaT* [58E]
quote [Vt] *tsitEErima* [291B]
quotient [N] *jagatis* [260A]

R

rabbi [N] *rabi* [13B]
rabbit (domestic) [N] *küülik* [234A]
race (genetic) [N] *raŞS* [58A]
race (cross-country) [N] *kroŞS* [58A]
rachitic [A] *rahhiitiline* [257D]
racial [A] *raşsiline* [257D]
racket (sport) [N] *reket* [229A]
radar [N] *radar* [229A]
radiance [N] *sära* [13A]
radiant [A] *heLge* [227B]
radiate [Vi] *kİİrgama* [348A]
[Vi] *õHkuma* [349G]
radiation [N] *kİİrgus* [260B]
radiator [N] *radiaaTor* [229A]
radical [A] *radikAAlne* [247]
radio [N] *rAAdio* [227A]
radish [N] *redis* [253]
radium [N] *rAAdium* [246]
radius [N] *rAAdius* [260A]
raffle [Vt] *lOOşima* [291A]
raft [N] *paRv* [63B]
raft [Vt] *parvetama* [349F]
rafter [N] *sarikas* [243A]
rag [N] *kalTs* [61B]
[N] *narTs* [61B]
rag [N] *närakas* [243A]
rage [N] *raEv* [61B]
rage [Vi] *märatsema* [349E]
[Vi] *raevutsema* [349E]
raid [N] *haarang* [234A]
railing [N] *reeling* [234A]
rain [N] *viHm* [49B]
rain [Vi] *sadama* [282]
rainfall [N] *sadu* [29]
rainy [A] *sajune* [251]
rainy [A] *vihmane* [251]
raise (lift) [Vt] *kergitama* [349F]
raise (grow) [Vt] *kasvatama* [349F]
raise an issue [Vt] *tõstatama* [349F]
raisin [N] *rosin* [231A]
rake [N] *reha* [13A]
rake [Vt] *rehitsema* [349E]
rally [Vi] *kOOnduma* [349H]
rally [Vt] *kOOndama* [349F]
rally (political) [N] *miiting* [234A]
rally (sport) [N] *raļli* [152]
ram [N] *jÄÄr* [53A]
[N] *oinas* [159B]
[N] *puKK* [58C]
rampart [N] *vaĻL* [58A]
rank [A] *väNge* [227B]
rapacious [A] *kiŞkjaliK* [62]
rape [Vt] *vägistama* [349F]
rapids [N] *kärestiK* [62]
rapier [N] *rapİİr* [58A]
rare [A] *haRv* [49B]
rarity [N] *haruldus* [260A]
rash [N] *lööve* [208A]
[N] *ohatis* [260A]
raspberry [N] *vaarikas* [243A]
rat [N] *roŢT* [58C]
rationalize [Vt] *ratsionalisEErima* [291B]
rattle [N] *kõristi* [225A]
rattle [Vi] *klobisema* [349C]
rattle [Vt] *klobistama* [349F]
[Vt] *põristama* [349F]
rattletrap [N] *logu* [13D]
ravage [Vt] *laaStama* [327B]
[Vt] *rüüStama* [327B]

rave [Vi] *mäSlema* [326G]
raven [N] *kAAren* [241A]
[N] *ronK* [53F]
raw [A] *toores* [161A]
ray [N] *kİİr* [82]
react [Vi] *reagEErima* [291B]
reaction [N] *reaktsiOOn* [58A]
reactionary [N] *reaktsionÄÄr* [58A]
[N] *tagurlane* [257C]
reactionary [A] *reaktsiooniline* [257D]
[A] *tagurliK* [62]
read [V] *lugema* [284]
readability [N] *loeTavus* [260A]
readable [A] *loeTav* [231A]
reader [N] *lugeja* [227A]
reader (book) [N] *lugemiK* [62]
readership [N] *lugejaskoNd* [106]
reading [N] *lugemine* [257E]
reading matter [N] *lektÜÜr* [58A]
ready (get) [Vi] *vaļmistuma* [349H]
realism [N] *realiSm* [58B]
realist [N] *realiSt* [58B]
realistic [A] *realiStliK* [62]
reality [N] *tegeliKKus* [260B]
[N] *tõElisus* [260A]
realize [Vt] *taiPama* [327D]
reason [N] *aru* [13A]
reason (intelligence) [N] *mõiStus* [260B]
reasonable [A] *mõiStliK* [62]
rebel [N] *mäSSaja* [227A]
rebel [Vi] *mäSSama* [327A]
rebellion [N] *mäSS* [61A]
rebellious [A] *mässuline* [257D]
recall [Vi] *mEEnuma* [349G]
recall [Vt] *meenutama* [349F]
recede [Vi] *kaugenema* [349D]
receipt [N] *kviiTung* [229A]
[N] *tähik* [234A]
receive [Vt] *sAAma* [266]
recent [A] *hiļjutine* [257A]
[A] *äşjane* [251]
receptacle [N] *anum* [231A]
recipe [N] *retsePt* [58B]
recipient [N] *sAAja* [227B]
[N] *saanu* [186]
recite [Vt] *deklamEErima* [291B]
[Vt] *eTlema* [326C]
recluse [N] *erak* [234A]
reclusive [A] *erakliK* [62]
recommend [Vt] *soovitama* [349F]
recommendation [N] *soovitus* [260A]
reconcile [Vt] *lepitama* [349F]
reconciliation [N] *lepitus* [260A]
reconstruct [Vt] *rekonstruEErima* [291B]
reconstruction [N] *rekonstruEErimine* [257E]
record [Vt] *jäädvustama* [349F]
record [N] *rekord* [229A]
record (sound) [N] *plaaŢ* [58E]
record [A] *rekordiline* [257D]
record (sounds) [Vt] *salvestama* [349F]
recording [N] *salvestamine* [257E]
recover [Vi] *toİbuma* [349G]
recover from illness [Vi] *kosuma* [269]
rectification [N] *õiendamine* [257E]
rectify [V] *õiendama* [349F]
rector [N] *reKtor* [229A]
recur [Vi] *koRduma* [349H]
recurrence [N] *koRdumine* [257E]
recurrent [A] *koRduv* [231A]
red [A] *punane* [251]
reddish [A] *punakas* [243A]
redecorate [Vt] *remoņTima* [291F]
redecorating [N] *remoņT* [58E]
redeem [Vt] *lunastama* [349F]
redness [N] *puna* [13A]
reduction in price [N] *aLLahiNdlus* [260B]
reed [N] *rOOg* [133]
reef [N] *kari* [13A]
[N] *rahu* [13A]
refer [Vt] *viiTama* [327E]
reference book [N] *teaTmiK* [62]
refinement [N] *vääristus* [260A]
reflect [Vt] *peegeldama* [349F]
reflected (be) [Vi] *peegelduma* [349H]
reflection [N] *peegeldus* [260A]
reform [N] *refoRm* [58B]
reform [Vt] *reformEErima* [291B]
[Vt] *refoRmima* [291C]
reformation [N] *reformatsiOOn* [58A]
reformer [N] *reformaaTor* [229A]
refrain [N] *refrÄÄn* [58A]
refresh [Vt] *karastama* [349F]
[Vt] *kosutama* [349F]
[Vt] *värskendama* [349F]
refreshing [A] *karastav* [231A]
[A] *kosutav* [231A]
refrigerate [Vt] *külmutama* [349F]
refrigeration [N] *külmutus* [260A]
refrigerator [N] *külmik* [234A]
refugee [N] *põgeniK* [62]
refusal [N] *kEEldumine* [257E]
refuse [N] *jääTmed (pl)* [179D]
refuse [Vi] *kEElduma* [349H]
regal [A] *kuningliK* [62]
regatta [N] *regaŢT* [58C]
regime [N] *režİİm* [58A]
regiment [N] *polK* [61F]
[N] *rügemeņT* [58E]
region [N] *kaņT* [58E]
register [N] *regiSter* [240A]
register [Vi] *registrEEruma* [349G]
register [Vt] *registrEErima* [291B]
register mail [Vt] *täHtima* [308B]
registrar [N] *registraaTor* [229A]
registration [N] *registratsiOOn* [58A]
[N] *registrEErimine* [257E]
registry [N] *registratUUr* [58A]
regret [N] *kahetsus* [260A]
regret [Vt] *kahetsema* [349E]
regular [A] *regulAArne* [247]
regularity [N] *regulAArsus* [260B]
regulation [N] *mÄÄrus* [260B]
regulations [N] *mÄÄrustiK* [62]
regulator [N] *regulaaTor* [229A]
rehabilitate [Vt] *rehabilitEErima* [291B]
rehabilitation [N] *rehabilitEErimine* [257E]
rehearsal [N] *prOOv* [58A]
rein [N] *ohi* [71A]
reject [N] *praaK* [58F]
rejoice [Vi] *juubeldama* [349F]
[Vi] *rõõmustama* [349F]
rejoicing [N] *juubeldus* [260A]
rejuvenate [Vt] *noorendama* [349F]
relate to [Vi] *suHtuma* [349H]
relationship [N] *suhe* [211B]
relationship (blood) [N] *sugulus* [260A]
relative [A] *relatİİvne* [247]
[A] *suHteline* [257D]
relative (blood) [N] *sugulane* [257C]
relativity [N] *relatİİvsus* [260B]
relax [Vi] *lõõgastuma* [349H]
relaxation [N] *lõõgastus* [260A]
relay [N] *relEE* [2]
release pollen [Vi] *toLmlema* [326B]
relic [N] *igand* [229A]
[N] *reliiKvia* [227A]
relief [N] *kergendus* [260A]
religion [N] *religiOOn* [58A]
[N] *usund* [229A]
religious [A] *uSkliK* [62]
[A] *usuline* [257D]
relinquish [Vt] *loovutama* [349F]
rely on [Vi] *tuginema* [349D]
remain [Vi] *jÄÄma* [266]
remains [N] *jäänus* [253]
remark [N] *märKus* [260B]

remedy [N] *arStim* [229A]
[N] *ravim* [229A]
remember [Vt] *mäletama* [349F]
remnant [N] *reŞt* [58B]
remote in time [A] *ammune* [251]
removal [N] *eemaldamine* [257E]
removal [N] *kõrvaldamine* [257E]
remove [Vt] *eemaldama* [349F]
[Vt] *kõrvaldama* [349F]
Renaissance [N] *renessanSS* [58G]
rendezvous [N] *koHtumine* [257E]
renew [Vi] *uuenema* [349D]
renew [Vt] *uuendama* [349F]
renewal [N] *uuendus* [260A]
renounce [Vi] *lOObuma* [349G]
renowned [A] *nimekas* [243A]
rent [N] *reņT* [58E]
[N] *ÜÜr* [58A]
rent [Vt] *reņTima* [291F]
[Vt] *ÜÜrima* [291A]
reorganize [Vt] *reorganisEErima* [291B]
repair [N] *parandus* [260A]
repair [Vt] *parandama* [349F]
[Vt] *remoņTima* [291F]
repairer [N] *parandaja* [227A]
repairs [N] *remoņT* [58E]
repatriate [Vt] *repatriEErima* [291B]
repay [Vt] *tasuma* [269]
repeat [Vt] *koRdama* [344]
repel [Vt] *tõRjuma* [291C]
repertoire [N] *repertuAAr* [58A]
repetition [N] *koRdamine* [257E]
report [N] *raport* [229A]
report [Vt] *raportEErima* [291B]
[Vt] *raporTima* [291F]
report (résumé) [Vt] *referEErima* [291B]
reporter [N] *reporTer* [229A]
reporting [N] *reportAAž* [58A]
represent [Vt] *esindama* [349F]
representative [N] *esindaja* [227A]
repress [Vt] *repressEErima* [291B]
repression [N] *repressiOOn* [58A]
reprimand [N] *noomitus* [260A]
reprimand [Vt] *nOOmima* [291A]
reproduce [Vt] *reprodutsEErima* [291B]
reproduction [N] *reproduktsiOOn* [58A]
reproof [N] *laiTus* [260B]
reptile [N] *rOOmaja* [227A]
repugnance [N] *vaţtikus* [260A]
repugnant [A] *vaţtik* [234A]
repulsive [A] *EEmaletõuKav* [231A]
[A] *jäļK* [58F]

reputation [N] *maine* [177B]
[N] *reputatsiOOn* [58A]
request [Vt] *paluma* [269]
requiem [N] *reeKviem* [246]
required [A] *nõuTav* [231A]
requirement [N] *nõue* [210B]
rescue [Vt] *pääStma* [297A]
rescuer [N] *pääStja* [227B]
research [N] *UUrimus* [260A]
researcher [N] *teAdur* [229A]
resemblance [N] *sarnasus* [260A]
resemble [Vi] *sarnanema* [349D]
reservation [N] *reservatsiOOn* [58A]
reserve [N] *reseRv* [58B]
reserve [Vt] *reservEErima* [291B]
reserve tickets [Vt] *bronEErima* [291B]
residence [N] *residenTs* [58B]
residue [N] *jääK* [58F]
resin [N] *vaiK* [61F]
resinous [A] *vaigune* [251]
resist [Vi] *tõrKuma* [291G]
resolute [A] *resoluuTne* [247]
resolution [N] *resolutsiOOn* [58A]
resort [N] *kUUrorT* [58E]
resound [Vi] *kajama* [269]
[Vi] *kõlama* [269]
resourceful [A] *leİdliK* [62]
respect [N] *auStus* [260B]
respect [Vt] *auStama* [349F]
respectability [N] *solİİdsus* [260B]
respectable [A] *solİİdne* [247]
respectful [A] *auStav* [231A]
responsibility [N] *vastutus* [260A]
responsible [A] *vastutav* [231A]
responsible for (be) [Vi] *vastutama* [349F]
rest [Vi] *lebama* [269]
rest [Vi] *puHkama* [348C]
restaurant [N] *restoran* [245]
restless [A] *püsimatu* [227A]
[A] *rahutu* [227A]
restlessness [N] *püsimatus* [260A]
[N] *rahutus* [260A]
restoration [N] *restauratsiOOn* [58A]
[N] *taaStamine* [257E]
restore [Vt] *eņnistama* [349F]
[Vt] *restaurEErima* [291B]
[Vt] *taaStama* [349F]
restorer [N] *restauraaTor* [229A]
restrain [Vt] *ohjeldama* [349F]
restrict [Vt] *kitsendama* [349F]
restriction [N] *kitsendus* [260A]
result [N] *resultaaT* [58E]

[N] *tulemus* [260A]
result from [Vi] *tulenema* [349D]
resuscitation unit [N] *reanimatsiOOn* [58A]
retch [Vi] *ööKima* [291G]
retention [N] *retentsiOOn* [58A]
reticule [N] *ridikül* [245]
retouch [Vt] *retušEErima* [291B]
[Vt] *retuŠŠima* [291D]
retreat [N] *tAAndumine* [257E]
retreat [Vi] *tAAnduma* [349H]
[Vi] *taganema* [349D]
return [Vi] *nAAsma* [296A]
return (give back) [Vt] *tagastama* [349F]
revenge [N] *revanŠ* [58B]
review [N] *retsensiOOn* [58A]
review (article) [Vt] *retsensEErima* [291B]
reviewer [N] *refereņT* [58E]
revile [V] *sõİmama* [327B]
revise [Vt] *redigEErima* [291B]
[Vt] *revidEErima* [291B]
revision [N] *revidEErimine* [257E]
revive [Vi] *elustuma* [349H]
revive [Vt] *elustama* [349F]
revolt [N] *revoļT* [58E]
revolution [N] *revolutsiOOn* [58A]
revolutionary [N] *revolutsionÄÄr* [58A]
revolve [Vi] *kEErlema* [326A]
[Vi] *pÖÖrlema* [326A]
revolver [N] *revoLver* [240A]
rheumatism [N] *jooKsva* [227B]
[N] *reuma* [152]
[N] *reumatiSm* [58B]
rhubarb [N] *rabaRber* [229A or 240A]
rhyme [N] *rİİm* [58A]
rhyme [V] *rİİmima* [291A]
rhythm [N] *rüTm* [58B]
rhythmic [A] *rütmiline* [257D]
rib [N] *ribi* [13B]
[N] *roie* [210D]
ribbon [N] *paEl* [50]
rice [N] *rİİs* [58A]
rich [A] *rikas* [159C]
rich (become) [Vi] *rikastuma* [349H]
rickets [N] *rahhiiT* [58E]
riddle [N] *mõistatus* [260A]
ride [N] *sõiT* [61E]
ride [Vi] *sõiTma* [297C]
ride horse-back [V] *ratsutama* [349F]
ridge [N] *hari* [68A]
[N] *seļjak* [234A]
ridicule [N] *pilge* [177F]
riding-school [N] *manEEž* [58A]

Riesling N *riisling* 229A
right N *õÏgus* 260B
right A *õÏge* 227B
right angel N *vinKel* 240A
rind of meat N *kamar* 231A
ring N *rõngas* 159B
ring Vt *rõngastama* 349F
ring (finger) N *sõrmus* 253
ring (bell) Vi *helisema* 349C
ring (bell) Vt *helistama* 349F
ringed snake N *naştik* 234A
rinse Vt *loputama* 349F
ripe A *küPs* 233B
A *vaĻmis* 244
ripen Vi *küPsema* 291C
Vi *vaĻmima* 349B
ripeness N *küPsus* 260B
ripple Vi *virvendama* 349F
rippling N *virvendus* 260A
rise Vi *kerKima* 349B
rise Vi *tõUsma* 296B
risk N *hasarT* 58E
N *riSk* 58B
risk Vt *riskEErima* 291B
Vt *riSkima* 291C
risky A *riskanTne* 247
ritual N *rituAAl* 58A
rival N *rivAAl* 58A
river N *jõgi* 42
river system N *jõgikoNd* 106
rivet N *neeŢ* 58E
rivet Vt *neeŢima* 291F
roach (fish) N *säRg* 141
road N *tEE* 2
roam Vi *hulKuma* 291G
roam Vi *uiTama* 327E
roam Vi *uiTma* 297C
roar Vi *möÏrgama* 345B
roast N *prAAḑ* 115
rob Vt *rÖÖvima* 291A
robber N *rÖÖvel* 240A
robbery N *rÖÖv* 58A
robe N *rÜÜ* 1
robe of office N *talAAr* 58A
robot N *robot* 229A
robust A *jõUline* 257D
A *rammus* 231A
rock N *rünK* 53F
rock V *kiigutama* 349F
rock Vi *kiiKuma* 291G
Vi *võnKuma* 291G
rock Vt *võngutama* 349F

rocket N *rakeŢT* 58C
rogue N *keĻm* 58B
roguery N *keĻmus* 260B
roguish A *keļmikas* 243A
roll N *ruĻL* 58A
roll Vi *vEErema* 291A
roll Vt *pööritama* 349F
Vt *ruĻLima* 291A
Vt *veeretama* 349F
roller N *vaļTs* 58B
roller (bird) N *sinirAAg* 96
romance N *romanSS* 58G
N *romaņtika* 227A
Romanian N *rumEEnlane* 257C
romantic N *romaņtik* 234A
romantic A *romaņtiline* 257D
romanticism N *romantiSm* 58B
romp Vi *mürama* 269
Vi *rüselema* 325
roof N *katus* 253
room N *rUUm* 58A
N *tuba* 38
roomy A *mahukas* 243A
A *ruumikas* 243A
root N *jUUr* 82
root (take) Vi *jUUrduma* 349H
rope N *köÏs* 143C
rose N *rOOş* 58A
rosemary N *rosmarÏIn* 58A
rough A *kare* 235
A *krobe* 235
A *krobeline* 257D
roughness N *karedus* 260A
roulade N *rulAAd* 58A
roulette N *ruleŢT* 58C
round N *tUUr* 58A
round A *ümmargune* 257A
round (in game) N *partÏÏ* 1
round (turn) N *tÏIr* 61A
round off Vt *ümardama* 349F
rounded A *ümar* 231A
roundness N *ümarus* 260A
rouse Vt *virgutama* 349F
route N *marSruuT* 58E
row N *rida* 35
N *rivi* 13A
row V *sõUdma* 316A
row Vi *aerutama* 349F
rowdy (be) Vi *käratsema* 349E
Vi *laaberdama* 349F
rower N *sõUdja* 227B
rub Vi *hÕÕrduma* 349H

rub Vt *hÕÕruma* 291A
rubber N *kuMM* 58A
N *kummi* 152
rubberize Vt *kummEErima* 291B
rubbish N *praHt* 116
ruby N *rubÏIn* 58A
rudder N *tÜÜr* 58A
rudimentary A *aLgeline* 257D
ruff Vt *krooKima* 291G
ruff (fish) N *kiiSk* 95B
rug N *vaiP* 49D
Ruhnu native N *ruHnlane* 257C
ruin Vt *laoStama* 349F
Vt *ruinEErima* 291B
ruination N *hukatus* 260A
ruined Vi *ruinEEruma* 349G
ruined (be) Vi *laoStuma* 349H
ruins N *varemed (pl)* 157
rule N *rEEgel* 240A
rule Vt *valitsema* 349E
rule (draw lines) Vt *linEErima* 291B
ruler N *valitseja* 227A
rum N *ruMM* 58A
rumble N *kõmin* 231A
N *mürin* 231A
rumble Vi *kõmisema* 349C
Vi *mühisema* 349C
Vi *mürisema* 349C
rumbling N *mühin* 231A
ruminant N *mäletseja* 227A
ruminate Vi *mäletsema* 349E
rummage V *sorima* 269
rummage Vi *tuHnima* 291C
rumour N *kUUldus* 260B
rumoured (be) Vi *kUUlduma* 349H
run N *jooKs* 61B
run Vi *jooKsma* 302
runes N *ruunid (pl)* 58A
runic song N *runo* 13A
runner (plant) N *võsund* 229A
runner (sled) N *jalas* 253
running A *jooKsev* 241A
rural community N *külakoNd* 106
rusk N *kuivik* 234A
Russian N *venelane* 257C
Russify Vt *venestama* 349F
russula (mushroom) N *pilvik* 234A
rust N *rooste* 177B
rust Vi *roostetama* 349F
rustle N *kahin* 231A
N *krabin* 231A
N *kõbin* 231A

[N] *sahin* [231A]
rustle [Vi] *kahisema* [349C]
[Vi] *krabisema* [349C]
[Vi] *sahisema* [349C]
rustle [Vt] *kahistama* [349F]
[Vt] *krabistama* [349F]
rustle [Vt] *sahistama* [349F]
rye [N] *rukis* [163A]

S

Saaremaa native [N] *sAArlane* [257C]
sable [N] *sOObel* [240A]
sabotage [N] *diversiOOn* [58A]
[N] *sabotAAž* [58A]
sabotage [Vt] *sabotEErima* [291B]
saboteur [N] *diversaņT* [58E]
saccharin [N] *sah(h)arİİn* [58A]
sack [N] *seKK* [58C]
sacrament [N] *sakrameņT* [58E]
sacred grove [N] *hİİs* [143B]
sacrifice [N] *oHver* [240A]
sacrifice [Vt] *ohverdama* [349F]
sad [A] *kuRb* [101B]
sad (become) [Vi] *kurvastuma* [349H]
saddle [N] *sadul* [231A]
saddle [Vt] *saduldama* [349F]
sadist [N] *sadiSt* [58B]
sadistic [A] *sadiStliK* [62]
safe [A] *ohutu* [227A]
safe (for valuables) [N] *seiF* [58A]
safety [N] *ohutus* [260A]
safety razor [N] *žileŢT* [58C]
saffron [N] *saFran* [229A]
sail [N] *puri* [76]
sail [Vi] *purjetama* [349F]
sailboat [N] *purjekas* [243A]
sailcloth [N] *puLdan* [229A]
sailor [N] *madrus* [253]
saint [N] *pühak* [234A]
salad [N] *salat* [229A]
sale [N] *müüK* [58F]
saleable [A] *mÜÜdav* [231A]
saliva [N] *ila* [13A]
salmon [N] *lõhe* [153]
[N] *lõhi* [18]
salt [N] *sOOl* [53A]
salt [Vt] *sOOlama* [327A]
salty [A] *soolane* [251]
salute [N] *saluuT* [58E]
salute [Vt] *salutEErima* [291B]
same [A] *sama* [14A]
sameness [N] *samasus* [260A]
sample [N] *näidis* [253]
sanatorium [N] *sanatOOrium* [246]
sanatorium [A] *sanatOOrne* [247]
sanction [N] *sanktsiOOn* [58A]
sanction [Vt] *sanktsionEErima* [291B]
sand [N] *lİİv* [49A]
sand [Vt] *liivatama* [349F]
sandal [N] *sandAAl* [58A]
[N] *sandaleŢT* [58C]
sandals [N] *rihmikud (pl)* [234A]
sandbank [N] *naSv* [49B]
sandy [A] *liivane* [251]
sanitary [A] *sanitAArne* [247]
sapper [N] *sapÖÖr* [58A]
sapphire [N] *safİİr* [58A]
sarcastic [A] *sarkastiline* [257D]
sarcastic (be) [Vi] *ironisEErima* [291B]
sardine [N] *sardİİn* [58A]
Satan [N] *sAAdan* [231A]
[N] *saaTan* [231A]
Satanism [N] *sataniSm* [58B]
satchel [N] *ranits* [231A]
satellite [N] *kAAslane* [257C]
[N] *satelliiT* [58E]
satiation [N] *küllastus* [260A]
satin [N] *satÄÄn* [58A]
satire [N] *satİİr* [58A]
satisfaction [N] *rahuldus* [260A]
satisfactory [A] *rahuldav* [231A]
satisfied (be) [Vi] *rahulduma* [349H]
satisfy [Vt] *rahuldama* [349F]
sauce [N] *kaste* [179C]
saucepan [N] *kaStrul* [229A]
sauna [N] *saUn* [49B]
saunter [Vi] *lonKima* [291G]
sausage [N] *vorSt* [58B]
savage [N] *meTslane* [257C]
save (money) [Vt] *sääStma* [297A]
savings [N] *sääSt* [61B]
Saviour [N] *lunastaja* [227A]
saw [N] *sAAg* [119]
saw [Vt] *sAAgima* [311]
saxophone [N] *saksofon* [245]
say [Vt] *üTlema* [338]
saying [N] *üTlus* [260B]
scab [N] *käRn* [53B]
scabby [A] *kärnane* [251]
scaffold [N] *teļling* [234A]
scale [N] *maStaaP* [58D]
[N] *skaala* [152]
scale (fish) [N] *soomus* [253]
scales (weight) [N] *kaalud (pl)* [61A]
scamp [N] *vemmal* [200]
scandal [N] *skandAAl* [58A]
scandalous [A] *skandAAlne* [247]
Scandinavian [N] *skandinAAvlane* [257C]
scanty [A] *vähene* [251]
scar [N] *aRm* [58B]
scarce [A] *naPP* [58C]
scarcity [N] *naPPus* [260B]
scare [N] *ehmatus* [260A]
scarf [N] *saĻL* [58A]
scarlet fever [N] *sarlakid (pl)* [229A]
scenario [N] *stsenAArium* [246]
scene [N] *stsEEn* [58A]
scent [Vt] *lõhnastama* [349F]
sceptic [N] *kaHtleja* [227A]
sceptical [A] *skeptiline* [257D]
schematic [A] *skemaatiline* [257D]
scheme [N] *sepitsus* [260A]
scheme [Vt] *sepitsema* [349E]
scholar [N] *õpetlane* [257C]
scholarship [N] *stipeŅdium* [246]
[N] *stiPP* [58C]
scholarship holder [N] *stipendiaaT* [58E]
school [N] *kOOļ* [58A]
school [Vt] *kooļitama* [349F]
school (disciples) [N] *kOOļkoNd* [106]
schottische [N] *reİnleNder* [240A]
science [N] *teAdus* [260B]
scientific [A] *teAdusliK* [62]
scientist [N] *teAdlane* [257C]
scissors [N] *käärid (pl)* [58A]
scold [Vi] *pragama* [269]
[Vi] *rİİdlema* [330A]
scoop [N] *koPP* [53C]
scorch [Vi] *kõRbema* [349B]
scorch [Vt] *kõrvetama* [349F]
score [N] *skOOr* [58A]
score in music [N] *partitUUr* [58A]
scorpion [N] *skorPion* [246]
Scot [N] *šoTlane* [257C]
scoundrel [N] *kaabakas* [243A]
[N] *lurjus* [253]
scout [N] *lUUraja* [227A]
scouting [N] *skauTlus* [260B]

scowl [Vi] *põrnitsema* [349E]
scrag [N] *roju* [13A]
scrap [N] *utİl* [58A]
scrape [Vt] *kaaPima* [291E]
[Vt] *kraaPima* [291E]
scratch [N] *kriimustus* [260A]
scratch [Vi] *siblima* [269]
scratch [Vt] *kraŢsima* [291C]
[Vt] *kriimustama* [349F]
[Vt] *sügama* [269]
scream [Vi] *kaRjuma* [291C]
screech [Vi] *kriiSkama* [348C]
screen [N] *ekrAAn* [58A]
[N] *siRm* [58B]
screen a film [Vt] *linastama* [349F]
screw [N] *kruvi* [17]
screw [Vt] *kruvima* [269]
screw-driver [N] *kruvits* [231A]
scribble [N] *kritseldus* [260A]
scribble [Vt] *kritseldama* [349F]
script writer [N] *stsenariSt* [58B]
scrub [Vt] *kÜÜrima* [291A]
[Vt] *nüHkima* [313B]
sculptor [N] *kujur* [229A]
[N] *skulPtor* [229A]
sculpture [N] *skulptUUr* [58A]
scythe [N] *vikat* [229A]
sea [N] *meri* [20]
sea-gull [N] *kajakas* [243A]
seal [N] *pitsat* [229A]
[N] *piTser* [229A]
seal [Vt] *pitsEErima* [291B]
seal (animal) [N] *hüljes* [197]
seam [N] *õMblus* [260B]
seamstress [N] *õMbleja* [227A]
season (spices) [Vt] *maitsestama* [349F]
season (year) [N] *sesOOn* [58A]
seat [N] *iste* [179C]
seaweed [N] *adru* [152]
second (another) [A] *teine* [258A]
second (time) [N] *sekuNd* [58B]
[N] *sekund* [229A]
secondary [A] *kõrvaline* [257D]
[A] *sekundAArne* [247]
secondary school [N] *gümnAAsium* [246]
secret [N] *saladus* [260A]
secret [A] *salajane* [257A]
secretariat [N] *sekretariaaT* [58E]
secretary [N] *sekretär* [245]
secretive [A] *salaliK* [62]
section [N] *sektsiOOn* [58A]
sector [N] *seKtor* [229A]
secular [A] *ilmaliK* [62]
sedative [N] *rahusti* [225A]
sedge [N] *taRn* [49B]
sediment [N] *sete* [177C]
seduce [Vt] *võrgutama* [349F]
see [V] *nägema* [289]
seed [N] *seeme* [183A]
seed [Vt] *seemendama* [349F]
seek [Vt] *oŢsima* [291C]
seem [Vi] *näİma* [261B]
[Vi] *tuNduma* [349H]
seeming [A] *näİliK* [62]
seethe [Vi] *kihisema* [349C]
[Vi] *puļbitsema* [349E]
seine [N] *nooT* [53E]
seize [Vt] *hAArama* [327A]
selection [N] *valimiK* [62]
self-confident [A] *iseteAdev* [241A]
self-service [N] *selve* [177B]
self-supporting [A] *isemajandav* [231A]
selfish [A] *isekas* [243A]
selfishness [N] *isekus* [260A]
sell [Vt] *mÜÜma* [264A]
seller [N] *mÜÜja* [227B]
semantics [N] *semantika* [227A]
semaphore [N] *semafor* [245]
semester [N] *semeSter* [240A]
seminar [N] *seminar* [245]
semolina [N] *manna* [152]
senate [N] *senat* [229A]
senator [N] *senaaTor* [229A]
send [Vt] *saaTma* [297C]
sender [N] *saaTja* [227B]
sending [N] *saaTmine* [257E]
senile [A] *raugaliK* [62]
senile (become) [Vi] *raugastuma* [349H]
seniority [N] *stAAž* [58A]
sensation [N] *kõmu* [13A]
[N] *sensatsiOOn* [58A]
sensational [A] *kõmuline* [257D]
sense [Vt] *aiStima* [291C]
sense (perception) [N] *aisting* [234A]
senseless [A] *mõTTetu* [227A]
senselessness [N] *mõTTetus* [260A]
sensible [A] *arukas* [243A]
sensitive [A] *tuNdliK* [62]
sensitivity [N] *tuNdliKKus* [260B]
sentence [N] *lause* [177B]
sentimental [A] *sentimentAAlne* [247]
sentimentality [N] *sentimentAAlsus* [260B]
sentry [N] *poŞt* [58B]
separate [Vi] *eralduma* [349H]
separate [Vt] *eraldama* [349F]
separation [N] *eraldamine* [257E]
September [N] *septeMber* [240A]
septet [N] *septeŢT* [58C]
sequel [N] *jäRg* [141]
sequin [N] *liTTer* [240B]
serenade [N] *serenAAd* [58A]
serge [N] *saRž* [58B]
sergeant [N] *sEErsanT* [58E]
series [N] *sari* [68A]
[N] *sEEria* [227A]
serious [A] *tõsine* [251]
seriousness [N] *tõsidus* [260A]
sermon [N] *juTlus* [260B]
servant [N] *tEEner* [240A]
[N] *tEEnija* [227A]
serve [Vt] *servEErima* [291B]
[Vt] *tEEnima* [291A]
serve (customer) [Vt] *teenindama* [349F]
serve (sport) [N] *paļling* [234A]
[N] *seRv* [58B]
serve (sport) [Vt] *paĻLima* [291A]
[Vt] *seRvima* [291C]
service [N] *teene* [177A]
[N] *teenus* [253]
sesame [N] *sEEsam* [229A]
session [N] *istung* [229A]
[N] *seŞS* [58A]
[N] *sessiOOn* [58A]
set [N] *kompleKt* [58B]
[N] *seŢT* [58C]
set astronomically [Vi] *lOOjuma* [349G]
set to music [Vt] *viisistama* [349F]
settle [Vi] *asuma* [269]
settlement [N] *asula* [227A]
settler [N] *asuniK* [62]
Setu (SE Estonian) [N] *setu* [152]
seven [N] *seitse* [179C]
seventh [N] *seiTsmendiK* [62]
seventh [A] *seiTsmes* [237C]
severe [A] *käre* [235]
sew [Vt] *õMblema* [329]
sewer [Vt] *kanalisEErima* [291B]
sewerage [N] *kanalisatsiOOn* [58A]
sex [N] *seKs* [58B]
sex (gender) [N] *sugu* [33]
sex appeal [N] *seksapİl* [58A]
sexologist [N] *seksuolOOg* [58A]
sextet [N] *seksteŢT* [58C]
sexual [A] *seksuAAlne* [247]
sexual intercourse [N] *suguühe* [211B]
shabby [A] *vilets* [231A]

shadow [N] *vari* [74]
shady [A] *varjukas* [243A]
[A] *varjuline* [257D]
shaft [N] *aİs* [50]
[N] *võĻL* [58A]
shake [N] *raputus* [260A]
shake [Vi] *raPPuma* [349G]
shake [Vt] *raputama* [349F]
shake (liquid) [Vi] *loKsuma* [291C]
shake (liquid) [Vt] *loksutama* [349F]
shallow [N] *madaliK* [62]
shaman [N] *šamAAn* [58A]
shame [N] *häbi* [13B]
shame [Vt] *häbistama* [349F]
shameful [A] *häbistav* [231A]
shameless [A] *häbitu* [227A]
shampoo [N] *šampOOn* [58A]
shank [N] *koİb* [101B]
[N] *põTk* [49B]
[N] *sÄÄr* [82]
shape [N] *kuju* [13A]
shape [Vt] *kujundama* [349F]
[Vt] *voRmima* [291C]
shape (take) [Vi] *kujunema* [349D]
shapeless [A] *vormitu* [227A]
share [N] *jagu* [31]
share (stock market) [N] *aKtsia* [227A]
share holder [N] *osaniK* [62]
shark [N] *haİ* [1]
sharp [A] *terav* [231A]
sharp (music) [N] *diEEs* [58A]
sharpen [Vi] *teravnema* [349D]
sharpen [Vt] *teravdama* [349F]
[Vt] *teritama* [349F]
sharpness [N] *teravus* [260A]
shatter [Vi] *purunema* [349D]
shatter [Vt] *purustama* [349F]
shave [Vt] *rasEErima* [291B]
shaver [N] *paRdel* [240A]
sheaf [N] *viHk* [131C]
shearing [N] *pügi* [34]
sheatfish [N] *säga* [13D]
sheath [N] *tuPP* [63C]
sheath-knife [N] *puŞS* [58A]
sheave [N] *seİb* [58B]
shed [N] *kUUr* [58A]
sheep [N] *lammas* [188]
sheet (book printing) [N] *pOOgen* [241A]
shelf [N] *riiul* [229A]
shelter [N] *varjend* [229A]
sherry [N] *šerri* [152]
shield [N] *kiļP* [58D]
shift [N] *nihe* [217C]
shift [Vi] *niHkuma* [349G]
shift [Vt] *nihutama* [349F]
Shiite [N] *šiiiT* [58E]
shimmer [Vi] *heļKima* [291G]
shine [N] *hİİlgus* [260B]
shine [Vi] *hİİlgama* [348A]
shingle (grit) [N] *riHv* [49B]
shingle (roof) [N] *siNdel* [240A]
shining [N] *hiile* [217A]
shining [A] *hİİlgav* [231A]
ship [N] *laEv* [49B]
shipowner [N] *laEvniK* [62]
shipping [N] *laevandus* [260A]
shirk [Vi] *vİİlima* [291A]
shirt [N] *särK* [58F]
shishkebab [N] *šašlõKK* [58C]
shit [N] *paSk* [95B]
[N] *siTT* [49C]
shit [V] *siTTuma* [291D]
shitty [A] *sitane* [251]
shiver [Vi] *lõdisema* [349C]
shiver (make) [Vt] *lõdistama* [349F]
shock [N] *šoKK* [58C]
[N] *vapustus* [260A]
shock [Vt] *vapustama* [349F]
shocked (be) [Vi] *vaPPuma* [349G]
shocking [A] *vapustav* [231A]
shoe [N] *kiNg* [53B]
shoe a horse [Vt] *rauTama* [349F]
shoe polish [N] *viKs* [58B]
shoot [Vt] *laSkma* [323]
shoot (plant) [N] *võsu* [13A]
shoot with bow [V] *aMbuma* [304]
shooting-range [N] *tİİr* [61A]
shop [N] *kauPlus* [260B]
shop [N] *äri* [13A]
shore [N] *kallas* [191]
shore dweller [N] *raNdlane* [257C]
short [A] *lühike(ne)* [257G]
short story [N] *noveĻL* [58A]
shortage [N] *pUUdus* [260B]
[N] *vähesus* [260A]
shorten [Vi] *lühenema* [349D]
shorten [Vt] *lühendama* [349F]
shorter [A] *lühem* [231A]
shorthand (write) [Vt] *stenografEErima* [291B]
shortish [A] *lüheldane* [257A]
shorts [N] *püksikud (pl)* [234A]
shot [N] *laSk* [131C]
shot of liquor [N] *naPs* [58B]
[N] *piŢs* [58B]
shoulder [N] *õLg* [95A]
shout [N] *hõise* [217C]
shout [N] *karjatus* [260A]
shout [V] *hõiKama* [327F]
shout for joy [Vi] *kilKama* [327F]
shovel [N] *küHvel* [240A]
shovel [N] *labidas* [243A]
shovel [Vt] *kühveldama* [349F]
show [Vt] *näiTama* [327E]
show-off [N] *keKs* [58B]
shower bath [N] *duŠŠ* [58C]
shred [N] *lemmes* [196]
shriek [N] *kiļjatus* [260A]
shriek [Vi] *kiĻjuma* [291C]
shriek (give) [Vi] *kiļjatama* [349F]
shrill [A] *kriiSkav* [231A]
shrimp [N] *kreveŢT* [58C]
Shrove-tide [N] *vaStlad (pl)* [241A]
shrubbery [N] *põõsastiK* [62]
shrug shoulders [Vt] *kehitama* [349F]
shudder [N] *judin* [231A]
shutter [N] *luuK* [58F]
shuttle [N] *süştik* [234A]
shy [A] *häbeliK* [62]
shy (be) [Vi] *võõrastama* [349F]
shyness [N] *häbeliKKus* [260B]
Siberian [N] *siberlane* [257C]
sick [A] *haİge* [227B]
sicken [Vi] *haigestuma* [349H]
sickle [N] *sirP* [58D]
sickly [A] *haİglane* [257C]
[A] *põdur* [231A]
[A] *tõbine* [251]
side [N] *küĻg* [141]
sieve [N] *sõEl* [49B]
sieve [Vt] *sõEluma* [291C]
sigh [N] *ohe* [217C]
sigh [Vi] *oHkama* [348C]
sight [N] *nägemine* [257E]
sight [Vt] *siLmama* [327B]
sign [N] *tähis* [253]
signal [N] *märK* [61F]
[N] *signAAl* [58A]
signal [Vt] *signalisEErima* [291B]
signboard [N] *siļT* [58E]
silage [N] *silo* [13A]
silence [N] *vaiKus* [260B]
silent [A] *vaiKiv* [231A]
silent (be) [Vi] *vaiKima* [350]
silhouette [N] *silueŢT* [58C]
silica [N] *silikaaT* [58E]
silicone [N] *räni* [13A]

silk [N] *sİİd* [58A]
silky [A] *siidine* [251]
silver [N] *hõbe* [235]
simmer [Vi] *podisema* [349C]
simple [A] *liHtne* [249]
simpleton [A] *loļlakas* [243A]
simplicity [N] *liHtsus* [260B]
simplification [N] *lihtsustamine* [257E]
simplify [Vt] *lihtsustama* [349F]
simulate [Vt] *simulEErima* [291B]
simultaneous game [N] *simultAAn* [58A]
sin [N] *paTT* [61C]
sin [Vi] *patustama* [349F]
sincere [A] *siiras* [159A]
sincerity [N] *sİİrus* [260B]
sinew [N] *kõõlus* [253]
sinful [A] *patune* [251]
sing [V] *laUlma* [292B]
singer [N] *laUlja* [227B]
singer at wedding [N] *kaasitaja* [227A]
single [A] *üksik* [234A]
singlet [N] *särgik* [234A]
singular [N] *aİnsus* [260B]
sink [N] *valamu* [227A]
sink [Vi] *vajuma* [269]
sip [Vt] *rüüPama* [327D]
sir [N] *sÖÖr* [58A]
sister [N] *sõsar* [231A]
[N] *õde* [25]
[N] *õEs* [256]
sister-in-law (wife's sister) [N] *käli* [13A]
sister-in-law (husband's sister) [N] *nadu* [27]
sisterly [A] *õEliK* [62]
sit down [Vi] *iStuma* [291C]
site [N] *ase* [157]
sitting [N] *seanSS* [58G]
sitting (be) [Vi] *iStuma* [291C]
situated (be) [Vi] *paiKnema* [349D]
situation [N] *situatsiOOn* [58A]
six [N] *kUUs* [143A]
sixth [N] *kuuendiK* [62]
sixth [A] *kuues* [238A]
size [N] *sUUrus* [260B]
sizzle [N] *sisin* [231A]
sizzle [Vi] *sisisema* [349C]
[Vi] *särisema* [349C]
skate [N] *uiSk* [131C]
skate [Vi] *uisutama* [349F]
skater [N] *uisutaja* [227A]
skein [N] *toKK* [58C]
[N] *viHt* [116]
skeleton [N] *luuStiK* [62]
[N] *skeleŢT* [58C]
sketch [N] *skiTs* [58B]
sketch [Vt] *skitsEErima* [291B]
sketchy [A] *visandliK* [62]
skewer [N] *varras* [193]
ski [N] *suuSk* [109]
ski [Vi] *suusatama* [349F]
skier [N] *suusataja* [227A]
skiing [N] *suusatamine* [257E]
skiing (downhill) [N] *slAAlom* [229A]
skilful [A] *osav* [231A]
skill [N] *osavus* [260A]
[N] *oSkus* [260B]
skilled [A] *oSkusliK* [62]
skin [N] *naHk* [95B]
skin [Vt] *nüļgima* [313A]
skin for tanning [N] *mäLv* [53B]
skip (hop about) [Vi] *keKsima* [291C]
skirt [N] *seelik* [234A]
skull [N] *koļju* [152]
[N] *kolP* [53D]
slack [A] *lodev* [231A]
slacken [Vi] *lõdvenema* [349D]
slacken [Vt] *lõdvendama* [349F]
slander [N] *laİm* [61B]
slander [Vt] *laİmama* [327B]
slang [N] *argOO* [1]
[N] *släNg* [58B]
slanting [A] *vildak* [234A]
[A] *vildakas* [243A]
[A] *vilTune* [257B]
slaughter [N] *taPP* [49C]
Slav [N] *slAAvlane* [257C]
slave [N] *ori* [71A]
slave [V] *oRjama* [327B]
slavery [N] *oRjus* [260B]
slavish [A] *orjaliK* [62]
sled [N] *kelK* [61F]
sled [Vi] *kelgutama* [349F]
sleep [N] *uni* [20]
sleep [Vi] *magama* [269]
sleepiness [N] *unisus* [260A]
sleepless [A] *unetu* [227A]
sleeplessness [N] *unetus* [260A]
sleepy [A] *unine* [251]
sleeve [N] *varrukas* [243A]
sleeveless undershirt [N] *maika* [152]
sleeves [N] *käİsed (pl)* [254]
sleigh [N] *regi* [41]
[N] *sAAņ* [58A]
sleigh-bell [N] *kuļjus* [253]
slender [A] *kõhnuke(ne)* [257G]
[A] *peenike(ne)* [257G]
[A] *sihvakas* [243A]
slenderness [N] *sihvakus* [260A]
sley [N] *pİİrd* [89A]
[N] *suga* [39]
slice [N] *lõiK* [61F]
slice [N] *vİİl* [61A]
[N] *viilukas* [243A]
slide [Vt] *libistama* [349F]
slide rule [N] *lükati* [225A]
slim [A] *sale* [235]
slime [N] *lima* [13A]
slimness [N] *saledus* [260A]
slimy [A] *limane* [251]
sling [N] *liNg* [61B]
slip [Vi] *libisema* [349C]
slip through [Vt] *poeTama* [349F]
slipper [N] *päŢT* [58C]
[N] *suŞS* [58A]
[N] *tuHvel* [240A]
slippery [A] *libe* [235]
sliver [N] *piNd* [129]
slogan [N] *loosung* [229A]
slop [N] *soļK* [58F]
slope [N] *kallak* [234A]
[N] *nõLv* [49B]
[N] *vEEr* [61A]
sloppiness [N] *lohakus* [260A]
sloppy [A] *lohakas* [243A]
slovenly [A] *räpane* [251]
slow [A] *aEglane* [257C]
sludge [N] *kõnTs* [49B]
slug [N] *näļKjas* [243B]
sluggard [N] *laiSkur* [229A]
sluggish [A] *pikaldane* [257A]
sluice [N] *lÜÜs* [58A]
slum [N] *agul* [229A]
slush [N] *lörTs* [58B]
sly [A] *kaval* [231A]
slyness [N] *kavalus* [260A]
smack [N] *laKs* [61B]
[N] *laksak* [234A]
smack (lips) [Vt] *matsutama* [349F]
small [A] *väiKe(ne)* [259]
small horn [N] *nukits* [231A]
smaller [A] *pisem* [231A]
smallpox [N] *rõUged (pl)* [227B]
smell [Vi] *lõHnama* [327B]
smell [Vt] *haiStma* [297A]
smell [Vt] *nuusutama* [349F]
smelt [N] *tiņT* [58E]
smile [N] *naeratus* [260A]

smile [Vi] *naeratama* [349F]
smirk [N] *muie* [216]
smirk [Vi] *muİgama* [345B]
smith [N] *sePP* [53C]
smock [N] *kiTTel* [240B]
smog [N] *sudu* [13C]
smoke [N] *suiTs* [61B]
smoke [Vi] *suiTsema* [291C]
smoke [Vt] *suitsetama* [349F]
smoke (cigarette) [V] *suitsetama* [349F]
smoker [N] *suitsetaja* [227A]
smoking [N] *suitsetamine* [257E]
smoky [A] *suitsune* [251]
smooth [A] *sile* [235]
smooth [Vt] *siluma* [269]
smoothness [N] *siledus* [260A]
smugly smile [Vi] *muhelema* [325]
snack [N] *sakusmeņT* [58E]
snail [N] *tigu* [32]
snake [N] *siUg* [134]
snake [N] *uŞS* [58A]
sneak [Vi] *hİİlima* [291A]
sneakers [N] *keţsid (pl)* [58B]
sneer [N] *irvitus* [260A]
sneer [Vi] *irvitama* [349F]
sneeze [N] *aevastus* [260A]
sneeze [Vi] *aevastama* [349F]
snigger [Vi] *kihistama* [349F]
snooty [A] *ninakas* [243A]
snore [N] *norin* [231A]
snore [Vi] *norisema* [349C]
[Vi] *norSkama* [348C]
snot [N] *taŢT* [58C]
snotty [A] *taţine* [251]
snotty (make) [V] *taţistama* [349F]
snout [N] *kOOn* [61A]
[N] *kärSS* [53G]
snow [N] *lumi* [21]
snowdrift [N] *haNg* [63B]
snowy [A] *lumine* [251]
soak [N] *ligu* [32]
soak [Vi] *liguma* [287]
soak [Vi] *ligunema* [349D]
soak [Vt] *leoTama* [349F]
soak in [Vi] *iMbuma* [349G]
soap [N] *seeP* [58D]
soapy [A] *seebine* [251]
sob [Vi] *nuuKsuma* [291C]
sober [A] *kaine* [177B]
sober up [Vi] *kainestuma* [349H]
sociable [A] *seļTsiv* [231A]
social [A] *seļTskoNdliK* [62]
[A] *sotsiAAlne* [247]
[A] *ühiskoNdliK* [62]
society [N] *ühiskoNd* [106]
society (organization) [N] *seļTs* [58B]
sociologist [N] *sotsiolOOg* [58A]
sociology [N] *sotsiolOOgia* [227A]
sock [N] *soKK* [58C]
sod [N] *mätas* [159C]
soda [N] *sooda* [152]
sodium [N] *naaTrium* [246]
sodomite [N] *sodomiiT* [58E]
sofa [N] *sohva* [152]
soft [A] *peHme* [227B]
soft drink [N] *limonAAd* [58A]
soften [Vi] *pehmenema* [349D]
soften [Vt] *pehmendama* [349F]
softener [N] *pehmendi* [225A]
softness [N] *peHmus* [260B]
soil [N] *muLd* [105]
soil [Vt] *soļKima* [291G]
solder [Vt] *tinutama* [349F]
soldier [N] *soldat* [229A]
[N] *sõdur* [229A]
sole [N] *taLd* [91]
sole [A] *ainus* [169]
sole [Vt] *tallutama* [349F]
solemn [A] *pühaliK* [62]
solemnity [N] *pühaliKKus* [260B]
solid [A] *taHke* [227B]
solidarity [N] *solidAArsus* [260B]
solitude [N] *üksindus* [260A]
solo [N] *soolo* [152]
soloist [N] *soliSt* [58B]
soluble [A] *lahustuv* [231A]
solution [N] *lahendus* [260A]
[N] *lahus* [253]
solve [Vt] *lahendama* [349F]
some [A] *mõni* [22]
[A] *mõningane* [257A]
some (a certain) [A] *miNgi* [225B]
somersault [N] *salto* [152]
son [N] *poEg* [113]
son-in-law [N] *väİ* [1]
sonant [A] *heliline* [257D]
song [N] *laUl* [61B]
songster [N] *laulik* [234A]
sonnet [N] *soneŢT* [58C]
sonny [N] *poju* [13A]
sonority [N] *kõlavus* [260A]
sonorous [A] *kõlav* [231A]
soot [N] *nõgi* [42]
[N] *taHm* [49B]
soothe [Vt] *leevendama* [349F]
soothsay [V] *aRbuma* [291C]
soothsayer [N] *aRbuja* [227A]
sooty [A] *tahmane* [251]
soporific [N] *uinuti* [225A]
soprano [N] *soPran* [229A]
sorcerer [N] *sorTs* [58B]
sorcery [N] *aSk* [95B]
sorority [N] *korporatsiOOn* [58A]
sorrel [N] *oblikas* [243A]
sorrow [N] *kuRbus* [260B]
sorrowful [A] *hale* [235]
sort [N] *sorT* [58E]
sort [Vt] *sortEErima* [291B]
[Vt] *sorTima* [291F]
soul [N] *hiNg* [63B]
sound [N] *heli* [13A]
[N] *kõla* [13A]
sound (language) [N] *häälik* [234A]
sound of bell [N] *helin* [231A]
soundless [A] *helitu* [227A]
[A] *kõlatu* [227A]
sounds (make) [Vi] *häälitsema* [349E]
soup [N] *suPP* [58C]
sour [A] *hapu* [152]
sour (become) [Vi] *haPnema* [349D]
sour (make) [Vt] *hapendama* [349F]
source [N] *aļlikas* [243A]
south [N] *lõuna* [178B]
south-east [N] *kagu* [13D]
south-west [N] *edel* [231A]
souvenir [N] *meene* [177A]
[N] *suvenİİr* [58A]
souvlaki [N] *šašlõKK* [58C]
sovereign [A] *suverÄÄnne* [247]
sow [N] *emis* [253]
sow [Vt] *küLvama* [327B]
sowing [N] *küĻv* [58B]
spacious [A] *avar* [231A]
spades (cards) [N] *pada* [13C]
Spaniard [N] *hispAAnlane* [257C]
spark [N] *säde* [157]
sparkle [Vi] *läiKima* [291G]
[Vi] *sädelema* [325]
[Vi] *särama* [269]
sparkling [A] *särav* [231A]
sparrow [N] *vaRblane* [257C]
sparse [A] *hõre* [235]
sparse (become) [Vi] *hõrenema* [349D]
sparse (make) [Vt] *hõrendama* [349F]
spatter [N] *pritse* [179C]
spatula [N] *spaaTel* [240A]

spawn [N] *kudu* [13C]
spawn [Vi] *kudema* [278]
speak [Vi] *kõnelema* [325]
speak [V] *rääKima* [291G]
speak hoarsely [Vi] *kähisema* [349C]
speak language badly [Vt] *purSSima* [291H]
speaker [N] *kõneleja* [227A]
speaker (parliament) [N] *spiiker* [229A]
spear [N] *oda* [13C]
special [A] *spetsiAAlne* [247]
specialist [N] *speŢs* [58B]
specialization [N] *spetsialisEErumine* [257E]
specialize [Vi] *spetsialisEEruma* [349G]
species [N] *liiK* [58F]
specific [A] *spetsiifiline* [257D]
specification [N] *täpsustus* [260A]
specify [Vt] *täpsustama* [349F]
speck [N] *täpe* [177C]
[N] *täpes* [161C]
speckled [A] *tähniline* [257D]
spectrum [N] *speKter* [240A]
speculate [Vt] *spekulEErima* [291B]
speculation [N] *spekulatsiOOn* [58A]
speculator [N] *spekulaņT* [58E]
speech [N] *kõne* [153]
speechless [A] *keeletu* [227A]
speed [N] *kİİrus* [260B]
speed up [Vi] *kiirenema* [349D]
speed up [Vt] *kiirendama* [349F]
spell [Vt] *vEErima* [291B]
spend (use up) [Vt] *kulutama* [349F]
spend time [Vt] *veeTma* [297C]
sperm [N] *sperma* [152]
sphere [N] *kera* [13A]
[N] *sfÄÄr* [58A]
spice [N] *vürTs* [58B]
spice [Vt] *vürtsitama* [349F]
spicy [A] *piPrane* [257B]
[A] *vürtsine* [251]
spider [N] *äMbliK* [62]
spike [N] *ora* [13A]
[N] *orK* [58F]
spin [Vi] *tİİrlema* [326A]
spin [Vt] *keTrama* [327E]
spinach [N] *spinat* [229A]
spinnaker [N] *spinnaker* [245]
spinner [N] *keTraja* [227A]
spinning-rod [N] *spinning* [234A]
spinning-wheel [N] *voKK* [58C]
spiral [N] *spirAAl* [58A]
spiral [A] *spirAAlne* [247]
spirit [N] *vaİm* [61B]
spirit alcohol [N] *piiritus* [260A]
spiritless [A] *tujutu* [227A]
spiritual [A] *hingeline* [257D]
[A] *vaİmne* [247]
spiritualism [N] *spiritualiSm* [58B]
spit [V] *sülitama* [349F]
spittle [N] *süĻg* [141]
splash [N] *pladin* [231A]
[N] *solin* [231A]
[N] *sulpsatus* [260A]
splash [Vi] *pladisema* [349C]
[Vi] *solisema* [349C]
[Vi] *solistama* [349F]
[Vi] *sulPsama* [327B]
spleen [N] *põRn* [49B]
splendid [A] *tore* [235]
splendour [N] *toredus* [260A]
splint [N] *lahas* [253]
splinter [N] *pilbas* [159D]
splinter [Vt] *killustama* [349F]
splinter of glass [N] *kiLd* [128]
splintered (become) [Vi] *killunema* [349D]
split [N] *lõHk* [131C]
split apart [Vi] *lõhenema* [349D]
split apart [Vt] *lõhestama* [349F]
spoil [Vi] *riKnema* [349D]
spoil [Vt] *riKKuma* [291D]
spoke [N] *kodar* [231A]
sponge [N] *käSn* [53B]
spontaneous [A] *spontAAnne* [247]
spool [N] *pOOl* [58A]
spoon [N] *lusikas* [243A]
sport [N] *sporT* [58E]
sporting [A] *sporTlasliK* [62]
sports [A] *sporTliK* [62]
sports (do) [Vi] *sporTima* [291F]
sportsperson [N] *sporTlane* [257C]
spot [N] *täPP* [58C]
spotlight [N] *prožeKtor* [229A]
spotted [A] *täpiline* [257D]
spout [N] *tila* [13A]
sprain [N] *nikastus* [260A]
sprain [Vt] *nikastama* [349F]
[Vt] *vÄÄnama* [327A]
sprat [N] *kilu* [13A]
[N] *sproŢT* [58C]
spray [Vt] *priŢsima* [291C]
spread out [Vi] *laİuma* [349G]
spread out [Vt] *laoTama* [349F]
spring [N] *vedru* [152]
spring [A] *kevadine* [257A]
spring (season) [N] *kevad* [233A]
spring (water) [N] *läte* [177C]
springy [A] *veTruv* [231A]
springy (be) [Vi] *vedrutama* [349F]
sprinkle [Vt] *piserdama* [349F]
sprinkler [N] *piserdi* [225A]
sprinter [N] *sprinTer* [229A]
sprout [N] *idu* [13C]
[N] *võrse* [177B]
sprout [Vi] *tärKama* [327F]
[Vi] *võRsuma* [349G]
spry [A] *tragi* [13D]
spur [N] *kannus* [253]
spurious [A] *vaļSk* [120B]
spurt [N] *purse* [217C]
spurt [Vi] *purSkuma* [349G]
spurt [Vt] *purSkama* [348C]
spy [N] *nuHk* [120B]
[N] *spiOOn* [58A]
spy [V] *spionEErima* [291B]
spy [Vt] *lUUrama* [327A]
[Vt] *nuHkima* [313B]
squabble [Vi] *purelema* [325]
squad [N] *salK* [61F]
square [N] *plaŢs* [58B]
[N] *väļjak* [234A]
square (geometry) [N] *ruuT* [61E]
squash [Vt] *lömastama* [349F]
squat [Vi] *kükitama* [349F]
squeak [Vi] *kriuKsuma* [291C]
[Vi] *piiksatama* [349F]
[Vi] *piuKsuma* [291C]
squeeze [Vt] *pigistama* [349F]
squid [N] *kalmAAr* [58A]
squire [N] *mõİsniK* [62]
squirm [Vi] *vingerdama* [349F]
squirrel [N] *orav* [231A]
stab [Vt] *torKama* [327F]
stability [N] *stabİİlsus* [260B]
stabilize [Vi] *stabilisEEruma* [349G]
stable [A] *stabİİlne* [247]
stadium [N] *stAAdion* [246]
staff (personnel) [N] *ametniKKoNd* [106]
stage [N] *lava* [14A]
stage [Vt] *lavastama* [349F]
stage (level) [N] *etaPP* [58C]
stage manager [N] *inspitsieņT* [58E]
stage production [N] *lavastus* [260A]
stage set [N] *dekoratsiOOn* [58A]
stage-setting [N] *kulişsid (pl)* [58A]
stagger [Vi] *tAAruma* [291A]
[Vi] *tuigerdama* [349F]
[Vi] *tuiKuma* [291G]

stagnation [N] *stagnatsiOOn* [58A]
stain [N] *laiK* [61F]
[N] *pleKK* [58C]
stained [A] *plekiline* [257D]
stained glass [N] *vitrAAž* [58A]
stairs [N] *trePP* [58C]
stake [N] *teivas* [187]
stall [N] *taĻL* [58A]
stallion [N] *täKK* [61C]
stammer [Vi] *kogelema* [325]
[Vi] *ökitama* [349F]
stamp [N] *temPel* [240A]
stamp [Vt] *tembeldama* [349F]
stamp (postage) [N] *marK* [58F]
stamp (with feet) [Vi] *tramPima* [291E]
stand [N] *steNd* [58B]
stand [Vi] *seİsma* [293B]
standard [N] *standard* [229A]
standard [A] *standaRdne* [247]
standardize [Vt] *normEErima* [291B]
[Vt] *noRmima* [291C]
[Vt] *standardisEErima* [291B]
standing [N] *seİs* [61B]
standstill [N] *seisak* [234A]
standstill (come to) [Vi] *seisatama* [349F]
stanza [N] *strooF* [58A]
staple (paper) [N] *kramP* [58D]
star [N] *täHt* [139]
star (actor)) [N] *stAAr* [58A]
starch [Vt] *tärgeldama* [349F]
stare at [Vt] *vaHtima* [308B]
stark [A] *jäiK* [49F]
starkness [N] *jäiKus* [260B]
starlet (sky) [N] *täheke(ne)* [257G]
start [Vi] *starTima* [291F]
start (sport) [N] *starT* [58E]
start doing [Vi] *haKKama* [327C]
start up [Vt] *käivitama* [349F]
starter [N] *starTer* [229A]
startle [Vt] *ehmatama* [349F]
startled (be) [Vi] *eHmuma* [349G]
[Vi] *koHkuma* [349G]
starve [Vi] *näĻgima* [349B]
starve [Vt] *näļjutama* [349F]
state [N] *riiK* [58F]
state [A] *riiKliK* [62]
state [Vt] *konstatEErima* [291B]
[Vt] *neņTima* [291F]
[Vt] *väiTma* [297C]
state of being [N] *olek* [234A]
statement [N] *väide* [177E]
station [N] *jAAm* [49A]
statistical [A] *statistiline* [257D]
statistics [N] *statistika* [227A]
status [N] *seisund* [229A]
[N] *staaTus* [260B]
stay for some time [Vi] *vİİbima* [349B]
steal [Vt] *varastama* [349F]
steam [N] *aUr* [61B]
steam [Vi] *aUrama* [327B]
steam in sauna [N] *leİl* [58B]
steamer [N] *aurik* [234A]
steamy [A] *aurune* [251]
steel [N] *teras* [253]
steep [A] *järSk* [131C]
steepness [N] *järSkus* [260B]
steer [Vt] *rOOļima* [291A]
[Vt] *tÜÜrima* [291A]
steering-wheel [N] *rOOļ* [58A]
stem [N] *vaRs* [144]
stem (grammar) [N] *tüvi* [18]
stencil [N] *šablOOn* [58A]
step [Vi] *aStuma* [291C]
step (footstep) [N] *saMM* [61A]
step (pace) [N] *aste* [177B]
step (stair) [N] *aste* [179C]
steppe [N] *stePP* [58C]
stereometry [N] *stereomeeTria* [227A]
stereophonic [A] *stereofooniline* [257D]
stereoscopic [A] *stereoskoopiline* [257D]
stereotypical [A] *trafareTne* [247]
sterile [A] *sterİİlne* [247]
sterility [N] *sterİİlsus* [260B]
sterilize [Vt] *sterilisEErima* [291B]
stern of ship [N] *aHter* [240A]
sternum [N] *mäLv* [63B]
stevedore [N] *lAAḑija* [227A]
stew [Vi] *haUduma* [349H]
stew [Vt] *hauTama* [349F]
steward [N] *stjuuard* [229A]
stewardess [N] *stjuardeSS* [58A]
stewed fruit [N] *kompoŢT* [58C]
stick [N] *kaigas* [159E]
[N] *kePP* [58C]
[N] *pulK* [53F]
stick (glue) [Vt] *kleePima* [291E]
stick (put) [Vt] *piStma* [297A]
sticker [N] *kleebis* [253]
stiff [A] *kaNge* [227B]
stiffness [N] *kaNgus* [260B]
still life [N] *natÜÜrmorT* [58E]
stimulate [Vt] *stimulEErima* [291B]
stimulus [N] *stİİmul* [229A]
sting [N] *astel* [173B]
sting (snake, insect) [Vt] *nõElama* [327B]
stinginess [N] *iHnsus* [260B]
[N] *kiţsidus* [260A]
stingy [A] *ihne* [177B]
[A] *kiţsi* [152]
stingy (be) [Vi] *koonerdama* [349F]
stink [N] *haİs* [61B]
[N] *leHk* [109]
stink [Vi] *haİsema* [291C]
stinking [A] *haİsev* [241A]
[A] *leHkav* [231A]
stirrup [N] *jalus* [253]
stitch [N] *piste* [177B]
stock [N] *foNd* [58B]
stock exchange [N] *böRs* [58B]
stocking [N] *suKK* [53C]
stomach [N] *magu* [31]
stone [N] *kivi* [17]
stones (broken) [N] *killustiK* [62]
stony [A] *kivine* [251]
stony spot [N] *raUn* [49B]
stool [N] *tabureŢ* [58H]
stoop [N] *kÜÜr* [61A]
stoop [Vi] *küürutama* [349F]
stop [N] *peaTus* [260B]
stop [Vi] *peaTuma* [349H]
stop [Vt] *peaTama* [349F]
stop up [Vt] *mäŢsima* [291C]
stop-watch [N] *stoPPer* [229A]
stopper [N] *suLgur* [229A]
storage [N] *hoİd* [123B]
store [N] *pOOḑ* [115]
storehouse [N] *aiT* [49E]
storekeeper [N] *pOOḑniK* [62]
storey in building [N] *korrus* [253]
storm [N] *toRm* [58B]
storm [Vi] *toRmama* [327B]
stormy [A] *tormiline* [257D]
[A] *tormine* [251]
story [N] *juTT* [61C]
stout [A] *kehakas* [243A]
[A] *tüse* [235]
stout (become) [Vi] *tüsenema* [349D]
stoutness [N] *tüsedus* [260A]
stove [N] *ahi* [74]
[N] *pliiT* [58E]
straight [A] *siRge* [227B]
straighten [Vi] *õgvenema* [349D]
straighten [Vt] *õgvendama* [349F]
strain [Vt] *pingutama* [349F]
strainer [N] *kuRn* [53B]
strait [N] *saLm* [63B]

[N] *väİn* [49B]
strand (yarn, rope) [N] *säie* [223]
strange [A] *imeliK* [62]
[A] *kummaline* [257D]
[A] *võõras* [159A]
stranger [N] *võõras* [159A]
strangle [Vt] *kägistama* [349F]
strategy [N] *stratEEgia* [227A]
straw [N] *kõRs* [144]
[N] *õĻg* [142A]
strawberry [N] *maasikas* [243A]
streak [N] *juŢT* [58C]
stream [N] *vOOlus* [260B]
stream (current) [Vi] *hOOvama* [327A]
street [N] *tänav* [231A]
streets (network) [N] *tänavastiK* [62]
strength [N] *jõUd* [127]
[N] *tugevus* [260A]
strengthen [Vi] *tugevnema* [349D]
strengthen [Vt] *tugevdama* [349F]
strenuous [A] *piNgeline* [257D]
[A] *piNgne* [249]
stress [N] *streŞS* [58A]
stress [Vt] *tooņitama* [349F]
stressed [A] *rõhuline* [257D]
stretch [N] *sirutus* [260A]
stretch [Vi] *ringutama* [349F]
[Vi] *sirutuma* [349H]
stretch [Vt] *sirutama* [349F]
stretch out [Vt] *venitama* [349F]
strew [Vt] *puiStama* [327B]
strict [A] *raNge* [227B]
strictness [N] *nõUdliKKus* [260B]
[N] *raNgus* [260B]
strike [N] *streiK* [58F]
strike [Vi] *streiKima* [291G]
striker [N] *streiKija* [227A]
striking [A] *rabav* [231A]
[A] *tabav* [231A]
string [N] *nÖÖr* [58A]
string [Vt] *lüKKima* [291D]
strip [N] *riba* [13B]
strip-tease [N] *striptİİs* [58A]
stripe [N] *triiP* [61D]
[N] *vööŢ* [58E]
striped [A] *triibuline* [257D]
[A] *vööďiline* [257D]
stroke (brain) [N] *insuļT* [58E]
stroke (pet) [Vt] *paiTama* [349F]
[Vt] *silitama* [349F]
stroll [Vi] *jalutama* [349F]
strong [A] *tugev* [231A]
stronghold [N] *kaņTs* [58B]
[N] *linnus* [253]
structural [A] *struktuuriline* [257D]
structure [N] *struktUUr* [58A]
struggle [N] *heiTlus* [260B]
struggle [Vi] *heiTlema* [326E]
struggle [Vi] *rabelema* [325]
stub [N] *juPP* [58C]
[N] *konTs* [61B]
stubborn [A] *joņnakas* [243A]
[A] *tõrges* [166B]
stubbornness [N] *joŅN* [58A]
stuck (become) [Vi] *takerduma* [349H]
student [N] *tudeng* [229A]
[N] *õpilane* [257C]
student body [N] *õpilaskoNd* [106]
student's cap [N] *teKKel* [240B]
studies [N] *õpingud (pl)* [234A]
studio [N] *ateljEE* [2]
[N] *stUUdio* [227A]
study [N] *kabineŢ* [58H]
study [Vt] *õPPima* [291D]
stuff [N] *krAAm* [58A]
stuff [Vt] *topistama* [349F]
stuffy [A] *uMbne* [247]
stumble [N] *komistus* [260A]
stumble [Vi] *komistama* [349F]
stump [N] *tüügas* [159E]
stump of tree [N] *käNd* [129]
stunt [N] *vigur* [229A]
stunts (do) [V] *vigurdama* [349F]
stupid [A] *loĻL* [58A]
[A] *rumal* [231A]
stupidity [N] *loĻLus* [260B]
[N] *rumalus* [260A]
sturdy [A] *toeKas* [243B]
sturgeon [N] *saMb* [87]
stutter [Vi] *kokutama* [349F]
style [N] *stİİl* [58A]
stylish [A] *moeKas* [243B]
[A] *stİİlne* [247]
stylistic [A] *stiililine* [257D]
stylistics [N] *stilistika* [227A]
subdue [Vt] *alistama* [349F]
subject matter [N] *süžEE* [2]
[N] *temaatika* [227A]
subjective [A] *subjektİİvne* [247]
submission [N] *alistumine* [257E]
submissive [A] *alistuv* [231A]
submit (surrender) [Vi] *alistuma* [349H]
subordinate [N] *alam* [231A]
[N] *aLLuv* [231A]
subordinate [Vt] *allutama* [349F]
subordinate oneself [Vi] *aLLuma* [349G]
subordination [N] *aLLuvus* [260A]
subscribe [Vt] *teĻLima* [291A]
subscriber [N] *aboneņT* [58E]
[N] *teĻLija* [227A]
subscription [N] *teĻLimine* [257E]
[N] *teĻLimus* [260A]
subsequent [A] *jäRgnev* [231A]
subside [Vi] *vaİbuma* [349G]
subsidy [N] *dotatsiOOn* [58A]
subsist [Vi] *elatuma* [349H]
substance [N] *aine* [177B]
[N] *matEEria* [227A]
[N] *ollus* [253]
substantial [A] *sisukas* [243A]
substitute [N] *asendaja* [227A]
substitute [Vt] *asendama* [349F]
subtlety [N] *pEEnsus* [260B]
subway [N] *metrOO* [1]
success [N] *edu* [13C]
[N] *menu* [13A]
[N] *õnnestumine* [257E]
succeed [Vi] *õnnestuma* [349H]
successful [A] *edukas* [243A]
[A] *menukas* [243A]
successor [N] *jäRglane* [257C]
such [A] *säärane* [251]
[A] *taOline* [257D]
suck [Vt] *imema* [269]
suck up to [Vi] *pugema* [284]
suckle [Vt] *imetama* [349F]
sue [Vt] *hagema* [269]
suffer [V] *kannatama* [349F]
suffer poor health [Vi] *virelema* [325]
sufferer [N] *kannataja* [227A]
suffice [Vi] *pİİsama* [327A]
sufficient [A] *pİİsav* [231A]
suffocate [Vi] *läMbuma* [349G]
suffocate [Vt] *lämmatama* [349F]
suffocating [A] *lämmatav* [231A]
suffocation [N] *läMbus* [260B]
sugar [N] *suHkur* [242A]
suit [N] *kostÜÜm* [58A]
suit [N] *ülikoNd* [106]
suit [Vi] *sobima* [269]
suitable [A] *paras* [156]
[A] *sobiv* [231A]
suitcase [N] *koHver* [240A]
[N] *sumadan* [245]
suite [N] *süiT* [58E]
sulk [Vi] *joŅNima* [291A]

Vi *tusatsema* 349E
sulky *A* *pahur* 231A
A *tusane* 251
sullen *A* *moRn* 58B
sulphur *N* *vÄÄvel* 240A
sum *N* *summa* 152
summary *N* *resümEE* 2
summary *A* *summAArne* 247
summer *N* *suvi* 18
summer cottage *N* *suvila* 227A
summery *A* *suvine* 251
summons *N* *läkitus* 260A
sun *N* *päiKe(ne)* 259
sun-bathe *V* *päevitama* 349F
sunbathe *Vt* *peesitama* 349F
sunflower seed *N* *sihvka* 152
sunset *N* *eha* 13A
N *loojang* 234A
sunshine *N* *päiKesepaiste* 177B
suntan *N* *päevitus* 260A
superficial *A* *pinnaline* 257D
superfluous *A* *ülearune* 251
superintendent *N* *komandaṇT* 58E
superior *N* *ülem* 231A
superiority *N* *paremus* 260A
supple *A* *nõTke* 227B
supplementary *A* *täiendav* 231A
supplier *N* *varustaja* 227A
supply *N* *varu* 13A
supply *Vt* *taRnima* 291C
Vt *varuma* 269
Vt *varustama* 349F
support *N* *toeTus* 260B
N *tugi* 43
support *Vt* *toeTama* 349F
supporter *N* *pOOldaja* 227A
N *toeTaja* 227A
suppose *Vt* *aRvama* 327B
Vt *oletama* 349F
supposition *N* *oletus* 260A
supreme *A* *ülim* 231A
sure *A* *kiNdel* 241A

surface *N* *piNd* 92
surgeon *N* *kiruRg* 58B
surgery *N* *kiruRgia* 227A
surgical *A* *kirurgiline* 257D
surpass *Vt* *ületama* 349F
surprise *N* *üllatus* 260A
surprise *Vt* *üllatama* 349F
surprised (be) *Vi* *üllatuma* 349H
surprising *A* *üllatusliK* 62
surround *Vt* *ümbritsema* 349E
surroundings *N* *üMbrus* 260B
survivor *N* *eLLujäänu* 186
N *jäänu* 186
suspect *Vt* *kahtlustama* 349F
suspenders *N* *traksid (pl)* 58B
suspicion *N* *kahtlustus* 260A
swallow *N* *pääsuke(ne)* 257G
swallow *Vt* *nEElama* 327A
swamp *N* *sOO* 5
swampy *A* *soİne* 252
swan *N* *luiK* 63E
swarm *Vi* *kihama* 269
swarthy *A* *tõmmu* 152
sway *Vi* *kõiKuma* 291G
sway *Vi* *õõTsuma* 291C
sway *Vt* *kõigutama* 349F
sway *Vt* *õõtsutama* 349F
swaying *N* *õõtsutus* 260A
swear *Vi* *vaNduma* 310
swear (cuss) *Vi* *ropendama* 349F
sweat *N* *higi* 13D
sweat *Vi* *higistama* 349F
sweater *N* *sviiTer* 240A
sweaty *A* *higine* 251
Swede *N* *rooTslane* 257C
sweep *Vt* *püHkima* 313B
sweepings *N* *püHkmed (pl)* 224
sweet *A* *magus* 231A
sweet-toothed *A* *maias* 159B
sweeten *Vt* *magustama* 349F
sweetheart *N* *aRmsam* 231A
swell *Vi* *paistetama* 349F

Vi *tuRsuma* 349G
swelling *N* *paistetus* 260A
swerve *Vi* *põiKama* 327F
swim *Vi* *ujuma* 269
swimmer *N* *ujuja* 227A
swimming-pool *N* *basseİn* 58B
swimming-pool *N* *ujula* 227A
swindler *N* *peţis* 253
swing *N* *kiiK* 63E
swing *Vi* *kiiKuma* 291G
swish *Vi* *vihisema* 349C
Swiss *N* *šveiTslane* 257C
switch *N* *lüliti* 225A
switch *Vt* *lülitama* 349F
switch (change) *N* *pööre* 179A
switch (rod) *N* *viTs* 51
switchboard *N* *kommutaaTor* 229A
sword *N* *mõõK* 49F
syllabify *Vt* *siļbitama* 349F
syllable *N* *siļP* 58D
symbol *N* *süMbol* 229A
symbolic *A* *sümbOOlne* 247
symbolize *Vt* *sümbolisEErima* 291B
symmetrical *A* *sümmeetriline* 257D
symmetry *N* *sümmeeTria* 227A
sympathetic *A* *sümpaaTne* 247
sympathy *N* *sümpaaTia* 227A
symphony *N* *sümfOOnia* 227A
symposium *N* *sümpOOsion* 246
symptom *N* *sümPtom* 229A
synod *N* *sinod* 229A
synonym *N* *sünonÜÜm* 58A
syntax *N* *süntaks* 229A
synthesis *N* *süntEEs* 58A
synthetic *A* *sünteetiline* 257D
syringe *N* *priŢs* 58B
syringe *N* *süstal* 170B
syrup *N* *siirup* 229A
system *N* *süstEEm* 58A
systematic *A* *süstemaatiline* 257D
systematize *Vt* *süstematisEErima* 291B

T

table *N* *laUd* 88A
table (chart) *N* *tabel* 229A
table guests *N* *laUdkoNd* 106
tablet *N* *tableŢT* 58C
tact *N* *taKt* 58B
tactful *A* *taktiline* 257D
tactical *A* *taktikaline* 257D

tactics *N* *taktika* 227A
tactless *A* *taktitu* 227A
tag *N* *lipik* 234A
tail *N* *häNd* 106
N *saba* 14B
tail (coat, dress) *N* *hõLm* 49B
tailed coat *N* *fraKK* 58C

tailor *N* *rätsep* 231A
take (carry off) *Vt* *viİma* 264A
take (pick up) *Vt* *võTma* 300
talc *N* *taļK* 58F
tale *N* *lugu* 33
talent *N* *taleṇT* 58E
talented *A* *aNdekas* 243A

talisman [N] *talisman* [245]
talk [N] *kõnelus* [260A]
[N] *referaaT* [58E]
talkative [A] *jutukas* [243A]
tall (grow) [Vi] *siRguma* [349G]
Tallinn native [N] *taĻLinlane* [257C]
tame [A] *taltsas* [159B]
tame [Vt] *taltsutama* [349F]
tampon [N] *tampOOn* [58A]
tan hide [Vt] *parKima* [291G]
tangerine [N] *mandarİİn* [58A]
tank [N] *paaK* [58F]
tanned (become) [Vi] *päevituma* [349H]
tanning of hide [N] *parK* [58F]
tap [N] *krAAņ* [58A]
tap [Vt] *koKsima* [291C]
tap-dance [Vi] *stePPima* [291D]
tape [N] *liņT* [58E]
tape [Vt] *liņdistama* [349F]
tape-record [Vt] *magnetofOOnima* [291A]
tape-recorder [N] *magnetofon* [245]
[N] *maKK* [58C]
tar [N] *tõRv* [49B]
tar [Vt] *tõRvama* [327B]
tariff [N] *tariiF* [58A]
tarpaulin [N] *preseņT* [58E]
tarry [A] *tõrvane* [251]
Tartu native [N] *tarTlane* [257C]
tassel [N] *tuPs* [61B]
tasselled [A] *tupsuline* [257D]
taste [N] *maitse* [177B]
taste [V] *maiTsema* [295]
[V] *maiTsma* [295]
tasteful [A] *maiTsekas* [243A]
tasteless [A] *maiTsetu* [227A]
tasty [A] *maiTsev* [241A]
Tatar [N] *tatarlane* [257C]
tatter [N] *näru* [13A]
[N] *räbal* [231A]
tattoo [Vt] *tätovEErima* [291B]
tavern [N] *kõrTs* [58B]
tavern keeper [N] *kõrTsmiK* [62]
tax [Vt] *maksustama* [349F]
taxation [N] *maksustamine* [257E]
taxi [N] *takso* [152]
tea [N] *tEE* [1]
teach [Vt] *õpetama* [349F]
teacher [N] *õpetaja* [227A]
teaching staff [N] *õpetajaskoNd* [106]
team (horses) [N] *rakend* [229A]
team (men's) [N] *mEEskoNd* [106]
team (mixed) [N] *võiStkoNd* [106]
team (women's) [N] *naİskoNd* [106]
tear [N] *rebestus* [260A]
tear [Vi] *kärisema* [349C]
[Vi] *rebenema* [349D]
tear [Vt] *käristama* [349F]
[Vt] *rebestama* [349F]
tear [Vt] *rebima* [269]
tear (crying) [N] *pisar* [231A]
tear at [Vt] *kiSkuma* [313B]
tear down [Vt] *lammutama* [349F]
tearable [A] *rebitav* [231A]
tease [Vt] *kiUsama* [327B]
[Vt] *naRRima* [291A]
teat [N] *nisa* [13A]
technical [A] *tehniline* [257D]
technical college [N] *tehnikum* [245]
technician [N] *tehnik* [234A]
technological [A] *tehnoloogiline* [257D]
technologist [N] *tehnolOOg* [58A]
technology [N] *tehnika* [227A]
[N] *tehnolOOgia* [227A]
teddy bear [N] *mõMM* [58A]
teem [Vi] *kubisema* [349C]
teenaged [A] *teİsmeline* [257D]
teflon [N] *teFlon* [229A]
telegram [N] *telegraMM* [58A]
telegraph [N] *telegraaF* [58A]
telegraph [Vt] *telegrafEErima* [291B]
telegraphist [N] *telegrafiSt* [58B]
telephone [N] *telefon* [245]
telephone [Vi] *helistama* [349F]
[Vi] *telefonEErima* [291B]
[Vi] *telefOOnima* [291A]
telescope [N] *kiiKer* [240A]
[N] *teleskooP* [58D]
television [N] *televisiOOn* [58A]
television set [N] *teler* [229A]
[N] *televİİsor* [229A]
telex [N] *teleks* [229A]
tell a story [Vt] *veStma* [297A]
temperament [N] *temperameņT* [58E]
temperamental [A] *temperamenTne* [247]
temperature [N] *temperatUUr* [58A]
temperature (take) [Vt] *krAAḑima* [291A]
tempest [N] *maru* [13A]
[N] *raju* [13A]
temple (head) [N] *oİm* [61B]
temple (worship) [N] *temPel* [240A]
tempo [N] *tempo* [152]
temporary [A] *ajutine* [257A]
temptation [N] *kiusatus* [260A]
tempting [A] *kiusatusliK* [62]
ten [N] *kümme* [183B]
ten or so [N] *kümmekoNd* [106]
ten-day period [N] *dekAAd* [58A]
tenant [N] *reņTniK* [62]
[N] *üüriline* [257D]
tend [V] *talitama* [349F]
tendency [N] *tendenTs* [58B]
tendentious [A] *tendenTsliK* [62]
tender (person) [N] *talitaja* [227A]
tender [A] *heLL* [53A]
[A] *õRn* [49B]
tenderness [N] *õRnus* [260B]
tending [N] *hOOļitsus* [260A]
[N] *talitus* [260A]
tennis [N] *teņnis* [253]
tenor [N] *tenor* [229A]
tens (20, 30, etc.) [N] *-kümmend* [184]
tense [A] *pinev* [231A]
tenseness [N] *pinevus* [260A]
tension [N] *pinge* [177B]
tent [N] *teļK* [58F]
tenth [N] *küMnendiK* [62]
tenth [A] *küMnes* [237C]
tercet [N] *tertseŢT* [58C]
term [N] *teRmin* [229A]
terminology [N] *terminolOOgia* [227A]
terra cotta [N] *terrakota* [152]
terrace [N] *terraŞS* [58A]
terrific [A] *kiHvt* [58B]
terrify [Vt] *kohutama* [349F]
territorial [A] *territoriAAlne* [247]
territory [N] *territOOrium* [246]
terror [N] *teRRor* [229A]
terrorist [N] *terroriSt* [58B]
terrorize [Vt] *terrorisEErima* [291B]
terry cloth [N] *frotEE* [2]
test [N] *teŞt* [58B]
testicle [N] *munand* [229A]
testify [Vt] *tuņnistama* [349F]
testimony [N] *tuņnistus* [260A]
Teutonic Order [N] *ordu* [152]
text [N] *teKst* [58B]
textbook [N] *õpik* [234A]
textile [N] *tekstİİl* [58A]
texture [N] *toİm* [63B]
thank [Vt] *tänama* [269]
thankful [A] *tänuliK* [62]
thanks [N] *tänu* [13A]
thaw [N] *sula* [13A]
theatre [N] *teaTer* [240A]
theatrical [A] *teatrAAlne* [247]
theft [N] *vaRgus* [260B]

theme [N] *teema* [152]
theologist [N] *teolOOg* [58A]
theoretic [A] *teoreetiline* [257D]
theory [N] *teOOria* [227A]
there [A] *seAlne* [247]
thermos [N] *termos* [253]
thesis [N] *tEEs* [58A]
thick [A] *jäme* [235]
thicket [N] *padrik* [234A]
[N] *rägastiK* [62]
[N] *tihnik* [234A]
thickness [N] *jämedus* [260A]
thief [N] *varas* [194]
thigh [N] *reİs* [143C]
thin [A] *kõHn* [49B]
[A] *õhuke(ne)* [257G]
thin (become) [Vi] *kõHnuma* [349G]
thin out [Vi] *harvenema* [349D]
thin out [Vt] *harvendama* [349F]
thing [N] *asi* [69A]
think [Vt] *mõTlema* [337]
thinner [A] *õhem* [231A]
third [N] *kolmandiK* [62]
third [A] *kolmas* [238A]
thirst [N] *janu* [13A]
thirsty (be) [Vi] *janunema* [349D]
this year's [A] *tänavune* [257A]
thistle [N] *ohakas* [243A]
thorn [N] *okas* [159C]
thorny [A] *oKKaline* [257D]
thorough [A] *põhjaliK* [62]
thoroughness [N] *põhjaliKKus* [260B]
thought [N] *mõte* [177C]
thoughtless [A] *mõTlematu* [227A]
thoughtlessness [N] *mõTlematus* [260A]
thousand [N] *tuhat* [239]
thousandth [A] *tuhandes* [237B]
thousandth [N] *tuhandiK* [62]
thrash [Vt] *koļKima* [291G]
thrashing [N] *koļK* [58F]
thread [N] *niiT* [58E]
thread (screw) [N] *viņT* [58E]
threat [N] *ähvardus* [260A]
threaten [Vt] *ähvardama* [349F]
three [N] *koLm* [63B]
threshold [N] *küņnis* [253]
thrilling [A] *hAArav* [231A]
thrive [Vi] *vohama* [269]
throat [N] *kurK* [61F]
[N] *kõri* [13A]
throb [Vi] *põKsuma* [291C]
[Vi] *tuKsuma* [291C]
throne [N] *trOOņ* [58A]
throw [N] *vise* [217C]
throw [Vt] *viSkama* [348C]
throw oneself [Vi] *viSkuma* [349G]
thrush [N] *rästas* [159B]
thud [N] *põnTs* [49B]
thumb [N] *pöial* [201]
thumbtack [N] *knopka* [152]
thunder [N] *kõU* [63B]
thunder [Vi] *müristama* [349F]
thunder-storm [N] *äiKe(ne)* [259]
thundering [N] *müristamine* [257E]
thyme [N] *tÜÜmian* [246]
Tibetan [N] *tiibetlane* [257C]
tick [Vi] *tiKsuma* [291C]
tick (insect) [N] *puuK* [58F]
ticket [N] *pilet* [229A]
ticket punch [N] *kompoSter* [240A]
tickle [N] *kõdi* [13C]
tickle [Vt] *kõdistama* [349F]
[Vt] *kõditama* [349F]
tidy up [Vt] *koristama* [349F]
tie [N] *liPs* [61B]
tie [Vt] *siduma* [281]
tie (railway) [N] *liiPer* [240A]
tiger [N] *tİİger* [240A]
tilt [Vt] *kallutama* [349F]
timber [N] *puiT* [61E]
time [N] *aEg* [98]
time-table [N] *graafik* [234A]
timid [A] *aRgliK* [62]
[A] *karTliK* [62]
[A] *peLgliK* [62]
timidity [N] *karTliKKus* [260B]
timidness [N] *aRgliKKus* [260B]
tin [N] *pleKK* [58C]
tin [N] *tina* [13A]
tin-foil [N] *fOOlium* [246]
[N] *staNNiol* [246]
tinder [N] *taEl* [49B]
tinge [N] *varjund* [229A]
tingle [Vi] *kihelema* [325]
tiniest [A] *pisim* [231A]
tinkle [N] *kõlin* [231A]
tinkle [Vi] *kõlisema* [349C]
tinkle [Vt] *kõlistama* [349F]
tinned food [N] *hoidis* [253]
tiny [A] *pisike(ne)* [257G]
tip [N] *oTs* [55]
[N] *tiPP* [61C]
tipsiness [N] *kiļK* [58F]
tirage [N] *tirAAž* [58A]
tire [N] *kuMM* [58A]
[N] *reHv* [58B]
tire [Vt] *väsitama* [349F]
tired (become) [Vi] *väsima* [269]
tiresome [A] *tüüTu* [227B]
tiring [A] *väsitav* [231A]
tissue [N] *kude* [26]
tit [N] *tiŞS* [58A]
title [N] *tiiTel* [240A]
titmouse [N] *tihane* [251]
toast [Vt] *röŞtima* [291C]
tobacco [N] *tubakas* [243A]
today's [A] *tänane* [251]
toddler [N] *mudilane* [257C]
toe [N] *varvas* [187]
toilet [N] *kloseŢT* [58C]
[N] *tualeŢT* [58C]
toilet (outhouse) [N] *käİmla* [227B]
tolerable [A] *talutav* [231A]
tolerance [N] *lePliKKus* [260B]
tolerant [A] *lePliK* [62]
tolerate [Vt] *saĻLima* [291A]
tomato [N] *tomat* [229A]
tomorrow [A] *hoMne* [247]
tone [N] *tOOņ* [58A]
tongue [N] *kEEl* [82]
tonne [N] *toŅN* [58A]
tonsil [N] *maNdel* [240A]
tonsillitis [N] *angİİn* [58A]
tool [N] *riiSt* [49B]
toot [V] *tuututama* [349F]
tooth [N] *hammas* [188]
[N] *pİİ* [1]
toothed [A] *haMbuline* [257D]
top (toy) [N] *vuRR* [58A]
top (tree) [N] *laTv* [49E]
top-hat [N] *siliNder* [240A]
topaz [N] *topAAs* [58A]
topical [A] *aktuAAlne* [247]
[A] *temaatiline* [257D]
topmost [A] *tiPmine* [257F]
torch [N] *pEErg* [131A]
[N] *tungal* [170B]
[N] *tõrvik* [234A]
torment [N] *pİİn* [49A]
torment [Vt] *pİİnama* [327A]
tormented (be) [Vi] *vaEvlema* [326B]
tormentor [N] *pİİnaja* [227A]
torte [N] *torT* [58E]
toss [Vt] *piLduma* [309]
toss and turn [Vi] *viSklema* [336]
total [A] *totAAlne* [247]

totter [Vi] *vanKuma* [291G]
touch [N] *puudutus* [260A]
touch [Vt] *kaTsuma* [291C]
[Vt] *puudutama* [349F]
touch up [Vt] *viimistlema* [351]
touching [A] *liigutav* [231A]
tough [A] *siTke* [227B]
tough (of meat) [A] *vinTske* [227B]
toughness [N] *siTkus* [260B]
tour [N] *turnEE* [2]
tourist [N] *turiSt* [58B]
tournament [N] *turnİİr* [58A]
tousle [Vt] *sasima* [269]
towel [N] *räţik* [234A]
tower [N] *toRn* [58B]
town [N] *alev* [229A]
town council [N] *rAAḑ* [115]
township [N] *vaLd* [91]
toy [N] *kaŅN* [58A]
[N] *lelu* [13A]
traceless [A] *jäļjetu* [227A]
tracing paper [N] *kaļka* [152]
track [N] *jäĻg* [141]
track (railway) [N] *roobas* [159D]
[N] *rööbas* [159D]
track-suit [N] *dreŞS* [58A]
tractor [N] *traKtor* [229A]
tractor driver [N] *traktoriSt* [58B]
trade-mark [N] *marK* [58F]
trade-unionist [N] *ametiühinglane* [257C]
tradition [N] *pärimus* [260A]
[N] *traditsiOOn* [58A]
traditional [A] *pärimusliK* [62]
[A] *traditsiooniline* [257D]
traffic [N] *liiKlus* [260B]
traffic light [N] *fOOr* [58A]
tragedy [N] *traagika* [227A]
[N] *tragÖÖdia* [227A]
tragic [A] *traagiline* [257D]
train [N] *roNg* [58B]
train [Vt] *trEEnima* [291A]
train (animal) [Vt] *dressEErima* [291B]
train station [N] *vaKsal* [229A]
trainee [N] *praktikaņT* [58E]
trainer [N] *trEEner* [229A]
trainer (animal) [N] *dressEErija* [227A]
training [N] *praktikum* [245]
[N] *treening* [234A]
[N] *treŅN* [58A]
[N] *õPPus* [260B]
training suit [N] *treeningud (pl)* [234A]
traitor [N] *reeTur* [229A]
tram [N] *traMM* [58A]
tramp [N] *päŢT* [58C]
trampoline [N] *tramplİİn* [58A]
transaction [N] *tehing* [234A]
transcribe [Vt] *transkribEErima* [291B]
transform [Vi] *mOOnduma* [349H]
transform [Vt] *mOOndama* [349F]
transformer [N] *transformaaTor* [229A]
translate [Vt] *tõļKima* [291G]
translation [N] *tõlge* [177F]
translator [N] *tõļKija* [227A]
transmit [Vt] *translEErima* [291B]
transplant [Vt] *sİİrdama* [341A]
transport [N] *tranSporT* [58E]
[N] *veOndus* [260B]
transport [Vt] *transporTima* [291F]
trap [N] *lõKs* [61B]
[N] *püünis* [253]
[N] *pÜÜs* [254]
trapeze [N] *trapets* [229A]
trash [N] *rämPs* [61B]
trauma [N] *trauma* [152]
travel [Vi] *reİsima* [291C]
traveller [N] *reİsija* [227A]
travelling [N] *reİsimine* [257E]
trawl [Vt] *trAAļima* [291A]
trawler [N] *trAAler* [229A]
tray [N] *kaņdik* [234A]
treacherous [A] *reeTliK* [62]
tread [V] *taLLama* [327A]
treasure [N] *aare* [211A]
treasurer [N] *laeKur* [229A]
treat [N] *koştitus* [260A]
treat [Vt] *koHtlema* [331B]
treat (medicine) [Vt] *ravima* [269]
treatment [N] *käsitlus* [260A]
treatment (cure) [N] *kUUr* [58A]
[N] *ravi* [13A]
treaty [N] *leping* [234A]
tree [N] *pUU* [7]
trellis [N] *võrestiK* [62]
tremble [N] *värin* [231A]
tremble [Vi] *vabisema* [349C]
[Vi] *värisema* [349C]
tremble (make) [Vt] *väristama* [349F]
trench [N] *kaevik* [234A]
tribe [N] *hõİm* [61B]
tribune [N] *tribÜÜn* [58A]
trick [N] *niPP* [58C]
[N] *triKK* [58C]
trickle [Vi] *nirisema* [349C]
tricolour [N] *trikolOOr* [58A]
trifle [N] *tühi-tähi* [71A]
trigger [N] *päästik* [234A]
trillion [N] *triĻjon* [229A]
trimmings [N] *garnitUUr* [58A]
trio [N] *trİo* [1]
trip [N] *reİs* [58B]
tripe [N] *ruPskid (pl)* [225B]
triplet [N] *koļmik* [234A]
trite [A] *šablooniline* [257D]
triumph [N] *triumF* [58A]
triumph [Vi] *triumfEErima* [291B]
trivial [A] *tühine* [251]
triviality [N] *köömes* [161A]
[N] *tühisus* [260A]
troll [N] *troĻL* [58A]
trolley bus [N] *troļli* [152]
[N] *troĻL* [58A]
[N] *troļlibuŞS* [58A]
trombone [N] *trombOOn* [58A]
troop [N] *liPkoNd* [106]
trophy [N] *trofEE* [2]
tropical [A] *troopiline* [257D]
tropics [N] *troopika* [227A]
trot [N] *sörK* [58F]
trot [Vi] *sörKima* [291G]
trouble [N] *häda* [13C]
[N] *tülin* [231A]
trouble [Vt] *vaEvama* [327B]
troublesome [A] *tülikas* [243A]
trough [N] *küna* [13A]
[N] *moĻd* [117]
troupe [N] *truPP* [58C]
trout [N] *foreĻL* [58A]
trowel [N] *kellu* [152]
trudge [Vi] *vaņTsima* [291C]
true [A] *tõEline* [257D]
trump [N] *trumP* [58D]
trump [V] *trumPama* [327D]
trumpet [N] *pasun* [231A]
[N] *trompet* [229A]
trunk (animal) [N] *loņT* [58E]
trunk (tree) [N] *tüvi* [18]
truss [N] *kubu* [24]
trust [N] *usaldus* [260A]
trust [Vt] *usaldama* [349F]
trustee [N] *voliniK* [62]
trustworthy [A] *usaldatav* [231A]
truth [N] *tõde* [25]
truth (earenestness) [N] *tõsi* [44]
truth (arrive at) [Vt] *tõdema* [269]
try [Vt] *prOOvima* [291A]
[Vt] *pÜÜdma* [316B]

try on [Vt] *paŞSima* [291A]
tub [N] *püŢT* [58C]
tuba [N] *tuuba* [152]
tube [N] *tUUb* [58A]
tube (pipe) [N] *toru* [13A]
tuber [N] *mugul* [231A]
tubercular [A] *tuberkulOOsne* [248]
tuberculosis [N] *tiisikus* [260A]
[N] *tuberkulOOS* [58A]
tuft [N] *tuŢT* [58C]
tuft of hair [N] *tuKK* [53C]
tug [Vt] *tirima* [269]
tulip [N] *tuĻP* [58D]
tulle [N] *tüĻL* [58A]
tumour [N] *kaSvaja* [227A]
tundra [N] *tuNdra* [227B]
tune [Vt] *häälestama* [349F]
tuner [N] *häälestaja* [227A]
tunnel [N] *tuNNel* [229A]
turd [N] *julK* [53F]
[N] *juŅN* [58A]
Turk [N] *türKlane* [257C]
turkey [N] *kalKun* [229A]
turn [N] *pöörang* [234A]
turn [Vi] *pÖÖrduma* [349H]
turn [Vt] *kÄÄnama* [327A]
[Vt] *pÖÖrama* [327A]
turn (in game) [N] *vOOr* [61A]
turn out to be [Vi] *osutuma* [349H]
turn over [Vt] *kaarutama* [349F]
turning [N] *pÖÖramine* [257E]
turnip [N] *kaaļikas* [243A]
[N] *naeris* [164B]
turpentine [N] *tärpentin* [245]
turquoise [N] *türkİİs* [58A]
tuxedo [N] *smoking* [229A or 234A]
twaddler [N] *jaUram* [229A]
tweezers [N] *näpits* [231A]
[N] *pintseŢT* [58C]
twig [N] *rAAg* [132]
twin [N] *kaksik* [234A]
twine [Vi] *põİmuma* [349G]
twine [Vt] *põİmima* [291C]
twist [N] *kEErd* [124A]
twist [Vt] *keerutama* [349F]
twitch [Vi] *tõMblema* [329]
twitter [V] *vidistama* [349F]
two [N] *kaKs* [149]
type [N] *tüüP* [58D]
type (write) [Vt] *tiPPima* [291D]
typhus [N] *tüüFus* [260B]
typical [A] *tüüpiline* [257D]
tyrannize [Vt] *türannisEErima* [291B]
tyranny [N] *türaŅNia* [227A]
tyrant [N] *türaŅN* [58A]

U

udder [N] *udar* [231A]
Udmurt [N] *udmurT* [58E]
ugliness [N] *inetus* [260A]
ugly [A] *inetu* [227A]
ugly face [N] *lõuSt* [49B]
Ukrainian [N] *ukraİnlane* [257C]
ulcer [N] *haavand* [229A]
ultimatum [N] *ultimaaTum* [229A]
ultramarine [N] *sine* [153]
ultramarine [A] *ultramarİİn* [58A]
unaccustomed [A] *haRjumatu* [227A]
unanimous [A] *solidAArne* [247]
unavoidable [A] *väļTimatu* [227A]
unbearable [A] *talumatu* [227A]
unbreakable [A] *muRdumatu* [227A]
uncertainty [N] *kiNdlusetus* [260A]
unchangeable [A] *muuTumatu* [227A]
uncle [N] *onu* [13A]
uncle (father's brother) [N] *leLL* [63A]
uncommon [A] *haruldane* [257A]
unconcealed [A] *vaRjamatu* [227A]
unconscious [A] *meelemärKusetu* [227A]
[A] *teAdvusetu* [227A]
unconsciousness [N] *teAdvusetus* [260A]
unconstrained [A] *suŅdimatu* [227A]
uncouth [A] *tahumatu* [227A]
undeniable [A] *saLgamatu* [227A]
underarm [N] *kaenal* [170B]
undergrowth [N] *võsa* [13A]
[N] *võsastiK* [62]
undermine [Vt] *minEErima* [291B]
underpants [N] *truşsikud (pl)* [234A]
undersigned [N] *aLLakirjutanu* [227A]
understand [Vt] *mõiStma* [297A]
understandable [A] *mõistetav* [231A]
understudy [N] *dublaņT* [58E]
undignified [A] *vääritu* [227A]
undulate [Vi] *lainetama* [349F]
uneasy [A] *kõhe* [235]
unemployed [A] *tööTu* [227B]
uneven [A] *konarliK* [62]
unexpected [A] *ooTamatu* [227A]
unfair [A] *ülekoHtune* [257B]
unfaithful [A] *trUUdusetu* [227A]
unfeeling [A] *tuNdetu* [227A]
unforgettable [A] *unustamatu* [227A]
ungrateful [A] *tänamatu* [227A]
unhappy [A] *õnnetu* [227A]
unhindered [A] *takistamatu* [227A]
uniform [N] *muNder* [240A]
[N] *voRm* [58B]
uniform [A] *üHtlane* [257C]
unimportant [A] *täHtsusetu* [227A]
union [N] *ühendus* [260A]
unit [N] *ühik* [234A]
[N] *üKsus* [260B]
unite [Vi] *ühinema* [349D]
unite [Vt] *ühendama* [349F]
united [A] *üHtne* [247]
unity [N] *üHtsus* [260B]
universal [A] *universAAlne* [247]
universe [N] *univeŖsum* [229A]
unjustified [A] *põhjendamatu* [227A]
[A] *õigustamatu* [227A]
unknown [A] *teAdmatu* [227A]
[A] *tuNdmatu* [227A]
unlimited [A] *pİİramatu* [227A]
unmarried [A] *vallaline* [257D]
unnavigable [A] *laevatamatu* [227A]
unprejudiced [A] *EElaRvamusetu* [227A]
unprepared [A] *eTTevaļmistamatu* [227A]
unravel [Vt] *harutama* [349F]
unrestrained [A] *ohjeldamatu* [227A]
unsalted [A] *mage* [235]
unseemly [A] *näoTu* [227B]
unshakable [A] *vanKumatu* [227A]
unskilled [A] *oSkamatu* [227A]
unsolvable [A] *lahendamatu* [227A]
unsteady [A] *kõiKuv* [231A]
unstressed [A] *rõhutu* [227A]
unsuitable [A] *sobimatu* [227A]
unsurpassable [A] *ületamatu* [227A]
untalented [A] *aNdetu* [227A]
untiring [A] *tüdimatu* [227A]
untiring [A] *väsimatu* [227A]
unwarranted [A] *tEEnimatu* [227A]
unwavering [A] *kõiKumatu* [227A]
upbringing [N] *kasvatus* [260A]
upheaval [N] *pööre* [211A]
upholster [Vt] *polsterdama* [349F]

uplands [N] *kõRgustiK* [62]
upper back [N] *turi* [71A]
uppermost [A] *ülemine* [257F]
upright [A] *püŞtine* [257B]
uproar [N] *kära* [13A]
[N] *möLL* [61A]
uproar (be in) [Vi] *möLLama* [327A]
uproot [Vt] *jUUrima* [291A]
upstart [N] *tõusik* [234A]
Uralic studies [N] *uralistika* [227A]
uranium [N] *urAAn* [58A]
urbanize [Vi] *linnastuma* [349H]
urbanize [Vt] *linnastama* [349F]
urchin [N] *jõmpsikas* [243A]
urgent [A] *edasilüKKamatu* [227A]
[A] *pakiline* [257D]
[A] *tuNgiv* [231A]
urinal [N] *pissuAAr* [58A]
urinate [Vi] *kusema* [272]
[Vi] *urinEErima* [291B]
urine [N] *kusi* [19]
[N] *urİİn* [58A]
urn [N] *uRn* [58B]
usage [N] *pruuK* [58F]
use [N] *tarvitus* [260A]
use (benefit) [N] *kasu* [13A]
use [Vt] *kasutama* [349F]
[Vt] *pruuKima* [291G]
[Vt] *tarvitama* [349F]
used book shop [N] *antikvariaaT* [58E]
useful [A] *kasuliK* [62]
usefulness [N] *kasuliKKus* [260B]
useless [A] *kasutu* [227A]
[A] *kõLbmatu* [227A]
[A] *taRbetu* [227A]
usual [A] *tavaline* [257D]
usurp [Vt] *anastama* [349F]
usurpation [N] *anastamine* [257E]
Utopia [N] *utooPia* [227A]
Utopian [A] *utoopiline* [257D]
utter [Vt] *laUsuma* [291C]

V

vacant [A] *vakanTne* [247]
vacation [N] *puHkus* [260B]
vacation [Vi] *suvitama* [349F]
vacationer [N] *puHkaja* [227A]
vacationer [N] *suvitaja* [227A]
vaccinate [Vt] *vaktsinEErima* [291B]
vaccination [N] *vaktsinatsiOOn* [58A]
vaccine [N] *vaktsİİn* [58A]
vacuum [N] *vaaKum* [229A]
[N] *vaaKuum* [246]
vagabond [N] *hulKur* [229A]
vagina [N] *vagiina* [152]
vain [A] *edev* [231A]
valerian [N] *palderjan* [245]
valid [A] *keHtiv* [231A]
valid (be) [Vi] *keHtima* [349B]
validate a ticket [Vt] *kompostEErima* [291B]
validity [N] *keHtivus* [260A]
[N] *maKsvus* [260B]
valley [N] *oRg* [131B]
valuable [A] *hinnaline* [257D]
[A] *väärTusliK* [62]
value [N] *väärTus* [260B]
value [Vt] *hiNdama* [343]
valve [N] *klaPP* [58C]
[N] *ventİİl* [58A]
vampire [N] *vampİİr* [58A]
van [N] *furgOOn* [58A]
vandal [N] *vandAAl* [58A]
vandalism [N] *vandaliSm* [58B]
vanguard [N] *avangaRd* [58B]
vanilla [N] *vaniļje* [152]
vanish [Vi] *haiHtuma* [349H]
vanity [N] *edevus* [260A]
variety show [N] *varietEE* [2]
varnish [N] *laKK* [58C]
[N] *värnits* [231A]
varnish [Vt] *laKKima* [291D]
vary [Vi] *variEEruma* [349G]
vary [Vt] *variEErima* [291B]
vase [N] *vAAş* [58A]
vaseline [N] *vaselİİn* [58A]
vat [N] *tõRs* [144]
vault [N] *võĻv* [58B]
vaulting [N] *võļvistiK* [62]
vegetable [A] *taİmne* [247]
vegetation [N] *taimestiK* [62]
vehicle [N] *sõiduk* [229A]
[N] *veoK* [229B]
veil [N] *lOOr* [58A]
veil [Vt] *lOOrima* [291A]
[Vt] *looritama* [349F]
vein [N] *sOOn* [82]
velvet [N] *samet* [229A]
[N] *velvet* [229A]
velvety [A] *sametine* [257A]
ventilate [Vt] *ventilEErima* [291B]
ventilation [N] *ventilatsiOOn* [58A]
venture [Vt] *söAndama* [349F]
Vepsian [N] *vePslane* [257C]
verandah [N] *veranda* [152]
verbal [A] *sõnaline* [257D]
[A] *verbAAlne* [247]
verdant [A] *haļjas* [159B]
verdant (be) [Vi] *haļjendama* [349F]
vermouth [N] *vermut* [229A]
verse [N] *saĻm* [58B]
[N] *saļmike(ne)* [257G]
[N] *värSS* [58G]
version [N] *teisend* [229A]
[N] *variaņT* [58E]
[N] *versiOOn* [58A]
vertical [A] *vertikAAlne* [247]
vessel [N] *nõU* [12]
vest [N] *veŞt* [58B]
veteran [N] *veteran* [245]
veto [N] *veto* [152]
viaduct [N] *viaduKt* [58B]
vibrate [V] *vibrEErima* [291B]
vibration [N] *vibratsiOOn* [58A]
[N] *võnge* [177F]
[N] *võnKumine* [257E]
vicar [N] *vikAAr* [58A]
victim [N] *oHver* [240A]
victorious [A] *võidukas* [243A]
victory [N] *võiT* [61E]
video monitor [N] *kuvar* [229A]
view [N] *vaade* [177E]
vigilance [N] *vaLvsus* [260B]
vigilant [A] *valvas* [165B]
vigorous [A] *priSke* [227B]
Viking [N] *viiking* [229A]
vile [A] *alatu* [227A]
villa [N] *villa* [152]
village [N] *küla* [13A]
village hop [N] *siMMan* [229A]
villainy [N] *alatus* [260A]
vine [N] *vääŢ* [58E]
vinegar [N] *ääḑikas* [243A]
violent (become) [Vi] *ägenema* [349D]
violet (colour) [A] *violeTne* [247]
violet (flower) [N] *kaņnike(ne)* [257G]
violin [N] *viiul* [229A]
viper [N] *madu* [27]
[N] *räşţik* [234A]

virgin [N] *neiTsi* [225B]
virtue [N] *vOOrus* [260B]
virtuosity [N] *virtuOOsliKKus* [260B]
virtuous [A] *vOOrusliK* [62]
virtuousness [N] *vOOrusliKKus* [260B]
Virumaa native [N] *virulane* [257C]
virus [N] *vİİrus* [260B]
visa [N] *viisa* [152]
viscountess [N] *vikonteSS* [58A]
visibility [N] *näHtavus* [260A]
visible [A] *näHtav* [231A]
visible (be) [Vi] *paiStma* [297A]
vision [N] *nägemus* [260A]
visit [Vi] *käİma* [264B]
visit [Vt] *külastama* [349F]
visitor [N] *külastaja* [227A]
visual [A] *näiTliK* [62]
[A] *visuAAlne* [247]
vital [A] *eluline* [257D]
vitamin [N] *vitamİİn* [58A]
vocation [N] *kuTsumus* [260A]
vodka [N] *vİİn* [49A]
voice [N] *hÄÄl* [82]
void [N] *tühik* [234A]
[N] *tühimiK* [62]
volcanic [A] *vulkaaniline* [257D]
volcano [N] *vulkAAn* [58A]
volt [N] *voļT* [58E]
volume (book) [N] *köide* [177E]
vomit [N] *okse* [177B]
vomit [V] *oksendama* [349F]
voracious [A] *ablas* [159D]
voracity [N] *aPlus* [260B]
Võrumaa native [N] *võrulane* [257C]
vote [V] *hääletama* [349F]
Vote [N] *vaḑjalane* [257C]
voter [N] *hääletaja* [227A]
[N] *valija* [227A]
voting [N] *hääletamine* [257E]
[N] *hääletus* [260A]
voucher [N] *taloNg* [58B]
vowel [N] *vokAAl* [58A]
vulcanize [Vt] *vulkanisEErima* [291B]
vulgar [A] *labane* [251]
[A] *vulgAArne* [247]
vulgarity [N] *labasus* [260A]
[N] *vulgAArsus* [260B]
vulgarize [Vt] *labastama* [349F]
vulva [N] *häbe* [157]

W

wad [N] *topend* [229A]
wade [Vi] *kaHlama* [327B]
[Vi] *sumama* [269]
wafer [N] *vaHvel* [240A]
wag (head) [Vt] *vangutama* [349F]
wag (tail) [Vt] *liputama* [349F]
wage war [Vi] *sõdima* [269]
wagon [N] *vanKer* [240A]
wagtail [N] *väStriK* [62]
waist [N] *piHt* [89B]
waistband [N] *väRvel* [240A]
wait [Vt] *ooTama* [327E]
wait on [Vt] *ümmardama* [349F]
waiter [N] *keLner* [229A]
waiting [N] *ooTamine* [257E]
wake (funeral) [N] *peİed (pl)* [177B]
waken [Vi] *ärKama* [327F]
waken [Vt] *äratama* [349F]
wakened (getting) [N] *äratus* [260A]
waking up [N] *ärKamine* [257E]
walk [Vi] *kõŅdima* [310]
[Vi] *käİma* [264B]
walkway [N] *käiK* [61F]
wall [N] *mÜÜr* [58A]
[N] *seİn* [50]
wall-paper [N] *tapeeŢ* [58E]
wall-paper [Vt] *tapeeŢima* [291F]
wallow [Vi] *püherdama* [349F]
walrus [N] *morSk* [109]
waltz [N] *vaļSS* [58G]
waltz [Vi] *vaļSSima* [291H]
wander [Vi] *räNdama* [343]
wanderer [N] *räNdur* [229A]
wanderings [N] *rännak* [234A]
want [N] *taHtmine* [257E]
want [Vt] *taHtma* [320]
war [N] *sõda* [36]
warble [Vi] *lõõritama* [349F]
ward (child) [N] *kasvandiK* [62]
warehouse [N] *ladu* [27]
wares [N] *kauP* [49D]
warlike [A] *sõjakas* [243A]
warm [A] *soE* [73]
warm [Vt] *soojendama* [349F]
warmer (become) [Vi] *soojenema* [349D]
warming [N] *soojendus* [260A]
warmth [N] *sOOjus* [260B]
warn [Vt] *hoiatama* [349F]
warning [N] *hoiatus* [260A]
warp [N] *lõİm* [63B]
wash [N] *pesu* [13A]
wash [Vt] *mõSkma* [322]
[Vt] *pesema* [272]
wash ashore [Vi] *uHtma* [320]
[Vi] *uHtuma* [308B]
wash-cloth [N] *nuuştik* [234A]
wasp [N] *herilane* [257C]
waste [Vt] *raiSkama* [348C]
waste (material) [N] *heide* [179D]
wasting [N] *raiSkamine* [257E]
watch (clock) [N] *UUr* [58A]
watch (guard) [N] *valve* [177B]
watchful [A] *valvakas* [243A]
water [N] *vesi* [46]
water (animals) [Vt] *jooTma* [297C]
water (plants) [Vt] *kaStma* [297A]
water-colour [N] *akvareĻL* [58A]
water-melon [N] *arbUUs* [58A]
waterfall [N] *koŞk* [142B]
waterlogged (become) [Vi] *veŢTima* [349B]
waterproof boots [N] *kalavinSkid (pl)* [225B]
watery [A] *vesine* [251]
watt [N] *vaŢT* [58C]
wave [N] *laine* [177B]
wave [Vt] *lehvitama* [349F]
wave of hand [N] *lehvitus* [260A]
waver [Vi] *ebalema* [349A]
waves [N] *lainetus* [260A]
wax [N] *vaha* [13A]
wax [Vt] *vahatama* [349F]
wax (floor, furniture) [Vt] *pOOnima* [291A]
way [N] *tEEkoNd* [106]
weak [A] *nõrK* [49F]
weaken [Vi] *nõrgenema* [349D]
[Vi] *nõrKema* [349B]
weaken [Vt] *nõrgendama* [349F]
weakness [N] *nõrKus* [260B]
weal [N] *vorP* [58D]
wealth [N] *riKKus* [260B]
[N] *vara* [13A]
weapon [N] *reLv* [53B]
wear out [Vi] *kuluma* [269]
weariness [N] *roİdumus* [260A]
[N] *tüdimus* [260A]
weary (become) [Vi] *roİduma* [349H]
weasel [N] *nirK* [58F]

weather [N] *iLm* [49B]
weave [Vt] *kuduma* [283]
[Vt] *punuma* [269]
weaver [N] *kaNgur* [242A]
[N] *kuduja* [227A]
weaving [N] *kudumine* [257E]
wedding [N] *pulmad (pl)* [53B]
wedge [N] *kİİl* [61A]
wedge [Vt] *kİİluma* [291A]
weed [Vt] *rohima* [269]
week [N] *nädal* [231A]
weigh [Vt] *kAAluma* [291A]
weight [N] *kAAl* [61A]
[N] *raSkus* [260B]
weight (scales) [N] *viHt* [116]
weightless [A] *kaalutu* [227A]
weighty [A] *kaalukas* [243A]
[A] *kAAluv* [231A]
weir [N] *mõRd* [93]
weld [Vt] *keevitama* [349F]
welder [N] *keevitaja* [227A]
well [N] *kaEv* [61B]
well-being [N] *hüvang* [234A]
werewolf [N] *soEnd* [229B]
west [N] *lÄÄş* [146]
wet [A] *mäRg* [112]
wet-nurse [N] *aMM* [63A]
wetland [N] *luHt* [104B]
whale [N] *vAAl* [49A]
what kind of [A] *miļline* [251]
wheat [N] *nisu* [13A]
wheel [N] *ratas* [159C]
wheel-barrow [N] *käru* [13A]
whet [Vt] *ihuma* [269]
[Vt] *luiSkama* [348C]
whetstone [N] *luiSk* [131C]
whey [N] *vadak* [234A]
which (ordinal) [A] *miTmes* [238B]
which of two [N] *kuMb* [102]
whimper [N] *virin* [231A]
whimper [Vi] *kiUnuma* [291C]
[Vi] *virisema* [349C]
whimpering [N] *viril* [231A]
whine [Vi] *viNguma* [291C]
whip [N] *nuuT* [58E]
[N] *piiTs* [49B]
whip (food) [Vt] *vahustama* [349F]
whip (punish) [Vt] *piitsutama* [349F]
whir [N] *vurin* [231A]
whir [Vi] *vurisema* [349C]
whir [Vt] *vuristama* [349F]
whirl [N] *pööris* [253]

whisk [N] *mäNd* [106]
[N] *viSpel* [240A]
whisk [Vt] *vispeldama* [349F]
whisk (sauna) [N] *viHt* [89B]
whisk in sauna [V] *viHtlema* [331B]
whisky [N] *viski* [152]
whisper [N] *sosin* [231A]
whisper [V] *sosistama* [349F]
whistle [N] *vile* [153]
whistle [V] *vilistama* [349F]
white [A] *vaLge* [227B]
white fish [N] *sİİg* [94B]
whiten [Vt] *valgendama* [349F]
whitener [N] *valgendi* [225A]
whitewash [Vt] *luPjama* [327D]
whitlow [N] *umme* [209]
whittle [Vt] *veStma* [297A]
whiz [N] *vuhin* [231A]
whiz [Vi] *vuhisema* [349C]
whoa (horse) [V] *ptruuTama* [349F]
whole [A] *kogu* [13D]
[A] *terve* [177B]
whole [N] *tervik* [234A]
whole wheat bread [N] *sepik* [234A]
wholesome [A] *tervisliK* [62]
whore [N] *hOOr* [53A]
whortleberry [N] *poHl* [53B]
[N] *sinikas* [243A]
wick [N] *taHt* [116]
wicked [A] *õEl* [231B]
wickedness [N] *õElus* [260B]
wide [A] *laİ* [49B]
wide-awake [A] *viRge* [227B]
widen [Vi] *laienema* [349D]
widen [Vt] *laiendama* [349F]
widening [N] *laiendus* [260A]
widening [N] *laienemine* [257E]
widow(er) [N] *leSk* [140B]
width [N] *laİus* [260B]
wiener [N] *sardeĻL* [58A]
[N] *vİİner* [229A]
wig [N] *parukas* [243A]
wild [A] *meţsik* [234A]
wild animal [N] *uluk* [229A]
will (desire) [N] *tahe* [211B]
will (testament) [N] *testameņT* [58E]
willow [N] *paju* [13A]
[N] *remmelgas* [243A]
wilt [Vi] *näRbuma* [349G]
win [V] *võiTma* [297C]
wince [N] *võpatus* [260A]
wince [Vi] *võpatama* [349F]

wind [N] *tUUl* [82]
wind [Vt] *kEErama* [327A]
wind [Vt] *kerima* [269]
windmill [N] *tuulik* [234A]
window [N] *aken* [172]
windy [A] *tuuline* [251]
wine [N] *veİn* [58B]
wing [N] *tİİb* [86A]
wink [N] *pilgutus* [260A]
winner [N] *võiTja* [227B]
winter [N] *tali* [66]
[N] *taĻv* [66]
winter [Vi] *taļvitama* [349F]
wintry [A] *taļvine* [251]
wire [N] *traaŢ* [58E]
wisdom [N] *tarKus* [260B]
wise [A] *tarK* [49F]
wish [N] *sOOv* [58A]
wish [Vt] *sOOvima* [291A]
wisp [N] *tuuŞt* [58B]
wit [N] *taiP* [61D]
[N] *vaimukus* [260A]
witch (shaman) [N] *nõİd* [88B]
witchcraft [N] *nõİdus* [260B]
withdraw [Vi] *eemalduma* [349H]
[Vi] *tõMbuma* [349G]
withdrawal [N] *eemaldumine* [257E]
wither [Vi] *närTsima* [349B]
witness [N] *tuņnistaja* [227A]
witty [A] *vaimukas* [243A]
wizard [N] *võlur* [229A]
wobble [Vi] *logisema* [349C]
woeful [A] *härras* [193]
wolf [N] *huņT* [58E]
[N] *susi* [47]
[N] *võsaviLLem* [229A]
woman [N] *naine* [258A]
womanly [A] *naiseliK* [62]
womb [N] *üSk* [109]
wonder [N] *imestus* [260A]
wonder at [V] *imestama* [349F]
wonder at [Vt] *uudistama* [349F]
woo [Vt] *kosima* [269]
wood anemone [N] *ülane* [251]
wooden [A] *puİne* [252]
wooer [N] *kosilane* [257C]
wool [N] *viLL* [49A]
woollen [A] *villane* [251]
word [N] *sõna* [14A]
word [Vt] *sõnastama* [349F]
wording [N] *sõnastus* [260A]
work [N] *tÖÖ* [8]

work [Vi] *tööTama* [349F]
work of art [N] *taies* [253]
work of art, literature [N] *teOs* [254]
worked up (get) [Vi] *ägestuma* [349H]
worker [N] *tÖÖline* [257D]
workers [N] *tÖÖliskoNd* [106]
workers' union [N] *ühing* [234A]
world of dead [N] *toonela* [227A]
worm-eaten (be) [Vi] *uşsitama* [349F]
worried [A] *mureliK* [62]
worry [N] *mure* [153]
worry [Vi] *muretsema* [349E]
worse [A] *halvem* [231A]
[A] *pahem* [231A]
worsen [Vi] *halvenema* [349D]
worsen [Vt] *halvendama* [349F]
worthless [A] *väärTusetu* [227A]
worthy [A] *vääriline* [257D]
wound [N] *hAAv* [49A]
wound [Vt] *hAAvama* [327A]
wrangle [Vi] *nägelema* [325]
wrap [Vt] *mäHkima* [313B]
[Vt] *mäŞSima* [291A]
wrapper [N] *ümbris* [253]
wrapping [N] *mähis* [253]
wreath [N] *päRg* [112]
wreathe [Vt] *päRgama* [347]
wreck [N] *vraKK* [58C]
wren [N] *käblik* [234A]
wrench [Vt] *kangutama* [349F]
wrestle [Vi] *mAAdlema* [326A]
wrestler [N] *mAAdleja* [227A]
wrestling [N] *mAAdlus* [260B]
wretchedness [N] *armetus* [260A]
wrinkle [N] *korTs* [61B]
wrinkle [Vt] *kortsutama* [349F]
wrinkle [Vt] *kirtsutama* [349F]
wrinkled (become) [Vi] *korTsuma* [349G]
wrist [N] *ranne* [221]
write [Vt] *kirjutama* [349F]
writer [N] *kirjutaja* [227A]
writer (author) [N] *kirjaniK* [62]
writhe [Vi] *vÄÄnlema* [326A]
writing [N] *kirjutus* [260A]
written [A] *kirjaliK* [62]
wrong [A] *vale* [153]

X

X-ray [N] *rönTgen* [229A]
xylophone [N] *ksülofon* [245]

Y

yacht [N] *jaHt* [116]
Yale lock [N] *snePPer* [240B]
Yankee [N] *jänki* [152]
yard [N] *õU* [63B]
yarn [N] *lõNg* [49B]
yawn [N] *haigutus* [260A]
yawn [Vi] *haigutama* [349F]
year [N] *aaSta* [227B]
year-old [A] *aaStane* [257B]
yearn [Vi] *igatsema* [349E]
yearning [N] *igatsus* [260A]
yeast [N] *päRm* [58B]
yell [Vi] *kisendama* [349F]
yellow [A] *kollane* [251]
yellow (turn) [V] *kolletama* [349F]
Yellow fish [N] *koger* [81B]
yellowish [A] *kollakas* [243A]
yelp [Vi] *kläHvima* [291C]
yesterday's [A] *eİlne* [247]
yield [N] *aŅd* [118]
yield [N] *saagikus* [260A]
yoke [N] *ike* [177C]
yolk [N] *rebu* [13B]
young [A] *nOOr* [82]
young man [N] *nooruk* [229A]
youth [N] *nOOrus* [260B]
youth (callow) [N] *noļK* [58F]
youthful [A] *nOOrusliK* [62]
youthfulness [N] *nOOrusliKKus* [260B]

Z

zeal [N] *õhin* [231A]
zebra [N] *sebra* [152]
zenith [N] *seniiT* [58E]
Zeppelin [N] *tsepelİİn* [58A]
zero [N] *nuĻL* [58A]
zigzag [N] *siKsaK* [58H]
zigzag [A] *siKsakiline* [257D]
zinc [N] *tsinK* [58F]
zither [N] *kannel* [205]
zodiac [N] *sodiaaK* [58F]
zone [N] *tsOOn* [58A]
[N] *vÖÖnd* [229B]
zoologist [N] *zoolOOg* [58A]
zoology [N] *zoolOOgia* [227A]

Lightning Source UK Ltd.
Milton Keynes UK
UKHW020910080921
390216UK00002B/188

9 780933 070424